Overloading, Overriding, Runtime Type, and Object Orientation

- State the benefits of encapsulation in object oriented design and write code that implements tightly encapsulated classes and the relationships "is a" and "has a".
- Write code to invoke overridden or overloaded methods and parental or overloaded constructors; and describe the effect of invoking these methods.
- Write code to construct instances of any concrete class including normal top level classes, inner classes, static inner classes, and anonymous inner classes.

Threads

- Write code to define, instantiate, and start new threads using both `java.lang.Thread` and `java.lang.Runnable`.
- Recognize conditions that might prevent a thread from executing.
- Write code using `synchronized`, `wait`, `notify`, and `notifyAll` to protect against concurrent access problems and to communicate between threads. Define the interaction between threads and between threads and object locks when executing `synchronized`, `wait`, `notify`, or `notifyAll`.

The *java.awt* Package

- Write code using `component`, `container`, and `LayoutManager` classes of the `java.awt` package to present a GUI with specified appearance and resize behavior, and distinguish the responsibilities of layout managers from those of containers.
- Write code to implement listener classes and methods, and in listener methods, extract information from the event to determine the affected component, mouse position, nature, and time of the event. State the event classname for any specified event listener interface in the `java.awt.event` package.

The *java.lang* Package

- Write code using the following methods of the `java.lang.Math` class: `abs`, `ceil`, `floor`, `max`, `min`, `random`, `round`, `sin`, `cos`, `tan`, `sqrt`.
- Describe the significance of the immutability of `String` objects.

The *java.util* Package

- Make appropriate selection of collection classes/interfaces to suit specified behavior requirements.

The *java.io* Package

- Write code that uses objects of the file class to navigate a file system.
- Write code that uses objects of the classes InputStreamReader and OutputStreamWriter to translate between Unicode and either platform default or ISO 8859-1 character encodings.
- Distinguish between conditions under which platform default encoding conversion should be used and conditions under which a specific conversion should be used.
- Select valid constructor arguments for FilterInputStream and FilterOutputStream subclasses from a list of classes in the `java.io` package.
- Write appropriate code to read, write and update files using FileInputStream, FileOutputStream, and RandomAccessFile objects.
- Describe the permanent effects on the file system of constructing and using FileInputStream, FileOutputStream, and RandomAccessFile objects.

Complete
Java 2 Certification

Second Edition

Complete
Java™ 2 Certification

Second Edition

Simon Roberts
Philip Heller
Michael Ernest

San Francisco • Paris • Düsseldorf • Soest • London

SYBEX

Associate Publisher: Richard Mills
Contracts and Licensing Manager: Kristine O'Callaghan
Acquisitions & Developmental Editor: Denise Santoro Lincoln
Editor: Pete Gaughan
Production Editor: Teresa L. Trego
Technical Editors: Natalie Levi, John Zukowski
Book Designer: Bill Gibson
Graphic Illustrator: Tony Jonick
Electronic Publishing Specialists: Bill Gibson, Nila Nichols
Proofreader: Laurie O'Connell
Indexer: Ted Laux
CD Technician: Keith McNeil
CD Coordinator: Kara Eve Schwartz
Cover Designer: Archer Design
Cover Photograph: Natural Selection

Library of Congress Card Number: 00-106195

ISBN: 0-7821-2825-4

Manufactured in the United States of America
10 9 8 7 6 5

Software License Agreement: Terms and Conditions

The media and/or any online materials accompanying this book that are available now or in the future contain programs and/or text files (the "Software") to be used in connection with the book. SYBEX hereby grants to you a license to use the Software, subject to the terms that follow. Your purchase, acceptance, or use of the Software will constitute your acceptance of such terms.

Software Support

The Software compilation is the property of SYBEX unless otherwise indicated and is protected by copyright to SYBEX or other copyright owner(s) as indicated in the media files (the "Owner(s)"). You are hereby granted a single-user license to use the Software for your personal, noncommercial use only. You may not reproduce, sell, distribute, publish, circulate, or commercially exploit the Software, or any portion thereof, without the written consent of SYBEX and the specific copyright owner(s) of any component software included on this media.

Warranty

In the event that the Software or components include specific license requirements or end-user agreements, statements of condition, disclaimers, limitations or warranties ("End-User License"), those End-User Licenses supersede the terms and conditions herein as to that particular Software component. Your purchase, acceptance, or use of the Software will constitute your acceptance of such End-User Licenses.

Disclaimer

By purchase, use or acceptance of the Software you further agree to comply with all export laws and regulations of the United States as such laws and regulations may exist from time to time.*Software Support*Components of the supplemental Software and any offers associated with them may be supported by the specific Owner(s) of that material but they are not supported by SYBEX. Information regarding any available support may be obtained from the Owner(s) using the information provided in the appropriate read.me files or listed elsewhere on the media.

Shareware

Should the manufacturer(s) or other Owner(s) cease to offer support or decline to honor any offer, SYBEX bears no responsibility. This notice concerning support for the Software is provided for your information only. SYBEX is not the agent or principal of the Owner(s), and SYBEX is in no way responsible for providing any support for the Software, nor is it liable or responsible for any support provided, or not provided, by the Owner(s).*Warranty*SYBEX warrants the enclosed media to be free of physical defects for a period of ninety (90) days after purchase. The Software is not available

from SYBEX in any other form or media than that enclosed herein or posted to *www.sybex.com*. If you discover a defect in the media during this warranty period, you may obtain a replacement of identical format at no charge by sending the defective media, postage prepaid, with proof of purchase to:

SYBEX Inc.
Customer Service Department
1151 Marina Village Parkway
Alameda, CA 94501
(510) 523-8233
Fax: (510) 523-2373
e-mail: info@sybex.com
WEB: HTTP://WWW.SYBEX.COM

After the 90-day period, you can obtain replacement media of identical format by sending us the defective disk, proof of purchase, and a check or money order for $10, payable to SYBEX.*Disclaimer*SYBEX makes no warranty or representation, either expressed or implied, with respect to the Software or its contents, quality, performance, merchantability, or fitness for a particular purpose. In no event will SYBEX, its distributors, or dealers be liable to you or any other party for direct, indirect, special, incidental, consequential, or other damages arising out of the use of or inability to use the Software or its contents even if advised of the possibility of such damage. In the event that the Software includes an online update feature, SYBEX further disclaims any obligation to provide this feature for any specific duration other than the initial posting.

Copy Protection

The exclusion of implied warranties is not permitted by some states. Therefore, the above exclusion may not apply to you. This warranty provides you with specific legal rights; there may be other rights that you may have that vary from state to state. The pricing of the book with the Software by SYBEX reflects the allocation of risk and limitations on liability contained in this agreement of Terms and Conditions.*Shareware Distribution*This Software may contain various programs that are distributed as shareware. Copyright laws apply to both shareware and ordinary commercial software, and the copyright Owner(s) retains all rights. If you try a shareware program and continue using it, you are expected to register it. Individual programs differ on details of trial periods, registration, and payment. Please observe the requirements stated in appropriate files.*Copy Protection*The Software in whole or in part may or may not be copy-protected or encrypted. However, in all cases, reselling or redistributing these files without authorization is expressly forbidden except as specifically provided for by the Owner(s) therein.

For my children, Emily and Bethan
—Simon

To Virginia, Karen, and Dave: friends who have supported my creativity.
—Philip

For Becky Day
—Michael

Acknowledgments

I would like to thank Annie Colvin, Mike Bridwell, Ray Moore, Gary Taylor, and Brian Couling—all of Sun Microsystems—who made it possible for me to work on the certification project in the first place. I would also like to thank Jari Paukku, Diane Hudlin, and Robert Pedigo, who have kept me involved. Finally, but by no means least, I'd like to thank Phil for his tremendous support when I needed it most.

—Simon Roberts

Thanks Kat! And thanks to everyone at Alberto's, and especially Gabriel Romero and Alicia Chacon.

—Philip Heller

My contribution to this book would not have been possible without the encouragement and support of John Varel, CEO of Synergistic Computer Solutions. John provided company time and moral support through both a hectic sales quarter and a frustrating string of illnesses, and I'm grateful for his energy and faith. My wife Heather listened as I recited text to ensure it sounded intelligible; more importantly, she put up with an absentee husband. Pete Royce had to get by without a full-time engineer, and yet remained positive about the whole thing. I especially want to thank Val Cramer of Sun Microsystems and Jerry Gilreath of FusionStorm. Without them as work partners during the day, I'd have had nothing left at night. Thank you both very much.

—Michael Ernest

The authors would also like to thank the people at Sybex: Richard Mills, Denise Santoro Lincoln, Pete Gaughan, Teresa Trego, Bill Gibson, Nila Nichols, Tony Jonick, Ted Laux, Keith McNeil, Kara Schwartz, and Liz Paulus.

Preface to the Second Edition

For a while it didn't seem to be moving at all, and I wondered if it ever would. Then it moved forward a few steps, wobbly but at least making progress. Then it was definitely on the move, and then it took off. It rose, stabilized, and soared.

As a matter of fact, I'm not talking about Java certification. I'm talking about a bird I can see through my office window. I mention the bird because one way to introduce a subject is to introduce something else to get people's attention, and then slyly switch over to what you're supposed to be talking about.

As a matter of fact, Java certification has acted a lot like that bird. It started slowly, finally took off, and now it has reached a really impressive height. I can't give you specific numbers, because for now Sun is treating all statistics regarding certification as confidential. I can't tell you how many people are taking the various exams, or what fraction of those people are passing. But if I can't give you hard numbers, I can still give you anecdotal evidence that indicates the growth of interest in Java certification.

First, sales of the previous edition of this book have been, well, gratifying. The other authors and I would like to express our sincere gratitude to all the readers who have previously bought the book, read it, and used it to gain their certification.

Second, other publishers are deciding that Java certification is big enough that they ought to get in the game. We have even seen at least one book that is as close as one can legally come to being a shameless imitation of ours. The sincerest form of flattery! We still believe we can give you the best information, because we designed the Programmer's and Developer's exams, and continue to maintain them.

Third, attendance at my "Fast-Track Java Platform Certification" seminar is growing by leaps and bounds... or, to continue the bird metaphor, it's growing by flaps and surges.

The fourth bit of evidence is a program that was announced at the June 1999 JavaOne conference. Four impressive companies joined with Sun in an initiative to endorse Java certification. The four companies are IBM, Oracle, Novell, and Netscape. The endorsements took the form of action, not just words and press releases. You can read about the details of this initiative in Appendix D, "The Certification Initiative for Enterprise Development." The big idea is that these companies, along with Sun, are throwing their considerable weight behind the proposition that people who claim to know how to program in Java should be able to prove it. This is in marked contrast to a hiring philosophy that was prevalent a few years ago, and has been rapidly losing popularity. The old hiring criterion was to see if the candidate's resume said "Java" on it somewhere. If the candidate passed this test, a cold mirror was held just in front of the candidate's mouth for a count of thirty seconds. Misty condensation on the mirror meant "hire;" no condensation meant "don't hire, this one isn't breathing." The test was every bit as reliable as a dowser's wand or a groundhog's shadow; friends in the medical profession assure me that even a person in a coma can still fog a mirror. But they can't write good code, no matter what anyone else says, and the five companies of the certification initiative are out to replace the mirror test with a much more difficult exam.

Finally, there is the attention that Sun has been paying to certification. They must know something we don't. The exam was completely rewritten in the middle of 2000. There has been no change to the style, depth, or balance of the questions; the only difference is that there is a whole new set of questions.

More than ever, *much* more than ever, Java certification is important.

What's New in This Edition?

We have kept the basic organization of the original book, but we have gone over the content of this book with a fine tooth comb. And we have added some new material that we think you're really going to like:

- We added a 50-question "Programmer's Final Exam." If you pass it, you are good and ready.

- We added 150 brand new questions to the tester on the CD-ROM.

- We greatly expanded our coverage of the Developer's Exam.

- We added a reference section on the certification alliance mentioned above.

Everybody who worked on this edition is extremely pleased with how it came out. We hope you enjoy reading it, enjoy taking the exams, greatly enjoy being told that you have passed, and boundlessly enjoy the career freedom that certification brings.

Philip Heller

September 2000

Mountain View, California

Contents at a Glance

Contents

Introduction

Hello! Come in, sit down, and make yourself at home. Please get comfortable; there are a lot of topics to cover in this book.

You have come here because you are ready. Ready to *get* ready, at least, which is practically the same thing. Now all that's left to do is the work.

And there is a lot of work to be done. Probably you heard that the 1.1 version of the exam was difficult. That was true; the Java 2 version is harder still, since it covers a few more topics. Not everybody passes—even on repeated attempts. We want to change these statistics. It wouldn't hurt to get a little help—and we're the ones to help.

Since this is, after all, the Introduction, allow us to introduce ourselves: Simon, Mike, and Phil. We are Java instructors by day, and by night we write.

What we teach (by day) are Java courses. When the 1.1 edition of this book was published, we wrote that among us we had taught Java to more than 1,000 people. By now the number is well into the thousands. We have been through our own certification process for instructors, and Sun trusts us to teach people the Java facts that Sun considers important. Recently, Simon has been developing new course material; Phil now teaches a two-day exam-preparation seminar. We want you to know all this because we want to be the ones you choose to help you pass the Certification Exam. We want you to know our credentials.

What we write (by night) are Java books. (Phil keeps talking about finishing his novel this year; we will just have to wait and see.) We wrote the *Java 1.1 Developer's Handbook* (Sybex, 1997) and we contributed to *Mastering Java 1.1* (Sybex, 1997). Then we wrote the *Java 1.1 Certification Study Guide*. Later, Sun released Java 2, so we rewrote everything. And now here we are, presenting the latest Java 2 version of the *Certification Study Guide*.

We thought we were the best team to write this book. Simon led the team that wrote all of the questions for the exam. Phil was a consultant for developing the exam and is one of the graders for the Developer's Exam, so he also has the inside view of things. And Mike, who wrote the chapters about the Developer's Exam, has been on the front lines of Java instruction for years.

Simon's unique position at Sun places a few restrictions on us. We can't give away any answers to the questions on the exam. (We wouldn't want to do that anyway; we want you to pass because you're good at Java, not because we slipped you a crib.) We had to make sure that the sample questions did not accidentally match any of the real test questions. It took a bit more work, but we think the benefit to you is tremendous: Everything in this book is here for a very good reason. If it's here, then it's here because we know you need to know about it. We understand that buying a book like this costs you money, reading it costs you time, and absorbing it costs you effort. We appreciate your investment, and we believe it will pay off.

If you read this book, absorb it, solve the practice questions at the end of each chapter, and work through the practice exam on the CD-ROM, you will be in the best possible position when you walk through the doors of your local testing center.

Let's just take care of a few standard formalities and then we can really get started.

Taking the Exam

You can take the Java Certification Exam whenever you like, by making an appointment with Sun Educational Services. Sun contracts with third-party test centers throughout the world, so hopefully you won't have to travel far. The cost of taking the exam is $150.

The U.S. telephone number for Sun Educational Services is (800) 422-8020; their URL is http://suned.sun.com. From there it will be easy to find the links you need. We hesitate to give more detailed instructions, because the site changes fairly often.

You can make an appointment for any time during regular business hours. When you make the appointment, ask how much time you will have. This is subject to change; on average, you'll be given two minutes per question. You will not be allowed to bring food or personal belongings into the test area. One piece of scratch paper is permitted; you will not be allowed to keep it after you have finished the exam. (See the end of Chapter 9, "Layout Managers," for a suggestion about how to use the scratch paper.) Most sites have security cameras.

You will be escorted to a cubicle containing a PC. The exam program will present you with randomly selected questions. Navigation buttons take you to the next or previous question for review and checking. When you have finished the test, the program will immediately present you with your score and a pass/fail indication. You will also be given feedback that indicates how well you performed in each of the dozen or so categories of the objectives. You will not be told which particular questions you got right or wrong.

Formalities of the Exam

There are no trick questions on the exam, but every question requires careful thought. The wording of the questions is highly precise; the exam has been reviewed not just by Java experts, but also by language experts whose task was to eliminate any possible ambiguity. All you have to worry about is knowing Java; your score will not depend on your ability to second-guess the examiners.

It is not a good idea to try to second-guess the question layout. For example, do not be biased toward answer C simply because C has not come up recently. The questions are taken from a pool and presented to you in a random order, so it is entirely possible to get a run of a particular option; it is also possible to get the answers neatly spread out.

Most of the questions are multiple choice. Of these, some have a single answer while others require you to select all the appropriate responses. The graphical user interface of the test system indicates which kind of answer you should supply. If a question only has one correct answer, you will be presented with radio buttons, so that selecting a second answer cancels the selection of a previous answer. With this kind of question, you have to select the most appropriate answer. If, on the other hand, you are presented with check boxes, then you may need to make more than one selection, so every possible answer has to be considered on its own merits—not weighed against the others.

You should be aware that where multiple answers are possible, you are being asked to make a decision about each answer, rather as though the question were five individual true/false questions. This requires more effort and understanding from you, because you have to get all the pieces correct. Fortunately, such questions will state how many correct answers there are. Think carefully, and always base your answer on your knowledge of Java.

The short-answer, type-in questions often cause undue concern. How are they marked? What happens if you omit a semicolon? These worries can stem from the knowledge that the questions are marked electronically and the belief that an answer might be marked wrong simply because the machine didn't have the sense to recognize a good variation of what it was programmed to accept.

As with all exam questions, you should be careful to answer precisely what is asked. However, you should also be aware that the system does accept a variety of different answers; it has been set up with all the variations that the examination panel considered to be reasonable.

Some of the type-in questions *do,* however, provide specific instructions concerning the format of the answer. Take this guidance seriously. If, for example, a question says, "Answer in the form `methodname()`," then your answer should be

```
method()
```

and not any of

```
object.method()
method();
method(a, b)
method
```

Some of the other answers might well be accepted, but programming is a precision job and you should be accustomed to following precise directions.

The test is taken using a windowed interface that can be driven almost entirely with the mouse. Many of the screens require scrolling; the scroll bar is on the right side of the screen. Always check the scroll bar so you can be sure you have read a question in its entirety. It would be a shame to get a question wrong because you didn't realize you needed to scroll down a few lines.

The exam contains about 60 questions. On average, this gives you a little more than two minutes per question. Some of the questions are easier than others, and undoubtedly there will be some that you can answer faster than others. However, you really do need to answer all the questions if you possibly can. The test system allows you to review your work after you reach the end. The system will explicitly direct your attention toward any multiple-choice questions that have no items selected. So if you find a particular question difficult, consider moving on and coming back to it later.

If you pass, you will be given a temporary certificate. A few weeks later you will receive by mail a permanent certificate, along with instructions for downloading an artwork sheet. The artwork shows the "Sun Certified Programmer for the Java™ 2 Platform" logo. By passing the exam (and signing an online license agreement), you have earned the right to display the logo. Printers know how to reproduce the artwork onto business cards, stationery, and so on. The lettering is legible (just barely, by people who eat carrots) down to a reduction of about 5/8" wide by 3/8" high.

Conventions Used in This Book

This book uses a number of conventions to present information in as readable a manner as possible. Tips, Notes, and Warnings, shown below, appear from time to time in the text in order to call attention to specific highlights.

This is a Tip. Tips contain specific programming information.

This is a Note. Notes contain important side discussions.

This is a Warning. Warnings call attention to bugs, design omissions, and other trouble spots.

This book takes advantage of several font styles. **Bold font** in text indicates something that the user types. A monospaced font is used for code, output, URLs, and file and directory names. A *monospaced italic font* is used for code variables mentioned in text.

These style conventions are intended to facilitate your learning experience with this book—in other words, to increase your chances of passing the exam.

Let's begin.

The Programmer's Exam

Chapter

1

Language Fundamentals

JAVA CERTIFICATION EXAM OBJECTIVES COVERED IN THIS CHAPTER:

✓ Identify correctly constructed source files, package declarations, import statements, class declarations (of all forms including inner classes), interface declarations and implementations (for *java.lang.Runnable* or other interface described in the test), method declarations (including the main method that is used to start execution of a class), variable declarations and identifiers.

✓ Identify all Java programming language keywords and correctly constructed identifiers.

✓ State the range of all primitive data types and declare literal values for *String* and all primitive types using all permitted formats, bases, and representations.

✓ Write code that declares, constructs, and initializes arrays of any base type using any of the permitted forms both for declaration and for initialization.

✓ State the effect of using a variable or array element of any kind when no explicit assignment has been made to it.

✓ State the correspondence between index values in the argument array passed to a main method and command line arguments.

✓ Determine the effect upon objects and primitive values of passing variables into methods and performing assignments or other modifying operations in that method.

✓ State the behavior that is guaranteed by the garbage collection system, and write code that explicitly makes objects eligible for collection.

This book is not an introduction to Java. Since you are preparing for certification, you are obviously already familiar with the fundamentals. The purpose of this chapter is to make sure you are 100 percent clear on those fundamentals covered by the Certification Exam objectives.

Source Files

All Java source files must end with the .java extension. A source file should generally contain, at most, one top-level public class definition; if a public class is present, the class name should match the unextended filename. For example, if a source file contains a public class called RayTraceApplet, then the file must be called RayTraceApplet.java. A source file may contain an unlimited number of non-public class definitions.

This is not actually a language requirement, but is an implementation requirement of many compilers, including the reference compilers from Sun. It is therefore unwise to ignore this convention since doing so limits the portability of your source files (but not, of course, your compiled files).

There are three *top-level* elements that may appear in a file. None of these elements is required. If they are present, then they must appear in the following order:

1. Package declaration

2. Import statements

3. Class definitions

The format of the package declaration is quite simple. The keyword package occurs first, and is followed by the package name. The package name is a series of elements separated by periods. When class files are created, they must be placed in a directory hierarchy that reflects their package names. You must therefore be careful that each component of your package name hierarchy is a legitimate directory name on all platforms. Therefore, you must not use characters such as the space, forward slash, backslash, or other symbols.

Import statements have a similar form, but you may import either an individual class from a package or the entire package. To import an individual class, simply place the fully qualified class name after the `import` keyword and finish the statement with a semicolon; to import an entire package simply add an asterisk to the end of the package name.

White space and comments may appear before or after any of these elements. For example, a file called `Test.java` might look like this:

```
1. // Package declaration
2. package exam.prepguide;
3.
4. // Imports
5. import java.awt.Button; // imports a specific class
6. import java.util.*;     // imports an entire package
7.
8. // Class definition
9. public class Test {...}
```

Sometimes you might have classes with the same name in two different packages, such as the Date classes in the packages java.util and java.sql. If you use the asterisk form of import—to import both entire packages—and then attempt to use a class simply called Date, you will get a compiler error reporting that this is ambiguous. You must either make an additional import, naming one or the other Date class explicitly, or you must refer to the class using its fully qualified name.

Keywords and Identifiers

The Java language specifies 51 keywords and other reserved words, which are listed in Table 1.1.

TABLE 1.1 Java Keywords and Reserved Words

abstract	const	final	instanceof	private	switch	void
boolean	continue	finally	int	protected	synchronized	volatile
break	default	float	interface	public	this	while
byte	do	for	long	return	throw	
case	double	goto	native	short	throws	
catch	else	if	new	static	transient	
char	extends	implements	null	strictfp	true	
class	false	import	package	super	try	

The words goto and const are reserved: Although they have no meaning in Java, programmers may not use them as identifiers.

An identifier is a word used by a programmer to name a variable, method, class, or label. Keywords and reserved words may not be used as identifiers. An identifier must begin with a letter, a dollar sign ($), or an underscore (_); subsequent characters may be letters, dollar signs, underscores, or digits. Some examples are:

```
1. foobar               // legal
2. BIGinterface         // legal: embedded keywords
3.                      // are OK.
4. $incomeAfterExpenses // legal
5. 3_node5              // illegal: starts with a digit
6. !theCase             // illegal: must start with
7.                      // letter, $, or _
```

Identifiers are case sensitive—for example, radius and Radius are distinct identifiers.

The exam is careful to avoid potentially ambiguous questions that require you to make purely academic distinctions between reserved words and keywords.

Primitive Data Types

Java's primitive data types are

- boolean
- char
- byte
- short
- int
- long
- float
- double

The apparent bit patterns of these types are defined in the Java language specification, and their effective sizes are listed in Table 1.2.

TABLE 1.2   Primitive Data Types and Their Effective Sizes

Type	Effective Representation Size (bits)	Type	Effective Representation Size (bits)
boolean	1	char	16
byte	8	short	16
int	32	long	64
float	32	double	64

Variables of type boolean may only take the values true and false.

The actual storage size and memory layout for these data items is not, in fact, required by the language specification. What is specified is the apparent behavior, so, for example, the effect of bit mask operations, shifts, and so on are entirely predictable at the Java level. If you write native code, you might find things are different from these tables. Importantly, this means that you cannot reliably calculate the amount of memory consumed by adding up data sizes. However, the exam is careful to avoid potentially ambiguous questions and only asks about variables from the Java language perspective, not the underlying implementation.

The four signed integral data types are

- byte
- short
- int
- long

Variables of these types are two's-complement numbers; their ranges are given in Table 1.3. Notice that for each type, the exponent of 2 in the minimum and maximum is one less than the size of the type.

TABLE 1.3 Ranges of the Integral Primitive Types

Type	Size	Minimum	Maximum
byte	8 bits	-2^7	$2^7 - 1$
short	16 bits	-2^{15}	$2^{15} - 1$
int	32 bits	-2^{31}	$2^{31} - 1$
long	64 bits	-2^{63}	$2^{63} - 1$

The char type is integral but unsigned. The range of a variable of type char is from 0 through $2^{16} - 1$. Java characters are in Unicode, which is a 16-bit encoding capable of representing a wide range of international characters. If the most significant nine bits of a char are all 0, then the encoding is the same as seven-bit ASCII.

The two floating-point types are:

- float

- double

These types conform to the IEEE 754 specification. Many mathematical operations can yield results that have no expression in numbers (infinity, for example). To describe such non-numerical situations, both doubles and floats can take on values that are bit patterns that do not represent numbers. Rather, these patterns represent non-numerical values. The patterns are defined in the Float and Double classes and may be referenced as follows (NaN stands for Not a Number):

- Float.NaN

- Float.NEGATIVE_INFINITY

- Float.POSITIVE_INFINITY

- Double.NaN

- Double.NEGATIVE_INFINITY

- Double.POSITIVE_INFINITY

The code fragment below shows the use of these constants:

```
1. double d = -10.0 / 0.0;
2. if (d == Double.NEGATIVE_INFINITY) {
3.    System.out.println("d just exploded: " + d);
4. }
```

In this code fragment, the test on line 2 passes, so line 3 is executed.

All the numerical primitive types (that is, all except boolean and char) are signed.

Literals

A *literal* is a value specified in the program source, as opposed to one determined at runtime. Literals can represent primitive or string variables, and may appear on the right side of assignments or in method calls. You cannot assign a value into a literal, so they cannot appear on the left side of an assignment.

boolean Literals

The only valid literals of `boolean` type are `true` and `false`. For example,

```
1. boolean isBig = true;
2. boolean isLittle = false;
```

char Literals

A `char` literal can be expressed by enclosing the desired character in single quotes, as shown here:

```
char c = 'w';
```

Of course, this technique only works if the desired character is available on the keyboard at hand. Another way to express a character literal is as a Unicode value specified using four hexadecimal digits, preceded by \u, with the entire expression in single quotes—for example,

```
char c1 = '\u4567';
```

Java supports a few escape sequences for denoting special characters:

- `'\n'` for new line
- `'\r'` for return
- `'\t'` for tab
- `'\b'` for backspace
- `'\f'` for formfeed
- `'\''` for single quote
- `'\"'` for double quote
- `'\\'` for backslash

Integral Literals

Integral literals may be expressed in decimal, octal, or hexadecimal. The default is decimal. To indicate octal, prefix the literal with 0 (zero). To indicate hexadecimal, prefix the literal with 0x or 0X; the hex digits may be upper- or lowercase. The value twenty-eight may thus be expressed six ways:

- 28
- 034
- 0x1c
- 0x1C
- 0X1c
- 0X1C

By default, an integral literal is a 32-bit value. To indicate a long (64-bit) literal, append the suffix L to the literal expression. (The suffix can be lowercase, but then it looks so much like a one that your readers are bound to be confused.)

Floating-Point Literals

A *floating-point* literal expresses a floating-point number. In order to be interpreted as a floating-point literal, a numerical expression must contain one of the following:

- A decimal point: 1.414
- The letter E or e, indicating scientific notation: 4.23E+21
- The suffix F or f, indicating a float literal: 1.828f
- The suffix D or d, indicating a double literal: 1234d

A floating-point literal with no F or D suffix defaults to double type.

When you assign the value of a literal to a variable, such as in short s = 9;, the compiler determines the size of the literal according to the target of the assignment. Therefore, the assignment just shown is OK. This contrasts with the handling of variable expressions such as short s1 = 9 + s;, which cause a compiler error because the size of the expression 9 + s is int, not short.

String Literals

A *string* literal is a sequence of characters enclosed in double quotes. For example,

```
String s = "Characters in strings are 16-bit Unicode.";
```

Java provides many advanced facilities for specifying non-literal string values, including a concatenation operator and some sophisticated constructors for the String class. These facilities are discussed in detail in Chapter 8, "The *java.lang* and *java.util* Packages."

Arrays

A Java *array* is an ordered collection of primitives, object references, or other arrays. Java arrays are homogeneous: Except as allowed by polymorphism, all elements of an array must be of the same type. That is, when you create an array you specify the element type, and the resulting array can contain only elements that are instances of that class or sub-classes of that class.

To create and use an array, you must follow three steps:

1. Declaration

2. Construction

3. Initialization

Declaration tells the compiler what the array's name is and what the type of its elements will be. For example,

```
1. int[] ints;
2. double[] dubs;
3. Dimension[] dims;
4. float[][] twoDee;
```

Lines 1 and 2 declare arrays of primitive types. Line 3 declares an array of object references (Dimension is a class in the java.awt package). Line 4 declares a two-dimensional array: that is, an array of arrays of floats.

The square brackets can come before or after the array variable name. This is also true, and perhaps most useful, in method declarations. A method that takes an array of doubles could be declared as `myMethod(double dubs[])` or as `myMethod(double[] dubs)`; a method that returns an array of doubles may be declared as either `double[] anotherMethod()` or as `double anotherMethod()[]`. In this last case, the first form is probably more readable.

Generally, placing the square brackets adjacent to the type, rather than following the variable or method, allows the type declaration part to be read as a single unit: "int array" or "float array", which might make more sense. However, C/C++ programmers will be more familiar with the form where the brackets are placed to the right of the variable or method declaration. Given the number of magazine articles that have been dedicated to ways to correctly interpret complex C/C++ declarations (perhaps you recall the "spiral rule"), it's probably not a bad thing that Java has modified the syntax for these declarations. Either way, you need to recognize both forms.

Notice that the declaration does not specify the size of an array. Size is specified at runtime, when the array is allocated via the new keyword. For example,

```
1. int[] ints;            // Declaration to the compiler
2. ints = new int[25];    // Run time construction
```

Since array size is not used until runtime, it is legal to specify size with a variable rather than a literal:

```
1. int size = 1152 * 900;
2. int[] raster;
3. raster = new int[size];
```

Declaration and construction may be performed in a single line:

```
1. int[] ints = new int[25];
```

When an array is constructed, its elements are automatically initialized to their default values. These defaults are the same as for object member variables. Numerical elements are initialized to zero; non-numerical elements are initialized to zero-like values, as shown in Table 1.4.

TABLE 1.4 Array Element Initialization Values

Element Type	Initial Value	Element Type	Initial Value
byte	0	short	0
int	0	long	0L
float	0.0f	double	0.0d
char	'\u0000'	boolean	false
object reference	null		

Arrays actually are objects, even to the extent that you can execute methods on them (mostly the methods of the Object class), although you cannot subclass the array class. Therefore this initialization is exactly the same as for other objects, and as a consequence you will see this table again in the next section.

If you want to initialize an array to values other than those shown in Table 1.4, you can combine declaration, construction, and initialization into a single step. The line of code below creates a custom-initialized array of five floats:

```
1. float[] diameters = {1.1f, 2.2f, 3.3f, 4.4f, 5.5f};
```

The array size is inferred from the number of elements within the curly braces.

Of course, an array can also be initialized by explicitly assigning a value to each element:

```
1. long[] squares;
2. squares = new long[6000];
3. for (int i = 0; i < 6000; i++) {
4.   squares[i] = i * i;
5. }
```

When the array is created at line 2, it is full of default values (0L); the defaults are immediately replaced. The code in the example works but can be improved. If the array size changes (in line 2), the loop counter will have to change (in line 3), and the program could be damaged if line 3 is not taken care of. The safest way to refer to the size of an array is to apply `.length` to the array name. Thus, our example becomes:

```
1. long[] squares;
2. squares = new long[6000];
3. for (int i = 0; i < squares.length; i++) {
4.   squares[i] = i * i;
5. }
```

Java's array indexes always start at 0.

Java allows you to create non-rectangular arrays. Because multi-dimensional arrays are simply arrays of arrays, each sub-array is a separate object, and there is no requirement that the dimension of each sub-array be the same. Of course, this type of array requires more care in handling, as you cannot simply iterate each sub-array using the same limits.

Class Fundamentals

Java is all about classes, and a review of the Certification Exam objectives will show that you need to be intimately familiar with them. Classes are discussed in detail in Chapter 6; for now there are a few fundamentals to examine.

The *main()* Method

The `main()` method is the normal entry point for Java applications. To create an application, you write a class definition that includes a `main()` method. To execute an application, type **java** at the command line, followed by the name of the class containing the `main()` method to be executed.

The signature for main() is

```
public static void main(String[] args)
```

The main() method is declared public by convention. However, it is a requirement that it be static so that it may be executed without the necessity of constructing an instance of the corresponding class.

The args array contains any arguments that the user might have entered on the command line. For example, consider the following command line:

```
% java Mapper France Belgium
```

With this command line, the args[] array has two elements: "France" in args[0], and "Belgium" in args[1]. Note that neither the class name ("Mapper") nor the command name ("java") appears in the array. Of course, the name args is purely arbitrary: Any legal identifier may be used, provided the array is a single-dimensional array of String objects.

Variables and Initialization

Java supports variables of two different lifetimes:

- A *member variable* of a class is created when an instance is created, and is destroyed when the object is destroyed. Subject to accessibility rules and the need for a reference to the object, member variables are accessible as long as the enclosing object exists.

- An *automatic variable* of a method (also known as a *method local*) is created on entry to the method, exists only during execution of the method, and therefore is only accessible during the execution of that method. (You'll see an exception to this when you look at inner classes, but don't worry about that for now.)

All member variables that are not explicitly assigned a value upon declaration are automatically assigned an initial value. The initialization value for member variables depends on the member variable's type. Values are listed in Table 1.5.

TABLE 1.5 Initialization Values for Member Variables

Element Type	Initial Value	Element Type	Initial Value
byte	0	short	0

TABLE 1.5   Initialization Values for Member Variables *(continued)*

Element Type	Initial Value	Element Type	Initial Value
int	0	long	0L
float	0.0f	double	0.0d
char	'\u0000'	boolean	false
object reference	null		

The values in Table 1.5 are the same as those in Table 1.4; member variable initialization values are the same as array element initialization values.

A member value may be initialized in its own declaration line:

```
1. class HasVariables {
2.    int x = 20;
3.    static int y = 30;
```

When this technique is used, non-static instance variables are initialized just before the class constructor is executed; here *x* would be set to 20 just before invocation of any HasVariables constructor. Static variables are initialized at class load time; here *y* would be set to 30 when the HasVariables class is loaded.

Automatic variables (also known as *local variables*) are not initialized by the system; every automatic variable must be explicitly initialized before being used. For example, this method will not compile:

```
1. public int wrong() {
2.    int i;
3.    return i+5;
4. }
```

The compiler error at line 3 is, "Variable i may not have been initialized." This error often appears when initialization of an automatic variable occurs at a lower level of curly braces than the use of that variable. For example, the method below returns the fourth root of a positive number:

```
1. public double fourthRoot(double d) {
2.    double result;
3.       if (d >= 0) {
```

```
4.          result = Math.sqrt(Math.sqrt(d));
5.      }
6.      return result;
7. }
```

Here the result is initialized on line 4, but the initialization takes place within the curly braces of lines 3 and 5. The compiler will flag line 6, complaining that "Variable `result` may not have been initialized." A common solution is to initialize `result` to some reasonable default as soon as it is declared:

```
1. public double fourthRoot(double d) {
2.   double result = 0.0;  // Initialize
3.     if (d >= 0) {
4.         result = Math.sqrt(Math.sqrt(d));
5.     }
6.     return result;
7. }
```

Now `result` is satisfactorily initialized. Line 2 demonstrates that an automatic variable may be initialized in its declaration line. Initialization on a separate line is also possible.

Argument Passing

When Java passes an argument into a method call, it is actually a *copy* of the argument that gets passed. Consider the following code fragment:

```
1. double radians = 1.2345;
2. System.out.println("Sine of " + radians +
3.                    " = " + Math.sin(radians));
```

The variable `radians` contains a pattern of bits that represents the number 1.2345. On line 2, a copy of this bit pattern is passed into the Java Virtual Machine's method-calling apparatus.

When an argument is passed into a method, changes to the argument value by the method do not affect the original data. Consider the following method:

```
1. public void bumper(int bumpMe) {
2.    bumpMe += 15;
3. }
```

Line 2 modifies a copy of the parameter passed by the caller. For example,

```
1. int xx = 12345;
2. bumper(xx);
3. System.out.println("Now xx is " + xx);
```

On line 2, the caller's *xx* variable is copied; the copy is passed into the bumper() method and incremented by 15. Since the original *xx* is untouched, line 3 will report that *xx* is still 12345.

This is still true when the argument to be passed is an object rather than a primitive. However, it is crucial for you to understand that the effect is very different. In order to understand the process, you have to understand the concept of the *object reference.*

Java programs do not deal directly with objects. When an object is constructed, the constructor returns a value—a bit pattern—that uniquely identifies the object. This value is known as a reference to the object. For example, consider the following code:

```
1. Button btn;
2. btn = new Button("Ok");
```

In line 2, the Button constructor returns a reference to the just-constructed button—not the actual button object or a copy of the button object. This reference is stored in the variable *btn*. In some implementations of the JVM, a reference is simply the address of the object; however, the JVM specification gives wide latitude as to how references may be implemented. You can think of a reference as simply a pattern of bits that uniquely identifies an individual object.

In most JVMs, the reference value is actually the address of an address. This second address refers to the real data. This approach, called double indirection, allows the garbage collector to relocate objects to reduce memory fragmentation.

When Java code appears to store objects in variables or pass objects into method calls, it is the object references that get stored or passed.

Consider this code fragment:

```
1. Button btn;
2. btn = new Button("Pink");
3. replacer(btn);
4. System.out.println(btn.getLabel());
5.
6. public void replacer(Button replaceMe) {
7.    replaceMe = new Button("Blue");
8. }
```

Line 2 constructs a button and stores a reference to that button in btn. In line 3, a copy of the reference is passed into the replacer() method. Before execution of line 7, the value in replaceMe is a reference to the Pink button. Then line 7 constructs a second button and stores a reference to the second button in replaceMe, thus overwriting the reference to the Pink button. However, the caller's copy of the reference is not affected, so on line 4 the call to btn.getLabel() calls the original button; the string printed out is "Pink".

You have seen that called methods cannot affect the original value of their arguments, that is, the values stored by the caller. However, when the called method operates on an object via the reference value that is passed to it, there are important consequences. If the method modifies the object via the reference, as distinguished from modifying the method argument—the reference—then the changes will be visible to the caller. For example,

```
1. Button btn;
2. btn = new Button("Pink");
3. changer(btn);
4. System.out.println(btn.getLabel());
5.
6. public void changer(Button changeMe) {
7.    changeMe.setLabel("Blue"));
```

8. }

In this example, the variable replaceMe is a copy of the reference *btn*, just as before. However, this time the code uses the copy of the reference to change the actual, original, object rather than trying to change the reference.

Since the caller's object is changed rather than the callee's reference, the change is visible and the value printed out by line 4 is "Blue."

Arrays are objects, meaning that programs deal with references to arrays, not with arrays themselves. What gets passed into a method is a copy of a reference to an array. It is therefore possible for a called method to modify the contents of a caller's array.

How to Create a Reference to a Primitive

This is a useful technique if you need to create the effect of passing primitive values by reference. Simply pass an array of one primitive element over the method call, and the called method can now change the value seen by the caller. Like this:

```
 1. public class PrimitiveReference {
 2.   public static void main(String args[]) {
 3.     int [] myValue = { 1 };
 4.     modifyIt(myValue);
 5.     System.out.println("myValue contains " +
 6.                         myValue[0]);
 7.   }
 8.   public static void modifyIt(int [] value) {
 9.     value[0]++;
10.   }
11.}
```

Garbage Collection

Most modern languages permit you to allocate data storage during a program run. In Java, this is done directly when you create an object with the new operation and indirectly when you call a method that has local variables or arguments. Method locals and arguments are allocated space on the stack and are discarded when the method exits, but objects are allocated space on the heap and have a longer lifetime. It is important to recognize that objects are always allocated on the heap, since even if they are created in a method using code like this:

```
public void aMethod() {
    MyClass mc = new MyClass();
}
```

the local variable mc is a reference, allocated on the stack, while the object to which that variable refers, an instance of MyClass, is allocated on the heap.

This section is concerned with recovery of space allocated on the heap. The problem of storage allocation on the heap is that the increased lifetime raises the question of when the storage can be released. Some languages require that you, the programmer, explicitly release the storage when you have finished with it. This approach has proven seriously error-prone, since you might easily release the storage too soon (causing corrupted data if any other reference to the data is still in use) or forget to release it altogether (causing a memory shortage). Java's garbage collection solves the first of these problems and greatly simplifies the second.

In Java, you never explicitly free memory that you have allocated; instead, Java provides automatic garbage collection. The runtime system keeps track of the memory that is allocated and is able to determine whether that memory is still useable. This work is usually done in the background by a low-priority thread that is referred to as the *garbage collector*. When the garbage collector finds memory that is no longer accessible from any live thread, it takes steps to release it back into the heap for re-use.

Garbage collection can be done in a number of different ways; each has advantages and disadvantages, depending upon the type of program that is running. A real-time control system, for example, needs to know that nothing will prevent it from responding quickly to interrupts; this requires a garbage collector that can work in small chunks or that can be interrupted easily. On the other hand, a memory-intensive program might work better with a garbage collector that stops the program from time to time but recovers memory more urgently as a result. At present, garbage collection is hardwired into the Java runtime system; most garbage collection algorithms use an approach that gives a reasonable compromise between speed of memory recovery and responsiveness. In the future, you will probably be able to plug in different garbage-collection algorithms or buy different JVMs with appropriate collection algorithms, according to your particular needs.

This all leaves one crucial question unanswered: When is storage recovered? The best you can answer is that storage is not recovered unless it is definitely no longer in use. That's it. Even though you are not using an object any longer, you cannot say if it will be collected in 1 millisecond, in 100 milliseconds—or even if it will be collected at all. There are methods, System.gc() and Runtime.gc(), that look as if they "run the garbage collector." Even these cannot be relied upon in general, since some other thread might prevent the garbage collection thread from running. In fact, the documentation for the gc() methods states:

> "Calling this method *suggests* that the Java Virtual Machine expends effort toward recycling unused objects." (author's italics)

How to Cause Leaks in a Garbage Collection System

There is an important consequence of the nature of automatic garbage collection: You can still get memory leaks. If you allow live, accessible references to unneeded objects to persist in your programs, then those objects cannot be garbage collected. Therefore, it may be a good idea to explicitly assign null into a variable when you have finished with it. This is particularly noticeable if you are implementing a collection of some kind. In this example, assume the array "storage" is being used to maintain the storage of a stack. This pop() method is inappropriate:

```
1. public Object pop() {
2.    return storage[index--];
3. }
```

If the caller of this pop() method abandons the popped value, it will not be eligible for garbage collection until the array element containing a reference to it is overwritten. This might take a long time. You can speed up the process like this:

```
1. public Object pop() {
2.    Object returnValue = storage[index];
3.    storage[index--] = null;
4.    return returnValue;
5. }
```

Chapter Summary

This chapter has covered quite a bit of ground, and a large variety of topics. The important points are:

- A source file's elements must appear in this order:

    1. Package declaration

    2. Import statements

    3. Class definitions

- There should be, at most, one public class definition per source file; the filename must match the name of the public class.

- An identifier must begin with a letter, a dollar sign, or an underscore; subsequent characters may be letters, dollar signs, underscores, or digits.

- Java has four signed integral primitive data types. These are `byte`, `short`, `int`, and `long`; all four types display the behavior of two's-complement representation.

- The two floating-point primitive data types are `float` and `double`.

- The `char` type is unsigned and represents a Unicode character.

- The `boolean` type may only take on the values `true` and `false`.

- Arrays must be (in order):

    1. Declared

    2. Constructed

    3. Initialized

- Default initialization is applied to both member variables and array elements, but not automatic variables. The default values are zero for numerical types, the null value for object references, the null character for `char`, and false for `boolean`.

- The `.length` member of an array gives the number of elements in the array.

- A class with a `main()` method can be invoked from the command line as a Java application. The signature for `main()` is `public static void main(String[] args)`. The `args[]` array contains all command-line arguments that appeared after the name of the application class.

- Method arguments are copies, not originals. For arguments of primitive data type, this means that modifications to an argument within a method are not visible to the caller of the method. For arguments of object type (including arrays), modifications to an argument value within a method are still not visible to the caller of the method; however, modifications in the object or array to which the argument refers *do* appear to the caller.

- Java's garbage collection mechanism may only recover memory that is definitely unused.

- It is not possible to force garbage collection reliably.

- It is not possible to predict when a piece of unused memory will be collected, only to say when it becomes *eligible* for collection.

- Garbage collection does not prevent memory leaks, which can still occur if unused references are not cleared to `null` or destroyed.

Test Yourself

1. A signed data type has an equal number of non-zero positive and negative values available.

    A. True

    B. False

2. Choose the valid identifiers from those listed below.

    A. BigOlLongStringWithMeaninglessName

    B. $int

    C. bytes

    D. $1

    E. finalist

3. Which of the following signatures are valid for the main() method entry point of an application?

    A. public static void main()

    B. public static void main(String arg[])

    C. public void main(String [] arg)

    D. public static void main(String[] args)

    E. public static int main(String [] arg)

4. If all three top-level elements occur in a source file, they must appear in which order?

A. Imports, package declaration, classes.

B. Classes, imports, package declarations.

C. Package declaration must come first; order for imports and class definitions is not significant.

D. Package declaration, imports, classes.

E. Imports must come first; order for package declaration and class definitions is not significant.

5. Consider the following line of code:

```
int[] x = new int[25];
```

After execution, which statement or statements are true?

A. x[24] is 0.

B. x[24] is undefined.

C. x[25] is 0.

D. x[0] is null.

E. x.length is 25.

6. Consider the following application:

```
1. class Q6 {
2.    public static void main(String args[]) {
3.       Holder h = new Holder();
4.       h.held = 100;
5.       h.bump(h);
6.       System.out.println(h.held);
7.    }
8. }
9.
10. class Holder {
11.    public int held;
12.    public void bump(Holder theHolder) {
13.       theHolder.held++; }
14.    }
15. }
```

What value is printed out at line 6?

A. 0

B. 1

C. 100

D. 101

7. Consider the following application:

```
1. class Q7 {
2.   public static void main(String args[]) {
3.     double d = 12.3;
4.     Decrementer dec = new Decrementer();
5.     dec.decrement(d);
6.     System.out.println(d);
7.   }
8. }
9.
10. class Decrementer {
11.   public void decrement(double decMe) {
12.     decMe = decMe - 1.0;
13,   }
14. }
```

What value is printed out at line 6?

A. 0.0

B. −1.0

C. 12.3

D. 11.3

8. How can you force garbage collection of an object?

A. Garbage collection cannot be forced.

B. Call System.gc().

C. Call System.gc(), passing in a reference to the object to be garbage-collected.

D. Call Runtime.gc().

E. Set all references to the object to new values (null, for example).

9. What is the range of values that can be assigned to a variable of type `short`?

   A. It depends on the underlying hardware.

   B. 0 through $2^{16} - 1$

   C. 0 through $2^{32} - 1$

   D. -2^{15} through $2^{15} - 1$

   E. -2^{31} through $2^{31} - 1$

10. What is the range of values that can be assigned to a variable of type `byte`?

    A. It depends on the underlying hardware.

    B. 0 through $2^{8} - 1$

    C. 0 through $2^{16} - 1$

    D. -2^{7} through $2^{7} - 1$

    E. -2^{15} through $2^{15} - 1$

Chapter

2

Operators and Assignments

JAVA CERTIFICATION EXAM OBJECTIVES COVERED IN THIS CHAPTER:

✓ Determine the result of applying any operator, including assignment operators and *instanceof*, to operands of any type, class, scope, or accessibility, or any combination of these.

✓ Determine the result of applying the *boolean equals(Object)* method to objects of any combination of the classes *java.lang.String*, *java.lang.Boolean*, and *java.lang.Object*.

✓ In an expression involving the operators &, |, &&, ||, and variables of known values state which operands are evaluated and the value of the expression.

Java provides a fully featured set of operators, most of which are taken fairly directly from C and C++. However, Java's operators differ in some important aspects from their counterparts in these other languages, and you need to understand clearly how Java's operators behave. This chapter describes all the operators: Some are described briefly, while others receive significantly more attention. Operators that sometimes cause confusion are described in detail. You will also learn about the behavior of expressions under conditions of arithmetic overflow.

Java's operators are shown in Table 2.1. They are listed in precedence order, with the highest precedence at the top of the table. Each group has been given a name for reference purposes; that name is shown in the left column of the table. Arithmetic and comparison operators are each split into two further subgroupings because they have different levels of precedence; we'll discuss these groupings later.

TABLE 2.1 Operators in Java, in Descending Order of Precedence

Category	Operators
Unary	++ -- + - ! ~ ()
Arithmetic	* / %
	+ -
Shift	<< >> >>>
Comparison	< <= > >= instanceof
	== !=
Bitwise	& ^ |
Short-circuit	&& ||
Conditional	?:
Assignment	= "op="

The rest of this chapter examines each of these operators, but before we start, let's consider the general issue of evaluation order.

Evaluation Order

In Java, unlike many other languages, the apparent order of evaluation of operands in an expression is fixed. Specifically, the result of any statement will be as if all operands are evaluated left to right, even if the order of execution of the operations is something different, or if some optimization makes other changes to the reality. This is most noticeable in the case of assignments. Consider this code fragment:

```
1. int [] a = { 4, 4 };
2. int b = 1;
3. a[b] = b = 0;
```

In this case, it might be unclear which element of the array is modified: What is the value of *b* used to select the array element, 0 or 1? An evaluation from left to right requires that the leftmost expression, a[b], be evaluated first, so it is a reference to the element a[1]. Next, *b* is evaluated, which is simply a reference to the variable called *b*. The constant expression 0 is evaluated next, which clearly does not involve any work. Now that the operands have been evaluated, the operations take place. This is done in the order specified by precedence and associativity. For assignments, associativity is right-to-left, so the value 0 is first assigned to the variable called *b* and then the value 0 is assigned into the last element of the array *a*.

The following sections examine each of these operators in turn.

Although Table 2.1 shows precedence order, the degree of detail shown is higher than the Certification Exam requires. (This order is, itself, not actually complete). It is generally better style to keep expressions simple and to use redundant parentheses to make it clear how any particular expression should be evaluated. This approach reduces the chance that less experienced programmers will find it difficult trying to read or maintain your code. Bear in mind that the code generated by the compiler will be the same despite redundant parentheses.

The Unary Operators

$\mathbf{T}$he first group of operators in Table 2.1 consists of the *unary operators*. Most operators take two operands. When you multiply, for example, you work with two numbers. Unary operators, on the other hand, take only a single operand and work just on that. Java provides seven unary operators:

- The increment and decrement operators: ++   --
- The unary plus and minus operators: +   -
- The bitwise inversion operator: ~
- The boolean complement operator: !
- The cast: ( )

Strictly speaking, the cast is not an operator. However, we discuss it as if it were for simplicity, because it fits well with the rest of our discussion.

The Increment and Decrement Operators: ++ and --

These operators modify the value of an expression by adding or subtracting 1. So, for example, if an `int` variable x contains 10, then ++x results in 11. Similarly --x, again applied when x contains 10, gives a value of 9. Since, in this case, the expression --x itself describes storage (the variable x), the resulting value is stored in x.

The preceding examples show the operators positioned before the expression. They can, however, be placed after the expression instead. To understand how the position of these operators affects their operation, you must appreciate the difference between the value stored by these operators and the result value they give. Both x++ and ++x cause the same result in x. However, the apparent value of the expression itself is different. For example, you could say y = x++; then the value assigned to y is the original value of x. If you say y = ++x; then the value assigned to y is 1 more than the original value of x. In both cases, the value of x is incremented by 1.

Let us look more closely at how the position of the increment and decrement operators affects their behavior. If one of these operators is to the left of an expression, then the value of the expression is modified *before* it takes part in the rest of the calculation. This is called pre-increment or pre-decrement, according to which operator is used. Conversely, if the operator is positioned to the right of an expression, then the value that is used in the rest of the calculation is the *original* value of that expression, and the increment or decrement only occurs after the expression has been calculated.

Table 2.2 shows the values of x and y, before and after particular assignments, using these operators.

TABLE 2.2 Examples of Pre-Modify and Post-Modify with the Increment and Decrement Operators

Initial Value of x	Expression	Final Value of y	Final Value of x
5	y = x++	5	6
5	y = ++x	6	6
5	y = x--	5	4
5	y = --x	4	4

The Unary Plus and Minus Operators: + and –

The unary operators + and – are distinct from the more common binary + and – operators, which are usually just referred to as + and – (add and subtract). Both the programmer and the compiler are able to determine which meaning these symbols should have in a given context.

Unary + has no effect on the value of its operand, but the expression is promoted to at least int. Unary – negates an expression. So, you might make a block of assignments like this:

```
1. x = -3;
2. y = +3;
3. z = -(y + 6);
```

In such an example, the only reasons for using the unary + operator are to make it explicit that y is assigned a positive value and perhaps to keep the code aligned more pleasingly. At line 3, notice that these operators are not restricted to literal values but can be applied to expressions equally well, so the value of z is initialized to –9.

The Bitwise Inversion Operator: ~

The ~ operator performs *bitwise inversion* on integral types.

For each primitive type, Java uses a virtual machine representation that is platform-independent. This means that the bit pattern used to represent a particular value in a particular variable type is always the same. This feature makes bit-manipulation operators even more useful, since they do not introduce platform dependencies. The ~ operator works by converting all the 1 bits in a binary value to 0s and all the 0 bits to 1s.

For example, applying this operator to a byte containing 00001111 would result in the value 11110000. The same simple logic applies, no matter how many bits there are in the value being operated on. This operator is often used in conjunction with shift operators (<<, >>, and >>>) to perform bit manipulation, for example when driving I/O ports.

The Boolean Complement Operator: *!*

The ! operator inverts the value of a `boolean` expression. So !true gives false and !false gives true.

This operator is often used in the test part of an `if()` statement. The effect is to change the value of the affected expression. In this way, for example, the body of the `if()` and `else` parts can be swapped. Consider these two equivalent code fragments:

```
1. public Object myMethod(Object x) {
2.   if (x instanceof String) {
3.     // do nothing
4.   }
5.   else {
6.     x = x.toString();
7.   }
8.   return x;
9. }
```

and

```
1. public Object myMethod(Object x) {
2.   if (!(x instanceof String)) {
3.     x = x.toString();
```

```
4.   }
5.   return x;
6. }
```

In the first fragment, a test is made at line 2, but the conversion and assignment, at line 6, occurs only if the test failed. This is achieved by the somewhat cumbersome technique of using only the `else` part of an `if/else` construction. The second fragment uses the complement operator so that the overall test performed at line 2 is reversed; it may be read as, "If it is false that x is an instance of a string" or more likely, "If x is not a string." Because of this change to the test, the conversion can be performed at line 3 in the situation that the test has succeeded; no `else` part is required, and the resulting code is cleaner and shorter.

This is a simple example, but such usage is common, and this level of understanding will leave you well armed for the Certification Exam.

The Cast Operator: *(type)*

Casting is used for explicit conversion of the type of an expression. This is only possible for plausible target types. The compiler and the runtime system check for conformance with typing rules, which are described below.

Casts can be applied to change the type of primitive values, for example forcing a `double` value into an `int` variable like this:

```
int circum = (int)(Math.PI * diameter);
```

If the cast, which is represented by the `(int)` part, were not present, the compiler would reject the assignment. This is because a `double` value, such as is returned by the arithmetic here, cannot be represented accurately by an `int` variable. The cast is the programmer's way to say to the compiler, "I know you think this is risky, but trust me—I'm an engineer." Of course, if the result loses value or precision to the extent that the program does not work properly, then you are on your own.

Casts can also be applied to object references. This often happens when you use containers, such as the `Vector` object. If you put, for example, `String` objects into a `Vector`, then when you extract them, the return type of the `elementAt()` method is simply `Object`. To use the recovered value as a `String` reference, a cast is needed, like this:

```
1. Vector v = new Vector();
2. v.add ("Hello");
3. String s = (String)v.get(0);
```

The cast here occurs at line 3, in the form (`String`). Although the compiler allows this cast, checks occur at runtime to determine if the object extracted from the `Vector` really is a `String`. Chapter 4 covers casting, the rules governing which casts are legal and which are not, and the nature of the runtime checks that are performed on cast operations.

Now that we have considered the unary operators, which have the highest precedence, we will discuss the five arithmetic operators.

The Arithmetic Operators

Next highest in precedence, after the unary operators, are the *arithmetic operators*. This group includes, but is not limited to, the four most familiar operators, which perform addition, subtraction, multiplication, and division. Arithmetic operators are split into two further subgroupings, as shown in Table 2.1. In the first group are *, /, and %; in the second group, at lower precedence, are + and –. The following sections discuss these operators and also what happens when arithmetic goes wrong.

The Multiplication and Division Operators: * and /

The operators * and / perform multiplication and division on all primitive numeric types and `char`. Integer division can generate an `Arithmetic-Exception` from a division by zero.

You probably understand multiplication and division quite well from years of rote learning at school. In programming there are, of course, some limitations imposed by the representation of numbers in a computer. These limitations apply to all number formats, from `byte` to `double`, but are perhaps most noticeable in integer arithmetic.

If you multiply or divide two integers, the result will be calculated using integer arithmetic in either `int` or `long` representation. If the numbers are large enough, the result will be bigger than the maximum number that can be represented, and the final value will be meaningless. For example, `byte` values can represent a range of –128 to +127, so if two particular bytes have the values 64 and 4, then multiplying them should, arithmetically, give a value of 256 (100000000 in binary—note there are nine digits in that value). Actually, when you store the result in a `byte` variable you will get a value of 0, since only the low-order eight bits of the result can be represented.

On the other hand, when you divide with integer arithmetic, the result is forced into an integer and, typically, a lot of information that would have formed a fractional part of the answer is lost. For example, 7 / 4 should give 1.75, but integer arithmetic will result in a value of 1. You therefore have a choice in many expressions: Multiply first and then divide, which risks overflow, or divide first and then multiply, which almost definitely loses precision. Conventional wisdom says that you should multiply first and then divide, because this at least might work perfectly, whereas dividing first almost definitely loses precision. Consider this example:

```
1. int a = 12345, b = 234567, c, d;
2. long e, f;
3.
4. c = a * b / b; // this should equal a, that is, 12345
5. d = a / b * b; // this should also equal a
6. System.out.println("a is " + a +
7.    "\nb is " + b +
8.    "\nc is " + c +
9.    "\nd is " + d);
10.
11. e = (long)a * b / b;
12. f = (long)a / b * b;
13. System.out.println(
14.    "\ne is " + e +
15.    "\nf is " + f);
```

The output from this code is:

```
a is 12345
b is 234567
c is -5965
d is 0

e is 12345
f is 0
```

Do not worry about the exact numbers in this example. The important feature is that in the case where multiplication is performed first, the calculation overflows when performed with int values, resulting in a nonsense answer. However, the result is correct if the representation is wide enough—as when using the long variables. In both cases, dividing first has a catastrophic effect on the result, regardless of the width of the representation.

The Modulo Operator: %

Although multiplication and division are generally familiar operations, the *modulo operator* is perhaps less well known. The modulo operator gives a value which is related to the remainder of a division. It is generally applied to two integers, although it can be applied to floating-point numbers, too. So, in school, we learned that 7 divided by 4 gives 1, remainder 3. In Java, we say x = 7 % 4;, and expect that x will have the value 3.

The previous paragraph describes the essential behavior of the modulo operator, but additional concerns appear if you use negative or floating-point operands. In such cases, follow this procedure: reduce the *magnitude* of the left operand by the *magnitude* of the right one. Repeat this until the magnitude of the result is less than the magnitude of the right operand. This result is the result of the modulo operator. Figure 2.1 shows some examples of this process.

FIGURE 2.1 Calculating the result of the modulo operator for a variety of conditions

<u>17 % 5</u>
17 − 5 → 12
12 − 5 → 7
7 − 5 → 2
2 < 5 so 17 % 5 = <u>2</u>

<u>21 % 7</u>
21 − 7 = 14
14 − 7 = 7
7 − 7 = 0
0 < 7 so 21 % 7 = <u>0</u>

<u>7.6 % 2.9</u>
7.6 − 2.9 = 4.7
4.7 − 2.9 = 1.8
1.8 < 2.9 so 7.6 % 2.9 = <u>1.8</u>

<u>−5 % 2</u>
Here, to reduce absolute value by 2, we must <u>add</u>
−5 + 2 = −3
−3 + 2 = −1
Absolute value of −1 is 1 and 1 < 2
so −5 % 2 = <u>−1</u>

<u>−5 % −2</u>
Again, we must reduce absolute value of −5 by the absolute value of −2 which is 2
−5 − (−2) = −3
−3 − (−2) = −1
so again, −5 % −2 = <u>−1</u>

Note that the sign of the result is entirely determined by the sign of the left operand. When the modulo operator is applied to floating-point types, the effect is to perform an integral number of subtractions, leaving a floating-point result that might well have a fractional part.

A useful rule of thumb for dealing with modulo calculations that involve negative numbers is this: Simply drop any negative signs from either operand and calculate the result. Then, if the original left operand was negative, negate the result. The sign of the right operand is irrelevant.

The modulo operation involves division during execution. Because of this, it can throw an `ArithmeticException` if applied to integral types and the second operand is zero.

Although you might not have learned about the modulo operator in school, you will certainly recognize the + and – operators. Although basically familiar, the + operator has some capabilities beyond simple addition.

The Addition and Subtraction Operators: + and –

The operators + and – perform addition and subtraction. They apply to operands of any numeric type but, uniquely, + is also permitted where either operand is a `String` object. In that case, the other operand is used to create a `String` object, whatever its original type. Creating a `String` object in this way is always possible, but the resulting text might be somewhat cryptic and perhaps only useful for debugging.

The + Operator in Detail

Java does not allow the programmer to perform operator overloading, but the + operator is overloaded by the language. This is not surprising, because in most languages that support multiple arithmetic types, the arithmetic operators (+, –, *, /, and so forth) are overloaded to handle these different types. Java, however, further overloads the + operator to support clear and concise *concatenation*—that is, joining together—of `String` objects. The use of + with `String` arguments also performs conversions, and these can be succinct and expressive if you understand them. First we will consider the use of the + operator in its conventional role of numeric addition.

Overloading is the term given when the same name is used for more than one piece of code, and the code that is to be used is selected by the argument or operand types provided. For example the `println()` method can be given a `String` argument or an `int`. These two uses actually refer to entirely different methods; only the name is re-used. Similarly, the + symbol is used to indicate addition of `int` values, but the exact same symbol is also used to indicate the addition of `float` values. These two forms of addition require entirely different code to execute; again, the operand types are used to decide which code is to be run. Operator overloading describes the ability to use the same operator with different operand types. Some languages, but not Java, allow the programmer to use operator overloading to define multiple uses of operators for their own types. Overloading is described in detail in Chapter 6.

Where the + operator is applied to purely numeric operands, its meaning is simple and familiar. The operands are added together to produce a result. Of course, some promotions might take place, according to the normal rules, and the result might overflow. Generally, however, numeric addition behaves as you would expect.

If overflow or underflow occurs during numeric addition or subtraction, then meaning is lost but no exception occurs. A more detailed description of behavior in arithmetic error conditions appears in a later section, "Arithmetic Error Conditions." Most of the new understanding to be gained about the + operator relates to its role in concatenating text.

Where either of the operands of a + expression is a `String` object, the meaning of the operator is changed from numeric addition to concatenation of text. In order to achieve this, both operands must be handled as text. If both operands are in fact `String` objects, this is simple. If, however, one of the operands is not a `String` object, then the non-`String` operand is converted to a `String` object before the concatenation takes place.

How Operands Are Converted to String Objects

Although a review of the certification objectives will show that the Certification Exam does not require it, it is useful in practice to know a little about how + converts operands to `String` objects. For object types, conversion to a `String` object is performed simply by invoking the `toString()` method of that object. The `toString()` method is defined in `java.lang.Object`, which is the root of the class hierarchy, and therefore all objects have a `toString()` method. Sometimes, the effect of the `toString()` method is to produce rather cryptic text that is only suitable for debugging output, but it definitely exists and may legally be called.

Conversion of an operand of primitive type to a `String` is typically achieved by using, indirectly, the conversion utility methods in the wrapper classes. So, for example, an `int` value is converted by the static method `Integer.toString()`.

The `toString()` method in the `java.lang.Object` class produces a `String` that contains the name of the object's class and some identifying value—typically its reference value, separated by the at symbol (@). For example, this might look like `java.lang.Object@1cc6dd`. This behavior is inherited by subclasses unless they deliberately override it. It is a good idea to define a helpful `toString()` method in all your classes, even if you do not require it as part of the class behavior. Code the `toString()` method so that it represents the state of the object in a fashion that can assist in debugging; for example, output the names and values of the main instance variables.

To prepare for the Certification Exam questions, and to use the + operator effectively in your own programs, you should understand the following points.

For a + expression with two operands of primitive numeric type, the result:

- Is of a primitive numeric type.

- Is at least `int`, because of normal promotions.

- Is of a type at least as wide as the wider of the two operands.

- Has a value calculated by promoting the operands to the result type, then performing the addition using that type. This might result in overflow or loss of precision.

For a + expression with any operand that is not of primitive numeric type:

- At least one operand must be a `String` object or literal, otherwise the expression is illegal.

- Any remaining non-`String` operands are converted to `String`, and the result of the expression is the concatenation of all operands.

To convert an operand of some object type to a `String`, the conversion is performed by invoking the `toString()` method of that object.

To convert an operand of a primitive type to a `String`, the conversion is performed by a static method in a wrapper class, such as `Integer` `.toString()`.

NOTE If you want to control the formatting of the converted result, you should use the facilities in the `java.text` package.

Now that you understand arithmetic operators and the concatenation of text using the + operator, you should realize that sometimes arithmetic does not work as intended—it could result in an error of some kind. The next section discusses what happens under such error conditions.

Arithmetic Error Conditions

We expect arithmetic to produce "sensible" results that reflect the mathematical meaning of the expression being evaluated. However, since the computation is performed on a machine with specific limits on its ability to represent numbers, calculations can sometimes result in errors. You saw, in the section on the multiplication and division operators, that overflow can easily occur if the operands are too large. In overflow, and other exceptional conditions, the following rules apply:

- Integer division by zero, including modulo (%) operation, results in an `ArithmeticException`.

- No other arithmetic causes any exception. Instead, the operation proceeds to a result, even though that result might be arithmetically incorrect.

- Floating-point calculations represent out-of-range values using the IEEE 754 infinity, minus infinity, and Not a Number (NaN) values. Named constants representing these are declared in both the `Float` and `Double` classes.

- Integer calculations, other than division by zero, that cause overflow or similar error, simply leave the final, typically truncated, bit pattern in the result. This bit pattern is derived from the operation and the number representation and might even be of the wrong sign. Because the operations and number representations do not depend upon the platform, neither do the result values under error conditions.

These rules describe the effect of error conditions, but there is some additional significance associated with the NaN values. NaN values are used to indicate that a calculation has no result in ordinary arithmetic, such as some calculations involving infinity or the square root of a negative number.

Comparisons with Not a Number

Some floating-point calculations can return a NaN. This occurs, for example, as a result of calculating the square root of a negative number. Two NaN values are defined in the `java.lang` package (`Float.NaN` and `Double.NaN`) and are considered non-ordinal for comparisons. This means that for *any* value of x, including NaN itself, all of the following comparisons will return false:

```
x < Float.NaN
x <= Float.NaN
x == Float.NaN
x > Float.NaN
x >= Float.NaN
```

In fact, the test

```
Float.NaN != Float.NaN
```

and the equivalent with `Double.NaN` return true, as you might deduce from the item above indicating that x `== Float.NaN` gives false even if x contains `Float.NaN`.

The most appropriate way to test for a NaN result from a calculation is to use the `Float.isNaN(float)` or `Double.isNaN(double)` static methods provided in the `java.lang` package.

The next section discusses a concept often used for manipulating bit patterns read from I/O ports: the shift operators <<, >>, and >>>.

The Shift Operators: <<, >>, and >>>

Java provides three *shift operators*. Two of these, << and >>, are taken directly from C/C++, but the third, >>>, is new.

Shifting is common in control systems, where it can align bits that are read from, or to be written to, I/O ports. It can also provide efficient integer multiplication or division by powers of two. In Java, because the bit-level representation of all types is defined and platform-independent, you can use shifting with confidence.

Fundamentals of Shifting

Shifting is, on the face of it, a simple operation: It involves taking the binary representation of a number and moving the bit pattern left or right. However, the unsigned right-shift operator >>> is a common source of confusion, probably because it does not exist in C and C++.

The shift operators may be applied to arguments of integral types only. In fact, they should generally be applied only to operands of either int or long type. This is a consequence of the effects of promotion in expressions (see "Arithmetic Promotions of Operands" later in this chapter). Figure 2.2 illustrates the basic mechanism of shifting.

FIGURE 2.2 The basic mechanisms of shifting

Original data			192		
in binary		00000000	00000000	00000000	11000000
Shifted left 1 bit	0	00000000	00000000	00000001	1000000?
Shifted right 1 bit		?0000000	00000000	00000000	01100000	0
Shifted left 4 bits	0000	00000000	00000000	00001100	0000????
Original data			−192		
in binary		11111111	11111111	11111111	01000000
Shifted left 1 bit	1	11111111	11111111	11111110	1000000?
Shifted right 1 bit		?1111111	11111111	11111111	10100000	0

The diagram in Figure 2.2 shows the fundamental idea of shifting, which involves moving the bits that represent a number to positions either to the left or right of their starting points. This is similar to people standing in line at a store checkout. As one moves forward, the person behind takes their place and so on to the end of the line. This raises two questions:

- What happens to the bits that "fall off" the end? The type of the result will have the same number of bits as the original value, but the result of a shift looks as if it might have more bits than that original.

- What defines the value of the bits that are shifted in? These are the bits that are marked by question marks in Figure 2.2.

The first question has a simple answer. Bits that move off the end of a representation are discarded.

In some languages, mostly assembly languages, an additional operation exists, called a *rotate*, that uses these bits to define the value of the bits at the other end of the result. Java, like most high-level languages, does not provide a rotate operation.

Shifting Negative Numbers

The second question, regarding the value of the bits that are shifted in, requires more attention. In the case of the left-shift << and the unsigned right-shift >>> operators, the new bits are set to zero. However, in the case of the signed right-shift >> operator, the new bits take the value of the most significant bit before the shift. Figure 2.3 shows this. Notice that where a 1 bit is in the most significant position before the shift (indicating a negative number), 1 bits are introduced to fill the spaces introduced by shifting. Conversely, when a 0 bit is in the most significant position before the shift, 0 bits are introduced during the shift.

This might seem like an arbitrary and unduly complex rule governing the bits that are shifted in during a signed right-shift operation, but there is a good reason for the rule. If a binary number is shifted left one position (and provided that none of the bits that move off the ends of a left-shift operation are lost), the effect of the shift is to double the original number. Shifts by more than one bit effectively double and double again, so the result is as if the number had been multiplied by 2, 4, 8, 16, and so on.

FIGURE 2.3   Signed right shift of positive and negative numbers

			192	
Original data				
in binary	00000000	00000000	00000000	11000000
Shifted right 1 bit	00000000	00000000	00000000	01100000
Shifted right 7 bits	00000000	00000000	00000000	00000001

			−192	
Original data				
in binary	11111111	11111111	11111111	01000000
Shifted right 1 bit	11111111	11111111	11111111	10100000
Shifted right 7 bits	11111111	11111111	11111111	11111110

If shifting the bit pattern of a number left by one position doubles that number, then you might reasonably expect that shifting the pattern right, which apparently puts the bits back where they came from, would halve the number, returning it to its original value. If the right shift results in 0 bits being added at the most significant bit positions, then for positive numbers, this division does result. However, if the original number was negative, then the assumption is false.

Notice that with the negative number in two's-complement representation, the most significant bits are 1s. In order to preserve the significance of a right shift as a division by two when dealing with negative numbers, we must bring in bits set to 1, rather than 0. This is how the behavior of the arithmetic right shift is determined. If a number is positive, its most significant bit is zero and when shifting right, more 0 bits are brought in. However, if the number is negative, its most significant bit is 1, and more 1 bits must be brought in when the shift occurs. This is illustrated in the examples in Figure 2.4.

There is a feature of the arithmetic right shift that differs from simple division by two. If you divide −1 by 2, the result will be 0. However, the result of arithmetic shift right of −1 right is −1. You can think of this as the shift operation rounding down, while the division rounds toward 0.

We now have two right-shift operators: one that treats the left integer argument as a bit pattern with no special arithmetic significance and another that attempts to ensure that the arithmetic equivalence of shifting right with division by powers of two is maintained.

FIGURE 2.4   Shifting positive and negative numbers right

		192		
Original data in binary	00000000	00000000	00000000	11000000
Shifted right 1 bit = 96 = 192 / 2	00000000	00000000	00000000	01100000
Shifted right 4 bits = 12 = 192 / 16 = 192 / 2⁴	00000000	00000000	00000000	00001100

$$= 12$$
$$= 192 / 16$$
$$= 192 / 2^4$$

		−192		
Original data in binary	11111111	11111111	11111111	01000000
Shifted right 1 bit = −96 = −192 / 2	11111111	11111111	11111111	10100000
Shifted right 4 bits = −12 = −192 / 16 = −192 / 2⁴	11111111	11111111	11111111	11110100

NOTE   Why does Java need a special operator for unsigned shift right, when neither C nor C++ required this? The answer is simple: Both C and C++ provide for unsigned numeric types, but Java does not. If you shift an unsigned value right in either C or C++, you get the behavior associated with the >>> operator in Java. However, this does not work in Java simply because the numeric types (other than char) are signed.

Reduction of the Right Operand

The right argument of the shift operators is taken to be the number of bits by which the shift should move. However, for shifting to behave properly, this value should be smaller than the number of bits in the result. That is, if the shift is being done as an int type, then the right operand should be less than 32. If the shift is being done as long, then the right operand should be less than 64.

In fact, the shift operators do not reject values that exceed these limits. However, shifts of ints use only the low-order 5 bits, and shifts of longs use only the low-order 6 bits, of the right operand. Mathematically, this reduces the supplied value modulo the number of bits. So, if you attempt to shift an int value by 33 bits, you will actually shift by only one bit. This produces an anomalous result. You would expect that shifting a 32-bit number by 33 bits would produce zero as a result (or possibly –1 in the signed right-shift case). However, because of the reduction of the right operand, this is not the case.

Why Java Reduces the Right Operand of Shift Operators, or "The Sad Story of the Sleepy Processor"

The first reason for reducing the number of bits to shift modulo the number of bits in the left operand is that many CPUs implement the shift operations in this way. Why should CPUs do this?

Some years ago, there was a powerful and imaginatively designed CPU that provided both shift and rotate operations and could shift by any number of bits specified by any of its registers. Since the registers were wide, this was a very large number, and as each bit position shifted took a finite time to complete, the effect was that you could code an instruction that would take minutes to complete.

One of the intended target applications of this particular CPU was in control systems, and one of the most important features of real-time control systems is the worst-case time to respond to an external event, known as the *interrupt latency*. Unfortunately, since a single instruction on this CPU was indivisible—so that interrupts could not be serviced until it was complete—execution of a large shift instruction effectively crippled the CPU. The next version of that CPU changed the implementations of shift and rotate so that the number of bits by which to shift or rotate was treated as being limited to the size of the target data item. This restored a sensible interrupt latency. Since then, many other CPUs have adopted reduction of the right operand.

Arithmetic Promotion of Operands

Arithmetic promotion of operands takes place before any binary operator is applied so that all numeric operands are at least int type. This has an important consequence for the unsigned right-shift operator when applied to values that are narrower than int.

The diagram in Figure 2.5 shows the process by which a byte is shifted right. First the byte is promoted to an int, which is done treating the byte as a signed quantity. Next, the shift occurs, and zero bits are indeed propagated into the top bits of the result—but these bits are not part of the original byte. When the result is cast down to a byte again, the high-order bits of that byte appear to have been created by a signed shift right, rather than an unsigned one. This is why you should generally not use the logical right-shift operator with operands smaller than an int: It is unlikely to produce the result you expected.

FIGURE 2.5   Unsigned right shift of a byte

Calculation for −64 >>> 4.

Original data (−64 decimal)				11000000
Promote to int gives:	11111111	11111111	11111111	11000000
Shift right unsigned 4 bits gives:	00001111	11111111	11111111	11111100
Truncate to byte gives:				11111100
Expected result was:				00001100

The Comparison Operators

*C*omparison operators— <, <=, >, >=, ==, and != —return a boolean result; the relation as written is either true or it is false. They are commonly used to form conditions, such as in if() statements or in loop control. There are three types of comparison: *Ordinal* comparisons test the relative value of numeric operands. *Object-type* comparisons determine whether the runtime type of an object is of a particular type or a subclass of that particular type. *Equality* comparisons test whether two values are the same and may be applied to values of non-numeric types.

Ordinal Comparisons with <, <=, >, and >=

The ordinal comparison operators are

- Less than: <

- Less than or equal to: <=

- Greater than: >

- Greater than or equal to: >=

These are applicable to all numeric types and to char and produce a boolean result.

So, for example, given these declarations,

```
int p = 9;
int q = 65;
int r = -12;
float f = 9.0F;
char c = 'A';
```

the following tests all return true:

```
p < q
f < q
f <= c
c > r
c >= q
```

Notice that arithmetic promotions are applied when these operators are used. This is entirely according to the normal rules, which will be discussed in Chapter 4. For example, although it would be an error to attempt to assign, say, the float value 9.0F to the char variable c, it is perfectly in order to compare the two. To achieve the result, Java promotes the smaller type to the larger type, hence the char value 'A' (represented by the Unicode value 65) is promoted to a float 65.0F. The comparison is then performed on the resulting float values.

Although the ordinal comparisons operate satisfactorily on dissimilar numeric types, including char, they are not applicable to any non-numeric types. They cannot take boolean or any class-type operands.

The *instanceof* Operator

The instanceof operator tests the class of an object at runtime. The left argument can be any object reference expression, usually a variable or an array element, while the right operand must be a class, interface, or array type. You cannot use a java.lang.Class object reference or a String representing the name of the class as the right operand.

This code fragment shows an example of how instanceof may be used. Assume that a class hierarchy exists with Person as a base class and Parent as a subclass.

```
1. public class Classroom {
2.    private Hashtable inTheRoom = new Hashtable();
3.    public void enterRoom(Person p) {
4.       inTheRoom.put(p.getName(), p);
5.    }
6.    public Person getParent(String name) {
7.       Object p = inTheRoom.get(name);
8.       if (p instanceof Parent) {
9.          return (Parent)p;
10.      }
11.      else {
12.         return null;
13.      }
14.   }
15. }
```

The method getParent() at lines 6–14 checks to see if the Hashtable contains a parent with the specified name. This is done by first searching the Hashtable for an entry with the given name and then testing to see if the entry that is returned is actually a Parent or not. The instanceof operator returns true if the class of the left argument is the same as, or is some subclass of, the class specified by the right operand.

The right operand may equally well be an interface. In such a case, the test determines if the object at the left argument implements the specified interface.

You can also use the instanceof operator to test whether a reference refers to an array. Since arrays are themselves objects in Java, this is natural enough, but the test that is performed actually checks two things: First, it checks if the object is an array, and then it checks if the element type of that array is some subclass of the element type of the right argument. This is a logical extension of the behavior that is shown for simple types and reflects the idea that an array of, say, Button objects is an array of Component objects, because a Button is a Component. A test for an array type looks like this:

```
if (x instanceof Component[])
```

Note, however, that you cannot simply test for "any array of any element type," as the syntax. This line is not legal:

```
if (x instanceof [])
```

Neither is it sufficient to test for arrays of Object element type like this:

```
if (x instanceof Object [])
```

since the array might be of a primitive base type, in which case the test will fail.

Although it is not required by the Certification Exam, you might find it useful to know that you can determine if an object is in fact an array, without regard to the base type. You can do this using the isArray() method of the Class class. For example, this test returns true if the variable myObject refers to an array: myObject.getClass().isArray().

If the left argument of the instanceof operator is a null value, the instanceof test simply returns false; it does not cause an exception.

The Equality Comparison Operators: == and !=

The operators == and != test for equality and inequality, respectively, returning a boolean value. For primitive types, the concept of equality is quite straightforward and is subject to promotion rules so that, for example, a float value of 10.0 is considered equal to a byte value of 10. For variables of object type, the "value" is taken as the reference to the object—typically, the memory address. You should not use these operators to compare the contents of objects, such as strings, because they will return true if two references refer to the same object, rather than if the two objects have an equivalent meaning.

To achieve a content or semantic comparison, for example, so that two different String objects containing the text "Hello" are considered equal, you must use the equals() method rather than the == or != operators.

To operate appropriately, the equals() method must have been defined for the class of the objects you are comparing. To determine whether it has, check the documentation supplied with the JDK or, for third-party classes, produced by javadoc. This should report that an equals() method is defined for the class and overrides equals() in some superclass. If this is not indicated, then you shou ld assume that the equals() method will not produce a useful content comparison. You also need to know that equals() is defined as accepting an Object argument, but the actual argument must be of the same type as the object upon which the method is invoked—that is, for x equals(y) the test y instanceof x must be true. If this is not the case, then equals() must return false.

The information in this warning is not required for the Certification Exam, but is generally of value when writing real programs. If you define an equals() method in your own classes, you should be careful to observe three rules, or else your classes might behave incorrectly in some specific circumstances. First, the argument to the equals() method is an Object; you must avoid the temptation to make the argument to equals() specific to the class you are defining. If you do this, you have overloaded the equals() method, not over-ridden it. This means that functionality in other parts of the Java APIs that depends upon the equals() method will fail. Most significantly, perhaps, lookup methods in containers, such as containsKey() and get() in the HashMap, will fail. The second rule is that the equals() method should be com-mutative: the result of x.equals(y) should always be the same as the result of y.equals(x). The final rule you must observe is that if you define an equals() method, you should also define a hashCode() method. This method should return the same value for objects that compare equal using the equals() method. Again, this behavior is needed to support the containers, and other classes. A minimal, but acceptable, behavior for the hashCode() method is simply to return 1. This removes any efficiency gains that hashing would give, forcing a HashMap to behave like a linked list when storing such objects, but at least the behavior is correct.

The Bitwise Operators: &, ^, and /

The *bitwise operators* &, ^, and | provide bitwise AND, eXclusive-OR (XOR), and OR operations, respectively. They are applicable to integral types. Collections of bits are sometimes used to save storage space where several `boolean` values are needed or to represent the states of a collection of binary inputs from physical devices.

The bitwise operations calculate each bit of their results by comparing the corresponding bits of the two operands on the basis of these three rules:

- For AND operations, 1 AND 1 produces 1. Any other combination produces 0.

- For XOR operations, 1 XOR 0 produces 1, as does 0 XOR 1. (All these operations are commutative.) Any other combination produces 0.

- For OR operations, 0 OR 0 produces 0. Any other combination produces 1.

The names AND, XOR, and OR are intended to be mnemonic for these operations. You get a 1 result from an AND operation if both the first operand *and* the second operand are 1. An XOR gives a 1 result if one *or* the other operand, but not both (this is the *eXclusivity*), is 1. In the OR operation, you get a 1 result if either the first operand *or* the second operand (*or* both) is 1. These rules are represented in Tables 2.3 through Table 2.5.

TABLE 2.3 The AND Operation

Op1	Op2	Op1 AND Op2
0	0	0
0	1	0
1	0	0
1	1	1

TABLE 2.4 The XOR Operation

Op1	Op2	Op1 XOR Op2
0	0	0
0	1	1
1	0	1
1	1	0

TABLE 2.5 The OR Operation

Op1	Op2	Op1 OR OP2
0	0	0
0	1	1
1	0	1
1	1	1

Compare the rows of each table with the corresponding rule for the operations listed in the bullets above. You will see that for the AND operation, the only situation that leads to a 1 bit as the result is when both operands are 1 bits. For XOR, a 1 bit results when one or other (but not both) of the operands is a 1 bit. Finally, for the OR operation, the result is a 1 bit, except when both operands are 0 bits. Now let's see how this works when applied to whole binary numbers, rather than just single bits. The approach can be applied to any size of integer, but we will look at bytes because they serve to illustrate the idea without putting so many digits on the page as to cause confusion. Consider this example:

```
          00110011
          11110000
    AND   --------
          00110000
```

Observe that each bit in the result above is calculated solely on the basis of the two bits appearing directly above it in the calculation. The next calculation looks at the least significant bit:

```
        0011001|1|
        1111000|0|
AND     -------|-|
        0011000|0|
```

This result bit is calculated as 1 and 0, which gives 0.

For the fourth bit from the left, see the following calculation:

```
        001|1|0011
        111|1|0000
AND     ---|-|----
        001|1|0000
```

This result bit is calculated as 1 AND 1, which gives 1. All the other bits in the result are calculated in the same fashion, using the two corresponding bits and the rules stated above.

Exclusive-OR operations are done by a comparable approach, using the appropriate rules for calculating the individual bits, as the following calculations show:

```
      |0|0110011              0011001|1|
      |1|1110000              1111000|0|
XOR   |-|-------      XOR     -------|-|
      |1|1000011              1100001|1|
```

All the highlighted bits are calculated as either 1 XOR 0 or as 0 XOR 1, producing 1 in either case.

```
        001|1|0011
        111|1|0000
XOR     ---|-|----
        110|0|0011
```

In the previous calculation, the result bits are 0 because both operand bits were 1.

```
        00110|0|11
        11110|0|00
XOR     -----|-|--
        11000|0|11
```

And above, the 0 operand bits also result in 0 result bits.

The OR operation again takes a similar approach, but with its own rules for calculating the result bits. Consider this example:

```
        00110011
        11110000
OR      --------
        11110011
```

Here, the two operand bits are 1 and 0, so the result is 1.

```
        00110011
        11110000
OR      --------
        11110011
```

While in the calculation above, both operand bits are 0, which is the condition that produces a 0 result bit for the OR operation.

Although programmers usually apply these operators to the bits in integer variables, it is also permitted to apply them to `boolean` operands.

Boolean Operations

The &, ^, and | operators behave in fundamentally the same way when applied to arguments of `boolean`, rather than integral, types. However, instead of calculating the result on a bit-by-bit basis, the `boolean` values are treated as single bits, with true corresponding to a 1 bit, and false to a 0 bit. The general rules discussed in the previous section may be modified like this when applied to `boolean` values:

- For AND operations, true AND true produces true. Any other combination produces false.

- For XOR operations, true XOR false produces true, false XOR true produces true. Other combinations produce false.

- For OR operations, false OR false produces false. Any other combination produces true.

These rules are represented in Tables 2.6 through Table 2.8.

TABLE 2.6   The AND Operation on Boolean Values

Op1	Op2	Op1 AND OP2
false	false	false

TABLE 2.6   The AND Operation on Boolean Values *(continued)*

Op1	Op2	Op1 AND OP2
false	true	false
true	false	false
true	true	true

TABLE 2.7   The XOR Operation on Boolean Values

Op1	Op2	Op1 XOR OP2
false	false	false
false	true	true
true	false	true
true	true	false

TABLE 2.8   The OR Operation on Boolean Values

Op1	Op2	Op1 OR OP2
false	false	false
false	true	true
true	false	true
true	true	true

Again, compare these tables with the rules stated in the bulleted list. Also compare them with Tables 2.3 through 2.5, which describe the same operations on bits. You will see that 1 bits are replaced by true, while 0 bits are replaced by false.

As with all operations, the two operands must be of compatible types. So, if either operand is of boolean type, both must be. Java does not permit you to cast any type to boolean; instead you must use comparisons or methods that return boolean values.

The next section covers the short-circuit logical operators. These operators perform logical AND and OR operations, but are slightly different in implementation from the operators just discussed.

The Short-Circuit Logical Operators

The short-circuit logical operators **&&** and **||** provide logical AND and OR operations on **boolean** types. Note that there is no XOR operation provided. Superficially, these are similar to the **&** and **|** operators with the limitation of only being applicable to **boolean** values and not integral types. However, the **&&** and **||** operations have a valuable additional feature: the ability to "short circuit" a calculation if the result is definitely known. This feature makes these operators central to a popular null-reference-handling idiom in Java programming. They can also improve efficiency.

The main difference between the **&** and **&&** and between the **|** and **||** operators is that the right operand might not be evaluated in the latter cases. We will look at how this happens in the rest of this section. This behavior is based on two mathematical rules that define conditions under which the result of a **boolean** AND or OR operation is entirely determined by one operand without regard for the value of the other:

- For an AND operation, if one operand is false, the result is false, without regard to the other operand.

- For an OR operation, if one operand is true, the result is true, without regard to the other operand.

To put it another way, for any **boolean** value X:

- false AND X = false

- true OR X = true

Given these rules, if the left operand of a `boolean` AND operation is false, then the result is definitely false, whatever the right operand. It is therefore unnecessary to evaluate the right operand. Similarly, if the left operand of a `boolean` OR operation is true, the result is definitely true and the right operand need not be evaluated.

Consider a fragment of code intended to print out a `String` if that `String` exists and is longer than 20 characters:

```
1. if (s != null) {
2.   if (s.length() > 20) {
3.     System.out.println(s);
4.   }
5. }
```

However, the same operation can be coded very succinctly like this:

```
1. if ((s != null) && (s.length() > 20)) {
2.   System.out.println(s);
3. }
```

If the `String` reference s is null, then calling the `s.length()` method would raise a `NullPointerException`. In both of these examples, however, the situation never arises. In the second example, avoiding execution of the `s.length()` method is a direct consequence of the short-circuit behavior of the `&&` operator. If the test (`s != null`) returns false (if s is in fact null), then the whole test expression is guaranteed to be false. Where the first operand is false, the `&&` operator does not evaluate the second operand, so in this case the sub-expression (`s.length() > 20`) is not evaluated.

Although these shortcuts do not affect the result of the operation, side effects might well be changed. If the evaluation of the right operand involves a side effect, then omitting the evaluation will change the overall meaning of the expression in some way. This behavior distinguishes these operators from the bitwise operators applied to `boolean` types. Consider these fragments:

```
//first example:
1. int val = (int)(2 * Math.random());
2. boolean test = (val == 0) || (++val == 2);
3. System.out.println("test = " +test+ "\nval = " + val);
//second example:
1. int val = (int)(2 * Math.random());
2. boolean test = (val == 0) | (++val == 2);
3. System.out.println("test = " +test+ "\nval = " + val);
```

The first example will sometimes print:

```
test = true
val = 0
```

and sometimes it will print:

```
test = true
val = 2
```

The second example will sometimes print:

```
test = true
val = 1
```

and sometimes it will print:

```
test = true
val = 2
```

The point is that in the case of the short circuit operator, if val starts out at zero, then the second part of the expression (++val...) is never executed, and *val* remains at 0. Alternatively, *val* starts at 1 and is incremented to 2. In the second case, the non-short circuit version, the increment always occurs, and *val* ends up as either 1 or 2, depending on the original value returned by the random() method. In all cases, the value of *test* is true, since either *val* starts out at 0, or it starts at 1 and the test (++val == 2) is true.

So, the essential points about the && and || operators are:

- They accept boolean operands.

- They only evaluate the right operand if the outcome is not certain based solely on the left operand. This is determined using the identities:

  - false AND X = false

  - true OR X = true

The next section discusses the ternary, or conditional, operator. Like the short-circuit logical operators, this operator may be less familiar than others, especially to programmers without a background in C or C++.

The Conditional Operator: *?:*

The *conditional* operator ?: (also known as the *ternary* operator, because it takes three operands) provides a way to code simple conditions into a single expression. The expression to the left of the ? is evaluated. If true, the result of the whole expression is the value of the sub-expression to the left of the colon; otherwise it is the value of the sub-expression to the right of the colon. The sub-expressions on either side of the colon must be assignment-compatible with the result type.

For example, if *a*, *b*, and *c* are `int` variables, and *x* is a `boolean`, then the statement `a = x ? b : c;` is directly equivalent to the textually longer version:

```
1. if (x) {
2.    a = b;
3. }
4. else {
5.    a = c;
6. }
```

Of course *x*, *a*, *b*, and *c* can all be complex expressions if you desire.

NOTE   Many people do not like the conditional operator, and in some companies its use is prohibited by the local style guide. This operator does keep source code more concise, but in many cases an optimizing compiler will generate equally compact and efficient code from the longer, and arguably more readable, if/else approach. One particularly effective way to abuse the conditional operator is to nest it, producing expressions of the form a = b ? c ? d : e ? f : g : h ? i : j ? k : l;. Whatever your feelings, or corporate mandate, you should at least be able to read this operator, as you will find it used by other programmers.

Here are the points you should review for handling conditional operators in an exam question, or to use it properly in a program. In an expression of the form `a = x ? b : c;`,

- The types of the expressions *b* and *c* should be compatible and are made identical through conversion.

- The type of the expression *x* should be `boolean`.
- The type of the expressions *b* and *c* should be assignment-compatible with the type of *a*.
- The value assigned to *a* will be *b* if *x* is true or will be *c* if *x* is false.

Now that we have discussed the conditional (ternary) operator, only one group of operators remains: the assignment operators.

The Assignment Operators

Assignment operators set the value of a variable or expression to a new value. Assignments are supported by a battery of operators. Simple assignment uses =. Operators such as += and *= provide compound "calculate and assign" functions. These compound operators take a general form *op*=, where *op* can be any of the binary non-boolean operators already discussed. In general, for any compatible expressions *x* and *y*, the expression x *op*= y is a shorthand for x = x *op* y. However, there are two differences you must know. First, be aware that side effects in the expression *x* are evaluated exactly once, not twice, as the expanded view might suggest. The second issue is that the assignment operators include an implicit cast. Consider this situation:

```
1. byte x = 2;
2. x += 3;
```

If this had been written using the longhand approach:

```
1. byte x = 2;
2. x = (byte)(x + 3);
```

The cast to byte would have been necessary since the result of an integer addition is at least an `int`. In the first case, using the assignment operator, this cast is implied. This is one of two situations where Java allows downcasting without explicit programmer intervention. (The other situation is in combined declaration and initialization.) Be sure to compare this with the general principles of assignment and casting laid out in Chapter 4, "Converting and Casting."

The statement x += 2; involves typing two fewer characters, but is otherwise no more effective than the longer version x = x + 2; and is neither more nor less readable. However, if *x* is a complex expression, such as target[temp.calculateOffset(1.9F) + depth++].item, it is definitely more readable to express incrementing this value by 2 using the += 2 form. This is because these operators define that the exact same thing will be read on the right side as is written to on the left side. So the maintainer does not have to struggle to decide whether the two complex expressions are actually the same, and the original programmer avoids some of the risk of mistyping a copy of the expression.

An Assignment Has Value

All the operators discussed to this point have produced a value as a result of the operation. The expression 1 + 2, for example, results in a value 3, which can then be used in some further way, perhaps assignment to a variable. The assignment operators in Java are considered to be operators because they have a resulting value. So, given three int variables *a*, *b*, and *c*, the statement a = b = c = 0; is entirely legal. It is executed from right to left, so that first 0 is assigned into the variable *c*. After it has been executed, the expression c = 0 takes the value that was assigned to the left side—that is, zero. Next, the assignment of *b* takes place, using the value of the expression to the right of the equals sign—again, zero. Similarly that expression takes the value that was assigned, so finally the variable *a* is also set to zero.

Although *execution order* is determined by precedence and associativity, *evaluation order* of the arguments is not. Be sure you understand the points made in the section "Evaluation Order" at the start of this chapter and, as a general rule, avoid writing expressions that are complex enough for these issues to matter. A sequence of simply constructed expressions will be much easier to read and is less likely to cause confusion or other errors than complex ones. Importantly, you are also likely to find that the compiler will make just as good a job of optimizing multiple simple expressions as it would a single, very complex one.

Chapter Summary

We have covered a lot of material in this chapter, so let's recap the key points.

The Unary Operators

The seven unary operators are ++, −−, +, −, !, ~, and (). Their key points are:

- The ++ and −− operators increment and decrement expressions. The position of the operator (either prefix or suffix) is significant.

- The + operator has no effect on an expression other than to make it clear that a literal constant is positive. The − operator negates an expression's value.

- The ! operator inverts the value of a `boolean` expression.

- The ~ operator inverts the bit pattern of an integral expression.

- The `(type)` operator is used to persuade the compiler to permit certain assignments that the programmer believes are appropriate, but that break the normal, rigorous rules of the language. Its use is subject to extensive checks at compile time and runtime.

The Arithmetic Operators

There are five arithmetic operators:

- Multiplication: *
- Division: /
- Modulo: %
- Addition and `String` concatenation: +
- Subtraction: −

The arithmetic operators can be applied to any numeric type. Also, the + operator performs text concatenation if either of its operands is a `String` object. Under the conditions where one operand in a + expression is a `String` object, the other is forced to be a `String` object, too. Conversions are performed as necessary. They might result in cryptic text, but they are definitely legal.

Under conditions of arithmetic overflow or similar errors, accuracy is generally lost silently. Only integer division by zero can throw an exception. Floating-point calculations can produce NaN—indicating Not a Number, that is, the expression has no meaning in normal arithmetic—or an infinity as their result under error conditions.

The Shift Operators

These are the key points about the shift operators:

- The <<, >>, and >>> operators perform bit shifts of the binary representation of the left operand.

- The operands should be an integral type, generally either `int` or `long`.

- The right operand is reduced `modulo` x, where x depends on the type of the result of the operation. That type is either `int` or `long`, smaller operands being subjected to promotion. If the left operand is assignment-compatible with `int`, then x is 32. If the left operand is a `long`, then x is 64.

- The << operator shifts left. Zero bits are introduced at the least significant bit position.

- The >> operator performs a signed, or arithmetic, right shift. The result has 0 bits at the most significant positions if the original left operand was positive, and has 1 bits at the most significant positions if the original left operand was negative. The result approximates dividing the left operand by two raised to the power of the right operand.

- The >>> operator performs an unsigned, or logical, right shift. The result has 0 bits at the most significant positions and might not represent a division of the original left operand.

The Bitwise Operators

There are three bitwise operators: &, ^, and |. They are usually named AND, eXclusive-OR (XOR), and OR, respectively. For these operators, the following points apply:

- In bitwise operations, each result bit is calculated on the basis of the two bits from the same, corresponding position in the operands.

- For the AND operation, a 1 bit results if the first operand bit and the second operand bit are both 1.

- For the XOR operation, a 1 bit results only if exactly one operand bit is 1.

- For the OR operation, a 1 bit results if either the first operand bit or the second operand bit is 1.

For boolean operations, the arguments and results are treated as single-bit values with true represented by 1 and false by 0.

The Assignment Operators

The key points about the assignment operators are:

- Simple assignment, using =, assigns the value of the right operand to the left operand.

- The value of an object is its reference, not its contents.

- The right operand must be a type that is assignment-compatible with the left operand. Assignment compatibility and conversions are discussed in detail in Chapter 4.

- The assignment operators all return a value, so that they can be used within larger expressions. The value returned is the value that was assigned to the left operand.

- The compound assignment operators, of the form *op*=, when applied in an expression like a *op*= b;, appear to behave like a = a *op* b;, except that the expression a and any of its side effects are evaluated only once.

Compound assignment operators exist for all binary, non-boolean operators: *=, /=, %=, +=, –=, <<=, >>=, >>>=, &=, ^=, and |=. We have now discussed all the operators that are provided by Java and all that remains are the test questions. Good luck!

Test Yourself

1. After execution of the code fragment below, what are the values of the variables *x*, *a*, and *b*?

    ```
    1. int x, a = 6, b = 7;
    2. x = a++ + b++;
    ```

    A. *x* = 15, *a* = 7, *b* = 8

    B. *x* = 15, *a* = 6, *b* = 7

    C. *x* = 13, *a* = 7, *b* = 8

    D. *x* = 13, *a* = 6, *b* = 7

2. Which of the following expressions are legal? (Choose one or more.)

    A. `int x = 6; x = !x;`

    B. `int x = 6; if (!(x > 3)) {}`

    C. `int x = 6; x = ~x;`

3. Which of the following expressions results in a positive value in *x*? (Choose one.)

    A. `int x = -1; x = x >>> 5;`

    B. `int x = -1; x = x >>> 32;`

    C. `byte x = -1; x = x >>> 5;`

    D. `int x = -1; x = x >> 5;`

4. Which of the following expressions are legal? (Choose one or more.)

    A. `String x = "Hello"; int y = 9; x += y;`

    B. `String x = "Hello"; int y = 9; if (x == y) {}`

    C. `String x = "Hello"; int y = 9; x = x + y;`

    D. `String x = "Hello"; int y = 9; y = y + x;`

    E. `String x = null;int y = (x != null) && (x.length() > 0) ? x.length() : 0;`

5. Which of the following code fragments would compile successfully and print "Equal" when run? (Choose one or more.)

A. `int x = 100; float y = 100.0F;if (x == y){`
`System.out.println("Equal");}`

B. `int x = 100; Integer y = new Integer(100);if (x == y)`
`{ System.out.println("Equal");}`

C. `Integer x = new Integer(100);Integer y = new`
`Integer(100);if (x == y) {`
`System.out.println("Equal");}`

D. `String x = new String("100");String y = new`
`String("100");if (x == y) {`
`System.out.println("Equal");}`

E. `String x = "100";String y = "100";if (x == y) {`
`System.out.println("Equal");}`

6. What results from running the following code?

```
1. public class Short {
2.    public static void main(String args[]) {
3.       StringBuffer s = new StringBuffer("Hello");
4.       if ((s.length() > 5) &&
5.          (s.append(" there").equals("False")))
6.          ; // do nothing
7.       System.out.println("value is " + s);
8.    }
9. }
```

A. The output: `value is Hello`

B. The output: `value is Hello there`

C. A compiler error at line 4 or 5

D. No output

E. A `NullPointerException`

7. What results from running the following code?

```
1. public class Xor {
2.   public static void main(String args[]) {
3.     byte b = 10; // 00001010 binary
4.     byte c = 15; // 00001111 binary
5.     b = (byte)(b ^ c);
6.     System.out.println("b contains " + b);
7.   }
8. }
```

A. The output: b contains 10

B. The output: b contains 5

C. The output: b contains 250

D. The output: b contains 245

8. What results from attempting to compile and run the following code?

```
1. public class Conditional {
2.   public static void main(String args[]) {
3.     int x = 4;
4.     System.out.println("value is " +
5.       ((x > 4) ? 99.99 : 9));
6.   }
7. }
```

A. The output: value is 99.99

B. The output: value is 9

C. The output: value is 9.0

D. A compiler error at line 5

9. What is the output of this code fragment?

```
1. int x = 3; int y = 10;
2. System.out.println(y % x);
```

A. 0

B. 1

C. 2

D. 3

10. What results from the following fragment of code?

```
1. int x = 1;
2. String [] names = { "Fred", "Jim", "Sheila" };
3. names[--x] += ".";
4. for (int i = 0; i < names.length; i++) {
5.    System.out.println(names[i]);
6. }
```

A. The output includes Fred. with a trailing period.

B. The output includes Jim. with a trailing period.

C. The output includes Sheila. with a trailing period.

D. None of the outputs show a trailing period.

E. An ArrayIndexOutOfBoundsException is thrown.

Chapter

3

Modifiers

JAVA CERTIFICATION EXAM OBJECTIVES COVERED IN THIS CHAPTER:

✓ Declare classes, inner classes, methods, instance variables, static variables, and automatic (method local) variables making appropriate use of all permitted modifiers (such as *public, final, static, abstract,* and so forth). State the significance of each of these modifiers both singly and in combination, and state the effect of package relationships on declared items qualified by these modifiers.

✓ Identify correctly constructed source files, package declarations, import statements, class declarations (of all forms including inner classes), interface declarations and implementations (for *java.lang.Runnable* or other interfaces described in the test), method declarations (including the main method that is used to start execution of a class), variable declarations and identifiers.

*M*odifiers are Java keywords that give the compiler information about the nature of code, data, or classes. Modifiers specify, for example, that a particular feature is static, final, or transient. (A *feature* is a class, a method, or a variable.) A group of modifiers, called *access modifiers*, dictate which classes are allowed to use a feature. Other modifiers can be used in combination to describe the attributes of a feature.

In this chapter you will learn about all of Java's modifiers as they apply to top-level classes. Inner classes are not discussed here, but are covered in Chapter 6.

Modifier Overview

The most common modifiers are the access modifiers: public, protected, and private. Access modifiers are covered in the next section. The remaining modifiers do not fall into any clear categorization. They are:

- final
- abstract
- static
- native
- transient
- synchronized
- volatile

Each of these modifiers is discussed in its own section.

The Access Modifiers

Access modifiers control which classes may use a feature. A class's features are:

- The class itself
- Its class variables
- Its methods and constructors

Note that, with rare exceptions, the only variables that may be controlled by access modifiers are class-level variables. The variables that you declare and use within a class's methods may not have access modifiers. This makes sense; a method variable can only be used within its method.

The access modifiers are:

- `public`

- `protected`

- `private`

The only access modifier permitted to non-inner classes is `public`; there is no such thing as a `protected` or `private` top-level class.

A feature may have at most one access modifier. If a feature has no access modifier, its access defaults to a mode that, unfortunately, has no standardized name. The default access mode is known variously as *friendly, package,* or *default*. In this book, we use the term *default*. Be aware that Sun is encouraging us to avoid the use of *friendly,* due to confusion with a somewhat similar concept in C++.

The following declarations are all legal (provided they appear in an appropriate context):

```
class Parser { ... }
public class EightDimensionalComplex { ... }
private int i;
Graphics offScreenGC;
protected double getChiSquared() { ... }
private class Horse { ... }
```

The following declarations are illegal:

```
public protected int x;
    // At most 1 access modifier
default Button getBtn() { ... }
    // "default" isn't a keyword
```

public

The most generous access modifier is `public`. A public class, variable, or method may be used in any Java program without restriction. An applet (a subclass of class `java.applet.Applet`) is declared as a public class so that it may be instantiated by browsers. An application declares its `main()` method to be public so that `main()` may be invoked from any Java runtime environment.

private

The least generous access modifier is `private`. Top-level (that is, not inner) classes may not be declared private. A private variable or method may only be used by an instance of the class that declares the variable or method. For an example of the private access modifier, consider the following code:

```
1.  class Complex {
2.    private double real, imaginary;
3.
4.    public Complex(double r, double i) {
5.      real = r; imaginary = i;
6.    }
7.    public Complex add(Complex c) {
8.      return new Complex(real + c.real,
9.      imaginary + c.imaginary);
10.   }
11. }
12.
13. class Client {
14.   void useThem() {
15.     Complex c1 = new Complex(1, 2);
16.     Complex c2 = new Complex(3, 4);
17.     Complex c3 = c1.add(c2);
18.     double d = c3.real;   // Illegal!
19.   }
20. }
```

On line 17, a call is made to `c1.add(c2)`. Object `c1` will execute the method, using object `c2` as a parameter. In line 8, `c1` accesses its own private variables as well as those of `c2`. There is nothing wrong with this. Declaring `real` and `imaginary` to be private means that they may only be accessed by instances of the `Complex` class, but they may be accessed by any instance of `Complex`. Thus `c1` may access its own `real` and `imaginary` variables, as well as the `real` and `imaginary` of any other instance of `Complex`. Access modifiers dictate which *classes*, not which *instances*, may access features.

Line 18 is illegal and will cause a compiler error. The error message says, "Variable real in class Complex not accessible from class Client." The private variable `real` may only be accessed by an instance of `Complex`.

Private data can be hidden from the very object that owns the data. If class `Complex` has a subclass called `SubComplex`, then every instance of `SubComplex` will inherit its own `real` and `imaginary` variables. Nevertheless, no instance of `SubComplex` can ever access those variables. Once again, the private features of `Complex` may only be accessed within the `Complex` class; an instance of a subclass is denied access. Thus, for example, the following code will not compile:

```
1. class Complex {
2.    private double real, imaginary;
3. }
4.
5.
6. class SubComplex extends Complex {
7.    SubComplex(double r, double i) {
8.      real = r;              // Trouble!
9.    }
10. }
```

In the constructor for class `SubComplex` (on line 8), the variable `real` is accessed. This line causes a compiler error, with a message that is very similar to the message of the previous example: "Undefined variable: real." The private nature of variable `real` prevents an instance of `SubComplex` from accessing one of its own variables!

Default

Default is the name of the access of classes, variables, and methods, if you don't specify an access modifier. A class's data and methods may be default, as well as the class itself. A class's default features are accessible to any class in the same package as the class in question.

Default is *not* a Java access keyword; it is simply a name that is given to the access level that results from not specifying an access modifier.

It would seem that default access is only of interest to people who are in the business of making packages. This is technically true, but actually everybody is always making packages, even if they aren't aware of it. The result of this behind-the-scenes package making is a degree of convenience for programmers that deserves investigation.

When you write an application that involves developing several different classes, you probably keep all your `.java` sources and all your `.class` class files in a single working directory. When you execute your code, you do so from that directory. The Java runtime environment considers that all class files in its current working directory constitute a package.

Imagine what happens when you develop several classes in this way and don't bother to provide access modifiers for your classes, data, or methods. These features are neither public, nor private, nor protected. They result in default access, which means they are accessible to any other classes in the package. Since Java considers that all the classes in the directory actually make up a package, all your classes get to access one anothers' features. This makes it easy to develop code quickly without worrying too much about access.

Now imagine what happens if you are deliberately developing your own package. A little extra work is required: You have to put a package statement in your source code, and you have to compile with the `-d` option. Any features of the package's classes that you do not explicitly mark with an access modifier will be accessible to all the members of the package, which is probably what you want. Fellow package members have a special relationship, and it stands to reason that they should get access not granted to classes outside the package. Classes outside the package may not access the default features, because the features are default, not public. Classes outside the package may subclass the classes in the package (you do something like this, for example, when you write an applet); however, even the subclasses may not access the default features, because the features are default, not protected or public. Figure 3.1 illustrates default access both within and outside a package.

FIGURE 3.1 Default access

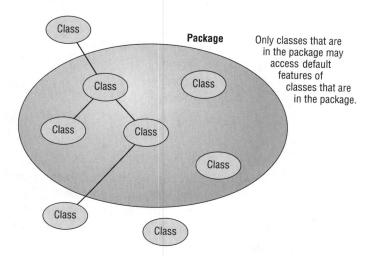

Package

Only classes that are in the package may access default features of classes that are in the package.

protected

The name *protected* is a bit misleading. From the sound of it, you might guess that protected access is extremely restrictive—perhaps the next closest thing to private access. In fact, protected features are even more accessible than default features.

Only variables and methods may be declared protected. A protected feature of a class is available to all classes in the same package, just like a default feature. Moreover, a protected feature of a class is available to all subclasses of the class that owns the protected feature. This access is provided even to subclasses that reside in a different package from the class that owns the protected feature.

As an example of the protected access modifier, consider the following code:

```
1. package sportinggoods;
2. class Ski {
3.    void applyWax() { . . . }
4. }
```

The `applyWax()` method has default access. Now consider the following subclass:

```
1. package sportinggoods;
2. class DownhillSki extends Ski {
3.   void tuneup() {
4.     applyWax();
5.     // other tuneup functionality here
6.   }
7. }
```

The subclass calls the inherited method `applyWax()`. This is not a problem as long as both the `Ski` and `DownhillSki` classes reside in the same package. However, if either class were to be moved to a different package, `DownhillSki` would no longer have access to the inherited `applyWax()` method, and compilation would fail. The problem would be fixed by making `applyWax()` protected on line 3:

```
1. package adifferentpackage;   // Class Ski now in
                                 // a different package
2. class Ski {
3.   protected void applyWax() { . . . }
4. }
```

Subclasses and Method Privacy

Java specifies that methods may not be overridden to be more private. For example, most applets provide an `init()` method, which overrides the do-nothing version inherited from the `java.applet.Applet` superclass. The inherited version is declared public, so declaring the subclass version to be private, protected, or default would result in a compiler error. The error message says, "Methods can't be overridden to be more private."

Figure 3.2 shows the legal access types for subclasses. A method with some particular access type may be overridden by a method with a different access type, provided there is a path in the figure from the original type to the new type.

FIGURE 3.2   Legal overridden method access

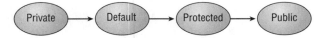

The rules for overriding can be summarized as follows:

- A private method may be overridden by a private, default, protected, or public method.
- A default method may be overridden by a default, protected, or public method.
- A protected method may be overridden by a protected or public method.
- A public method may only be overridden by a public method.

Figure 3.3 shows the illegal access types for subclasses. A method with some particular access type may not be shadowed by a method with a different access type, if there is a path in the figure from the original type to the new type.

FIGURE 3.3   Illegal overridden method access

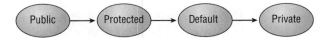

The illegal overriding combinations can be summarized as follows:

- A default method may not be overridden by a private method.
- A protected method may not be overridden by a default or private method.
- A public method may not be overridden by a protected, default, or private method.

Summary of Access Modes

To summarize, Java's access modes are:

- `public`: A public feature may be accessed by any class.
- `protected`: A protected feature may only be accessed by a subclass of the class that owns the feature or by a member of the same package as the class that owns the feature.

- default: A default feature may only be accessed by a class from the same package as the class that owns the feature.

- private: A private feature may only be accessed by the class that owns the feature.

Other Modifiers

The rest of this chapter covers Java's other modifiers: final, abstract, static, native, transient, synchronized, and volatile. (Transient and volatile are not mentioned in the Certification Exam objectives, so they are just touched on briefly in this chapter.)

Java does not care about order of appearance of modifiers. Declaring a class to be public final is no different from declaring it final public. Declaring a method to be protected static has the same effect as declaring it static protected.

Not every modifier can be applied to every kind of feature. Table 3.1, at the end of this chapter, summarizes which modifiers apply to which features.

final

The final modifier applies to classes, methods, and variables. The meaning of final varies from context to context, but the essential idea is the same: Final features may not be changed.

A final class may not be subclassed. For example, the code below will not compile, because the java.lang.Math class is final:

```
class SubMath extends java.lang.Math { }
```

The compiler error says, "Can't subclass final classes."

A final variable may not be modified once it has been assigned a value. In Java, final variables play the same role as consts in C++ and #define'd constants in C. For example, the java.lang.Math class has a final variable, of type double, called *PI*. Obviously, pi is not the sort of value that should be changed during the execution of a program.

If a final variable is a reference to an object, it is the reference that must stay the same, not the object. This is shown in the code below:

```
1.  class Walrus {
2.      int weight;
3.      Walrus(int w) { weight = w; }
4.  }
5.
6.  class Tester {
7.      final Walrus w1 = new Walrus(1500);
8.      void test() {
9.        w1 = new Walrus(1400);      // Illegal
10.       w1.weight = 1800;           // Legal
11.     }
12. }
```

Here the final variable is *w1*, declared on line 7. Since it is final, *w1* may not receive a new value; line 9 is illegal. However, the data inside *w1* is not final, and line 10 is perfectly legal. In other words,

- You may *not* change a final object reference variable.

- You *may* change data owned by an object that is referred to by a final object reference variable.

A final method may not be overridden. For example, the following code will not compile:

```
1. class Mammal {
2.     final void getAround() { }
3. }
4.
5. class Dolphin extends Mammal {
6.     void getAround() { }
7. }
```

Dolphins get around in a very different way from most mammals, so it makes sense to try to override the inherited version of **getAround()**. However, **getAround()** is final, so the only result is a compiler error at line 6 that says, "Final methods can't be overridden."

abstract

The abstract modifier can be applied to classes and methods. A class that is abstract may not be instantiated (that is, you may not call its constructor).

Abstract classes provide a way to defer implementation to subclasses. Consider the class hierarchy shown in Figure 3.4.

FIGURE 3.4 A class hierarchy with abstraction

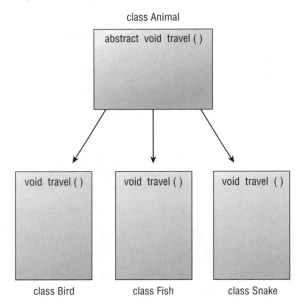

class Animal

abstract void travel ( )

void travel ( )   void travel ( )   void travel ( )

class Bird   class Fish   class Snake

The designer of class Animal has decided that every subclass should have a travel() method. Each subclass has its own unique way of traveling, so it is not possible to provide travel() in the superclass and have each subclass inherit the same parental version. Instead, the Animal superclass declares travel() to be abstract. The declaration looks like this:

```
abstract void travel();
```

At the end of the line is a semicolon where you would expect to find curly braces containing the body of the method. The method body—its implementation—is deferred to the subclasses. The superclass only provides the method name and signature. Any subclass of `Animal` must provide an implementation of `travel()` or declare itself to be abstract. In the latter case, implementation of `travel()` is deferred yet again, to a subclass of the subclass.

If a class contains one or more abstract methods, the compiler insists that the class must be declared abstract. This is a great convenience to people who will be using the class: They only need to look in one place (the class declaration) to find out if they are allowed to instantiate the class directly or if they have to build a subclass.

In fact, the compiler insists that a class must be declared abstract if any of the following conditions is true:

- The class has one or more abstract methods.

- The class inherits one or more abstract method (from an abstract parent) for which it does not provide implementations.

- The class declares that it implements an interface but does not provide implementations for every method of that interface.

These three conditions are very similar to one another. In each case, there is an incomplete class. Some part of the class's functionality is missing and must be provided by a subclass.

In a way, `abstract` is the opposite of `final`. A final class, for example, may not be subclassed; an abstract class *must* be subclassed.

static

The `static` modifier can be applied to variables, methods, and even a strange kind of code that is not part of a method. You can think of static features as belonging to a class, rather than being associated with an individual instance of the class.

The following example shows a simple class with a single static variable:

```
1. class Ecstatic{
2.    static int x = 0;
3.    Ecstatic() { x++; }
4. }
```

Variable *x* is static; this means that there is only one *x*, no matter how many instances of class `Ecstatic` might exist at any moment. There might be one

Ecstatic instance, or many, or even none; yet there is always precisely one x. The four bytes of memory occupied by x are allocated when class Ecstatic is loaded. The initialization to zero (line 2) also happens at class-load time. The static variable is incremented every time the constructor is called, so it is possible to know how many instances have been created.

There are two ways to reference a static variable:

- Via a reference to any instance of the class

- Via the class name

The first method works, but it can result in confusing code and is considered bad form. The following example shows why:

```
1. Ecstatic e1 = new Ecstatic();
2. Ecstatic e2 = new Ecstatic();
3. e1.x = 100;
4. e2.x = 200;
5. reallyImportantVariable = e1.x;
```

If you didn't know that x is static, you might think that reallyImportant-Variable gets set to 100 in line 5. In fact, it gets set to 200, because e1.x and e2.x refer to the same (static) variable.

A better way to refer to a static variable is via the class name. The following code is identical to the code above:

```
1. Ecstatic e1 = new Ecstatic();
2. Ecstatic e2 = new Ecstatic();
3. Ecstatic.x = 100;    // Why did I do this?
4. Ecstatic.x = 200;
5. reallyImportantVariable = Ecstatic.x;
```

Now it is clear that line 3 is useless, and the value of reallyImportant-Variable gets set to 200 in line 5. Referring to static features via the class name rather than an instance results in source code that more clearly describes what will happen at runtime.

Methods, as well as data, can be declared static. Static methods are not allowed to use the non-static features of their class (although they are free to access the class's static data and call its other static methods). Thus static methods are not concerned with individual instances of a class. They may be invoked before even a single instance of the class is constructed. Every Java

application is an example, because every application has a `main()` method
that is static:

```
1. class SomeClass {
2.    static int i = 48;
3.    int j = 1;
4.
5.    public static void main(String args[]) {
6.       i += 100;
7.       // j *= 5; Lucky for us this is commented out!
8.    }
9. }
```

When this application is started (that is, when somebody types `java
SomeClass` on a command line), no instance of class `SomeClass` exists. At
line 6, the i that gets incremented is static, so it exists even though there are
no instances. Line 7 would result in a compiler error if it were not commented out, because j is non-static.

Non-static (or *instance*) methods have an implicit variable named `this`,
which is a reference to the object executing the method. In non-static code,
you can refer to a variable or method without specifying which object's variable or method you mean. The compiler assumes you mean `this`. For example, consider the code below:

```
1. class Xyzzy {
2.    int w;
3.
4. void bumpW() {
5.       w++;
6.    }
7. }
```

On line 5, the programmer has not specified which object's w is to be incremented. The compiler assumes that line 5 is an abbreviation for `this.w++;`.

With static methods, there is no `this`. If you try to access an instance variable or call an instance method within a static method, you will get an error
message that says, "Undefined variable: `this`." The concept of "the instance
that is executing the current method" does not mean anything, because there

is no such instance. Like static variables, static methods are not associated with any individual instance of their class.

If a static method needs to access a non-static variable or call a non-static method, it must specify which instance of its class owns the variable or executes the method. This situation is familiar to anyone who has ever written an application with a GUI:

```
1.   import java.awt.*;
2.
3.   public class MyFrame extends Frame {
4.     MyFrame() {
5.       setSize(300, 300);
6.     }
7.
8.     public static void main(String args[]) {
9.       MyFrame theFrame = new MyFrame();
10.      theFrame.setVisible(true);
11.    }
12.  }
```

In line 9, the static method `main()` constructs an instance of class `MyFrame`. In the next line, that instance is told to execute the (non-static) method `setVisible()`. This technique bridges the gap from static to non-static, and it is frequently seen in applications.

A static method may not be overridden to be non-static. The code below, for example, will not compile:

```
1. class Cattle {
2.   static void foo() {}
3. }
4.
5. class Sheep extends Cattle {
6.   void foo() {}
7. }
```

The compiler flags line 6 with the message, "Static methods can't be overridden." If line 6 were changed to `static void foo() { }`, then compilation would succeed.

To summarize static methods:

- A static method may only access the static data of its class; it may not access non-static data.

- A static method may only call the static methods of its class; it may not call non-static methods.

- A static method has no `this`.

- A static method may not be overridden to be non-static.

Static Initializers

It is legal for a class to contain static code that does not exist within a method body. A class may have a block of initializer code that is simply surrounded by curly braces and labeled `static`. For example,

```
1.    public class StaticExample {
2.      static double d=1.23;
3.
4.      static {
5.        System.out.println("Static code: d=" + d++);
6.      }
7.
8.      public static void main(String args[]) {
9.        System.out.println("main: d = " + d++);
10.     }
11.   }
```

Something seems to be missing from line 4. You might expect to see a complete method declaration there: `static void printAndBump()`, for example, instead of just `static`. In fact, line 4 is perfectly valid; it is known as *static initializer* code. The code inside the curlies is executed exactly once, at the time the class is loaded. At class-load time, all static initialization (such as line 2) and all free-floating static code (such as lines 4–6) are executed in order of appearance within the class definition.

Free-floating initializer code should be used with caution, as it can easily be confusing and unclear. The compiler supports multiple initializer blocks within a class, but there is never a good reason for having more than one such block.

native

The native modifier can refer only to methods. Like the abstract keyword, native indicates that the body of a method is to be found elsewhere. In the case of abstract methods, the body is in a subclass; with native methods, the body lies entirely outside the Java Virtual Machine, in a library.

Native code is written in a non-Java language, typically C or C++, and compiled for a single target machine type. (Thus Java's platform independence is violated.) People who port Java to new platforms implement extensive native code to support GUI components, network communication, and a broad range of other platform-specific functionality. However, it is rare for application and applet programmers to need to write native code.

One technique, however, is of interest in light of the last section's discussion of static code. When a native method is invoked, the library that contains the native code ought to be loaded and available to the Java Virtual Machine; if it is not loaded, there will be a delay. The library is loaded by calling System.loadLibrary ("library_name") and, to avoid a delay, it is desirable to make this call as early as possible. Often programmers will use the technique shown in the code sample below, which assumes the library name is MyNativeLib:

```
1. class NativeExample {
2.    native void doSomethingLocal(int i);
3.
4.    static {
5.      System.loadLibrary("MyNativeLib");
6.    }
7. }
```

Notice the native declaration on line 2, which declares that the code that implements doSomethingLocal() resides in a local library. Lines 4–6 are static initializer code, so they are executed at the time that class NativeExample is loaded; this ensures that the library will be available by the time somebody needs it.

Callers of native methods do not have to know that the method is native. The call is made in exactly the same way as if it were non-native:

```
1. NativeExample natex;
2. natex = new NativeExample();
3. natex.doSomethingLocal(5);
```

Many common methods are native, including the `clone()` and `notify()` methods of the `Object` class.

transient

The `transient` modifier applies only to variables. A transient variable is not stored as part of its object's persistent state.

Many objects (specifically, those that implement the `Serializable` or `Externalizable` interfaces) can have their state serialized and written to some destination outside the Java Virtual Machine. This is done by passing the object to the `writeObject()` method of the `ObjectOutputStream` class. If the stream is chained to a `FileOutputStream`, then the object's state is written to a file. If the stream is chained to a socket's `OutputStream`, then the object's state is written to the network. In both cases, the object can be reconstituted by reading it from an `ObjectInputStream`.

There will be times when an object will contain extremely sensitive information. Consider the following class:

```
1. class WealthyCustomer
2. extends Customer implements Serializable {
3.    private float $wealth;
4.    private String accessCode;
5. }
```

Once an object is written to a destination outside the JVM, none of Java's elaborate security mechanisms is in effect. If an instance of this class were to be written to a file or to the Internet, somebody could snoop the access code. Line 4 should be marked with the `transient` keyword:

```
1. class WealthyCustomer
2. extends Customer implements Serializable {
3.    private float $wealth;
4.    private transient String accessCode;
5. }
```

Now the value of `accessCode` will not be written out during serialization.

synchronized

The synchronized modifier is used to control access to critical code in multi–threaded programs. Multithreading is an extensive topic in its own right and is covered in Chapter 7.

volatile

The last modifier is volatile. It is mentioned here only to make our list complete, as it is not mentioned in the exam objectives and is not yet in common use. Only variables may be volatile; declaring them so indicates that such variables might be modified asynchronously, so the compiler takes special precautions. Volatile variables are of interest in multiprocessor environments.

Modifiers and Features

Not all modifiers can be applied to all features. Top-level classes may not be protected. Methods may not be transient. Static is so general that you can apply it to free-floating blocks of code.

Table 3.1 shows all the possible combinations of features and modifiers. Note that classes here are strictly top-level (that is, not inner) classes. (Inner classes are covered in Chapter 6.)

TABLE 3.1   All Possible Combinations of Features and Modifiers

Modifier	Class	Variable	Method	Constructor	Free-Floating Block
public	yes	yes	yes	yes	no
protected	no	yes	yes	yes	no
(default)*	yes	yes	yes	yes	yes
private	no	yes	yes	yes	no
final	yes	yes	yes	no	no

TABLE 3.1   All Possible Combinations of Features and Modifiers *(continued)*

Modifier	Class	Variable	Method	Constructor	Free-Floating Block
abstract	yes	no	yes	no	no
static	no	yes	yes	no	yes
native	no	no	yes	no	no
transient	no	yes	no	no	no
volatile	no	yes	no	no	no
synchronized	no	no	yes	no	yes

* *default* is not a modifier; it is just the name of the access if no modifier is specified.

Chapter Summary

Java's access modifiers are:

- public
- protected
- private

If a feature does not have an access modifier, its access is "default." Java's other modifiers are:

- final
- abstract
- static
- native
- transient
- synchronized
- volatile

Test Yourself

1. Which of the following declarations are illegal? (Choose one or more.)

   A. `default String s;`

   B. `transient int i = 41;`

   C. `public final static native int w();`

   D. `abstract double d;`

   E. `abstract final double hyperbolicCosine();`

2. Which one of the following statements is true?

   A. An abstract class may not have any final methods.

   B. A final class may not have any abstract methods.

3. What is the *minimal* modification that will make this code compile correctly?

```
1. final class Aaa
2. {
3.     int xxx;
4.     void yyy() { xxx = 1; }
5. }
6.
7.
8. class Bbb extends Aaa
9. {
10.     final Aaa finalref = new Aaa();
11.
12.     final void yyy()
13.     {
14.         System.out.println("In method yyy()");
15.         finalref.xxx = 12345;
16.     }
17. }
```

A. On line 1, remove the `final` modifier.

B. On line 10, remove the `final` modifier.

C. Remove line 15.

D. On lines 1 and 10, remove the `final` modifier.

E. The code will compile as is. No modification is needed.

4. Which one of the following statements is true?

A. Transient methods may not be overridden.

B. Transient methods must be overridden.

C. Transient classes may not be serialized.

D. Transient variables must be static.

E. Transient variables are not serialized.

5. Which one statement is true about this application?

```
1. class StaticStuff
2. {
3.      static int x = 10;
4.
5.      static { x += 5; }
6.
7.      public static void main(String args[])
8.      {
9.           System.out.println("x = " + x);
10.     }
11.
12.     static {x /= 5; }
13. }
```

A. Lines 5 and 12 will not compile, because the method names and return types are missing.

B. Line 12 will not compile, because you can only have one static initializer.

C. The code compiles, and execution produces the output x = 10.

D. The code compiles, and execution produces the output x = 15.

E. The code compiles, and execution produces the output x = 3.

6. Which one statement is true about this code?

```
1. class HasStatic
2. {
3.     private static int x = 100;
4.
5.     public static void main(String args[])
6.     {
7.         HasStatic hs1 = new HasStatic();
8.         hs1.x++;
9.         HasStatic hs2 = new HasStatic();
10.        hs2.x++;
11.        hs1 = new HasStatic();
12.        hs1.x++;
13.        HasStatic.x++;
14.        System.out.println("x = " + x);
15.    }
16. }
```

A. Line 8 will not compile, because it is a static reference to a private variable.

B. Line 13 will not compile, because it is a static reference to a private variable.

C. The program compiles, and the output is x = 102.

D. The program compiles, and the output is x = 103.

E. The program compiles, and the output is x = 104.

7. Given the code shown, and making no other changes, which access modifiers (`public`, `protected`, or `private`) can legally be placed before aMethod() on line 3? If line 3 is left as it is, which keywords can legally be placed before aMethod() on line 8?

```
1. class SuperDuper
2. {
3.     void aMethod() { }
4. }
5.
6. class Sub extends SuperDuper
7. {
8.     void aMethod() { }
9. }
```

8. Which modifier or modifiers should be used to denote a variable that should not be written out as part of its class's persistent state? (Choose the shortest possible answer.)

A. `private`

B. `protected`

C. `private protected`

D. `transient`

E. `private transient`

The next two questions concern the following class definition:

```
1. package abcde;
2.
3. public class Bird {
4.    protected static int referenceCount = 0;
5.    public Bird() { referenceCount++; }
6.    protected void fly() { /* Flap wings, etc. */ }
7.    static int getRefCount() { return referenceCount; }
8. }
```

9. Which one statement is true about class `Bird` above and class `Parrot` below?

```
1. package abcde;
2.
3. class Parrot extends abcde.Bird {
4.    public void fly() {
5.       /* Parrot-specific flight code. */
6.    }
7.    public int getRefCount() {
8.       return referenceCount;
9.    }
10. }
```

A. Compilation of `Parrot.java` fails at line 4, because method `fly()` is protected in the superclass, and classes Bird and Parrot are in the same package.

B. Compilation of `Parrot.java` fails at line 4, because method `fly()` is protected in the superclass and public in the subclass, and methods may not be overridden to be more public.

C. Compilation of `Parrot.java` fails at line 7, because method `getRefCount()` is static in the superclass, and static methods may not be overridden to be non-static.

D. Compilation of `Parrot.java` succeeds, but a runtime exception is thrown if method `fly()` is ever called on an instance of class Parrot.

E. Compilation of `Parrot.java` succeeds, but a runtime exception is thrown if method `getRefCount()` is ever called on an instance of class `Parrot`.

10. Which one statement is true about class `Bird` above and class `Nightingale` below?

```
1. package singers;
2.
3. class Nightingale extends abcde.Bird {
4.    Nightingale() { referenceCount++; }
5.
6.    public static void main(String args[]) {
7.      System.out.print("Before: " + referenceCount);
8.      Nightingale florence = new Nightingale();
9.      System.out.println(" After: " + referenceCount);
10.     florence.fly();
11.   }
12. }
```

A. The program will compile and execute. The output will be
Before: 0   After: 2

B. The program will compile and execute. The output will be
Before: 0   After: 1

C. Compilation of `Nightingale` will fail at line 4, because static members cannot be overridden.

D. Compilation of `Nightingale` will fail at line 10, because method `fly()` is protected in the superclass.

E. Compilation of `Nightingale` will succeed, but an exception will be thrown at line 10, because method `fly()` is protected in the superclass.

Chapter

4

Converting and Casting

JAVA CERTIFICATION EXAM OBJECTIVE COVERED IN THIS CHAPTER:

✓ Determine the result of applying any operator, including assignment operators, *instanceof*, and casts, to operands of any type, class, scope, or accessibility, or any combination of these.

Every Java variable has a type. Primitive data types include `int`, `long`, and `double`. Object reference data types may be classes (such as `Vector` or `Graphics`) or interfaces (such as `LayoutManager` or `Runnable`). There can also be arrays of primitives, objects, or arrays.

This chapter discusses the ways that a data value can change its type. Values can change type either explicitly or implicitly; that is, either they change at your request or at the system's initiative. Java places a lot of importance on type, and successful Java programming requires that you be aware of type changes.

Explicit and Implicit Type Changes

You can explicitly change the type of a value by *casting*. To cast an expression to a new type, just prefix the expression with the new type name in parentheses. For example, the following line of code retrieves an element from a vector, casts that element to type `Button`, and assigns the result to a variable called `btn`:

```
Button btn = (Button) (myVector.elementAt(5));
```

Of course, the sixth element of the vector must be capable of being treated as a `Button`. There are compile-time rules and runtime rules that must be observed. This chapter will familiarize you with those rules.

There are situations in which the system implicitly changes the type of an expression without your explicitly performing a cast. For example, suppose you have a variable called `myColor` that refers to an instance of `Color`, and you want to store `myColor` in a vector. You would probably do the following:

```
myVector.add(myColor);
```

There is more to this code than meets the eye. The `add()` method of class `Vector` is declared with a parameter of type `Object`, not of type `Color`. As the argument is passed to the method, it undergoes an implicit type change. Such automatic, non-explicit type changing is known as *conversion*. Conversion, like casting, is governed by rules. Unlike the casting rules, all conversion rules are enforced at compile time.

The number of casting and conversion rules is rather large, due to the large number of cases to be considered. (For example, can you cast a `char` to a `double`? Can you convert an interface to a final class? Yes to both of these, as it happens.) The good news is that most of the rules accord with common sense, and most of the combinations can be generalized into rules of thumb. By the end of this chapter, you will know when you can explicitly cast, and when the system will implicitly convert on your behalf.

Primitives and Conversion

The two broad categories of Java data types are primitives and objects. *Primitive* data types are `ints`, `floats`, `booleans`, and so on. (There are eight primitive data types in all; see Chapter 1 for a complete explanation of Java's primitives.) *Object* data types (or more properly, *object reference* data types) are the hundreds of classes and interfaces provided with the JDK, plus the infinitude of classes and interfaces to be invented by Java programmers.

Both primitive values and object references can be converted and cast, so there are four general cases to consider:

- Conversion of primitives
- Casting of primitives
- Conversion of object references
- Casting of object references

The simplest topic is implicit conversion of primitives. All conversion of primitive data types takes place at compile time; this is because all the information needed to determine whether or not the conversion is legal is available at compile time.

There are three contexts or situations in which conversion of a primitive might occur:

- Assignment
- Method call
- Arithmetic promotion

The following sections deal with each of these contexts in turn.

Primitive Conversion: Assignment

Assignment conversion happens when you assign a value to a variable of a different type from the original value. For example:

```
1. int i;
2. double d;
```

```
3. i = 10;
4. d = i;  // Assign an int value to a double variable
```

Obviously, *d* cannot hold an integer value. At the moment that the fourth line of code is executed, the integer 10 that is stored in variable *i* gets converted to the double-precision value 10.0000000000000 (remaining zeros omitted for brevity).

The code above is perfectly legal. Some assignments, on the other hand, are illegal. For example, the following code will not compile:

```
1. double d;
2. short s;
3. d = 1.2345;
4. s = d;   // Assign a double value to a short variable
```

This code will not compile. (The error message says "Incompatible type for =.") The compiler recognizes that trying to cram a double value into a short variable is like trying to pour a quart of coffee into an eight-ounce teacup, as shown in Figure 4.1. It can be done (that is, the larger-to-smaller value assignment can be done; the coffee thing is impossible), but you must use an explicit cast, which will be explained in the following section.

FIGURE 4.1   Illegal conversion of a quart to a cup, with loss of data

The general rules for primitive assignment conversion can be stated as follows:

- A boolean may not be converted to any other type.

- A non-boolean may be converted to another non-boolean type, provided the conversion is a *widening conversion*.

- A non-boolean may not be converted to another non-boolean type, if the conversion would be a *narrowing conversion*.

Widening conversions change a value to a type that accommodates a wider range of values than the original type can accommodate. In most cases, the new type has more bits than the original and can be visualized as being "wider" than the original, as shown in Figure 4.2.

FIGURE 4.2 Widening conversion of a positive value

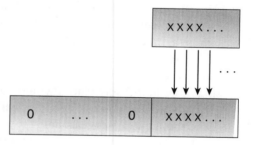

Widening conversions do not lose information about the magnitude of a value. In the first example in this section, an int value was assigned to a double variable. This was legal, because doubles are, so to speak, "wider" than ints, so there is room in a double to accommodate the information in an int. Java's widening conversions are:

- From a byte to a short, an int, a long, a float, or a double

- From a short to an int, a long, a float, or a double

- From a char to an int, a long, a float, or a double

- From an int to a long, a float, or a double

- From a long to a float or a double

- From a float to a double

Figure 4.3 illustrates all the widening conversions. The arrows can be taken to mean "can be widened to." To determine whether it is legal to convert from one type to another, find the first type in the figure and see if you can reach the second type by following the arrows.

FIGURE 4.3 Widening conversions

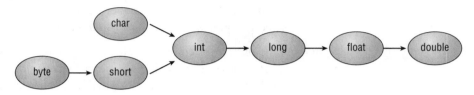

The figure shows, for example, that it is perfectly legal to assign a byte value to a float variable, because you can trace a path from byte to float by following the arrows (byte to short to int to long to float). You cannot, on the other hand, trace a path from long to short, so it is not legal to assign a long value to a short variable.

Figure 4.3 is easy to memorize. The figure consists mostly of the numeric data types in order of size. The only extra piece of information is char, but that goes in the only place it could go: a 16-bit char "fits inside" a 32-bit int. (Note that you can't convert a byte to a char or a char to a short, even though it seems reasonable to do so.)

Any conversion between primitive types that is not represented by a path of arrows in Figure 4.3 is a *narrowing conversion*. These conversions lose information about the magnitude of the value being converted, and are not allowed in assignments. It is geometrically impossible to portray the narrowing conversions in a graph like Figure 4.3, but they can be summarized as follows:

- From a byte to a char
- From a short to a byte or a char
- From a char to a byte or a short
- From an int to a byte, a short, or a char
- From a long to a byte, a short, a char, or an int
- From a float to a byte, a short, a char, an int, or a long
- From a double to a byte, a short, a char, an int, a long, or a float

You do not really need to memorize this list. It simply represents all the conversions not shown in Figure 4.3, which is easier to memorize.

Assignment Conversion, Little Primitives, and Literal Values

Java's assignment conversion rule is sometimes inconvenient when a literal value is assigned to a primitive. By default, a numeric literal is either a `double` or an `int`, so the following line of code generates a compiler error:

```
float f = 1.234;
```

The literal value 1.234 is a `double`, so it cannot be assigned to a `float` variable.

One might assume that assigning a literal `int` to some narrower integral type (`byte`, `short`, or `char`) would fail to compile in a similar way. For example, it would be reasonable to assume that all of the following lines generate compiler errors:

```
byte  b = 1;
short s = 2;
char  c = 3;
```

In fact, all three of the lines above compile without error. The reason is that Java relaxes its assignment conversion rule when a literal `int` value is assigned to a narrower primitive type (`byte`, `short`, or `char`) provided the literal value falls within the legal range of the primitive type.

This relaxation of the rule only applies when the assigned value is an integral literal. Thus the second line of the following code will *not* compile: `int i = 12; byte b = i;`

Primitive Conversion: Method Call

Another kind of conversion is *method-call conversion*. A method-call conversion happens when you pass a value of one type as an argument to a method that expects a different type. For example, the `cos()` method of the `Math` class expects a single argument of type `double`. Consider the following code:

```
1. float frads;
2. double d;
3. frads = 2.34567f;
4. d = Math.cos(frads);   // Pass float to method
                          // that expects double
```

The `float` value in `frads` is automatically converted to a `double` value before it is handed to the `cos()` method. Just as with assignment conversions, there are strict rules that govern which conversions are allowed and which conversions will be rejected by the compiler. The code below quite reasonably generates a compiler error (assuming there is a vector called `myVector`):

```
1. double d = 12.0;
2. Object ob = myVector.elementAt(d);
```

The compiler error message says, "Incompatible type for method. Explicit cast needed to convert double to int." This means that the compiler can't convert the `double` argument to a type that is supported by a version of the `elementAt()` method. It turns out that the only version of `elementAt()` is the version that takes an integer argument. Thus a value may be passed to `elementAt()` only if that value is an `int` or can be converted to an `int`.

Fortunately, the rule that governs which method-call conversions are permitted is the same rule that governs assignment conversions. Widening conversions (as shown in Figure 4.3) are permitted; narrowing conversions are forbidden.

Primitive Conversion: Arithmetic Promotion

The last kind of primitive conversion to consider is *arithmetic promotion*. Arithmetic-promotion conversions happen within arithmetic statements, while the compiler is trying to make sense out of many different possible kinds of operand.

Consider the following fragment:

```
1. short s = 9;
2. int i = 10;
```

```
3. float f = 11.1f;
4. double d = 12.2;
5. if (-s * i  >=  f / d)
6.    System.out.println(">>>>");
7. else
8.    System.out.println("<<<<");
```

The code on line 5 multiplies a negated `short` by an `int`; then it divides a `float` by a `double`; finally it compares the two results. Behind the scenes, the system is doing extensive type conversion to ensure that the operands can be meaningfully incremented, multiplied, divided, and compared. These conversions are all widening conversions. Thus they are known as *arithmetic-promotion conversions*, because values are "promoted" to wider types.

The rules that govern arithmetic promotion distinguish between unary and binary operators. *Unary* operators operate on a single value. *Binary* operators operate on two values. Figure 4.4 shows Java's unary and binary arithmetic operators.

FIGURE 4.4   Unary and binary arithmetic operators

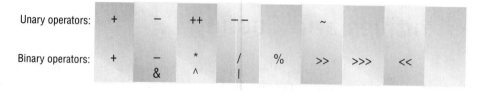

For unary operators, two rules apply, depending on the type of the single operand:

- If the operand is a `byte`, a `short`, or a `char`, it is converted to an `int` (unless the operator is `++` or `--`, in which case no conversion happens).

- Else there is no conversion.

For binary operators, there are four rules, depending on the types of the two operands:

- If one of the operands is a `double`, the other operand is converted to a `double`.

- Else if one of the operands is a `float`, the other operand is converted to a `float`.

- Else if one of the operands is a long, the other operand is converted to a long.

- Else both operands are converted to ints.

With these rules in mind, it is possible to determine what really happens in the code example given at the beginning of this section:

1. The short s is promoted to an int and then negated.

2. The result of step 1 (an int) is multiplied by the int i. Since both operands are of the same type, and that type is not narrower than an int, no conversion is necessary. The result of the multiplication is an int.

3. Before dividing float f by double d, f is widened to a double. The division generates a double-precision result.

4. The result of step 2 (an int) is to be compared to the result of step 3 (a double). The int is converted to a double, and the two operands are compared. The result of a comparison is always of type boolean.

Primitives and Casting

So far, this chapter has shown that Java is perfectly willing to perform widening conversions on primitives. These conversions are implicit and behind the scenes; you don't need to write any explicit code to make them happen.

Casting means explicitly telling Java to make a conversion. A casting operation may widen or narrow its argument. To cast, just precede a value with the parenthesized name of the desired type. For example, the following lines of code cast an int to a double:

```
1. int i = 5;
2. double d = (double)i;
```

Of course, the cast is not always necessary. The following code, in which the cast has been omitted, would do an assignment conversion on i, with the same result as the example above:

```
1. int i = 5;
2. double d = i;
```

Casts are required when you want to perform a narrowing conversion. Such conversion will never be performed implicitly; you have to program an explicit cast to convince the compiler that what you really want is a narrowing conversion. Narrowing runs the risk of losing information; the cast tells the compiler that you accept the risk.

For example, the following code generates a compiler error:

```
1. short s = 259;
2. byte b = s;    // Compiler error
3. System.out.println("s = " + s + ", b = " + b);
```

The compiler error message for the second line will say (among other things), "Explicit cast needed to convert short to byte." Adding an explicit cast is easy:

```
1. short s = 259;
2. byte b = (byte)s;      // Explicit cast
3. System.out.println("b = " + b);
```

When this code is executed, the number 259 (binary 100000011) must be squeezed into a single byte. This is accomplished by preserving the low-order byte of the value and discarding the rest. The code prints out the (perhaps surprising) message:

```
b = 3
```

The 1 bit in bit position 8 gets discarded, leaving only 3, as shown in Figure 4.5. Narrowing conversions can result in radical value changes; this is why the compiler requires you to cast explicitly. The cast tells the compiler, "Yes, I really want to do it."

FIGURE 4.5 Casting a short to a byte

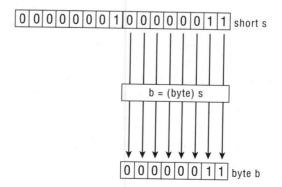

Casting a value to a wider value (as shown in Figure 4.3) is always permitted but never required; if you omit the cast, an implicit conversion will be performed on your behalf. However, explicitly casting can make your code a bit more readable. For example,

```
  1. int i = 2;
  2. double radians;
     .        // Hundreds of
     .        // lines of
     .        // code
600. radians = (double)i;
```

The cast in the last line is not required, but it serves as a good reminder to any readers (including yourself) who might have forgotten the type of `radians`.

There are two simple rules that govern casting of primitive types:

- You can cast any non-`boolean` type to any other non-`boolean` type.

- You cannot cast a `boolean` to any other type; you cannot cast any other type to a `boolean`.

Note that while casting is ordinarily used when narrowing, it is perfectly legal to cast when widening. The cast is unnecessary, but provides a bit of clarity.

Object Reference Conversion

Object reference variables, like primitive values, participate in assignment conversion, method-call conversion, and casting. (There is no arithmetic promotion of object references, since references cannot be arithmetic operands.) Object reference conversion is more complicated than primitive conversion, because there are more possible combinations of old and new types—and more combinations mean more rules.

Reference conversion, like primitive conversion, takes place at compile time, because the compiler has all the information it needs to determine whether the conversion is legal. Later you will see that this is not the case for object casting.

The following sections examine object reference assignment, method-call, and casting conversions.

Object Reference Assignment Conversion

Object reference assignment conversion happens when you assign an object reference value to a variable of a different type. There are three general kinds of object reference type:

- A class type, such as `Button` or `FileWriter`
- An interface type, such as `Cloneable` or `LayoutManager`
- An array type, such as `int[][]` or `TextArea[]`

Generally speaking, assignment conversion of a reference looks like this:

```
1. Oldtype x = new Oldtype();
2. Newtype y = x;    // reference assignment conversion
```

This is the general format of an assignment conversion from an `Oldtype` to a `Newtype`. Unfortunately, `Oldtype` can be a class, an interface, or an array; `Newtype` can also be a class, an interface, or an array. Thus there are nine (= 3 × 3) possible combinations to consider. Figure 4.6 shows the rules for all nine cases.

FIGURE 4.6   The rules for object reference assignment conversion

Converting `Oldtype` to `Newtype`:

	`Oldtype` is a class	`Oldtype` is an interface	`Oldtype` is an array
`Newtype` is a class	`Oldtype` must be a subclass of `Newtype`	`Newtype` must be `Object`	`Newtype` must be `Object`
`Newtype` is an interface	`Oldtype` must implement interface `Newtype`	`Oldtype` must be a subinterface of `Newtype`	`Newtype` must be `Cloneable` or `Serializable`
`Newtype` is an array	Compiler error	Compiler error	`Oldtype` must be an array of some object reference type that can be converted to whatever `Newtype` is an array of

It would be difficult to memorize the nine rules shown in Figure 4.6. Fortunately, there is a rule of thumb.

Recall that with primitives, conversions were permitted, provided they were widening conversions. The notion of widening does not really apply to references, but there is a similar principle at work. In general, object reference conversion is permitted when the direction of the conversion is "up" the inheritance hierarchy; that is, the old type should inherit from the new type. This rule of thumb does not cover all nine cases, but it is a helpful way to look at things.

The rules for object reference conversion can be stated as follows:

- An interface type may only be converted to an interface type or to `Object`. If the new type is an interface, it must be a superinterface of the old type.

- A class type may be converted to a class type or to an interface type. If converting to a class type, the new type must be a superclass of the old type. If converting to an interface type, the old class must implement the interface.

- An array may be converted to the class `Object`, to the interface `Cloneable` or `Serializable`, or to an array. Only an array of object reference types may be converted to an array, and the old element type must be convertible to the new element type.

To illustrate these rules, consider the inheritance hierarchy shown in Figure 4.7 (assume there is an interface called `Squeezable`).

FIGURE 4.7 A simple class hierarchy

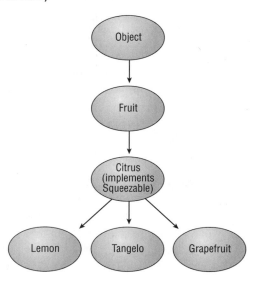

As a first example, consider the following code:

```
1. Tangelo tange = new Tangelo();
2. Citrus cit = tange;
```

This code is fine. A `Tangelo` is being converted to a `Citrus`. The new type is a superclass of the old type, so the conversion is allowed. Converting in the other direction ("down" the hierarchy tree) is not allowed:

```
1. Citrus cit = new Citrus();
2. Tangelo tange = cit;
```

This code will result in a compiler error.

What happens when one of the types is an interface?

```
1. Grapefruit g = new Grapefruit();
2. Squeezable squee = g;    // No problem
3. Grapefruit g2 = squee;   // Error
```

The second line ("No problem") changes a class type (`Grapefruit`) to an interface type. This is correct, provided `Grapefruit` really implements `Squeezable`. A glance at Figure 4.7 shows that this is indeed the case, because `Grapefruit` inherits from `Citrus`, which implements `Squeezable`. The third line is an error, because an interface can never be implicitly converted to any reference type other than `Object`.

Finally, consider an example with arrays:

```
1. Fruit fruits[];
2. Lemon lemons[];
3. Citrus citruses[] = new Citrus[10];
4. for (int i = 0; i < 10; i++) {
5.    citruses[i] = new Citrus();
6. }
7. fruits = citruses;     // No problem
8. lemons = citruses;     // Error
```

Line 7 converts an array of `Citrus` to an array of `Fruit`. This is fine, because `Fruit` is a superclass of `Citrus`. Line 8 converts in the other direction and fails, because `Lemon` is not a superclass of `Citrus`.

Object Method-Call Conversion

Fortunately, the rules for method-call conversion of object reference values are the same as the rules described above for assignment conversion of objects. The general rule of thumb is that converting to a superclass is permitted and converting to a subclass is not permitted. The specific, formal rules were given in a bulleted list in the previous section and are shown again here:

- An interface type may only be converted to an interface type or to Object. If the new type is an interface, it must be a superinterface of the old type.

- A class type may be converted to a class type or to an interface type. If converting to a class, the new type must be a superclass of the old type. If converting an interface type, the old class must implement the interface.

- An array may be converted to the class Object, to the interface Cloneable or Serializable, or to an array. Only an array of object reference types may be converted to an array, and the old element type must be convertible to the new element type.

To see how the rules make sense in the context of method calls, consider the extremely useful Vector class. You can store anything you like in a Vector (anything non-primitive, that is) by calling the method add (Object ob). For example, the code below stores a Tangelo in a vector:

```
1. Vector myVec = new Vector();
2. Tangelo tange = new Tangelo();
3. myVec.add (tange);
```

The tange argument will automatically be converted to type Object. The automatic conversion means that the people who wrote the Vector class didn't have to write a separate method for every possible type of object that anyone might conceivably want to store in a vector. This is fortunate: The Tangelo class was developed years after the invention of the Vector, so the developer of the Vector class could not possibly have written specific Tangelo-handling code. An object of any class (and even an array of any type) can be passed into the single add (Object ob) method.

Object Reference Casting

Object reference casting is like primitive casting: By using a cast, you convince the compiler to let you do a conversion that otherwise might not be allowed.

Any kind of conversion that is allowed for assignments or method calls is allowed for explicit casting. For example, the following code is legal:

```
1. Lemon lem = new Lemon();
2. Citrus cit = (Citrus)lem;
```

The cast is legal, but not needed; if you leave it out, the compiler will do an implicit assignment conversion. The power of casting appears when you explicitly cast to a type that is not allowed by the rules of implicit conversion.

To understand how object casting works, it is important to understand the difference between objects and object reference variables. Every object (well, nearly every object because there are some obscure cases) is constructed via the **new** operator. The argument to **new** determines for all time the true class of the object. For example, if an object is constructed by calling **new** Color(222, 0, 255), then throughout that object's lifetime its class will be Color.

Java programs do not deal directly with objects. They deal with *references* to objects. For example, consider the following code:

```
Color purple = new Color(222, 0, 255);
```

The variable purple is not an object; it is a reference to an object. The object itself lives in memory somewhere in the Java Virtual Machine. The variable purple contains something similar to the address of the object. This address is known as a *reference* to the object. The difference between a reference and an object is illustrated in Figure 4.8. References are stored in variables, and variables have types that are specified by the programmer at compile time. Object reference variable types can be classes (such as Graphics or FileWriter), interfaces (such as Runnable or LayoutManager), or arrays (such as int[][] or Vector[]).

FIGURE 4.8 Reference and object

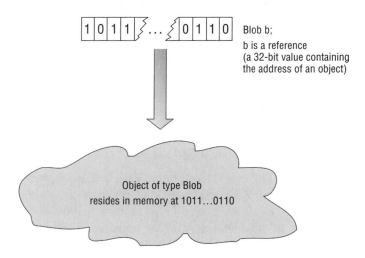

Blob b;
b is a reference
(a 32-bit value containing
the address of an object)

Object of type Blob
resides in memory at 1011...0110

While an object's class is unchanging, it may be referenced by variables of
many different types. For example, consider a stack. It is constructed by calling `new Stack()`, so its class really is `Stack`. Yet at various moments during
the lifetime of this object, it may be referenced by variables of type `Stack` (of
course), or of type `Vector` (because `Stack` inherits from `Vector`), or of type
`Object` (because everything inherits from `Object`). It may even be referenced by
variables of type `Serializable`, which is an interface, because the `Stack` class
implements the `Serializable` interface. This situation is shown in Figure 4.9.

FIGURE 4.9 Many variable types, one class

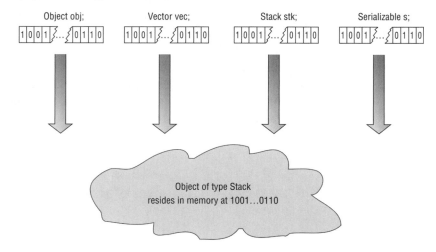

Object obj;   Vector vec;   Stack stk;   Serializable s;

Object of type Stack
resides in memory at 1001...0110

The type of a reference variable is obvious at compile time. However, the class of an object referenced by such a variable cannot be known until runtime. This lack of knowledge is not a shortcoming of Java technology; it results from a fundamental principle of computer science. The distinction between compile-time knowledge and runtime knowledge was not relevant to our discussion of conversions; however, the difference becomes important with reference value casting. The rules for casting are a bit broader than those for conversion. Some of these rules concern reference type and can be enforced by the compiler at compile time; other rules concern object class and can only be enforced during execution.

There is no escaping the fact that there are quite a few rules governing object casting. The good news is that most of the rules cover obscure cases. You might as well start by seeing the big picture in all its complicated glory, but after this glimpse you will be presented with a few simple ideas that will see you through most common situations.

For object reference casting, there are not three but *four* possibilities for both the old type and the new type. Each type can be a non-final class, a final class, an interface, or an array. The first round of rule enforcement happens at compile time. Most of the compile-time rules are summarized in the imposing Figure 4.10.

FIGURE 4.10   Compile-time rules for object reference casting

	Oldtype is a non-final class	Oldtype is a final class	Oldtype is an interface	Oldtype is an array
Newtype is a non-final class	Oldtype must extend Newtype, or vice versa	Oldtype must extend Newtype	Always OK	Newtype must be Object
Newtype is a final class	Newtype must extend Oldtype	Oldtype and Newtype must be the same class	Newtype must implement Cloneable or Serializable	Compiler error
Newtype is an interface	Always OK	Oldtype must implement interface Newtype	Always OK	Compiler error
Newtype is an array	Oldtype must be Object not Newtype	Compiler error	Compiler error	Oldtype must be an array of some type that can be cast to whatever Newtype is an array of.

Newtype nt; Oldtype ot; nt = (newtype)ot;

Assuming that a desired cast survives compilation, a second check must occur at runtime. The second check determines whether the class of the object being cast is compatible with the new type. Here, *compatible* means that the class can be converted according to the conversion rules discussed in the previous two sections.

What a baffling collection of rules! For sanity's sake, bear in mind that only a few of the situations covered by these rules are commonly encountered in real life. (For instance, there are cases when it is not okay to have interfaces for both the old and new types, but these cases are extremely obscure.) A few rules of thumb and some examples should help to clarify things.

First, to simplify dealing with the compile-time rules, bear in mind the following facts about casting from Oldtype to Newtype:

- When both Oldtype and Newtype are classes, one class must be a subclass of the other.

- When both Oldtype and Newtype are arrays, both arrays must contain reference types (not primitives), and it must be legal to cast an element of Oldtype to an element of Newtype.

- You can always cast between an interface and a non-final object.

As for the runtime rules, remember that the conversion to Newtype must actually be possible. The following rules of thumb cover the most common cases:

- If Newtype is a class, the class of the expression being converted must be Newtype or must inherit from Newtype.

- If Newtype is an interface, the class of the expression being converted must implement Newtype.

It is definitely time for some examples! Look once again at the Fruit/Citrus hierarchy that you saw earlier in this chapter 6, which is repeated in Figure 4.11

FIGURE 4.11   Fruit hierarchy (reprise)

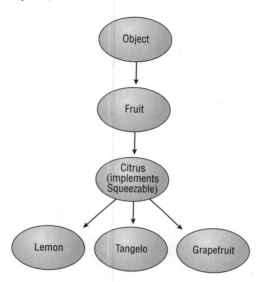

First, consider the following code:

```
1. Grapefruit g, g1;
2. Citrus c;
3. Tangelo t;
4. g = new Grapefruit(); // Class is Grapefruit
5. c = g;                // Legal assignment conversion,
                         // no cast needed
6. g1 = (Grapefruit)c;   // Legal cast
7. t = (Tangelo)c;       // Illegal cast
                         // (throws an exception)
```

This code has four references but only one object. The object's class is Grapefruit, because it is Grapefruit's constructor that gets called on line 4. The assignment c = g on line 5 is a perfectly legal assignment conversion ("up" the inheritance hierarchy), so no explicit cast is required. In lines 6 and 7, the Citrus is cast to a Grapefruit and to a Tangelo. Recall that for casting between class types, one of the two classes (it doesn't matter which one) must be a subclass of the other. The first cast is from a Citrus to its subclass Grapefruit; the second cast is from a Citrus to its subclass Tangelo. Thus both casts are legal—at compile time. The compiler cannot determine the class of the object referenced by c, so it accepts both casts and lets fate determine the outcome at runtime.

When the code is executed, eventually the Java Virtual Machine attempts to execute line 6: g1 = (Grapefruit)c; The class of c is determined to be Grapefruit, and there is no objection to converting a Grapefruit to a Grapefruit.

Line 7 attempts (at runtime) to cast c to type Tangelo. The class of c is still Grapefruit, and a Grapefruit cannot be cast to a Tangelo. In order for the cast to be legal, the class of c would have to be Tangelo itself or some subclass of Tangelo. Since this is not the case, a runtime exception (java.lang.ClassCastException) is thrown.

Now take an example where an object is cast to an interface type. Begin by considering the following code fragment:

```
1. Grapefruit g, g1;
2. Squeezable s;
3. g = new Grapefruit();
4. s = g;        // Convert Grapefruit to Squeezable (OK)
5. g1 = s;       // Convert Squeezable to Grapefruit
                 // (Compile error)
```

This code will not compile. Line 5 attempts to convert an interface (Squeezable) to a class (Grapefruit). It doesn't matter that Grapefruit implements Squeezable. Implicitly converting an interface to a class is never allowed; it is one of those cases where you have to use an explicit cast to tell the compiler that you really know what you're doing. With the cast, line 5 becomes

```
5. g1 = (Grapefruit)s;
```

Adding the cast makes the compiler happy. At runtime, the Java Virtual Machine checks whether the class of s (which is Grapefruit) can be converted to Grapefruit. It certainly can, so the cast is allowed.

For a final example, involving arrays, look at the code below:

```
1. Grapefruit g[];
2. Squeezable s[];
3. Citrus c[];
4. g = new Grapefruit[500];
```

```
5. s = g;              // Convert Grapefruit array to
                       // Squeezable array (OK)
6. c = (Citrus[])s;    // Cast Squeezable array to Citrus
                       // array (OK)
```

Line 6 casts an array of Squeezables (s) to an array of Citruses (c). An array cast is legal if casting the array element types is legal (and if the element types are references, not primitives). In this example, the question is whether a Squeezable (the element type of array s) can be cast to a Citrus (the element type of the cast array). The previous example showed that this is a legal cast.

Chapter Summary

Primitive values and object references are very different kinds of data. Both can be converted (implicitly) or cast (explicitly). Primitive type changes are caused by

- Assignment conversion

- Method-call conversion

- Arithmetic-promotion conversion

- Explicit casting

Primitives may only be converted if the conversion widens the data. Primitives may be narrowed by casting, as long as neither the old nor the new type is boolean.

Object references may be converted or cast; the rules that govern these activities are extensive, as there are many combinations of cases to be covered. In general, going "up" the inheritance tree may be accomplished implicitly through conversion; going "down" the tree requires explicit casting. Object reference type changes are caused by:

- Assignment conversion

- Method-call conversion

- Explicit casting

Test Yourself

1. Which of the following statements is correct? (Choose one.)

   A. Only primitives are converted automatically; to change the type of an object reference, you have to do a cast.

   B. Only object references are converted automatically; to change the type of a primitive, you have to do a cast.

   C. Arithmetic promotion of object references requires explicit casting.

   D. Both primitives and object references can be both converted and cast.

   E. Casting of numeric types may require a runtime check.

2. Which one line in the following code will not compile?

   ```
   1. byte b = 5;
   2. char c = '5';
   3. short s = 55;
   4. int i = 555;
   5. float f = 555.5f;
   6. b = s;
   7. i = c;
   8. if (f > b)
   9.    f = i;
   ```

3. Will the following code compile?

   ```
   1. byte b = 2;
   2. byte b1 = 3;
   3. b = b * b1;
   ```

4. In the code below, what are the possible types for variable `result`?
(Choose the most complete true answer.)

```
1. byte b = 11;
2. short s = 13;
3. result = b * ++s;
```

A. byte, short, int, long, float, double

B. boolean, byte, short, char, int, long, float, double

C. byte, short, char, int, long, float, double

D. byte, short, char

E. int, long, float, double

5. Consider the following class:

```
1.   class Cruncher {
2.     void crunch(int i) {
3.       System.out.println("int version");
4.     }
5.     void crunch(String s) {
6.       System.out.println("String version");
7.     }
8.
9.     public static void main(String args[]) {
10.      Cruncher crun = new Cruncher();
11.      char ch = 'p';
12.      crun.crunch(ch);
13.    }
14.  }
```

Which of the statements below is true? (Choose one.)

A. Line 5 will not compile, because `void` methods cannot be overridden.

B. Line 12 will not compile, because there is no version of `crunch()` that takes a `char` argument.

C. The code will compile but will throw an exception at line 12.

D. The code will compile and produce the following output:
`int version`

E. The code will compile and produce the following output:
`String version`

6. Which of the statements below is true? (Choose one.)

A. Object references can be converted in assignments but not in method calls.

B. Object references can be converted in method calls but not in assignments.

C. Object references can be converted in both method calls and assignments, but the rules governing these conversions are very different.

D. Object references can be converted in both method calls and assignments, and the rules governing these conversions are identical.

E. Object references can never be converted.

7. Consider the following code. Which line below will not compile?

```
1. Object ob = new Object();
2. String stringarr[] = new String[50];
3. Float floater = new Float(3.14f);
4.
5. ob = stringarr;
6. ob = stringarr[5];
7. floater = ob;
8. ob = floater;
```

Questions 8–10 refer to the class hierarchy shown in Figure 4.12.

FIGURE 4.12   Class hierarchy for questions 8, 9, and 10

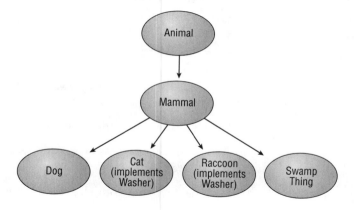

8. Consider the following code:

```
1. Dog        rover, fido;
2. Animal     anim;
3.
4. rover = new Dog();
5. anim = rover;
6. fido = (Dog)anim;
```

Which of the statements below is true? (Choose one.)

A. Line 5 will not compile.

B. Line 6 will not compile.

C. The code will compile but will throw an exception at line 6.

D. The code will compile and run.

E. The code will compile and run, but the cast in line 6 is not required and can be eliminated.

9. Consider the following code:

```
1. Cat sunflower;
2. Washer wawa;
3. SwampThing pogo;
4.
5. sunflower = new Cat();
6. wawa = sunflower;
7. pogo = (SwampThing)wawa;
```

Which of the statements below is true? (Choose one.)

A. Line 6 will not compile; an explicit cast is required to convert a Cat to a Washer.

B. Line 7 will not compile, because you cannot cast an interface to a class.

C. The code will compile and run, but the cast in line 7 is not required and can be eliminated.

D. The code will compile but will throw an exception at line 7, because runtime conversion from an interface to a class is not permitted.

E. The code will compile but will throw an exception at line 7, because the runtime class of wawa cannot be converted to type SwampThing.

10. Consider the following code:

```
1. Raccoon rocky;
2. SwampThing pogo;
3. Washer w;
4.
5. rocky = new Raccoon();
6. w = rocky;
7. pogo = w;
```

Which of the following statements is true? (Choose one.)

A. Line 6 will not compile; an explicit cast is required to convert a Raccoon to a Washer.

B. Line 7 will not compile; an explicit cast is required to convert a Washer to a SwampThing.

C. The code will compile and run.

D. The code will compile but will throw an exception at line 7, because runtime conversion from an interface to a class is not permitted.

E. The code will compile but will throw an exception at line 7, because the runtime class of w cannot be converted to type SwampThing.

Chapter

5

Flow Control and Exceptions

JAVA CERTIFICATION EXAM OBJECTIVES COVERED IN THIS CHAPTER:

✓ Write code using *if* and *switch* statements and identify legal argument types for these statements.

✓ Write code using all forms of loops including labeled and unlabeled use of *break* and *continue*, and state the values taken by loop control variables during and after loop execution.

✓ Write code that makes proper use of exceptions and exception handling clauses (*try, catch, finally*) and declares methods and overriding methods that throw exceptions.

Flow control is a fundamental facility of almost any programming language. Sequence, iteration, and selection are the major elements of flow control, and Java provides these in forms that are familiar to C and C++ programmers. Additionally, Java provides for exception handling.

Sequence control is provided simply by the specification that, within a single block of code, execution starts at the top and proceeds toward the bottom. Iteration is catered for by three styles of loop: the `for()`, `while()`, and `do` constructions. Selection occurs when either the `if()`/`else` or `switch()` construct is used.

Java omits one common element of flow control: the idea of a goto statement. When Java was being designed, the team responsible did some analysis of a large body of existing code and determined that there were two situations where the use of goto was appropriate in new code: when code breaks out of nested loops, and the handling of exception conditions or errors. The designers left out goto and, in its place, provided alternative constructions to handle these particular conditions. The `break` and `continue` statements that control the execution of loops were extended to handle nested loops, and formalized exception handling was introduced, using ideas similar to those of C++.

This chapter discusses the flow-control facilities of Java. We will look closely at the exception mechanism, since this is an area that commonly causes some confusion. But first, we will discuss the loop mechanisms.

The Loop Constructs

Java provides three loop constructions. Taken from C and C++, these are the `while()`, `do`, and `for()` constructs. Each provides the facility for repeating the execution of a block of code until some condition occurs. We will discuss the `while()` loop, which is perhaps the simplest, first.

The *while()* Loop

The general form of the `while()` loop is

```
1. while (boolean_condition)
2.    repeated_statement_or_block
```

In such a construct, the element `boolean_condition` can be any expression that returns a `boolean` result. Notice that this differs from C and C++, where a variety of types may be used: In Java you can *only* use a `boolean` expression. Typically, you might use a comparison of some kind, such as `x > 5`.

The `repeated_statement_or_block` will be executed again and again as long as the `boolean_condition` is true. If the condition never becomes false, then the loop will repeat forever. In practice, this really means that the loop will repeat until the program is stopped or the machine is turned off.

Notice that we've described the loop body as a "repeated statement or block." There are two important points about this. The first is one of coding style, and as such is not directly related to the Programmer's Exam (although it might be relevant to the Developer's Exam when you take that). The second is the strict interpretation of the language specification, and as such might be needed in the Programmer's Exam. The two issues are related, so we will discuss them over the next few paragraphs.

The first point is that you would be well advised always to write a *block* to contain the code for the body of a loop or an `if()` statement. That is, always use a pair of braces so your code will look like this:

```
1. while (boolean_condition) {
2.     statement(s);
3. }
```

even where you only have a single statement inside the loop. The reason for this is that you will find many situations where you will change from a single line to multiple lines, and if the braces are in position already, that is one less thing to forget. One typical situation where this arises is when you add debug output to the middle of a loop to see how many times the loop is executed. It's very frustrating to realize after twenty minutes of messing about that the loop was executed ten times although the message was printed only on exit from the loop. It's perhaps worse to see the message printed ten times, but to have moved the proper body of the loop outside of it entirely.

The second point is that, from the position of strict correctness, you need to know that a single statement without braces is allowed in loops and `if` statements. So the following code is correct and prints "five times" 5 times, but "once" only once:

```
1.   int i = 0;
2.   while (i++ < 5)
3.     System.out.println("five times");
4.   System.out.println("once");
```

It is highly unlikely that you will be presented with code that uses a single, non-blocked, statement as the body of a loop or the conditional part of an if statement, but if you do, you need to recognize how it will behave, and that it is not incorrect.

The exact position of the opening curly brace that marks a block of code is a matter of near-religious contention. Some programmers put it at the end of a line, as in most of the examples in this book. Others put it on a line by itself. Provided it is otherwise placed in the correct sequence, it does not matter how many space, tab, and newline characters are placed before or after the opening curly brace. In other words, this positioning is not relevant to syntactic correctness. You should be aware, however, that the style used in presenting the exam questions, as well as that used for the code in the developer-level exam, is the style shown here, where the opening brace is placed at the end of the line.

Observe that if the `boolean_condition` is already `false` when the loop is first encountered, then the body of the loop will never be executed. This relates to the main distinguishing feature of the do loop, which we will discuss next.

The *do* Loop

The general form of the do loop is

```
1. do
2.    repeated_statement_or_block
3. while (boolean_condition);
```

This is similar to the `while()` loop just discussed, and as before, it is best to have a loop body formed with a block:

```
1. do {
2.    do_something
3.    do_more
4. } while (boolean_condition);
```

Again, repetition of the loop is terminated when the `boolean_condition` becomes false. The significant difference is that this loop always executes the body of the loop at least once, since the test is performed at the end of the body.

In general, the `do` loop is probably less frequently used than the `while()` loop, but the third loop format is perhaps the most common. The third form is the `for()` loop, which we will discuss next.

The *for()* Loop

A common requirement in programming is to perform a loop so that a single variable is incremented over a range of values between two limits. This is frequently provided by a loop that uses the keyword `for`. Java's `while()` loop can achieve this effect, but it is most commonly achieved using the `for()` loop. However, as with C and C++, using the `for()` loop is more general than simply providing for iteration over a sequence of values.

The general form of the `for()` loop is

```
1. for (statement ; condition ; expression)
2.    loop_body
```

Again, a block should normally be used as the `loop_body` part, like this:

```
1. for (statement ; condition ; expression) {
2.    do_something
3.    do_more
4. }
```

The keys to this loop are in the three parts contained in the brackets following the `for` keyword:

- The `statement` is executed immediately before the loop itself is started. It is often used to set up starting conditions. You will see shortly that it can also contain variable declarations.

- The `condition` must be a boolean expression and is treated exactly the same as in the `while()` loop. The body of the loop will be executed repeatedly until the condition ceases to be true. As with the `while()` loop, it is possible that the body of a `for()` loop might never be executed. This occurs if the condition is already false at the start of the loop.

- The `expression` (short for "iteration expression") is executed immediately after the body of the loop, just before the test is performed again. Commonly, this is used to increment a loop counter.

If you have already declared an `int` variable `x`, you can code a simple sequence counting loop like this:

```
1. for (x = 0; x < 10; x++) {
2.    System.out.println("value is " + x);
3. }
```

This would result in 10 lines of output, starting with

```
value is 0
```

and ending with

```
value is 9
```

In fact, because `for()` loops commonly need a counting variable, you are allowed to declare variables in the `statement` part. The scope of such a variable is restricted to the statement or block following the `for()` statement and the `for()` part itself. This protects loop counter variables from interfering with each other and prevents leftover loop count values from accidental re-use. This results in code like this:

```
1. for (int x = 0; x < 10; x++) {
2.    System.out.println("value is " + x);
3. }
```

It might be useful to look at the equivalent of this code implemented using a `while()` loop:

```
1. {
2.    int x = 0;
3.    while (x < 10) {
4.       System.out.println("value is " + x);
5.       x++;
6.    }
7. }
```

This version reinforces a couple of points. First, the scope of the variable `x`, declared in the `statement` part of the `for()` loop, is restricted to the loop and its control parts (that is, the `statement`, `condition`, and `expression`). Second, the `expression` is executed after the rest of the loop body, effectively before control comes back to the test condition.

Empty *for()* Loops

Any part of a `for()` loop's control may be omitted if you wish. Omitting the test is equivalent to a perpetually true test, so the construct:

```
for(;;) {
```

creates a loop that repeats forever.

The *for()* Loop and the Comma Separator

The `for()` loop allows the use of the comma separator in a special way. The `statement` and `expression` parts described previously can actually contain a sequence of expressions rather than just a single one. If you want such a sequence, you should separate those expressions, not with a semicolon (which would be mistaken as the separator between the three parts of the `for()` loop control structure) but with a comma. This behavior is borrowed from C and C++, where the comma is an operator, but in Java the comma serves only as a special case separator for conditions where the semicolon would be unsuitable. This example demonstrates:

```
1. int j, k;
2. for (j = 3, k = 6; j + k < 20; j++, k +=2) {
3.    System.out.println("j is " + j + " k is " + k);
4. }
```

Note that while you can use the comma to separate several expressions, you cannot mix expressions with variable declarations, nor can you have multiple declarations of different types. So these would be illegal:

```
1. int i = 7;
2. for (i++, int j = 0; i < 10; j++) { } // illegal!
```

```
1. for (int i = 7, long j = 0; i < 10; j++) { } // illegal!
```

A final note on this issue is that the use of the comma to separate multiple declarations of a single type is allowed, like this:

```
1. for (int i = 7, j = 0; i < 10; j++) { }
```

which declares two `int` variables, *i* and *j*, and initializes them to 7 and 0 respectively. This, however, is a standard feature of declarations, and is not specific to the `for()` loop.

We have now discussed the three loop constructions in their basic forms. The next section looks at more advanced flow control in loops, specifically the use of the `break` and `continue` statements.

The *break* and *continue* Statements in Loops

Sometimes you need to abandon execution of the body of a loop—or perhaps a number of nested loops. The Java development team recognized this situation as a legitimate use for a goto statement. Java provides two statements, `break` and `continue`, which can be used instead of goto to achieve this effect.

Using *continue*

Suppose you have a loop that is processing an array of items that each contain two `String` references. The first `String` is always non-null, but the second might not be present. To process this, you might decide that you want, in pseudocode, something along these lines:

```
for each element of the array
  process the first String
  if the second String exists
    process the second String
  endif
endfor
```

You will recognize that this can be coded easily by using an `if` block to control processing of the second `String`. However, you can also use the `continue` statement like this:

```
1. for (int i = 0; i < array.length; i++) {
2.    // process first string
3.    if (array[i].secondString == null) {
4.      continue;
5.    }
6.    // process second string
7. }
```

In this case, the example is sufficiently simple so that you probably do not see any advantage over using the `if()` condition to control the execution of the second part. If the second `String` processing was long, and perhaps heavily indented in its own right, you might find that the use of `continue` was slightly simpler visually.

The real strength of `continue` is that it is able to skip out of multiple levels of loop. Suppose our example, instead of being two `String` objects, had been two-dimensional arrays of char values. Now we will need to nest our loops. Consider this sample:

```
1. mainLoop: for (int i = 0; i < array.length; i++) {
2.    for (int j = 0; j < array[i].length; j++) {
3.       if (array[i][j] == '\u0000') {
4.          continue mainLoop;
5.       }
6.    }
7. }
```

Notice particularly the label `mainLoop` that has been applied to the `for()` on line 1. The fact that this is a label is indicated by the trailing colon. You typically apply labels of this form to the opening loop statements: `while()`, `do`, or `for()`.

Here, when the processing of the second array comes across a zero value, it abandons the whole processing not just for the inner loop, but for the current object in the main array. This is equivalent to jumping to the statement `i++` in the first `for()` statement.

You might still think that this is not really any advantage over using `if()` statements, but imagine that further processing was done between lines 4 and 5 and that finding the zero character in the array was required to avoid that further processing, too. To achieve that without using `continue`, you would have to set a flag in the inner loop and use that to abandon the outer loop processing. It can be done, but it is rather messy.

Using *break*

The `break` statement, when applied to a loop, is somewhat similar to the `continue` statement. However, instead of prematurely completing the current iteration of a loop, `break` causes the entire loop to be abandoned. Consider this example:

```
1. for (int j = 0; j < array.length; j++) {
2.    if (array[j] == null) {
3.       break; //break out of inner loop
4.    }
5.    // process array[j]
6. }
```

In this case, instead of simply skipping some processing for `array[j]` and proceeding directly to processing `array[j+1]`, this version quits the entire inner loop as soon as a `null` element is found.

You can also use labels on `break` statements, and as before, you must place a matching label on one of the enclosing blocks. The `break` and `continue` statements provide a convenient way to make parts of a loop conditional, especially when used in their labeled formats.

> In fact, labels may be applied to any statements, and break can be used to jump out of any labeled block, whether that block is the body of a loop statement or not. This actually makes the break statement a close imitation of a full fledged goto. In the Certification Exam, you will not be expected to use break for any purpose other than jumping out of loops. In daily programming, you should probably avoid using it for any other purpose too.

The next section discusses the `if()`/`else` and `switch()` constructions, which provide the normal means of implementing conditional code.

The Selection Statements

Java provides a choice of two selection constructs. These are the `if()`/`else` and `switch()` mechanisms. You can easily write simple conditional code for a choice of two execution paths based on the value of a `boolean` expression using `if()`/`else`. If you need more complex choices between multiple execution paths, and if an appropriate argument is available to control the choice, then you can use `switch()`; otherwise you can use either nests or sequences of `if()`/`else`.

The *if()*/*else* Construct

The `if()`/`else` construct takes a `boolean` argument as the basis of its choice. Often you will use a comparison expression to provide this argument, for example:

```
1. if (x > 5) {
2.   System.out.println("x is more than 5");
3. }
```

This sample executes line 2, provided the test (x > 5) in line 1 returns true. Notice that we used a block even though there is only a single conditional line, just as we suggested you should generally do with the loops discussed earlier.

Also, you can use an else part to give code that is executed under the conditions that the test returns false. For example,

```
1. if (x > 5) {
2.    System.out.println("x is more than 5");
3. }
4. else {
5.    System.out.println("x is not more than 5");
6. }
```

Beyond this, you can use if()/else in a nested fashion, refining conditions to more specific, or narrower, tests at each point.

The if()/else construction makes a test between only two possible paths of execution, although you can create nests or sequences to select between a greater range of possibilities. The next section discusses the switch() construction, which allows a single value to select between multiple possible execution paths.

The *switch()* Construct

If you need to make a choice between multiple alternative execution paths, and the choice can be based upon an int value, you can use the switch() construct. Consider this example:

```
1. switch (x) {
2.    case 1:
3.       System.out.println("Got a 1");
4.       break;
5.    case 2:
6.    case 3:
7.       System.out.println("Got 2 or 3");
8.       break;
9.    default:
10.      System.out.println("Not a 1, 2, or 3");
11.      break;
12. }
```

Note that, although you cannot determine the fact by inspection of this code, the variable x must be either byte, short, char, or int. It must not be long, either of the floating-point types, boolean, or an object reference. Strictly, we say that the value must be "assignment compatible" with int.

The comparison of values following case labels with the value of the expression supplied as an argument to switch() determines the execution path. The arguments to case labels must be constants, or at least a constant expression that can be fully evaluated at compile time. You cannot use a variable or expression involving variables.

Each case label takes only a single argument, but when execution jumps to one of these labels, it continues downward until it reaches a break statement. This occurs even if it passes another case label or the default label. So in the example shown above, if x has the value 2, execution goes through lines 1, 5, 6, 7, and 8, and continues beyond line 12. This requirement for break to indicate the completion of the case part is important. More often than not, you do not want to omit the break, as you do not want execution to "fall through." However, to achieve the effect shown in the example, where more than one particular value of x causes execution of the same block of code, you use multiple case labels with only a single break.

The default statement is comparable to the else part of an if()/else construction. Execution jumps to the default statement if none of the explicit case values matches the argument provided to switch(). Although the default statement is shown at the end of the switch() block in the example (and this is both a conventional and reasonably logical place to put it), there is no rule that requires this placement.

Now that we have examined the constructions that provide for iteration and selection under normal program control, we will look at the flow of control under exception conditions—that is, conditions when some runtime problem has arisen.

Exceptions

Sometimes when a program is executing, something occurs that is not quite normal from the point of view of the goal at hand. For example, a user might enter an invalid filename; a file might contain corrupted data; a network link could fail; or there could be a bug in the program that causes it to try to make an illegal memory access, such as referring to an element beyond the end of an array.

Circumstances of this type are called *exception* conditions in Java and are represented using objects. A subtree of the class hierarchy starting with the class java.lang.Throwable is dedicated to describing them.

The process of an exception "appearing" either from the immediate cause of the trouble, or because a method call is abandoned and passes the exception up to its caller, is called *throwing* an exception in Java. You will hear other terms used, particularly an exception being *raised*.

If you take no steps to deal with an exception, execution jumps to the end of the current method. The exception then appears in the caller of that method, and execution jumps to the end of the calling method. This continues until execution reaches the "top" of the affected thread, at which point the thread dies.

Flow of Control in Exception Conditions

Using *try{} catch() {}*

To intercept, and thereby control, an exception, you use a try/catch/finally construction. You place lines of code that are part of the normal processing sequence in a try block. You then put code to deal with an exception that might arise during execution of the try block in a catch block. If there are multiple exception classes that might arise in the try block, then several catch blocks are allowed to handle them. Code that must be executed no matter what happens can be placed in a finally block. Let's take a moment to consider an example:

```
1.  int x = (int)(Math.random() * 5);
2.  int y = (int)(Math.random() * 10);
3.  int [] z = new int[5];
4.  try {
5.    System.out.println("y/x gives " + (y/x));
6.    System.out.println("y is "
7.     + y + " z[y] is " + z[y]);
8.  }
9.  catch (ArithmeticException e) {
10.   System.out.println("Arithmetic problem " + e);
11. }
12. catch (ArrayIndexOutOfBoundsException e) {
13.   System.out.println("Subscript problem " + e);
14. }
```

In this example, an exception is possible at line 5 and at line 6. Line 5 has the potential to cause a division by 0, which in integer arithmetic results in an `ArithmeticException` being thrown. Line 6 will sometimes throw an `ArrayIndexOutOfBoundsException`.

If the value of *x* happens to be 0, then line 5 will result in the construction of an instance of the `ArithmeticException` class that is then thrown. Execution continues at line 9, where the variable *e* takes on the reference to the newly created exception. At line 10, the message printed includes a description of the problem, which comes directly from the exception itself. A similar flow occurs if line 5 executes without a problem but the value of *y* is 5 or greater, causing an out-of-range subscript in line 6. In that case, execution jumps directly to line 12.

In either of these cases, where an exception is thrown in a `try` block and is caught by a matching `catch` block, the exception is considered to have been handled: Execution continues after the last `catch` block as if nothing had happened. If, however, there is no `catch` block that names either the class of exception that has been thrown or a class of exception that is a parent class of the one that has been thrown, then the exception is considered to be unhandled. In such conditions, execution generally leaves the method directly, just as if no `try` had been used.

Table 5.1 summarizes the flow of execution that occurs in the exception handling scenarios discussed up to this point. You should not rely on this table for exam preparation, because it is only describes the story so far. You will find a more complete study reference in the summary at the end of this chapter.

TABLE 5.1 Outline of Flow in Simple Exception Conditions

Exception	*try {}*	Matching *catch() {}*	Behavior
No	N/A	N/A	Normal flow
Yes	No	N/A	Method terminates
Yes	Yes	No	Method terminates
Yes	Yes	Yes	1. Terminate try {} block
			2. Execute body of matching catch block
			3. Continue normal flow after catch blocks

Using *finally*

The generalized exception-handling code has one more part to it than you saw in the last example. This is the `finally` block. If you put a `finally` block after a `try` and its associated `catch` blocks, then once execution enters the `try` block, the code in that `finally` block will definitely be executed whatever the circumstances—well, nearly definitely. If an exception arises with a matching `catch` block, then the `finally` block is executed after the `catch` block. If no exception arises, the `finally` block is executed after the `try` block. If an exception arises for which there is no appropriate `catch` block, then the `finally` block is executed after the `try` block.

The circumstances that can prevent execution of the code in a `finally` block are:

- An exception arising in the `finally` block itself

- The death of the thread

- The use of `System.exit()`

- Turning off the power to the CPU

Notice that an exception in the `finally` block behaves exactly like any other exception; it can be handled via a `try/catch`. If no `catch` is found, then control jumps out of the method from the point at which the exception is raised, perhaps leaving the `finally` block incompletely executed.

Catching Multiple Exceptions

When you define a `catch` block, that block will catch exceptions of the class specified, including any exceptions that are subclasses of the one specified. In this way, you can handle categories of exceptions in a single `catch` block. If you specify one exception class in one particular `catch` block and a parent class of that exception in another `catch` block, you can handle the more specific exceptions—those of the subclass—separately from others of the same general parent class. Under such conditions these rules apply:

- A more specific `catch` block must precede a more general one in the source. Failure to meet this ordering requirement causes a compiler error.

- Only one `catch` block, that is the first applicable one, will be executed.

Now let's look at the overall framework for `try`, multiple `catch` blocks, and `finally`:

```
 1. try {
 2.   // statements
 3.   // some are safe, some might throw an exception
 4. }
 5. catch (SpecificException e) {
 6.   // do something, perhaps try to recover
 7. }
 8. catch (OtherException e) {
 9.   // handling for OtherException
10. }
11. catch (GeneralException e) {
12.   // handling for GeneralException
13. }
14. finally {
15.   // code that must be executed under
16.   // successful or unsuccessful conditions.
17. }
18. // more lines of method code
```

In this example, `GeneralException` is a parent class of `Specific-Exception`. Several scenarios can arise under these conditions:

- No exceptions occur.

- A `SpecificException` occurs.

- A `GeneralException` occurs.

- An entirely different exception occurs, which we will call an `UnknownException`.

If no exceptions occur, execution completes the `try` block, lines 1–4, and then proceeds to the `finally` block, lines 14–17. The rest of the method, line 18 onward, is then executed.

If a `SpecificException` occurs, execution abandons the `try` block at the point the exception is raised and jumps into the `SpecificException catch` block. Typically, this might result in lines 1 and 2, then 5, 6, and 7 being executed. After the `catch` block, the `finally` block and the rest of the method are executed, lines 14–17 and line 18 onward.

If a `GeneralException` that is not a `SpecificException` occurs, then execution proceeds out of the `try` block, into the `GeneralException catch` block at lines 11–13. After that `catch` block, execution proceeds to the `finally` block and the rest of the method, just as in the last example.

If an `UnknownException` occurs, execution proceeds out of the `try` block directly to the `finally` block. After the `finally` block is completed, the rest of the method is abandoned. This is an uncaught exception; it will appear in the caller just as if there had never been any `try` block in the first place.

Now that we have discussed what happens when an exception is thrown, let's proceed to how exceptions are thrown and the rules that relate to methods that might throw exceptions.

Throwing Exceptions

The last section discussed how exceptions modify the flow of execution in a Java program. We will now continue by examining how exceptions are issued in the first place, and how you can write methods that use exceptions to report difficulties.

The *throw* Statement

Throwing an exception, in its most basic form, is simple. You need to do two things. First, you create an instance of an object that is a subclass of `java.lang.Throwable`. Next you use the `throw` keyword to actually throw the exception. These two are normally combined into a single statement like this:

```
throw new IOException("File not found");
```

There is an important reason why the `throw` statement and the construction of the exception are normally combined. The exception builds information about the point at which it was created, and that information is shown in the stack trace when the exception is reported. It is convenient if the line reported as the origin of the exception is the same line as the `throw` statement, so it is a good idea to combine the two parts, and `throw new xxx()` becomes the norm.

The *throws* Statement

You have just seen how easy it is to generate and throw an exception; however, the overall picture is more complex. First, as a general rule, Java requires that any method that might throw an exception must declare the fact. In a way, this is a form of enforced documentation, but you will see that there is a little more to it than just that.

If you write a method that might throw an exception (and this includes unhandled exceptions that are generated by other methods called from your method), then you must declare the possibility using a `throws` statement. For example, the (incomplete) method shown here can throw a `MalformedURLException` or an `EOFException`.

```
1. public void doSomeIO(String targetUrl)
2.    throws MalformedURLException, EOFException {
3.    // new URL might throw MalformedURLException
4.    URL url = new URL(targetUrl);
5.    // open the url and read from it...
6.    // set flag 'completed' when IO is successful
7.    //....
8.    // so if we get here with completed == false,
9.    // we got unexpected end of file.
10.   if (!completed) {
11.      throw new EOFException("Invalid file contents");
12.   }
13. }
```

Line 11 demonstrates the use of the `throw` statement—it is usual for a `throw` statement to be conditional in some way; otherwise the method has no way to complete successfully. Line 2 shows the use of the `throws` statement. In this case, there are two distinct exceptions listed that the method might throw under different failure conditions. The exceptions are given as a comma-separated list.

The section "Catching Multiple Exceptions" earlier in this chapter explained that the class hierarchy of exceptions is significant in `catch` blocks. The hierarchy is also significant in the `throws` statement. In this example, line 2 could be shortened to `throws IOException`. This is because both `MalformedURLException` and `EOFException` are subclasses of `IOException`.

It is important to recognize that declaring that a method throws an exception does not mean the method will fail with that exception, only that it might do so. In fact, it is perfectly legitimate—and in some situations that you will see later, actually necessary—to make such declarations, even though they appear to be redundant.

Checked Exceptions

So far we have discussed throwing exceptions and declaring methods that might throw exceptions. We have said that any method that throws an exception should use the `throws` statement to declare the fact. The whole truth is slightly subtler than that.

The class hierarchy that exists under the class `java.lang.Throwable` is divided into three parts. One part contains the errors, which are `java.lang.Error` and all subclasses. Another part is called the runtime exceptions, which are `java.lang.RuntimeException` and all its subclasses. The third part contains the checked exceptions, which are all subclasses of `java.lang.Exception` (except for `java.lang.RuntimeException` and its subclasses). Figure 5.1 shows this diagrammatically.

FIGURE 5.1   Categories of exceptions

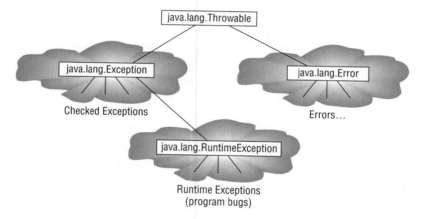

You might well ask why the hierarchy is divided up and what these various names mean.

The *checked exceptions* describe problems that can arise in a correct program, typically difficulties with the environment such as user mistakes or I/O problems. For example, attempting to open a socket can fail if the remote machine does not exist, is not responding, or is not providing the requested service. Neither of these problems indicates a programming error; it's more likely to be a problem with the machine name (the user mistyped it) or with the remote machine (perhaps it is incorrectly configured). Because these conditions can arise at any time, in a commercial-grade program you must write code to handle and recover from them. In fact, the Java compiler checks that you have indeed stated what is to be done when they arise, and it is because of this checking that they are called checked exceptions.

Runtime exceptions typically describe program bugs. You could use a runtime exception as deliberate flow control, but it would be an odd way to design code and rather poor style. Runtime exceptions generally arise from things like out-of-bounds array accesses, and normally these would be avoided by a correctly coded program. Because runtime exceptions should never arise in a correct program, you are not required to handle them. After all, it would only clutter your program if you had to write code that your design states should never be executed.

Errors generally describe problems that are sufficiently unusual, and sufficiently difficult to recover from, that you are not required to handle them. They might reflect a program bug, but more commonly they reflect environmental problems, such as running out of memory. As with runtime exceptions, Java does not require that you state how these are to be handled.

An approach to program design and implementation that is highly effective in producing robust and reliable code is known as *programming by contract*. Briefly, this approach requires clearly defined responsibilities for methods and the callers of those methods. For example, a square-root method could require that it must be called only with a non-negative argument. If called with a negative argument, the method would react by throwing an exception, since the contract between it and its caller has been broken. This approach simplifies code, since methods only attempt to handle properly formulated calls. It also brings bugs out into the open as quickly as possible, thereby ensuring they get fixed. You should use runtime exceptions to implement this approach, as it is clearly inappropriate for the caller to have to check for programming errors; the programmer should fix them.

It *is* appropriate to catch runtime exceptions at the top of a program, but not to try to continue. You should make a best effort to save the current state of the program's data so that the program can attempt to load that data when restarted. If you simply allow the program to "bomb out", your users will be rightly annoyed at the loss of all their work. Be careful, however, to avoid the temptation to write the data over the original file. This is because you know something in your program is broken, although you don't know what. It might be that the program's data is already damaged, and by overwriting the original file, you might lose not only the user's work, but also their recovery point.

Checking Checked Exceptions

We have stated that of the three categories of exceptions, the checked exceptions make certain demands of the programmer: You are obliged to state how the exception is to be handled. In fact you have two choices. You can put a `try` block around the code that might throw the exception and provide a corresponding `catch` block that will apply to the exception in question. This handles the exception so it effectively goes away. Alternatively, you might decide that if this exception occurs, your method cannot proceed and should be abandoned. In this case, you do not need to provide the `try/catch` construction, but you must instead make sure that the method declaration includes a `throws` part that informs potential callers that the exception might arise. Notice that by insisting that the method be declared in this way, the responsibility for handling the exception is explicitly passed to the caller of the method, which must then make the same choice—whether to declare or handle the exception. The following example demonstrates this choice:

```
1.  public class DeclareOrHandle {
2.    // This method makes no attempt to recover from the
3.    // exception, rather it declares that it might
4.    // throw it and uses no try block
5.    public void declare(String s) throws IOException {
6.      URL u = new URL(s); // might throw IOException
7.      // do things with the URL object u...
8.    }
9.
10.   // This method handles the exception that might
11.   // arise when it calls the method declare().
12.   // Therefore, it does not throw any exceptions
13.   // and so does not use any throws declaration
14.   public void handle(String s) {
15.     boolean success = false;
16.     while (!success) {
17.       try {
18.         declare(s);  // might throw an IOException
19.         // execute this if declare() succeeded
20.         success = true;
```

```
21.        }
22.        catch (IOException e) {
23.          // Advise user that String s is somehow
24.          // unusable and ask for a new one
25.        }
26.      } // end while loop, exits when success is true
27.    }
28. }
```

The method `declare()` does not attempt to handle the exception that might arise during construction of the URL object. Instead, the `declare()` method states that it might throw the exception. By contrast, the `handle()` method uses a `try/catch` construction to ensure that control remains inside the `handle()` method itself until it becomes possible to recover from the problem.

We have now discussed the handling of exceptions and the constructions that allow you to throw exceptions of your own. Before we finish with exceptions, we must consider a rule relating to overriding methods and exceptions. The next section discusses this rule.

Exceptions and Overriding

When you extend a class and override a method, Java insists that the new method cannot be declared as throwing checked exceptions of classes other than those that were declared by the original method. Consider these examples (assume they are declared in separate source files; the line numbers are simply for reference):

```
1. public class BaseClass {
2.    public void method() throws IOException {
3.    }
4. }
5.
6. public class LegalOne extends BaseClass {
7.    public void method() throws IOException {
8.    }
9. }
10.
11. public class LegalTwo extends BaseClass {
12.    public void method() {
13.    }
```

```
14. }
15.
16. public class LegalThree extends BaseClass {
17.     public void method()
18.     throws EOFException, MalformedURLException {
19.     }
20. }
21.
22. public class IllegalOne extends BaseClass {
23.     public void method()
24.     throws IOException, IllegalAccessException {
25.     }
26. }
27.
28. public class IllegalTwo extends BaseClass {
29.     public void method()
30.     throws Exception {
31.     }
32. }
```

Notice that the original method() in BaseClass is declared as throwing IOException. This allows it, and any overriding method defined in a subclass, to throw an IOException or any object that is a subclass of IOException. Overriding methods may not, however, throw any checked exceptions that are not subclasses of IOException.

Given these rules, you will see that line 7 in LegalOne is correct, since method() is declared exactly the same way as the original that it overrides. Similarly, line 18 in LegalThree is correct, since both EOFException and MalformedURLException are subclasses of IOException—so this adheres to the rule that nothing may be thrown that is not a subclass of the exceptions already declared. Line 12 in LegalTwo is correct, since it throws no exceptions and therefore cannot throw any exceptions that are not subclasses of IOException.

The methods at lines 23 and 29 are not permissible, since both of them throw checked exceptions that are not subclasses of IOException. In IllegalOne, IllegalAccessException is a subclass of Exception; in IllegalTwo, Exception itself is a superclass of IOException. Both IllegalAccessException and Exception are checked exceptions, so the methods that attempt to throw them are illegal as overriding methods of `method()` in `BaseClass`.

The point of this rule relates to the use of base class variables as references to objects of subclass type. Chapter 4 explains that you can declare a variable of a class X and then use that variable to refer to any object that is of class X or any subclass of X.

Imagine that in the examples just described, you had declared a variable `myBaseObject` of class `BaseClass`; you can use it to refer to objects of any of the classes `LegalOne`, `LegalTwo`, and `LegalThree`. (You couldn't use it to refer to objects of class `IllegalOne` or `IllegalTwo`, since those objects cannot be created in the first place: Their code won't compile.) The compiler imposes checks on how you call `myBaseObject.method()`. Those checks ensure that for each call, you have either enclosed the call in a `try` block and provided a corresponding `catch` block or you have declared that the calling method itself might throw an `IOException`. Now suppose that at runtime the variable `myBaseObject` was used to refer to an object of class `IllegalOne`. Under these conditions, the compiler would still believe that the only exceptions that must be dealt with are of class `IOException`. This is because it believes that `myBaseObject` refers to an object of class `BaseClass`. The compiler would therefore not insist that you provide a `try/catch` construct that catches the `IllegalAccessException`, nor that you declare the calling method as throwing that exception. This means that if the class `IllegalOne` were permitted, then overriding methods would be able to bypass the enforced checks for checked exceptions.

Because an overriding method cannot throw more exceptions than were declared for the original method, it is important to consider the likely needs of subclasses whenever you define a class. Recall from the earlier section "The *throws* Statement" that it is entirely permissible to declare that a method throws an exception even if no code exists to actually throw that exception. Now that you know an overriding method must not throw exceptions that were not declared in the parent method, you will recognize that some parent classes need to declare exceptions in methods that do not in fact throw any exceptions. For example, the `InputStream` class cannot, of itself, actually throw any exceptions, since it doesn't interact with real devices that could fail. However, it is used as the base class for a whole hierarchy of classes that do interact with physical devices: `FileInputStream` and so forth. It is important that the `read()` methods of those subclasses be able to throw exceptions, so the corresponding `read()` methods in the `Input-Stream` class itself must be declared as throwing `IOException`.

We have now looked at all the aspects of exception handling that you will need to prepare for the Certification Exam and to make effective use of exceptions in your programs.

Chapter Summary

Loop Constructs

- Three loop constructs are provided: `while()`, `do`, and `for()`.

- Each loop statement is controlled by an expression that must be of `boolean` type.

- In both `while()` and `for()`, the test occurs at the "top" of the loop, so the body might not be executed at all.

- In `do`, the test occurs at the end of the loop so the body of the loop definitely executes at least once.

- The `for()` loop takes three elements in its brackets. The first is executed once only, before the loop starts. Typically you might use it for initializing the loop or for declaring a loop counter variable. The second element must be `boolean`, and is the loop control test. The third is executed at the end of the loop body, just prior to performing the test.

- The first element in the brackets of a `for()` construction can declare a variable. In that case, the scope of the variable is restricted to the control parts in the brackets, and the following statement. The following statement is often a block in its own right, in which case the variable remains in scope throughout that block.

- All three parts of the `for()` construction are optional. If the test is missing, it is treated as perpetually true.

- The `continue` statement causes the current iteration of the loop to be abandoned. Flow restarts at the bottom of the loop. For `while()` and `do`, this means the test is executed next. For the `for()` loop, the third statement in the parentheses is executed, followed by the test.

- The `break` statement abandons the loop altogether; the test is not performed on the way out.

- Both `break` and `continue` can take a label that causes them to skip out of multiple levels of nested loop. The matching label must be placed at the head of a loop and is indicated by using an identifier followed by a colon (`:`).

Selection Statements

- The if() statement takes a boolean argument.

- The else part is optional after if().

- The switch() statement takes an argument that is assignment-compatible to int (that is, one of byte, short, char, or int).

- The argument to case must be a constant or constant expression that can be calculated at compile time.

- The case label takes only a single argument. To create a list of values that lead to the same point, use multiple case statements and allow execution to "fall through."

- The default label may be used in a switch() construction to pick up execution where none of the explicit cases match.

Flow in Exception Handling

- An exception causes a jump to the end of the enclosing try block even if the exception occurs within a method called from the try block, in which case the called method is abandoned.

- If any of the catch blocks associated with the try block that just terminated specifies an exception class that is the same as, or a parent class of, the exception that was thrown, then execution proceeds to the first such catch block. The exception is now considered handled. If no appropriate catch block is found, the exception is considered unhandled.

- Regardless of whether or not an exception occurred, or whether or not it was handled, execution proceeds next to the finally block associated with the try block, if such a finally block exists.

- If there was no exception, or if the exception was handled, execution continues after the finally block.

- If the exception was unhandled, the process repeats, looking for the next enclosing try block. If the search for a try block reaches the top of the method-call hierarchy (that is, the point at which the thread was created), then the thread is killed and a message and stack trace is dumped to System.err.

Exception Throwing

- To throw an exception, use the construction `throw new XXXException();`.

- Any object that is of class `java.lang.Exception`, or any subclass of `java.lang.Exception` except subclasses of `java.lang.RuntimeException`, is a checked exception.

- In any method that contains lines that might throw a checked exception, you must either handle the exception using a `try/catch` construct, or declare that the method throws the exception using a `throws` construct in the declaration of the method.

- A method cannot throw any `Throwable` other than `RuntimeException`, `Error`, and subclasses of these, unless a `throws` declaration is attached to the method to indicate that this might happen.

- A method that declares an exception need not include code to throw that exception.

- An overriding method may not throw a checked exception unless the overridden method also throws that exception or a superclass of that exception.

Test Yourself

1. Consider the following code:

```
1. for (int i = 0; i < 2; i++) {
2.    for (int j = 0; j < 3; j++) {
3.       if (i == j) {
4.          continue;
5.       }
6.       System.out.println("i = " + i + " j = " + j);
7.    }
8. }
```

Which lines would be part of the output?

A. i = 0 j = 0

B. i = 0 j = 1

C. i = 0 j = 2

D. i = 1 j = 0

E. i = 1 j = 1

F. i = 1 j = 2

2. Consider the following code:

```
1. outer: for (int i = 0; i < 2; i++) {
2.    for (int j = 0; j < 3; j++) {
3.       if (i == j) {
4.          continue outer;
5.       }
6.       System.out.println("i = " + i + " j = " + j);
7.    }
8. }
```

Which lines would be part of the output?

A. i = 0 j = 0

B. i = 0 j = 1

C. i = 0 j = 2

D. i = 1 j = 0

E. i = 1 j = 1

F. i = 1 j = 2

3. Which of the following are legal loop constructions? (Choose one or more.)

A.
```
1. while (int i < 7) {
2.    i++;
3.    System.out.println("i is " + i);
4. }
```

B.
```
1. int i = 3;
2. while (i) {
3.    System.out.println("i is " + i);
4. }
```

C.
```
1. int j = 0;
2. for (int k = 0; j + k != 10; j++, k++) {
3.    System.out.println("j is " + j + " k is " + k);
4. }
```

D.
```
1. int j = 0;
2. do {
3.    System.out.println("j is " + j++);
4.    if (j == 3) { continue loop; }
5. } while (j < 10);
```

4. What would be the output from this code fragment?

```
1.  int x = 0, y = 4, z = 5;
2.  if (x > 2) {
3.    if (y < 5) {
4.      System.out.println("message one");
5.    }
6.    else {
7.      System.out.println("message two");
8.    }
9.  }
10. else if (z > 5) {
11.   System.out.println("message three");
12. }
13. else {
14.   System.out.println("message four");
15. }
```

A. message one

B. message two

C. message three

D. message four

5. Which statement is true about the following code fragment?

```
1.  int j = 2;
2.  switch (j) {
3.    case 2:
4.      System.out.println("value is two");
5.    case 2 + 1:
6.      System.out.println("value is three");
7.      break;
8.    default:
9.      System.out.println("value is " + j);
10.     break;
11. }
```

A. The code is illegal because of the expression at line 5.

B. The acceptable types for the variable j, as the argument to the `switch()` construct, could be any of `byte`, `short`, `int`, or `long`.

C. The output would be only the text `value is two`.

D. The output would be the text `value is two` followed by the text `value is three`.

E. The output would be the text `value is two`, followed by the text `value is three`, followed by the text `value is 2`.

6. Consider the following class hierarchy and code fragment:

```
                    java.lang.Exception
                            \
                    java.io.IOException
                       /            \
java.io.StreamCorruptedException        java.net.MalformedURLException
```

```
1. try {
2.    // assume s is previously defined
3.    URL u = new URL(s);
4.    // in is an ObjectInputStream
5.    Object o = in.readObject();
6.    System.out.println("Success");
7. }
8. catch (MalformedURLException e) {
9.    System.out.println("Bad URL");
10. }
11. catch (StreamCorruptedException e) {
12.    System.out.println("Bad file contents");
13. }
14. catch (Exception e) {
15.    System.out.println("General exception");
16. }
17. finally {
18.    System.out.println("doing finally part");
19. }
20. System.out.println("Carrying on");
```

What lines are output if the constructor at line 3 throws a `MalformedURLException`?

A. Success

B. Bad URL

C. Bad file contents

D. General exception

E. Doing finally part

F. Carrying on

7. Consider the following class hierarchy and code fragment:

```
                      java.lang.Exception
                             \
                        java.io.IOException
                         /               \
 java.io.StreamCorruptedException    java.net.MalformedURLException
```

```
1. try {
2.    // assume s is previously defined
3.    URL u = new URL(s);
4.    // in is an ObjectInputStream
5.    Object o = in.readObject();
6.    System.out.println("Success");
7. }
8. catch (MalformedURLException e) {
9.    System.out.println("Bad URL");
10. }
11. catch (StreamCorruptedException e) {
12.    System.out.println("Bad file contents");
13. }
14. catch (Exception e) {
15.    System.out.println("General exception");
16. }
17. finally {
18.    System.out.println("Doing finally part");
19. }
20. System.out.println("Carrying on");
```

What lines are output if the methods at lines 3 and 5 complete successfully without throwing any exceptions?

A. Success

B. Bad URL

C. Bad file contents

D. General exception

E. Doing finally part

F. Carrying on

8. Consider the following class hierarchy and code fragment:

```
                java.lang.Throwable
               /                    \
    java.lang.Error          java.lang.Exception
           /                          \
java.lang.OutOfMemoryError      java.io.IOException
                               /                    \
    java.io.StreamCorruptedException    java.net.MalformedURLException
```

```
1. try {
2.     // assume s is previously defined
3.     URL u = new URL(s);
4.     // in is an ObjectInputStream
5.     Object o = in.readObject();
6.     System.out.println("Success");
7. }
8. catch (MalformedURLException e) {
9.     System.out.println("Bad URL");
10. }
11. catch (StreamCorruptedException e) {
12.     System.out.println("Bad file contents");
13. }
14. catch (Exception e) {
15.     System.out.println("General exception");
16. }
17. finally {
18.     System.out.println("Doing finally part");
19. }
20. System.out.println("Carrying on");
```

What lines are output if the method at line 5 throws an OutOfMemoryError?

A. Success

B. Bad URL

C. Bad file contents

D. General exception

E. Doing finally part

F. Carrying on

9. Which *one* of the following fragments shows the *most* appropriate way to throw an exception? Assume that any undeclared variables have been appropriately declared elsewhere and are in scope and have meaningful values.

A.
```
1. Exception e = new IOException("File not found");
2. if (!f.exists()) { // f is a File object
3.    throw e;
4. }
```

B.
```
1. if (!f.exists()) { // f is a File object
2.    throw new IOException("File " + f.getName() +
      " not found");
3. }
```

C.
```
1. if (!f.exists()) {
2.    throw IOException;
3. }
```

D.
```
1. if (!f.exists()) {
2.    throw "File not found";
3. }
```

E.
```
1. if (!f.exists()) { // f is a File object
2.    throw new IOException();
3. }
```

10. The method `risky()` might throw a `java.io.IOException`, `java
.lang.RuntimeException`, or `java.net.MalformedURLException`
(which is a subclass of `java.io.IOException`). Appropriate imports
have been declared for each of those exceptions. Which of the following
classes and sets of classes are legal? (Choose one or more.)

A.
```
1. public class SomeClass {
2.    public void aMethod() {
3.       risky();
4.    }
5. }
```

B.
```
1. public class SomeClass {
2.    public void aMethod() throws
3.       IOException {
4.       risky();
5.    }
6. }
```

C.
```
1. public class SomeClass {
2.    public void aMethod() throws
3.       RuntimeException {
4.       risky();
5.    }
6. }
```

D.
```
1.  public class SomeClass {
2.     public void aMethod() {
3.        try {
4.           risky();
5.        }
6.        catch (IOException e) {
7.           e.printStackTrace();
8.        }
9.     }
10. }
```

E.

```
1. public class SomeClass {
2.    public void aMethod()
3.       throws MalformedURLException {
4.       try { risky(); }
5.       catch (IOException e) {
6.          // ignore it
7.       }
8.    }
9. }
10.
11. public class AnotherClass
12.    extends SomeClass {
13.    public void aMethod()
14.       throws java.io.IOException {
15.       super.aMethod();
16.    }
17. }
```

Chapter

6

Objects and Classes

JAVA CERTIFICATION EXAM OBJECTIVES COVERED IN THIS CHAPTER:

✓ State the benefits of encapsulation in object-oriented design, and write code that implements tightly encapsulated classes and the relationships "is a" and "has a."

✓ State the legal return types for any method given the declarations of all related methods in this or parent classes.

✓ Write code to invoke overridden or overloaded methods and parental or overloaded constructors; and describe the effect of invoking these methods.

✓ Declare classes, inner classes, methods, instance variables, static variables, and automatic (method local) variables, making appropriate use of all permitted modifiers (such as *public, final, static, abstract,* and so forth). State the significance of each of these modifiers both singly and in combination, and state the effect of package relationships on declared items qualified by these modifiers.

✓ Write code to construct instances of any concrete class, including normal top-level classes, inner classes, static inner classes, and anonymous inner classes.

✓ Identify correctly constructed source files, package declarations, import statements, class declarations (of all forms, including inner classes), interface declarations and implementations (for *java.lang.Runnable* or other interface described in the test), method declarations (including the *main* method that is used to start execution of a class), variable declarations, and identifiers.

This chapter discusses the object-oriented features of Java. Good coding in Java requires a sound understanding of the object-oriented (OO) paradigm, and this in turn requires a good grasp of the language features that implement objects and classes. The many benefits of object orientation have been the subject of considerable public debate, but for most programmers these benefits have not been realized. In most cases, the reason the promise has not been fulfilled is simply that programmers have not been writing objects. Instead, many programmers have been writing hybrid applications with a mixture of procedural and object-oriented code. Unfortunately, such an approach has given rise, not to *some* of the benefits of OO, but instead to *all* the disadvantages of both styles.

Benefits of Object-Oriented Implementation

Beginning with the 1.2 examination, you are required to understand the benefits of object-oriented design. These benefits accrue from two particular features of the OO paradigm. The first of these, and perhaps the most important, is the notion of an abstract data type; the second and perhaps better-known is the extensibility provided by inheritance.

Abstract Data Types

An abstract data type is really just a fancy name for a well-encapsulated aggregate of data and behavior. Consider the primitive data types of any programming language you have ever used. You do not know how these data items are stored and, for the most part, you do not care. What matters are the operations that you can perform on these data items and the boundary conditions within which you can expect those operations to work properly. These primitive types are in fact abstract data types, albeit not user-defined.

Your first goal in defining a good class should be to clearly state the operations that can be applied to instances of that class. Next, consider how to represent the state of the instance, keeping in mind that this should be done only with variables of private accessibility. All behavior should be accessed only via methods. By insisting that the variables inside an object are inaccessible outside the object, you ensure that the nature of those variables is irrelevant outside the object. This in turn means that you can freely change the nature of the storage, for maintenance purposes, for performance improvement, or for any other reason.

Sometimes, perhaps as a consequence of the way you have stored the state in a class, boundary conditions must be applied to its methods. A boundary condition is a limit on the range of arguments for which a method can operate properly. As examples, a square-root function cannot operate conventionally on a negative number; an add operation cannot operate if both of its arguments are more than half the maximum representable range for the operation's return type.

When you encounter a boundary condition that results from your choice of storage format, you must make a choice. If you consider that the boundary conditions are reasonable, then you should do two things. First, document the boundary condition. Next, test the boundary conditions at the entry to the method and, if the boundary condition has been exceeded, throw a runtime exception of some kind. Alternatively, you might decide that the boundary condition is not acceptable, in which case you should redesign the storage used in the class.

Now, consider this: If you had allowed access to any of the variables used to represent the object state, then redefining the way the object's state is stored would immediately cause any other code that uses these variables to have to be rewritten. However, by using only private member variables, we have insisted that all interaction with this object is made through methods and never by direct variable access—so we have eliminated this problem. In consequence, we are able to redesign our internal storage freely and, provided the signatures of all the methods remain the same, no other code needs to change.

Sometimes you will realize that the methods you have provided for a class are inadequate. This is not usually a problem, either. You may add new methods to freely provide additional functionality. No client code will break, provided the methods that were already provided remain available, with the same signatures and the same semantics. The only issues that might arise during maintenance are if you realize that a method you have defined has a fundamentally flawed prototype. This should not happen often, since it implies that the operation you defined for the class was conceptually flawed in some way.

Encapsulation and Perceived Efficiency

Many programmers have such deep-seated concerns about performance that they cannot bring themselves to force all access to their objects to be made through methods, and they resist creating classes with entirely private member variables. There are several reasons why this is an unwise approach. First, fully encapsulated classes are more likely to be used correctly, especially if boundary conditions are properly flagged with exceptions—therefore, code using them is more likely to be correct. Second, bug fixes and maintenance changes are less likely to break the program as a whole, since the effects of the change are confined to the affected class. These reasons fall into the broad heading of "Would your customer prefer a slow program that works and is delivered on time (and that can be made faster later) or a program that is delivered late, works incorrectly, but runs quickly?"

There are more reasons why fully encapsulated classes are the right way to start out a design. An optimizing virtual machine such as Sun's HotSpot can transparently optimize simple variable access methods by "inlining." This approach allows the program all the robustness, reliability, and maintainability that results from full encapsulation, while giving the runtime performance associated with direct variable access. Furthermore, if you decide that a program's slow performance is attributable to the use of private variables and accessor/mutator methods, then changing the variable to be more accessible does not require any changes to the rest of the code, either inside or outside the class. On the other hand, if you have code that fails to run properly as a result of making direct variable access, you will find that reducing the accessibility of the relevant variable will require considerable collateral changes in many other pieces of code (all code that makes such direct access).

Reuse

We have discussed how tight encapsulation can make code that is more reliable and robust. Now we will consider the second most significant advantage of object-oriented programming: code reuse.

Writing good, encapsulated classes usually requires more work in the initial stages than would have been required to produce the same functionality with a traditional programming approach. While this is true, you will normally find that using rigorous OO techniques will actually reduce the overall time required to produce finished code. This happens for two reasons. The first is that the robust classes you produce actually require less time to integrate into the final program and less time to fix bugs. The second is that with careful design you can reuse classes even in some circumstances that are different from the original intent of the class.

This reuse is actually possible in two ways, using either composition (the "has a" relation) or inheritance (the "is a" relation). Composition is probably safer and easier to control, although inheritance—perhaps because it is perceived as "pure OO"—seems to be more interesting and appealing to most programmers.

The Java certification exam does not require you to discuss details of object-oriented design techniques or the relative merits and weaknesses of composition versus inheritance. However, you should appreciate one significant sequence of facts: If a class is well encapsulated, it will be easier to reuse successfully. The more a class is reused, the better tested it will be and the fewer bugs it will have. Better-tested, less-buggy classes are easier to reuse. This sequence leads to a positive spiral of quality since the better the class, the easier and safer it becomes to reuse. All this comes from tight encapsulation.

Now that we've discussed why you would want to write object-oriented code, let's look at how this is achieved.

Implementing Object-Oriented Relationships

This section is not intended to discuss object-oriented design; rather, it considers the implementation of classes for which you have been given a basic description.

There are two clauses that are commonly used when describing a class in plain English: "is a" and "has a." As a working simplification, these are used to describe the superclass and member variables, respectively. For example, consider this description:

"A home is a house that has a family and a pet."

This description would give rise to the outline of a Java class in this form:

```
1. public class Home extends House {
2.    Family inhabitants;
3.    Pet thePet;
4. }
```

Notice the direct correspondence between the "is a" clause and the extends clause. In this example, there is also a direct correspondence between the items listed after "has a" and the member variables. Such a correspondence is representative in simple examples and in a test situation; however, you should be aware that in real examples there are other ways that you can provide a class with attributes. Probably the most important of these alternatives is the approach taken by Java Beans, which is to supply accessor and mutator methods that operate on private data members.

WARNING   The example shown is simplified to focus on the knowledge and understanding that is required by the exam. In a real situation, the variables should generally be private (or at least some specific rationale should apply to whatever accessibility they have) and some methods will be needed in the class.

Overloading and Overriding

As you construct classes and add methods to them, there are circumstances when you will want to reuse the same name for a method. There are two ways that you can do this with Java. Reusing the same method name with different arguments and perhaps a different return type is known as *overloading*. Using the same method name with identical arguments and return type is known as *overriding*.

A method name can be reused anywhere, as long as certain conditions are met:

- In an unrelated class, no special conditions apply and the two methods are not considered related in any way.

- In the class that defines the original method, or a subclass of that class, the method name can be reused if the argument list differs in terms of the type of at least one argument. This is overloading. It is important to realize that a difference in return type alone is insufficient to constitute an overload and is illegal.

- In a strict subclass of the class that defines the original method, the method name can be reused with identical argument types and order and with identical return type. This is overriding. In this case, additional restrictions apply to the accessibility of, and exceptions that may be thrown by, the method.

In general, a class is considered to be a subclass of itself. That is, if classes A, B, and C are defined so that C extends B, and B extends A, then the subclasses of A are A, B, and C. The term *strict subclass* is used to describe the subclasses excluding the class itself. So the strict subclasses of A are only B and C.

Now let's take a look at these ideas in detail. First, we will consider overloading method names.

Overloading Method Names

In Java, a method is uniquely identified by the combination of its fully qualified class name, method name, and the exact sequence of its argument types. Overloading is the reuse of a method name in the one class or subclass for a different method. This is not related to object orientation, although there is a purely coincidental correlation that shows that object-oriented languages are more likely to support overloading. Notice that overloading is essentially a trick with names, hence this section's title is "Overloading Method Names" rather than "Overloading Methods." The following are all different methods:

```
1. public void aMethod(String s) { }
```

```
2. public void aMethod() { }
3. public void aMethod(int i, String s) { }
4. public void aMethod(String s, int i) { }
```

These methods all have identical return types and names, but their argument lists are different either in the types of the arguments that they take or in the order. Only the argument types are considered, not their names, so a method such as

```
public void aMethod(int j, String name) { }
```

would *not* be distinguished from the method defined in line 3 above.

What Is Overloading For?

Why is overloading useful? There are times when you will be creating several methods that perform closely related functions under different conditions. For example, imagine methods that calculate the area of a triangle. One such method might take the Cartesian coordinates of the three vertices and another might take the polar coordinates. A third method might take the lengths of all three sides, while a fourth might take three angles and the length of one side. These would all be performing the same essential function, and so it is entirely proper to use the same name for the methods. In languages that do not permit overloading, you would have to think up four different method names, such as:

```
areaByCoord(Point p, Point q, Point r)
areaByPolarCoord(PolarPt p, PolarPt q, PolarPt r)
areaBySideLengths(int l1, int l2, int l3)
areaByAnglesAndASide(int l1, int angle1, int angle2, int
angle3)
```

Overloading is really nothing new. Almost every language that has a type system has used overloading in a way, although most have not allowed the programmer free use of it. Consider the arithmetic operators +, -, *, and /. In most languages, these can be used with integer or floating-point operands. The actual implementation of, say, multiplication for integer and floating-point operands generally involves completely different code, and yet the compiler permits the same symbol to be used. Because the operand types are different, the compiler can decide which version of the operation should be used. This is known as operator overloading and is the same principle as method overloading.

So it is quite useful, for thinking up method names and for improving program readability, to be able to use one method name for several related methods requiring different implementations. However, you should restrict your use of overloaded method names to situations where the methods really are performing the same basic function with different data sets. Methods that perform different jobs should have different names.

One last point to consider is the return type of an overloaded method. The language treats methods with overloaded names as totally different methods, and as such they *can* have different return types (you will see shortly that overriding methods do not have this freedom). However, if two methods are performing the same job with different data sets, shouldn't they produce the same result type? Generally this is true, and you should expect overloaded methods to be defined with the same result types. There is one particular condition, however, under which it is clearly sensible to define different return types for overloaded methods. This is the situation where the return type is derived from the argument type and is exactly parallel with the arithmetic operators discussed earlier. If you define three methods called addUp() that take two arguments, both int, both float, or both double, then it is entirely reasonable for the method to return int, float, or double in line with its arguments.

Invoking Overloaded Methods

When you write multiple methods that perform the same basic function with different arguments, you often find that it would be useful to call one of these methods as support for another version. Consider a method called printRightJustified() that is to be provided in versions that take a String or an int value. The version that takes an int could most easily be coded so that it converts the int to a String and then calls the version that operates on String objects.

You can do this easily. Remember that the compiler decides which method to call simply by looking at the argument list and that the various overloaded methods are in fact unrelated. All you have to do is write the method call exactly as normal—the compiler will do the rest. Consider this example:

```
1. public class RightJustify {
2.   // Declare a String of 80 spaces
3.   private static final String padding =
4.     "                    " +
5.     "                    " +
```

```
6.      "                      " +
7.      "                      ";
8.    public static void print(String s, int w) {
9.      System.out.print(
10.       padding.substring(0, w - s.length()));
11.     System.out.print(s);
12.   }
13.   public static void print(int i, int w) {
14.     print("" + i, w);
15.   }
16. }
```

At line 14 the `int` argument is converted to a `String` object by adding it to an empty `String`. The method call at this same line is then seen by the compiler as a call to a method called `print()` that takes a `String` as the first argument, which results in selection of the method at line 8.

To summarize, these are the key points about overloading methods:

- The identity of a method is determined by the combination of its fully qualified class, its name, and the type, order, and count of arguments in the argument list.

- Two or more methods in the same class (including methods inherited from a superclass) with the same name but different argument lists are called overloaded.

- Methods with overloaded names are effectively independent methods—using the same name is really just a convenience to the programmer. Return type, accessibility, and exception lists may vary freely.

- Overloaded methods may call one another simply by providing a normal method call with an appropriately formed argument list.

Now that we have considered overloading thoroughly, let's look at overriding.

Method Overriding

You have just seen that overloading is essentially a trick with names, effectively treating the argument list as part of the method identification. Overriding is somewhat more subtle, relating directly to subclassing and hence to the object-oriented nature of a language.

When you extend one class to produce a new one, you inherit and have access to all the non-private methods of the original class. Sometimes, however, you might need to modify the behavior of one of these methods to suit your new class. In this case, you actually want to redefine the method, and this is the essential purpose of overriding.

There are a number of key distinctions between overloading and overriding:

- Overloaded methods supplement each other; an overriding method (largely) replaces the method it overrides.

- Overloaded methods can exist, in any number, in the same class. Each method in a parent class can be overridden at most once in any one subclass.

- Overloaded methods must have *different* argument lists; overriding methods must have argument lists of *identical* type and order (otherwise they are simply treated as overloaded methods).

- The return type of an overloaded method may be chosen freely; the return type of an overriding method must be *identical* to that of the method it overrides.

What Is Overriding For?

Overloading allows multiple implementations of the same essential functionality to use the same name. Overriding, on the other hand, modifies the implementation of a particular piece of behavior for a subclass.

Consider a class that describes a rectangle. Imaginatively, we'll call it `Rectangle`. We're talking about an abstract rectangle here, so there is no visual representation associated with it. This class has a method called `setSize()`, which is used to set width and height values. In the `Rectangle` class itself, the implementation of the `setSize()` method simply sets the value of the private width and height variables for later use. Now imagine we create a `DisplayedRectangle` class that is a subclass of the original `Rectangle`. Now, when the `setSize()` method is called, we need to arrange a new behavior. Specifically, the width and height variables must be changed, but also the visual representation must be redrawn. This is achieved by overriding.

If you define a method that has exactly the same name and exactly the same argument types as a method in a parent class, then you are overriding the method. Under these conditions, the method must also have the identical return type to that of the method it overrides. Consider this example:

```
1. class Rectangle {
2.    int x, y, w, h;
3.
4.    public void setSize(int w, int h) {
5.       this.w = w; this.h = h;
6.    }
7. }
8. class DisplayedRectangle extends Rectangle {
9.    public void setSize(int w, int h) {
10.      this.w = w; this.h = h;
11.      redisplay(); // implementation
12.   }
13.   public void redisplay() {
14.      // implementation not shown
15.   }
16. }
17.
18. public class TestRectangle {
19.    public static void main(String args[]) {
20.       Rectangle [] recs = new Rectangle[4];
21.       recs[0] = new Rectangle();
22.       recs[1] = new DisplayedRectangle();
23.       recs[2] = new DisplayedRectangle();
24.       recs[3] = new Rectangle();
25.       for (int r=0; r<4; r++) {
26.          int w = ((int)(Math.random() * 400));
27.          int h = ((int)(Math.random() * 200));
28.          recs[r].setSize(w, h);
29.       }
30.    }
31. }
```

Clearly this example is incomplete, since no code exists to cause the display of the DisplayedRectangle objects, but it is complete enough for us to discuss.

At line 20, the array *recs* is created as an array of `Rectangle` objects, yet at lines 21–24 the array is used to hold not only two instances of `Rectangle` but also two instances of `DisplayedRectangle`. Subsequently, when the `setSize()` method is called, it will be important that the code that is executed should be the code associated with the actual object referred to by the array element, rather than always being the code of the `Rectangle` class. This is actually exactly what Java does, and this is the essential point of overriding methods. It is as if you ask an object to perform certain behavior, and that object makes its own interpretation of that request. This is a point that C++ programmers should take particular note of, as it differs significantly from the default behavior of overriding methods in that language.

In order for any particular method to override another correctly, some requirements must be met. Some of these have been mentioned before in comparison with overloading, but all are listed here for completeness:

- The method name and the type and order of arguments must be identical to those of a method in a parent class. If this is the case, then the method is an attempt to override the corresponding parent class method and the remaining points listed here must be adhered to, or a compiler error arises. If these criteria are not met, then the method is not an attempt to override and the following rules are irrelevant.

- The return type must be identical.

- The accessibility must not be more restricted than the original method.

- The method must not throw checked exceptions of classes that are not possible for the original method.

The first two points have been covered, but the last two are new. The accessibility of an overriding method must not be less than that of the method it overrides, simply because it is considered to be the replacement method in conditions like those of the rectangles example earlier. So, imagine that the `setSize()` method of `DisplayedRectangle` was inaccessible from the `main()` method of the `TestRectangle` class. The calls to `recs[1].setSize()` and `recs[2].setSize()` would be illegal, but the compiler would be unable to determine this, since it only knows that the elements of the array are `Rectangle` objects. The `extends` keyword literally requires that the subclass be an extension of the parent class: If methods could be removed from the class, or made less accessible, then the subclass would not be a simple extension, but would potentially be a reduction. Under those conditions, the idea of treating `DisplayedRectangle` objects as being `Rectangle` objects when used as method arguments or elements of a collection would be severely flawed.

A similar logic gives rise to the final rule relating to checked exceptions. Checked exceptions are those that the compiler ensures are handled in the source you write. As with accessibility, it must be possible for the compiler to make correct use of a variable of the parent class even if that variable really refers to an object of a derived class. For checked exceptions, this means that an overriding method must not be able to throw exceptions that would not be thrown by the original method. Chapter 5 discusses checked exceptions and this rule in more detail.

Late Binding or Virtual Method Invocation

Normally, when a compiler for a non-object-oriented language comes across a method (or function or procedure) invocation, it determines exactly what target code should be called and builds machine language to represent that call. In an object-oriented language, this is not possible since the proper code to invoke is determined based upon the class of the object being used to make the call, not the type of the variable. Instead, code is generated that will allow the decision to be made at runtime. This delayed decision making is variously referred to as *late binding* (binding is one term for the job a linker does when it glues various bits of machine code together to make an executable program file) or *virtual method invocation*.

Java's Virtual Machine has been designed from the start to support an object-oriented programming system, so there are machine-level instructions for making method calls. The compiler only needs to prepare the argument list and produce one method invocation instruction; the job of identifying and calling the proper target code is performed by the Virtual Machine.

If the Virtual Machine is to be able to decide what actual code should be invoked by a particular method call, it must be able to determine the class of the object upon which the call is based. Again, the Virtual Machine design has supported this from the beginning. Unlike traditional languages or runtime environments, every time the Java system allocates memory, it marks that memory with the type of the data that it has been allocated to hold. This means that given any object, and without regard to the type associated with the reference variable acting as a handle to that object, the runtime system can determine the real class of that object by inspection. This is the basis of the `instanceof` operator, which allows you to program a test to determine the actual class of an object at runtime. The `instanceof` operator is described in Chapter 2.

Invoking Overridden Methods

When we discussed overloading methods, you saw how to invoke one version of a method from another. It is also useful to be able to invoke an overridden method from the method that overrides it. Consider that when you write an overriding method, that method entirely replaces the original method. However, sometimes you only wish to add a little extra behavior and want to retain all the original behavior. This can be achieved, although it requires a small trick of syntax to perform. Look at this example:

```
1. class Rectangle {
2.   private int x, y, w, h;
3.   public String toString() {
4.     return "x = " + x + ", y = " + y +
5.       ", w = " + w + ", h = " + h;
6.   }
7. }
8. class DecoratedRectangle extends Rectangle {
9.   private int borderWidth;
10.   public String toString() {
11.     return super.toString() + ", borderWidth = " +
12.     borderWidth;
13.   }
14. }
```

At line 11 the overriding method in the DecoratedRectangle class uses the parental toString() method to perform the greater part of its work. Since the variables x, y, w, and h in the Rectangle class are marked as private, it would have been impossible for the overriding method in DecoratedRectangle to achieve its work directly.

A call of the form super.xxx() always invokes the behavior that would have been used if the current overriding method had not been defined. It does not matter whether the parental method is defined in the immediate superclass or in some ancestor class further up the hierarchy: super invokes the version of this method that is "next up the tree." Be aware that you cannot bypass a level in the hierarchy. That is, if three classes, A, B, and C, all define a method m(), and they are all part of a hierarchy—so that B extends A and C extends B—then the method m() in class C *cannot* directly invoke the method m() in class A.

To summarize, these are the key points about overriding methods:

- A method that has an identical name, and identical number, types, and order of arguments as a method in a parent class is an overriding method.

- Each parent class method may be overridden at most once in any one subclass. (That is, you cannot have two identical methods in the same class.)

- An overriding method must return exactly the same type as the method it overrides.

- An overriding method must not be less accessible than the method it overrides.

- An overriding method must not throw any checked exceptions that are not declared for the overridden method.

- An overridden method is completely replaced by the overriding method unless the overridden method is deliberately invoked from within the subclass.

- An overridden method can be invoked from within the subclass using the construction `super.xxx()`, where `xxx()` is the method name. Methods that are overridden more than once (by chains of subclasses) are not directly accessible.

There is quite a lot to think about in overriding methods, so you might like to have a break before you move on to the next topic: constructors.

Constructors and Subclassing

Inheritance generally makes the code and data that are defined in a parent class available for use in a subclass. This is subject to accessibility controls so that, for example, private items in the parent class are not directly accessible in the methods of the subclass, even though they exist. In fact, constructors are not inherited in the normal way but must be defined for each class in the class itself.

When you write code to construct an instance of any particular class, you write code of the form `new MyClass(arg, list);`. In these conditions there must be a constructor defined for MyClass, and that constructor must take arguments of the types (or some superclass) of the variables arg and list. In the case of a constructor, it is insufficient for this to have been defined in the parent class; rather, a constructor is generally available for a class only if it is explicitly defined in that class. The exception to this is the default constructor. The default constructor takes no arguments and is created by the compiler if no other constructors are defined for the class. The default constructor is not inherited; it is created for you by the compiler if, and only if, you do not provide *any* other constructors in the source of the particular class.

Often you will define a constructor that takes arguments and will want to use those arguments to control the construction of the parent part of the object. You can pass control to a constructor in the parent class by using the keyword super(). To control the particular constructor that is used, you simply provide the appropriate arguments. Consider this example:

```
1. class Base {
2.   public Base(String s) {
3.     // initialize this object using s
4.   }
5.   public Base(int i) {
6.     // initialize this object using i
7.   }
8. }
9.
10. class Derived extends Base {
11.   public Derived(String s) {
12.     // pass control to Base constructor at line 2
13.     super(s);
14.   }
15.   public Derived(int i) {
16.     // pass control to Base constructor at line 5
17.     super(i);
18.   }
19. }
```

The code at lines 13 and 17 demonstrate the use of `super()` to control the construction of the parent class part of an object. The definitions of the constructors at lines 11 and 15 select an appropriate way to build the parental part of themselves by invoking `super()` with an argument list that matches one of the constructors for the parent class. It is important to know that the superclass constructor must be called before any reference is made to any part of this object. This rule is imposed to guarantee that nothing is ever accessed in an uninitialized state. Generally the rule means that if `super()` is to appear at all in a constructor, then it must be the first statement.

Although the example shows the invocation of parental constructors with argument lists that match those of the original constructor, this is not a requirement. It would be perfectly acceptable, for example, if line 17 had read:

```
17.    super("Value is " + i);
```

This would have caused control to be passed to the constructor at line 2, which takes a `String` argument, rather than the one at line 5.

Overloading Constructors

Although you have just seen that constructors are not inherited in the same way as methods, the overloading mechanisms apply quite normally. In fact, the example discussing the use of `super()` to control the invocation of parental constructors showed overloaded constructors. You saw earlier how you could invoke one method from another that overloads its name simply by calling the method with an appropriate parameter list. There are also times when it would be useful to invoke one constructor from another. Imagine you have a constructor that takes five arguments and does considerable processing to initialize the object. You wish to provide another constructor that takes only two arguments and sets the remaining three to default values. It would be nice to avoid re-coding the body of the first constructor and instead simply set up the default values and pass control to the first constructor. This is possible using a small trick of syntax.

Usually you would invoke a method by using its name followed by an argument list in parentheses, and you would invoke a constructor by using the keyword `new`, followed by the name of the class, followed again by an argument list in parentheses. This might lead you to try to use the `new ClassName(args)` construction to invoke another constructor of your own class. Unfortunately, although this is legal syntax, it results in an entirely separate object being created. The approach Java takes is to provide another meaning for the keyword `this`. Look at this example:

```
1. public class AnyClass {
2.    public AnyClass(int a, String b, float c, Date d) {
3.       // complex processing to initialize
4.       // based on arguments
5.    }
6.    public AnyClass(int a) {
7.       this(a, "default", 0.0F, new Date());
8.    }
9. }
```

The constructor at line 6 takes a single argument and uses that, along with three other default values, to call the constructor at line 2. The call itself is made using the `this()` construction at line 7. As with `super()`, `this()` must be positioned as the first statement of the constructor.

We have said that any use of either `super()` or `this()` in a constructor must be placed at the first line. Clearly, you cannot put both on the first line. In fact, this is not a problem. If you write a constructor that has neither a call to `super(...)` nor a call to `this(...)`, then the compiler automatically inserts a call to the parent class constructor with no arguments. If an explicit call to another constructor is made using `this(...)`, then the superclass constructor is not called until the other constructor runs. It is permitted for that other constructor to start with a call to either `this(...)` or `super(...)`, if desired. Java insists that the object is initialized from the top of the class hierarchy downward; that is why the call to `super(...)` or `this(...)` must occur at the start of a constructor. Actually, there is an important consequence of a point just made. We just said that if there is no call to either `this(...)` or `super(...)` then the compiler puts in a call to the no-argument constructor in the parent. This means that if you try to extend a class that does not have a no-argument constructor, then you *must* explicitly call `super(...)` with one of the argument forms that are supported by constructors in the parent class.

Let's summarize the key points about constructors before we move on to inner classes:

- Constructors are not inherited in the same way as normal methods. You can only create an object if a constructor with an argument list that matches the one your `new` call provides is defined in the class itself.

- If you define no constructors at all in a class, then the compiler provides a default that takes no arguments. If you define even a single constructor, this default is not provided.

- It is common to provide multiple overloaded constructors, that is, constructors with different argument lists. One constructor can call another using the syntax `this(arguments…)`.

- A constructor delays running its body until the parent parts of the class have been initialized. This commonly happens because of an implicit call to `super()` added by the compiler. You can provide your own call to `super(arguments…)` to control the way the parent parts are initialized. If you do this, it must be the first statement of the constructor.

- A constructor can use overloaded constructor versions to support its work. These are invoked using the syntax `this(arguments…)` and if supplied, this call must be the first statement of the constructor. In such conditions, the initialization of the parent class is performed in the overloaded constructor.

Inner Classes

The material we have looked at so far has been part of Java since its earliest versions. Inner classes are a feature added with the release of JDK 1.1. Inner classes, which are sometimes called *nested classes*, can give your programs additional clarity and make them more concise.

Fundamentally, an *inner class* is the same as any other class, but is declared inside (that is, between the opening and closing curly braces of) some other class. In fact, you can declare nested classes in any block, including blocks that are part of a method. Classes defined inside a method differ slightly from the more general case of inner classes that are defined as members of a class; we'll look at these differences in detail later. For now, when we refer to a "member class," we mean a class that is *not* defined in a method, but simply in a class. In this context the use of the term "member" is closely parallel to its use in the context of member variables and member methods.

The complexity of inner classes relates to scope and access, particularly access to variables in enclosing scopes. Before we consider these matters, let's look at the syntax of a basic inner class, which is really quite simple. Consider this example:

```
1.  public class OuterOne {
2.     private int x;
3.     public class InnerOne {
4.        private int y;
5.        public void innerMethod() {
6.           System.out.println("y is " + y);
7.        }
8.     }
9.     public void outerMethod() {
10.       System.out.println("x is " + x);
11.    }
12.    // other methods...
13. }
```

In this example, there is no obvious benefit in having declared the class called InnerOne as an inner class; so far we are only looking at the syntax. When an inner class is declared like this, the enclosing class name becomes part of the fully qualified name of the inner class. In this case, the two classes' full names are OuterOne and OuterOne.InnerOne. This format is reminiscent of a class called InnerOne declared in a package called OuterOne. This point of view is not entirely inappropriate, since an inner class belongs to its enclosing class in a fashion similar to the way a class belongs to a package. It is illegal for a package and a class to have the same name, so there can be no ambiguity.

WARNING

Although the dotted representation of inner class names works for the declaration of the type of an identifier, it does not reflect the file name of the class. If you try to load this class using the Class.forName() method, the call will fail. On the disk, and from the point of view of the Class class and class loaders, the name of the class is actually OuterOne$InnerOne. The dollar-separated name is also used if you print out the class name by using the methods getClass().getName() on an instance of the inner class. You probably recall that classes are located in directories that reflect their package names. The dollar-separated convention is adopted for inner class names to ensure that there is no ambiguity on the disk between inner classes and package members. It also reduces conflicts with filing systems that treat the dot character as special, perhaps limiting the number of characters that can follow it.

Although for the purpose of naming there is some organizational benefit in being able to define a class inside another class, this is not the end of the story. Objects that are instances of the inner class generally retain the ability to access the members of the outer class. This is discussed in the next section.

The Enclosing *this* Reference and Construction of Inner Classes

When an instance of an inner class is created, there must normally be a preexisting instance of the outer class acting as context. This instance of the outer class will be accessible from the inner object. Consider this example, which is expanded from the earlier one:

```
1. public class OuterOne {
2.    private int x;
3.    public class InnerOne {
4.       private int y;
5.       public void innerMethod() {
6.          System.out.println("enclosing x is " + x);
7.          System.out.println("y is " + y);
8.       }
9.    }
10.   public void outerMethod() {
```

```
11.        System.out.println("x is " + x);
12.    }
13.    public void makeInner() {
14.        InnerOne anInner = new InnerOne();
15.        anInner.innerMethod();
16.    }
17.    // other methods...
18. }
```

You will see two changes in this code when you compare it to the earlier version. First, innerMethod() now outputs not just the value of *y*, which is defined in InnerOne, but also, at line 6, it outputs the value of *x*, which is defined in OuterOne. The second change is that in lines 13–16, there is code that creates an instance of the InnerOne class and invokes innerMethod() upon it.

The accessibility of the members of the enclosing class is crucial and very useful. It is possible because the inner class actually has a hidden reference to the outer class instance that was the current context when the inner class object was created. In effect, it ensures that the inner class and the outer class belong together, rather than the inner instance being just another member of the outer instance.

Sometimes you might want to create an instance of an inner class from a static method, or in some other situation where there is no this object available. The situation arises in a main() method or if you need to create the inner class from a method of some object of an unrelated class. You can achieve this by using the new operator as though it were a member method of the outer class. Of course you still must have an instance of the outer class. The following code, which is a main() method in isolation, could be added to the code seen so far to produce a complete example:

```
1. public static void main(String args[]) {
2.   OuterOne.InnerOne i = new OuterOne().new InnerOne();
3.   i.innerMethod();
4. }
```

From the point of view of the inner class instance, this use of two new statements on the same line is a compacted way of doing this:

```
1. public static void main(String args[]) {
```

```
2.    OuterOne o = new OuterOne();
3.    OuterOne.InnerOne i = o.new InnerOne();
4.    i.innerMethod();
5. }
```

If you attempt to use the new operation to construct an instance of an inner class without a prefixing reference to an instance of the outer class, then the implied prefix this. is assumed. This behavior is identical to that which you find with ordinary member accesses and method invocations. As with member access and method invocation, it is important that the this reference be valid when you try to use it. Inside a static method there is no this reference, which is why you must take special efforts in these conditions.

Member Classes

To this point, we have not distinguished between classes defined directly in the scope of a class—that is, "member classes" and classes defined inside of methods. There are important distinctions between these two scopes that you will need to have clear in your mind when you sit for the Certification Exam. First, we'll look at the features that are unique to member classes.

Access Modifiers

Members of a class, whether they be variables, methods, or nested classes, may be marked with modifiers that control access to those members. This means that member classes can be marked private, public, protected, or default access. The meaning of these access modifiers is the same for member classes as it is for other members, and therefore we'll not spend time on those issues here. Instead, refer to Chapter 3, "Modifiers," if you need to revisit these concepts.

Static Inner Classes

Just like any other member, a member inner class may be marked static. When applied to a variable, static means that the variable is associated with the class, rather than with any particular instance of the class. When applied to an inner class, the meaning is similar. Specifically, a static inner class does *not* have any reference to an enclosing instance. Because of this, methods of a static inner class cannot use the keyword this (either implied or explicit) to access instance variables of the enclosing class; those methods can, however, access `static` variables of the enclosing class. This is just the same as the rules that apply to `static` methods in ordinary classes. As you would expect, you can create an instance of a `static` inner class without the need for a current instance of the enclosing class. The syntax for this construction is very simple, just use the long name of the inner class—that is, the name that includes the name of the outer class, as in the highlighted part of line 5:

```
1. public class MyOuter {
2.   public static class MyInner {
3.   }
4.   public static void main(String [] args) {
5.     MyInner aMyInner = new MyOuter.MyInner();
6.   }
7. }
```

The net result is that a `static` inner class is really just a top-level class with a modified naming scheme. In fact, you can use `static` inner classes as an extension to packaging.

Not only can you declare a class inside another class, but you can also declare a class inside a method of another class. We will discuss this next.

Classes Defined Inside Methods

In the opening of this chapter, we said that nested classes can be declared in any block, and that this means you can define a class inside a method. This is superficially similar to what you have already seen, but in this case there are three particular points to be considered.

The first point is that anything declared inside a method is not a member of the class, but is local to the method. The immediate consequence is that classes declared in methods are private to the method and cannot be marked with any access modifier, neither can they be marked as `static`. If you think about this, you'll recognize that these are just the same rules as for any variable declaration you might make in a method.

The second point is that an object created from an inner class within a method can have some access to the variables of the enclosing method. We'll look at how this is done, and the restrictions that apply to this access in a moment.

Finally, it is possible to create an anonymous class—literally, a class with no specified name—and this can be very eloquent when working with event listeners. We will discuss this after covering the rules governing access from an inner class to method variables in the enclosing blocks.

Accessing Method Variables

The rule that governs access to the variables of an enclosing method is simple. Any variable, either a local variable or a formal parameter, can be accessed by methods within an inner class, provided that variable is marked final. A final variable is effectively a constant, so this might seem to be quite a severe restriction, but the point is simply this: An object created inside a method is likely to outlive the method invocation. Since local variables and method arguments are conventionally destroyed when their method exits, these variables would be invalid for access by inner class methods after the enclosing method exits. By allowing access only to final variables, it becomes possible to copy the values of those variables into the object itself, thereby extending their lifetimes. The other possible approaches to this problem would be writing to two copies of the same data every time it got changed or putting method local variables onto the heap instead of the stack. Either of these approaches would significantly degrade performance.

Let's look at an example:

```
1.  public class MOuter {
2.    private int m = (int)(Math.random() * 100);
3.    public static void main(String args[]) {
4.      MOuter that = new MOuter();
5.      that.go((int)(Math.random() * 100),
6.        (int)(Math.random() * 100));
7.    }
8.
9.    public void go(int x, final int y) {
10.     int a = x + y;
11.     final int b = x - y;
12.     class MInner {
13.       public void method() {
14.         System.out.println("m is " + m);
15. //        System.out.println("x is " + x); //Illegal!
```

```
16.              System.out.println("y is " + y);
17. //           System.out.println("a is " + a); //Illegal!
18.              System.out.println("b is " + b);
19.        }
20.     }
21.
22.     MInner that = new MInner();
23.     that.method();
24.   }
25. }
```

In this example, the class MInner is defined in lines 12–20 (in bold). Within it, method() has access to the member variable m in the enclosing class (as with the previous examples) but also to the final variables of method() itself. The commented-out code on lines 15 and 17 would be illegal, because it attempts to refer to non-final variables in method(); if these were included in the source proper, they would cause compiler errors.

Anonymous Classes

Some classes that you define inside a method do not need a name. A class defined in this way without a name is called an *anonymous class*. Anonymous classes can be declared to extend another class or to implement a single interface. The syntax does not allow you to do both at the same time, nor to implement more than one interface explicitly (of course, if you extend a class and the parent class implements interfaces, then so does the new class). If you declare a class that implements a single explicit interface, then it is a direct subclass of java.lang.Object.

Since you do not know the name of an anonymous inner class, you cannot use the new keyword in the usual way to create an instance of that class. In fact, the definition, construction, and first use (often in an assignment) of an anonymous class all occur in the same place. The next example shows a typical creation of an anonymous inner class that implements a single interface, in this case ActionListener. The essential parts of the declaration and construction are in bold on lines 3 through to 7.

```
1. public void aMethod() {
2.   theButton.addActionListener(
3.     new ActionListener() {
```

```
4.          public void actionPerformed(ActionEvent e) {
5.             System.out.println("The action has occurred");
6.          }
7.       }
8.    );
9. }
```

In this fragment the variable used at line 2, `theButton`, is a reference to a `Button` object. Notice that the action listener attached to the button is defined in lines 3–7. The entire declaration forms the argument to the `addActionListener()` method call at line 2; the closing parenthesis that completes this method call is on line 8.

The declaration and construction both start on line 3. Notice that the name of the interface is used immediately after the new keyword. This pattern is used for both interfaces or classes. The class has no visible name of its own in the source, but is referred to simply using the class or interface name from which the new anonymous class is derived. The effect of this syntax is to state that you are defining a class and you do not want to think up a name for that class. Further, the class implements the specified interface or extends the specified class without using the either the `implements` or `extends` keywords.

An anonymous class gives you a convenient way to avoid having to think up trivial names for classes, but the facility should be used with care. Clearly, you cannot instantiate objects of this class anywhere except in the code shown. Further, anonymous classes should be small. If the class defines methods other than those of a simple, well-known interface such as an AWT event listener, it probably should not be anonymous. Similarly, if the class has methods containing more than one or two lines of straightforward code or if the entire class has more than about ten lines, it probably should not be anonymous. These are not absolute rules; rather, the point here is that if you do not give the class a name, you have only the "self-documenting" nature of the code itself to explain what it is for. If, in fact, the code is not simple enough to be genuinely self-documenting, then you probably should give it a descriptive name.

Construction and Initialization of Anonymous Inner Classes

You need to understand a few points about the construction and initialization of anonymous inner classes to succeed in the Certification Exam and in real life. Let's have a look at these issues.

As you have already seen, the class is instantiated and declared in the same place. This means that anonymous inner classes are unique to method scopes; you cannot have anonymity with a member class.

You cannot define any specific constructor for an anonymous inner class. This is a direct consequence of the fact that you do not specify a name for the class, and therefore you cannot use that name to specify a constructor. However, an inner class can be constructed with arguments under some conditions, and an inner class can have an initializer if you wish.

Anonymous Class Declarations

As we have already seen, the central theme of the code that declares and constructs an anonymous inner class is:

```
new Xxxx() { /* class body. */ }
```

where Xxxx is a class or interface name. It is important to grasp that code of this form is an *expression* that returns a reference to an object. This means that the code above is incomplete by itself but can be used wherever you can use an object reference. For example, you might assign the reference to the constructed object into a variable, like this:

```
Xxxx AnXxxx = new Xxxx () { /* class body. */ };
```

Notice that you must be sure to make a complete statement, including the closing semicolon. Alternatively, you might use the reference to the constructed object as an argument to a method call. In that case, the overall appearance is like this:

```
someMethod(new Xxxx () { /* class body. */ });
```

Passing Arguments into the Construction of an Anonymous Inner Class

If the anonymous inner class extends another class, and that parent class has constructors that take arguments, then you can arrange for one of these constructors to be invoked by specifying the argument list to the construction of the anonymous inner class. An example follows.

```
// Assume this code appears in some method
Button b = new Button("Anonymous Button") {
  // behavior for the button
};
// do things with the button b...
...
```

In this situation, the compiler will build a constructor for your anonymous inner class that effectively invokes the superclass constructor with the argument list provided, something like this:

```
// This is not code you write! This exemplifies what the
// compiler creates internally when asked to compile
// something like the previous anonymous example
class AnonymousButtonSubclass extends Button {
  public AnonymousButtonSubclass(String s) {
    super(s);
  }
}
```

Note that this isn't the actual code that would be created—specifically, the class name is made up—but it conveys the general idea.

Initializing an Anonymous Inner Class

Sometimes you will want to perform some kind of initialization when an inner class is constructed. In normal classes, you would create a constructor. In an anonymous inner class, you cannot do this, but you can use the initializer feature that was added to the language at JDK 1.1. If you provide an unnamed block in class scope, then it will be invoked as part of the construction process, like this:

```
public MyClass {
  { // initializer
    System.out.println("Creating an instance");
  }
}
```

This is true of any class, but the technique is particularly useful with anonymous inner classes, where it is the only tool you have that provides some control over the construction process.

A Complex Example of Anonymous Inner Classes

Now let's look at a complete example following the pattern of the earlier example using a Button. This example uses two anonymous inner classes, one nested inside the other, an initializer, and a constructor that takes an argument:

```
1.  import java.awt.*;
2.  import java.awt.event.*;
3.
4.  public class X extends Frame {
5.    public static void main(String args[]) {
6.      X x = new X();
7.      x.pack();
8.      x.setVisible(true);
9.    }
10.
11.   private int count;
12.
13.   public X() {
14.     final Label l = new Label("Count = " + count);
15.     add(l, BorderLayout.SOUTH);
16.
17.     add(
18.       new Button("Hello " + 1) {
19.         { // initializer
20.           addActionListener(
21.             new ActionListener() {
22.               public void actionPerformed(
23.                 ActionEvent ev) {
24.                 count++;
25.                 l.setText("Count = " + count);
26.               }
```

```
27.                 }
27.               );
29.             }
30.         }, BorderLayout.NORTH
31.       );
32.     }
33. }
```

Lines 19–29 form the initializer, and actually set up a listener on the Button. The listener is itself another anonymous inner class; as we said earlier, you can arbitrarily nest these things. Notice how the label variable declared at line 14 is final; this allows it to be accessed from the inner classes, and specifically from the listener defined in the initializer of the first anonymous inner class.

Chapter Summary

We have covered a lot of material in this chapter, but all of it is important. Let's look again at the key points.

Object-Oriented Design and Implementation

- Tightly encapsulated class designs make for more robust and reusable code. Code reuse involves code retesting, which further improves reliability and robustness.

- Tightly encapsulated classes hide their state variables from outside interference, typically marking all member variables as private and providing appropriate methods for operating on the state.

- Code reuse can be achieved by simply reusing classes, by composition (the "has a" relation) or by inheritance (the "is a" relation).

- The "is a" relation is implemented by inheritance, using the Java keyword extends.

- The "has a" relation is implemented by providing the class with member variables.

Overloading and Overriding

- A method can have the same name as another method in the same class, providing it forms either a valid overload or override.

- A valid overload differs in the number or type of its arguments. Differences in argument names are not significant. A different return type is permitted, but it is not sufficient by itself to distinguish an overloading method.

- Methods that overload a name are different methods and can coexist in a single class.

- Both overloaded and overloading methods are accessed simply by providing the correct argument types for the method call.

- A valid override has identical argument types and order, identical return type, and is not less accessible than the original method. The overriding method must not throw any checked exceptions that were illegal for the original method.

- An overriding method completely replaces the original method unless the derived class makes specific reference to that original method using the `super.xxx()` construction.

- An overriding method cannot be defined in the same class as the method it overrides; rather, it must be defined in a subclass.

- The `super.xxx()` mechanism gives access to an overridden method from within the subclass that defines the overriding method.

- An overridden method is not accessible outside the overriding class. Virtual method invocation otherwise insures that the behavior associated with the object class (not with the variable type) will be the behavior that occurs.

Constructors and Subclassing

- Constructors are not inherited into subclasses; you must define each form of constructor that you require.

- A class that has no constructors defined in the source is given exactly one constructor. This is the default constructor; it takes no arguments and is of `public` accessibility.

- A constructor can call upon other constructors in its class to help with its work. The `this()` construction does this. If you use the `this()` mechanism, it must occur at the start of the constructor.

- A constructor can call a specific constructor of the parent class by using the `super()` mechanism. If you use the `super()` mechanism, it must occur at the start of the constructor.

- If you do not provide any call to either `super()` or `this()` in a constructor, then the compiler creates a call to `super()` for you.

- If you extend a class that has no zero argument constructor, or if that constructor is not accessible in your subclass, then you cannot allow the default call to `super()` since it will fail. In these conditions, you must explicitly call a superclass constructor that you do have access to using an appropriate form of `super()`.

Inner Classes

- A class can be declared in any scope. Classes defined in other classes, including those defined in methods, are called inner classes.

- An inner class in class scope can have any accessibility, including `private`. However, an inner class declared local to a block (for example, in a method), must not have any access modifier. Such a class is effectively private to the block.

- Inner classes defined local to a block may not be `static`.

- Classes defined in methods can be anonymous, in which case they must be instantiated at the same point they are defined.

- Inner classes, unless `static`, have an implicit reference to the enclosing instance. The enclosing instance must be provided to the `new` call that constructs the inner class. In many cases, inner classes are constructed inside instance methods of the enclosing class, in which case `this.new` is implied by `new`.

- Inner classes have access to the variables of the enclosing class instance. Static inner classes can only access the static members of the enclosing class. Also, inner classes defined in method scope have read access to `final` variables of the enclosing scope.

- Anonymous inner classes may implement interfaces or extend other classes.

- Anonymous inner classes cannot have any explicit constructors.

That's it for classes. This summary includes a great deal of information condensed into terminology, so be sure to review the sections of this chapter if you are unsure about any point. Otherwise, you're ready to move on to the test questions. Good luck!

Test Yourself

1. Consider this class:

    ```
    1. public class Test1 {
    2.    public float aMethod(float a, float b) {
    3.    }
    4.
    5. }
    ```

    Which of the following methods would be legal if added (individually) at line 4?

    A. `public int aMethod(int a, int b) { }`

    B. `public float aMethod(float a, float b) { }`

    C. `public float aMethod(float a, float b, int c) throws Exception { }`

    D. `public float aMethod(float c, float d) { }`

    E. `private float aMethod(int a, int b, int c) { }`

2. Consider these classes, defined in separate source files:

    ```
    1. public class Test1 {
    2.    public float aMethod(float a, float b) throws
    3.    IOException {
    4.    }
    5. }
    ```

    ```
    1. public class Test2 extends Test1 {
    2.
    3. }
    ```

Which of the following methods would be legal (individually) at line 2 in class `Test2`?

A. `float aMethod(float a, float b) { }`

B. `public int aMethod(int a, int b) throws Exception { }`

C. `public float aMethod(float a, float b) throws Exception { }`

D. `public float aMethod(float p, float q) { }`

3. You have been given a design document for a veterinary registration system for implementation in Java. It states:

"A pet has an owner, a registration date, and a vaccination-due date. A cat is a pet that has a flag indicating whether it has been neutered, and a textual description of its markings."

Given that the `Pet` class has already been defined, which of the following fields would be appropriate for inclusion in the `Cat` class as members?

A. `Pet thePet;`

B. `Date registered;`

C. `Date vaccinationDue;`

D. `Cat theCat;`

E. `boolean neutered;`

F. `String markings;`

4. You have been given a design document for a veterinary registration system for implementation in Java. It states:

"A pet has an owner, a registration date, and a vaccination-due date. A cat is a pet that has a flag indicating if it has been neutered, and a textual description of its markings."

Given that the `Pet` class has already been defined and you expect the `Cat` class to be used freely throughout the application, how would you make the opening declaration of the `Cat` class, up to but not including the first opening brace? Use only these words and spaces: `boolean`, `Cat`, `class`, `Date`, `extends`, `Object`, `Owner`, `Pet`, `private`, `protected`, `public`, `String`.

5. Consider the following classes, declared in separate source files:

```
1. public class Base {
2.    public void method(int i) {
3.       System.out.println("Value is " + i);
4.    }
5. }
```

```
1. public class Sub extends Base {
2.    public void method(int j) {
3.       System.out.println("This value is " + j);
4.    }
5.    public void method(String s) {
6.       System.out.println("I was passed " + s);
7.    }
8.    public static void main(String args[]) {
9.       Base b1 = new Base();
10.       Base b2 = new Sub();
11.       b1.method(5);
12.       b2.method(6);
13.    }
14. }
```

What output results when the main method of the class Sub is run?

A. Value is 5
Value is 6

B. This value is 5
This value is 6

C. Value is 5
This value is 6

D. This value is 5
Value is 6

E. I was passed 5
I was passed 6

6. Consider the following class definition:

```
1. public class Test extends Base {
2.     public Test(int j) {
3.     }
4.     public Test(int j, int k) {
5.         super(j, k);
6.     }
7. }
```

Which of the following are legitimate calls to construct instances of the Test class?

A. Test t = new Test();

B. Test t = new Test(1);

C. Test t = new Test(1, 2);

D. Test t = new Test(1, 2, 3);

E. Test t = (new Base()).new Test(1);

7. Consider the following class definition:

```
1. public class Test extends Base {
2.    public Test(int j) {
3.    }
4.    public Test(int j, int k) {
5.       super(j, k);
6.    }
7. }
```

Which of the following forms of constructor must exist explicitly in the definition of the Base class?

A. Base() { }

B. Base(int j) { }

C. Base(int j, int k) { }

D. Base(int j, int k, int l) { }

8. Which of the following statements are true? (Choose one or more.)

A. An inner class may be declared private.

B. An inner class may be declared static.

C. An inner class defined in a method should always be anonymous.

D. An inner class defined in a method can access all the method local variables.

E. Construction of an inner class may require an instance of the outer class.

9. Consider the following definition:

```
1. public class Outer {
2.    public int a = 1;
3.    private int b = 2;
4.    public void method(final int c) {
5.       int d = 3;
6.       class Inner {
7.          private void iMethod(int e) {
8.
9.          }
10.      }
11.   }
12. }
```

Which variables may be referenced correctly at line 8?

A. *a*

B. *b*

C. *c*

D. *d*

E. *e*

10. Which of the following statements are true? (Choose one or more.)

A. Given that Inner is a non-static class declared inside a public class Outer, and appropriate constructor forms are defined, an instance of Inner may be constructed like this:

```
new Outer().new Inner()
```

B. If an anonymous inner class inside the class Outer is defined to implement the interface ActionListener, it may be constructed like this:

```
new Outer().new ActionListener()
```

C. Given that Inner is a non-static class declared inside a public class Outer and appropriate constructor forms are defined, an instance of Inner may be constructed in a static method like this:

```
new Inner()
```

D. An anonymous class instance that implements the interface MyInterface may be constructed and returned from a method like this:

```
1. return new MyInterface(int x) {
2.     int x;
3.     public MyInterface(int x) {
4.        this.x = x;
5.     }
6. };
```

Chapter 7

Threads

JAVA CERTIFICATION EXAM OBJECTIVES COVERED IN THIS CHAPTER:

✓ Write code to define, instantiate, and start new threads using both *java.lang.Thread* and *java.lang.Runnable*.

✓ Recognize conditions that might prevent a thread from executing.

✓ Write code using *synchronized*, *wait*, *notify*, and *notifyAll* to protect against concurrent access problems and to communicate between threads. Define the interaction between threads and between threads and object locks when executing *synchronized*, *wait*, *notify*, and *notifyAll*.

Threads are Java's way of making a single Java Virtual Machine look like many machines, all running at the same time. This effect, usually, is an illusion: There is only one JVM and most often only one CPU; but the CPU switches among the JVM's various projects to give the impression of multiple CPUs.

Java provides you with tools for creating and managing threads. Threads are a valuable tool for simplifying program design, allowing unrelated or loosely related work to be programmed separately, while still executing concurrently. There are system threads that work behind the scenes on your behalf, listening for user input and managing garbage collection. The best way to cooperate with these facilities is to understand what threads really are.

The Certification Exam objectives require that you be familiar with Java's thread support, including the mechanisms for creating, controlling, and communicating between threads.

Thread Fundamentals

Java's thread support resides in three places:

- The `java.lang.Thread` class
- The `java.lang.Object` class
- The Java language and virtual machine

Most (but definitely not all) support resides in the Thread class. In Java, every thread corresponds to an instance of the Thread class. These objects can be in various states: at any moment, at most one object is executing per CPU, while others might be waiting for resources, or waiting for a chance to execute, or sleeping, or dead.

In order to demonstrate an understanding of threads, you need to be able to answer a few questions:

- When a thread executes, what code does it execute?
- What states can a thread be in?
- How does a thread change its state?

The next few sections will look at each of these questions in turn.

What a Thread Executes

To make a thread execute, you call its start() method. This registers the thread with a piece of system code called the *thread scheduler*. The scheduler might be part of the JVM or of the host operating system. The scheduler determines which thread is actually running on each available CPU at any given time. Note that calling your thread's start() method doesn't immediately cause the thread to run; it just makes it *eligible* to run. The thread must still contend for CPU time with all the other threads. If all is well, then at some point in the future the thread scheduler will permit your thread to execute.

During its lifetime, a thread spends some time executing and some time in any of several non-executing states. In this section, you can ignore (for the moment) the questions of how the thread is moved between states. The question at hand is: When the thread gets to execute, what does it execute?

The simple answer is that it executes a method called run(). But which object's run() method? You have two choices:

- The thread can execute its own run() method.

- The thread can execute the run() method of some other object.

If you want the thread to execute its own run() method, you need to subclass the Thread class and give your subclass a run() method. For example,

```
1. public class CounterThread extends Thread {
2.   public void run() {
3.     for (int i = 1; i <= 10; i++) {
4.       System.out.println("Counting: " + i);
5.     }
6.   }
7. }
```

This run() method just prints out the numbers from 1 to 10. To do this in a thread, you first construct an instance of CounterThread and then invoke its start() method:

```
1. CounterThread ct = new CounterThread();
2. ct.start();        // start(), not run()
```

What you *don't* do is call run() directly; that would just count to 10 in the current thread. Instead, you call start(), which the CounterThread class inherits from its parent class, Thread. The start() method registers the thread (that is, ct) with the thread scheduler; eventually the thread will execute, and at that time its run() method will be called.

If you want your thread to execute the run() method of some object other than itself, you still need to construct an instance of the Thread class. The only difference is that when you call the Thread constructor, you have to specify which object owns the run() method that you want. To do this, you invoke an alternate form of the Thread constructor:

```
public Thread(Runnable target)
```

The Runnable interface describes a single method:

```
public void run();
```

Thus you can pass any object you want into the constructor, provided it implements the Runnable interface (so that it really does have a run() method for the thread scheduler to invoke).

Having constructed an instance of Thread, you proceed as before: You invoke the start() method. As before, this registers the thread with the scheduler, and eventually the run() method of the target will be called.

For example, the following class has a run() method that counts down from 10 to 1:

```
1. public class DownCounter implements Runnable {
2.    public void run() {
3.       for (int i = 10; 1 >= 1; i--) {
4.          System.out.println("Counting Down: " + i);
5.       }
6.    }
7. }
```

This class does not extend Thread. However, it has a run() method, and it declares that it implements the Runnable interface. Thus any instance of the DownCounter class is eligible to be passed into the alternative (non-default) constructor for Thread:

```
1. DownCounter dc = new DownCounter();
2. Thread t = new Thread(dc);
3. t.start();
```

This section has presented two strategies for constructing threads. Superficially, the only difference between these two strategies is the location of the run() method. The second strategy, where a runnable target is passed into the constructor, is perhaps a bit more complicated in the case of the simple examples we have considered. However, there are good reasons why you might choose to make this extra effort. The run() method, like any other member method, is allowed to access the private data, and call the private methods, of the class of which it is a member. Putting run() in a subclass of Thread may mean that the method cannot access features it needs (or cannot access those features in a clean, reasonable manner).

Another reason that might persuade you to implement your threads using Runnables rather than subclassing Thread is the single implementation inheritance rule. If you write a subclass of Thread, it cannot be a subclass of anything else; but using Runnable, you can subclass whatever other parent class you choose.

Finally, from an object-oriented point of view, a subclass of Thread combines two unrelated functionalities: the support for multithreading that is inherited from the Thread superclass, and the execution behavior provided by the run() method. These functionalities are not very closely related, so good object-oriented discipline suggests that they exist in two separate classes. In the jargon of objected-oriented analysis, if you create a class that extends Thread, you're saying that your class "is a" thread. If you create a class that implements Runnable, you're saying that your class "is associated with" a thread.

To summarize, there are two approaches to specifying which run() method will be executed by a thread:

- Subclass Thread. Define your run() method in the subclass.

- Write a class that implements Runnable. Define your run() method in that class. Pass an instance of that class into your call to the Thread constructor.

When Execution Ends

When the run() method returns, the thread has finished its task and is considered *dead*. There is no way out of this state. Once a thread is dead, it may not be started again; if you want the thread's task to be performed again, you have to construct and start a new thread instance. The dead thread continues to exist; it is an object like any other object, and you can still access its data and call its methods. You just can't make it run again. In other words,

- You *can't* restart a dead thread.

- You *can* call the methods of a dead thread.

The Thread methods include a method called stop(), which forcibly terminates a thread, putting it into the dead state. This method is deprecated since JDK 1.2, because it can cause data corruption or deadlock if you kill a thread that is in a critical section of code. The stop() method is therefore no longer part of the Certification Exam. Instead of using stop(), if a thread might need to be killed from another thread, you should call interrupt() on it from the killing method.

Although you can't restart a dead thread, if you use runnables, you can submit the old Runnable instance to a new thread. However, it is generally poor design to constantly create, use, and discard threads, because constructing a Thread is a relatively heavyweight operation, involving significant kernel resources. It is better to create a pool of reusable worker threads that can be assigned chores as needed. This is discussed further in Chapter 17 (in the Developer's Exam part of the book).

Thread States

When you call start() on a thread, the thread does not run immediately. It goes into a "ready-to-run" state and stays there until the scheduler moves it to the "running" state. Then the run() method is called. In the course of executing run(), the thread may temporarily give up the CPU and enter some other state for a while. It is important to be aware of the possible states a thread might be in and of the triggers that can cause the thread's state to change.

The thread states are:

Running The state that all threads aspire to

Various waiting states Waiting, Sleeping, Suspended, Blocked

Ready Not waiting for anything except the CPU

Dead All done

Figure 7.1 shows the non-dead states. Notice that the figure does not show the Dead state.

FIGURE 7.1   Living thread states

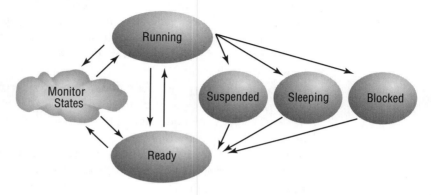

At the top of Figure 7.1 is the Running state. At the bottom is the Ready state. In between are the various not-ready states. A thread in one of these intermediate states is waiting for something to happen; when that something eventually happens, the thread moves to the Ready state, and eventually the thread scheduler will permit it to run again. Note that the methods associated with the Suspended state are now deprecated; you will not be tested on this state or its associated methods in the exam. For this reason, we will not discuss them in any detail in this book.

The arrows between the bubbles in Figure 7.1 represent state transitions. Be aware that only the thread scheduler can move a ready thread into the CPU.

Later in this chapter, you will examine in detail the various waiting states. For now, the important thing to observe in Figure 7.1 is the general flow: A running thread enters an intermediate state for some reason; later, whatever the thread was waiting for comes to pass, and the thread enters the Ready state; later still, the scheduler grants the CPU to the thread. The exceptions to this general flow involve synchronized code and the `wait()` / `notify()` sequence; the corresponding portion of Figure 7.1 is depicted as a vague bubble labeled "Monitor States." These monitor states are discussed later in this chapter, in the section "Monitors, *wait()*, and *notify()*."

Thread Priorities

Every thread has a *priority*, an integer from 1 to 10; threads with higher priority get preference over threads with lower priority. The priority is considered by the thread scheduler when it decides which ready thread should execute. The scheduler generally chooses the highest-priority waiting thread. If there is more than one waiting thread, the scheduler chooses one of them. There is no guarantee that the thread chosen will be the one that has been waiting the longest.

The default priority is 5, but all newly created threads have their priority set to that of the creating thread. To set a thread's priority, call the setPriority() method, passing in the desired new priority. The getPriority() method returns a thread's priority. The code fragment below increments the priority of thread theThread, provided the priority is less than 10. Instead of hardcoding the value 10, the fragment uses the constant MAX_PRIORITY. The Thread class also defines constants for MIN_PRIORITY (which is 1), and NORM_PRIORITY (which is 5).

```
1. int oldPriority = theThread.getPriority();
2. int newPriority = Math.min(oldPriority+1,
3.    Thread.MAX_PRIORITY);
4. theThread.setPriority(newPriority);
```

The specifics of how thread priorities affect scheduling are platform-dependent. The Java specification states that threads must have priorities, but it does not dictate precisely what the scheduler should do about priorities. This vagueness is a problem: Algorithms that rely on manipulating thread priorities might not run consistently on all platforms.

Controlling Threads

Thread control is the art of moving threads from state to state. You control threads by triggering state transitions. This section examines the various pathways out of the Running state. These pathways are:

- Yielding

- Suspending and then resuming

- Sleeping and then waking up
- Blocking and then continuing
- Waiting and then being notified

Yielding

A thread can offer to move out of the virtual CPU by *yielding*. A call to the `yield()` method causes the currently executing thread to move to the Ready state if the scheduler is willing to run any other thread in place of the yielding thread. The state transition is shown in Figure 7.2.

FIGURE 7.2   Yield

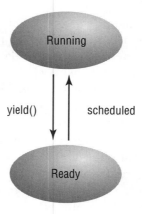

A thread that has yielded goes into the Ready state. There are two possible scenarios. If any other threads are in the Ready state, then the thread that just yielded might have to wait a while before it gets to execute again. However, if there are no other waiting threads, then the thread that just yielded will get to continue executing immediately. Note that most schedulers do not stop the yielding thread from running in favor of a thread of lower priority.

The `yield()` method is a static method of the `Thread` class. It always causes the currently executing thread to yield.

Yielding allows a time-consuming thread to permit other threads to execute. For example, consider an applet that computes a 300×300 pixel image using a ray-tracing algorithm. The applet might have a "Compute" button and an "Interrupt" button. The action event handler for the "Compute" button would create and start a separate thread, which would call a traceRays() method. A first cut at this method might look like this:

```
1. private void traceRays() {
2.    for (int j = 0; j < 300; j++) {
3.      for (int i = 0; i < 300; i++) {
4.        computeOnePixel(i, j);
5.      }
6.    }
7. }
```

There are 90,000 pixel color values to compute. If it takes 0.1 second to compute the color value of one pixel, then it will take two and a half hours to compute the complete image.

Suppose after half an hour the user looks at the partial image and realizes that something is wrong. (Perhaps the viewpoint or zoom factor is incorrect.) The user will then click the "Interrupt" button, since there is no sense in continuing to compute the useless image. Unfortunately, the thread that handles GUI input might not get a chance to execute until the thread that is executing traceRays() gives up the CPU. Thus the "Interrupt" button will not have any effect for another two hours.

If priorities are implemented meaningfully in the scheduler, then lowering the priority of the ray-tracing thread will have the desired effect, ensuring that the GUI thread will run when it has something useful to do. However, this is not reliable between platforms (although it is a good course of action anyway, since it will do no harm). The reliable approach is to have the ray-tracing thread periodically yield. If there is no pending input when the yield is executed, then the ray-tracing thread will not be moved off the CPU. If, on the other hand, there is input to be processed, the input-listening thread will get a chance to execute.

The ray-tracing thread can have its priority set like this:

```
rayTraceThread.setPriority(Thread.NORM_PRIORITY-1);
```

The traceRays() method listed above can yield after each pixel value is computed, after line 4. The revised version looks like this:

```
1. private void traceRays() {
2.    for (int j = 0; j < 300; j++) {
```

```
3.        for (int i = 0; i < 300; i++) {
4.          computeOnePixel(i, j);
5.          Thread.yield();
6.        }
7.      }
8.    }
```

Suspending

Suspending a thread is a mechanism that allows any arbitrary thread to make another thread unready for an indefinite period of time. The suspended thread becomes ready when some other thread resumes it. This might feel like a useful mechanism, but it is very easy to cause deadlock in a program using these methods, since a thread has no control over when it is suspended (the control comes from outside the thread) and it might be in a critical section, holding an object lock at the time. The exact effect of suspend() and resume() is much better implemented using wait() and notify().

The suspend() and resume() methods are deprecated as of the Java 2 release and have no place in the Java 2 version of the Certification Exam, so we will not discuss them any further.

Sleeping

A *Sleeping* thread passes time without doing anything and without using the CPU. A call to the sleep() method requests the currently executing thread to cease executing for (approximately) a specified amount of time. There are two ways to call this method, depending on whether you want to specify the sleep period to millisecond precision or to nanosecond precision:

- public static void sleep(long milliseconds) throws InterruptedException

- public static void sleep(long milliseconds, int nanoseconds) throws InterruptedException

Note that sleep(), like yield(), is static. Both methods operate on the currently executing thread.

The state diagram for Sleeping is shown in Figure 7.3. Notice that when the thread has finished sleeping, it does not continue execution. As you would expect, it enters the Ready state and will only execute when the thread scheduler allows it to do so. For this reason, you should expect that a `sleep()` call will block a thread for at least the requested time, but it might block for much longer. This suggests that very careful thought should be given to your design before you expect any meaning from the nanosecond accuracy version of the `sleep()` method.

FIGURE 7.3 The Sleeping state

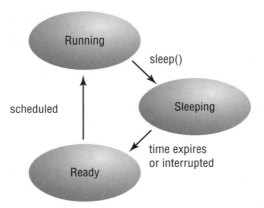

The `Thread` class has a method called `interrupt()`. A Sleeping thread that receives an `interrupt()` call moves immediately into the Ready state; when it gets to run, it will execute its `InterruptedException` handler.

Blocking

Many methods that perform input or output have to wait for some occurrence in the outside world before they can proceed; this behavior is known as *blocking*. A good example is reading from a socket:

```
1. try {
2.    Socket sock = new Socket("magnesium", 5505);
3.    InputStream istr = sock.getInputStream();
4.    int b = istr.read();
5. }
```

```
6. catch (IOException ex) {
7.   // Handle the exception
8. }
```

If you aren't familiar with Java's socket and stream functionality, don't worry: It's all covered in Chapter 13. The discussion here is uncomplicated.

It looks like line 4 reads a byte from an input stream that is connected to port 5505 on a machine called "magnesium." Actually, line 4 *tries* to read a byte. If a byte is available (that is, if magnesium has previously written a byte), then line 4 can return immediately and execution can continue. If magnesium has not yet written anything, however, the `read()` call has to wait. If magnesium is busy doing other things and takes half an hour to get around to writing a byte, then the `read()` call has to wait for half an hour.

Clearly, it would be a serious problem if the thread executing the `read()` call on line 4 remained in the Running state for the entire half hour. Nothing else could get done. In general, if a method needs to wait an indeterminable amount of time until some I/O occurrence takes place, then a thread executing that method should graciously step out of the Running state. All Java I/O methods behave this way. A thread that has graciously stepped out in this fashion is said to be *blocked*. Figure 7.4 shows the transitions of the Blocked state.

FIGURE 7.4 The Blocked state

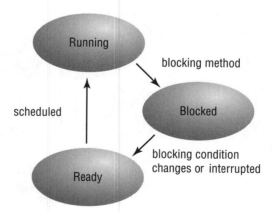

In general, if you see a method with a name that suggests that it might do nothing until something becomes ready—for example, waitForInput() or waitForImages()—you should expect that the caller thread might be blocked, thus losing the CPU, when the method is called. You do not need to know about all APIs to make this assumption; this is a general principle of APIs, both core and third-party, in a Java environment.

A thread can also become Blocked if it fails to acquire the lock for a monitor or if it issues a wait() call. Locks and monitors are explained in detail later in this chapter, beginning in the section "Monitors, *wait()*, and *notify()*." Internally, most blocking for I/O, like the read() calls just discussed, is implemented using wait() and notify() calls.

Monitor States

Figure 7.5 (which is just a rerun of Figure 7.1) shows all the thread-state transitions. The intermediate states on the right side of the figure (Suspended, Sleeping, and Blocked) have been discussed in previous sections. The Monitor states are drawn all alone on the left side of the figure to emphasize that they are very different from the other intermediate states.

FIGURE 7.5 Thread states (reprise)

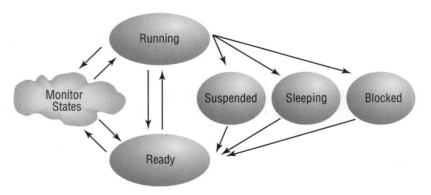

The wait() method puts an executing thread into the *Waiting* state, and the notify() and notifyAll() methods move waiting threads out of the

Waiting state. However, these methods are very different from suspend(), resume(), and yield(). For one thing, they are implemented in the Object class, not in Thread. For another, they may only be called in synchronized code. The Waiting state, and the associated issues and subtleties, are discussed in the final sections of this chapter. But first, there is one more topic to look at concerning thread control.

Scheduling Implementations

Historically, two approaches have emerged for implementing thread schedulers:

- Preemptive scheduling
- Time-sliced or round-robin scheduling

So far, the facilities described in this chapter have been preemptive. In preemptive scheduling, there are only two ways for a thread to leave the Running state without explicitly calling a thread-scheduling method such as wait() or suspend():

- It can cease to be ready to execute (by calling a blocking I/O method, for example).
- It can get moved out of the CPU by a higher-priority thread that becomes ready to execute.

With time slicing, a thread is only allowed to execute for a limited amount of time. It is then moved to the Ready state, where it must contend with all the other ready threads. Time slicing insures against the possibility of a single high-priority thread getting into the Running state and never getting out, preventing all other threads from doing their jobs. Unfortunately, time slicing creates a non-deterministic system; at any moment, you can't be certain which thread is executing or for how long it will continue to execute.

It is natural to ask which implementation Java uses. The answer is that it depends on the platform; the Java specification gives implementations a lot of leeway.

Monitors, *wait()*, and *notify()*

A *monitor* is an object that can block and revive threads. The concept is simple, but it takes a bit of work to understand what monitors are good for and how to use them effectively.

The reason for having monitors is that sometimes a thread cannot perform its job until an object reaches a certain state. For example, consider a class that handles requests to write to standard output:

```
1. class Mailbox {
2.    public boolean    request;
3.    public String     message;
4. }
```

The intention of this class is that a client can set `message` to some value, then set `request` to `true`:

```
1. myMailbox.message = "Hello everybody.";
2. myMailbox.request = true;
```

There must be a thread that checks `request`; on finding it `true`, the thread should write `message` to `System.out`, and then set `request` to `false`. (Setting `request` to `false` indicates that the mailbox object is ready to handle another request.) It is tempting to implement this thread like this:

```
1. public class Consumer extends Thread {
2.    private Mailbox myMailbox;
3.
4.    public Consumer(Mailbox box) {
5.       this.myMailbox = box;
6.    }
7.
8.    public void run() {
9.       while (true) {
10.         if (myMailbox.request) {
11.            System.out.println(myMailbox.message);
12.            myMailbox.request = false;
13.         }
```

```
14.
15.        try {
16.           sleep(50);
17.        }
18.        catch (InterruptedException e) { }
19.     }
20.  }
```

The consumer thread loops forever, checking for requests every 50 milli-seconds. If there is a request (line 10), the consumer writes the message to standard output (line 11) and then sets `request` to `false` to show that it is ready for more requests.

The `Consumer` class may look fine at first glance, but it has two serious problems:

- The `Consumer` class accesses data internal to the `Mailbox` class, intro-ducing the possibility of corruption. On a time-sliced system, the con-sumer thread could just possibly be interrupted between lines 10 and 11. The interrupting thread could just possibly be a client that sets `message` to its own message (ignoring the convention of checking `request` to see if the handler is available). The consumer thread would send the wrong message.

- The choice of 50 milliseconds for the delay can never be ideal. Some-times 50 milliseconds will be too long, and clients will receive slow ser-vice; sometimes 50 milliseconds will be too frequent, and cycles will be wasted. A thread that wants to send a message has a similar dilemma if it finds the `request` flag set: The thread should back off for a while, but for how long? There is no good answer to this question.

Ideally, these problems would be solved by making some modifications to the `Mailbox` class:

- The mailbox should be able to protect its data from irresponsible cli-ents.

- If the mailbox is not available—that is, if the `request` flag is already set—then a client consumer should not have to guess how long to wait before checking the flag again. The handler should tell the client when the time is right.

Java's monitor support addresses these issues by providing the following resources:

- A lock for each object

- The synchronized keyword for accessing an object's lock

- The wait(), notify(), and notifyAll() methods, which allow the object to control client threads

The sections below describe locks, synchronized code, and the wait(), notify(), and notifyAll() methods, and show how these can be used to make thread code more robust.

The Object Lock and Synchronization

Every object has a *lock*. At any moment, that lock is controlled by, at most, one single thread. The lock controls access to the object's synchronized code. A thread that wants to execute an object's synchronized code must first attempt to acquire that object's lock. If the lock is available—that is, if it is not already controlled by another thread—then all is well. If the lock is under another thread's control, then the attempting thread goes into the Seeking Lock state and only becomes ready when the lock becomes available. When a thread that owns a lock passes out of the synchronized code, the thread automatically gives up the lock. All this lock-checking and state-changing is done behind the scenes; the only explicit programming you need to do is to declare code to be synchronized.

Figure 7.6 shows the Seeking Lock state. This figure is the first state in our expansion of the Monitor States, as depicted in Figure 7.5.

FIGURE 7.6 The Seeking Lock state

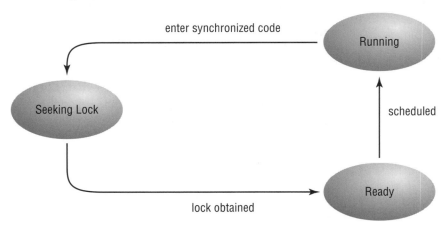

There are two ways to mark code as synchronized:

- Synchronize an entire method by putting the synchronized modifier in the method's declaration. To execute the method, a thread must acquire the lock of the object that owns the method.

- Synchronize a subset of a method by surrounding the desired lines of code with curly brackets ({}) and inserting the expression synchronized(someObject) before the opening curly. This technique allows you to synchronize the block on the lock of any object at all, not necessarily the object that owns the code.

The first technique is by far the more common; synchronizing on any object other than the object that owns the synchronized code can be extremely dangerous. The Certification Exam requires you to know how to apply the second technique, but the exam does not make you think through complicated scenarios of synchronizing on external objects. The second technique is discussed at the very end of this chapter.

Synchronization makes it easy to clean up some of the problems with the Mailbox class:

```
1. class Mailbox {
2.    private boolean    request;
3.    private String     message;
4.
5.    public synchronized void
6.    storeMessage(String message) {
7.      request = true;
8.      this.message = message;
9.    }
10.
11.    public synchronized String retrieveMessage() {
12.      request = false;
13.      return message;
14.    }
15. }
```

Now the request flag and the message string are private, so they can only be modified via the public methods of the class. Since storeMessage() and retrieveMessage() are synchronized, there is no danger of a message-producing thread corrupting the flag and spoiling things for a message-consuming thread, or vice versa.

The Mailbox class is now safe from its clients, but the clients still have problems. A message-producing client should only call storeMessage() when the request flag is false; a message-consuming client should only call retrieveMessage() when the request flag is true. In the Consumer class of the previous section, the consuming thread's main loop polled the request flag every 50 milliseconds. (Presumably a message-producing thread would do something similar.) Now the request flag is private, so you must find another way.

It is possible to come up with any number of clever ways for the client threads to poll the mailbox, but the whole approach is backwards. The mailbox becomes available or unavailable based on changes of its own state. The mailbox should be in charge of the progress of the clients. Java's wait() and notify() methods provide the necessary controls, as you will see in the next section.

wait() and notify()

The wait() and notify() methods provide a way for a shared object to pause a thread when it becomes unavailable to that thread, and to allow the thread to continue when appropriate. The threads themselves never have to check the state of the shared object.

An object that controls its client threads in this manner is known as a monitor. In strict Java terminology, a monitor is any object that has some synchronized code. To be really useful, most monitors make use of wait() and notify() methods. So the Mailbox class is already a monitor; it just is not quite useful yet.

Figure 7.7 shows the state transitions of wait() and notify().

FIGURE 7.7 The monitor states

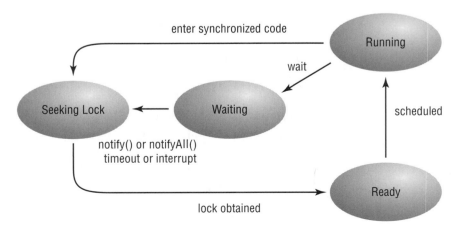

Both wait() and notify() must be called in synchronized code. A thread that calls wait() releases the virtual CPU; at the same time, it releases the lock. It enters a pool of waiting threads, which is managed by the object whose wait() method got called. Every object has such a pool. The code below shows how the Mailbox class's retrieveMessage() method could be modified to begin taking advantage of calling wait().

```
1. public synchronized String retrieveMessage() {
2.    while (request == false) {
3.      try {
4.        wait();
5.      } catch (InterruptedException e) { }
6.    }
7.    request = false;
8.    return message;
9. }
```

Now consider what happens when a message-consuming thread calls this method. The call might look like this:

```
myMailbox.retrieveMessage();
```

When a message-consuming thread calls this method, the thread must first acquire the lock for myMailbox. Acquiring the lock could happen immediately, or it could incur a delay if some other thread is executing any of the synchronized code of myMailbox. One way or another, eventually the consumer thread has the lock and begins to execute at line 2. The code first checks the request flag. If the flag is not set, then myMailbox has no message for the thread to retrieve. In this case the wait() method is called at line 4 (it can throw an InterruptedException, so the try/catch code is required, and the while will re-test the condition). When line 4 executes, the consumer thread ceases execution; it also releases the lock for myMailbox and enters the pool of waiting threads managed by myMailbox.

The consumer thread has been successfully prevented from corrupting the myMailbox monitor. Unfortunately, it is stuck in the monitor's pool of waiting threads. When the monitor changes to a state where it can provide the consumer with something to do, then something will have to be done to get the consumer out of the Waiting state. This is done by calling notify()

when the monitor's request flag becomes `true`, which only happens in the `storeMessage()` method. The revised `storeMessage()` looks like this:

```
1. public synchronized void
2. storeMessage(String message) {
3.   this.message = message;
4.   request = true;
5.   notify();
6. }
```

On line 5, the code calls `notify()` just after changing the monitor's state. What `notify()` does is to arbitrarily select one of the threads in the monitor's waiting pool and move it to the Seeking Lock state. Eventually that thread will acquire the mailbox's lock and can proceed with execution.

Now imagine a complete scenario. A consumer thread calls `retrieveMessage()` on a mailbox that has no message. It acquires the lock and begins executing the method. It sees that the request flag is `false`, so it calls `wait()` and joins the mailbox's waiting pool. (In this simple example, there are no other threads in the pool.) Since the consumer has called `wait()`, it has given up the lock. Later, a message-producing thread calls `storeMessage()` on the same mailbox. It acquires the lock, stores its message in the monitor's instance variable, and sets the `request` flag to `true`. The producer then calls `notify()`. At this moment only one thread is in the monitor's waiting pool: the consumer. So the consumer gets moved out of the waiting pool and into the Seeking Lock state. Now the producer returns from `storeMessage()`; since the producer has exited from synchronized code, it gives up the monitor's lock. Later the patient consumer re-acquires the lock and gets to execute; once this happens, it checks the request flag and (finally!) sees that there is a message available for consumption. The consumer returns the message; upon return it automatically releases the lock.

To briefly summarize this scenario: a consumer tried to consume something, but there was nothing to consume, so the consumer waited. Later a producer produced something. At that point there was something for the consumer to consume, so the consumer was notified; once the producer was done with the monitor, the consumer consumed a message.

NOTE As Figure 7.7 shows, a waiting thread has ways to get out of the Waiting state that do not require being notified. One version of the wait() call takes an argument that specifies a timeout in milliseconds; if the timeout expires, the thread moves to the Seeking Lock state, even if it has not been notified. No matter what version of wait() is invoked, if the waiting thread receives an interrupt() call, it moves immediately to the Seeking Lock state.

This example protected the consumer against the possibility that the monitor might be empty; the protection was implemented with a wait() call in retrieveMessage() and a notify() call in storeMessage(). A similar precaution must be taken in case a producer thread wants to produce into a monitor that already contains a message. To be robust, storeMessage() needs to call wait(), and retrieveMessage() needs to call notify(). The complete Mailbox class looks like this:

```
1.  class Mailbox {
2.     private boolean   request;
3.     private String    message;
4.
5.     public synchronized void
6.     storeMessage(String message) {
7.       while(request == true) {
8.          // No room for another message
9.          try {
10.            wait();
11.         } catch (InterruptedException e) { }
12.      }
13.      request = true;
14.      this.message = message;
15.      notify();
16.   }
17.
18.    public synchronized String retrieveMessage() {
19.      while(request == false) {
20.         // No message to retrieve
21.         try {
```

```
22.          wait();
23.        } catch (InterruptedException e) { }
24.      }
25.      request = false;
26.      notify();
27.      return message;
28.    }
29. }
```

 By synchronizing code and judiciously calling wait() and notify(), monitors such as the Mailbox class can ensure the proper interaction of client threads and protect shared data from corruption.

Here are the main points to remember about wait():

- The calling thread gives up the CPU.

- The calling thread gives up the lock.

- The calling thread goes into the monitor's waiting pool.

Here are the main points to remember about notify():

- One arbitrarily chosen thread gets moved out of the monitor's waiting pool and into the Seeking Lock state.

- The thread that was notified must re-acquire the monitor's lock before it can proceed.

The Class Lock

It is clear by now that every object (that is, every instance of every class) has a lock. Every class also has a lock. The class lock controls access to all synchronized static code in the class. Consider the following example:

```
class X {
  static int x, y;
  static synchronized void foo() {
    x++;
    y++;
  }
}
```

When the foo() method is called (for example, with the code X.foo()), the invoking thread must acquire the class lock for the X class. Ordinarily, when a thread attempts to call a non-static synchronized method, the thread must acquire the lock of the current object; the current object is referenced by this in the scope of the method. However, there is no this reference in a static method, because there is no current object.

If Java did not provide class locks, there would be no built-in way to synchronize static code, and no way to protect shared static data such as *x* and *y* in the example above.

Beyond the Pure Model

The mailbox example of the previous few sections has been a very simple example of a situation involving one producer and one consumer. In real life things are not always so simple. You might have a monitor that has several methods that do not purely produce or purely consume. All you can say in general about such methods is that they cannot proceed unless the monitor is in a certain state and they themselves can change the monitor's state in ways that could be of vital interest to the other methods.

The notify() method is not precise: You cannot specify which thread is to be notified. In a mixed-up scenario such as the one described above, a thread might alter the monitor's state in a way that is useless to the particular thread that gets notified. In such a case, the monitor's methods should take two precautions:

- Always check the monitor's state in a while loop rather than an if statement.

- After changing the monitor's state, call notifyAll() rather than notify().

The first precaution means that you should *not* do the following:

```
1. public synchronized void mixedUpMethod() {
2.    if (i<16 || f>4.3f || message.equals("UH-OH") {
3.      try { wait(); } catch (InterruptedException e) { }
4.    }
5.
6.    // Proceed in a way that changes state, and then...
7.    notify();
8. }
```

The danger is that sometimes a thread might execute the test on line 2, then notice that *i* is (for example) 15, and have to wait. Later, another thread might change the monitor's state by setting *i* to -23444, and then call notify(). If the original thread is the one that gets notified, it will pick up where it left off, even though the monitor is not in a state where it is ready for mixedUpMethod().

The solution is to change mixedUpMethod() as follows:

```
1. public synchronized void mixedUpMethod() {
2.     while (i<16 || f>4.3f || message.equals("UH-OH") {
3.         try { wait(); } catch (InterruptedException e) { }
4.     }
5.
6.     // Proceed in a way that changes state, and then...
7.     notifyAll();
8. }
```

The monitor's other synchronized methods should be modified in a similar manner.

Now when a waiting thread gets notified, it does not assume that the monitor's state is acceptable. It checks again, in the while-loop check on line 2. If the state is still not conducive, the thread waits again.

On line 7, having made its own modifications to the monitor's state, the code calls notifyAll(); this call is like notify(), but it moves *every* thread in the monitor's waiting pool to the Seeking Lock state. Presumably every thread's wait() call happened in a loop like the one on lines 2–4, so every thread will once again check the monitor's state and either wait or proceed. Note that if a monitor has a large number of waiting threads, calling notifyAll() can cost a lot of time.

Using a while loop to check the monitor's state is a good idea even if you are coding a pure model of one producer and one consumer. After all, you can never be sure that somebody won't try to add an extra producer or an extra consumer.

Deadlock

The term *deadlock* describes another class of situations that might prevent a thread from executing. In general terms, if a thread blocks because it is waiting for a condition, and something else in the program makes it impossible for that condition to arise, then the thread is said to be deadlocked.

Deadlock conditions can arise for many reasons, but there is one classic example of the situation that is easy to understand. Because it is used as the standard example, this situation has a special name of its own: "deadly embrace."

Imagine a thread is trying to obtain exclusive use of two locks that are encapsulated in objects a and b. First the thread gets the lock on object a, then it proceeds to try to get the lock on object b. This sounds innocent enough, but now imagine that another thread already holds the lock on object b. Clearly, the first thread cannot proceed until the second thread releases the lock on object b.

Now for the nasty part: imagine that the other thread, while holding the lock on object b, is trying to get the lock on object a. This situation is now hopeless. The first thread holds the lock on object a and cannot proceed without the lock on object b. Further, the first thread cannot release the lock on object a until it has obtained the lock on object b. At the same time, the second thread holds the lock on object b and cannot release it until it obtains the lock on object a.

Let's have a look at code that could cause this situation:

```
1. public class Deadlock implements Runnable {
2.    public static void main(String [] args)  {
3.      Object a = "Resource A";
4.      Object b = "Resource B";
5.      Thread t1 = new Thread(new Deadlock(a, b));
6.      Thread t2 = new Thread(new Deadlock(b, a));
7.      t1.start();
8.      t2.start();
9.    }
10.
11.   private Object firstResource;
12.   private Object secondResource;
13.
14.   public Deadlock(Object first, Object second) {
15.     firstResource = first;
16.     secondResource = second;
17.   }
18.
19.   public void run() {
```

```
20.      for (;;) {
21.        System.out.println(
22.          Thread.currentThread().getName() +
23.          " Looking for lock on " + firstResource);
24.
25.        synchronized (firstResource) {
26.          System.out.println(
27.            Thread.currentThread().getName() +
28.            " Obtained lock on " + firstResource);
29.
30.          System.out.println(
31.            Thread.currentThread().getName() +
32.            " Looking for lock on " + secondResource);
33.
34.          synchronized (secondResource) {
35.            System.out.println(
36.              Thread.currentThread().getName() +
37.              " Obtained lock on " + secondResource);
38.            // simulate some time consuming activity
39.            try { Thread.sleep(100); }
40.            catch (InterruptedException ex) {}
41.          }
42.        }
43.      }
44.    }
45. }
```

In this code, the resources are locked at lines 25 and 34. Notice that, although the same code executes in both threads, the references firstResource and secondResource actually refer to different objects in both threads. This is because of the way the two Deadlock instances are constructed on lines 5 and 6.

When run, the exact behavior is non-deterministic, because of differences in thread scheduling between executions. Commonly, however, the output will look something like this:

```
Thread-0 Looking for lock on Resource A
Thread-0 Obtained lock on Resource A
```

```
Thread-1 Looking for lock on Resource B
Thread-0 Looking for lock on Resource B
Thread-1 Obtained lock on Resource B
Thread-1 Looking for lock on Resource A
```

If you study this output, you will see that the first thread ("Thread-0") holds the lock on Resource A and is trying to obtain the lock on Resource B. Meanwhile, the second thread ("Thread-1") holds the lock on Resource B—which prevents the first thread from ever executing. Further, the second thread is waiting for Resource A and can never proceed because that will never be released by the first thread.

It is useful to realize that if both threads were looking for the locks in the same order, then the deadly embrace situation would never occur. However, it can be very difficult to arrange for this ordering solution in situations where the threads are disparate parts of the program. Indeed, looking at the variables used in this example, you will see that it can sometimes be very difficult to recognize an ordering problem like this even if the code is all in one place.

Strange Ways to Synchronize

There are two ways to synchronize code that have not been explained yet. They are hardly common and generally should not be used without a very compelling reason. The two approaches are:

- Synchronizing on the lock of a different object
- Synchronizing on the lock of a class

It was briefly mentioned in an earlier section ("The Object Lock and Synchronization") that you can synchronize on the lock of any object. Suppose, for example, that you have the following class, which is admittedly a bit contrived:

```
1. class StrangeSync {
2.    Rectangle rect = new Rectangle(11, 13, 1100, 1300);
3.    void doit() {
4.       int x = 504;
5.       int y = x / 3;
6.       rect.width -= x;
```

```
7.      rect.height -= y;
8.   }
9. }
```

If you add the synchronized keyword at line 3, then a thread that wants to execute the doit() method of some instance of StrangeSync must first acquire the lock for that instance. That may be exactly what you want. However, perhaps you only want to synchronize lines 6 and 7, and perhaps you want a thread attempting to execute those lines to synchronize on the lock of rect, rather than on the lock of the current executing object. The way to do this is shown below:

```
 1. class StrangeSync {
 2.   Rectangle rect = new Rectangle(11, 13, 1100, 1300);
 3.   void doit() {
 4.     int x = 504;
 5.     int y = x / 3;
 6.     synchronized(rect) {
 7.       rect.width -= x;
 8.       rect.height -= y;
 9.     }
10.   }
11. }
```

The code above synchronizes on the lock of some arbitrary object (specified in parentheses after the synchronized keyword on line 6), rather than synchronizing on the lock of the current object. Also, the code above synchronizes just two lines, rather than an entire method.

It is difficult to find a good reason for synchronizing on an arbitrary object. However, synchronizing only a subset of a method can be useful; sometimes you want to hold the lock as briefly as possible, so that other threads can get their turn as soon as possible. The Java compiler insists that when you synchronize a portion of a method (rather than the entire method), you have to specify an object in parentheses after the synchronized keyword. If you put this in the parentheses, then the goal is achieved: You have synchronized a portion of a method, with the lock using the lock of the object that owns the method.

So your options are:

- To synchronize an entire method, using the lock of the object that owns the method. To do this, put the `synchronized` keyword in the method's declaration.

- To synchronize part of a method, using the lock of an arbitrary object. Put curly brackets around the code to be synchronized, preceded by `synchronized(theArbitraryObject)`.

- To synchronize part of a method, using the lock of the object that owns the method. Put curly brackets around the code to be synchronized, preceded by `synchronized(this)`.

Classes, as well as objects, have locks. A class lock is used for synchronizing the static methods of a class. The Certification Exam objectives do not reflect a great emphasis on class locks.

Chapter Summary

A Java thread scheduler can be preemptive or time-sliced, depending on the design of the JVM. No matter which design is used, a thread becomes eligible for execution ("Ready") when its `start()` method is invoked. When a thread begins execution, the scheduler calls the `run()` method of the thread's target (if there is a target) or the `run()` method of the thread itself (if there is no target). The target must be an instance of a class that implements the `Runnable` interface.

In the course of execution, a thread can become ineligible for execution for a number or reasons: A thread can suspend, or sleep, or block, or wait. In due time (one hopes!), conditions will change so that the thread once more becomes eligible for execution; then the thread enters the Ready state and eventually can execute.

When a thread returns from its `run()` method, it enters the Dead state and cannot be restarted.

You might find the following lists to be a useful summary of Java's threads.

- Scheduler implementations:
  - Preemptive
  - Time-sliced
- Constructing a thread:
  - `new Thread()`: no target; thread's own `run()` method is executed
  - `new Thread(Runnable target)`: target's `run()` method is executed
- Non-runnable thread states:
  - Suspended: caused by `suspend()`, waits for `resume()`
  - Sleeping: caused by `sleep()`, waits for timeout
  - Blocked: caused by various I/O calls or by failing to get a monitor's lock, waits for I/O or for the monitor's lock
  - Waiting: caused by `wait()`, waits for `notify()` or `notifyAll()`
  - Dead: caused by `stop()` or returning from `run()`, no way out

Test Yourself

1. Which one statement below is true concerning the following code?

```
1. class Greebo extends java.util.Vector
2.    implements Runnable {
3.      public void run(String message) {
4.        System.out.println("in run() method: " +
5.        message);
6.    }
7. }
8.
9. class GreeboTest {
10.    public static void main(String args[]) {
12.      Greebo g = new Greebo();
13.      Thread t = new Thread(g);
14.      t.start();
15.    }
16. }
```

A. There will be a compiler error, because class Greebo does not correctly implement the Runnable interface.

B. There will be a compiler error at line 13, because you cannot pass a parameter to the constructor of a Thread.

C. The code will compile correctly but will crash with an exception at line 13.

D. The code will compile correctly but will crash with an exception at line 14.

E. The code will compile correctly and will execute without throwing any exceptions.

244 Chapter 7 · Threads

2. Which one statement below is always true about the following application?

```
1.  class HiPri extends Thread {
2.    HiPri() {
3.      setPriority(10);
4.    }
5.
6.    public void run() {
7.      System.out.println(
8.        "Another thread starting up.");
9.      while (true) { }
10.   }
11.
12.   public static void main(String args[]) {
13.     HiPri hp1 = new HiPri();
14.     HiPri hp2 = new HiPri();
15.     HiPri hp3 = new HiPri();
16.     hp1.start();
17.     hp2.start();
18.     hp3.start();
19.   }
20. }
```

A. When the application is run, thread hp1 will execute; threads hp2 and hp3 will never get the CPU.

B. When the application is run, all three threads (hp1, hp2, and hp3) will get to execute, taking time-sliced turns in the CPU.

C. Either A or B will be true, depending on the underlying platform.

3. True or False: A thread wants to make a second thread ineligible for execution. To do this, the first thread can call the yield() method on the second thread.

A. True

B. False

4. A thread's `run()` method includes the following lines:

```
1. try {
2.    sleep(100);
3. } catch (InterruptedException e) { }
```

Assuming the thread is not interrupted, which one of the following statements is correct?

A. The code will not compile, because exceptions may not be caught in a thread's `run()` method.

B. At line 2, the thread will stop running. Execution will resume in, at most, 100 milliseconds.

C. At line 2, the thread will stop running. It will resume running in exactly 100 milliseconds.

D. At line 2, the thread will stop running. It will resume running some time after 100 milliseconds have elapsed.

5. A monitor called `mon` has 10 threads in its waiting pool; all these waiting threads have the same priority. One of the threads is `thr1`. How can you notify `thr1` so that it alone moves from the Waiting state to the Ready state?

A. Execute `notify(thr1);` from within synchronized code of `mon`.

B. Execute `mon.notify(thr1);` from synchronized code of any object.

C. Execute `thr1.notify();` from synchronized code of any object.

D. Execute `thr1.notify();` from any code (synchronized or not) of any object.

E. You cannot specify which thread will get notified.

6. If you attempt to compile and execute the application listed below, will it ever print out the message In xxx?

```
1. class TestThread3 extends Thread {
2.   public void run() {
3.     System.out.println("Running");
4.     System.out.println("Done");
5.   }
6.
7.   private void xxx() {
8.     System.out.println("In xxx");
9.   }
10.
11.   public static void main(String args[]) {
12.     TestThread3 ttt = new TestThread3();
13.     ttt.xxx();
14.     ttt.start();
12.   }
13. }
```

A. Yes

B. No

7. True or False: A Java monitor must either extend Thread or implement Runnable.

A. True

B. False

Chapter

8

The *java.lang* and *java.util* Packages

JAVA CERTIFICATION EXAM OBJECTIVES COVERED IN THIS CHAPTER:

✓ Determine the result of applying the *boolean equals(Object)* method to objects of any combination of the classes *java.lang.String, java.lang.Boolean,* and *java.lang.Object*.

✓ Write code using the following methods of the *java.lang.Math* class: *abs, ceil, floor, max, min, random, round, sin, cos, tan, sqrt*.

✓ Describe the significance of the immutability of *String* objects.

✓ Make appropriate selection of collection classes/interfaces to suit specified behavior requirements.

The java.lang package contains classes that are central to the operation of the Java language and environment. Very little can be done without the String class, for example, and the Object class is completely indispensable. The Java compiler automatically imports all the classes in the package into every source file.

This chapter examines some of the most important classes of the java.lang package:

- Object
- Math
- The wrapper classes
- String
- StringBuffer

In addition, this chapter also covers the collection classes of the java.util package.

The *Object* Class

The Object class is the ultimate ancestor of all Java classes. If a class does not contain the extends keyword in its declaration, the compiler builds a class that extends directly from Object.

All the methods of Object are inherited by every class. Three of these methods (wait(), notify(), and notifyAll()) support thread control; they are discussed in detail in Chapter 7. Two other methods, equals() and toString(), provide little functionality on their own. The intention is that programmers who develop reusable classes can override equals() and toString() in order to provide class-specific useful functionality.

The signature of equals() is

```
public boolean equals(Object object)
```

The method is supposed to provide "deep" comparison, in contrast to the "shallow" comparison provided by the == operator. To see the difference between the two types of comparison, consider the java.util.Date class, which represents a moment in time. Suppose you have two references of type

Date: *d1* and *d2*. One way to compare these two is with the following line of code:

```
if (d1 == d2)
```

The comparison will be true if the reference in *d1* is equal to the reference in *d2*. Of course, this is only the case when both variables refer to the same object.

Sometimes you want a different kind of comparison. Sometimes you don't care whether *d1* and *d2* refer to the same Date object. Sometimes you *know* they are different objects; what you care about is whether the two objects, which encapsulate day and time information, represent the same moment in time. In this case, you don't want the shallow reference-level comparison of ==; you need to look deeply into the objects themselves. The way to do it is with the equals() method:

```
if (d1.equals(d2))
```

The version of equals() provided by the Object class is not very useful; in fact, it just does an == comparison. All classes should override equals() so that it performs a useful comparison. That is just what most of the standard Java classes do: they compare the relevant instance variables of two objects.

The purpose of the toString() method is to provide a string representation of an object's state. This is especially useful for debugging.

The toString() method is similar to equals() in that the version provided by the Object class is not especially useful. (It just prints out the object's class name, followed by a hash code.) Many JDK classes override toString() to provide more useful information. Java's string concatenation facility makes use of this method, as you will see later in this chapter, in the "String Concatenation the Easy Way" section.

The *Math* Class

Java's Math class contains a collection of methods and two constants that support mathematical computation. The class is final, so you cannot extend it. The constructor is private, so you cannot create an instance. Fortunately, the methods and constants are static, so they can be accessed through the class name without having to construct a Math object. (See Chapter 3 for an explanation of Java's modifiers, including final, static, and private.)

The two constants of the Math class are Math.PI and Math.E. They are declared to be public, static, final, and double.

The methods of the Math class cover a broad range of mathematical functionality, including trigonometry, logarithms and exponentiation, and rounding. The intensive number-crunching methods are generally native, to take advantage of any math-acceleration hardware that might be present on the underlying machine.

The Certification Exam requires you to know about the methods shown in Table 8.1.

TABLE 8.1 Methods of the Math Class

Method	Returns
int abs(int i)	absolute value of *i*
long abs(long l)	absolute value of *l*
float abs(float f)	absolute value of *f*
double abs(double d)	absolute value of *d*
double ceil(double d)	the smallest integer that is not less than *d* (returns as a double)
double floor(double d)	the largest integer that is not greater than *d* (returns as a double)
int max(int i1, int i2)	greater of *i1* and *i2*
long max(long l1, long l2)	greater of *l1* and *l2*
float max(float f1, float f2)	greater of *f1* and *f2*
double max(double d1, double d2)	greater of *d1* and *d2*
int min(int i1, int i2)	smaller of *i1* and *i2*
long min(long l1, long l2)	smaller of *l1* and *l2*
float min(float f1, float f2)	smaller of *f1* and *f2*
double min(double d1, double d2)	smaller of *d1* and *d2*

TABLE 8.1 Methods of the Math Class *(continued)*

Method	Returns
`double random()`	random number >= 0.0 and <1.0
`int round(float f)`	closest `int` to *f*
`long round(double d)`	closest `long` to *d*
`double sin(double d)`	sine of *d*
`double cos(double d)`	cosine of *d*
`double tan(double d)`	tangent of *d*
`double sqrt(double d)`	square root of *d*

The Wrapper Classes

Each Java primitive data type has a corresponding *wrapper class*. A wrapper class is simply a class that encapsulates a single, immutable value. For example, the `Integer` class wraps up an `int` value, and the `Float` class wraps up a `float` value. The wrapper class names do not perfectly match the corresponding primitive data type names. Table 8.2 lists the primitives and wrappers.

TABLE 8.2 Primitives and Wrappers

Primitive Data Type	Wrapper Class
`boolean`	`Boolean`
`byte`	`Byte`
`char`	`Character`
`short`	`Short`
`int`	`Integer`

TABLE 8.2 Primitives and Wrappers *(continued)*

Primitive Data Type	Wrapper Class
long	Long
float	Float
double	Double

All the wrapper classes can be constructed by passing the value to be wrapped into the appropriate constructor. The code fragment below shows how to construct an instance of each wrapper type:

```
 1. boolean   primitiveBoolean = true;
 2. Boolean   wrappedBoolean =
 3.                new Boolean(primitiveBoolean);
 4.
 5. byte      primitiveByte = 41;
 6. Byte      wrappedByte = new Byte(primitiveByte);
 7.
 8. char      primitiveChar = 'M';
 9. Character wrappedChar = new Character(primitiveChar);
10.
11. short     primitiveShort = 31313;
12. Short     wrappedShort = new Short(primitiveShort);
13.
14. int       primitiveInt = 12345678;
15. Integer   wrappedInt = new Integer(primitiveInt);
16.
17. long      primitiveLong = 12345678987654321L;
18. Long      wrappedLong = new Long(primitiveLong);
19.
20. float     primitiveFloat = 1.11f;
21. Float     wrappedFloat = new Float(primitiveFloat);
22.
23. double    primitiveDouble = 1.11111111;
24. Double    wrappedDouble =
25.                new Double(primitiveDouble);
```

There is another way to construct any of these classes, with the exception of `Character`. You can pass into the constructor a string that represents the value to be wrapped. Most of these constructors throw `NumberFormat-Exception`, because there is always the possibility that the string will not represent a valid value. Only `Boolean` does not throw this exception: the constructor accepts any `String` input, and wraps a `true` value if the string (ignoring case) is `"true"`. The code fragment below shows how to construct wrappers from strings:

```
1. Boolean wrappedBoolean = new Boolean("True");
2. try {
3.    Byte wrappedByte = new Byte("41");
4.    Short wrappedShort = new Short("31313");
5.    Integer wrappedInt = new Integer("12345678");
6.    Long wrappedLong = new Long("12345678987654321");
7.    Float wrappedFloat = new Float("1.11f");
8.    Double wrappedDouble = new Double("1.11111111");
9. }
10. catch (NumberFormatException e) {
11.    System.out.println("Bad Number Format");
12. }
```

The values wrapped inside two wrappers of the same type can be checked for equality by using the `equals()` method discussed in the previous section. For example, the code fragment below checks two instances of `Double`:

```
1. Double d1 = new Double(1.01055);
2. Double d2 = new Double("1.11348");
3. if (d1.equals(d2)) {
4.    // Do something.
5. }
```

After a value has been wrapped, it may eventually be necessary to extract it. For an instance of `Boolean`, you can call `booleanValue()`. For an instance of `Character`, you can call `charValue()`. The other six classes extend from the abstract superclass `Number`, which provides methods to retrieve the wrapped value as a `byte`, a `short`, an `int`, a `long`, a `float`, or a `double`. In other words, the value of any wrapped number can be retrieved as any numeric type. The retrieval methods are:

- `public byte byteValue()`

- `public short shortValue()`
- `public int intValue()`
- `public long longValue()`
- `public float floatValue()`
- `public double doubleValue()`

The wrapper classes are useful whenever it would be convenient to treat a piece of primitive data as if it were an object. A good example is the `Vector` class, which is a dynamically growing collection of objects of arbitrary type. The method for adding an object to a vector is

```
public void add(Object ob)
```

Using this method, you can add any object of any type to a vector; you can even add an array (you saw why in Chapter 4). You cannot, however, add an `int`, a `long`, or any other primitive to a vector. There are no special methods for doing so, and `add(Object ob)` will not work because there is no automatic conversion from a primitive to an object. Thus, the code below will not compile:

```
1. Vector vec = new Vector();
2. boolean boo = false;
3. vec.addElement(boo);  // Illegal
```

The solution is to wrap the boolean primitive, as shown below:

```
1. Vector vec = new Vector();
2. boolean boo = false;
3. Boolean wrapper = new Boolean(boo);
4. vec.add(wrapper);  // Legal
```

The wrapper classes are useful in another way: they provide a variety of utility methods, most of which are static. For example, the static method `Character.isDigit(char ch)` returns a `boolean` that tells whether the character represents a base-10 digit. All the wrapper classes except `Character` have a static method called `valueOf(String s)`, which parses a string and constructs and returns a wrapper instance of the same type as the class whose method was called. So, for example, `Long.valueOf("23L")` constructs and returns an instance of the `Long` class that wraps the value 23.

All wrapper classes have an inconvenient feature: the values they wrap are immutable. After an instance is constructed, the encapsulated value cannot be changed. It is tempting to try to subclass the wrappers, so that the sub-classes inherit all the useful functionality of the original classes, while offering mutable contents. Unfortunately, this strategy doesn't work, because the wrapper classes are final.

To summarize the major facts about the primitive wrapper classes:

- Every primitive type has a corresponding wrapper class type.

- All wrapper types can be constructed from primitives; all except `Character` can also be constructed from strings.

- Wrapped values can be tested for equality with the `equals()` method.

- Wrapped values can be extracted with various `XXXValue()` methods. All six numeric wrapper types support all six numeric `XXXValue()` methods.

- Wrapper classes provide various utility methods, including the static `valueOf()` methods, which parse an input string.

- Wrapped values cannot be modified.

Strings

Java uses the `String` and `StringBuffer` classes to encapsulate strings of characters. Java uses 16-bit Unicode characters in order to support a broader range of international alphabets than would be possible with traditional 8-bit characters. Both strings and string buffers contain sequences of 16-bit Unicode characters. The next several sections examine these two classes, as well as Java's string concatenation feature.

The *String* Class

The `String` class contains an immutable string. Once an instance is created, the string it contains cannot be changed. There are numerous forms of constructor, allowing you to build an instance out of an array of `bytes` or `chars`, a subset of an array of `bytes` or `chars`, another string, or a string buffer. Many of these constructors give you the option of specifying a character encoding, specified as a string; however, the Certification Exam does not require you to know the details of character encodings.

Probably the most common string constructor simply takes another string as its input. This is useful when you want to specify a literal value for the new string:

```
String s1 = new String("immutable");
```

An even easier abbreviation could be:

```
String s1 = "immutable";
```

It is important to be aware of what happens when you use a `String` literal ("immutable" in both examples). Every string literal is represented internally by an instance of `String`. Java classes may have a pool of such strings. When a literal is compiled, the compiler adds an appropriate string to the pool. However, if the same literal already appeared as a literal elsewhere in the class, then it is already represented in the pool. The compiler does not create a new copy; instead, it uses the existing one from the pool. This saves on memory and can do no harm. Since strings are immutable, there is no way that a piece of code can harm another piece of code by modifying a shared string.

Earlier in this chapter, you saw how the `equals()` method can be used to provide a deep equality check of two objects. With strings, the `equals()` method does what you would expect: it checks the two contained collections of characters. The code below shows how this is done:

```
1. String s1 = "Compare me";
2. String s2 = "Compare me";
3. if (s1.equals(s2)) {
4.    // whatever
5. }
```

Not surprisingly, the test at line 3 succeeds. Given what you know about how `String` literals work, you can see that if line 3 is modified to use the `==` comparison, as shown below, the test still succeeds:

```
1. String s1 = "Compare me";
2. String s2 = "Compare me";
3. if (s1 == s2)) {
4.    // whatever
5. }
```

The == test is true because *s2* refers to the String in the pool that was created in line 1. Figure 8.1 shows this graphically.

FIGURE 8.1 Identical literals

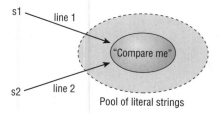

Pool of literal strings

You can also construct a String by explicitly calling the constructor, as shown below; however, this causes extra memory allocation for no obvious advantage.

```
String s2 = new String("Constructed");
```

When this line is compiled, the String literal "Constructed" is placed into the pool. At runtime, the new String() statement is executed and a fresh instance of String is constructed, duplicating the String in the literal pool. Finally, a reference to the new String is assigned to *s2*. Figure 8.2 shows the chain of events.

FIGURE 8.2 Explicitly calling the String constructor

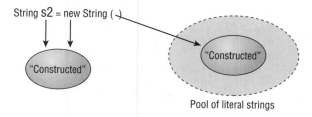

Pool of literal strings

Figure 8.2 shows that explicitly calling new String() results in the existence of two objects, one in the literal pool and the other in the program's space.

You have just seen that if you create a new String instance at runtime, it will not be in the pool but really will be a new and distinct object. You can arrange for your new String to be placed into the pool for possible reuse, or to reuse an existing identical String from the pool, by using the intern() method of the String class. In programs that use a great many strings that might be similar, this can reduce memory requirements. More importantly, in programs that make a lot of String equality comparisons, ensuring that all strings are in the pool allows you to use the == reference comparison in place of the slower equals() method.

There are several convenient methods in the String class; some of these methods perform a transformation on a string. For example, toUpperCase() converts all the characters of a string to uppercase. It is important to remember that the original string is not modified. That would be impossible, since strings are immutable. What really happens is that a new string is constructed and returned. Generally, this new string will not be in the pool unless you explicitly call intern() to put it there.

The methods listed below are just some of the most useful methods of the String class. There are more methods than those listed here, and some of those listed have overloaded forms that take different inputs. This list includes all the methods that you are required to know for the Certification Exam, plus a few additional useful ones:

- char charAt(int index): This returns the indexed character of a string, where the index of the initial character is 0.

- String concat(String addThis): This returns a new string consisting of the old string followed by addThis.

- int compareTo(String otherString): This performs a lexical comparison; it returns an int that is less than 0 if the current string is less than otherString, equal to 0 if the strings are identical, and greater than 0 if the current string is greater than otherString.

- boolean endsWith(String suffix): This returns true if the current string ends with suffix; otherwise it returns false.

- boolean equals(Object ob): This returns true if ob instanceof String and the string encapsulated by ob matches the string encapsulated by the executing object.

- boolean equalsIgnoreCase(String s): This is like equals(), but the argument is a String and the comparison ignores case.

- `int indexOf(int ch)`: This returns the index within the current string of the first occurrence of `ch`. Alternative forms return the index of a string and begin searching from a specified offset.

- `int lastIndexOf(int ch)`: This returns the index within the current string of the last occurrence of `ch`. Alternative forms return the index of a string and end searching at a specified offset from the end of the string.

- `int length()`: This returns the number of characters in the current string.

- `String replace(char oldChar, char newChar)`: This returns a new string, generated by replacing every occurrence of `oldChar` with `newChar`.

- `boolean startsWith(String prefix)`: This returns true if the current string begins with `prefix`; otherwise it returns false. Alternate forms begin searching from a specified offset.

- `String substring(int startIndex)`: This returns the substring, beginning at `startIndex` of the current string and extending to the end of the current string. An alternate form specifies starting and ending offsets.

- `String toLowerCase()`: This converts the executing object to lowercase and returns a new string.

- `String toString()`: This returns the executing object.

- `String toUpperCase()`: This converts the executing object to uppercase and returns a new string.

- `String trim()`: This returns the string that results from removing whitespace characters from the beginning and ending of the current string.

The code below shows how to use two of these methods to "modify" a string. The original string is " 5 + 4 = 20". The code first strips off the leading blank space, then converts the addition sign to a multiplication sign.

```
1. String s = "  5 + 4 = 20";
2. s = s.trim();              // "5 + 4 = 20"
3. s = s.replace('+', 'x');   // "5 x 4 = 20"
```

After line 3, *s* refers to a string whose appearance is shown in the line 3 comment. Of course, the modification has not taken place within the original string. Both the `trim()` call in line 2 and the `replace()` call of line 3 construct and return new strings; the address of each new string in turn gets assigned to the reference variable *s*. Figure 8.3 shows this sequence graphically.

FIGURE 8.3 Trimming and replacing

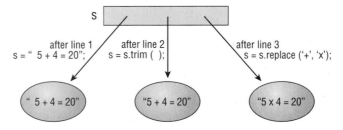

Figure 8.3 shows that the original string only seems to be modified. It is actually replaced, because strings are immutable. If much modification is required, then this becomes very inefficient, as it stresses the garbage collector cleaning up all the old strings and it takes time to copy the contents of the old strings into the new ones. The next section discusses a class that helps alleviate these problems because it represents a mutable string: the `StringBuffer` class.

The *StringBuffer* Class

An instance of Java's `StringBuffer` class represents a string that can be dynamically modified.

The most commonly used constructor takes a `String` instance as input. You can also construct an empty string buffer (probably with the intention of adding characters to it later). An empty string buffer can have its initial capacity specified at construction time. The three constructors are:

- `StringBuffer()`: This constructs an empty string buffer.

- `StringBuffer(int capacity)`: This constructs an empty string buffer with the specified initial capacity.

- `StringBuffer(String initialString)`: This constructs a string buffer that initially contains the specified string.

A string buffer has a `capacity`, which is the longest string it can represent without needing to allocate more memory. A string buffer can grow beyond this as necessary, so usually you do not have to worry about capacity.

The list below presents some of the methods that modify the contents of a string buffer. All of them return the original string buffer itself.

- `StringBuffer append(String str)`: This appends `str` to the current string buffer. Alternative forms support appending primitives and character arrays; these are converted to strings before appending.

- `StringBuffer append(Object obj)`: This calls `toString()` on `obj` and appends the result to the current string buffer.

- `StringBuffer insert(int offset, String str)`: This inserts `str` into the current string buffer at position `offset`. There are numerous alternative forms.

- `StringBuffer reverse()`: This reverses the characters of the current string buffer.

- `StringBuffer setCharAt(int offset, char newChar)`: This replaces the character at position `offset` with `newChar`.

- `StringBuffer setLength(int newLength)`: This sets the length of the string buffer to `newLength`. If `newLength` is less than the current length, the string is truncated. If `newLength` is greater than the current length, the string is padded with null characters.

The code below shows the effect of using several of these methods in combination.

```
1. StringBuffer sbuf = new StringBuffer("12345");
2. sbuf.reverse();            // "54321"
3. sbuf.insert(3, "aaa");     // "543aaa21"
4. sbuf.append("zzz");        // "543aaa21zzz"
```

The method calls above actually modify the string buffer they operate on (unlike the `String` class example of the previous section). Figure 8.4 graphically shows what this code does.

FIGURE 8.4 Modifying a StringBuffer

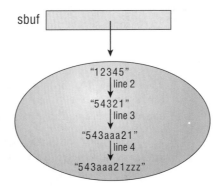

One last string buffer method that bears mentioning is toString(). You saw earlier in this chapter that every class has one of these methods. Not surprisingly, the string buffer's version just returns the encapsulated string, as an instance of class String. You will see in the next section that this method plays a crucial role in string concatenation.

String Concatenation the Easy Way

The concat() method of the String class and the append() method of the StringBuffer class glue two strings together. An easier way to concatenate strings is to use Java's overloaded + operator. String concatenation with the + operator and the arithmetic operations are situations in which Java provides built-in operator overloading. However, don't forget that you, the programmer, cannot define additional operator overloads.

String concatenation is useful in many situations—for example, in debugging print statements. So, to print the value of a double called radius, all you have to do is this:

```
System.out.println("radius = " + radius);
```

This technique also works for object data types. To print the value of a `Dimension` called `dimension`, all you need is:

```
System.out.println("dimension = " + dimension);
```

It is important to understand how the technique works. At compile time, if either operand of a + operator (that is, if what appears on either side of a + sign) is a `String` object, then the compiler recognizes that it is in a *string context*. In a string context, the + sign is interpreted as calling for string concatenation, rather than arithmetic addition.

A string context is simply a run of additions, where one of the operands is a string. For example, if variable *a* is a string, then the following partial line of code is a string context, regardless of the types of the other operands:

```
a + b + c
```

The Java compiler treats the code above as if it were the following:

```
new
StringBuffer().append(a).append(b).append(c).toString();
```

If any of the variables (*a*, *b*, or *c*) is a primitive, the `append()` method computes an appropriate string representation. For an object variable, the `append()` method uses the string returned from calling `toString()` on the object. The conversion begins with an empty string buffer, then appends each element in turn to the string buffer, and finally calls `toString()` to convert the string buffer to a string.

The code below implements a class with its own `toString()` method.

```
1. class Abc {
2.    private int a;
3.    private int b;
4.    private int c;
5.
6.    Abc(int a, int b, int c) {
7.      this.a = a;
8.      this.b = b;
9.      this.c = c;
10.   }
11.
```

```
12.    public String toString() {
13.       return "a = " + a + ", b = " + b + ", c = " + c;
14.    }
15. }
```

Now the `toString()` method (lines 12–14) can be used by any code that wants to take advantage of string concatenation. For example,

```
Abc theAbc = new Abc(11, 13, 48);
System.out.println("Here it is: " + theAbc);
```

The output is:

```
Here it is: a = 11, b = 13, c = 48
```

To summarize, the sequence of events for a string context is:

1. An empty string buffer is constructed.

2. Each argument in turn is concatenated to the string buffer, using the `append()` method.

3. The string buffer is converted to a string with a call to `toString()`.

That is all you need to know about string manipulation for the Certification Exam, and probably all you need to know to write effective and efficient code, too. Next, we're going to look at collections.

The Collections API

Many programs need to keep track of groups of related data items. The most basic mechanism for doing this is the array. Although they are extremely useful for many purposes, arrays have some inherent limitations. They only provide a very simple mechanism for storing and accessing data. Moreover, their capacity must be known at construction time; there is no way to make an array bigger or smaller. Java has always had arrays and also some additional classes, such as the `Vector` and `Hashtable` classes, to allow you to manipulate groups of objects. Since JDK 1.2, however, there is a significant feature to support much more generalized collection management: the Collections API. The Certification Exam objectives now require that you have a grasp of the concepts of this new functionality.

The Collections API is a mechanism for manipulating object references. While arrays are capable of storing primitives or references, collections are not. If you need to take advantage of collection functionality to manipulate primitives, you have to wrap the primitives in the wrapper classes that were presented earlier in this chapter.

The Collections API is often referred to as a *framework*. That is, the classes have been designed with a common abstraction of data container behavior in mind, ensuring uniform semantics wherever possible. At the same time, each implemented collection type is free to optimize its own operations. The factory class `java.util.Collections` supplements support for these types, which are discussed below, with a variety of static helper and factory methods. These methods support operations such as synchronizing the container, establishing immutability, executing binary searches, and so on. With these classes in place, programmers are no longer required to build their own basic data structures from scratch.

Collection Types

There are several different collections. They vary, for example, in the storage mechanisms used, in the way they can access data, and in the rules about what data might be stored. The Collections API provides a variety of interfaces and some concrete implementation classes, covering these variations.

There is a general interface, `java.util.Collection`, that defines the basic framework for collections. This interface stipulates the methods that allow you to add items, remove items, determine if items are in the collection, and count the number of items in the collection. A collection is sometimes known as a *bag* or a *multiset*. A simple collection places no constraints on the type, order, or repetition of elements within the collection.

Some collections are ordered; that is, there is a clear notion of one item following another. A collection of this kind is commonly known as a *list* or a *sequence*. In some lists, the order is the order in which items are added to the collection; in others, the elements themselves are assumed to have a natural order, and that order is understood by the list. In the Java Collections API, the interface `java.util.List` defines a basic framework for collections of this sort.

If a collection imposes the specific condition that it cannot contain the same value more than once, then it is known as a *set*. The interface `java.util.Set` defines the basic framework for this type of collection. In some sets, the null value is a legitimate entry, but if it is allowed, null can only occur once in a set.

The final type of specialized behavior directly supported by the Collections API is known as a *map*. A map uses a set of key values to look up, or index, the stored data. For example, if you store an object representing a person, then as the key value you could either use that person's name or some other unique identifier such as a social security number or employee i.d. number. Maps are particularly appropriate for implementing small online databases, especially if the data being stored will usually be accessed via the unique identifier. It is a requirement for a map that the key be unique, and for this reason if you were storing data about a person in a map, the name would not make a very good key since it is quite possible for two people to have the same name.

Let's take a moment to recap these points:

- A collection has no special order and does not reject duplicates.

- A list is ordered and does not reject duplicates.

- A set has no special order but rejects duplicates.

- A map supports searching on a key field, values of which must be unique.

Of course, it is possible for combinations of these behaviors to be meaningful. For example, a map might also be ordered. However, the Certification Exam only requires you to understand these four fundamental types of collection.

The storage associated with any one collection can be implemented in many ways, but the Collections API implements the four methods that are most widely used: an array, a linked list, a tree, or a hash table. Each of these techniques has benefits and constraints. Let's consider these benefits and constraints for each storage technique in turn.

Array storage tends to be fast to access, but it is relatively inefficient as the number of elements in the collection grows or if elements need to be inserted or deleted in the middle of a list. These limitations occur because the array itself is a fixed sequence. Adding or removing elements in the middle requires that all the elements from that point onward must be moved up or down by one position. Adding more data once the array is full requires a whole new array to be allocated, and the entire contents copied over to the new array.

Another limitation of an array is that it provides no special search mechanism. Despite these weaknesses, an array can still be an appropriate choice for data that are ordered, do not change often, and do not need to be searched much.

A *linked list* allows elements to be added to, or removed from, the collection at any location in the container, and allows the size of the collection to grow arbitrarily without the penalties associated with array copying. This improvement occurs because each element is an individual object that refers to the next (and sometimes previous, in a double-linked list) element in the list. However, it is significantly slower to access by index than an array, and still provides no special search mechanism. Because linked lists can insert new elements at arbitrary locations, however, they can apply ordering very easily, making it a simple (if not always efficient) matter to search a subset, or range, of data.

A *tree*, like a linked list, allows easy addition and deletion of elements and arbitrary growth of the collection. Unlike a list, trees insist on a means of ordering. In fact, constructing a tree requires that there be some comparison mechanism to the data being stored—although this can be created artificially in some cases. A tree will usually provide more efficient searching than either an array or a linked list, but this benefit may be obscured if unevenly distributed data is being stored.

A *hash table* requires that some unique identifying key can be associated with each data item, which in turn provides efficient searching. Hashes still allow a reasonably efficient access mechanism and arbitrary collection growth. Hashing may be inappropriate for small data sets, however, since there is typically some overhead associated with calculating the hash values and maintaining the more complex data structure associated with this type of storage. Without a sufficiently large number of elements that would justify the operational costs, the overhead of a hashing scheme may cancel out or outweigh the benefits of indexed access.

To work properly in the various collection types, data items may need to exhibit certain specific behavior. If you wish to search for an item, for example, that item's class must correctly implement the `equals()` method. Searching in ordered collections may also require that the data implement the interface `java.lang.Comparable`, which defines `compareTo()`, a method for determining the inherent order of two items of the same type. Most implementations of `Map` will also require a correct implementation of the `hashCode()` method. It is advisable to keep these three methods in mind whenever you define a new class, even if you do not anticipate storing instances of this class in collections.

Collection Implementations in the API

A variety of concrete implementation classes are supplied in the Collections API to implement the interfaces Collection, List, Set, and Map, using different storage types. Some of them are listed here:

HashMap/Hashtable These two classes are very similar, using hash-based storage to implement a map. The Hashtable has been in the Java API since the earliest releases, and the HashMap was added at JDK 1.2. The main difference between the two is that Hashtable does not allow the null value to be stored, although it makes some efforts to support multithreaded use.

Note that the List and Set interfaces extend the Collection interface. The Map interface does not extend Collection.

HashSet This is a set, so it does not permit duplicates and it uses hashing for storage.

LinkedList This is an implementation of a list, based on a linked-list storage.

TreeMap This class provides an ordered map. The elements must be orderable, either by implementing the Comparable interface or by providing a Comparator class to perform the comparisons.

TreeSet This class provides an ordered set, using a tree for storage. As with the TreeMap, the elements must have an order associated with them.

Vector This class, which has been in the Java API since the first release, implements a list using an array internally for storage. The array is dynamically reallocated as necessary, as the number of items in the vector grows.

Collections and Code Maintenance

There is no such thing as the "best implementation" of a collection. Using any kind of collection involves several kinds of overhead penalty: memory usage, storage time, retrieval time. No implementation can optimize all three of these features. So instead of looking for the best list or the best hash table or the best set, it is more reasonable to look for the most appropriate list, set, or hash table implementation for a particular programming situation.

As a program evolves, its data collections tend to grow. A collection that was created to hold a little bit of data may later be required to hold a large amount of data, while still providing reasonable response time. It is prudent from the outset to design code in such a way that it is easy to substitute one collection implementation type for another. Java's collections framework makes this easy because of its emphasis on interfaces. This section presents a typical scenario.

Imagine a program that maintains data about shoppers who are uniquely identified by their e-mail addresses. Such a program might use a `Shopper` class, with instances of this class stored in some kind of hash table, keyed by e-mail address. Suppose that when the program is first written, it is known that there are, and always will be, only three shoppers. The code fragment listed below constructs one instance for each shopper and stores the data in a hashmap; then the map is passed to various methods for processing:

```
1. private void getShoppers() {
2.    Shopper sh1 = getNextShopper();
3.    String email1 = getNextEmail();
4.    Shopper sh2 = getNextShopper();
5.    String email2 = getNextEmail();
6.    Shopper sh3 = getNextShopper();
7.    String email3 = getNextEmail();
8.
9.    Map map = new HashMap();   // Very important!
10.   map.put(sh1, email1);
11.   map.put(sh2, email2);
12.   map.put(sh3, email3);
13.
14.   findDesiredProducts(map);
15.   shipProducts(map);
16.   printInvoices(map);
17.   collectMoney(map);
18. }
```

Note the declaration of map on line 9. The reference type is Map, not HashMap (the interface, rather than the class). This is a very important difference whose value will become clear later on. The four processing methods do not much concern us here. Just consider their declarations:

```
private void findDesiredProducts(Map map) { ... }
private void shipProducts (Map map) { ... }
private void printInvoices (Map map) { ... }
private void collectMoney (Map map) { ... }
```

Imagine that each of these methods passes the hash map to other subordinate methods, which pass it to still other methods; our program has a large number of processing methods. Note that the argument types will be Map, not HashMap (again, the interface, rather than the class).

As development proceeds, suppose it becomes clear that the getShoppers() method should return the map's keys (which are the shoppers' e-mail addresses) in a sorted array. Since there are, and always will be, only three shoppers, there are and always will be only three keys to sort; the easiest implementation is therefore as follows:

```
1.  private String[] getShoppers() {  // New return type
2.    Shopper sh1 = getNextShopper();
3.    String email1 = getNextEmail();
4.    Shopper sh2 = getNextShopper();
5.    String email2 = getNextEmail();
6.    Shopper sh3 = getNextShopper();
7.    String email3 = getNextEmail();
8.
9.    Map map = new HashMap();
10.   map.put(sh1, email1);
11.   map.put(sh2, email2);
12.   map.put(sh3, email3);
13.
14.   findDesiredProducts(map);
15.   shipProducts(map);
16.   printInvoices(map);
17.   collectMoney(map);
18.
```

```
19.    // New sorting code.
20.    String[] sortedKeys = new String[3];
21.    if (email1.compareTo(email2) < 0  &&
22.        email1.compareTo(email3) < 0) {
23.       sortedKeys[0] = email1;
24.       if (email2.compareTo(email3) < 0)
25.          sortedKeys[1] = email2;
26.       else
27.          sortedKeys[2] = email3;
28.    }
29.    else if (email2.compareTo(email3) < 0) {
30.       sortedKeys[0] = email2;
31.       if (email1.compareTo(email3) < 0)
32.          sortedKeys[1] = email1;
33.       else
34.          sortedKeys[2] = email3;
35.    }
36.    else {
37.       sortedKeys[0] = email3;
38.       if (email1.compareTo(email2) < 0)
39.          sortedKeys[1] = email1;
40.       else
41.       sortedKeys[2] = email2;
42.    }
43.    return sortedKeys;
44. }
```

The added code is fairly lengthy: 26 lines.

Never believe a spec that says that the size of anything is and always will be small.

Predictably, as soon as the code is developed and debugged, someone will decide that the program needs to be expanded to accommodate twenty shoppers instead of the original three. The new requirement suggests the need for a separate sorting algorithm, in its own separate method. The new method will be called `sortStringArray()`. The next evolution of `getShoppers()` looks like this:

```
1.  private String[] getShoppers() {
2.    String[] keys = new String[20];
3.    Map map = new HashMap()
4.    for (int i=0; i<20; i++) {
5.      Shopper s = getNextShopper();
6.      keys[i] = getNextEmail();
7.      map.put(keys[i], s);
8.    }
9.
10.   findDesiredProducts(map);
11.   shipProducts(map);
12.   printInvoices(map);
13.   collectMoney(map);
14.
15.   sortStringArray(keys);
16.   return keys;
17. }
```

This code is much more modular and compact. However, it is still not mature. The next requirement is that it has to be able to handle any number of shoppers, even a very large number. At first glance, the solution seems very simple: just pass the number of shoppers in to the method, as shown below:

```
1.  private String[] getShoppers(int nShoppers) {
2.    String[] keys = new String[nShoppers];
3.    Map map = new HashMap()
4.    for (int i = 0; i < nShoppers; i++) {
5.      Shopper s = getNextShopper();
6.      keys[i] = getNextEmail();
7.      map.put(keys[i], s);
8.    }
9.
10.   findDesiredProducts(map);
11.   shipProducts(map);
```

```
12.    printInvoices(map);
13.    collectMoney(map);
14.
15.    sortStringArray(keys);
16.    return keys;
17. }
```

This code seems fine until the number of shoppers crosses some threshold. Then the amount of time spent sorting the keys (in method `sortStringArray()`, called on line 15) becomes prohibitive. Now is the time when the collections framework shows its true value. In particular, we are about to see the value of referencing the map with variables of type `Map`, rather than `HashMap` (the interface, rather than the class).

Since the sorting method is now the bottleneck, it is reasonable to wonder whether there is a different kind of map that can solve the performance problem. It is time for a quick look at the API pages for the classes that implement the `Map` interface. One finds that there is a suitable alternative: the `TreeMap` class. This implementation maintains its keys in sorted order and has a method for returning them in sorted order. Since the keys are always sorted, there seems to be zero overhead for sorting. Actually, the situation is not quite so good. There must be some extra overhead (hopefully slight) in the `put()` method, when the `TreeMap` stores a new key. Before deciding that `TreeMap` is the right class to use, it is important to ascertain that storing and retrieving data in the new collection will not cost an unreasonable amount of time, even if the map is very large.

First, what is the current cost of storing and retrieving in a `HashMap`? The API page for `HashMap` says that storage and retrieval take constant time, no matter what the size of the map might be. This is ideal; hopefully, the performance of a `TreeMap` will also be constant. If it is not constant, it must still be acceptable when the data collection is large.

The API page for `TreeMap` says that the class "provides guaranteed $\log(n)$ time cost" for various operations, including storage and retrieval. This means that the time to store and retrieve data grows with the logarithm of the size of the data set. Figure 8.5 shows a graph of the logarithm function.

FIGURE 8.5 The logarithm function

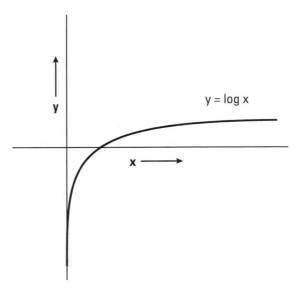

The graph in the figure rises steadily, but at an ever-decreasing rate. The cost for accessing a large tree map is only slightly greater than the cost for accessing a small one. Logarithmic overhead is almost as good as constant overhead; it is certainly acceptable for the current application.

Apparently the `TreeMap` class is a very good substitute for the original `HashMap` class. Now we see how easy it is to replace one collection implementation with another. Because all references to the hash table are of type `Map` (the interface) rather than type `HashMap` (the class), there is only one line of code that needs to be modified: the line in which the hash table is constructed. That line originally was:

```
Map map = new HashMap();
```

All that is required is to call a different constructor:

```
Map map = new TreeMap();
```

Many data processing methods pass references to the hash table back and forth among themselves. Not one of these methods needs to be modified at all. In fact, the only major change that needs to be made is to dispense with the `sortStringArray()` method and the call to it, substituting the tree map's intrinsic functionality. This modification is not directly relevant to the main point of this example, which is how easy it is to replace one collection type with another. However, it is instructive to see how the modification is accomplished. The final code looks like this:

```
1. private String[] getShoppers(int nShoppers) {
2.    Map map = new TreeMap()
3.    for (int i=0; i< nShoppers; i++) {
4.       map.put(getNextEmail(), getNextShopper());
5.    }
6.
7.    findDesiredProducts(map);
8.    shipProducts(map);
9.    printInvoices(map);
10.   collectMoney(map);
11.
12.   String[] keys = new String[nShoppers];
13.   Iterator iter = map.keySet().iterator();
14.   int i = 0;
15.   while (iter.hasNext())
16.      keys[i++] = (String)iter.next();
17.   return keys;
18. }
```

An iterator is an object that returns the elements of a collection one by one. Here the iterator on line 13 returns the elements of the hash table's key set. Since the hash table is an instance of TreeMap, the key set is guaranteed to be sorted.

This example has shown the importance of referencing collections with variables of interface rather than class type. If you do this, replacing one collection type with another type becomes trivially easy.

Summary of Collections

The essential points in this section have been:

- Collections impose no order, nor restrictions, on content duplication.
- Lists maintain an order (possibly inherent in the data, possibly externally imposed).
- Sets reject duplicate entries.
- Maps use unique keys to facilitate lookup of their contents.

For storage:

- Using arrays makes insertion, deletion, and growing the store more difficult.

- Using a linked list supports insertion, deletion, and growing the store, but makes indexed access slower.

- Using a tree supports insertion, deletion, and growing the list. Indexed access is slow, but searching is faster.

- Using hashing supports insertion, deletion, and growing the store. Indexed access is slow, but searching is particularly fast. However, hashing requires the use of unique keys for storing data elements.

Chapter Summary

The java.lang package contains classes that are indispensable to Java's operation, so all the classes of the package are automatically imported into all source files. Some of the most important classes in the package are:

- Object

- Math

- The wrapper classes

- String

- StringBuffer

In a string context, addition operands are appended in turn to a string buffer, which is then converted to a string; primitive operands are converted to strings, and objects are converted by having their toString() methods invoked.

The java.util package contains many utilities, but for the Certification Exam, the Collections API is of interest. Collections provide ways to store and retrieve data in a program. Different types of collection provide different rules for storage, and different collection implementations optimize different access and update behaviors.

Test Yourself

1. Given a string constructed by calling s = new String("xyzzy"), which of the calls listed below modify the string? (Choose all that apply.)

   A. s.append("aaa");

   B. s.trim();

   C. s.substring(3);

   D. s.replace('z', 'a');

   E. s.concat(s);

   F. None of the above

2. Which one statement is true about the code below?

```
1. String s1 = "abc" + "def";
2. String s2 = new String(s1);
3. if (s1 == s2)
4.    System.out.println("== succeeded");
5. if (s1.equals(s2))
6.    System.out.println(".equals() succeeded");
```

   A. Lines 4 and 6 both execute.

   B. Line 4 executes, and line 6 does not.

   C. Line 6 executes, and line 4 does not.

   D. Neither line 4 nor line 6 executes.

3. Suppose you want to write a class that offers static methods to compute hyperbolic trigonometric functions. You decide to subclass `java.lang.Math` and provide the new functionality as a set of static methods. Which one statement below is true about this strategy?

   A. The strategy works.

   B. The strategy works, provided the new methods are public.

   C. The strategy works, provided the new methods are not private.

   D. The strategy fails, because you cannot subclass `java.lang.Math`.

   E. The strategy fails, because you cannot add static methods to a subclass.

4. Which one statement is true about the code fragment below?

```
1. import java.lang.Math;
2. Math myMath = new Math();
3. System.out.println("cosine of 0.123 = " +
4.    myMath.cos(0.123));
```

   A. Compilation fails at line 2.

   B. Compilation fails at line 3 or 4.

   C. Compilation succeeds, although the import on line 1 is not necessary. During execution, an exception is thrown at line 3 or 4.

   D. Compilation succeeds. The import on line 1 is necessary. During execution, an exception is thrown at line 3 or 4.

   E. Compilation succeeds, and no exception is thrown during execution.

5. Which one statement is true about the code fragment below?

```
1. String s = "abcde";
2. StringBuffer s1 = new StringBuffer("abcde");
3. if (s.equals(s1))
4.    s1 = null;
5. if (s1.equals(s))
6.    s = null;
```

A. Compilation fails at line 1, because the `String` constructor must be called explicitly.

B. Compilation fails at line 3, because *s* and *s1* have different types.

C. Compilation succeeds. During execution, an exception is thrown at line 3.

D. Compilation succeeds. During execution, an exception is thrown at line 5.

E. Compilation succeeds. No exception is thrown during execution.

6. True or False: In the code fragment below, after execution of line 1, sbuf references an instance of the `StringBuffer` class. After execution of line 2, sbuf still references the same instance.

```
1. StringBuffer sbuf = new StringBuffer("abcde");
2. sbuf.insert(3, "xyz");
```

A. True

B. False

7. True or False: In the code fragment below, after execution of line 1, sbuf references an instance of the `StringBuffer` class. After execution of line 2, sbuf still references the same instance.

```
1. StringBuffer sbuf = new StringBuffer("abcde");
2. sbuf.append("xyz");
```

A. True

B. False

8. True or False: In the code fragment below, line 4 is executed.

```
1. String s1 = "xyz";
2. String s2 = "xyz";
3. if (s1 == s2)
4.    System.out.println("Line 4");
```

A. True

B. False

9. True or False: In the code fragment below, line 4 is executed.

```
1. String s1 = "xyz";
2. String s2 = new String(s1);
3. if (s1 == s2)
4.    System.out.println("Line 4");
```

A. True

B. False

10. Which would be most suitable for storing data elements that must not appear in the store more than once, if searching is not a priority?

A. Collection

B. List

C. Set

D. Map

E. Vector

Chapter

9

Layout Managers

JAVA CERTIFICATION EXAM OBJECTIVE COVERED IN THIS CHAPTER:

✓ Write code using component, container, and layout manager classes of the *java.awt* package to present a GUI with specified appearance and resize behavior, and distinguish the responsibilities of layout managers from those of containers.

Java's layout manager approach to graphical user interfaces is a novelty. Many GUI systems encourage GUI programmers to think in terms of precise specification of the size and location of interface components. Java changes all that. The Abstract Window Toolkit (AWT) provides a handful of layout managers, each of which implements its own layout policy. In Java, you create a GUI by choosing one or more layout managers and letting them take care of the details.

When you started working with layout managers, you probably had two impressions:

- You no longer bore the burden of specifying the exact position and dimensions of each component.

- You no longer had the power to specify the exact position and dimensions of each component.

Some people enjoy working with layout managers, and others resent them. They are here to stay, so the job at hand is to master this feature of the language. Acquiring this competence requires three things:

- An understanding of why Java uses layout managers

- An understanding of the layout policies of the more basic layout managers

- Some practice

The next section explains why Java uses layout managers. Then, after some intervening theory about how layout managers work, the last sections of this chapter describe Java's five layout managers: Flow, Grid, Border, Card, and GridBag.

In the versions of the exam prior to the Java 2 Platform, the objectives related explicitly to the Flow, Grid, and Border layout managers. However, the objectives were modified with the release of the Java 2 Platform edition of the exam, and since then all AWT layout managers are possible candidates for questions.

Although this chapter is long, there are relatively few questions on this topic in the exam. Furthermore, those questions tend to discuss qualitative aspects of the layout managers more than quantitative ones. This is particularly true of the more complex layouts.

Why Java Uses Layout Managers

There are two reasons why Java's AWT uses layout managers. The first reason is a bit theoretical, and you may or may not find yourself convinced by it. The second reason is thoroughly practical.

The theory lies in the position that precise layout (that is, specification in pixels of each component's size and position) is a repetitious and often-performed task; therefore, according to the principles of object-oriented programming, layout functionality ought to be encapsulated into one or more classes to automate the task. Certainly the layout managers eliminate a lot of development tedium. Many programmers dislike the idea of layout managers at first, but come to appreciate them more and more as tedious chores are eliminated.

The practical reason for having layout managers stems from Java's platform independence. In Java, AWT components borrow their behavior from the window system of the underlying hardware on which the Java Virtual Machine is running. Thus on a Macintosh, an AWT button looks like any other Mac button; on a Motif platform, a Java button looks like any other Motif button; and so on. The problem here is that buttons and other components have different sizes when instantiated on different platforms.

For example, consider the button that is constructed by the following line of code:

```
Button b = new Button("OK");
```

In a simple test, this button was 32 pixels wide by 21 pixels high on a typical Windows machine, but was 22 pixels high on a Motif platform, even though the same font was used for each. The difference seems small until you consider the effect such a difference would have on a column of many buttons. Most components vary somewhat in size from platform to platform. If Java encouraged precise pixel-level sizing and positioning, there would be a lot of Java GUIs that looked exquisite on their platform of origin—and terrible, or even unusable, on other hosts.

There is no guarantee that fonts with identical names will truly be 100 percent identical from platform to platform; there could be minute differences. Therefore, Java cannot even guarantee that two Strings drawn with the same text and font will display at the same size across platforms. Similarly, there is no way to achieve size consistency among components, which have to deal with font differences and with decoration differences.

How Layout Managers Solve the Problem

The essence of the problem you face when designing a GUI for a Java program is that you don't know how big each graphic element will be when the program runs. This problem is addressed by giving you a way to specify layouts with relative specifications, such as "this component is below that one," "this component is the same width as that one," "this component goes along the top." Such specifications are meaningful even without knowledge of the component sizes and can be put together in a way that allows a neat and similar layout even when the program runs with radically different GUI component sizes.

To implement this approach, Java delegates layout work to layout managers. The rest of this chapter investigates what layout managers are and explores those that are part of the AWT.

Layout Manager Theory

There are five layout-manager classes in the AWT toolkit. You might expect that there would be a common abstract superclass, called something like LayoutManager, from which these five layout managers would inherit common functionality. In fact, the common ancestor is java.awt.LayoutManager, but this is an interface, not a class, because the layout managers are so different from one another that they have nothing in common except a handful of method names. (There is also a java.awt.LayoutManager2 interface, which the GridBag, Border, and Card layout managers implement.)

Layout managers work in partnership with containers. To understand layout managers, it is important to understand what a container is and what happens when a component gets inserted into a container. The next two sections explore these topics; the information is not directly addressed by the Certification Exam, but some relevant theory at this point will make it much easier to understand the material that is required for the exam.

Containers and Components

Containers are Java components that can contain other components. There is a `java.awt.Container` class which, like `java.awt.Button` and `java.awt.Choice`, inherits from the `java.awt.Component` superclass. This inheritance relationship is shown in Figure 9.1.

FIGURE 9.1 Inheritance of java.awt.Container

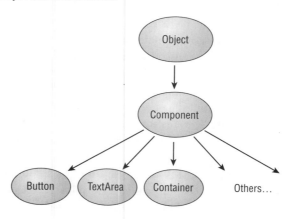

In older JDKs, the `Container` class was `abstract`, but now it isn't; its most commonly used concrete subclasses are `Applet`, `Frame`, and `Panel`, as shown in Figure 9.2. (Note that `Applet` is a subclass of `Panel`.)

FIGURE 9.2 Common subclasses of java.awt.Container

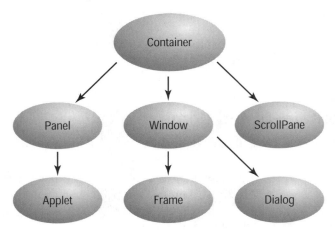

Java GUIs reside in applets or in frames. For simple applets, you just put your components in your applet; for simple applications, you just put your components in your frame. (In both cases, you might wonder how the components end up where they do; layout managers are lurking in the background, taking care of details.) For more complicated GUIs, it is convenient to divide the applet or frame into smaller regions. These regions might constitute, for example, a toolbar or a matrix of radio buttons. In Java, GUI subregions are implemented most commonly with the Panel container. Panels, just like applets and frames, can contain other components: buttons, canvases, check boxes, scroll bars, scroll panes, text areas, text fields, and of course other panels. Complicated GUIs sometimes have very complicated containment hierarchies of panels within panels within panels, and so on, down through many layers of containment.

In most OO windowing systems, including Java, the term *hierarchy* is ambiguous. When discussing classes, hierarchy refers to the structure of inheritance from superclass to subclass. When discussing GUIs, hierarchy can refer to the containment structure of GUI components, such as applets, frames, panels, buttons and so on.

The GUI in Figure 9.3 is a moderate-size frame for specifying a color. You can see at a glance that the panel contains labels, scroll bars, text fields, and buttons. You have probably guessed that the frame also contains some panels, even though they cannot be seen. In fact, the frame contains five panels. Each of the six containers (the five panels, plus the frame itself) has its own layout manager—there are four instances of Grid layout managers, one Flow layout manager, and one Border layout manager. Don't worry if you're not yet familiar with any of these managers— they will all be discussed shortly.

FIGURE 9.3   A GUI with several levels of containment

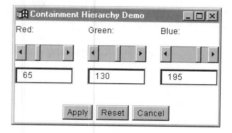

Figure 9.4 schematically shows the frame's containment hierarchy. A Java GUI programmer must master the art of transforming a proposed GUI into a workable and efficient containment hierarchy. This is a skill that comes with experience, once the fundamentals are understood. The Java Programmer's Certification Exam does not require you to develop any complicated containments, but it does require you to understand the fundamentals.

FIGURE 9.4   Containment hierarchy

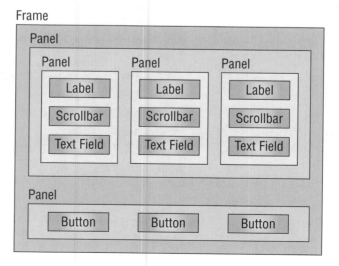

The code that implements the color chooser in Figure 9.3 is listed below:

```
1. import java.awt.*;
2.
3. public class Hier extends Frame {
4.    Hier() {
5.       super("Containment Hierarchy Demo");
6.       setBounds (20, 20, 300, 180);
7.       setLayout(new BorderLayout(0, 25));
8.
9.       // Build upper panel with 3 horizontal "strips".
10.      String strings[] = {"Red:", "Green:", "Blue:"};
11.      Panel bigUpperPanel = new Panel();
12.      bigUpperPanel.setLayout(
13.        new GridLayout(1, 3, 20, 0));
14.      for (int i=0; i<3; i++) {
15.        // Add strips.
16.        // Each strip is a panel within bigUpperPanel.
17.        Panel levelPanel = new Panel();
18.        levelPanel.setLayout(
19.          new GridLayout(3, 1, 0, 10));
20.        levelPanel.add(new Label(strings[i]));
21.        levelPanel.add(new Scrollbar(
22.          Scrollbar.HORIZONTAL, i, 10, 0, 255));
23.        levelPanel.add(new TextField("0"));
24.        bigUpperPanel.add(levelPanel);
25.      }
26.      add(bigUpperPanel, BorderLayout.CENTER);
27.
28.      // Build lower panel containing 3 buttons.
29.      Panel lowerPanel = new Panel();
30.      lowerPanel.add(new Button("Apply"));
31.      lowerPanel.add(new Button("Reset"));
32.      lowerPanel.add(new Button("Cancel"));
33.      add(lowerPanel, BorderLayout.SOUTH);
34.    }
35. }
```

As you can see from the listing, there is no code anywhere that specifies exactly where the labels, scroll bars, text fields, buttons, or panels should go. Instead, there are several calls (lines 7, 13, and 19) to layout manager constructors. Those new layout managers are set as the managers for the corresponding containers in lines 7, 12, and 18, respectively. The lower panel constructed in line 28 uses its default layout manager, so it is not necessary to give it a new one.

A component inside a container receives certain properties from the container. For example, if a component is not explicitly assigned a font, it uses the same font that its container uses. The same principle holds true for foreground and background color. Layout managers, however, are different. A panel's default layout manager is always Flow. An applet's default layout manager is also always Flow. A frame's default layout manager is always Border.

After each panel is constructed and assigned an appropriate layout manager, the panel is populated with the components it is to contain. For example, the lower panel, constructed in line 29, is populated with buttons in lines 30, 31, and 32. Finally, the now-populated panel is added to the container that is to hold it (line 33).

The `add()` method call in line 33 does not specify which object is to execute the call. That is, the form of the call is `add(params)`, and not `someObject.add(params)`. In Java, every non-static method call is executed by some object; if you don't specify one, Java assumes that you intended the method to be executed by `this`. So line 33 is executed by the instance of `Hier`, which is the outermost container in the hierarchy. Line 26, which adds the big upper panel, is similar: No executing object is explicitly specified in the `add()` call, so the panel is added to `this`.

In lines 20, 21, 23, 30, 31, and 32, a container is specified to execute the `add()` call. In those lines, components are added to intermediate containers.

Each panel in the sample code is built in four steps:

1. Construct the panel.

2. Give the panel a layout manager.

3. Populate the panel.

4. Add the panel to its own container.

When a container is constructed (step 1), it is given a default layout manager. For panels, the default is a flow layout manager, and step 2 can be skipped if this is the desired manager. In step 3, populating the panel involves constructing components and adding them to the panel; if any of these components is itself a panel, steps 1–4 must be executed recursively.

A container delegates to its layout manager the job of determining where components will be placed and (optionally) how they will be resized. If the container is subsequently resized, the layout manager again lays out the container's components (probably with different results, since it has a different area to work with). This "conference" between the container and the layout manager is the subject of the next section.

Component Size and Position

Components know where they are and how big they are. That is to say, the java.awt.Component class has instance variables called x, y, *width*, and *height*. The x and y variables specify the position of the component's upper-left corner (as measured from the upper-left corner of the container that contains the component), and *width* and *height* are in pixels. Figure 9.5 illustrates the x, y, *width*, and *height* of a text area inside a panel inside an applet.

A component's position and size can be changed by calling the component's setBounds() method. (In releases of the JDK before 1.1, the method was called reshape(); this has been deprecated in favor of setBounds().) It seems reasonable to expect that the following code, which calls setBounds() on a button, would create an applet with a fairly big button:

```
1. import java.awt.Button;
2. import java.applet.Applet;
3.
4. public class AppletWithBigButton extends Applet {
5.   public void init() {
6.     Button b = new Button("I'm enormous!");
7.         // Should make button really big
8.     b.setBounds(3, 3, 333, 333);
9.     add(b);
10.   }
11. }
```

If you have tried something like this, you know that the result is disappointing. A screen shot appears in Figure 9.6.

FIGURE 9.5   Position and size

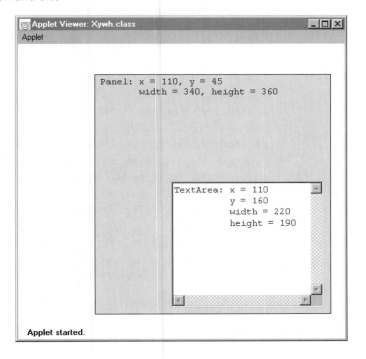

FIGURE 9.6   A disappointing button

It seems that line 7 should force the button to be 333 pixels wide by 333 pixels tall. In fact, the button is just the size it would be if line 7 were omitted or commented out.

Line 7 has no effect because after it executes, the button is added to the applet (line 9). Eventually (after a fairly complicated sequence of events), the applet calls on its layout manager to enforce its layout policy on the button. The layout manager decides where and how big the button should be; in this case, the layout manager wants the button to be just large enough to accommodate its label. When this size has been calculated, the layout manager calls setBounds() on the button, clobbering the work you did in line 7.

In general, it is futile to call setBounds() on a component, because layout managers always get the last word; that is, their call to setBounds() happens after yours. There are ways to defeat this functionality, but they tend to be complicated, difficult to maintain, and not in the spirit of Java. Java's AWT toolkit wants you to let the layout managers do the layout work. Java impels you to use layout managers, and the Certification Exam expects you to know the layout policies of all the AWT layout managers. These policies are covered in the next several sections.

Layout Policies

Every Java component has *a preferred size*. The preferred size expresses how big the component would like to be, barring conflict with a layout manager. Preferred size is generally the smallest size necessary to render the component in a visually meaningful way. For example, a button's preferred size is the size of its label text, plus a little border of empty space around the text, plus the shadowed decorations that mark the boundary of the button. Thus a button's preferred size is "just big enough."

Preferred size is platform-dependent, since component boundary decorations vary from system to system.

When a layout manager lays out its container's child components, it has to balance two considerations: the layout policy and each component's preferred size. First priority goes to enforcing layout policy. If honoring a component's preferred size would mean violating the layout policy, then the layout manager overrules the component's preferred size.

Understanding a layout manager means understanding where it will place a component, and also how it will treat a component's preferred size. The next several sections discuss the layout managers: FlowLayout, GridLayout, BorderLayout, CardLayout, and GridBagLayout. These are the layout managers that you must know for the Certification Exam.

The Flow Layout Manager

The Flow layout manager arranges components in horizontal rows. It is the default manager type for panels and applets, so it is usually the first layout manager that programmers encounter. It is a common experience for new Java developers to add a few components to an applet and wonder how they came to be arranged so neatly. The following code is a good example:

```
1. import java.awt.*;
2. import java.applet.Applet;
3.
4. public class NeatRow extends Applet {
5.    public void init() {
6.       Label label = new Label("Name:");
7.       add(label);
8.       TextField textfield = new TextField("Beowulf");
9.       add(textfield);
10.       Button button = new Button("OK");
11.       add(button);
12.    }
13. }
```

The resulting applet is shown in Figure 9.7.

FIGURE 9.7 Simple applet using Flow layout manager

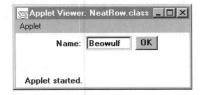

If the same three components appear in a narrower applet, as shown in Figure 9.8, there is not enough space for all three to fit in a single row. The Flow layout manager fits as many components as possible into the top row and spills the remainder into a second row. The components always appear, left to right, in the order in which they were added to their container.

FIGURE 9.8 A narrower applet using Flow layout manager

If the applet is thinner still, as in Figure 9.9, then the Flow layout manager creates still another row.

FIGURE 9.9 A very narrow applet using Flow layout manager

Within every row, the components are evenly spaced, and the cluster of components is centered. The alignment (sometimes called "justification") of the clustering can be controlled by passing a parameter to the FlowLayout constructor. The possible values are FlowLayout.LEFT, FlowLayout.CENTER, and FlowLayout.RIGHT. The applet listed below explicitly constructs a Flow layout manager to right-justify four buttons:

```
1. import java.awt.*;
2. import java.applet.Applet;
3.
4. public class FlowRight extends Applet {
```

```
 5.    public void init() {
 6.      setLayout(new FlowLayout(FlowLayout.RIGHT));
 7.      for (int i = 0; i < 4; i++) {
 8.        add(new Button("Button #" + i));
 9.      }
10.    }
11. }
```

Figure 9.10 shows the resulting applet with a wide window.

FIGURE 9.10   A right-justifying Flow layout manager

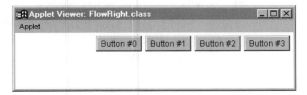

Figure 9.11 uses the same layout manager and components as Figure 9.10, but the applet is narrower.

FIGURE 9.11   A narrow right-justifying Flow layout manager

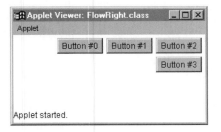

By default, the Flow layout manager leaves a gap of five pixels between components in both the horizontal and vertical directions. This default can be changed by calling an overloaded version of the FlowLayout constructor, passing in the desired horizontal and vertical gaps. All layout managers have this capability. Gaps are not covered in the Certification Exam, but they are certainly good to know about. A small gap modification can greatly improve a GUI's appearance. In the sample program in this chapter's section titled "Containers and Components," gaps were used in lines 7, 13, and 19.

The Grid Layout Manager

The Flow layout manager always honors a component's preferred size. The Grid layout manager takes the opposite extreme: When it performs a layout in a given space, it ignores a component's preferred size.

The Grid layout manager subdivides its territory into a matrix of rows and columns. The number of rows and number of columns are specified as parameters to the manager's constructor:

```
public GridLayout(int nRows, int nColumns)
```

Each row and each column in a Grid layout will be the same size; the overall area available to the layout is divided equally between the number of rows and between the number of columns.

The code listed below uses a Grid layout manager to divide an applet into five rows and three columns, and then puts a component in each grid cell:

```
1.  import java.awt.*;
2.  import java.applet.Applet;
3.
4.  public class ThreeByFive extends Applet {
5.    public void init() {
6.      setLayout(new GridLayout(5, 3));
7.      for (int row=0; row<5; row++) {
8.        add(new Label("Label " + row));
9.        add(new Button("Button " + row));
10.       add(new TextField("TextField " + row));
11.     }
12.   }
13. }
```

Note that the constructor in line 6 yields five rows and three columns, not the other way around. After so many years of programming with Cartesian coordinates, it is probably second nature for most programmers to specify horizontal sorts of information before the comma, and vertical sorts of information after the comma. The GridLayout constructor uses "row-major" notation, which is sometimes confusing for humans.

If you specify zero for either rows or columns, then the Grid will size itself based on the number of components and the other dimension.

As you can see in Figure 9.12, every component in the applet is exactly the same size. Components appear in the order in which they were added, from left to right, row by row.

FIGURE 9.12   Grid layout

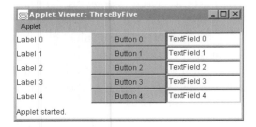

If the same components are to be laid out in a taller, narrower applet, then every component is proportionally taller and narrower, as shown in Figure 9.13.

FIGURE 9.13   Tall, narrow Grid layout

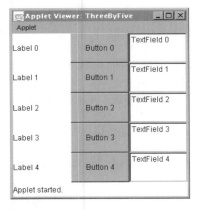

Grid layout managers behave strangely when you have them manage very few components (that is, significantly fewer than the number of rows times the number of columns) or very many components (that is, more than the number of rows times the number of columns).

The Border Layout Manager

The Border layout manager is the default manager for frames, so sooner or later application programmers are certain to come to grips with it. It enforces a very useful layout policy, but it is possibly less intuitive than either the Flow or Grid managers.

The Flow layout manager always honors a component's preferred size; the Grid layout manager never does. The Border layout manager does something in between.

The Border layout manager divides its territory into five regions. The names of these regions are North, South, East, West, and Center. Each region may be empty or may contain one component (that is, no region is *required* to contain a component, but the regions can only contain one component).

The component at North gets positioned at the top of the container, and the component at South gets positioned at the bottom. The layout manager honors the preferred height of the North and South components, and forces them to be exactly as wide as the container.

The North and South regions are useful for toolbars, status lines, and any other controls that ought to be as wide as possible, but no higher than necessary. Figure 9.14 shows an applet that uses a Border layout manager to position a toolbar at North and a status line at South. The font of the status line is set large to illustrate that the height of each of these regions is dictated by the preferred height of the component in the region. The panel that contains the toolbar buttons has its background set gray so you can see where it is. (For simplicity, the toolbar is just a panel containing a few buttons; remember we said that you can only put a single component in each region? Well, if that component is a Container, then you can get multiple components displayed.)

FIGURE 9.14 Border layout for toolbar and status line

Figure 9.15 shows what happens if the same code is used but the applet is larger. Notice that the toolbar is still at the top, and the status line is still at the bottom. The toolbar and the status line are as tall as they were in Figure 9.14, and they are automatically as wide as the applet itself.

FIGURE 9.15 Larger Border layout for toolbar and status line

The code that produced these screen shots appears below:

```
1.  import java.awt.*;
2.  import java.applet.Applet;
3.
4.  public class ToolStatus extends Applet {
5.    public void init() {
6.      setLayout(new BorderLayout());
7.
8.      // Build, populate, and add toolbar.
9.      Panel toolbar = new Panel();
10.     toolbar.setLayout(
11.       new FlowLayout(FlowLayout.LEFT));
12.     toolbar.setBackground(Color.lightGray);
13.     toolbar.add(new Button("This"));
14.     toolbar.add(new Button("Is"));
15.     toolbar.add(new Button("The"));
16.     toolbar.add(new Button("Toolbar"));
17.     add(toolbar, BorderLayout.NORTH);
18.
19.     // Add status line.
20.     TextField status = new TextField("Status.");
```

```
21.      status.setFont(
22.        new Font( "Monospaced", Font.BOLD, 48));
23.      add(status, BorderLayout.SOUTH);
24.    }
25. }
```

Notice that in lines 17 and 23, an overloaded form of the add() method is used. The border layout is not affected by the order in which you add components. Instead, you must specify which of the five regions will receive the component you are adding. The overloaded version of add() takes two parameters—first the component being added, and second an Object. Proper use of the Border layout manager requires that the second parameter be a constant defined in the BorderLayout class itself. The five constants that you should know about are:

- BorderLayout.NORTH

- BorderLayout.SOUTH

- BorderLayout.EAST

- BorderLayout.WEST

- BorderLayout.CENTER

An alternative technique, which exists for backward compatibility with the version of border layout that came with JDK 1.0.x, is to use a String to specify the name of the region; the valid values for this string are:

- "North"

- "South"

- "East"

- "West"

- "Center"

The string must be spelled exactly as shown above. It is a good idea to use the defined constants rather than the strings, because if you misspell the name of a constant, the compiler will let you know. (On the other hand, in JDK 1.2, if you use a misspelled String literal, a runtime exception will be thrown; in earlier versions, the component simply doesn't show up at all.)

The East and West regions are the opposite of North and South: In East and West, a component gets to be its preferred width but has its height constrained. Here a component extends vertically up to the bottom of the North component (if there is one) or to the top of the container (if there is no North component). A component extends down to the top of the South component (if there is one) or to the bottom of the container (if there is no South component). Figures 9.16 through 9.19 show applets that use a Border layout manager to lay out two scroll bars, one at East and one at West. In Figure 9.16, there are no components at North or South to contend with.

FIGURE 9.16 East and West

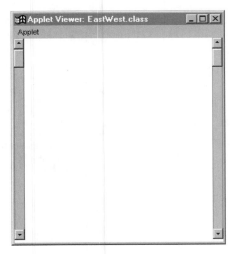

In Figure 9.17, there is a label at North.

In Figure 9.18, there is a label at South. The label has white text on black background so that you can see exactly where the South region is.

FIGURE 9.17 East and West, with North

FIGURE 9.18 East and West, with South

In Figure 9.19, there are labels at both North and South. The labels have white text on black background so that you can see exactly where the North and South regions are.

FIGURE 9.19   East and West, with both North and South

The code that generated these four applets is listed below—there is only one program. The code, as shown, generates Figure 9.19 (both North and South); lines 22 and 28 were judiciously commented out to generate the other figures:

```
1. import java.awt.*;
2. import java.applet.Applet;
3.
4. public class EastWest extends Applet {
5.    public void init() {
6.      setLayout(new BorderLayout());
7.
8.      // Scrollbars at East and West.
9.      Scrollbar sbRight = new Scrollbar(
10.       Scrollbar.VERTICAL);
11.      add(sbRight, BorderLayout.EAST);
12.      Scrollbar sbLeft = new Scrollbar(
13.       Scrollbar.VERTICAL);
14.      add(sbLeft, BorderLayout.WEST);
15.
16.      // Labels at North and South.
```

```
17.        Label labelTop = new Label("This is North");
18.        labelTop.setFont(new Font(
19.           "Serif", Font.ITALIC, 36));
20.        labelTop.setForeground(Color.white);
21.        labelTop.setBackground(Color.black);
22.        add(labelTop, BorderLayout.NORTH);
23.        Label labelBottom = new Label("This is South");
24.        labelBottom.setFont(new Font(
25.           "Monospaced", Font.BOLD, 18));
26.        labelBottom.setForeground(Color.white);
27.        labelBottom.setBackground(Color.black);
28.        add(labelBottom, BorderLayout.SOUTH);
29.    }
30. }
```

The fifth region that a Border layout manager controls is called Center.
Center is simply the part of a container that remains after North, South,
East, and West have been allocated. Figure 9.20 shows an applet with buttons at North, South, East, and West, and a panel at Center. The panel is the
white region.

FIGURE 9.20 The Center region

The code that generated Figure 9.20 is listed below:

```
1. import java.awt.*;
2. import java.applet.Applet;
```

```
3.
4. public class Center extends Applet {
5.    public void init() {
6.        setLayout(new BorderLayout());
7.        add(new Button("N"), BorderLayout.NORTH);
8.        add(new Button("S"), BorderLayout.SOUTH);
9.        add(new Button("E"), BorderLayout.EAST);
10.       add(new Button("W"), BorderLayout.WEST);
11.       Panel p = new Panel();
12.       p.setBackground(Color.white);
13.       add(p, BorderLayout.CENTER);
14.    }
15. }
```

In line 13, the white panel is added to the Center region. When adding a component to Center, it is legal, but very unwise, to omit the second parameter to the add() call. In the Java 2 platform, the Border layout manager will assume that you mean Center; however, in older versions, the behavior was unpredictable, and typically resulted in the component being entirely invisible. Generally, it is easier for other people to understand your code if you explicitly specify the region, as in line 13 above.

Figures 9.21 and 9.22 show what happens to the Center region in the absence of various regions. The applets are generated by commenting out line 7 (for Figure 9.21) and lines 8–10 (for Figure 9.22). The figures show that Center (the white panel) is simply the area that is left over after space has been given to the other regions.

FIGURE 9.21   Center, no North

FIGURE 9.22 Center, no South, East, or West

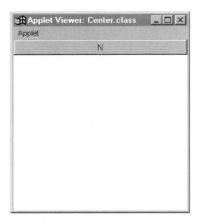

The Card Layout Manager

The Card layout manager lays out its components in time rather than in space. At any moment, a container using a Card layout manager is displaying one or another of its components; all the other components are unseen. A method call to the Card layout manager can tell it to display a different component. All the components (which are usually panels) are resized to occupy the entire container. The result is similar to a tabbed panel without the tabs.

When you use a Card layout, you have a couple of options for controlling which component is displayed and when. The Card layout gives the components that it manages a sequence, and you can ask it to display the first or last component in that sequence explicitly. In addition, you can ask for the next or previous component in the sequence. In this way, you can cycle through the components very easily.

The second way to control component display is to give each component a name. If you take this approach, the Card layout allows you to select the component to be displayed using that name. This is very much like an API equivalent of selecting a pane from a tabbed pane based on the label that it displays.

Adding Components to a Card Layout

To add components to a Card layout, you simply add them to the appropriate container. This is like any other.layout. You need to be aware of two things that influence the exact way that you add your components. First, the order that you add the components determines the order in which they will be cycled by the Card layout, should you choose to use this feature. Second, if you want to select particular components for display using the "by name" feature mentioned in the previous paragraph, then you must supply a name when adding the component. (Rather obviously, the name should not be shared by any other component in the same container.)

To add a component with a name, simply use the String object that represents that name in the second argument of the add method, like this:

```
Panel p = new Panel();
p.setLayout(new CardLayout());
Button b = new Button("A Component");
p.add(b, "Button-B");
```

If you examine the API for the Container class, you'll see that there is another add method that takes a String as the first argument, and the Component as the second. You can use this, and it works. However, that method, while not actually deprecated in JDK 1.2, does carry a note that the newer add() method—with an Object as the second argument—is strongly preferred.

Selecting the Displayed Component

The Card layout manager provides five methods that may be used to select the particular component that is displayed. These are:

- void first(Container)
- void last(Container)
- void next(Container)
- void previous(Container)
- void show(Container, String)

The first four of these methods are straightforward; first and last cause the display to select the first or last added component respectively. Similarly, the methods next and previous cause the displayed component to be cycled based on the order in which the components were originally added to the container.

The final method, show, selects a particular component based on the textual name that was given to the component when the component was added to the container. To use this, naturally, you must provide a name to the component. This is done by using the method

```
add(Component, Object)
```

to add the component to its container and ensuring that the names given to the components are unique for that container.

Let's have a look at an example, note the emboldened lines particularly:

```
1.  import java.awt.*;
2.  import java.awt.event.*;
3.
4.  public class Card extends Panel {
5.      private Panel cardPanel = new Panel();
6.      private CardLayout cardLayout = new CardLayout();
7.
8.      private Panel controlPanel = new Panel();
9.
10.     private Button firstButton = new Button("First");
11.     private Button lastButton = new Button("Last");
12.     private Button nextButton = new Button("Next");
13.     private Button prevButton = new Button("Prev");
14.     private TextField selectText = new TextField();
15.
16.     public Card() {
17.         setLayout(new BorderLayout());
18.
19.         cardPanel.setLayout(cardLayout);
20.
21.         Panel p = new Panel();
22.         p.setLayout(new BorderLayout());
23.         p.add(new Label("This is panel One"),
24.                 BorderLayout.CENTER);
25.         p.add(new Button("Dummy"),
26.                 BorderLayout.WEST);
```

```
27.        cardPanel.add(p, "1");
28.
29.      p = new Panel();
30.      p.setLayout(new BorderLayout());
31.      p.add(new Label("This is panel Two"),
32.            BorderLayout.CENTER);
33.      p.add(new Button("Don't press this"),
34.            BorderLayout.NORTH);
35.        cardPanel.add(p, "2");
36.
37.      p = new Panel();
38.      p.setLayout(new BorderLayout());
39.      p.add(new Label("This is panel Three"),
40.            BorderLayout.CENTER);
41.      p.add(new Button("Don't press this Either"),
42.            BorderLayout.SOUTH);
43.        cardPanel.add(p, "3");
44.
45.      p = new Panel();
46.      p.setLayout(new BorderLayout());
47.      p.add(new Label("This is panel Four"),
48.            BorderLayout.CENTER);
49.      p.add(new Button("Another"),
50.            BorderLayout.EAST);
51.        cardPanel.add(p, "4");
52.
53.      add(cardPanel, BorderLayout.CENTER);
54.
55.      firstButton.addActionListener(
56.        new ActionListener() {
57.          public void actionPerformed(ActionEvent e){
58.            cardLayout.first(cardPanel);
59.          }
60.        }
61.      );
62.
```

```
63.      lastButton.addActionListener(
64.        new ActionListener() {
65.          public void actionPerformed(ActionEvent e){
66.            cardLayout.last(cardPanel);
67.          }
68.        }
69.      );
70.
71.      nextButton.addActionListener(
72.        new ActionListener() {
73.          public void actionPerformed(ActionEvent e){
74.            cardLayout.next(cardPanel);
75.          }
76.        }
77.      );
78.
79.      prevButton.addActionListener(
80.        new ActionListener() {
81.          public void actionPerformed(ActionEvent e){
82.            cardLayout.previous(cardPanel);
83.          }
84.        }
85.      );
86.
87.      selectText.addActionListener(
88.        new ActionListener() {
89.          public void actionPerformed(ActionEvent e){
90.            cardLayout.show(cardPanel,
91.                            selectText.getText());
92.          }
93.        }
94.      );
95.
96.      Panel cp1 = new Panel();
97.      Panel cp2 = new Panel();
98.      cp1.add(firstButton);
```

```
 99.        cp1.add(prevButton);
100.        cp1.add(nextButton);
101.        cp1.add(lastButton);
102.
103.        cp2.add(new Label("Enter Panel Number: "));
104.        cp2.add(selectText);
105.
106.        controlPanel.setLayout(new BorderLayout());
107.        controlPanel.add(cp1, BorderLayout.NORTH);
108.        controlPanel.add(cp2, BorderLayout.SOUTH);
109.
110.        add(controlPanel, BorderLayout.SOUTH);
111.    }
112.
113.    public static void main(String args[]) {
114.        Frame f = new Frame("CardLayout Example");
115.        Card card = new Card();
116.        f.add(card, BorderLayout.CENTER);
117.        f.pack();
118.        f.setVisible(true);
119.    }
120. }
```

Although this is a somewhat lengthy example, you'll see that the bulk of it relates to creating the various panels that are displayed by the Card layout and to creating the controls that allow the user to select particular panels in the running program. The lines that are really of interest here are the creation and installation of the layout manager at line 19, the four calls to the add method at lines 27, 35, 43, and 51, and the calls to first, last, next, previous, and show methods at lines 58, 66, 74, 82, and 90/91, respectively.

The GridBag Layout Manager

GridBag is by far the most powerful layout manager. It can perform the work of the Flow, Grid, and Border layouts if appropriately programmed, and is capable of much more besides, often without the need for nesting multiple panels so often required with the other layout managers.

The GridBag layout divides its container into an array of cells, but (unlike the cells of a Grid layout manager) different cell rows can have different heights, and different cell columns can have different widths. A component can occupy part or all of a region that is based on either a single cell or a rectangle made up of multiple cells. A GridBag layout manager requires a lot of information to know where to put a component. A helper class called `GridBagConstraints` is used to hold all the layout position information. When you add a component, you use the `add(Component, Object)` version of the `add()` method, passing an instance of `GridBagConstraints` as the `Object` parameter.

Designing a Layout with GridBag

Although the GridBag layout is very powerful, it has been considered very hard to use. This seems to stem mostly from two things. First, the supplied documentation, while precise and complete from a technical point of view, does not describe much more than the API. What is noticeably missing is an explanation of the principles of operation. The second reason for difficulty is that some aspects of the control of the GridBag layout are rather confused. Specifically, you will notice that the row and column sizing controls are typically mixed in with the individual component controls. To make easy and confident use of the GridBag layout, you need to first understand the principles that drive it and then worry about the API that you must use.

Three levels of control are applied to a GridBag layout to make up the final layout in the container. The sizes of the various rows and columns, along with the way they stretch when the container is resized, must be considered. Also, the cell, or cells, that provides the target space for each component is determined. The final control determines how each component is stretched to fit or, if it isn't, how the component is positioned, within the target space.

The API governing each of these aspects is all built into a single mechanism, based around the `GridBagConstraints` class. This can be confusing, so we will discuss each of the principles of control separately as far as possible. As we do so, we will describe how the API controls this behavior. Finally, we will look at the interactions between these various controls and distill some generalizations that will be useful to you both when designing layouts and when answering examination questions.

Controlling the Rows and Columns

There are three aspects to the row and column behavior of a GridBag layout. The first is the number of rows and columns present. Typically, this is determined by the number of rows and columns that you ask to add components into. So, for example, if you place components at X coordinates 0, 1, 2, and 3, then you will find four columns in the container.

In fact, there is another way to specify that you want a particular number of rows or columns. The GridBag layout has two public variables called `columnWidths` and `rowHeights`. These are arrays of `int` values. If the `columnWidths` array contains four elements, then there will be (at least) four columns in the layout. The `rowHeights` affects the row count similarly. If you use these arrays, then the layout will contain at least as many rows as the size of the `rowHeights` array, and similarly the column count will be influenced by the size of the `columnWidths` array.

The next aspect is the default size of a row or column. The default height of a row is normally the preferred height of the tallest component in the row. Similarly, the default width of a column is the width of the widest component in the column. If you provided either or both of the `columnWidths` or `rowHeights` arrays, then if the value specified in the array for that particular row or column is greater than that calculated from the components, the array value will be used instead. That's easy enough, isn't it?

The final aspect of rows and columns is the stretchiness that occurs when the container is resized. This is governed by a property called *weight*. The rest of this section discusses row and column count, size, and weight.

Let's look at a trivial example that demonstrates controlling both the number of columns and the default size of those columns (it's rather hard to avoid having both at the same time, of course). The following example code creates a GridBag layout of three rows and three columns:

```
1.  import java.awt.*;
2.
3.  public class GB1 extends Panel {
4.    private Panel tallPanel = new Panel();
5.    private Panel tallPanel2 = new Panel();
6.
7.    public GB1() {
8.      tallPanel.setLayout(new GridLayout(3, 1));
9.      tallPanel.add(new Button("Press"));
```

```
10.        tallPanel.add(new Button("Any"));
11.        tallPanel.add(new Button("One"));
12.
13.        tallPanel2.setLayout(new GridLayout(3, 1));
14.        tallPanel2.add(new Button("Don't"));
15.        tallPanel2.add(new Button("Press"));
16.        tallPanel2.add(new Button("These"));
17.
18.        setLayout(new GridBagLayout());
19.
20.        GridBagConstraints c = new GridBagConstraints();
21.        c.gridx = 0; c.gridy = 0;
22.        add(new Button("topleft"), c);
23.        c.gridx = 1;
24.        add(new Button("topmiddle"), c);
25.        c.gridx = 2;
26.        add(new Button("topright"), c);
27.
28.        c.gridx = 0; c.gridy = 1;
29.        add(new Button("lefthandsidemiddle"), c);
30.        c.gridx = 1;
31.        add(tallPanel, c);
32.
33.        c.gridy = 2; // note, sets _y_
34.        add(new Button("bottomcenter"), c);
35.        c.gridx = 2;
36.        add(tallPanel2, c);
37.    }
38.
39.    public static void main(String args[]) {
40.        Frame f = new Frame("GridBag 1 example");
41.        f.add(new GB1());
42.        f.pack();
43.        f.setVisible(true);
44.    }
45. }
```

This program code results in a display like the one in Figure 9.23.

FIGURE 9.23   Trivial GridBagLayout example 1

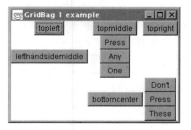

Notice how each component that is added is positioned using a GridBagConstraints object—actually the same object, but with different values. The GridBagConstraints object is used to specify all the controlling parameters for a GridBag layout, and is provided each time a component is added. The GridBag layout itself copies the values, so it's quite all right to reuse the constraints object for each component that you add.

Let's look at the behavior for a moment. We've said that this example produces three rows and three columns, and yet it might not be entirely obvious where those row and column boundaries are. The diagram in Figure 9.24 shows these boundaries.

FIGURE 9.24   Row and column boundaries in trivial GridBagLayout example 1

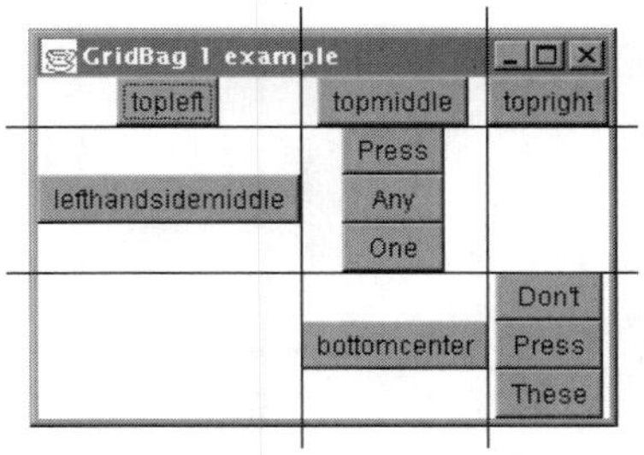

You will see that there are two cells of the layout that are unused, these are at 0, 2 (the bottom-left corner) and 2, 1 (right side, halfway down). That is not a problem, because the GridBag layout calculates the number of rows and columns on the basis of the most extreme cells that are used.

Each component in this layout was positioned explicitly using the gridx and gridy elements of the GridBagConstraints object. You do not always have to work quite this hard, but for now, it is much easier to understand what is happening if you do. Therefore, we will continue to use this approach for a while longer.

Notice that each row has a height, determined by the tallest component that it contains; similarly, the width of each row is based on the widest column. For components that are smaller in one dimension or the other than the space available to them, you'll see that the component is left at its natural size and is placed in the middle of the available space. Although this is the default, you will see later how to change this behavior, too.

So, the remaining question to address at this point is what happens if the container is resized. Well, we didn't specify any stretchiness for these rows and columns, so in fact all that happens is that the space is wasted—actually, it is distributed evenly around the layout as a whole. This is shown in Figure 9.25.

FIGURE 9.25   Trivial GridBagLayout example 1 with enlarged window

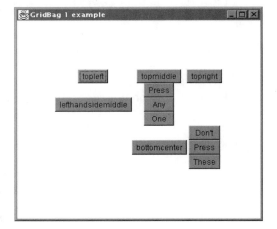

Commonly, you will want to make use of this extra space, and in fact there are two steps to doing this. Remember we just said that components that are smaller than the available cell just sit in the middle of the available space? Well, if we manage to enlarge the space, we must also change that behavior. We'll look at that in a while, but for now, let's look at how to enlarge the space. We will modify the program so that the bottom row and right-most column are allocated all the available space when the container is enlarged. To do this, we specify a non-zero value for the *weight* applied to the row and column.

The curious thing about weight is that it is specified using the members `weightx` and `weighty` in the `GridBagConstraints` object, so a value is specified for every component. This is odd, because the value applies to the *row* or *column,* not to the individual component. The way to deal with this is simply to be careful to specify a `weightx` in only one component in each column (`weightx` controls horizontal stretchiness) and a `weighty` in only one component in each row. So, we will modify our earlier example so that the right column and bottom row stretch to use up the available space. Rather than reprint the entire program to show the two areas of modification, we'll just show you the parts that relate to adding components to the layout:

```
20.      GridBagConstraints c = new GridBagConstraints();
21.      c.gridx = 0; c.gridy = 0;
22.      add(new Button("topleft"), c);
23.      c.gridx = 1;
24.      add(new Button("topmiddle"), c);
25.      c.gridx = 2;
26.      c.weightx = 1.0; // this is a stretchy column
27.      add(new Button("topright"), c);
28.      c.weightx = 0.0; // no other column stretches
29.
30.      c.gridx = 0; c.gridy = 1;
31.      add(new Button("lefthandsidemiddle"), c);
32.      c.gridx = 1;
33.      add(tallPanel, c);
34.
35.      c.gridy = 2; // note, sets _y_
36.      add(new Button("bottomcenter"), c);
37.      c.gridx = 2;
38.      c.weighty = 1.0; // this is a stretchy row
39.      add(tallPanel2, c);
40.      c.weighty = 0.0; // no other row streches
```

You'll see the components added at lines 27 and 39 have had weight applied to them. Don't forget: although this weight is carried on the back of a component, it applies to the row or column being added to and *not* to the component. So, at line 27, we're really setting a `weightx` value of 1 on column 2 (the last column), and similarly at line 39, we're setting a `weighty` value on row 2.

The effect of this, after enlarging the window, and with the grid boundary lines added, is shown in Figure 9.26.

FIGURE 9.26 Trivial GridBagLayout example with weights applied and enlarged window

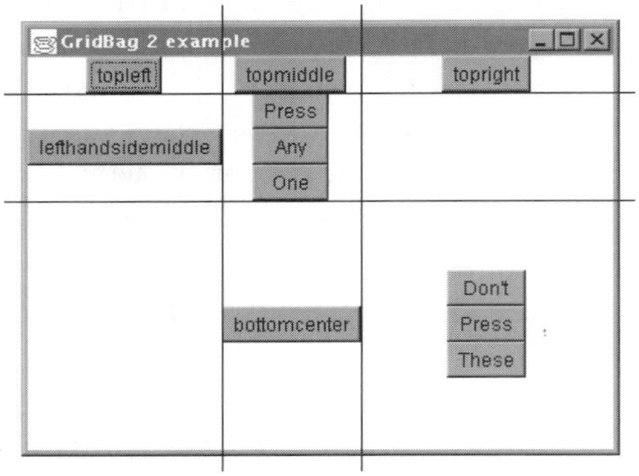

There are two remaining questions here. First, what is the significance of the value "1.0" that was set as the weight—what would be the effect of other values? Second, how can we make more than one row or column stretch? It turns out that these two questions are related. If we apply weight values to more than one row or column, then the available space is divided among those rows or columns. Exactly how it is divided is determined by the values given for weights.

The weight values you specify represent a *proportion* of the whole space; the width (in the case of columns) gained is the ratio of a column's weight to the total of all column weights. If you have three columns with weights of 9, 9, and 18, respectively, then the first two will get one-fourth of the total width gain each: 9 / (9 + 9 + 18). The third column will get one-half of the extra space for itself. Similarly, if you specify the same weight for each (7, 7, and 7, for instance), then each column will gain one-third of the total space gained. The same calculations hold true for vertical stretch by rows.

Weights can be any number. They do not have to add to 1.0 or 100, but it is generally reasonable to use weights that add to 100 (or thereabouts) so that you can consider the values as percentages. Just bear in mind that this is not required.

Although it is most usual to see weights for rows and columns being set by using a `GridBagConstraints` object when a component is added, this is neither the only, nor perhaps the best, way to achieve this. Instead, you can use the public variables `rowWeights` and `columnWeights` to do this. These variables are both arrays of `double` values, and will act as minimum weights for each row or column. If you think about it, it really makes very little sense from a style point of view to specify weights for a row or column by means of data passed when adding a component to a cell.

Using the `rowWeights` and `columnWeights` arrays has two advantages. First, it makes much more sense to set the weights this way. Second, and more importantly, it allows a weight to be set on a row or column that might not have any one component uniquely in that row or column. Using these arrays in conjunction with the `rowHeights` and `columnWidths` arrays allows you to simplify the code of many layouts and also to avoid the use of dummy components (a technique you sometimes see used in complex Grid-Bag layouts).

We seem to have spent a long time on this discussion already, so let's summarize what we've learned so far:

- The number of rows and columns in a GridBag layout is the greater of the number of cells that are used, or the size of the `rowHeights` and `columnWidths` arrays if these exist.

- The default size of each row and column is the size of its tallest or widest component, respectively, or the value in the relevant entry in the `rowHeights` or `columnWidths` array if the array exists and specifies a larger size than the default would otherwise be.

- Stretchiness of rows and columns is controlled by weight.

- Stretchiness is applied using the `weightx` (for a column) and `weighty` (for a row) values of the `GridBagConstraints` object, or by using the `rowWeights` and `columnWeights` arrays.

- Although `weightx` and `weighty` values exist for every component that is added, the values are really meant for the row or column to which the component is added, not the component itself. You should set a non-zero value for *at most one* component per row and one per column. (Note that you might have a component with both `weightx` and `weighty` set; rows and columns are independent things.) Using the `rowWeights` and `columnWeights` arrays can simplify this considerably.

- The amount of stretch in a row or column is calculated as the total stretch divided up in the same ratio as the individual weight values relative to the total weight for that axis. In math terms, if the weights are *w1*, *w2*, and *w3*, and the total stretch available is *s*, then the stretch applied to each column will be *s1*, *s2*, and *s3* where s1 = s × w1 / (w1 + w2 + w3) and s2 = s × w2 / (w1 + w2 + w3) and s3 = s × w3 / (w1 + w2 + w3).

The next aspect we will look at is how a component is positioned when the target region in which it is located is larger than the component itself.

Controlling Component Position and Stretch in a Cell

You saw in the previous example that a component that occupies an over-sized cell is normally placed in the center of the space, at its preferred size. Both these features are controllable. Using a feature called anchor, you can control where the component is placed within its available space. Using a feature called fill, you can determine whether a component stretches to fill the available space, either horizontally, vertically, or both. Let's look at a bunch of examples. We will start with this code:

```
1. import java.awt.*;
2.
3. public class GB3 extends Panel {
4.   public GB3() {
5.     Font f = new Font("Serif", 0, 36);
6.     setFont(f);
7.     setLayout(new GridBagLayout());
8.     GridBagConstraints c = new GridBagConstraints();
9.
10.    c.gridx = 0; c.gridy = 0;
11.    add(new Button("TL"), c);
12.    c.gridx = 1;
13.    add(new Button("Top Middle"), c);
14.    c.gridx = 2;
15.    add(new Button("TR"), c);
16.
17.    c.gridx = 0; c.gridy = 1;
18.    add(new Button("ML"), c);
```

```
19.        c.gridx = 2;   // note skipped over x=1, y=1
20.        add(new Button("MR"), c);
21.
22.        c.gridx = 0; c.gridy = 2;
23.        add(new Button("BL"), c);
24.        c.gridx = 1;
25.        add(new Button("Bottom Middle"), c);
26.        c.gridx = 2;
27.        add(new Button("BR"), c);
28.
29.        Button b = new Button("x");
30.        b.setFont(new Font("SansSerif", 0, 10));
31.
32.        c.gridx = 1; c.gridy = 1;
33.        add(b, c);
34.    }
35.
36.    public static void main(String args[]) {
37.        Frame f = new Frame("GridBag Example 3");
38.        f.add(new GB3(), BorderLayout.CENTER);
39.        f.pack();
40.        f.setVisible(true);
41.    }
42. }
```

When run, this produces an output as shown in Figure 9.27. Notice that the little button in the middle simply lies in the center of the space available to it.

FIGURE 9.27   GridBagLayout example showing unfilled, centered component

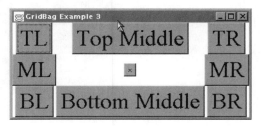

Now let's look at the positions that this component can occupy if we set different anchor values for it. The names of the anchor values are based on compass point names and are defined in the GridBagConstraints class as: NORTH, SOUTH, EAST, WEST, NORTHWEST, SOUTHWEST, NORTHEAST, SOUTHEAST, and CENTER. The default value for anchor, and the one exemplified in Figure 9.27, is CENTER. Now we'll make a small modification to the example program to see what we get if we change this anchor value. The modified programs are almost identical to the one above, except that an additional constraint value is set on the small button to define the anchor, like this:

```
32.      c.gridx = 1; c.gridy = 1;
33.      c.anchor = GridBagConstraints.NORTHWEST;
34.      add(b, c);
```

Figures 9.28, 9.29, and 9.30 show anchor values of NORTHWEST, SOUTHEAST, and EAST respectively. The effect of anchor will be clear enough from these three examples without showing them all.

FIGURE 9.28 GridBagLayout example showing unfilled component with NORTHWEST anchor

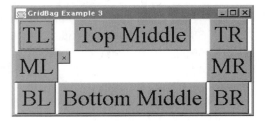

FIGURE 9.29 GridBagLayout example showing unfilled component with SOUTHEAST anchor

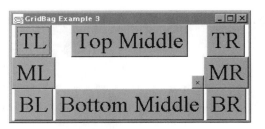

FIGURE 9.30 GridBagLayout example showing unfilled component with EAST anchor

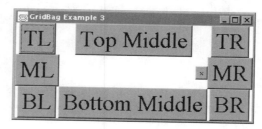

Now let's examine the `fill` feature. We'll start with the same code as we used before, but instead of setting anchor values for the small button, we will set fill values. There are four fill values to choose from, and as with anchor values, they are defined in the `GridBagConstraints` class. The values are called NONE (the default), HORIZONTAL, VERTICAL, and BOTH. So, let's make this change to the earlier example:

```
32.     c.gridx = 1; c.gridy = 1;
33.     c.fill = GridBagConstraints.HORIZONTAL;
34.     add(b, c);
```

Notice that the anchor value has been dropped entirely, so that it has reverted to the default value of CENTER. This time the effect we get is as in Figure 9.31.

FIGURE 9.31 GridBagLayout example showing component with HORIZONTAL fill

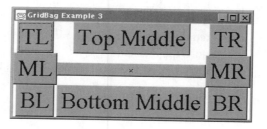

Figures 9.32 and 9.33 respectively show what happens if we change the fill to VERTICAL and BOTH.

FIGURE 9.32   GridBagLayout example showing component with VERTICAL fill

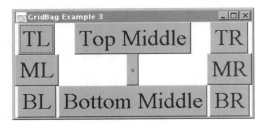

FIGURE 9.33   GridBagLayout example showing component with BOTH fill

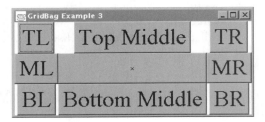

If you stop and think for a moment, you will see that the effects of `fill` somewhat nullify the effects of `anchor`. That is, if a component is stretched to fill its cell horizontally, then the anchor cannot move it left, right, or center. Similarly, if the component fills its cell vertically, then trying to anchor it to the top, middle, or bottom is similarly meaningless. So, if you have a fill of `HORIZONTAL`, then anchor values of `WEST`, `CENTER`, or `EAST` would all produce the same effect. If the fill is `BOTH`, the anchor value has no effect, and would most sensibly be left as default (`CENTER`).

Although this part has not been as lengthy as the first GridBag part, it's probably still appropriate to summarize what we've learned:

- The anchor value determines how a component is positioned when it is smaller than the cell it occupies.

- Values for `anchor` are available to specify each of the four corners of the rectangular cell, the middle of each of the four sides of the rectangular cell, or the center of the cell.

- The values of anchor are constants defined in the GridBag-Constraints class. Eight of the anchor names are compass point names (NORTH, SOUTHEAST, and so on), and the ninth is CENTER.

- The fill value controls how a component is stretched when its preferred size is smaller than the cell it has been given to occupy.

- Values for fill are constants defined in the GridBagConstraints class and are NONE, HORIZONTAL, VERTICAL, and BOTH. They specify no stretching, horizontal stretching, vertical stretching, or stretching in both directions, respectively.

- If a component is filling horizontally, then the left-right aspect of anchor is ineffective. If a component is filling vertically, the up-down aspect of anchor is ineffective. A component that is filling in both directions will not react to any anchor setting.

Now let's look at how components can have cells that extend over multiple rows and or columns.

Controlling the Cell Size for a Component

When you design a GUI using a GridBag layout, you sometimes find that some components do not fit neatly into a simple grid, and yet, there is still the general idea of rows and columns within the layout. Consider the layout in Figure 9.34.

FIGURE 9.34 GridBagLayout example showing components overlapping multiple rows and columns

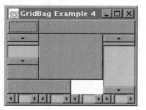

This example has, in fact, five rows and four columns, although several of the components extend over more than one of each. Figure 9.35 has been modified to show the boundaries of the rows and columns more clearly.

FIGURE 9.35 GridBagLayout example showing boundaries of rows and columns

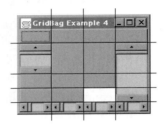

To achieve this effect of component cells that span multiple rows and or columns, the GridBagConstraints object provides fields called gridwidth and gridheight. Let's have a look at the code that produced this example and you will see these fields in action.

```
1. import java.awt.*;
2.
3. public class GB4 extends Panel {
4.   public GB4() {
5.     setLayout(new GridBagLayout());
6.     GridBagConstraints c = new GridBagConstraints();
7.
8.     // show entire cell region for all components
9.     c.fill = GridBagConstraints.BOTH;
10.
11.    c.gridx = 0; c.gridy = 0;
12.    c.gridwidth = 1;
13.    c.gridheight = 1;
14.    add(new Button(), c);
15.
16.    c.gridx = 1; c.gridy = 0;
17.    c.gridwidth = 3;
18.    c.gridheight = 1;
19.    add(new Button(), c);
20.
```

```
21.        c.gridx = 0; c.gridy = 1;
22.        c.gridwidth = 1;
23.        c.gridheight = 1;
24.        add(new Scrollbar(Scrollbar.VERTICAL,
25.              0, 10, 0, 100), c);
26.
27.        c.gridx = 1; c.gridy = 1;
28.        c.gridwidth = 2;
29.        c.gridheight = 2;
30.        add(new Button(), c);
31.
32.        c.gridx = 3; c.gridy = 1;
33.        c.gridwidth = 1;
34.        c.gridheight = 3;
35.        add(new Scrollbar(Scrollbar.VERTICAL,
36.              0, 10, 0, 250), c);
37.
38.        c.gridx = 0; c.gridy = 2;
39.        c.gridwidth = 1;
40.        c.gridheight = 1;
41.        add(new Button(), c);
42.
43.        c.gridx = 0; c.gridy = 3;
44.        c.gridwidth = 2;
45.        c.gridheight = 1;
46.        add(new Button(), c);
47.
48.        c.gridx = 0; c.gridy = 4;
49.        c.gridwidth = 1;
50.        c.gridheight = 1;
51.        add(new Scrollbar(Scrollbar.HORIZONTAL,
52.              0, 10, 0, 100), c);
53.
54.        c.gridx = 1; c.gridy = 4;
55.        c.gridwidth = 1;
56.        c.gridheight = 1;
```

```
57.        add(new Scrollbar(Scrollbar.HORIZONTAL,
58.               0, 10, 0, 100), c);
59.
60.        c.gridx = 2; c.gridy = 4;
61.        c.gridwidth = 1;
62.        c.gridheight = 1;
63.        add(new Scrollbar(Scrollbar.HORIZONTAL,
64.               0, 10, 0, 100), c);
65.
66.        c.gridx = 3; c.gridy = 4;
67.        c.gridwidth = 1;
68.        c.gridheight = 1;
69.        add(new Scrollbar(Scrollbar.HORIZONTAL,
70.               0, 10, 0, 100), c);
71.
72.    }
73.
74.    public static void main(String args[]) {
75.        Frame f = new Frame("GridBag Example 4");
76.        f.add(new GB4(), BorderLayout.CENTER);
77.        f.pack();
78.        f.setVisible(true);
79.    }
80. }
```

First of all, notice that at line 9 the fill has been set to BOTH and is left at this setting for all uses of the GridBagConstraints object. This means that all components will be stretched to fill their cells; this is the case even if the cell extends over multiple rows or columns. In this way, you can see more easily where the boundaries of the cells are.

The next point about this code is that it is considerably longer than it needs to be. This is because for every component that is added, the settings of gridx, gridy, gridwidth, and gridheight are explicitly set just before the add() method is called. This is done even when a value is not being changed, simply to make it easier to see exactly what each value is set to without having to scan up and down too far.

Compare the code with the screen shot in Figure 9.35. You will see the correspondence between `gridwidth` and the number of columns a component spans, and between `gridheight` and the number of rows a component spans. For example, the right button at the top of the layout is created by lines 16–19 of the code. At line 17, `gridwidth` is set to 3, and Figure 9.35 shows that the button does indeed extend across three columns in total.

Similarly, the large central button is set up by lines 27–30. Notice that the `gridwidth` and `gridheight` values are set to 2. Figure 9.35 shows that the button is two columns wide and two rows high.

One aspect warrants further mention. At row 3, column 2 (zero based) there is a blank space. This is perfectly acceptable, although it is unlikely to happen in a real GUI layout. If you work through all the positions, `gridwidth` and `gridheight` values, you will see that there is no component that has been placed in, or overlaps, that region.

That's about it for spanning multiple rows and columns:

- The `gridwidth` field specifies that a component's cell should extend horizontally over several columns.

- The `gridheight` field specifies that a component's cell should extend vertically over several rows.

It's not really very difficult, even if it has seemed that way before. Now let's look at a convenient shorthand mechanism that the GridBag layout offers.

GridBag's Shorthand

Two features you will undoubtedly have seen used in GridBag layout examples are RELATIVE and REMAINDER. These provide a shorthand mechanism designed to reduce the typing needed when coding a GridBag layout. They can also make maintenance of some types of layout simpler.

If you think back to the earlier examples, you will recall seeing many lines setting values for `gridx` and `gridy`. Very often, the value being set was greater by one than the current value; this is often the case in real layouts too. If you add your components in an orderly fashion, then you will be likely to set up the component in row zero, column zero first, then do column one, column two, and so on. You could achieve this by using code like this:

```
c.gridx++;
```

instead of the explicit numeric assignment that was used.

In many cases, if you are filling a layout completely, from top-left to bottom-right, one row at a time, then the shorthand mechanism of RELATIVE and REMAINDER will help. Let's look at a simple example:

```
1. import java.awt.*;
2.
3. public class GB5 extends Panel {
4.
5.    public GB5() {
6.       setLayout(new GridBagLayout());
7.       GridBagConstraints c = new GridBagConstraints();
8.       c.fill = GridBagConstraints.BOTH;
9.       c.weightx = 1;
10.
11.      add(new Button("1"), c);
12.      add(new Button("2"), c);
13.      add(new Button("3"), c);
14.      add(new Button("4"), c);
15.      c.gridwidth = GridBagConstraints.REMAINDER;
16.      add(new Button("5"), c);
17.      c.gridwidth = 1;
18.      c.weightx = 0;
19.
20.      add(new Button("A"), c);
21.      add(new Button("B"), c);
22.      add(new Button("C"), c);
23.      c.gridwidth = GridBagConstraints.REMAINDER;
24.      add(new Button("D"), c);
25.      c.gridwidth = 1;
26.
27.      add(new Button("a"), c);
28.      c.gridwidth = GridBagConstraints.RELATIVE;
29.      add(new Button("b"), c);
30.      c.gridwidth = GridBagConstraints.REMAINDER;
31.      add(new Button("c"), c);
32.      c.gridwidth = 1;
33.
```

```
34.    }
35.
36.    public static void main(String args[]) {
37.       Frame f = new Frame("GridBag Example 5");
38.       GB5 gb5 = new GB5();
39.       f.add(gb5, BorderLayout.CENTER);
40.       f.pack();
41.       f.setVisible(true);
42.    }
43. }
```

The output of this program is shown in Figure 9.36.

FIGURE 9.36   GridBagLayout example using RELATIVE/REMAINDER shorthands

Notice that when the `GridBagConstraints` object is constructed, its values are mostly left constant. Notably, we never set any value for `gridx` or `gridy` in the whole program; in fact, these values remain at their default—RELATIVE—throughout the whole program. It's important to realize that the x and y control in this example is done entirely with the `gridwidth` value.

We use the value REMAINDER in the `gridwidth` field to indicate the last component on each line. After each line end, we set `gridwidth` back to 1, because failing to do this would cause every component to be on a line of its own for the rest of the layout.

The button labeled "b" is interesting too. You will see that we set a value for `gridwidth` of RELATIVE for this button. The effect is that it fills up the space from its own starting point to the start of the last column. The documentation describes this as the component being the "last but one." This effect can be very useful when you are creating a workspace area and want to have either a row of buttons underneath it, or down the right side, such as might be used for a toolbar.

Clearly, this way of using the grid bag can make the code much simpler, although in some layouts, it might still be easier to read if you explicitly state the x and y coordinate values for each component as you add it. You will have to use your judgment on this point.

Now we have covered the essentials of the grid bag that you will need for the exam, and have learned to use this powerful tool so you can create almost any rectangular layout imaginable. There remain a couple of other options for creating layouts. Although these are not exam topics, this section would be incomplete if we did not mention them.

Other Layout Options

The Certification Exam only requires you to know how to create GUI layouts using AWT layout managers. However, it is useful to know a little bit about the other options. If you are in a situation where Flow, Grid, Border, Card, and GridBag will not create the layout you need, your choices are:

- To find a layout manager from another source
- To create your own layout manager
- To use no layout manager

Finding a third-party layout manager might be simple or hard, depending upon the particular behavior you want. Several have been described in books, and more are available as freeware, as shareware, or in commercial graphics libraries for Java.

It is beyond the scope of this book to show you how to concoct your own layout manager, but for simple layout policies it is not especially difficult to do so. The advantage of creating a custom layout manager over setting a container's layout manager to null is that you no longer have to write code to detect resizing of the container; you just have to write code to implement the layout policy, and the system will make the right calls at the right time. Writing your own layout manager class involves implementing the Layout-Manager interface (or possibly the LayoutManager2 interface). For a good reference with examples on how to do this, see *Java 2 Developer's Handbook* (Sybex, 1999).

You always have the option of using no layout manager at all. To do this, just call

```
myContainer.setLayout(null);
```

If a container has no layout manager, it honors each component's x, y, width, and height values. Thus, you can call setBounds() on a component, add() it to a container which has no layout manager, and have the component end up where you expect it to be. This is certainly tempting, but we hope that the first part of this chapter has convinced you that layout managers are simple and efficient to work with. Moreover, if your container resides in a larger container (a frame, for example) that gets resized, your layout may need to be redone to save components from being overlaid or clipped away. People who set a container's layout manager to null find that they have to write code to detect when the container resizes, and more code to do the right thing when resizing occurs. This ends up being more complicated than creating your own layout manager.

Improving Your Chances

More than any other Java-related topic, layout managers require you to use your ability to visualize in two dimensions. Whether you are taking the Certification Exam or designing a real GUI, you should spend time with pencil and paper visualizing your thoughts. Pay particular attention to resize behavior; draw each layout in its default size, and then again in an enlarged size. This will help you understand which components need to grow with extra space, and which do not. In the exam, you will be given a blank sheet of scratch paper, or perhaps a reusable tablet such as a white sheet of plastic and a dry erase marker. In some centers you might be allowed to bring blank paper into your test cubicle, but you will have to hand it in when you leave.

Chapter Summary

Layout managers provide a layer of geometrical support that relieves you of having to specify the size and position of each GUI component you create. The tradeoff is that you have to be aware of the layout policy implemented by each of the various layout managers. You are forced to think in terms of policy, rather than absolute width, height, and position.

This chapter has discussed the five AWT layout managers: Flow, Grid, Border, Card, and GridBag.

Test Yourself

1. A Java program creates a check box using the code listed below. The program is run on two different platforms. Which of the statements following the code are true? (Choose one or more.)

```
1. Checkbox cb = new Checkbox("Autosave");
2. Font f = new Font("Courier", Font.PLAIN, 14);
3. cb.setFont(f);
```

   A. The check box will be the same size on both platforms, because Courier is a standard Java font.

   B. The check box will be the same size on both platforms, because Courier is a fixed-width font.

   C. The check box will be the same size on both platforms, provided both platforms have identical 14-point plain Courier fonts.

   D. The check box will be the same size on both platforms, provided both platforms have identical check-box decorations.

   E. There is no way to guarantee that the check boxes will be the same size on both platforms.

2. What is the result of attempting to compile and execute the following
application under JDK 1.2 or later?

```
1.  import java.awt.*;
2.
3.  public class Q2 extends Frame {
4.     Q2() {
5.        setSize(300, 300);
6.        Button b = new Button("Apply");
7.        add(b);
8.     }
9.
10.    public static void main(String args[]) {
11.       Q2 that = new Q2();
12.       that.setVisible(true);
13.    }
14. }
```

A. There is a compiler error at line 11, because the constructor on line
4 is not public.

B. The program compiles but crashes with an exception at line 7,
because the frame has no layout manager.

C. The program displays an empty frame.

D. The program displays the button, using the default font for the button label. The button is just large enough to encompass its label.

E. The program displays the button, using the default font for the
button label. The button occupies the entire frame.

3. What is the result of compiling and running the following application?

```
1. import java.awt.*;
2.
3. public class Q3 extends Frame {
4.   Q3() {
5.     // Use Grid layout manager.
6.     setSize(300, 300);
7.     setLayout(new GridLayout(1, 2));
8.
9.     // Build and add 1st panel.
10.     Panel p1 = new Panel();
11.     p1.setLayout(
12.       new FlowLayout(FlowLayout.RIGHT));
13.     p1.add(new Button("Hello"));
14.     add(p1);
15.
16.     // Build and add 2nd panel.
17.     Panel p2 = new Panel();
18.     p2.setLayout(
19.       new FlowLayout(FlowLayout.LEFT));
20.     p2.add(new Button("Goodbye"));
21.     add(p2);
22.   }
23.
24.   public static void main(String args[]) {
25.     Q3 that = new Q3();
26.     that.setVisible(true);
27.   }
28. }
```

A. The program crashes with an exception at line 7, because the frame's default layout manager cannot be overridden.

B. The program crashes with an exception at line 7, because a `Grid` layout manager must have at least two rows and two columns.

C. The program displays two buttons, which are just large enough to encompass their labels. The buttons appear at the top of the frame. The "Hello" button is just to the left of the vertical midline of the frame; the "Goodbye" button is just to the right of the vertical midline of the frame.

D. The program displays two large buttons. The "Hello" button occupies the entire left half of the frame, and the "Goodbye" button occupies the entire right half of the frame.

E. The program displays two buttons, which are just wide enough to encompass their labels. The buttons are as tall as the frame. The "Hello" button is just to the left of the vertical midline of the frame; the "Goodbye" button is just to the right of the vertical midline of the frame.

4. What is the result of compiling and running the following application?

```
1. import java.awt.*;
2.
3. public class Q4 extends Frame {
4.   Q4() {
5.     // Use Grid layout manager.
6.     setSize(300, 300);
7.     setLayout(new GridLayout(3, 1));
8.
9.     // Build and add 1st panel.
10.    Panel p1 = new Panel();
11.    p1.setLayout(new BorderLayout());
12.    p1.add(new Button("Alpha"),
13.      BorderLayout.NORTH);
14.    add(p1);
15.
16.    // Build and add 2nd panel.
17.    Panel p2 = new Panel();
18.    p2.setLayout(new BorderLayout());
19.    p2.add(new Button("Beta"),
20.      BorderLayout.CENTER);
21.    add(p2);
22.
23.    // Build and add 3rd panel.
24.    Panel p3 = new Panel();
25.    p3.setLayout(new BorderLayout());
26.    p3.add(new Button("Gamma"),
27.      BorderLayout.SOUTH);
28.    add(p3);
29.  }
30.
31.  public static void main(String args[]) {
32.    Q4 that = new Q4();
33.    that.setVisible(true);
34.  }
35. }
```

A. Each button is as wide as the frame and is just tall enough to encompass its label. The "Alpha" button is at the top of the frame. The "Beta" button is in the middle. The "Gamma" button is at the bottom.

B. Each button is as wide as the frame. The "Alpha" button is at the top of the frame and is just tall enough to encompass its label. The "Beta" button is in the middle of the frame; its height is approximately one-third the height of the frame. The "Gamma" button is at the bottom of the frame and is just tall enough to encompass its label.

C. Each button is just wide enough and just tall enough to encompass its label. All three buttons are centered horizontally. The "Alpha" button is at the top of the frame. The "Beta" button is in the middle. The "Gamma" button is at the bottom.

D. Each button is just wide enough to encompass its label. All three buttons are centered horizontally. The "Alpha" button is at the top of the frame and is just tall enough to encompass its label. The "Beta" button is in the middle of the frame; its height is approximately one-third the height of the frame. The "Gamma" button is at the bottom of the frame and is just tall enough to encompass its label.

E. Each button is as tall as the frame and is just wide enough to encompass its label. The "Alpha" button is at the left of the frame. The "Beta" button is in the middle. The "Gamma" button is at the right.

5. You would like to compile and execute the following code. After the frame appears on the screen (assuming you get that far), you would like to resize the frame to be approximately twice its original width and approximately twice its original height. Which of the statements following the code is correct? (Choose one.)

```
1. import java.awt.*;
2.
3. public class Q5 extends Frame {
4.    Q5() {
5.       setSize(300, 300);
6.       setFont(new Font("SanSerif", Font.BOLD, 36));
7.       Button b = new Button("Abracadabra");
8.       add(b, BorderLayout.SOUTH);
9.    }
10.
11.   public static void main(String args[]) {
12.      Q5 that = new Q5();
13.      that.setVisible(true);
14.   }
15. }
```

A. Compilation fails at line 8, because the frame has not been given a layout manager.

B. Before resizing, the button appears at the top of the frame and is as wide as the frame. After resizing, the button retains its original width and is still at the top of the frame.

C. Before resizing, the button appears at the bottom of the frame and is as wide as the frame. After resizing, the button retains its original width and is the same distance from the top of the frame as it was before resizing.

D. Before resizing, the button appears at the bottom of the frame and is as wide as the frame. After resizing, the button is as wide as the frame's new width and is still at the bottom of the frame.

E. Before resizing, the button appears at the bottom of the frame and is as wide as the frame. After resizing, the button retains its original width and is about twice as tall as it used to be. It is still at the bottom of the frame.

6. The following code builds a GUI with a single button. Which one statement is true about the button's size?

```
1.  import java.awt.*;
2.
3.  public class Q6 extends Frame {
4.    Q6() {
5.      setSize(500, 500);
6.      setLayout(new FlowLayout());
7.
8.      Button b = new Button("Where am I?");
9.      Panel p1 = new Panel();
10.     p1.setLayout(
11.       new FlowLayout(FlowLayout.LEFT));
12.     Panel p2 = new Panel();
13.     p2.setLayout(new BorderLayout());
14.     Panel p3 = new Panel();
15.     p3.setLayout(new GridLayout(3, 2));
16.
17.     p1.add(b);
18.     p2.add(p1, BorderLayout.NORTH);
19.     p3.add(p2);
20.     add(p3);
21.   }
22.
23.   public static void main(String args[]) {
24.     Q6 that = new Q6();
25.     that.setVisible(true);
26.   }
27. }
```

    A. The button is just wide enough and tall enough to encompass its label.

    B. The button is just wide enough to encompass its label; its height is the entire height of the frame.

    C. The button is just tall enough to encompass its label; its width is the entire width of the frame.

    D. The button is just wide enough to encompass its label, and its height is approximately half the frame's height.

    E. The button's height is approximately half the frame's height. Its width is approximately half the frame's width.

7. An application has a frame that uses a Border layout manager. Why is it probably not a good idea to put a vertical scroll bar at North in the frame?

    A. The scroll bar's height would be its preferred height, which is not likely to be high enough.

    B. The scroll bar's width would be the entire width of the frame, which would be much wider than necessary.

    C. Both A and B.

    D. Neither A nor B. There is no problem with the layout as described.

8. What is the default layout manager for an applet? for a frame? for a panel?

9. True or false: If a frame uses a Grid layout manager and does not contain any panels or other containers, then all the components within the frame are the same width and height.

    A. True

    B. False

10. True or false: If a frame uses its default layout manager and does not contain any panels, then all the components within the frame are the same width and height.

    A. True

    B. False

11. True or false: With a Border layout manager, the component at Center gets all the space that is left over, after the components at North and South have been considered.

    A. True

    B. False

12. True or false: With a Grid layout manager, the preferred width of each component is honored, while height is dictated; if there are too many components to fit in a single row, additional rows are created.

    A. True

    B. False

13. For each of the following descriptions, select the layout manager or managers to which the description applies:

    A. Uses rows and columns of potentially unequal sizes.

    B. Constrains all components to the same sizes.

    C. Can resize some components along one axis while leaving them unchanged along the other when the container is resized on both axes.

    D. Can leave all component sizes unchanged regardless of container size changes.

    E. Can align components that are separated by other components that do not share the same alignment.

    F. Can simulate at least two other layout managers.

    G. Lays components so only one is visible at a time.

Chapter

10

Events

**JAVA CERTIFICATION EXAM OBJECTIVE
COVERED IN THIS CHAPTER:**

✓ Write code to implement listener classes and methods, and in
   listener methods, extract information from the event to
   determine the affected component, mouse position, nature,
   and time of the event. State the event classname for any
   specified event listener interface in the *java.awt.event* package.

Java's original "outward rippling" event model proved to have some shortcomings. A new "event delegation" model was introduced in release 1.1 of the JDK. Both models are supported in Java 2, but eventually the old model will disappear. For now, all methods that support the old event model are deprecated.

The two models are mutually incompatible. A Java program that uses both models is likely to fail, with events being lost or incorrectly processed. This chapter reviews the new model in detail; you will not be tested on the old model.

Motivation for the Event Delegation Model

Certain flaws in the original event model became apparent after Java had been in the world long enough for large programs to be developed.

The major problem was that an event could only be handled by the component that originated the event or by one of the containers that contained the originating component. This restriction violated one of the fundamental principles of object-oriented programming: Functionality should reside in the most appropriate class. Often the most appropriate class for handling an event is not a member of the originating component's containment hierarchy.

Another drawback of the original model was that a large number of CPU cycles were wasted on uninteresting events. Any event in which a program had no interest would ripple all the way through the containment hierarchy before eventually being discarded. The original event model provided no way to disable processing of irrelevant events.

In the event delegation model, a component may be told which object or objects should be notified when the component generates a particular kind of event. If a component is not interested in an event type, then events of that type will not be propagated.

The delegation model is based on four concepts:

- Event classes
- Event listeners
- Explicit event enabling
- Adapters

The Event Class Hierarchy

The event delegation model defines a large number of new event classes. The hierarchy of event classes that you need to know for the exam is shown in Figure 10.1. Most of the event classes reside in the `java.awt.event` package.

FIGURE 10.1   Event class hierarchy

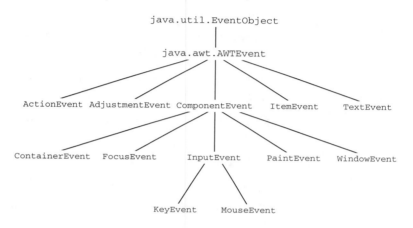

All classes belong to `java.awt.event` package unless otherwise noted.

The topmost superclass of all the new event classes is `java.util.Event-Object`. It is a very general class, with only one method of interest:

- `Object getSource()`: returns the object that originated the event

One subclass of `EventObject` is `java.awt.AWTEvent`, which is the superclass of all the delegation model event classes. Again, there is only one method of interest:

- `int getID()`: returns the ID of the event

An event's ID is an `int` that specifies the exact nature of the event. For example, an instance of the `MouseEvent` class can represent one of seven occurrences: a click, a drag, an entrance, an exit, a move, a press, or a release.

Each of these possibilities is represented by an `int`: `MouseEvent.MOUSE_CLICKED`, `MouseEvent.MOUSE_DRAGGED`, and so on.

The subclasses of `java.awt.AWTEvent` represent the various event types that can be generated by the various AWT components, and contain all necessary information relating to the activity that triggered the event. The non-superclass event types (i.e., those that are actually fired by components) are:

- `ActionEvent`: generated by activation of components

- `AdjustmentEvent`: generated by adjustment of adjustable components such as scroll bars

- `ContainerEvent`: generated when components are added to or removed from a container

- `FocusEvent`: generated when a component receives or loses input focus

- `ItemEvent`: generated when an item is selected from a list, choice, or check box

- `KeyEvent`: generated by keyboard activity

- `MouseEvent`: generated by mouse activity

- `PaintEvent`: generated when a component is painted

- `TextEvent`: generated when a text component is modified

- `WindowEvent`: generated by window activity (such as iconifying or de-iconifying)

The `InputEvent` superclass has a `getWhen()` method that returns the time when the event took place; the return type is `long`. The `MouseEvent` class has `getX()` and `getY()` methods that return the position of the mouse within the originating component at the time the event took place; the return types are both `int`.

Semantic Events

Java's events fall into two categories: *low-level* events and *semantic* events, although this distinction is not obvious from the class structure shown in Figure 10.1. A *semantic* event consists of a group of low-level input events, performed by the user in a specific sequence.

The AWT's semantic events are:

- `ActionEvent`
- `AdjustmentEvent`
- `ItemEvent`
- `TextEvent`

All other event types are low-level events.

Semantic events support the illusion that a GUI component on the screen is actually a mechanical input device. For example, when we speak of the `Button` class, we always speak in terms of *pushing a button,* when in reality we never do any such thing. What's on the screen is not at button at all, but only a picture of a button. In reality, we move the mouse in such a way that the mouse pointer ends up inside the button's territory of the screen. Then we press down on one of the mouse buttons; this "arms" the picture of the button. Then we are free to move the mouse, as long as the pointer is inside the picture of the button at the moment we raise our finger from the mouse button. The situation is best represented by a state diagram, as shown in Figure 10.2. Initially the button is in its quiescent state.

The figure shows that a fair amount of low-level mouse movement and clicking goes into the creation of a single button Action event. The state diagram is orchestrated by hidden functionality within the `Button` class. The important point to note here is that the ingredient low-level events are completely hidden from the programmer; there is no way for you to be notified when the low-level events take place. You can only know when the button has sent an Action event, meaning that the mouse button, having previously been pressed while the pointer was inside the picture of the button, has been released, while the pointer is still or again inside the picture of the button.

FIGURE 10.2   Button states

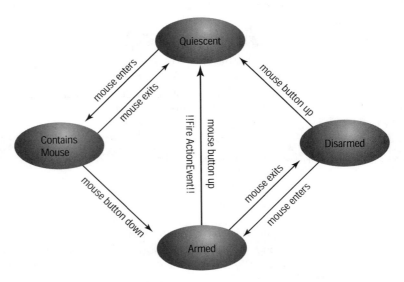

Adjustment and Item events are similar to Action events: the components that originate these events swallow the raw events that make up the semantic events, and there is no way to receive notification when the raw events take place. Text events are a bit different. A Text event says that the contents of a text component have changed. The contents may have changed because a keyboard key has gone down and then up; in this case, it *is* possible to receive notification of the low-level Key events.

Event Listeners

There are two ways to handle the events listed previously. The first way is to delegate event handling to a listener object; the second is to explicitly enable the originating component to handle its own events. This section discusses the more common approach of creating event listeners. The next section, "Explicit Event Enabling," discusses the alternative approach.

An *event listener* is an object to which a component has delegated the task of handling a particular kind of event. When the component experiences input, an event of the appropriate type is constructed; the event is then passed as the parameter to a method call on the listener. A listener must implement the interface that contains the event-handling method.

For example, consider a button in an applet. When the button is clicked, an Action event is to be sent to an instance of class MyActionListener. The code for MyActionListener is as follows:

```
1. class MyActionListener implements ActionListener {
2.   public void actionPerformed(ActionEvent ae) {
3.     System.out.println("Action performed.");
4.   }
5. }
```

The class implements the ActionListener interface, thus guaranteeing the presence of an actionPerformed() method. The applet code looks like this:

```
1. public class ListenerTest extends Applet {
2.   public void init() {
3.     Button btn = new Button("OK");
4.     MyActionListener myAL = new MyActionListener();
5.     btn.addActionListener(myAL);
6.     add(btn);
7.   }
8. }
```

On line 4, an instance of MyActionListener is created. On line 5, this instance is set as one of the button's Action listeners. The code follows a standard formula for giving an Action listener to a component; the formula can be summarized as follows:

1. Create a listener class that implements the ActionListener interface.

2. Construct the component.

3. Construct an instance of the listener class.

4. Call addActionListener() on the component, passing in the listener object.

In all, there are 11 listener types, each represented by an interface. Table 10.1 lists the listener interfaces, along with the interface methods and the addXXXListener() methods.

TABLE 10.1   Listener Interfaces and Their Methods

Interface	Interface Methods	Add Method
ActionListener	actionPerformed (ActionEvent)	addAction Listener()
AdjustmentListener	adjustmentValueChanged (AdjustmentEvent)	addAdjustment Listener()
ComponentListener	componentHidden (ComponentEvent)	addComponent Listener()
	componentMoved (ComponentEvent)	
	componentResized (ComponentEvent)	
	componentShown (ComponentEvent)	
ContainerListener	componentAdded (ContainerEvent)	addContainer Listener()
	componentRemoved (ContainerEvent)	
FocusListener	focusGained (FocusEvent)	addFocus Listener()
	focusLost(FocusEvent)	
ItemListener	itemStateChanged (ItemEvent)	addItem Listener()
KeyListener	keyPressed(KeyEvent)	addKeyListener()
	keyReleased(KeyEvent)	
	keyTyped(KeyEvent)	
MouseListener	mouseClicked(Mouse Event)	addMouseListener()
	mouseEntered(Mouse Event)	
	mouseExited(Mouse Event)	

TABLE 10.1 Listener Interfaces and Their Methods *(continued)*

Interface	Interface Methods	Add Method
	mousePressed(Mouse Event)	
	mouseReleased(MouseEvent)	
MouseMotionListener	mouseDragged(Mouse Event)	addMouseMotion Listener()
	mouseMoved(Mouse Event)	
TextListener	textValueChanged (TextEvent)	addTextListener()
WindowListener	windowActivated (WindowEvent)	addWindowListener()
	windowClosed(Window Event)	
	windowClosing(Window Event)	
	windowDeactivated (WindowEvent)	
	windowDeiconified (WindowEvent)	
	windowIconified (WindowEvent)	
	windowOpened (WindowEvent)	

A component may have multiple listeners for any event type. There is no guarantee that listeners will be notified in the order in which they were added. There is also no guarantee that all listener notification will occur in the same thread; thus, listeners must take precautions against corrupting shared data.

An event listener may be removed from a component's list of listeners by calling a removeXXXListener() method, passing in the listener to be removed. For example, the code below removes Action listener al from button btn:

```
btn.removeActionListener(al);
```

The techniques described in this section represent the standard way to handle events in the delegation model. Event delegation is sufficient in most situations; however, there are times when it is preferable for a component to handle its own events, rather than delegating its events to listeners. The next section describes how to make a component handle its own events.

Explicit Event Enabling

There is an alternative to delegating a component's events. It is possible to subclass the component and override the method that receives events and dispatches them to listeners. For example, components that originate Action events have a method called processActionEvent(ActionEvent), which dispatches its Action event to each Action listener. The following code implements a subclass of Button that overrides processActionEvent():

```
1. class MyBtn extends Button   {
2.    public MyBtn(String label) {
3.      super(label);
4.      enableEvents(AWTEvent.ACTION_EVENT_MASK);
5.    }
6.
7.    public void processActionEvent(ActionEvent ae) {
8.      System.out.println(
9.        "Processing an action event.");
10.     super.processActionEvent(ae);
11.   }
12. }
```

On line 4, the constructor calls enableEvents(), passing in a constant that enables processing of Action events. Each of the 11 listener types has a corresponding XXX_EVENT_MASK constant defined in the AWTEvent class, and corresponding `processXXXEvent()` methods; these are listed in Table 10.2. (Event processing is automatically enabled when event listeners are added, so if you restrict yourself to the listener model, you never have to call `enableEvents()`.)

Line 7 is the beginning of the subclass's version of the `processActionEvent()` method. Notice the call on line 10 to the super-class' version. This call is necessary because the superclass's version is responsible for calling `actionPerformed()` on the button's Action listeners; without line 10, registered Action listeners would be ignored.

TABLE 10.2   Event Masks and Their Methods

Mask	Method
AWTEvent.ACTION_EVENT_MASK	processActionEvent()
AWTEvent.ADJUSTMENT_EVENT_MASK	processAdjustmentEvent()
AWTEvent.COMPONENT_EVENT_MASK	processComponentEvent()
AWTEvent.CONTAINER_EVENT_MASK	processContainerEvent()
AWTEvent.FOCUS_EVENT_MASK	processFocusEvent()
AWTEvent.ITEM_EVENT_MASK	processItemEvent()
AWTEvent.KEY_EVENT_MASK	processKeyEvent()
AWTEvent.MOUSE_EVENT_MASK	processMouseEvent()
AWTEvent.MOUSE_MOTION_EVENT_MASK	processMouseMotionEvent()
AWTEvent.TEXT_EVENT_MASK	processTextEvent()
AWTEvent.WINDOW_EVENT_MASK	processWindowEvent()

Of course, you can always make a component subclass handle its own events by making the subclass an event listener of itself, as shown in the listing below:

```
1. class MyBtn extends Button
2.    implements ActionListener {
```

```
3.   public MyBtn(String label) {
4.     super(label);
5.     addActionListener(this);
6.   }
7.
8.   public void actionPerformed(ActionEvent ae) {
9.     // Handle the event here.
10.  }
11. }
```

The only difference between this strategy and the `enableEvents()` strategy is the order in which event handlers are invoked. When you explicitly call `enableEvents()`, the component's `processActionEvent()` method will be called before any Action listeners are notified. When the component subclass is its own event listener, there is no guarantee as to order of notification.

The strategy of explicitly enabling events for a component can be summarized as follows:

1. Create a subclass of the component.

2. In the subclass constructor, call `enableEvents(AWTEvent.XXX_EVENT_MASK)`.

3. Provide the subclass with a `processXXXEvent()` method; this method should call the superclass' version before returning.

Adapters

If you look at Table 10.1, which lists the methods of the 11 event listener interfaces, you will see that several of the interfaces have only a single method, while others have several methods. The largest interface, `WindowListener`, has seven methods.

Suppose you want to catch iconified events on a frame. You might try to create the following class:

```
1. class MyIkeListener implements WindowListener {
2.   public void windowIconified(WindowEvent we) {
3.     // Process the event.
```

```
4.    }
5. }
```

Unfortunately, this class will not compile. The `WindowListener` interface defines seven methods, and class `MyIkeListener` needs to implement the other six before the compiler will be satisfied.

Typing in the remaining methods and giving them empty bodies is tedious. The `java.awt.event` package provides seven *adapter* classes, one for each listener interface that defines more than just a single method. An adapter is simply a class that implements an interface by providing do-nothing methods. For example, the `WindowAdapter` class implements the `WindowListener` interface with seven do-nothing methods. Our example can be modified to take advantage of this adapter:

```
1. class MyIkeListener extends WindowAdapter {
2.    public void windowIconified(WindowEvent we) {
3.      // Process the event.
4.    }
5. }
```

Table 10.3 lists all the adapter classes, along with the event-listener interfaces that they implement.

TABLE 10.3   Adapter Classes and Their Interfaces

Adapter Class	Listener Interface
ComponentAdapter	ComponentListener
ContainerAdapter	ContainerListener
FocusAdapter	FocusListener
KeyAdapter	KeyListener
MouseAdapter	MouseListener
MouseMotionAdapter	MouseMotionListener
WindowAdapter	WindowListener

Action Commands

Of all the event types that we have examined in this chapter, Action events are the simplest. When you find out that a scroll bar has sent an Adjustment event, the obvious question is, "Now what is the scroll bar's value?" When you find out that the mouse has been clicked, it is natural to wonder, "What are the mouse's x and y coordinates?" But when you find out that a button has sent an Action event, there doesn't seem to be any additional information to seek; the button has been clicked, and that seems to be all there is to know.

However, there is an extra piece of information associated with an Action event. This information is a string, known as an *Action command*. You can extract an Action event's Action command with the getActionCommand() method.

If an Action event was sent by a textfield, getActionCommand() returns the current contents of the textfield. (A textfield sends an Action event when the user types the Enter key.) If an Action event was sent by a button, the default behavior is for getActionCommand() to return the string that is the button's label. However, you can explicitly set a button's Action command by calling its setActionCommand(String) method, as shown below:

```
button btn = new Button("Hola");
btn.setActionCommand("Hello");
```

The benefit of Action commands for buttons is apparent when a button's Action listener needs to decide how to react to an Action event. It is common for a single listener to act as a listener for several components; in our context, a single object might be an Action listener for several or many buttons. In this situation, the object's actionPerformed() method must begin by determining which button was hit. The following code fragment is typical:

```
public void actionPerformed(ActionEvent e) {
  Button btn = (Button)e.getSource();
  if (btn == okBtn)
    doOkStuff();
  else if (btn == cancelBtn)
    doCancelStuff();
  else
    doApplyStuff();
}
```

Unfortunately, this method needs access to okBtn and cancelBtn, which perhaps ought to be private members of the class that created them. One solution is to pass references to the required buttons into the constructor for the listener; however, such coupling and duplication are always poor object-oriented design, and should be avoided whenever possible. Another approach is to have the listener be an inner class within the class that creates the buttons; this solution is fine, as long as no other classes need to use the listener class. (And also as long as the source code does not become unwieldy.)

In early versions of Java, before the introduction of inner classes and Action commands, people commonly wrote event handlers that used the kind of approach listed below:

```
String s = theEventSourceButton.getLabel();
if (s.equals("OK"))
  doOkStuff();
else if (s.equals("Cancel"))
  doCancelStuff();
else
  doApplyStuff();
```

This structure avoids coupling, but it introduces two serious maintenance problems. First, the code no longer works if the buttons' labels change (perhaps due to rephrasing or spelling correction). Second, the code cannot be internationalized.

The solution is to associate an Action command with each button, independent of the button's label. Typically, the Action command is the button's label in the English language version of the program. The button's label itself depends on the locale in which the program is running, and is often read from a resource bundle. Our example would be modified so that the buttons are constructed as follows:

```
Button okBtn =
  new Button(getInternationalizedOK());
okBtn.setActionCommand("OK");
okBtn.addActionListener(myActionListenerInstance);
Button cancelBtn =
  new Button(getInternationalizedCancel());
cancelBtn.setActionCommand("Cancel");
```

```
cancelBtn.addActionListener(myActionListenerInstance);
Button applyBtn =
  new Button(getInternationalizedApply());
applyBtn.setActionCommand("Apply");
applyBtn.addActionListener(myActionListenerInstance);
```

Now the listener's `actionPerformed()` method can figure out what button what was clicked, as follows:

```
public void actionPerformed(ActionEvent e) {
  String s = e.getActionCommand();
  if (s.equals("OK"))
    doOkStuff();
  else if (s.equals("Cancel"))
    doCancelStuff();
  else
    doApplyStuff();
}
```

Chapter Summary

The event delegation model allows you to designate any object as a listener for a component's events. A component may have multiple listeners for any event type. All listeners must implement the appropriate interface. If the interface defines more than one method, the listener may extend the appropriate adapter class.

A component subclass may handle its own events by calling `enableEvents()`, passing in an event mask. With this strategy, a `processXXXEvent()` method is called before any listeners are notified.

Test Yourself

1. True or False: The event delegation model, introduced in release 1.1 of the JDK, is fully compatible with the 1.0 event model.

   A. True

   B. False

2. Which statement or statements are true about the code listed below?

```
1. public class MyTextArea extends TextArea {
2.    public MyTextArea(int nrows, int ncols) {
3.       enableEvents(AWTEvent.TEXT_EVENT_MASK);
4.    }
5.
6.    public void processTextEvent(TextEvent te) {
7.       System.out.println("Processing a text event.");
8.    }
9. }
```

   A. The source code must appear in a file called MyTextArea.java.

   B. Between lines 2 and 3, a call should be made to super(nrows, ncols) so that the new component will have the correct size.

   C. At line 6, the return type of processTextEvent() should be declared boolean, not void.

   D. Between lines 7 and 8, the following code should appear:
   return true;

   E. Between lines 7 and 8, the following code should appear:
   super.processTextEvent(te);

3. Which statement or statements are true about the code listed below?

```
1. public class MyFrame extends Frame {
2.    public MyFrame(String title) {
3.      super(title);
4.      enableEvents(AWTEvent.WINDOW_EVENT_MASK);
5.    }
6.
7.    public void processWindowEvent(WindowEvent e) {
8.      System.out.println(
9.          "Processing a window event.");
10.   }
11. }
```

A. Adding a Window listener to an instance of MyFrame will result in a compiler error.

B. Adding a Window listener to an instance of MyFrame will result in the throwing of an exception at runtime.

C. Adding a Window listener to an instance of MyFrame will result in code that compiles cleanly and executes without throwing an exception.

D. A Window listener added to an instance of MyFrame will never receive notification of Window events.

4. Which statement or statements are true about the code fragment listed below? (Assume that classes F1 and F2 both implement the FocusListener interface.)

```
1. TextField tf = new TextField("Not tricky");
2. FocusListener flis1 = new F1();
3. FocusListener flis2 = new F2();
4. tf.addFocusListener(flis1);
5. tf.addFocusListener(flis2);
```

A. Lines 2 and 3 generate compiler errors.

B. Line 5 throws an exception at runtime.

C. The code compiles cleanly and executes without throwing an exception.

5. Which statement or statements are true about the code fragment listed below? (Assume that classes F1 and F2 both implement the FocusListener interface.)

```
1. TextField tf = new TextField("Not tricky");
2. FocusListener flis1 = new F1();
3. FocusListener flis2 = new F2();
4. tf.addFocusListener(flis1);
5. tf.addFocusListener(flis2);
6. tf.removeFocusListener(flis1);
```

A. Lines 2 and 3 generate compiler errors.

B. Line 6 generates a compiler error.

C. Line 5 throws an exception at runtime.

D. Line 6 throws an exception at runtime.

E. The code compiles cleanly and executes without throwing an exception.

6. Which statement or statements are true about the code fragment listed below?

```
1. class MyListener
2. extends MouseAdapter implements MouseListener {
3.    public void mouseEntered(MouseEvent mev) {
4.       System.out.println("Mouse entered.");
5.    }
6. }
```

A. The code compiles without error and defines a class that could be used as a Mouse listener.

B. The code will not compile correctly, because the class does not provide all the methods of the MouseListener interface.

C. The code compiles without error. The words implements MouseListener can be removed from line 2 without affecting the code's behavior in any way.

D. The code compiles without error. During execution, an exception will be thrown if a component uses this class as a Mouse listener and receives a mouse-exited event.

7. Which statement or statements are true about the code fragment listed below? (Hint: The `ActionListener` and `ItemListener` interfaces each define a single method.)

```
1. class MyListener implements
2.    ActionListener, ItemListener {
3.    public void actionPerformed(ActionEvent ae) {
4.       System.out.println("Action.");
5.    }
6.
7.    public void itemStateChanged(ItemEvent ie) {
8.       System.out.println("Item");
9.    }
10. }
```

   A. The code compiles without error and defines a class that could be used as an Action listener or as an Item listener.

   B. The code generates a compiler error on line 2.

   C. The code generates a compiler error on line 7.

8. Which statement or statements are true about the code fragment listed below?

```
1. class MyListener extends MouseAdapter, KeyAdapter {
2.    public void mouseClicked(MouseEvent mev) {
3.       System.out.println("Mouse clicked.");
4.    }
5.
6.    public void keyPressed(KeyEvent kev) {
7.       System.out.println("KeyPressed.");
8.    }
9. }
```

   A. The code compiles without error and defines a class that could be used as a Mouse listener or as a Key listener.

   B. The code generates a compiler error on line 1.

   C. The code generates a compiler error on line 6.

9. A component subclass that has executed `enableEvents()` to enable processing of a certain kind of event cannot also use an adapter as a listener for the same kind of event.

   A. True

   B. False

10. Assume that the class `AcLis` implements the `ActionListener` interface. The code fragment below constructs a button and gives it four Action listeners. When the button is pressed, which Action listener is the first to get its `actionPerformed()` method invoked?

```
1.  Button btn = new Button("Hello");
2.  AcLis a1 = new AcLis();
3.  AcLis a2 = new AcLis();
4.  AcLis a3 = new AcLis();
5.  AcLis a4 = new AcLis();
6.  btn.addActionListener(a1);
7.  btn.addActionListener(a2);
8.  btn.addActionListener(a3);
9.  btn.addActionListener(a4);
10. btn.removeActionListener(a2);
11. btn.removeActionListener(a3);
12. btn.addActionListener(a3);
13. btn.addActionListener(a2);
```

   A. a1 gets its `actionPerformed()` method invoked first.

   B. a2 gets its `actionPerformed()` method invoked first.

   C. a3 gets its `actionPerformed()` method invoked first.

   D. a4 gets its `actionPerformed()` method invoked first.

   E. It is impossible to know which listener will be first.

Chapter

11

Components

Components are Java's building blocks for creating graphical user interfaces. Some component types, such as buttons and scroll bars, are used directly for GUI control. Other kinds of components (those that inherit from the `Container` class) provide spatial organization.

GUIs are an important part of any program. Java's Abstract Window Toolkit (AWT) provides extensive functionality. Chapter 9 discussed how to organize GUI components in two-dimensional space. Chapter 10 looked at how to respond to user input. This chapter reviews components.

While this chapter, and the two chapters that follow it, do not directly address topics that are explicitly mentioned in the Java Certification Exam objectives, this material is essential to a full understanding of the subjects you need to know for the exam. You need to know that the Programmer's Exam does not refer to Swing components; rather, Swing is required when you write a GUI in the Developer's Exam.

Components in General

Java's components are implemented by the many subclasses of the `java.awt.Component` and `java.awt.MenuComponent` superclasses. There are 19 non-superclass components in all, and you should know the basics of all the component classes. One way to organize this fairly large number of classes is to divide them into categories:

- Visual components

- Container components

- Menu components

These category names are not official Java terminology, but they serve to organize a fairly large number of component classes. This chapter discusses 19 classes: 11 visual components, 4 containers, and 4 menu components.

Several methods are implemented by all the visual and container components, by virtue of inheritance from `java.awt.Component`. (The menu components extend from `java.awt.MenuComponent`, so they do not inherit the same superclass functionality.) These methods are discussed below.

getSize()

The `getSize()` method returns the size of a component. The return type is `Dimension`, which has public data members `height` and `width`.

setForeground() and *setBackground()*

The `setForeground()` and `setBackground()` methods set the foreground and background colors of a component. Each method takes a single argument, which is an instance of `java.awt.Color`. Chapter 12 discusses how to use the `Color` class.

Generally, the foreground color of a component is used for rendering text, and the background color is used for rendering the non-textual area of the component. Thus a label with blue as its foreground color and black as its background color will show up as blue text on a black background.

The last paragraph describes how things are supposed to be, but some components on some platforms resist having their colors changed. This is particularly so on older versions of Java runtime, so if you are writing applets for use in general browsers, you should be careful to test as many browsers as you can and write code that gives the best compromise in most cases.

If you do not explicitly set a component's foreground or background color, the component uses the foreground and background color of its immediate container. Thus, if you have an applet whose foreground color is white and whose background color is red, and you add a button to the applet without calling `setForeground()` or `setBackground()` on the button, then the button's label will be white on red.

setFont()

The `setFont()` method determines the font that a component will use for rendering any text that it needs to display. The method takes a single argument, which is an instance of `java.awt.Font`. Chapter 12 discusses how to use the Font class.

If you do not explicitly set a component's font, the component uses the font of its container, in the same way that the container's foreground and background colors are used if you do not explicitly call `setForeground()` or `setBackground()`. Thus, if you have an applet whose font is 48-point bold Serif, and you add a check box to the applet without calling `setFont()` on the check box, you will get a check box whose label appears in 48-point bold Serif.

setEnabled()

The setEnabled() method takes a single argument of type boolean. If this argument is true, then the component has its normal appearance. If the argument is false, then the component is grayed out and does not respond to user input. This method replaces the 1.0 methods enable() and disable(), which are deprecated.

setSize() and setBounds()

These methods set a component's geometry—or rather, they *attempt* to set geometry. They replace the deprecated 1.0 methods resize() and reshape(). The setSize() method takes two int arguments: width and height; an overloaded form takes a single Dimension object. The setBounds() method attempts to set the position and size. Position is specified relative to the component's container or, in the case of a top-level window, relative to the screen. One form of the setBounds() method takes four int arguments: x, y, width, and height; an overloaded form takes a single Rectangle object.

If you have tried calling these methods, you know that it is usually futile. Chapter 9 explains that the size and position that you attempt to give a component is overruled by a layout manager. In fact, these two methods exist mostly for the use of layout managers. The major exception to this rule is the Frame class, which is not under the thumb of a layout manager and is perfectly willing to have you set its size or bounds. This is explained below in the "*Frame*" section.

setVisible()

This method takes a boolean argument that dictates whether the component is to be seen on the screen. This method is generally used for frames. Again, this method is explained in detail in the "*Frame*" section later in this chapter.

The Visual Components

The visual components are the ones that users can actually see and interact with. The 11 visual components are:

- Button

- Canvas
- Checkbox
- Choice
- FileDialog
- Label
- List
- ScrollPane
- Scrollbar
- TextArea
- TextField

To use one of these components in a GUI, you first create an instance by calling the appropriate constructor. Then you add the component to a container. Adding a component to a container is decidedly non-trivial; in fact, this topic was covered in Chapter 9. For the sake of this chapter, you will be asked to take it on faith that the components shown in the screen shots below have all been added to their containing applets in straightforward ways.

The next eleven sections show you how to construct each of the visual components. Of course, to really learn how to use components, you also have to know how to position them (see Chapter 9) and how to receive event notification from them (see Chapter 10).

Not all forms of the component constructors are given; the intention here is not to provide you with an exhaustive list (you can always refer to the API pages for that), but to expose you to what will be helpful for the Certification Exam, and to give you a foundation for general programming.

All the screen shots in this chapter were taken from a Windows 95 platform. Component appearance varies from machine to machine. All the applets were assigned a 24-point italic Serif font; most of the components were not sent setFont() method calls but rather inherited this font from their containment hierarchy.

Button

The Button class, of course, implements a push button. The button shown in Figure 11.1 was constructed with the following line of code:

```
new Button("Apply");
```

FIGURE 11.1   A button

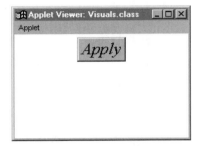

This constructor takes a string parameter that specifies the text of the button's label. When a button is pushed, it sends an Action event. Action events, and indeed the entire event delegation model, are explained in detail in Chapter 10.

Canvas

A *canvas* is a component that has no default appearance or behavior. You can subclass Canvas to create custom drawing regions, work areas, components, and so on. Canvases receive input events from the mouse and the keyboard; it is up to the programmer to transform those inputs into a meaningful look and feel.

The default size (or, more properly, the *preferred size*, as you saw in Chapter 9) of a canvas is uselessly small. One way to deal with this problem is to use a layout manager that will resize the canvas. Another way is to call setSize() on the canvas yourself; canvases are a rare case where this might actually work because the values you send into the setSize() method become the canvases' preferred size. Figure 11.2 shows a canvas that was created with the following code:

```
1. Canvas canv = new Canvas();
2. canv.setBackground(Color.black);
3. canv.setSize(100, 50);
```

FIGURE 11.2   A canvas

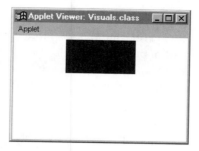

Canvases send Mouse, MouseMotion, and Key events, which are explained in Chapter 10.

Checkbox

A *check box* is a two-state button. The two states are true (checked) and false (not checked). The two basic forms of the Checkbox constructor are

```
Checkbox(String label)
Checkbox(String label, boolean initialState)
```

If you do not specify an initial state, the default is false. Two methods support getting (reading) and setting the state of a check box:

- boolean getState()

- void setState(boolean state)

Figure 11.3 shows a check box in the true state.

FIGURE 11.3   A check box

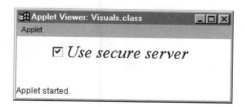

The use of setXxx() and getXxx() methods in pairs (as in getState() and setState() here) is a feature of the Beans style. This naming convention is part of the way that Bean builder tools are able to "wire up" general objects. You'll notice that the set/get convention occurs a lot, particularly in AWT components, which are themselves Java Beans.

Check boxes can be grouped together into check-box groups, which have radio behavior. With radio behavior, only one member of a check-box group can be true at any time; selecting a new member changes the state of the previously selected member to false. Many window systems (Motif and Next-Step, for example) implement radio groups as components in their own right. In Java, the java.awt.CheckboxGroup class is *not* a component; it is simply a non-visible class that organizes check boxes. This means that Java imposes no restrictions on the spatial relationships among members of a check-box group. If you wanted to, you could put one member of a group in the upper-left corner of a frame, another member in the lower-right corner, and a third member in a different frame altogether. Of course, the result would probably be contrary to both reason and most GUI style guides.

To use a check-box group, you first create an instance of CheckboxGroup, and then pass the instance as a parameter to the Checkbox constructor for each of the radio buttons (Checkbox objects) you want to create. The code below adds three radio-type check boxes to a check-box group called cbg. The result is shown in Figure 11.4.

```
1. CheckboxGroup cbg = new CheckboxGroup();
2. add(new Checkbox("Cinnamon", false, cbg));
3. add(new Checkbox("Nutmeg", false, cbg));
4. add(new Checkbox("Allspice", true, cbg));
```

FIGURE 11.4 Check boxes with radio behavior

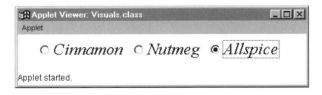

Two methods of the CheckboxGroup class support getting and setting the currently selected member of the group:

- Checkbox getSelectedCheckbox()

- void setSelectedCheckbox(Checkbox newSelection)

Check boxes send Item events (explained in Chapter 10) when they are selected.

Choice

A *choice* is a pull-down list, as shown in Figure 11.5. This figure shows two choices, both of which present the same options. The choice on the left is in its normal state; the choice on the right has been mouse-clicked.

FIGURE 11.5 Two choices

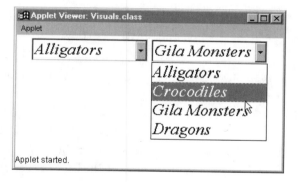

To create a choice, first call the constructor, and then populate the choice by repeatedly calling addItem(). The code fragment below shows how to create one of the choices shown in Figure 11.5.

```
1. Choice ch1 = new Choice();
2. ch1.addItem("Alligators");
3. ch1.addItem("Crocodiles");
4. ch1.addItem("Gila Monsters");
5. ch1.addItem("Dragons");
```

Choices, like check boxes, send Item events when they are selected. Item events are explained in Chapter 10.

FileDialog

The `FileDialog` class presents a file open or file save dialog. The appearance of these dialogs varies greatly from platform to platform. A file dialog is modal, which means input from the dialog's parent frame will be directed exclusively to the dialog, as long as the dialog remains visible on the screen. The dialog is automatically removed when the user specifies a file or clicks the Cancel button.

The most useful `FileDialog` constructor has the following form:

`FileDialog(Frame parent, String title, int mode)`

The dialog's parent is the frame over which the dialog will appear. The title string appears in the dialog's title bar (on most platforms). The mode should be either `FileDialog.LOAD` or `FileDialog.SAVE`.

After the user has specified a file, the name of the file or its directory can be retrieved with the following methods:

- `String getFile()`

- `String getDirectory()`

The code fragment below constructs a file dialog and displays it above frame f. After the user has specified a file, the file name is retrieved and displayed.

```
1. FileDialog fidi =
2.    new FileDialog(f, "Choose!", FileDialog.LOAD);
3. fidi.setVisible(true);
4. System.out.println(fidi.getFile());
```

Label

The simplest visible AWT component is probably the *label*. Labels are not generally used to respond to user input, nor to send out events.

There are three ways to construct a label:

- `Label()`

- `Label(String text)`

- `Label(String text, int alignment)`

The default alignment for labels is to the left. To set the alignment, use the third form of the constructor and pass in one of the following:

- `Label.LEFT`

- `Label.CENTER`
- `Label.RIGHT`

Two methods support getting and setting the text of a label:

- `String getText()`
- `void setText(String newText)`

If you use the no-arguments version of the label constructor, you will undoubtedly want to setText() at some point.

Figure 11.6 shows a label that was created with the following call:
`new Label("I'm a label, Mabel");`

FIGURE 11.6 A label

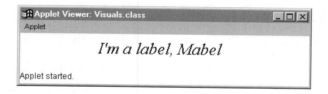

List

A *list* is a collection of text items, arranged vertically. If a list contains more items than it can display, it automatically acquires a vertical scroll bar. There are three forms of constructor:

- `List()`
- `List(int nVisibleRows)`
- `List(int nVisibleRows, boolean multiSelectOk)`

The number of visible rows (parameter `nVisibleRows`) specifies the preferred height of a list in rows. The first version of the constructor does not specify a number of visible rows but produces a default preferred height of four rows. Of course, in many cases the actual height of a list will be dictated by a layout manager.

If the version of the third constructor is used and `multiSelectOk` is true, then the list permits multiple selection. If multiple selection is not enabled, then selecting a new item causes the old selected item to be deselected.

The code listed below creates the list shown in Figure 11.7:

```
1. List list = new List(4, true);
2. list.add("Augustus");
3. list.add("Tiberius");
4. list.add("Caligula");
5. list.add("Claudius");
6. list.add("Nero");
7. list.add("Otho");
8. list.add("Galba");
```

The list has seven items but only four visible rows, so a scroll bar is automatically provided to give access to the bottom three items. Multiple selection is enabled, as shown in the figure; here, both of the barbarian (non-Roman) emperors are selected.

FIGURE 11.7 A scrolled list with multiple selection

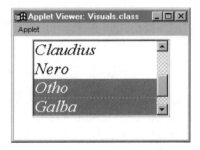

The `List` class provides a large number of support methods. A partial list of these methods appears below. The methods are intended to give you a feel for how the `List` class operates.

- `void add(String text)`: adds an item to the bottom of the list

- `void add(String text, int index)`: inserts an item at the specified index

- `String getItem(int index)`: returns the item at the specified index

- `int getItemCount()`: returns the number of items in the list

- `int getRows()`: returns the number of visible lines in the list

- `int getSelectedIndex()`: returns the index of the currently selected item (the list should be in single-selection mode)

- `int[] getSelectedIndexes()`: returns an array containing the index of every currently selected item (the list should be in multiple-selection mode)

- `String getSelectedItem()`: returns a string that reflects the currently selected item (the list should be in single-selection mode)

- `String[]getSelectedItems()`: returns an array containing a string for every currently selected item (the list should be in multiple-selection mode)

Selecting an item in a list causes the list to send an Item event; double-clicking an item sends an Action event.

ScrollPane

The `ScrollPane` is an extremely useful class that was introduced in Java 1.1. A scroll pane can contain a single component, which may be taller or wider than the scroll pane itself. If the contained component is larger than the scroll pane, then the default behavior of the scroll pane is to acquire horizontal and/ or vertical scroll bars as needed.

There are two constructors for this class:

- `ScrollPane()`: constructs a scroll pane with default scroll bar behavior

- `ScrollPane(int scrollbarPolicy)`: constructs a scroll pane with the specified scroll bar behavior

If you use the second form of the constructor, then `scrollbarPolicy` should be one of:

- `ScrollPane.SCROLLBARS_AS_NEEDED`

- `ScrollPane.SCROLLBARS_ALWAYS`

- `ScrollPane.SCROLLBARS_NEVER`

The code listed below creates a scroll pane with default (as-needed) scroll bar behavior. The scroll pane contains a very large button, so the scroll bars will definitely be needed.

```
1. ScrollPane spane = new ScrollPane();
2. Button reallyBigButton =
3.    new Button("What big teeth you have, Grandmother");
4. reallyBigButton.setFont(new Font("Serif", Font.ITALIC,
   80));
5. spane.add(reallyBigButton);
```

Figure 11.8 shows the resulting scroll pane.

FIGURE 11.8   A scroll pane

As a general rule, and just like other containers, events that originate in the region of a scroll pane are sent to the contained component.

Scrollbar

The scroll bar component that adjusts lists and scroll panes is available as a component in its own right. There are three constructors:

- `Scrollbar()`: constructs a vertical scroll bar
- `Scrollbar(int orientation)`: constructs a scroll bar with the specified orientation
- `Scrollbar(int orientation, int initialValue, int sliderSize, int minValue, int maxValue)`: constructs a scroll bar with the specified parameters

For constructors that take an orientation parameter, this value should be one of:

- `Scrollbar.HORIZONTAL`
- `Scrollbar.VERTICAL`

In the third form of the constructor, the `sliderSize` parameter is a bit confusing. The Java terminology for the piece of the scroll bar that slides is the *slider*, which in itself is confusing because in some window systems the entire component is called a slider. The `sliderSize` parameter controls the size of the slider, but not in pixel units. The units of `sliderSize` are the units defined by the spread between the minimum and maximum value of the scroll bar.

For example, consider a horizontal scroll bar whose minimum value is 600 and maximum value is 700. The spread covered by the scroll bar is the difference between these two numbers, or 100. A `sliderSize` value of 50 would represent half the spread, and the slider would be half the width of the scroll bar. A `sliderSize` value of 10 would represent one-tenth the spread, and the slider would be one-tenth the width of the scroll bar.

If the scroll bar's minimum and maximum were 1,400 and 1,500, the spread would still be 100; a `sliderSize` value of 50 would still represent half the spread, and the slider would still be half the width of the scroll bar. A `sliderSize` value of 10 would still result in a slider one-tenth the width of the scroll bar.

The code below creates a horizontal scroll bar with a range from 600 to 700. The initial value is 625. The slider size is 25 out of a range of 700 − 600 = 100, so the slider should be one-fourth the width of the scroll bar. Figure 11.9 shows that this is indeed the case.

```
Scrollbar sbar = new
    Scrollbar(Scrollbar.HORIZONTAL, 625, 25, 600, 700);
```

Scroll bars generate Adjustment events, which are explained in Chapter 10.

FIGURE 11.9 A horizontal scroll bar

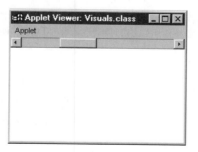

TextField and *TextArea*

The TextField and TextArea classes implement one-dimensional and two-dimensional components for text input, display, and editing. Both classes extend from the TextComponent superclass, as shown in Figure 11.10.

FIGURE 11.10   Inheritance of TextField and TextArea

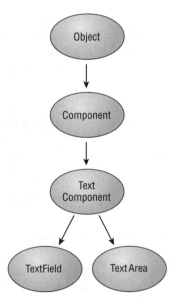

Both classes have a variety of constructors, which offer the option of specifying or not specifying an initial string or a preferred size. The constructors that do not specify a preferred size are most appropriate for situations where a layout manager will ignore the component's preferred size.

The constructors for TextField are:

- TextField(): constructs an empty text field
- TextField(int nCols): constructs an empty text field with the specified number of columns
- TextField(String text): constructs a text field whose initial content is text

- TextField(String text, int nCols): constructs a text field whose initial content is text, with the specified number of columns

The constructors for TextArea are:

- TextArea(): constructs an empty text area

- TextArea(int nRows, int nCols): constructs an empty text area with the specified number of rows and columns

- TextArea(String text): constructs a text area whose initial content is text

- TextArea(String text, int nRows, int nCols): constructs a text area whose initial content is text, with the specified number of rows and columns

- TextArea(String text, int nRows, int nCols, int scrollbarPolicy): same as above, but the scroll bar placement policy is determined by the last parameter, which should be one of the following:

  - TextArea.SCROLLBARS_BOTH

  - TextArea.SCROLLBARS_NONE

  - TextArea.SCROLLBARS_HORIZONTAL_ONLY

  - TextArea.SCROLLBARS_VERTICAL_ONLY

For both classes, there are some surprising issues to the number-of-columns parameter.

First, the number of columns is a measure of width in terms of columns of text, *as rendered in a particular font.* A 25-column text area with a tiny font will be very narrow, while a 5-column text area with a huge font will be extremely wide.

Next, there is the problem of proportional fonts. For a fixed-width font, it is obvious what the column width should be. For a proportional font, the column width is taken to be the average of all the font's character widths. This average is a simple average of all the characters in the set; it does not take into account frequency of character use, so, in most cases, text components that contain largely lowercase letters will display more than the requested number of characters.

A final issue is the question of what happens when a user types beyond the rightmost character column in one of these components. In both cases, the visible text scrolls to the left. The insertion point remains in place, at the rightmost column. The component now contains more text than it can display, so scrolling is required. Text areas support scroll bars. Text fields can be scrolled using the ← and → keys.

Both classes inherit some functionality from their common superclass, `TextComponent`. These methods include:

- `String getSelectedText()`: returns the currently selected text

- `String getText()`: returns the text contents of the component

- `void setEditable(boolean editable)`: if `editable` is true, permits the user to edit the component; if false, the user can still navigate using the arrow keys, but cannot alter the text

- `void setText(String text)`: sets the text contents of the component

A common experience among beginning AWT programmers who need, for example, to retrieve the contents of a text field, is to look for some promising name among the methods listed on the API page for `TextField`. There is nothing promising to be found there, and suddenly text fields seem useless. The problems, of course, are inheritance and the way the documentation is laid out: The desired methods are available, but they are inherited from `TextComponent` and are documented on a different page. If you know that a class must implement a certain method (because you have heard that it does, or because you remember using the method long ago, or because the class would otherwise be useless), don't give up if you don't find what you want in the class's list of methods. Look in the section titled "Methods inherited from class XXX" (or if you are using 1.1 API pages, follow the superclass hierarchy links near the top of the page).

The code below creates three text fields. Each is five columns wide, but they all use different fonts. (The fonts are all 24 points, so differences will be subtle.)

```
1. TextField tf1 = new TextField(5);
2. tf1.setFont(new Font("Serif", Font.PLAIN, 24));
3. tf1.setText("12345");
4. TextField tf2 = new TextField(5);
5. tf2.setFont(new Font("SansSerif", Font.PLAIN, 24));
```

```
6. tf2.setText("12345");
7. TextField tf3 = new TextField(5);
8. tf3.setFont(new Font("Monospaced", Font.PLAIN, 24));
9. tf3.setText("12345");
```

Figure 11.11 shows the text fields. Surprisingly, only four characters appear in each field (although the dot near the right of the first field looks suspiciously like the truncated tail of the "5"). This is not a bug. The fields really are five columns wide, but some of the space is taken up by leading and inter-character whitespace.

FIGURE 11.11   Three text fields

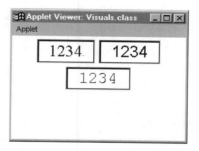

The code below implements three text areas, each with six rows and five columns. Again, each component has a different family of 24-point fonts. (The font name appears in the first row of each component.) The first two fonts are proportional, so a lot more *i*'s than *w*'s can fit into a row. Again, the components really do have five columns, but whitespace reduces the number of visible characters.

```
1. TextArea ta1 = new TextArea(6, 5);
2. ta1.setFont(new Font("Serif", Font.PLAIN, 24));
3. ta1.setText("Serif\n12345\nabcde\niiiiiiiiii\nWWWWW");
4. TextArea ta2 = new TextArea(6, 5);
5. ta2.setFont(new Font("SansSerif", Font.PLAIN, 24));
6. ta2.setText("Sans\n12345\nabcde\niiiiiiiiii\nWWWWW");
7. TextArea ta3 = new TextArea(6, 5);
8. ta3.setFont(new Font("Monospaced", Font.PLAIN, 24));
9. ta3.setText("Mono\n12345\nabcde\niiiiiiiiii\nWWWWW");
```

Figure 11.12 shows the resulting text areas.

FIGURE 11.12   Three text areas

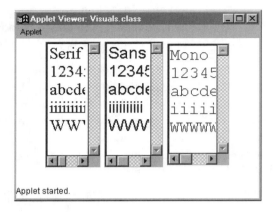

Both text fields and text areas generate Text and Key events. Additionally, text fields generate Action events on receipt of an Enter keystroke.

The Container Components

The four non-superclass container component classes are

- `Applet`
- `Frame`
- `Panel`
- `Dialog`

Technically, `ScrollPane` is also a container, because it inherits from the `Container` superclass, but it does not present the issues that the other four do. Figure 11.13 shows the inheritance hierarchy of these classes.

Containers are components capable of holding other components within their boundaries. Every screen shot so far in this chapter has shown an applet acting as a container for the component being illustrated. Adding components to containers requires interacting with layout managers; this entire topic was covered in depth in Chapter 9.

FIGURE 11.13   Inheritance of Container components

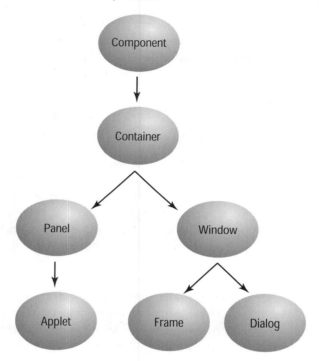

Applet

The only issue that needs attention here is the problem of resizing. Applets, by virtue of inheriting from Component, have setSize() and setBounds() methods. Applets typically exist in browsers. Changing the size of an applet might be permitted or forbidden by the applet's browser, and during the development cycle you cannot know which brand of browser will be running your applet. The easiest browser for development is the applet viewer, which allows resizing of applets. It is common for an applet to have a temporary setSize() call in its init() method, because this provides an easy way to play with different sizes. If you use this technique, remember to delete the setSize() call before final delivery and set the size in your HTML tag.

Frame

A *frame* is an independent window, decorated by the underlying window system and capable of being moved around on the screen independent of other GUI windows. Any application that requires a GUI must use one or more frames to contain the desired components.

There are only two forms of the `Frame` constructor:

- `Frame()`: constructs a frame with an empty title bar

- `Frame(String title)`: constructs a frame with the specified title

When a frame is constructed, it has no size and is not displayed on the screen. To give a frame a size, call one of the inherited methods `setSize()` or `setBounds()`. (If you call `setBounds()`, the x and y parameters tell the frame where it will appear on the screen.) Once a frame has been given a size, you can display it by calling `setVisible(true)`.

To remove an unwanted frame from the screen, you can call `setVisible(false)`. This does not destroy the frame or damage it in any way; you can always display it again by calling `setVisible(true)`.

When you are finished with a frame, you need to recycle its non-memory resources. (Memory will be harvested by the garbage collector.) Non-memory resources are system-dependent; suffice it to say that it takes a lot to connect a Java GUI to an underlying window system. On a Unix/Motif platform, for example, a frame's non-memory resources would include at least one file descriptor and X window.

To release the non-memory resources of a frame, just call its `dispose()` method. The code below builds and displays a 500×350 frame; 30 seconds later the frame is removed from the screen and disposed.

```
1. // Construct and display
2. Frame f = new Frame("This is a frame");
3. f.setBounds(10, 10, 500, 350);
4. f.setVisible(true);
5.
6. // Delay
7. try {
8.    Thread.sleep(30*1000);
9. } catch (InterruptedException e) { }
10.
11. // Remove and dispose
12. f.setVisible(false);
13. f.dispose();
```

If an applet attempts to display a frame, the applet confers with the browser's security manager. All browsers have security managers, and these managers generally impose this restriction on frames: Display of the frame is permitted, but the frame contains a label that marks the frame as "untrusted." The rationale is that the frame might have been displayed by an applet that was loaded from the Internet, so any sensitive information entered into the frame's components might possibly be transmitted to parties of dubious moral fiber. Programmers often ask whether the message can be avoided. The answer is that this is up to the person running the browser, not the person providing the applet. Because this is a security issue, this is the way it should be.

Panel

Applets and frames serve as top-level or outermost GUI components. *Panels* provide an intermediate level of spatial organization for GUIs. You are free to add all the components of a GUI directly into an applet or a frame, but you can provide additional levels of grouping by adding components to panels and adding panels to a top-level applet or frame. This process is recursive: The components that you add to panels can themselves be panels, and so on, to whatever depth of containment you like. Getting components to go exactly where you want them within a panel was the subject of the oft-mentioned Chapter 9.

Dialog

A *dialog* is a pop-up window that typically accepts user input in response to a specific question. The window manager often uses slightly different decoration for dialogs, perhaps omitting the ability to iconize or maximize them. Dialogs may optionally be made modal, in which case input cannot be directed at the application's main frame while the dialog is visible. Java does not support system modal dialogs—that is, dialogs that freeze up the whole of the rest of the display; such a concept is inappropriate in a user application running on a truly multitasking system. The `Dialog` class is the superclass of the `FileDialog` class. The default layout manager for a dialog is Border layout.

The Menu Components

Java supports two kinds of menus: pull-down and pop-up. The Certification Exam does not cover pop-up menus.

Pull-down menus are accessed via a menu bar, which may contain multiple menus. Menu bars may only appear in frames. (Therefore pull-down menus also may only appear in frames.)

> If this requirement is a problem for an application that you are writing, Swing might provide a solution. In Swing, menus are components like any other and may be positioned wherever you like. For the Programmer's Exam, however, you are not expected to know about Swing.

To create a frame with a menu bar containing a pull-down menu, you need to go through the following steps:

1. Create a menu bar and attach it to the frame.

2. Create and populate the menu.

3. Attach the menu to the menu bar.

To create a menu bar, just construct an instance of the `MenuBar` class. To attach it to a frame, pass it into the frame's `setMenuBar()` method.

To create a menu, construct an instance of the `Menu` class. The most common constructor takes a string that is the menu's label; this label appears on the menu bar. There are four kinds of elements that can be mixed and matched to populate a menu:

- Menu items

- Check-box menu items

- Separators

- Menus

A menu item is an ordinary textual component available on a menu. The basic constructor for the `MenuItem` class is

```
MenuItem(String text)
```

where `text` is the label of the menu item. A menu item is very much like a button that happens to live in a menu. Like buttons, menu items generate Action events.

A check-box menu item looks like a menu item with a check box to the left of its label. When a check-box menu item is selected, the check box changes its state. The basic constructor for the `CheckboxMenuItem` class is

```
CheckboxMenuItem(String text)
```

where `text` is the label of the item. A check-box menu item is very much like a check box that happens to live in a menu; you can read and set an item's state by calling `getState()` and `setState()` just as you would with a plain check box. Check-box menu items generate Item events.

A separator is just a horizontal mark used for visually dividing a menu into sections. To add a separator to a menu, call the menu's `addSeparator()` method.

When you add a menu to another menu, the first menu's label appears in the second menu, with a pull-right icon. Pulling the mouse to the right causes the sub-menu to appear.

After a menu is fully populated, you attach it to a menu bar by calling the menu bar's `add()` method. If you want the menu to appear in the Help menu position to the right of all other menus, call instead the `setHelpMenu()` method.

The code below creates and displays a frame with a menu bar and two menus. The first menu contains one of each kind of menu constituent (menu item, check-box menu item, separator, and submenu). The second menu is a Help menu and just contains two menu items.

```
1.  Frame        frame;
2.  MenuBar      bar;
3.  Menu         fileMenu, subMenu, helpMenu;
4.
5.  // Create frame and install menu bar.
6.  frame = new Frame("Menu demo");
7.  frame.setSize(400, 300);
8.  bar = new MenuBar();
9.  frame.setMenuBar(bar);
10.
11. // Create submenu.
12. subMenu = new Menu("Pull me");
13. subMenu.add(new MenuItem("Sub-This"));
14. subMenu.add(new MenuItem("Sub-That"));
```

```
15.
16. // Create and add file menu.
17. fileMenu = new Menu("File");
18. fileMenu.add(new MenuItem("New"));
19. fileMenu.add(new MenuItem("Open"));
20. fileMenu.addSeparator();
21. fileMenu.add(
22.   new CheckboxMenuItem("Print Preview Mode"));
23. fileMenu.add(subMenu);
24. bar.add(fileMenu);
25.
26. // Create help menu.
27. helpMenu = new Menu("Help");
28. helpMenu.add(new MenuItem("Contents ..."));
29. helpMenu.add(new MenuItem("About this program ..."));
30. bar.setHelpMenu(helpMenu);
31.
32. // Now that the frame is completely built, display it
33. frame.setVisible(true);
```

Figure 11.14 shows the frame with the File menu and the submenu visible; Figure 11.15 shows the frame with the Help menu visible.

FIGURE 11.14   Frame with file menu and submenu

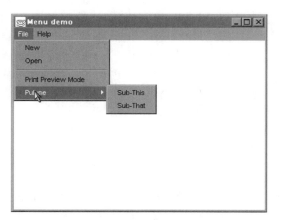

FIGURE 11.15   Frame with help menu

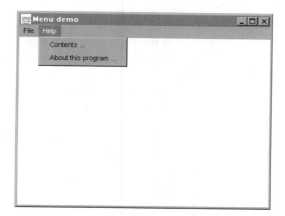

Chapter Summary

This chapter has introduced three categories of components:

- Visual components
- Container components
- Menu components

Visual components are the components that the user interacts with. Container components contain other components. Menu components support menus in frames.

Test Yourself

1. A text field is constructed and then given a foreground color of white and a 64-point bold serif font. The text field is then added to an applet that has a foreground color of red, background color of blue, and 7-point plain sans-serif font. Which one statement below is true about the text field?

   A. Foreground color is black, background color is white, font is 64-point bold serif.

   B. Foreground color is red, background color is blue, font is 64-point bold serif.

   C. Foreground color is red, background color is blue, font is 7-point bold serif.

   D. Foreground color is white, background color is blue, font is 7-point bold serif.

   E. Foreground color is white, background color is blue, font is 64-point bold serif.

2. You have a check box in a panel; the panel is in an applet. The applet contains no other components. Using setFont(), you give the applet a 100-point font, and you give the panel a 6-point font. Which statement or statements below are correct?

   A. The check box uses a 12-point font.

   B. The check box uses a 6-point font.

   C. The check box uses a 100-point font.

   D. The check box uses the applet's font, because you can't set a font on a panel.

   E. The check box uses the panel's font, because you did not explicitly set a font for the check box.

3. You have a check box in a panel; the panel is in an applet. The applet contains no other components. Using `setFont()`, you give the applet a 100-point font. Which statement or statements below are correct?

   A. The check box uses a 12-point font.

   B. The check box uses a 6-point font.

   C. The check box uses a 100-point font.

   D. The check box uses the applet's font.

   E. The check box uses the panel's font, because you did not explicitly set a font for the check box.

4. You want to construct a text area that is 80 character-widths wide and 10 character-heights tall. What code do you use?

   A. `new TextArea(80, 10)`

   B. `new TextArea(10, 80)`

5. You construct a list by calling `new List(10, false)`. Which statement or statements below are correct? (Assume that layout managers do not modify the list in any way.)

   A. The list has 10 items.

   B. The list supports multiple selection.

   C. The list has up to 10 visible items.

   D. The list does not support multiple selection.

   E. The list will acquire a vertical scroll bar if needed.

6. A text field has a variable-width font. It is constructed by calling new TextField("iiiii"). What happens if you change the contents of the text field to "wwwww"? (Bear in mind that i is one of the narrowest characters, and w is one of the widest.)

   A. The text field becomes wider.

   B. The text field becomes narrower.

   C. The text field stays the same width; to see the entire contents you will have to scroll by using the ← and → keys.

   D. The text field stays the same width; to see the entire contents you will have to scroll by using the text field's horizontal scroll bar.

7. Which of the following may a menu contain? (Choose all that apply.)

   A. A separator

   B. A Checkbox

   C. A Menu

   D. A Button

   E. A Panel

8. Which of the following may contain a menu bar? (Choose all that apply.)

   A. A panel

   B. A frame

   C. An applet

   D. A menu bar

   E. A menu

9. Your application constructs a frame by calling `Frame f = new Frame();`, but when you run the code, the frame does not appear on the screen. What code will make the frame appear? (Choose one.)

   A. `f.setSize(300, 200);`

   B. `f.setFont(new Font("SansSerif", Font.BOLD, 24));`

   C. `f.setForeground(Color.white);`

   D. `f.setVisible(true);`

   E. `f.setSize(300, 200); f.setVisible(true);`

10. True or False: The `CheckboxGroup` class is a subclass of the `Component` class.

   A. True

   B. False

Chapter

12

Painting

Chapter 11 discussed the various components of the AWT toolkit. Many types of AWT components (buttons and scroll bars, for example) have their appearance dictated by the underlying window system. Other component types—notably applets, frames, panels, and canvases—have no intrinsic appearance. If you use any of these classes other than simply as containers and want your component to look at all useful, you will have to provide the code that implements the component's appearance.

Java's painting mechanism provides the way for you to render your components. The mechanism is robust, and if you use it correctly you can create good, scaleable, reusable code. The best approach is to understand how Java's painting really works. The fundamental concepts of painting are:

- The `paint()` method and the graphics context
- The GUI thread and the `repaint()` method
- Spontaneous painting
- Painting to images

This chapter will take you through the steps necessary to understand and apply these concepts. And while the topics covered here are not explicitly mentioned in any of the Java 2 platform exam objectives, you may well find this information useful or essential. Also, the objectives of the 1.1 exam did mention these topics, so if you plan on taking that exam, be particularly sure to understand this chapter.

The *paint()* Method and the Graphics Context

Most programmers encounter the `paint()` method in the early chapters of an introductory Java book. The applet listed below is a simple example of this method:

```
1. import java.applet.Applet;
2. import java.awt.*;
3.
4. public class SimplePaint extends Applet {
5.   public void paint(Graphics g) {
6.     g.setColor(Color.black);
```

```
7.      g.fillRect(0, 0, 300, 300);
8.      g.setColor(Color.white);
9.      g.fillOval(30, 30, 50, 50);
10.  }
11. }
```

Figure 12.1 shows a screen shot of this applet.

FIGURE 12.1   A very simple painting applet

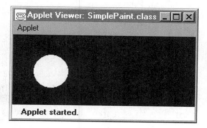

One interesting point about this applet is that no explicit calls are made to the `paint()` method; the method is simply *provided*. The environment seems to do a good job of calling `paint()` at the right moment. Exactly when the environment chooses to call `paint()` is the subject of "Spontaneous Painting," later in this chapter. For now, the topic at hand is the `paint()` method itself.

Painting on a component is accomplished by making calls to a *graphics context*, which is an instance of the `Graphics` class. A graphics context knows how to render onto a single target. The three media a graphics context can render onto are:

- Components

- Images

- Printers

Most of this chapter discusses graphics contexts that render onto components; at the end of the chapter is a section that discusses how to render onto an image. Printing—that is, producing hard copy—is not discussed, since it is not a topic of the Certification Exam.

Any kind of component can be associated with a graphics context. The association is permanent; a context cannot be reassigned to a new component. Although you can use graphics contexts to paint onto any kind of component, it is unusual to do so with components that already have an appearance. Buttons, choices, check boxes, labels, scroll bars, text fields, and text areas do not often require programmer-level rendering. Most often, these components just use the version of `paint()` that they inherit from the `Component` superclass. This version does nothing; the components are rendered by the underlying window system. However, there are four classes of "blank" components that have no default appearance and will show up as empty rectangles, unless they are subclassed and given `paint()` methods. These four component classes are:

- `Applet`
- `Canvas`
- `Frame`
- `Panel`

If you look at line 5 of the applet code sample earlier in this section, you will see that a graphics context is passed into the `paint()` method. When you subclass a component class and give the subclass its own `paint()` method, the environment calls that method at appropriate times, passing in an appropriate instance of `Graphics`.

The four major operation categories provided by the `Graphics` class are:

- Selecting a color
- Selecting a font
- Drawing and filling
- Clipping

Selecting a Color

Colors are selected by calling the `setColor()` method. The required argument is an instance of the `Color` class. There are 13 predefined colors, accessible as static final variables of the `Color` class. (The variables are themselves instances of the `Color` class, which makes some people uneasy, but Java has no trouble with such things.) The predefined colors are:

- `Color.black`
- `Color.blue`
- `Color.cyan`

- Color.darkGray

- Color.gray

- Color.green

- Color.lightGray

- Color.magenta

- Color.orange

- Color.pink

- Color.red

- Color.white

- Color.yellow

If you want a color that is not on this list, you can construct your own. There are several versions of the Color constructor; the simplest is:

```
Color(int redLevel, int greenLevel, int blueLevel)
```

The three parameters are intensity levels, on a scale of 0 to 255, for the primary colors. The colors are additive, which means they mix like light, not like paint. So:

- new Color(0, 0, 0) is black because it is the absence of any light

- new Color(255, 0, 0) is red because you are only including red hue.

- new Color(255, 255, 255) is white, all colors of light shining at once.

The code fragment below lists the first part of a paint() method that sets the color of its graphics context to pale green:

```
1. public void paint(Graphics g) {
2.    Color c = new Color(170, 255, 170);
3.    g.setColor(c);
         . . .
```

After line 3 above, all graphics will be painted in pale green, until the next g.setColor() call. Calling g.setColor() does not change the color of anything that has already been drawn; it only affects *subsequent* operations.

Selecting a Font

Setting the font of a graphics context is like setting the color: Subsequent string-drawing operations will use the new font, while previously drawn strings are not affected.

Before you can set a font, you have to create one. The constructor for the Font class looks like this:

```
Font(String fontname, int style, int size)
```

The first parameter is the name of the font. Font availability is platform-dependent. You can get a list of available font names, returned as an array of strings, by calling the getFontList() method on your toolkit like this:

```
String fontnames[] =
Toolkit.getDefaultToolkit().getFontList();
```

There are three font names that are platform independent and that you are encouraged to use:

- "Serif"
- "SansSerif"
- "Monospaced"

On 1.0.*x* releases of the JDK these were called, respectively, "TimesRoman", "Helvetica", and "Courier". However, you should use the new names unless you might be running on old platforms.

The style parameter of the Font constructor should be made up of the following three ints:

- Font.PLAIN
- Font.BOLD
- Font.ITALIC

The code fragment below sets the font of graphics context gc to 24-point bold sans serif:

```
1. Font f = new Font("SansSerif", Font.BOLD, 24);
2. gc.setFont(f);
```

You can specify combinations of styles, for example a bold italic font, by passing the sum of the styles, like this:

```
Font.BOLD + Font.ITALIC
```

as the style parameter to the Font constructor.

Drawing and Filling

All the rendering methods of the Graphics class specify pixel coordinate positions for the shapes they render. Every component has its own coordinate space, with the origin in the component's upper-left corner, x increasing to the right and y increasing downward. Figure 12.2 shows the component coordinate system.

FIGURE 12.2 The component coordinate system

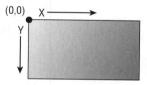

The GraphicsContext class does not have an extensive repertoire of painting methods. (Sophisticated rendering is handled by extended APIs such as 2D, 3D, and Animation.) The methods in the GraphicsContext class that you need to know about are:

- drawLine()
- drawRect() and fillRect()
- drawOval() and fillOval()
- drawArc() and fillArc()
- drawPolygon() and fillPolygon()
- drawPolyline()
- drawString()
- drawImage()

These methods are covered in detail in the next several sections.

drawLine()

The drawLine() method draws a line from point (x0, y0) to point (x1, y1). The method's signature is:

```
public void drawLine(int x0, int y0, int x1, int y1);
```

Figure 12.3 shows a simple applet whose paint() method makes the following call:

```
g.drawLine(20, 120, 100, 50);
```

FIGURE 12.3 *drawLine()*

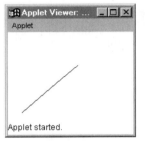

drawRect() and fillRect()

The drawRect() and fillRect() methods, respectively, draw and fill rectangles. The methods' signatures are:

```
public void drawRect(int x, int y, int width, int height);
public void fillRect(int x, int y, int width, int height);
```

The *x* and *y* parameters are the coordinates of the upper-left corner of the rectangle. Notice that the last two parameters are *width* and *height*, not the coordinates of the opposite corner. Width and height must be positive numbers, or nothing will be drawn. (This is true of all graphics-context methods that take a width and a height.)

Figure 12.4 shows a simple applet whose paint() method makes the following call:

```
g.drawRect(20, 20, 100, 80);
```

FIGURE 12.4   *drawRect()*

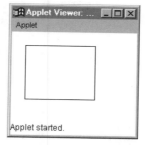

Figure 12.5 shows a simple applet whose `paint()` method makes the following call:

```
g.fillRect(20, 20, 100, 80);
```

FIGURE 12.5   *fillRect()*

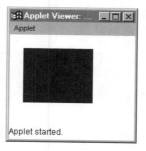

drawOval() and fillOval()

The `drawOval()` and `fillOval()` methods, respectively, draw and fill ovals. An oval is specified by a rectangular bounding box. The oval lies inside the bounding box and is tangent to each of the box's sides at the midpoint, as shown in Figure 12.6. To draw a circle, use a square bounding box. Note that the painting only draws foreground pixels, not background, so the space inside the bounding box but outside the oval is left unchanged.

FIGURE 12.6   Bounding box for an oval

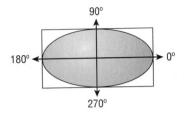

The two oval-drawing methods require you to specify a bounding box in exactly the same way that you specified a rectangle in the `drawRect()` and `fillRect()` methods:

```
public void drawOval(int x, int y, int width, int height);
public void fillOval(int x, int y, int width, int height);
```

Here *x* and *y* are the coordinates of the upper-left corner of the bounding box, and *width* and *height* are the width and height of the box.

Figure 12.7 shows a simple applet whose `paint()` method makes the following call:

```
g.drawOval(10, 10, 150, 100);
```

FIGURE 12.7   *drawOval()*

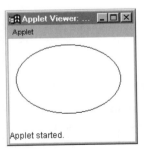

Figure 12.8 shows an applet whose `paint()` method calls

```
g.fillOval(10, 10, 150, 100);
```

FIGURE 12.8 *fillOval()*

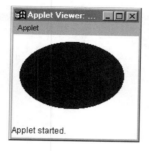

drawArc() and *fillArc()*

An *arc* is a segment of an oval. To specify an arc, you first specify the oval's bounding box, just as you do with drawOval() and fillOval(). You also need to specify the starting and ending points of the arc, which you do by specifying a starting angle and the angle swept out by the arc. Angles are measured in degrees. For the starting angle, 0 degrees is to the right, 90 degrees is upward, and so on, increasing counterclockwise, as shown in Figure 12.6.

A filled arc is the region bounded by the arc itself and the two radii from the center of the oval to the endpoints of the arc.

The method signatures are:

```
public void drawArc(int x, int y, int width, int height,
                    int startDegrees, int arcDegrees);
public void fillArc(int x, int y, int width, int height,
                    int startDegrees, int arcDegrees);
```

Figure 12.9 shows an application whose paint() method calls

```
g.drawArc(10, 10, 150, 100, 45, 135);
```

and

```
g.drawRect(10, 10, 150, 100);
```

FIGURE 12.9 *drawArc()*

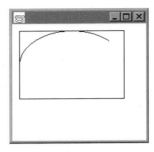

Figure 12.10 shows an application whose `paint()` method calls

`g.fillArc(10, 10, 150, 100, 45, 135);`

and

`g.drawRect(10, 10, 150, 100);`

FIGURE 12.10 *fillArc()*

drawPolygon and *fillPolygon*

A *polygon* is a closed figure with an arbitrary number of vertices. The vertices are passed to the drawPolygon() and fillPolygon() methods as two int arrays. The first array contains the x coordinates of the vertices; the second array contains the y coordinates. A third parameter specifies the number of vertices. The method signatures are:

```
public void drawPolygon(int xs[], int ys[], int
numPoints);
public void fillPolygon(int xs[], int ys[], int
numPoints);
```

Figure 12.11 shows an applet whose paint() method calls

```
1. int polyXs[] = {20, 150, 150};
2. int polyYs[] = {20, 20,  120};
3. g.drawPolygon(polyXs, polyYs, 3);
```

FIGURE 12.11 *drawPolygon()*

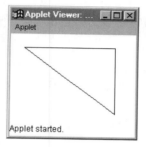

Figure 12.12 shows an applet whose paint() method calls

```
1. int polyXs[] = {20, 150, 150};
2. int polyYs[] = {20, 20,  120};
3. g.fillPolygon(polyXs, polyYs, 3);
```

FIGURE 12.12 *fillPolygon()*

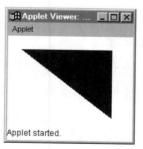

drawPolyline()

A *polyline* is similar to a polygon, but it is open rather than closed: There is no line segment connecting the last vertex to the first. The parameters to drawPolyline() are the same as those to drawPolygon(): a pair of int arrays representing vertices and an int that tells how many vertices there are. There is no fillPolyline() method, since fillPolygon() achieves the same result.

The signature for drawPolyline() is

```
public void drawPolyline(int xs[], int ys[],
                         int numPoints);
```

Figure 12.13 shows an applet whose paint() method calls

1. int polyXs[] = {20, 150, 150};
2. int polyYs[] = {20, 20, 120};
3. g.drawPolyline (polyXs, polyYs, 3);

FIGURE 12.13 *drawPolyline()*

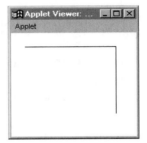

drawString()

The drawString() method paints a string of text. The signature is:

```
public void drawString(String s, int x, int y);
```

The *x* and *y* parameters specify the left edge of the baseline of the string. Characters with descenders (g, j, p, q, and y in most fonts) extend below the baseline.

The fact that text coordinates are relative to the baseline is important. In a simple test, for example, you might try to draw a string at (0, 0), expecting it to appear at the top-left of the space. However, because of the baseline, you will only see the descenders of the string—which might mean that you see nothing at all.

By default, a graphics context uses the font of the associated component. However, you can set a different font by calling the graphics context's `setFont()` method, as you saw in the section "Selecting a Font."

Figure 12.14 shows an applet whose `paint()` method calls

```
1. Font font = new Font("Serif", Font.PLAIN, 24);
2. g.setFont(font);
3. g.drawString("juggle quickly", 20, 50);
4. g.setColor(Color.darkGray);
5. g.drawLine(20, 50, 150, 50);
```

FIGURE 12.14 *drawString()*

The string in line 3 contains five descender characters. Lines 4 and 5 draw the baseline, so you can see it in relation to the rendered string.

drawImage()

An `Image` is an off-screen representation of a rectangular collection of pixel values. Java's image support is complicated, and a complete description would go well beyond the scope of this book. The last section of this chapter,

"Images," discusses what you need to know about creating and manipulating images.

For now, assume that you have somehow obtained an image (that is, an instance of class `java.awt.Image`) that you want to render to the screen using a certain graphics context. The way to do this is to call the graphics context's `drawImage()` method, which has the following signature:

```
boolean drawImage(Image im, int x, int y, ImageObserver
observer);
```

There are other versions of the method, but this is the most common form. Obviously, *im* is the image to be rendered, and *x* and *y* are the coordinates within the destination component of the upper-left corner of the image. The image observer must be an object that implements the `ImageObserver` interface.

Image observers are part of Java's complicated image-support system; the point to remember is that your image observer can always be the component into which you are rendering the image. For a complete discussion of images, please refer to the *Java 2 Developer's Handbook* (Sybex, 1999).

Clipping

Most calls that programmers make on graphics contexts involve color selection or drawing and filling. A less common operation is *clipping*. Clipping is simply restricting the region that a graphics context can modify.

Every graphics context—that is, every instance of the `Graphics` class—has a *clip region*, which defines all or part of the associated component. When you call one of the `drawXXX()` or `fillXXX()` methods of the `Graphics` class, only those pixels that lie within the graphics context's clip region are modified. The default clip region for a graphics context is the entire visible region of the associated component. There are methods that retrieve and modify a clip region.

In a moment you will see an example of clipping, but to set things up, consider the following `paint()` method:

```
1. public void paint(Graphics g) {
2.    for (int i = 10; i < 500; i += 20)
```

```
3.       for (int j = 10; j < 500; j += 20)
4.           g.fillOval(i, j, 15, 15);
5. }
```

This method draws a polka-dot pattern. Consider what happens when this is the `paint()` method of an applet that is 300 pixels wide by 300 pixels high. Because the loop counters go all the way up to 500, the method attempts to draw outside the bounds of the applet. This is not a problem, because the graphics context by default has a clip region that coincides with the applet itself. Figure 12.15 shows the applet.

FIGURE 12.15   Applet with default clipping

To set a rectangular clip region for a graphics context, you can call the `setClip (x, y, width, height)` method, passing in four `int`s that describe the position and size of the desired clip rectangle. For example, the code above could be modified as follows:

```
1. public void paint(Graphics g) {
2.    g.setClip(100, 100, 100, 100);
3.    for (int i = 10; i < 500; i += 20) {
4.      for (int j = 10; j < 500; j += 20) {
5.          g.fillOval(i, j, 15, 15);
```

```
6.      }
7.    }
8.  }
```

Now painting is clipped to a 100 × 100 rectangle in the center of the 300 × 300 applet, as Figure 12.16 shows.

FIGURE   12.16   Applet with specified clipping

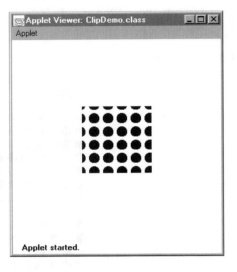

Clipping is good to know about in its own right. Clipping also comes into play when the environment needs to repair exposed portions of a component, as described in "Spontaneous Painting," later in this chapter.

Painting a Contained Component

If an applet or a frame contains components that have their own `paint()` methods, then all the `paint()` methods will be called by the environment when necessary. For example, if a frame contains a panel and a canvas, then at certain times the environment will call the frame's `paint()`, the panel's `paint()`, and the canvas' `paint()`.

The code listed below implements a frame that contains a panel and a canvas. The frame uses a Grid layout manager with three rows and one column. The panel is added to the frame first, so it appears in the top third of the frame. The canvas is added second, so it appears in the middle third. Since there is no component in the last grid cell, what you see in the bottom third of the frame is the frame itself (that is, you see whatever the frame itself draws in its own `paint()` method).

The panel draws concentric rectangles. The canvas draws concentric ovals. The frame draws text.

```
1.  import java.awt.*;
2.
3.  public class ThingsInFrame extends Frame {
4.    public ThingsInFrame() {
5.      super("Panel and Canvas in a Frame");
6.      setSize(350, 500);
7.      setLayout(new GridLayout(3, 1));
8.      add(new RectsPanel());
9.      add(new OvalsCanvas());
10.   }
11.
12.   public static void main(String args[]) {
13.     ThingsInFrame tif = new ThingsInFrame();
14.     tif.setVisible(true);
15.   }
16.
17.   public void paint(Graphics g) {
18.     Rectangle bounds = getBounds();
19.     int y = 12;
20.     while (y < bounds.height) {
21.       g.drawString(
22.         "frame frame frame frame frame frame", 60, y);
23.       y += 12;
24.     }
25.   }
26. }
27.
28.
29. class RectsPanel extends Panel {
30.   public RectsPanel() {
```

```
31.        setBackground(Color.lightGray);
32.      }
33.
34.      public void paint(Graphics g) {
35.        Rectangle bounds = getBounds();
36.        int x = 0;
37.        int y = 0;
38.        int w = bounds.width - 1;
39.        int h = bounds.height - 1;
40.        for (int i = 0; i < 10; i++) {
41.          g.drawRect(x, y, w, h);
42.          x += 10;
43.          y += 10;
44.          w -= 20;
45.          h -= 20;
46.        }
47.      }
48.  }
49.
50.
51.  class OvalsCanvas extends Canvas {
52.      public OvalsCanvas() {
53.        setForeground(Color.white);
54.        setBackground(Color.darkGray);
55.      }
56.
57.      public void paint(Graphics g) {
58.        Rectangle bounds = getBounds();
59.        int x = 0;
60.        int y = 0;
61.        int w = bounds.width - 1;
62.        int h = bounds.height - 1;
63.        for (int i = 0; i < 10; i++) {
64.          g.drawOval(x, y, w, h);
65.          x += 10;
66.          y += 10;
```

```
67.        w -= 20;
68.        h -= 20;
69.      }
70.    }
71.  }
```

Figure 12.17 shows the frame that results from this code.

FIGURE 12.17 A frame with contained components

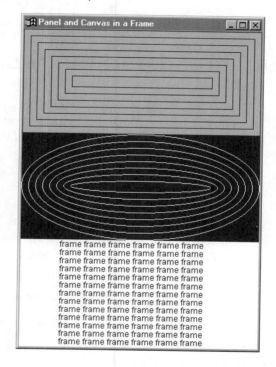

On line 31, the constructor for RectsPanel called setBackground().
On lines 53 and 54, the constructor for OvalsCanvas called both
setForeground() and setBackground(). The screen shot in Figure 12.17
shows that the foreground and background colors seem to have taken effect
without any effort on the part of the paint() methods. The environment is
not only making paint() calls at the right times; it is also doing the right
thing with the foreground and background colors.

The next several sections discuss what the environment is really up to. But first, to summarize what you have learned so far about the paint() method and the graphics context:

- A graphics context is dedicated to a single component.

- To paint on a component, you call the graphics context's drawXXX() and fillXXX() methods.

- To change the color or font of graphics operations, you call the graphics context's setColor() or setFont() methods, respectively.

The GUI Thread and the *repaint()* Method

In Chapter 7, you reviewed Java's facilities for creating and controlling threads. The runtime environment creates and controls its own threads that operate behind the scenes, and one of these threads is responsible for GUI management.

This GUI thread is the environment's tool for accepting user input events and (more importantly for this chapter) for calling the paint() method of components that need painting.

Calls to paint() are not all generated by the environment. Java programs can of course make their own calls, either directly (which is not recommended) or indirectly (via the repaint() method). The next two sections cover the two ways that paint() calls can be generated:

- Spontaneous painting, initiated by the environment

- Program-initiated painting

Spontaneous Painting

Spontaneous painting is not an official Java term, but it gets the point across. Some painting happens all by itself, with no impetus from the program. For example, as every introductory Java book explains, when a browser starts up an applet, shortly after the init() method completes, a call is made to the paint() method. Also, when part or all of a browser or a frame is covered by another window and then becomes exposed, a call is made to the paint() method.

It is the GUI thread that executes these calls to paint(). Every applet, and every application that has a GUI, has a GUI thread. The GUI thread spontaneously calls paint() whenever all or part of a component needs redrawing:

- After exposure

- After de-iconification

- After first display

- When a browser returns to a previously displayed page containing an applet, provided the applet is at least partially visible

When the GUI thread calls paint(), it must supply a graphics context, since the paint() method's input parameter is an instance of the Graphics class. An earlier section ("Clipping") discussed the fact that every graphics context has a clip region. The GUI thread makes sure that the graphics contexts that get passed to paint() have their clip regions appropriately set. Most often, the default clip region is appropriate. (Recall that the default clip region is the visible part of the component.) However, when a component is exposed, the clip region is set to be just that portion of the component that requires repair. If only a small piece of the component was exposed, then the clip region ensures that no time is wasted drawing pixels that are already the correct color. If an exposed region is non-rectangular, then multiple calls to paint() might occur, with the clip region of each successively building up to ensure that the whole exposed area gets repainted eventually.

The *repaint()* Method

There are times when the program, not the environment, should initiate painting. This can happen for several reasons, such as in response to input events, or if the time has arrived for the next frame in an animation to be displayed, or perhaps the program is displaying a scrolling graph in real time and the next time segment has come up. This kind of painting may be called program-initiated painting.

Since you can get a reference to a component's graphics using the method getGraphics(), it is tempting to believe that you can simply draw to a component from any convenient method. Generally, this approach is seriously flawed. This section introduces the limitations of the approach, and describes the proper, consistent, and reliable approach that you should use for drawing.

Suppose you have an applet that wants to draw a red dot at the point of the most recent mouse click. The remainder of the applet should be yellow. Assume that the applet is handling its own mouse events. You might consider creating an event handler like this:

```
1. public void mouseClicked(MouseEvent e) {
2.    Graphics g = getGraphics();
3.    g.setColor(Color.yellow);
4.    g.fillRect(0, 0, getSize().width, getSize().height);
5.    g.setColor(Color.red);                         // Red dot
6.    g.fillOval(e.getX() - 10, e.getY() - 10, 20, 20);
7. }
```

If this applet ever gets covered and exposed, the GUI thread will call paint(). Unfortunately, paint() does not know about the red circle that was drawn in mouseClicked(), so the red circle will not be repaired. The proper place for *all* drawing operations is in paint(), or in methods called from paint(); this technique ensures that the GUI thread will be able to repair exposure damage. The GUI thread expects paint() to be able to correctly reconstruct the screen at any arbitrary moment.

One possible way to achieve this is to remove all drawing code from event handlers and other arbitrary methods and place that code into the paint() method. Next, when a method needs to draw, arrange for it to write to variables that describe the desired drawing, so that those variables are accessible to the paint() method and can be used by the paint() method to perform the drawing. Now when the paint() method gets called, whether by one of your general methods, or by the GUI thread, it can draw whatever was originally intended. In our example, mouseClicked() might be modified as shown below, assuming that the class has instance variables *mouseX* and *mouseY*:

```
1. public void mouseClicked(MouseEvent e) {
2.    mouseX = e.getX();
3.    mouseY = e.getY();
4.    Graphics g = getGraphics();
5.    paint(g);
6. }
```

The corresponding `paint()` method would be as follows:

```
1. public void paint(Graphics g) {
2.    g.setColor(Color.yellow);     // Yellow background
3.    g.fillRect(0, 0, getSize().width, getSize().height);
4.    g.setColor(Color.red);        // Red dot
5.    g.fillOval(mouseX - 10, mouseY - 10, 20, 20);
6. }
```

At first sight this looks much better; if a dot gets covered and exposed, the damage will be repaired automatically. Two more problems remain, however, and these are a bit subtler than the spontaneous painting issue. The first problem is that the GUI thread is calling the `paint()` method as and when it needs to—remember that this occurs when exposure needs to be handled. This can cause thread interaction issues. To be fair, you will see that you might have to handle some of these issues anyway, even when using the preferred approach, since the `paint()` method will use data that you are modifying in other threads. However, you will minimize the problems if you allow `paint()` to be called only in the GUI thread.

The second problem is one of CPU usage. Consider this scenario: Your program is getting regular notification that it should update the display with the next frame of an animation or similar continuously moving graphic. Also suppose that the drawing is complex and time-consuming. If you simply call the whole `paint()` method, you might be only part way through the drawing when the next frame trigger occurs. This would result in your program spending, or trying to spend, all its time drawing. Further, the drawing would get further and further behind where it should be.

These problems can be dealt with very simply by using the preferred method of handling program-initiated drawing. The idea is that the main program maintains a data set that describes the drawing that should be presented to the user, but does not directly call the drawing routines. Instead, the program requests that the GUI thread should run the painting routines, in broadly the same way that thread would do if it were handling exposure. The GUI thread uses the data set presented by the main program to decide what and how to draw.

To support this approach, the GUI system provides a method called `repaint()`. This method is defined in the component class, and so is available on anything visible in a GUI. When you call this method, you are issuing a request to the GUI thread that it should perform the painting system routines. The GUI thread does so within a reasonable time scale, although this might be limited by other high-priority thread activity.

This approach ensures that the thread interactions between the GUI thread and user threads are minimized. You must, naturally, ensure that your data set is never used by the GUI thread while that data is in an inconsistent state. However, this can be achieved quite easily using either synchronization or a double buffering technique. We'll look at double buffering later in this chapter.

Another consequence of this behavior is that, no matter how much drawing the program tries to do, the system generally remains synchronized with the current frame. This happens because if you call the `repaint()` method ten times, for example, before the GUI thread is able to service the first call, then the result will be a single execution of the painting system. Therefore, in overload conditions, the painting system automatically skips frames that the host CPU simply cannot deal with. This means that the programmer can write code that reliably gets the best available video performance on a given platform, but still works tolerably well on any other platform. Let's have a look at the kind of code that implements this scheme:

```
1. public void mouseClicked(MouseEvent e) {
2.    mouseX = e.getX();
3.    mouseY = e.getY();
4.    repaint();
5. }
6.
7. public void paint(Graphics g) {
8.    g.setColor(Color.red);
9.    g.fillOval(mouseX - 10, mouseY - 10, 20, 20);
10. }
```

Notice the `repaint()` call at line 4 which has replaced the direct handling of painting. Now, regardless of how frequently the event handler is called, calls to `paint()` will not outstrip the system's ability to draw, and the program cannot fall increasingly behind.

The code above shows the essence of the preferred approach to program-initiated drawing. The main program stores information in instance variables and then calls the `repaint()` method. The `repaint()` method requests that the GUI thread draws the screen. The GUI thread uses the paint() method to do the drawing, and that method should perform the drawing according to the information in the instance variables. The benefits of this approach are:

- The screen is correctly repaired when the environment spontaneously calls paint().

- The thread interactions, between foreground threads trying to draw and the GUI thread, are controlled and predictable.

- The Virtual Machine is never overwhelmed by painting.

- When all code is written this way, there are no surprises for other programmers trying to debug the code.

Although this approach works well, there is a situation where still further improvement is needed: animation. If you use the approach exactly as described, you will probably notice that an animation flickers unpleasantly while it runs.

Smooth Animation

One feature of the default behavior of the repainting mechanism that you might not always want is that the system clears your drawing area as part of the preparation to respond to your call to repaint(). This can make animations and other real-time drawings flicker unpleasantly. It turns out that when you call repaint(), the GUI thread doesn't call paint(); instead it calls the update() method. The default behavior of update() is to do two things: clear the background and then call paint(). Like this:

```
public void update(Graphics g) {
  // width and height are default access instance variables
  g.clearRect(0, 0, width, height);
  paint(g);
}
```

You might reasonably ask why repaint() starts by clearing the window if this causes flickering. Well, in many cases, drawings are done using lines, rectangles, ovals, and so forth drawn on a background. If you are trying to make a spinning stick, you need to remove the old line before you draw the new one. Another way to think about this is to consider that if you are trying to draw a new drawing, you should first erase the old one.

So, how can we arrange for the new drawing to appear without having to clear the whole display first? You simply need to find another way to remove the old drawing. The general approach is to ensure that you draw the whole drawing—both background and foreground—each time you draw a frame. If you can arrange this, then you don't need to clear the component, and the flickering goes away.

To prevent the component being cleared before `paint()` is called, you simply override the `update()` method so that it calls `paint()` directly, as shown below:

```
1. public void update(Graphics g) {
2.   paint(g);
3. }
```

This is a standard technique and works perfectly, provided that your `paint()` method does indeed refresh all the pixels of the display. One particularly easy way to handle this is to use an off-screen image to store a drawing of what should be shown on the display. This technique isn't always the most efficient, in either speed or memory terms, but it is simple, easy to implement, and generally well understood by Java programmers. The next section looks at images, and how to use them to implement this technique.

Images

*I*mages are off-screen representations of rectangular pixel patterns. There are three things you can do with images:

- Create them

- Modify them

- Draw them to the screen or to other images

There are two ways to create an image. You can create an empty one, or you can create one that is initialized from a GIF, JPEG, XBM, or (since JDK 1.3) PNG file.

To create an empty image, call the `createImage()` method of the `Component` class and pass in the desired width and height. For example, the following line creates an image called im1 that is 400 pixels wide by 250 pixels high; it might appear in the init() method of an applet:

```
Image im1 = createImage(400, 250);
```

An image can be created based on the information in a .gif or a .jpeg file. The Applet and Toolkit classes both have a method called getImage(), which has two common forms:

```
getImage(URL fileURL)
getImage(URL dirURL, String path)
```

The first form takes a URL that refers to the desired image file. The second form takes a URL that references a directory and the path of the desired image file, relative to *that* directory. The code fragment below shows an applet's init() method; it loads an image from a file that resides in the same server directory as the page that contains the applet:

```
1. public void init() {
2.    Image im =
3.       getImage(getDocumentBase(), "thePicture.gif");
4. }
```

If you load an image from a file, you might want to modify it. If you create an image, you will definitely want to modify it, since such an image will be blank at creation. Fortunately, images have graphics contexts. All you need to do is obtain a graphics context for the image you wish to modify and make the calls that were discussed earlier in this chapter in "Drawing and Filling." To obtain a graphics context, just call getGraphics(). The code below implements an applet whose init() method creates an image and then obtains a graphics context in order to draw a blue circle on a yellow background. The applet's paint() method renders the image onto the screen using the drawImage() method, which is documented earlier in this chapter:

```
1. import java.applet.Applet;
2. import java.awt.*;
3.
4. public class PaintImage extends Applet {
5.    private Image im;
6.
```

```
7.   public void init() {
8.      im = createImage(300, 200);
9.      Graphics imgc = im.getGraphics();
10.     imgc.setColor(Color.yellow);
11.     imgc.fillRect(0, 0, 300, 200);
12.     imgc.setColor(Color.blue);
13.     imgc.fillOval(50, 50, 100, 100);
14.  }
15.
16.  public void paint(Graphics g) {
17.     g.drawImage(im, 25, 80, this);
18.  }
19. }
```

Notice that in lines 9–13, imgc is a graphics context that draws to the off-screen image im. In lines 16–17, g is a graphics context that draws to the applet's screen.

There are three caveats that you need to be aware of when using images. They both relate to the timing of when you try to create them. First, you cannot call the getImage() method of an applet before the init() method of that applet is called. If you do, you will receive a null pointer exception, since the method depends upon the AppletContext object that is provided to the applet by the browser in which it is running. To avoid this problem, don't put calls to getImage in constructors or initializers of applets. Second, if you have an Applet that is not running in a browser, then there will be no AppletContext object, and the getImage() method will not work. You can get images in Applications using the Toolkit object. Third, if you use the createImage() method of a component, the component must have been "realized"—that is, actually displayed—before you call that method.

Double Buffering Using Images

You are not required to understand techniques of double buffering for the Certification Exam. However, this is a standard approach used to provide smooth animation, and understanding it adds to your understanding of the correct way to handle program-initiated drawing. For these reasons, in addition to general completeness, we will discuss this.

To perform double buffering using images, and thereby remove flickering from animations and other real time drawings, is very easy. Look at the example:

```
1. import java.awt.*;
2.
3. public class DB extends Canvas {
4.     private Image [] backing = new Image[2];
5.     private int imageToDraw = 0;
6.     private int imageNotDraw = 1;
7.
8.     public void update(Graphics g) {
9.       paint(g);
10.    }
11.
12.    public synchronized void paint(Graphics g) {
13.       g.drawImage(backing[imageToDraw], 0, 0, this);
14.    }
15.
16.    public void addNotify() {
17.      super.addNotify();
18.      backing[0] = createImage(400, 400);
19.      backing[1] = createImage(400, 400);
20.      setSize(400, 400);
21.      new Thread(
22.        new Runnable() {
23.          private int direction = 1;
24.          private int position = 0;
25.          public void run() {
26.            for (;;) {
27.              try {
28.                Thread.sleep(10);
29.              }
30.              catch (InterruptedException ex) {
31.                // ignore
```

```
32.                    }
33.                    Graphics g =
34.                        backing[imageNotDraw].getGraphics();
35.                    g.clearRect(0, 0, 400, 400);
36.                    g.drawOval(position, 200 - position,
37.                            400 - (2 * position),7
38.                            2 * position);
39.                    synchronized(DB.this) {
40.                        int temp = imageNotDraw;
41.                        imageNotDraw = imageToDraw;
42.                        imageToDraw = temp;
43.                    }
44.                    position += direction;
45.                    if (position > 199) {
46.                        direction = -1;
47.                    }
48.                    else if (position < 1) {
49.                        direction = 1;
50.                    }
51.                    repaint();
52.                }
53.            }
54.        }
55.    ).start();
56.  }
57.
58.  public static void main(String args[]) {
59.      Frame f = new Frame("Double Buffer");
60.      f.add(new DB(), BorderLayout.CENTER);
61.      f.pack();
62.      f.setVisible(true);
63.  }
64. }
```

Notice that, at line 9, the body of the update() method has been modified so that it simply calls the paint() method. The paint() method simply
consists of a single line that copies the current stored image to the display.

The `addNotify()` method of a Component sets up the component ready for display. After the call to `super.addNotify()` in line 17, the DB object is fully realized but still hidden from view. This allows the calls to `createImage()` in lines 18 and 19 to operate properly.

In the background thread, based on the `Runnable` anonymous inner class created between lines 22 and 54, the animation is performed by alternately drawing the next step of the animation into the currently-unused background image. When the next image has been prepared, lines 39 through 43 swap the current used and unused images; line 51 then requests that the display be updated from the (newly changed) current image. Since both the `paint()` method, and the manipulation of the current used and unused images, are protected by synchronization, it is impossible for the program to start updating an image while it is currently being drawn.

Chapter Summary

The `paint()` method provides a graphics context for drawing. The functionality of the graphics context (class `Graphics`) includes:

- Selecting a color
- Selecting a font
- Drawing and filling
- Clipping

Calls to `paint()` can be generated spontaneously by the system, under four circumstances:

- After exposure
- After de-iconification
- After first display
- When a browser returns to a previously displayed page containing an applet (applets only)

In all cases, the clip region of the graphics context will be set appropriately.

When a program wants to draw on the screen, it should store appropriate state information in instance variables and then call `repaint()`. This schedules a call to `update()`, which by default clears the component to its background color and then calls `paint()`.

Images can be created from scratch or loaded from external files. An image can be modified by using a graphics context.

Test Yourself

1. How would you set the color of a graphics context *g* to cyan?

   A. `g.setColor(Color.cyan);`

   B. `g.setCurrentColor(cyan);`

   C. `g.setColor("Color.cyan");`

   D. `g.setColor("cyan");`

   E. `g.setColor(new Color(cyan));`

2. The code below draws a line. What color is the line?

   ```
   1. g.setColor(Color.red.green.yellow.red.cyan);
   2. g.drawLine(0, 0, 100, 100);
   ```

   A. Red

   B. Green

   C. Yellow

   D. Cyan

   E. Black

3. What does the following code draw?

   ```
   1. g.setColor(Color.black);
   2. g.drawLine(10, 10, 10, 50);
   3. g.setColor(Color.red);
   4. g.drawRect(100, 100, 150, 150);
   ```

   A. A red vertical line that is 40 pixels long and a red square with sides of 150 pixels

   B. A black vertical line that is 40 pixels long and a red square with sides of 150 pixels

   C. A black vertical line that is 50 pixels long and a red square with sides of 150 pixels

D. A red vertical line that is 50 pixels long and a red square with sides of 150 pixels

E. A black vertical line that is 40 pixels long and a red square with sides of 100 pixels

4. In the illustration shown, which shape (A or B) is drawn by the following line of code?

```
g.fillArc(10, 10, 100, 100, 0, 90);
```

A)
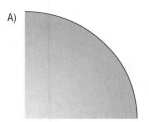

B)
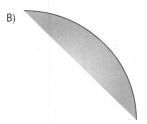

5. Which of the statements below are true? (Choose one or more.)

A. A polyline is always filled.

B. A polyline cannot be filled.

C. A polygon is always filled.

D. A polygon is always closed.

E. A polygon may be filled or not filled.

6. True or False: When the GUI thread calls `paint()` in order to repair exposure damage, the `paint()` method must determine what was damaged and set its clip region appropriately.

   A. True

   B. False

7. Your `mouseDragged()` event handler and your `paint()` method look like this:

```
1. public void mouseDragged(MouseEvent e) {
2.    mouseX = e.getX();
3.    mouseY = e.getY();
4.    repaint();
5. }
6.
7. public void paint(Graphics g) {
8.    g.setColor(Color.cyan);
9.    g.drawLine(mouseX, mouseY, mouseX+9, mouseY+9);
10. }
```

   You want to modify your code so that the cyan lines accumulate on the screen, rather than getting erased every time `repaint()` calls `update()`. You know that your program's window will never be obscured, minimized, nor otherwise damaged. What is the simplest way to proceed?

   A. On line 4, replace `repaint()` with `paint()`.

   B. On line 4, replace `repaint()` with `update()`.

   C. After line 7, add this: `super.update(g);`

   D. Add the following method:
   `public void update(Graphics g) {paint(g);}`

8. What code would you use to construct a 24-point bold serif font?

   A. `new Font(Font.SERIF, 24, Font.BOLD);`

   B. `new Font("Serif", 24, "Bold");`

   C. `new Font("Bold", 24, Font.SERIF);`

   D. `new Font("Serif", Font.BOLD, 24);`

   E. `new Font(Font.SERIF, "Bold", 24);`

9. What does the following `paint()` method draw?

```
1. public void paint(Graphics g) {
2.   g.drawString("question #9", 10, 0);
3. }
```

   A. The string "question #9", with its top-left corner at 10, 0

   B. A little squiggle coming down from the top of the component, a little way in from the left edge

10. What does the following `paint()` method draw?

```
1. public void paint(Graphics g) {
2.   g.drawOval(100, 100, 44);
3. }
```

   A. A circle at (100, 100) with radius of 44

   B. A circle at (100, 44) with radius of 100

   C. A circle at (100, 44) with radius of 44

   D. The code does not compile.

Chapter

13

Input and Output

Java supports input and output with a flexible set of stream classes. File I/O requires a bit of additional support, which Java provides in the File and RandomAccessFile classes. Socket I/O is supported by the Socket and ServerSocket classes.

All I/O operations into and out of a Java Virtual Machine are contingent on approval by the security manager. By default, most browsers forbid all file access and nearly all socket I/O, so the classes discussed in this chapter are generally for use in applications.

All the classes discussed in this chapter reside in the java.io and java.net packages.

As with Chapters 11 and 12, the information discussed here is not explicitly mentioned in the objectives, but should be considered essential background.

File Input and Output

Java's File and RandomAccessFile classes provide functionality for navigating the local file system, describing files and directories, and accessing files in non-sequential order. (Accessing files sequentially is done with streams, readers, and writers, which are described later in this chapter.)

Text Representation and UTF

Java uses two kinds of text representation:

- Unicode for internal representation of characters and strings

- UTF for input and output

Unicode uses 16 bits to represent each character. If the high-order 9 bits are all zeros, then the encoding is simply standard ASCII, with the low-order byte containing the character representation. Otherwise, the bits represent a character that is not represented in 7-bit ASCII. Java's char data type uses Unicode encoding, and the String class contains a collection of Java chars.

When Unicode text is to be written to a file or to a network, it is common practice to write something more compact than a sequence of 16-bit characters. Java supports this practice. Unicode is capable of very efficient data compression. The outside-the-computer format for Unicode is known as *UTF*. There is a common misconception that UTF stands for "Unicode Transmission Format." In fact, it is an abbreviation for "UCS Transformation Format," and UCS in turn stands for "Universal Character Set." But don't worry: you will not be tested on your knowledge of these abbreviations.

UTF encoding uses as many bits as needed to encode a character: fewer bits for languages with smaller writing systems, more bits for the larger, mostly Asian, systems. Since every character can be represented, UTF is a truly global encoding scheme.

The *File* Class

The java.io.File class represents the name of a file or directory that might exist on the host machine's file system. The simplest form of the constructor for this class is:

```
File(String pathname);
```

It is important to know that constructing an instance of File does not create a file on the local file system. Calling the constructor simply creates an instance that encapsulates the specified string. Of course, if the instance is to be of any use, most likely it should encapsulate a string that represents an existing file or directory, or one that will shortly be created. However, at construction time no checks are made.

There are two other versions of the File constructor:

```
File(String dir, String subpath);
File(File dir, String subpath);
```

Both versions require you to provide a directory and a relative path (the subpath argument) within that directory. In one version you use a string to specify the directory; in the other, you use an instance of File. (Remember that the File class can represent a directory as well as a file.) You might, for example, execute the following code on a Unix machine:

```
1. File f1 =
2.   new File("/tmp", "xyz"); // Assume /tmp is a dir
3. File f2 = new File(f1, "Xyz.java");
```

You might execute the following code on a Windows platform:

```
1. File f1 =
2.    new File("C:\\a");    // Assume C:\a is a dir
3. File f2 = new File(f1, "Xyz.java");
```

(In line 2, the first backslash is an escape character that ensures that the second backslash is accepted literally.)

Of course, there is no theoretical reason why you could not run the first example on a Windows machine and the second example on a Unix platform. Up to this point, you are doing nothing more than constructing objects that encapsulate strings. In practice, however, there is nothing to be gained from using the wrong pathname semantics.

After constructing an instance of File, you can make several method calls on it. Some of these calls simply do string manipulation on the file's pathname, while others access or modify the local file system.

The major methods that support navigation are:

- boolean exists(): This returns true if the file or directory exists; otherwise it returns false.

- String getAbsolutePath(): This returns the absolute (i.e., not relative) path of the file or directory.

- String getCanonicalPath(): This returns the canonical path of the file or directory. This is similar to getAbsolutePath(), but the symbols . and .. are resolved.

- String getName(): This returns the name of the file or directory. The name is the last element of the path.

- String getParent(): This returns the name of the directory that contains the File.

- boolean isDirectory(): This returns true if the File object describes a directory that exists on the file system.

- boolean isFile(): This returns true if the File object describes a file that exists on the file system.

- String[] list(): This returns an array containing the names of the files and directories within the File. The File must describe a directory, not a file.

Some non-navigation methods are:

- boolean canRead(): This returns true if the file or directory may be read.

- boolean canWrite(): This returns true if the file or directory may be modified.

- boolean delete(): This attempts to delete the file or directory.

- long length(): This returns the length of the file.

- boolean mkdir(): This attempts to create a directory whose path is described by the File.

- boolean renameTo(File newname): This renames the file or directory. It returns true if the renaming succeeded, otherwise it returns false.

The program listed below uses some of the navigation methods to create a recursive listing of a directory. The application expects the directory to be specified in the command line. The listing appears in a text area within a frame.

```
1.  import java.awt.*;
2.  import java.io.File;
3.
4.  public class Lister extends Frame {
5.    TextArea      ta;
6.
7.    public static void main(String args[]) {
8.      // Get path or dir to be listed.
9.      // Default to cwd if no command line arg.
10.     String path = ".";
11.     if (args.length >= 1)
12.       path = args[0];
13.
14.     // Make sure path exists and is a directory.
15.     File f = new File(path);
16.     if (!f.isDirectory()) {
17.       System.out.println(path +
18.         " doesn't exist or not dir");
19.       System.exit(0);
```

```
20.      }
21.
22.      // Recursively list contents.
23.      Lister lister = new Lister(f);
24.      lister.setVisible(true);
25.    }
26.
27.    Lister(File f) {
28.      setSize(300, 450);
29.      ta = new TextArea();
30.      ta.setFont(new Font(
31.               "Monospaced", Font.PLAIN, 14));
32.      add(ta, BorderLayout.CENTER);
33.      recurse(f, 0);
34.    }
35.
36.    // Recursively list the contents of dirfile.
37.    // Indent 5 spaces for each level of depth.
38.
39.    void recurse(File dirfile, int depth) {
40.      String contents[] = dirfile.list();
41.      // For each child ...
42.      for (int i=0; i<contents.length; i++) {
43.        // Indent
44.        for (int spaces=0; spaces<depth; spaces++)
45.          ta.append("     ");
46.        // Print name
47.        ta.append(contents[i] + "\n");
48.        File child = new File(dirfile, contents[i]);
49.        if (child.isDirectory())
50.          // Recurse if dir
51.          recurse(child, depth+1);
52.      }
53.    }
54. }
```

Figure 13.1 shows a sample of this program's output.

FIGURE 13.1   Sample listing

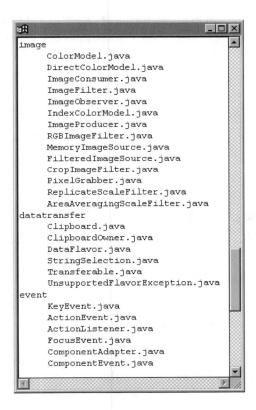

The program first checks for a command-line argument (lines 10–12). If one is supplied, it is assumed to be the name of the directory to be listed; if there is no argument, the current working directory will be listed. Note the call to isDirectory() on line 16. This call returns true only if path represents an existing directory.

After establishing that the thing to be listed really is a directory, the code constructs an instance of Lister, which makes a call to recurse(), passing in the File to be listed in the parameter dirfile.

The recurse() method makes a call to list() (line 40) to get a listing of the contents of the directory. Each file or subdirectory is printed (line 47) after appropriate indentation (five spaces per level, lines 44 and 45). If the child is a directory (tested on line 45), its contents are listed recursively.

The Lister program shows one way to use the methods of the File class to navigate the local file system. These methods do not modify the contents of files in any way; to modify a file you must use either the RandomAccess-File class or Java's stream, reader, and writer facilities. All these topics are covered in the sections that follow, but first, here is a summary of the key points concerning the File class:

- An instance of File describes a file or directory.

- The file or directory might or might not exist.

- Constructing/garbage collecting an instance of File has no effect on the local file system.

The *RandomAccessFile* Class

One way to read or modify a file is to use the java.io.RandomAccessFile class. This class presents a model of files that is incompatible with the stream/reader/writer model described later in this chapter. The stream/reader/writer model was developed for general I/O, while the RandomAccessFile class takes advantage of a particular behavior of files that is not found in general I/O devices.

With a random-access file, you can seek to a desired position within a file, and then read or write a desired amount of data. The RandomAccessFile class provides methods that support seeking, reading, and writing.

The constructors for the class are:

- RandomAccessFile(String file, String mode)
- RandomAccessFile(File file, String mode)

The mode string should be either "r" or "rw." Use "r" to open the file for reading only, and use "rw" to open for both reading and writing.

The second form of the constructor is useful when you want to use some of the methods of the File class before opening a random-access file, so that you already have an instance of File at hand when it comes time to call the RandomAccessFile constructor. For example, the code fragment below constructs an instance of File in order to verify that the string path represents a file that exists and may be written. If this is the case, the RandomAccess-File constructor is called; otherwise an exception is thrown.

```
1. File file = new File(path);
2. if (!file.isFile()   ||
3.      !file.canRead()  ||
4.      !file.canWrite()) {
5.    throw new IOException()
6. }
```

When the named file does not exist, constructing a `RandomAccessFile` is different from constructing an ordinary `File`. In this situation, if the random-access file is constructed in read-only mode, a `FileNotFoundException` is thrown. If the random-access file is constructed in read-write mode, then a zero-length file is created.

After a random-access file is constructed, you can seek to any byte position within the file and then read or write. Pre-Java systems (the C standard I/O library, for example) have supported seeking to a position relative to the beginning of the file, the end of the file, or the current position within the file. Java's random-access files only support seeking relative to the beginning of the file, but there are methods that report the current position and the length of the file, so you can effectively perform the other kinds of seek as long as you are willing to do the arithmetic.

The methods that support seeking are:

- `long getFilePointer() throws IOException`: This returns the current position within the file, in bytes. Subsequent reading and writing will take place starting at this position.

- `long length() throws IOException`: This returns the length of the file, in bytes.

- `void seek(long position) throws IOException`: This sets the current position within the file, in bytes. Subsequent reading and writing will take place starting at this position. Files start at position 0.

The code listed below is a subclass of `RandomAccessFile` that adds two new methods to support seeking from the current position or the end of the file. The code illustrates the use of the methods listed above.

```
1. class GeneralRAF extends RandomAccessFile {
2.    public GeneralRAF(File path, String mode)
3.       throws IOException {
```

```
4.        super(path, mode);
5.      }
6.
7.    public GeneralRAF(String path, String mode)
8.       throws IOException {
9.         super(path, mode);
10.     }
11.
12.   public void seekFromEnd(long offset)
13.      throws IOException {
14.        seek(length() - offset);
15.   }
16.
17.   public void seekFromCurrent(long offset)
18.      throws IOException {
19.        seek(getFilePointer() + offset);
20.   }
21. }
```

The whole point of seeking, of course, is to read from or write to a desired position within a file. All the reading and writing methods advance the current file position. Files are ordered collections of bytes, and the RandomAccess-File class has several methods that support reading and writing of bytes. However, the bytes in a file often combine to represent richer data formats. For example, two bytes could represent a Unicode character; four bytes could represent a float or an int.

The more common methods that support byte reading and writing are:

- int read() throws IOException: This returns the next byte from the file (stored in the low-order eight bits of an int) or −1 if at end of file.

- int read(byte dest[]) throws IOException: This attempts to read enough bytes to fill array dest[]. It returns the number of bytes read, or −1 if the file was at end of file.

- int read(byte dest[], int offset, int len) throws IOException: This attempts to read len bytes into array dest[], starting at offset. It returns the number of bytes read, or −1 if the file was at end of file.

- void write(int b) throws IOException: This writes the low-order byte of b.

- void write(byte b[]) throws IOException: writes all of byte array b[].

- void write(byte b[], int offset, int len) throws IOException: This writes len bytes from byte array b[], starting at offset.

Random-access files support reading and writing of all primitive data types. Each read or write operation advances the current file position by the number of bytes read or written. Table 13.1 presents the various primitive-oriented methods, all of which throw IOException.

TABLE 13.1   Random-Access File Methods for Primitive Data Types

Read Method	Write Method
boolean readBoolean()	void writeBoolean(boolean b)
byte readByte()	void writeByte(int b)
short readShort()	void writeShort(int s)
char readChar()	void writeChar(int c)
int readInt()	void writeInt(int i)
long readLong()	void writeLong(long l)
float readFloat()	void writeFloat(float f)
double readDouble()	void writeDouble(double d)
int readUnsignedByte()	None
int readUnsignedShort()	None
String readLine()	None
String readUTF()	void writeUTF(String s)

There are several more random-access file methods to support reading and writing of not-quite-primitive data types. These methods deal with unsigned bytes, unsigned shorts, lines of text, and UTF strings, as shown in Table 13.1.

When a random-access file is no longer needed, it should be closed:

```
void close() throws IOException
```

The `close()` method releases non-memory system resources associated with the file.

To summarize, random-access files offer the following functionality:

- Seeking to any position within a file

- Reading and writing single or multiple bytes

- Reading and writing groups of bytes, treated as higher-level data types

- Closing

Streams, Readers, and Writers

Java's stream, reader, and writer classes view input and output as ordered sequences of bytes. Of course, dealing strictly with bytes would be tremendously bothersome, because data appears sometimes as `bytes`, sometimes as `ints`, sometimes as `floats`, and so on. You have already seen how the `RandomAccessFile` class allows you to read and write all of Java's primitive data types. The `readInt()` method, for example, reads four bytes from a file, pieces them together, and returns an `int`. Java's general I/O classes provide a similar structured approach:

- A low-level output stream receives bytes and writes bytes to an output device.

- A high-level filter output stream receives general-format data, such as primitives, and writes bytes to a low-level output stream or to another filter output stream.

- A writer is similar to a filter output stream but is specialized for writing Java strings in units of Unicode characters.

- A low-level input stream reads bytes from an input device and returns bytes to its caller.

- A high-level filter input stream reads bytes from a low-level input stream, or from another filter input stream, and returns general-format data to its caller.

- A reader is similar to a filter input stream but is specialized for reading UTF strings in units of Unicode characters.

The stream, reader, and writer classes are not very complicated. The easiest way to review them is to begin with the low-level streams.

Low-Level Streams

Low-level input streams have methods that read input and return the input as bytes. *Low-level output streams* have methods that are passed bytes, and write the bytes as output. The FileInputStream and FileOutputStream classes are excellent examples.

The two most common file input stream constructors are:

- FileInputStream(String pathname)

- FileInputStream(File file)

After a file input stream has been constructed, you can call methods to read a single byte, an array of bytes, or a portion of an array of bytes. The functionality is similar to the byte-input methods you have already seen in the RandomAccessFile class:

- int read() throws IOException: This returns the next byte from the file (stored in the low-order eight bits of an int) or –1 if at end of file.

- int read(byte dest[]) throws IOException: This attempts to read enough bytes to fill array dest[]. It returns the number of bytes read or –1 if the file was at end of file.

- int read(byte dest[], int offset, int len) throws IOException: This attempts to read len bytes into array dest[], starting at offset. It returns the number of bytes read or –1 if the file was at end of file.

The code fragment below illustrates the use of these methods by reading a single byte into byte b, then enough bytes to fill byte array bytes[], and finally 20 bytes into the first 20 locations of byte array morebytes[].

```
1. byte b;
2. byte bytes[] = new byte[100];
3. byte morebytes[] = new byte[50];
4. try {
5.    FileInputStream fis = new FileInputStream("fname");
6.    b = (byte) fis.read();            // Single byte
7.    fis.read(bytes);                  // Fill the array
8.    fis.read(morebytes, 0, 20);       // 1st 20 elements
9.    fis.close();
10. }
11. catch (IOException e) { }
```

The FileInputStream class has a few very useful utility methods:

- int available() throws IOException: This returns the number of bytes that can be read without blocking.

- void close() throws IOException: This releases non-memory system resources associated with the file. A file input stream should always be closed when no longer needed.

- long skip(long nbytes) throws IOException: This attempts to read and discard nbytes bytes. Returns the number of bytes actually skipped.

It is not surprising that file output streams are almost identical to file input streams. The commonly used constructors are:

- FileOutputStream(String pathname)

- FileOutputStream(File file)

There are methods to support writing a single byte, an array of bytes, or a subset of an array of bytes:

- void write(int b) throws IOException: This writes the low-order byte of b.

- `void write(byte bytes[])` throws `IOException`: This writes all members of byte array `bytes[]`.

- `void write(byte bytes[], int offset, int len)` throws `IOException`: This writes `len` bytes from array `bytes[]`, starting at `offset`.

The `FileOutputStream` class also has a `close()` method, which should always be called when a file output stream is no longer needed.

In addition to the two classes described above, the `java.io` package has other low-level input and output stream classes:

- `InputStream` and `OutputStream`: These are the superclasses of the other low-level stream classes. They can be used for reading and writing network sockets.

- `ByteArrayInputStream` and `ByteArrayOutputStream`: These classes read and write arrays of bytes. Byte arrays are certainly not hardware I/O devices, but the classes are useful when you want to process or create sequences of bytes.

- `PipedInputStream` and `PipedOutputStream`: These classes provide a mechanism for synchronized communication between threads.

High-Level Filter Streams

It is all very well to read bytes from input devices and write bytes to output devices, if bytes are the unit of information you are interested in. However, more often than not the bytes to be read or written constitute higher-level information such as an `int` or a `string`.

Java supports high-level I/O with high-level streams. The most common of these (and the ones covered in this chapter) extend from the super-classes `FilterInputStream` and `FilterOutputStream`. *High-level input streams* do not read from input devices such as files or sockets; rather, they read from other streams. *High-level output streams* do not write to output devices, but to other streams.

A good example of a high-level input stream is the data input stream. There is only one constructor for this class:

- `DataInputStream(InputStream instream)`

The constructor requires you to pass in an input stream. This instance might be a file input stream (because FileInputStream extends Input-Stream), an input stream from a socket, or any other kind of input stream. When the instance of DataInputStream is called on to deliver data, it will make some number of read() calls on instream, process the bytes, and return an appropriate value. The commonly used input methods of the DataInputStream class are:

- boolean readBoolean() throws IOException
- byte readByte() throws IOException
- char readChar () throws IOException
- double readDouble () throws IOException
- float readFloat () throws IOException
- int readInt() throws IOException
- long readLong() throws IOException
- short readShort() throws IOException
- String readUTF() throws IOException

There is, of course, a close() method.

When creating chains of streams, it is recommended that you close all streams when you no longer need them, making sure to close in the reverse of the order in which the streams were constructed.

The code fragment below illustrates a small input chain:

```
1. try {
2.     // Construct the chain
3.     FileInputStream fis = new FileInputStream("fname");
4.     DataInputStream dis = new DataInputStream(fis);
5.
6.     // Read
7.     double d = dis.readDouble();
8.     int i = dis.readInt();
9.     String s = dis.readUTF();
```

```
10.
11.   // Close the chain
12.   dis.close();          // Close dis first, because it
13.   fis.close();          // was created last
14. }
15. catch (IOException e) { }
```

Figure 13.2 shows the hierarchy of the input chain.

FIGURE 13.2   A chain of input streams

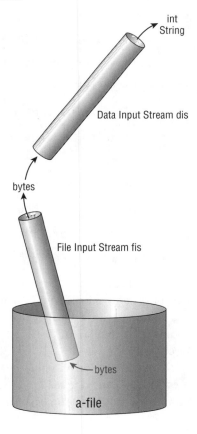

The code expects that the first eight bytes in the file represent a double, the next four bytes represent an int, and the next who-knows-how-many bytes represent a UTF string. This means that the code that originally created the file must have been writing a double, an int, and a UTF string. The file need not have been created by a Java program, but if it was, the easiest approach would be to use a data output stream.

The DataOutputStream class is the mirror image of the DataInput-Stream class. The constructor is:

- DataOutputStream(OutputStream ostream)

The constructor requires you to pass in an output stream. When you write to the data output stream, it converts the parameters of the write methods to bytes, and writes them to ostream. The commonly used output methods of the DataOutputStream class are:

- void writeBoolean(boolean b) throws IOException

- void writeByte(int b) throws IOException

- void writeBytes(String s) throws IOException

- void writeChar(int c) throws IOException

- void writeDouble(double d) throws IOException

- void writeFloat(float b) throws IOException

- void writeInt(int i) throws IOException

- void writeLong(long l) throws IOException

- void writeShort(int s) throws IOException

- void writeUTF(String s) throws IOException

All these methods convert their input to bytes in the obvious way, with the exception of writeBytes(), which writes out only the low-order byte of each character in its string. As usual, there is a close() method. Again, chains of output streams should be closed in reverse order from their order of creation.

With the methods listed above in mind, you can now write code that creates a file like the one read in the previous example. In that example, the file contained a double, an int, and a String. The file might be created as follows:

```
1. try {
2.     // Create the chain
3.     FileOutputStream fos = new FileOutputStream("txt");
```

```
4.    DataOutputStream dos = new DataOutputStream(fos);
5.
6.    // Write
7.    dos.writeDouble(123.456);
8.    dos.writeInt(55);
9.    dos.writeUTF("The moving finger writes");
10.
11.   // Close the chain
12.   dos.close();
13.   fos.close();
14. }
15. catch (IOException e) { }
```

In addition to data input streams and output streams, the java.io package offers several other high-level stream classes. The constructors for all high-level input streams require you to pass in the next-lower input stream in the chain; this will be the source of data read by the new object. Similarly, the constructors for the high-level output streams require you to pass in the next-lower output stream in the chain; the new object will write data to this stream. Some of the high-level streams are listed below:

- BufferedInputStream and BufferedOutputStream: These classes have internal buffers so that bytes can be read or written in large blocks, thus minimizing I/O overhead.

- PrintStream: This class can be asked to write text or primitives. Primitives are converted to character representations. The System.out and System.err objects are examples of this class.

- PushbackInputStream: This class allows the most recently read byte to be put back into the stream, as if it had not yet been read. This functionality is very useful for certain kinds of parsers.

It is possible to create stream chains of arbitrary length. For example, the code fragment below implements a data input stream that reads from a buffered input stream, which in turn reads from a file input stream:

```
1. FileInputStream f = new FileInputStream("text");
2. BufferedInputStream b = new BufferedInputStream(f);
3. DataInputStream d = new DataInputStream(b);
```

The chain that this code creates is shown in Figure 13.3.

FIGURE 13.3 A longer chain

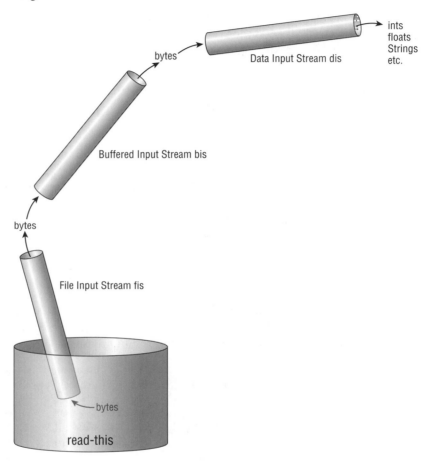

Readers and Writers

Readers and *writers* are like input and output streams: The low-level varieties communicate with I/O devices, while the high-level varieties communicate with low-level varieties. What makes readers and writers different is that they are exclusively oriented to Unicode characters.

A good example of a low-level reader is the `FileReader` class. Its commonly used constructors are:

- `FileReader(String pathname)`
- `FileReader(File file)`

Of course, any file passed into these constructors must genuinely contain UTF strings.

The corresponding writer is the `FileWriter` class:

- `FileWriter(String pathname)`
- `FileWriter(File file)`

The other low-level reader and writer classes are:

- `CharArrayReader` and `CharArrayWriter`: These classes read and write `char` arrays.

- `PipedReader` and `PipedWriter`: These classes provide a mechanism for thread communication.

- `StringReader` and `StringWriter`: These classes read and write strings.

The low-level readers all extend from the abstract `Reader` superclass. This class offers the now-familiar trio of `read()` methods for reading a single `char`, an array of `chars`, or a subset of an array of `chars`. Note, however, that the unit of information is now the `char`, not the `byte`. The three methods are:

- `int read() throws IOException`: This returns the next `char` (stored in the low-order 16 bits of the `int` return value) or −1 if at end of input.

- `int read(char dest[]) throws IOException`: This attempts to read enough `chars` to fill array `dest[]`. It returns the number of `chars` read or −1 if at end of input.

- `int read(char dest[], int offset, int len) throws IOException`: This attempts to read `len` chars into array `dest[]`, starting at `offset`. It returns the number of `chars` read or −1 if at end of input.

The low-level writers all extend from the abstract `Writer` superclass. This class provides methods that are a bit different from the standard trio of `write()` methods:

- `void write(int ch) throws IOException`: writes the `char` that appears in the low-order 16 bits of `ch`

- `void write(String str) throws IOException`: writes the string called `str`

- `void write(String str, int offset, int len) throws IOException`: writes the substring of `str` that begins at `offset` and has length `len`

- `void write(char chars[]) throws IOException`: writes the `char` array `chars[]`

- `void write(char chars[], int offset, int len) throws IOException`: writes `len` chars from array `chars[]`, beginning at `offset`

The high-level readers and writers all inherit from the `Reader` or `Writer` superclass, so they also support the methods listed above. As with high-level streams, when you construct a high-level reader or writer you pass in the next-lower object in the chain. The high-level classes are:

- `BufferedReader` and `BufferedWriter`: These classes have internal buffers so that data can be read or written in large blocks, thus minimizing I/O overhead. They are similar to buffered input streams and buffered output streams.

- InputStreamReader and OutputStreamWriter: These classes convert between streams of bytes and sequences of Unicode characters. By default, the classes assume that the streams use the platform's default character encoding; alternative constructors provide any desired encoding.

- LineNumberReader: This class views its input as a sequence of lines of text. A method called readLine() returns the next line, and the class keeps track of the current line number.

- PrintWriter: This class is similar to PrintStream, but it writes chars rather than bytes.

- PushbackReader: This class is similar to PushbackInputStream, but it reads chars rather than bytes.

The code fragment below chains a line number reader onto a file reader. The code prints each line of the file, preceded by a line number.

```
1. try {
2.    FileReader fr = new FileReader("data");
3.    LineNumberReader lnr = new LineNumberReader(fr);
4.    String s;
5.
6.    while ((s = lnr.readLine()) != null) {
7.       System.out.println(lnr.getLineNumber() +
8.       ": " + s);
9.    }
10.   lnr.close();
11.   fr.close();
12. }
13. catch (IOException x) { }
```

Figure 13.4 shows the reader chain implemented by this code.

FIGURE 13.4 A chain of readers

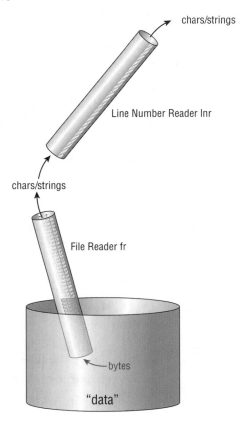

Encodings

The preceding discussion has carefully avoided a crucial point. Consider a file reader, which reads bytes from a file and returns strings of Unicode. How does the reader know how to translate an 8-bit character on the disk into a 16-bit character inside the JVM? Similarly, how does a file writer know how to translate a 16-bit Unicode character into an 8-bit byte?

The whole idea of readers and writers is that they connect the world inside the Java Virtual Machine, where characters are strictly 16-bit Unicode, to the external world, where text is historically presented as ordered sequences of bytes. Bytes represent different characters depending on where they appear in the world. There are only 256 bit combinations available in a byte; different languages and cultures map these combinations to different characters, and thus to different Unicode values. Readers and writers are sensitive to these linguistic and cultural differences.

An *encoding* is a mapping between eight-bit characters and Unicode. Figure 13.5 shows a few of the encodings that have been established by the Unicode Consortium. The figure is not drawn to scale. Note that some encodings are quite small (Greek requires only 144 Unicode values), while some are huge (more than 50,000 values for various Chinese, Japanese, and Korean characters; in the eight-bit world, such a character is represented by a sequence of multiple bytes).

FIGURE 13.5 Selected character encodings

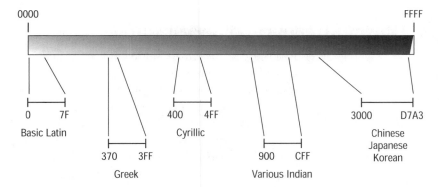

For an informative look at all Unicode mappings, see http://www.unicode.org. This is an outstanding Web site, with a minimum of extraneous graphic design and a maximum of well-organized, clearly presented information.

Most modern operating systems know what part of the world they are operating in—they are given this information when they are installed. The machine's locale is accessible to the Java Virtual Machine. By default, the encoding used by a reader or writer is the one appropriate to the machine's locale. However, readers and writers have forms of constructors that allow you to specify any desired locale. (A locale is specified by providing a string that identifies it.)

When the data written by a writer is to be read within the same locale, there is no need to consider what encoding to use; the default encoding will be appropriate. On the other hand, it may be that the data will cross a locale boundary. The writer might be connected to a socket, which communicates with a machine in a different locale. Or perhaps the writer is writing to a file on a floppy disk that will be carried across a boundary. In such cases the people involved must agree on an encoding; the common practice is to use the U.S. ASCII encoding. For programmers in the United States, this is conveniently the default. For others, it is necessary to specify this encoding when constructing readers and writers. The strings that denote encoding names are determined by standards committees, so they are not especially obvious or informative. For example, the U.S. ASCII encoding name is not "USASCII" as you might expect, but rather "ISO8859-1".

Object Streams and Serialization

Low-level streams, whether they are connected to disk files or to networks, provide byte-oriented I/O. Data input and output streams, when chained to low-level streams, provide a mechanism for reading and writing the other Java primitive data types: short, int, long, char, boolean, float, and double. Data input and output streams can also read and write Java strings. What is missing is a way to read and write general Java objects. This functionality is provided by object streams. These are not covered in the Programmer's Exam, but they are extremely useful, and knowledge of them will round out your understanding of Java's I/O. Moreover, if you intend to take the Developer's Exam, object streams are one option for your communication protocol.

Serialization is the process of breaking down a Java object and writing it out somewhere. The code fragment below shows how to serialize a Vector to a disk file:

```
1. try {
2.   FileOutputStream fos =
3.     new FileOutputStream("xx.ser");
4.   ObjectOutputStream oos =
5.     new ObjectOutputStream(fos);
6.   oos.writeObject(myVector);
7.   oos.close();
```

```
8.     fos.close();
9.  }
10. catch (IOException e) { }
```

There is much more to this code than meets the eye. What exactly gets transmitted when an object is serialized? First, be aware that only data is sent; the definition of the object's class is not serialized. Moreover, only certain data is sent. Static fields are not; neither are fields marked with the *transient* keyword. All other fields become part of the serialized object, whether they are primitives or object references.

This raises an interesting question. What should happen to object references? Consider the hypothetical Vector that is serialized on line 4 in the code sample above. Vectors contain references to other objects. Some of those objects may in turn contain references to still other objects, as illustrated in Figure 13.6. What should happen to such a network of referenced objects?

FIGURE 13.6 A network of objects

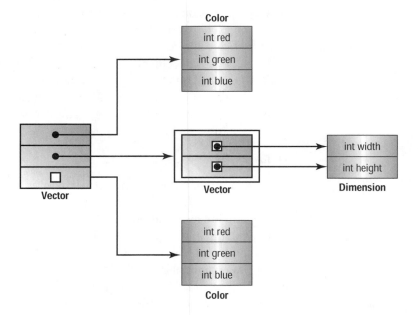

Fortunately, Java's object streams do the right thing (that is, the obvious and convenient thing): they recursively serialize all referenced objects. Thus when the Vector shown in Figure 13.6 is passed to an `ObjectOutput-Stream`, the data fields of two Vectors, two Points, and one Dimension are written out.

Reading a serialized object is straightforward. The code fragment below shows how to read the Vector shown in Figure 13.6, assuming it was written with the code fragment listed above.

```
1. try {
2.    FileInputStream fis = new FileInputStream ("xx.ser");
3.    ObjectInputStream ois = new ObjectInputStream (fis);
4.    Vector vec = (Vector)(ois.readObject());
5.    int b = ((Color)(vec.elementAt(2))).getBlue();
6.    ois.close();
7.    fis.close();
8. }
9. catch (IOException e) { }
```

Note the cast in line 4, which is required because the return type of `readObject()` is `Object`. Line 5 demonstrates how the elaborate connections among referenced objects are maintained during serialization and restored when the serialized object is read back.

Not every object is eligible for serialization. It makes no sense to serialize certain objects, such as file output streams or running threads. The argument type for the `writeObject()` method of `ObjectOutputStream` is not `Object` but `Serializable`. `Serializable` is an interface with the following surprising definition:

```
public interface Serializable { }
```

The interface contains no method signatures at all! An empty interface such as `Serializable` is known as a *tagging interface*. In order to make a class eligible for serialization, you have to tag it (or one of its superclasses) by stating that it implements `Serializable`. No other work is required; you do not have to implement any special methods. Most core Java classes implement the tagging interface, but `Object` does not. Thus, if you create a subclass of `Object` that you wish to have eligible for serialization, you will have to explicitly mark it as `implements Serializable`. This arrangement guarantees that classes are not by default serializable; programmers have to exert one quantum of deliberate effort to make their classes serializable.

Sockets

The Programmer's Exam objectives do not explicitly mention socket I/O, and the topic is beyond the scope of the exam. However, it is extremely useful to know about sockets, since they form the underlying infrastructure of many technologies, including object streams and RMI (Remote Method Invocation). If you are planning to eventually take the Developer's Exam, be aware that part of your project is required to use either object streams or RMI. Even if you do not plan to take the Developer's Exam in the near future, you may find the following information useful, as it rounds out what you learned in the previous section "Streams, Readers, and Writers."

A *socket* is an endpoint for TCP/IP communication. TCP/IP is a "reliable" protocol based on sending packets of binary data from one machine to another via a network. (It is tempting to say, "from one *computer* to another," but these days non-computer devices such as telephones and personal data assistants are also participating in TCP/IP communication. Many of these non-computer devices are powered by Java.)

The term *reliable* has a specific meaning in the context of network communication: it means that all data packets will eventually be delivered to the recipient, and will be delivered in the correct order. Reliability makes sockets ideal for situations where perfect delivery of data is the primary consideration. In some applications, such as live streaming audio or video, the performance cost of reliability is excessive, and faster, less reliable protocols should be considered.

A good metaphor for a TCP/IP interaction is a telephone call. With telephone communication, one person initiates the call. After the other person answers the phone, both parties communicate symmetrically, using similar equipment. Either person may hang up at any time. With TCP/IP communication, one machine (the client) takes the initiative to contact the other machine (the server). After communication is established, each machine uses an instance of the Socket class to provide input and output resources. At any time, either machine may terminate the connection.

It is reasonable to expect that a server machine may wish to provide more than one kind of service. For example, a server may wish to provide a time/date service, a stock-quote service, and an HTTP daemon (HTTPD) service. There needs to be a mechanism for distinguishing among service destinations on a single server. Ports are the abstraction that supports this mechanism.

Even if a server only has one physical network connection, it creates the illusion of offering a large number of connection destinations. These different destinations are known as *ports*, and each is identified with an integer. For example, HTTP daemons typically offer service on port 80. Figure 13.7 illustrates a server that offers time/date, stock-quote, and HTTPD services, each on its own port.

FIGURE 13.7 A TCP/IP server offering three services

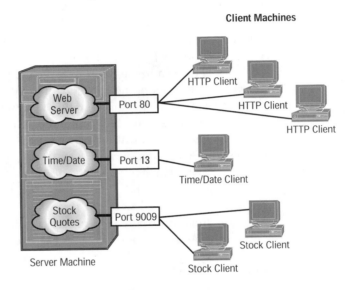

Thus, a server machine does not just offer a service. It offers a service on a particular port; or it may offer several or many services, each on its own port. A client machine does not just connect to a server; it connects to a port on a server. Figure 13.7 shows the HTTP service being offered on port 80, the Time/Date service on port 13, and the Stock Quote service on port 9009. Notice that multiple clients are permitted on a port; this is where the telephone-call metaphor breaks down. On the server, each client connection is represented by a Socket instance.

When a client wants to connect to a server, it creates an instance of java.io.Socket. The most common form of the constructor takes two arguments: the hostname of the server machine, and the desired port number. For example:

```
Socket sock = new Socket("brightwind", 9898);
```

The code above attempts to construct a socket that connects to port 9898 on server "brightwind." An `IOException` will be thrown if something goes wrong: if, for example, brightwind is not really offering a service on port 9898, or if brightwind's network hardware is down. The call to the `Socket` constructor blocks until the connection is established or an exception is thrown; if the server is popular, it could take a while for the constructor to return.

After you obtain a socket, you can retrieve from it an input stream and an output stream for reading and writing:

```
Socket sock = new Socket("brightwind", 9898);
InputStream is = sock.getInputStream();
OutputStream os = sock.getOutputStream();
```

These streams are similar to file input and file output streams. The only real difference is that they read and write the network, rather than a disk file. The input stream has three `read()` methods that return a byte, an array of bytes, and a portion of an array of bytes. The output stream has three `write()` methods that write out a byte, an array of bytes, and a portion of an array of bytes. Figure 13.8 shows a socket and its connections to internal software and the external world.

FIGURE 13.8   A socket

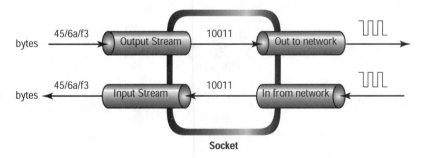

As with file input and output streams, the streams provided by a socket are of limited usefulness. Dealing with network bytes is every bit as clunky as dealing with disk bytes. Fortunately, the high-level filter streams that were introduced earlier in this chapter can be used with *any* variety of low-level I/O stream. Thus, as shown in the code fragment below, you can chain a

DataOutputStream onto a socket's output stream, and a DataInputStream onto a socket's input stream. The other subclasses of FilterInputStream and FilterOutputStream can be chained in a similar way.

```
1. try {
2.    Socket sock = new Socket(brightwind, 9898);
3.    InputStream is = sock.getInputStream();
4.    DataInputStream dis = new DataInputStream(is);
5.    int i = dis.readInt();
6.    double d = dis.readDouble();
7.    OutputStream os = sock.getOutputStream();
8.    DataOutputStream dos = new DataOutputStream(os);
9.    dos.writeUTF("Hello web world.");
10.   dos.writeBoolean(false);
11.   dos.close();
12.   os.close();
13. }
14. catch (IOException e) { }
```

Figure 13.9 shows high-level filter streams chained to a socket's input and output streams.

FIGURE 13.9   A socket with filter streams

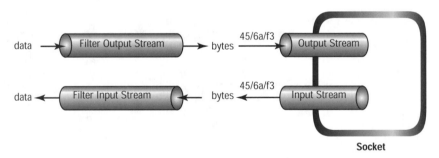

Chapter Summary

This chapter has covered several big ideas of Java's I/O support:

- Inside a Java Virtual Machine, text is represented by 16-bit Unicode characters and strings. For I/O, text may be represented by UTF strings. If text is to be translated between classical 8-bit and Unicode 16-bit representations, then an encoding must be provided.

- The File class is useful for navigating the local file system.

- The RandomAccessFile class lets you read and write at arbitrary places within a file.

- Input streams, output streams, readers, and writers provide a mechanism for creating input and output chains. Input and output streams operate on bytes; readers and writers operate on chars. The low-level classes interact directly with the outside world; Higher-level classes communicate with low-level classes and with other higher-level classes. Two of the most sophisticated higher-level classes are ObjectOutputStream and ObjectInputStream, which write and read entire objects.

Test Yourself

1. Which of the statements below are true? (Choose none, some, or all.)

    A. UTF characters are all 8 bits.

    B. UTF characters are all 16 bits.

    C. UTF characters are all 24 bits.

    D. Unicode characters are all 16 bits.

    E. Bytecode characters are all 16 bits.

    F. None of the above.

2. Which of the statements below are true? (Choose none, some, or all.)

    A. When you construct an instance of `File`, if you do not use the file-naming semantics of the local machine, the constructor will throw an `IOException`.

    B. When you construct an instance of `File`, if the corresponding file does not exist on the local file system, one will be created.

    C. When an instance of `File` is garbage collected, the corresponding file on the local file system is deleted.

    D. None of the above.

3. True or False: The `File` class contains a method that changes the current working directory.

    A. True

    B. False

4. True or False: It is possible to use the `File` class to list the contents of the current working directory.

    A. True

    B. False

5. How many bytes does the following code write to file `dest`?

```
1. try {
2.     FileOutputStream fos = new FileOutputStream("dest");
3.     DataOutputStream dos = new DataOutputStream(fos);
4.     dos.writeInt(3);
5.     dos.writeDouble(0.0001);
6.     dos.close();
7.     fos.close();
8. }
9. catch (IOException e) { }
```

A. 2

B. 8

C. 12

D. 16

E. The number of bytes depends on the underlying system.

6. What does the following code fragment print out at line 9?

```
1. FileOutputStream fos = new FileOutputStream("xx");
2. for (byte b=10; b<50; b++)
3.     fos.write(b);
4. fos.close();
5. RandomAccessFile raf = new RandomAccessFile("xx", "r");
6. raf.seek(10);
7. int i = raf.read();
8. raf.close()
9. System.out.println("i = " + i);
```

A. The output is i = 30.

B. The output is i = 20.

C. The output is i = 10.

D. There is no output because the code throws an exception at line 1.

E. There is no output because the code throws an exception at line 5.

7. A file is created with the following code:

```
1. FileOutputStream fos = new FileOutputStream("datafile");
2. DataOutputStream dos = new DataOutputStream(fos);
3. for (int i=0; i<500; i++)
4.   dos.writeInt(i);
```

You would like to write code to read back the data from this file. Which solutions listed below will work?

A. Construct a `FileInputStream`, passing the name of the file. Onto the `FileInputStream`, chain a `DataInputStream`, and call its `readInt()` method.

B. Construct a `FileReader`, passing the name of the file. Call the file reader's `readInt()` method.

C. Construct a `PipedInputStream`, passing the name of the file. Call the piped input stream's `readInt()` method.

D. Construct a `RandomAccessFile`, passing the name of the file. Call the random access file's `readInt()` method.

E. Construct a `FileReader`, passing the name of the file. Onto the `FileReader`, chain a `DataInputStream`, and call its `readInt()` method.

8. True or False: Readers have methods that can read and return `floats` and `doubles`.

A. True

B. False

9. You execute the code below in an empty directory. What is the result?

```
1. File f1 = new File("dirname");
2. File f2 = new File(f1, "filename");
```

A. A new directory called `dirname` is created in the current working directory.

B. A new directory called `dirname` is created in the current working directory. A new file called `filename` is created in directory `dirname`.

C. A new directory called di rname and a new file called fi lename are created, both in the current working directory.

D. A new file called fi lename is created in the current working directory.

E. No directory is created, and no file is created.

10. What is the result of attempting to compile and execute the code fragment below? Assume that the code fragment is part of an application that has write permission in the current working directory. Also assume that before execution, the current working directory does *not* contain a file called datafile.

```
1. try {
2.    RandomAccessFile raf = new
3.       RandomAccessFile("datafile" ,"rw");
4.    BufferedOutputStream bos = new
5.       BufferedOutputStream(raf);
6.    DataOutputStream dos = new
7.       DataOutputStream(bos);
8.    dos.writeDouble(Math.PI);
9.    dos.close();
10.   bos.close();
11.   raf.close();
12. }
13. catch (IOException e) { }
```

A. The code fails to compile.

B. The code compiles, but throws an exception at line 4.

C. The code compiles and executes, but has no effect on the local file system.

D. The code compiles and executes; afterward, the current working directory contains a file called datafile.

The Developer's Exam

Chapter

14

Taking the Developer's Exam

The first thing you should know about the Java 2 Developer's Exam is that it is practical rather than objective. In an industry where certification testing almost always boils down to multiple-choice questions, term/definition matching, short answers, and true/false statements—the mainstays of evaluating competence cost-effectively—practical exams are rare. But there are good reasons for them beyond cost. In a timed multiple-choice test, for example, the answer to each question can be "normalized," or designed so it not only provides the correct answer but also elicits it, unambiguously, with the right question. The average response time (difficulty level) can be assessed in trials, so that the candidate faces a reasonable number of questions for the time allotted, receives the same opportunity as everyone else, and so on.

In a practical exam, the test candidate aims for a more general result: "Make this thing work." A few application vendors use such exams for their resellers or field engineers as a test of applied skills, but typically the time given in such cases is liberal or even left to the candidate's discretion. Certain skills or resources, such as keyboard thinking, that a timed, restricted environment might negate or prohibit become more useful, allowing some candidates greater comfort while under stress to perform. These exams are not evenhanded in the sense of being rigidly standardized and always applied under the same conditions, but at the same time, each candidate is generally free to draw upon familiar tools to solve a problem. Of course, there is a catch. Practical exams, particularly project assignments, have more requirements to fulfill and depend on a broader range of skills—rather than knowledge and reasoning—to fulfill them. Candidates must rehearse the kinds of skills expected in field situations and similar to the ones the practical test suggests. Moreover, as is often true in the field, process matters just as much as the finished product. Guessing strategies are far less helpful.

For people who prefer projects over knowledge-based examinations, the Developer's Exam is ideal (although you still must pass the Programmer's Exam as a prerequisite). Because it is broad in scope and because there are few industry exams like it, we will review the concepts and expectations of the exam in some detail. We'll use a scenario similar to the one the Developer's Exam offers as a guide to understanding what is required and how to approach the test—by breaking down its component parts and building them into a working whole. The certification process at this level costs a few hundred dollars, so it is certainly worth your while to assess your readiness.

Are You Ready for the Exam?

You can deduce from the guides to the Programmer's Exam in this book that Sun does not want to confer pro forma certifications. The candidates for that exam are expected to know the core libraries, operators, and compile-time and runtime behaviors well enough to recognize flawed code when they read it and to anticipate the errors such code will generate. In an era when many of us use the compiler to point out flaws in our code, that's a skill that may require honing at first. Most programmers don't set out to write lots of flawed code and see what happens; however, they accomplish this readily in everyday practice. But it is everyday practice that will best complement the use of this guide.

Again, this Certification Exam is a practical one. The test challenges your ability to use Java in conjunction with the skills, experience, and discipline required of any competent programmer. If Java has been your sole focus for more than a year and you have a bit more experience on development projects using Java or some other language—ideally an object-oriented one—little of what you see in the programming assignment or follow-up exam should be too surprising. Even if some requirements represent new territory, there's no time limit, so the opportunity to learn one or two things as you go should not represent a hardship.

It should therefore come as no surprise that getting the code to execute correctly merely initiates the grading process. Professional developers must be able to justify their designs, recognize strengths and weaknesses in their solutions, translate those principles correctly into code, and document their work clearly for the benefit of future programmers and maintainers. In that spirit, this guide focuses on strategy and design choices more than fully coded solutions, in order to demonstrate the various tasks the exam presents and provide a conceptual model for developing the solution. Your ability to write the code is assumed, and in fact, several code exercises are left to the reader as preparatory exercises.

The reason code-level solutions are not always included is simple: The exam itself has as many right answers as there are justifiable ways of solving them. The exam does not hint at or beg for an ideal solution. Rather, you must design and implement the assignment project in a manner sufficient to you. The code must pass a functional test, which, as anyone might guess, cannot verify all possible solutions. Finally, you must explain how your code works in two ways: by demonstrating knowledge of some other approaches and by explaining what benefits and penalties derive from the one applied.

If you are confident in your experience and only want a feel for the structure of the assignment, feel free to browse the chapters now and get the lay of the land. Chapter 15 introduces a sample project (we will say more about this in a bit) and offers a means for analyzing and breaking down the requirements. Chapters 16 through 18 each address the major topics—the database/server, networking, and creating a client module. Chapters 19 through 23 go over the exam again, but in more detail and less overview, using a different sample assignment. Chapter 24 poses several questions to stimulate your thinking about design. The focus in this final chapter is oriented toward tenable design. Of course, you are free to write an implementation as practice; it is certainly less expensive to practice here than on the exam itself.

Listed below are a few general questions to spur your thinking as you assess your readiness:

- Do you write Java code three or more days a week?

- How many applications have you completed based only on written instructions?

- Name one or two principles of effective user interface design.

- How many threaded applications have you written? Client-server? Database-oriented?

- Recall your last experience of being assigned an incomplete project, including undocumented code and missing source files. How did you work through those problems?

- What risks are involved with a remote client locking a record on a database?

- For storing data in memory, when does it make sense to use an array? A `Vector`? A `Hashtable`? A `List`?

- What are the relative merits of using Remote Method Invocation (RMI), object serialization, or some ad hoc data format for network communication?

- How is a two-tier client-server scheme different from three-tier?

Some of these questions are the basis for discussion in the following chapters. If they seem intimidating, review the following chapters with some care.

The exam may prove to be quite a challenge if many of the discussions you see ahead are unfamiliar. Precise knowledge of Java's core operations and class libraries, which is required to pass the Programmer's Exam, will carry you some of the way. The single best preparation for getting certified as a Developer, however, is meaningful experience with Java development, ideally by completing tasks put to you by someone else. We cannot emphasize enough the value of good programming habits and experience in taking on a moderately complex programming task with only written instructions for guidance and no real-world pressure to finish (other than forfeiting the registration fee).

Sun offers a five-day course, called Java Programming Language Workshop, which is well suited to preparing students for this certification. The course is numbered SL-285; the course description can be viewed by pointing your browser to http://suned.sun.com/courses/SL-285.html.

Sun also offers courses specific to major areas of the exam, but these are not defined as certification courses. You may also wish to browse SL-320, GUI Construction with Swing and JFC, and SL-301, Distributed Programming with Java, which treats RMI in detail.

Formalities of the Exam

The Developer's Certification Exam has two parts: a project assignment and a follow-up exam. The assignment describes a programming task that starts with some code supplied with the project description; you are then asked to finish the intended project. Some portions of the final code are to be written from scratch, some must extend or apply provided interfaces or classes, and some must modify incomplete or rudimentary classes. The requirements will also indicate areas of the application that you are not required to finish; to keep the test within reasonable limits, no one will be asked to create a robust, user-tolerant, business-grade application using the code provided. In fact, solving more problems than the assignment requires may actually create problems in examining your work. To keep testing simple, the assignment constrains some areas by disallowing certain approaches (for example, CORBA) or by simply limiting them (say, RMI or object serialization). As further discouragement against going too far afield, a solution that works but duplicates resources readily available in the core libraries may be scored lower.

The follow-up exam, which takes place in a timed and proctored test facility, has at least three aspects. The objective aspect deals with knowledge of Java's features and libraries. For example, you might be asked to list some data structures useful for storing an indeterminate number of runtime objects and then asked to explain the advantages each of those structures offers relative to the others. The practical aspect of the exam focuses on your knowledge and understanding of your own code (yes, this is a check to make sure you've done the work), asking you to offer one or two cases where you made a certain choice and what you decided on. Finally, in the subjective aspect, you may be asked to justify that choice. Perhaps you did not pick the fastest or most efficient data structure. What did you pick, and why? The right answer, in this last case, will be one that demonstrates that your choices were made in a conscious and reasonable way, regardless of whether the grader of the test might have done the same thing. It's important to bear in mind that this is not an exercise in anticipating what Sun wants Java programmers to think. You should not second-guess your own judgment if your design suits you.

Nonetheless, the reality of open-ended practical exams is that grading can become subjective. Process does matter. So while getting your application to run properly doesn't guarantee certification, it's a bare minimum for getting to that point. But it isn't worthwhile to dwell for very long on the idea of "subjective grading." There are a few compensating factors:

- The weight allotted to each part of the assignment evaluation, and the categories of evaluation, are included in the assignment.

- The time limit of the exam is the life of the exam's administration.

- This guide will help you to broaden your inquiry into the skills needed to succeed.

Downloading the Assignment

Once you pay the registration fee for the Developer's Exam, Sun will enter your name in their Certification Database; you may have to wait a day for this to process.

Full details on the Developer's Exam for Java 2 are available by browsing http://suned.sun.com/usa/cert_test.html or by calling Sun Educational Services at (800) 422-8020.

Once the assignment is ready, you can download it by logging in to the database through your browser. Be sure to save the downloaded bundle to a backup right away; the site is not set up to allow repeated downloads. The bundle you receive will include the project description, some source and class files, and instructions for submitting the finished work back to Sun.

You'll need your assigned student ID as a password. The login page is located at http://www.galton.com/~sun. You can verify your Programmer's Exam score and certification here as well. While you are there, you may also want to check the contact information this database has for you and make sure it is correct.

Taking the Follow-up Exam

Sun does not review your assignment until you complete the essay examination. This portion requires an additional fee payable to Sun, which will issue you an exam voucher. The voucher is used to reserve testing space at any Sylvan Prometric center, which administers the exam. As seating is limited in most centers, and the exams are scheduled ahead of time for download to a testing computer, reservations are essential (call 1-800-795-3926). The time limit is 90 minutes. See the above section "Formalities of the Exam" for an overview of what this exam is like.

The finished assignment will be relatively complex, and you will not have the luxury of bringing any notes into the exam room. It's a good idea to submit the assignment as soon as you have it working and to take the follow-up quickly thereafter, while the code is still fresh in your mind.

What the Assignment Covers

Chapter 15 illustrates, through a mock assignment, what the actual project might address. In short, you'll be asked to take an existing database scheme and enhance its features by adding one or more new functions. The database may require support for user access (local, remote, or both), concurrent users, and a client GUI to facilitate ease-of-use. To accomplish these tasks—to integrate them and design something flexible enough to make future improvements easy to implement—requires a practical command of these areas:

- TCP/IP networking
- I/O streams
- Swing
- The AWT event model
- Object serialization
- RMI
- javadoc
- Packages
- Threads
- Interfaces

Some of the elements listed here may not appear on the exam or may have already been established for you; familiarity in that topic area may be all that you need. For example, one or two interfaces may be provided that you are simply required to implement. On other elements, the assignment may dictate how you may apply these elements to the project, typically to help standardize the grading process or to ensure that the finished code compiles.

How the Assignment and Exam Are Graded

Review of the assignment begins once the follow-up exam is completed and forwarded to a Sun-appointed grader. The grader tests the submitted application code by hand; failure to clear this phase automatically concludes the evaluation. If you have tested your code before submitting it, however, this step should be a formality. The grader then examines the source code along with the answers given in the follow-up exam. Good source-writing style, adequate documentation, clarity of design, judicious use of the core libraries, and the consistency of the follow-up essays with the assignment all fall under review.

Sun estimates that grading takes four weeks from the date they receive the follow-up exam. The values assigned to each part of the grading criteria are listed in the downloaded assignment documentation, but here are the general parameters:

- API-style documentation; proper use of comment code

- Use of standard library features and algorithms

- Applying conventional object-oriented programming techniques

- GUI meets requirements, follows principles for effective human–computer interaction

- Event-handling mechanisms are appropriate

- Data operations are threadsafe

- Code layout is clear, maintainable, and consistent and follows expected formatting guidelines

JDK 1.2 Specifics

If you have taken the Developer's Exam for JDK 1.1, the structure of the exam does not change that much for you in this version. The change from Java 1.1 to 2, however, is a different matter. The new additions, such as Swing, add considerable depth and richness to areas where the JDK had been perceived as anemic. Improvements to existing facilities are broad as well. The following list describes those areas most relevant to the exam, including topics that will be required to complete the exam.

Swing

Swing is required for writing the client GUI. Swing's dependence on the AWT Component class, layout managers, and event-handling structure means that skill with those elements is still necessary (we include discussions of important topics on both packages). If you have paid relatively little attention to Swing so far, bear in mind that it is more than a larger library of widgets unencumbered by the AWT native-peer component strategy. The internal architecture of Swing components is quite different from the AWT; this design pattern is widely referred to as a Model-View-Controller (MVC) implementation. For the sake of argument, we refer to this structure as "View-Controller-Model" or "model-delegate" because we believe these clarify the relations between the pieces.

To make the inclusion of Swing meaningful and to make grading manageable, the requirements for building the GUI will be more general than in previous test versions. Rather than build a menu that looks exactly like the one pictured or decipher which layout managers are involved in a picture of a sample frame resizing, you will assume responsibility for good design. These points are also discussed in Chapters 18 and 21. You will still control your aesthetic choices, in addition to demonstrating your knowledge of the components available.

Collections

Java 2 has stepped up considerably in its offering of container classes in java.util. The package now includes several classes, initially made available as an add-on to the JDK 1.1, called the Collections framework. This framework abstracts the major operations of all container classes and provides a mechanism for, among other things, moving data from one container type to another with very little programming effort. Vector and Hashtable have been retrofitted into the Collections scheme as well, and a new class, Arrays, now supports methods for sorting, filling, and treating an array like a list. The Enumeration interface has an eventual successor, Iterator, which maps back to the container, offering a tighter binding during most element-level operations. Certain other classes like Dictionary are still around but slated for oblivion.

One key issue to examine with respect to these classes is how to implement multithreading. There are at least two schools of thought on performance and multithreading. One school suggests that serializing access to these containers—which requires a single method call—offers credible performance. Other imminent developments to increase VM performance on lower-level operations will justify trading optimal performance designs for the ease of maintaining synchronized-container code. The other school wants to realize the full efficiency of multithreaded performance wherever it can. Synchronizing on the container is fine for small structures with few records, but as the data scales to large proportions, the only feasible solution to keeping performance high is record-level access.

We cover the issues concerning both camps in Chapters 16 and 17.

Data Formatting for Communications

The assignment will require that you fashion some means for communicating between the server and the client. The only constant principle in the exam, with respect to networking, is that the client must operate in a separate VM from the server and the back-end application it supports. There are really three choices to consider: use serialization, RMI, or a combination of the two. In the guide, these techniques will be demonstrated simply and on their own, to help illustrate their differences and to stimulate further thinking on which approach offers the greatest advantage for a given task. Much like the discussion surrounding containers and multithreading, this design approach can mostly be reduced to choosing flexibility or ease of coding and maintenance, along a few lines.

Object serialization and RMI have both undergone important changes. Given the practical limits and expectations of testing, it is unlikely most of these new features will be involved in completing the programming assignment.

The change history for the Java Object Serialization Specification is available with the documentation download. From the base docs directory, the path to the index is docs/guide/serialization/index.html. The documents are also available online. Put http://java.sun.com/products/jdk/1.2/ in front of the previous path to access it.

On the slight chance that the assignment requires an "activatable" object (a new RMI extension) or a custom socket factory to enable protocols like SSL, the JDK tutorials are both detailed and populated with sample code.

These tutorials are recommended for experienced RMI users, however, so they are worth reviewing in advance. Remember that the aim of the Developer's Exam is to test your skills on a reasonably sized problem set, not to make you write code on every new feature. Examples of RMI implementations with and without activation appear in Chapter 22.

Browse `docs/guide/rmi/index.html` relative to a local or online documentation set, as shown above, for details on RMI enhancements.

With that qualification in mind, the follow-up exam may be an ideal place to express awareness of these features and apply that awareness to your justification of a design solution for the project assignment. If knowing that distributed garbage collection or the ability to activate an RMI server from a remote VM is reason enough to design a solution that can take advantage of them, then by all means proceed. In open-ended assignments such as this one, some developers will go beyond the stated requirements of the exam to write something "meaningful." That is OK to a point—that point being to make sure the grader can certify your code, so long as the effort is qualified by correct facts and justified by the proper view in the follow-up exam. In Chapter 17, however, the discussion will stay focused on the modest boundaries of completing the project to satisfaction.

Documentation and *javadoc*

There are five additional documentation tags in Java 2 to be aware of. Three, in particular, help to document object serialization code for those who employ object serialization in their designs.

@link   Links a name (package, class, interface, constructor, field, method) to a label, or hyperlinked text. Unlike the @see tag, {link} formats the label where it occurs in the comment code, instead of moving it to a "See Also" subheading.

@serial   For use in documenting a field that is already serialized.

@serialData   For use in documenting the order and type of objects in a serial stream. Recommended particularly for use with `writeObject()`, `readObject()`, `writeExternal()`, and `readExternal()` calls.

@serialField   For use in documenting objects of type `ObjectStreamField`, a descriptor class that identifies the characteristics of a each serializable field for a given class.

@throws   Synonymous with the `@exception` tag, provided for semantic convenience.

Not to be left behind in the quest for ubiquitous flexibility and choice, `javadoc` now supports a pluggable output scheme called *doclets*, intended for technical writers who want to target another document format, such as XML, for their standard. Expect no requirement in this area, but there's lots of online information on the subject. Browse `http://java.sun.com/products/jdk/1.2/docs/tooldocs/javadoc/` for more.

Chapter

15

Assignment: Room Reservation System

This chapter describes a programming assignment similar in style to the actual project assignment. The assignment itself is intended to be neither a mystery nor an exercise in reading between the lines of the project description. The scenario is provided as a motivation to write the code and offer a basis for justifying your implementation.

At the same time, you should not try to infer much beyond what you see on the page. No portion of the exam will ask, for instance, whether you considered this or that aspect of the business case given when you devised your threading model. On the other hand, you should know whether your code fares well or poorly if, say, the data model scales from one or two hundred to tens of thousands of records.

Structure of the Assignment

The stated objectives of the Developer's Exam will read something like the following:

- Write an application program using Java 2, with the following component parts:

  - A user interface utilizing specified component elements and conforming to general principles of human interaction.

  - A network connection, using a specified protocol, to connect to an information server that supplies the data for display in the user interface.

  - A multithreaded, threadsafe network server, which connects to a previously specified Java database.

  - An application created by extending the functionality of a previously written piece of code, for which only limited documentation is available. This application may take the form of a flat-file database or some other application that can be modeled simply in pure Java.

- List some of the significant design choices to be made during the implementation of the application.

- List some of the main advantages and disadvantages of each of these design choices.

- Briefly justify choices made in terms of the comparison of design and implementation objectives with the advantages and disadvantages of each.

Our purpose here is simply to familiarize you with the conditions of the exam. It starts out with some nearly completed code for a database scheme, based on a business scenario. Your job is broken down into a series of tasks, which may include some or all of the following:

- Supply the "missing feature" to the database scheme; this may be a field-level search capability, a sort routine to support advanced queries, or possibly a record-locking mechanism.

- Write a debugging or conversion tool that will output the current contents into human-readable text and/or import a valid text file into the data format.

- Implement the network protocol without benefit of the underlying source. This "protocol" may be nothing more than the pre-compiled interface file and an API-style HTML page made available.

- Write a GUI-based client to access the database. Count on using only Swing components. Since we can certainly expect to display records, a JTable is an obvious consideration.

Certain variations may occur from one assignment to the next, and certain underlying files may vary accordingly. This step is a check against sharing with or receiving assignment files and tasks from other candidates, as there is no time limit and no way to monitor the work before submission.

In short, the assignment's test of functional proficiency is in completing a project with multiple, interrelated tasks, despite any limitations imposed by the initial code. The test of overall proficiency is in writing code that is clear, concise, and relatively easy to interpret through its generated API documentation. One aim the candidate should have in mind is to produce code that a less-experienced programmer could read and maintain with a working knowledge of the language and the use of standard Java references and conventions.

The actual Developer's Exam assignment will provide scoring criteria, instructions for submitting the exam, and other administrative details that this book does not cover. Those sections relevant to our discussion are:

- A business scenario to create the assignment's context

- Some project specifics to stimulate thoughts on design

- An overall project goal

- A requirements breakdown for each portion of the assignment

Business Scenario

Mobile Conferencing Services is a startup firm that leases meeting rooms by the day. The meeting rooms vary in type, number, and housing facility from location to location, and are currently available to subscribing customers by calling a sales rep and making a reservation. In response to customer requests for faster service, Mobile Conferencing wants to automate their reservation process. They ultimately want to develop an on-site kiosk where their representatives and clients can reserve and confirm meeting rooms and dates. Clients have also expressed interest in being able to schedule rooms from their desks, home offices, or hotel rooms. To provide that level of service but avoid the cost of an expensive network infrastructure, the company wants to explore using the Internet, but prefers to develop a dedicated client tool.

Mobile Conferencing's current IT employee has already written a rudimentary database scheme in Java, as a way to familiarize himself with the language and prove Java's usability for the overall development effort. This scheme was suitable for stub-testing. However, inexperience with object-oriented development and more urgent projects have made it necessary for him to outsource the next phase of development. Mindful of the cost of outside development, the company president wants the project to incorporate all the code written so far. Meanwhile, the IT "staff" will be engaged in a rollout of desktop systems at several remote facilities, so a developer who can work independently, using only written instructions as a guide, is a must.

Project Specifics

To make the exam manageable and testable, some advisories that narrow the scope of the assignment may appear in or after the scenario. Here are a likely set of constraints as a part of the business rationale.

Through the client tool, the user should be able to determine, for any one location, how many rooms are available, what type of meeting rooms that facility has, and the daily lease rate. In this phase of the project, each facility will offer one type of room, all at the same lease rate, and customer information will not be included. User/password login validation will be implemented at a later date.

The initial database schema assumes single-user access to the kiosk (and therefore the local database) at one time. Strong customer demand for remote access to the reservation tool has added a requirement for a network server to front the database. The developer will have to devise the protocol for network communications and implement it from scratch. Since funding for this phase of the project is limited, the company expresses no technological preference for the implementation method.

Like many startups, Mobile Conferencing is unsure of its future growth projections. Currently they have as many as four dozen rooms at one site and about 100 sites. They may decide to host all databases on a single server at some point, using their current kiosks as remote clients.

In discussing interface design meetings, the IT staff expressed dissatisfaction with the limited components available in the AWT library. They avoided third-party libraries to keep the code in-house. The project was finally shelved until Swing could be fully reviewed. Now that Swing is ready, they want certain components included in the interface. They also intend to review the completed GUI to ensure they can easily maintain and extend it.

Code and APIs Provided

The code supplied with the project assignment will largely consist of concrete code, rather than a skeletal design that must first be implemented. With respect to the database scheme, this means that certain choices, such as the underlying Collections type, will be predetermined, along with the fundamental methods for reading from and writing to the database. Method signatures for the enhancements you are required to add may already be defined as well. You may have to subclass the code provided or add the missing code to it, so we'll address both situations in the next chapter.

An implementation-independent schema might look like this:

```
public interface DataBase {
    public Field[] getFields();
    public int recordTotal();
    public Record getRecord(int recID);
    public Record[] find(String matchItem);
    public void addRecord(String [] newData);
    public void modifyRecord(Record changes);
    public void deleteRecord(Record delete);
    public void close();
}
```

This prototype view is for the sake of illustration. Obviously, we cannot define important constructors or protected methods—which could nonetheless be designed independent of implementation—in an interface; but we wanted to keep this preview tight and defer fleshing out an abstract or concrete class until the next chapter. Even though you won't have to develop schema code of your own, you can see in the above interface what a simple Java schema might amount to. The object types' names are self-explanatory. Those who want more flexibility may balk at defining an `int` for a record number in `getRecord()`. We could of course specify `recID` as an `Object`, arguing that it makes more sense to use a wrapper class to get an `int`. Alternatively, we might overload `getRecord()` in a concrete subclass and call the provided method signature from there. These are both useful observations to apply to the follow-up exam, so keep a critical eye toward such factors as you consider how you will complete the project. Chapter 16 includes a walkthrough of building the initial database scheme, then provides a method for fulfilling the current requirements, as a guide for anticipating the problems you'll inherit from the supplied code.

The project will also incorporate a package structure to logically divide the functional areas of the project. Packaging should pose no particular difficulties with respect to the scope of existing code; you should observe the vanilla rules of encapsulation unless there is an unavoidable reason to do otherwise (performance or the ease of direct field access are not good reasons to offer). In case you are consulting a variety of materials to prepare for the exam, note that the terms "friendly" and "package private" both refer to the same thing: a field, method, or class with no explicit scope keyword; that is, with *default* access. "Package private" is far more descriptive, but the term "friendly," something of a holdover from Java's applet-mania days, still gets some use. Certain classes that must be developed may already be named in the assignment to assure consistent grading.

Functional Goals

The next three chapters concern themselves with delving into the design and implementation issues for each major assignment task. Below we offer an overview of the strategic choices you will need to make before jumping into writing the code.

Write a User Interface

The user interface has two tasks. The first is to provide users with an interactive tool that they can learn easily. An interface should draw on a user's experience with other client interfaces by providing a clear, familiar visual layout with predictable graphic elements. The graphics library toolkit must supply the visual aesthetics and appeal that invite clicking or scrolling, but the GUI developer still must deploy them properly. It is just as easy today to frustrate or confuse a user with poor layout or uncoordinated graphic elements as it ever was. A random survey of a several dozen business and personal Web sites will demonstrate the point.

For the purposes of building the GUI client for this project, keeping things simple and following the instructions provided should be sufficient. In fact, if the project instructions are very precise, dictating the behavior on resizing and which components to use, the task actually gets easier. There are only so many layout managers that don't resize a component along with the parent container (FlowLayout or possibly GridBagLayout) and only so many ways to ensure that another component gets all the horizontal space its container has to offer but only as much vertical space as it requires (BorderLayout).

Even with Swing, only certain components recommend themselves if the instructions are very specific. If they aren't, keep things simple. There are four facilities you can provide to promote interaction with the user:

- Menu choices

- Widgets that toggle a feature or initiate action when clicked

- Important data fields a user is inclined to treat as a widget

- Keystroke combinations to match core menu choices, especially file and edit operations

Chapter 18 focuses on describing how the Swing framework clarifies the structure for adding multiple types of access to the same underlying events and data models associated with each component type. Studying the data models of those Swing components we are most likely to use will supplement that discussion.

This brings us to the second task of the user interface: to handle data flow so that graphic presentation is consistent with the exchange of data between client and server programs. Although the AWT supports this well through event handling, Swing components separate the data and display objects from each other so that the programmer has a little bit more to understand about the internals of a Swing component, but ultimately can complete the objectives with a bit more elegance and in fewer lines of code. In practice, this means the data model of a Swing component will rely heavily on the client code, while the display model will rely on the data model's view of what the client retrieves.

The foundation for this elegance in the Swing package is a variation on a design pattern known as Model-View-Controller (MVC). In this pattern, the model is state data. In a JList component, for example, the *Model* comprises all the elements contained by the component internally, along with their current states. The *View* refers to any perspective of that model; for a human user, the view is the graphic representation of a list—all or some of the elements, limited by the viewing area's constraints, with selected elements highlighted and the rest not. The *Controller* (event handler) is then responsible for updating the Model's state.

The conventional relation among these three actors is triangular. With respect to Swing, there's really only one View we are concerned with, and that's the GUI. The Model's data updates the View as expected. The View, by way of an event object, passes state-change information to the Controller, which in turn updates the Model. Given the user-centric approach we take to GUI development, saying "view-controller-model" seems a little more intuitively clear, but that still isn't quite what Swing does.

Put another way, the View is the screen, or the "read-only" attribute of every Swing component. Using the data contained in the Model that expresses the visual state of the component, the View applies its set of drawing instructions and rules for component behavior to render what the user sees. Users may of course form the impression that they are manipulating the View when they click a button or resize a frame, but the View's only responsibility is to paint its share of the screen with information provided by the Model. Gathering and interpreting user input are actions the Controller performs. The Controller has nothing the user may read, even though it accepts all user input to the component. This makes it easy to confuse the two actors; because they often share pixel space on-screen, the intuitive guess is that the View itself presents the graphic layer and accepts all change requests sent to it.

It's important to outline these issues early so that we can see how Swing makes it easy to support multiple views with the same data model or possibly just change the view if the current one doesn't satisfy. Once you get your data model the way you want it, there's no need to revise it. Managing appearances is a completely separate task.

Enable Network Access (Client-Server)

Building the connection between client and server for this assignment is perhaps the most straightforward—if potentially most tedious—portion of the overall exercise. Unless the plans for the project assignment change at the last minute, each candidate will have the option of using object serialization to communicate across the wire or using Remote Method Invocation (RMI) as a transport. Like many other choices in object-oriented development, making this decision boils down to an accurate analysis of the given requirements and forecast of how the application is best suited for future growth. A concrete implementation (straight serialization) can be done quickly, but if there are frequent changes to what goes on the stream, the cost of ongoing maintenance may be high. A more flexible, open-ended architecture will make maintenance less of a problem over the long run, but if no changes are in the plan, is the initial effort up front justified? These are real-world considerations that don't influence this testing environment much, since the time spent to complete the project is up to each candidate.

For the purpose of staking out territory for these two choices, though, it's worth saying here that object serialization as a stand-alone technique is vulnerable to some amount of criticism. The developer has to define the objects that will go over the stream and their order for each request, and ensure that client and server adhere to that format. Protocols such as HTTP, FTP, Telnet, and others operate this way, but in these cases a community of developers has agreed on how standard services will work. This makes it possible for everyone to implement their own applications, while fully expecting they will work with any other application built to the standard. Any standardized browser should be able to contact any HTTP server and expect the service to function correctly.

For small or custom applications this is not much of a problem, unless you plan to build on top of it, tie it in to other applications that perform a supplementary service, or make a wholesale changes to the protocol when new services need to be added. Maintaining backward compatibility complicates the matter, particularly if the client and server are developed independently. Barring some shrewd design choices, foresight, and luck, maintaining an independent protocol may be a dead-end for design over time. Then again, depending on the circumstances, these problems may be safe to ignore.

RMI is Sun's approach to distributed computing among Java VMs. Its feature set continues to develop rapidly as the user community demands increasingly sophisticated operations from it. The idea of RMI is to make the network imposed between client and server seem like a semantic detail, requiring one extra layer of handling compared to operations taking place within a single VM. This means the actions of two separate VMs have to be coordinated. The client and server code must be developed in tandem and kept in sync.

RMI uses object serialization to marshal data between VMs, so objects that use RMI still must implement the java.io.Serializable interface. *Marshalling* is the term Java uses to describe converting an object first into its component arguments, then into a serialized byte stream suitable for transport over the network.

When running, the RMI server exports objects that are available to clients at a well-known port; the client only has to know where to ask and what to ask for, using stub references to call on each server-side object it wants.

RMI's built-in "wire protocol," or *transport*, then handles the exchange between the two VMs.

RMI has technical limitations of its own. Because the execution trace moves back and forth between VMs, debugging client-server problems can be difficult. More importantly, when dealing with a multithreaded server, care must be taken that the single channel between the client VM and server VM does not block on a thread that prevents the server side from completing a related process via an update() call. This typically entails some kind of thread-moderating process. It is also possible for the client to get an object from the server and pass it back so that the server considers it a remote object, not a local one. This is similar to having phone calls forwarded to an office that then forwards them back, incurring a usage charge each way. It will work, but the cost will continue to add up until someone notices.

These, of course, are consequences of incorrect implementation. The chief point is that RMI may add a noticeable amount of complexity. As with any design choice, the benefits should be clear and compelling before adopting it.

Add Features to an Existing Database

The work required here will depend largely on the code provided with the project assignment. There are several ways a simple database scheme could be implemented, centering on what structure is used to store the data. Each approach will pose some ground-level obstacles to ensuring threadsafe operation. Our discussion will examine several of these angles, taking a comprehensive view as the best preparation.

Assuming the assignment may pose some feature to be implemented at the record-object level, there will be another strategic decision to make—similar to the one between object serialization and RMI. There are several ways to ensure a data store will not be corrupted by multiple accesses; the two broad approaches are synchronizing on the data structure itself and designing a threading scheme that synchronizes at the record level. The latter approach is of course far more efficient and levies a proportionally greater burden on the developer to design it correctly.

The central consideration is scalability. Serializing access to the entire data store, while effectively guaranteeing data integrity, erodes performance as the record count and user demand (threaded access) increase. But against a database with no thread safety, the vulnerability to corruption also increases. Let's say Thread A is totaling a column of fields, which requires accessing that field in each record. Thread B enters the data store to insert a record. If no mechanism for thread safety is available to order these processes, the resulting behavior is uncertain. If Thread B inserts a record that Thread A has not accessed yet, then Thread A will include that value in its sum once it gets there. But if Thread B inserts a record in an area that Thread A has already passed by, Thread A will omit the value, and its record count will be off by one. If Thread A enters a record that Thread B is in the middle of writing, the result is uncertain. This problem is termed a *race condition*, suggesting that one thread is "racing" to finish before another can cause trouble.

In a small bank with two tellers, it might be far easier on the bank if it closes while each teller balances their cash drawer in turn, and the impact on customer service might be negligible. But in a large branch with a dozen tellers, the same policy would generate no small number of complaints. Each kind of bank must take into account the way it intends to operate and structure its procedures accordingly. Where threading and data are concerned, a "one size fits all" approach to data access could mean over-developed code at one end of the scale and unacceptable performance on the other.

In the following chapter, we'll review the potential container strategies for a data scheme built in Java, then focus on one to further explore these two approaches to thread safety.

Other Requirements

The following elements address how the grader appointed by Sun will review the source code and documentation submitted with your working program. In the assignment documentation you receive, the relative weight of each category will be provided.

Adhere to Supplied Naming

Following the naming scheme given for packages, classes, and methods primarily ensures that the grader will check the code properly. Beyond that, there is no set limit on the number of support classes that may be created for the finished assignment. Choose names for any such classes you supply that evoke their purpose or type. Naming subclasses so that they refer to the parent helps to create an immediate association for the code reader and is good policy where it is practical.

Stress Readability

Java Software recommends a few conventions for programmers to follow. These guidelines promote a common visual appearance for source code that makes it easier for other programmers to identify the elements and form a clear impression of the code's operation. Some guidelines to bear in mind are:

- Begin all class names with an uppercase letter.

- Begin all method and field names with a lowercase letter.

- Use mixed case for multiple-word names (like `getResourceAsStream()`).

- Avoid one-character field names (o, l, i, and e) beyond temporary variables in a loop.

- Indent three or four spaces per code block. (We use smaller indents in this book to avoid line breaks.)

- Avoid using multiple `System.out.print()` calls to concatenate a long string. Use the + operator instead and span the strings over multiple lines.

As with any coding style, the key is a consistent application of form the intended readers know. One habit we have seen in sample code on the Web is beginning class names with a lowercase letter. While legal, it can make a class reference hard to distinguish from a variable in a long code list. Avoid this practice.

Use *javadoc*-Style Comments

The source code bundled with the download will include `javadoc`-ready comments. Employing the same style and format in the code you submit should offer some form of immunity. If you intend to use object serialization on its own, you might apply the three serial tags that are new with Java 2. Note that `javadoc` now supports HTML output for API overview and package-level documentation by including properly named files in the same directory as the source. `javadoc`'s command-line argument options have expanded considerably and are worth a look.

New tags and other changes to javadoc are included with the documentation bundle for JDK 2, which can be downloaded from http://java.sun.com/ products/. If installed locally, the relative path to javadoc is docs/tooldocs/ solaris/javadoc.html.

Don't Comment the Obvious

Good form is part of the grading process, as is your best understanding of the level of information other programmers need to know to grasp your code quickly. Anyone who is going to read source code for meaning—as opposed to seeing what it looks like—will find a comment on an assignment operation or what object type a method returns distracting rather than helpful. Limit source file commentary to complex operations that may be unclear from the code block itself or to defining the role of methods that contribute to a larger design scheme. javadoc commentary should inform the API browser what service each documented field and method offers.

Use Standard Design Patterns

Design patterns describe a relation within a class or among several classes that serve a fundamental purpose to applications without regard to their "domain." The JDK makes ample use of design patterns throughout its core libraries: Swing uses a variation of the MVC pattern to support multiple graphic views of one data model. The Applet class uses an Observer pattern to monitor any Image instances it may contain. These abstractions also allow developers to communicate their ideas in terms of architecture, rather than implementation. Once consensus is achieved on the structure of an application, the individual programmers can then focus on building the elements needed to complete it.

Design patterns by themselves are not magic. They simply express a consistently useful approach to some common problem. It's quite likely that some experienced programmers use them without knowing their given names. But knowing these patterns by name and structure can greatly reduce the time it takes to recognize the tools that use them. Classes like java.net.ContentHandlerFactory, for example, embed the design model directly in their names. If you know what a Factory design is good for, you'll be able to identify a factory class's role quickly and put it to use. Other classes, such as `java.util.Observer` and `Observable`, get their names directly from the patterns they implement, so the pattern-aware programmer can save time otherwise spent researching classes and reading method lists. It is worth your while to research the patterns most commonly used and learn to apply them to your projects.

Chapter

16

Enhancing and Extending the Database

This chapter discusses the first part of the project assignment by tracing the design steps for building a small database application. The specific objective is to design a model suitable to the scenario presented in the last chapter and to build enough code to illustrate one implementation. Based on our own development, we will be able to anticipate some of the issues the project assignment will present. After that walk-through, we'll encounter several issues in extending the application—for example, securing the database from the hazards of concurrent access ("thread safety").

The assignment may contain a requirement that the candidate cannot (or may not) solve in an ideal way. The idea behind this condition is to require each candidate to weigh the relative merits of the remaining choices. It is possible that none of them will be programmatically attractive, which is arguably real-world enough. To simulate that less than perfect environment, we will also discuss some likely constraints on enhancing our own code and possible work-arounds, along with their costs and benefits.

Two-Tier Databases

This chapter does not assume you know a lot about databases or have studied the Java Database Connectivity (JDBC) API. This chapter concentrates on an application structure that adheres to a simple *client-server* architecture. In a client-server structure, the database system is integrated with or running in the same process space as the mechanism that handles client requests and serves data back. The next few paragraphs cover common terms relating to database design and structure, and they supply a context to aid our approach to design.

The most widely used database model today is the *relational* database. Relational databases are composed of multiple *tables* of information. A single table comprises any number of *records* of a specific kind. A table stores each record in its own *row*, which consists of ordered *fields* of data. Each field is, in turn, defined by its *column*, which declares what *type* of data it will store and the maximum space (*width*) available to each field in the column.

Relational design, as the name suggests, makes it possible to declare relations between tables that share columns of the same type. For example, one table of baseball players might be used to show current batting statistics. Each player belongs to a team, of course, but it would be cumbersome to include all the information associated with the player's team in this same table. In a relational design, we might create a second table that is *keyed* on team names. When we look up player data, we will see the team name. The database programmer may then allow us to drill down to team data by using this key to call on the second table.

This arrangement of data has several potential benefits. For example, highly redundant field data can be replaced by lookup references to another table. On a more sophisticated level, a database programmer can develop new relations from existing tables to meet a new user requirement. This functionality comes at the price of substantial complexity, certainly enough to justify the vast industry behind relational database management systems (RDBMS) seen on the market today. In fact, the JDBC API merely addresses a vendor-neutral way to incorporate an existing RDBMS package into a Java application.

For the purposes of discussing the project assignment, we will use a "flat" data model in this chapter. The database model offered in the project is *two-tiered* in structure. Simply put, this means that the server and database portions of the project are integrated and running on the same virtual machine. The user (*client*) runs on a separate VM, which might be located on the same machine or a remote machine accessible via a network. This relation between the two processes is one variation of the client-server computing model.

The explosion of commercial interest in the Internet over the last few years has brought the *three-tier* (alternatively, *n-tier*) model into more widespread use, particularly in areas where client interaction is intense and response times are critical. This arrangement logically separates the server component from the database and allows the server component to focus on managing client demands so that the database can be optimized for storage and retrieval performance. The advantages of *n*-tier models extend in several potential directions. A common strategy is to deploy multiple servers between the clients and the back-end application. The server portion may spend more time interpreting or preparing client requests than submitting them. In this case, having multiple servers speaking to one database may be the best solution. If there is some concern that the server application could crash and take the database with it, this separation also achieves some amount of data protection.

A few servers could also be needed to support a wide variety of request types that the servers must then route to the correct data server. This could easily be the case for the Mobile Conferencing scenario described in the previous chapter. We might prefer to build multiple distributed databases but access them through a common server. The server itself then handles the various incoming requests, making maintenance and updating easier, and avoiding any elaborate client-side coding for determining which database to connect to. *n*-tier architectures provide a wealth of other strategies on top of these more common approaches, including the introduction of architectural concepts such as *application partitioning,* a means for moving application demand loads from one server to another as a form of load-balancing. Many companies interested in adjusting for the volatility of Internet demand look to these schemes as a way of expanding their ability to serve customers without bringing systems down to refit their hardware; as with many strategies for increasing flexibility, the key is advance planning and design.

Designing a Basic Scheme

A flat data model simply implies that the scheme for organizing data records is largely, if not completely, self-describing. Relational or other data-indexing schemes can be very powerful, but they impose complexities, not the least of which is a separate language to access the scheme's feature set. A flat file is ideal for small databases that do not require a complete subsystem to facilitate searching and/or organizing data.

There are only so many meaningful ways to write a scheme that is little more than the data itself. Some of the most common types include the following:

- An ASCII-based file of human-readable information, in which the rules for delimiting or parsing data are often hard-coded in the application logic or self-evident in the layout of the file itself.

- A binary file, written with an encoded definition of its own structure, called a header or *metadata*, followed by data records adhering to that structure.

- Multiple data files indexed by a control file. Schemes of this type (such as a browser's disk cache) often use the file system's directory structure as a ready-made structure for facilitating searches.

- A data structure that resides completely in memory but is saved to a file on regular intervals.

Simple text files are, of course, easiest to read and edit directly. Binary files can be read faster, obscure the contained information (which may or may not be desirable), and are ideal for arbitrary or "random" access.

Using Interfaces

Establishing the design by writing interfaces has multiple advantages. One advantage is that writing only the abstractions first helps to determine what actions and class relations are necessary without committing to a specific means of achieving them. Interfaces achieve the broadest sense of polymorphic behavior, because they supply the definition of the behavior that is wanted but not the means to implement behavior. They can also provide a bridge for using the same underlying data in several concrete classes that share the same high-level design, in the same way Java 2's Collections framework allows several container types to store one set of data.

One risk in any development effort that begins with concrete coding is the potential for implementation obstacles that cost as much to throw away as they do to solve. Once in that regrettable situation of facing a rewrite, there is the further risk of scrapping otherwise useful design elements because the specific code in which they are obscured failed to work. By using an interface design at the start, the possibilities for implementation remain open and some investment is preserved.

The simplest structure we have to create is a field type. A field is a member in a record that contains one type of data. The type and width of the field are defined by a column, which is the representation of one field type across multiple records. To leave open the possibilities of using the column in some meaningful way, we decide to define it abstractly:

```
/**
 * GenericColumn describes the behavior of a general
 * data column.
 *
 * @author Mobile Conferencing IT
 */
public interface GenericColumn {

  /**
   * getTitle() returns the name of the column.
```

```
     *
     * @returns String - the name assigned to the column
     */
    public String getTitle();


    /**
     * getWidth() gives the maximum length one column
     * entry can take.
     *
     * @return int - the width allotted to any entry.
     */
    public int getWidth();
}
```

A record consists of an ordered set of fields, each of which is described by a column. Given the simplicity of our scheme, we decide somewhat arbitrarily that we want records to be able to report their own organization; therefore, we need a method to return the list of columns the record contains. A record will also have to have some form of unique identification within the table. The identification type should not be limited to a primitive such as int, in case the data container implemented allows a non-numeric ID:

```
    /**
     * GenericRecord defines any record that knows its own
     * schema and the unique identifier given to it in a
     * table.
     *
     * @author Mobile Conferencing IT
     */
    public interface GenericRecord {

        /**
         * getSchema() returns the list of columns that
         * compose a record.
         *
         * @returns GenericColumn[] - the abstract type of a
         * column that reports its name and width.
```

```
 * @see GenericColumn
 */
public GenericColumn[] getSchema();

/**
 * getID() returns the Object representation of the
 * class used to store a record's unique ID.
 *
 * @returns java.lang.Object
 */
public Object getID();
}
```

Defining a field—a cell that is part of every record—can be tricky in this scheme. Following simple rules of thumb may not always determine a best choice. We can say every field has a column; the phrase "has a" then signifies that a field object should include a column member in its class definition. On the other hand, a field "is a" kind of column—one with a single row—which suggests that subclassing makes intuitive sense. Rather than commit to a design choice for either one, we'll leave the decision to a subsequent stage of development.

You may also be wondering whether a method like `getData()` should be included in the interface. There are at least two schools of thought on this matter. A minimalist approach suggests the interface should only declare methods that this type must support for the benefit of other classes. Assuming we only want to publicly define our records within our framework by their schema and unique ID, this interface is arguably sufficient... for now. We may determine later that `GenericRecord` should enforce `getData()`— if for no other reason than to ensure consistent naming and type return—and simply include it. The need to apply further methods to the interface is therefore compelled by demonstration rather than intuition. If we do include `getData()` now, we will have to decide on (and fix) its return type. The benefit is that we can start drawing on this part of the interface right away, since a record's data could then be returned through its abstract type. The only real question is whether to defer specifying `getData()` until the best implementation presents itself, or to put it in now and worry about any needed changes to its signature later.

Finally, we want to define a `DataBase` interface, to specify the real work. As a description of data control, it must account for the following tasks:

- Manipulating records: adding, modifying, deleting
- Counting records
- Finding a record by a field value contained there
- Saving data to a backing store
- Knowing the scheme of the database

The `DataBase` interface shown below declares all the methods we want to ensure are employed. By describing them here, we document the methods other programmers may rely on when they write related or dependent classes.

```
/**
 * DataBase outlines the basic services required of any
 * implementing database.
 *
 * @author Mobile Conferencing IT
 */
public interface DataBase {

    /**
     * recordTotal() should return the number of records
     * currently residing in the database.
     *
     * @returns long - number of database records
     * currently stored.
     */
    public long recordTotal();

    /**
     * getRecord() returns the Record matching a unique
     * ID. The ID value and type are determined by the
     * implementing class.
     *
```

```
 * @param Object - a key or ID value in an object
 * wrapper.
 * @returns String[] - the full record matched to
 * the unique ID.
 */
public String[] getRecord(Object ID);

/**
 * find() searches through the available records and
 * returns all records that match Column data to the
 * String provided.
 *
 * @param String - a text value that matches data in
 * a Record.
 * @returns String[][] - an array of matching Record
 * objects.
 */
public String[][] find(String matchItem);

/**
 * add() accepts a String array which is assumed to
 * conform to the Record type in use.  Means for
 * handling an improper parameter is left to
 * implementation.  Client validation or
 * exception-handling are possible avenues.
 *
 * @param String[] - Data values conforming to the
 * record scheme.
 */
public void add(String[] newData);

/**
 * modify() allows Record update.
 *
 * @param Object - the key or wrapped ID of the
 * original Record.
 * @param String[] - the original Record with
 * updated values.
```

```
     */
    public void modify(Object ID, String[] changes);

    /**
     * deleteRecord() removes a Record from the
     * database.
     *
     * @param Object - ID of the object to be removed.
     */
    public void delete(Object ID);

    /**
     * Commit current state of database to file.
     */
    public void save();

    /**
     * listScheme() allows caller to see the layout
     * of a Record.
     *
     * @returns GenericColumn[] - Ordered list of column
     * names and widths used in the current scheme.
     */
    public GenericColumn[] listScheme();
}
```

Part of the task in reading code that's been given to you, particularly in a test situation, is to read for what's missing as well as what's explicitly troublesome. In the previous case, there is something missing, something that is a potential trap to your interface: None of the previous methods throw exceptions. Unlike adding methods to an interface, which is a matter of adding on and then tracing through any existing implementations, adding exceptions later on is not a simple option. Consider the following:

```
public interface Commit {
    public void save();
}
```

```
public class Persistent implements Commit {
  public void save() throws CommitException { }
}
```

The class will not compile under the rule that an overriding method cannot add to a parent method's declared list of exceptions. Therefore, an interface that provides a series of process-sensitive methods must include the semantics of those exceptions up front. Otherwise, implementing the interface becomes very awkward. An interface's methods must also be public, and overriding methods cannot further restrict a method's scope. If a developer were forced to work under such constraints, it would still be possible to include some kind of precondition within each method that disallowed access to all but the instance itself. Having done that, the developer could then supply other new public methods that throw the required exceptions, but this would be a seriously compromised and confusing implementation at best. If we want to support exception handling, we must incorporate it at the design level. Backtracking, in this regard, is not difficult, but it does involve revising all implemented methods, which can be tedious. For further discussion on why the interface should not throw generic exceptions, see the "Issues in Implementation" section later in this chapter.

Using Abstract Classes

In designing and reviewing a set of interfaces over time, it is likely that some new requirements will emerge and others will boil out. The effort to achieve efficient abstractions can also get lost in generalities, with lots of methods taking `Object` parameters and returning `Object` types. In extreme cases, so many options are left completely open that it becomes unclear how to implement the model meaningfully or how to avoid constant casting and type checking down the line.

By the same token, anticipating a concrete solution can also cause problems in design. Adding methods that point overtly to one implementation may obscure the interface's usefulness to a feasible set of alternatives. Moreover, an interface that tempts developers to null-code methods in order to get at what they want becomes, at best, tedious. Unless the interface methods are specifically designed to be ignored safely (such as the listener classes in `java.awt.event`), the implementing class may be of limited use.

A good way to remain partial to abstractions while nailing down some important details is to write an abstract class. Since abstract classes can include constructors and non-`public` methods and add or defer method implementations as desired, they are an effective means for signaling insights and intended approaches to a given design. An ideal use for an abstract class models the style of abstract implementations shown throughout the JDK. In the bulk of those implementations, the abstract class implements some amount of code that all its subclasses can use. But, one or more of those implemented methods then call on the abstract methods in the class, which the developer must implement in order to complete the subclass for use. The `Component` class is in the AWT stock example of this technique. However, abstract classes needn't be confined to this toolkit-oriented interpretation of their use.

Partial coding gives us a way to address the previously raised question about whether to write a `Field` class that subclasses a column or includes an object of that type. Using an abstract class, we could have it both ways. The following example leaves out any additional abstract methods that might be useful, such as package-private methods for setting the width or title, to keep the illustration simple. Comment code is also omitted for this and other brief examples:

```
public abstract class ModelColumn
implements GenericColumn {
  private String title;
  private int width;

  ModelColumn(String name, int width) {
    title = name;
    this.width = width;
  }

  public String getTitle() {
    return title;
  }

  public int getWidth() {
    return width;
  }
  ...
}
```

With the constructor and methods already written, a concrete version of Column, suitable for use in a Field class, is trivial.

```
public class Column extends ModelColumn {

  public Column(String name, int width) {
    super(name, width);
  }
}
public class Field implements Serializable {
  private String datum;
  private Column col;

  public Field(String datum) {
    this.datum = datum;
  }
}
```

Or Field could simply use a Column in one of its constructors and extend the abstract class.

```
public class Field
  extends ModelColumn implements Serialiazable {
  private String datum;

  public Field(Column col, String datum) {
    super(col.getTitle(), col.getWidth());
    this.datum = datum;
  }

  public Field(String column, int width, String datum) {
    super(column, width);
    this.datum = datum;
  }
}
```

Abstract classes are also useful for pointing out implementation strategies that, by definition, an interface cannot convey. Any developer who wants to implement `DataBase`, for example, will write a constructor to read in an existing data file. It may be less obvious to create a second constructor in order to create new data files as needed and self-document the layout data files must conform to.

```
public abstract class ModelDatabase implements DataBase {

  public ModelDatabase(String datafile) {
    FileInputStream fis = new FileInputStream(datafile);
    // Read metadata or index from datafile
    // Verify file integrity
    // Read in records
  }

  public ModelDatabase(String file, GenericColumn[]
  newScheme) {
    // Read in newScheme array
    // Use newScheme metrics to determine metadata
    FileOutputStream fos = new FileOutputStream(file);
    // Write metadata to newfile
  }
  ...
  protected String[] getMetadata(){ }
  void close();
}
```

This skeleton code illustrates the most likely implementation of a backing store for a database: reading information to and from files. Just as important, it describes a way to create a new data file and automatically build its metadata. Now the developer does not have to track these details; a short program to generate new data files is reduced to passing a name for a file and the columns it will contain.

These two sections that illustrate interfaces and abstract classes are by no means complete. They are merely intended to suggest that some conceptual work before writing an application can help to clarify common elements. The result may be the development of a more flexible framework that can be applied to other problems, or simply recognition that certain well-known patterns have emerged through conceptual realization and can be applied with better understanding now that the application goals have been laid out.

More importantly, well-designed applications promote more effective maintenance. Programmers assigned to maintain an existing application can read its interfaces first to cleanly separate issues of design from implementation in their own minds. Code reuse, with respect to other projects, is not always a practical objective, particularly for tasks such as this project assignment. Nonetheless, maintenance is not a great factor in this test either, aside from defending your code as maintainable. Where they are practical, worth the effort, and justifiable in the time required to design them, interfaces offer a lot of benefit.

Issues in Implementation

The fact that we had no assignment code in hand gave us a means to introduce the use of design abstractions. We can anticipate what a simple database application might look like simply by considering what elements are required and by avoiding the specifics of implementation other than surveying common tactics. A variety of articles is available on the Web; they address specific techniques in great detail.

The actual code you receive will spell things out soon enough. There are enough variations to make a comprehensive discussion here fairly tedious and not necessarily helpful; there is no assurance the assignment will even center on using a low-level database. In that area, each candidate must rely on their general experience to adapt to the assignment specifics as best they can.

Our focus here is the general set of implementation problems the exam will pose, which should revolve around one or more of the following topical areas:

- Exception handling
- Design flaws
- Thread safety
- Supporting new features

Thread safety will almost certainly be a central issue in all assignment variations, and the exam objectives will certainly influence other potential problem areas, such as writing in new features or dealing with deliberate design flaws. Nonetheless, we'll handle these topics point by point, referring to the potential impact on thread safety and its server counterpart, concurrent access, as we go.

Exception Handling

Exceptions in Java define the conditions in normal program operation that would otherwise interrupt execution, based on non-routine circumstances. There are as many as four objectives to pursue when dealing with aberrant but non-fatal processing in a program:

- Determine whether modifying the existing code will eliminate the problem.

- Inform the user.

- Save the data whenever possible.

- Offer the user a choice of subsequent action.

A fundamental exception type might preclude one or more of these objectives being met. Other exceptions may be benign and require no action from the user. If normal operation can be resumed with no threat to data loss, the exception might be noted in a log for someone who maintains the application. But the user should not be alerted to circumstances beyond their control and that do not affect their work. Beyond these two cases, however, a robust program will provide any user with clear problem reports, data safety, and the courses of action open to them.

The parent class of all these operations is `Throwable`. From `Throwable`, there are three major branches in which exception classes are defined:

- `Error`

- `RuntimeException`

- `Exception`

Descendants of `Error` represent system- or VM-level interruptions (such as `OutOfMemoryError`) in which the question of recovering user access is probably a moot point. It is possible to briefly catch some of these exception types, but what level of service is then available may be indeterminate. These classes are therefore intended simply to name the specific error, when possible, and provide a stack trace of execution as an aid to ruling out fundamental bugs in the underlying VM or other low-level resource.

`RuntimeException` subclasses define type violations and other faults that cannot be trapped at compile-time, such as a `NullPointerException`. The VM will use these classes to specify the fault type, so they are not types a programmer should intentionally throw. While they can be caught, it's a fundamental mistake to conditionally handle problems that originate with faulty code. Consider the following:

```java
public class MathWhiz {
  ...
  public long add (String num1, String num2) {
    long n1 = Integer.parseInt(num1);
    long n2 = Integer.parseInt(num2);
    return (n1 + n2);
  }

  public static void main(String args[]) {
    MathWhiz mw = new MathWhiz();
    try {
      mw.add("3","FOOD");
    }
    catch(NumberFormatException nfe) {
    ...
    }
  }
}
```

This is not a subtle example, but it illustrates the burden placed on a `catch` clause that would attempt to rectify the situation. This clause could report the error by name, but the VM already provides that service. It could report the specific input values that were used when the exception was thrown, but that merely shifts attention from the problem to its symptoms. Finally, the catch code could perform the work expected of the original method, but that would merely underscore how poorly the original method handles its assigned task. Runtime exception conditions should be traced and solved, and be treated as program bugs. Any handling in this regard can only be considered a short-term hack that must be applied each time the class is used.

Classes that directly extend `Exception` lie between system faults and code flaws, usually dealing with events that reflect the necessary risks of the activities they relate to. Dealing with stream or thread operations, as two examples, require some means for anticipating `IOException` and `InterruptedException` objects, respectively. When a method executes a "risky" operation, it has the option of dealing with it, by catching the potential exception, or deferring its handling to a calling method, by throwing (or rethrowing) the exception. The key criterion is the portion of the resulting program that is best able to inform the user, preserve data integrity, and provide alternatives to the intended operation, including repeat attempts.

Every exception object knows three things: its name, the trace of execution leading to the point where it was constructed from the top of its thread, and any data that was passed to its constructor (usually a `String`). An exception's name is provided by its `toString()` method, which is useful when a `try` block only captures a parent exception. It is therefore always a good idea to develop a family of exceptions for any application of substance, much as a list of error codes is compiled for an elaborate C program. Often these exceptions simply add a naming scheme for context. Extending `Exception` is all that's required. To support message passing, the parent class of an application's exception hierarchy then provides two constructors: one to accept a `String` message and a default that either requires no message or passes along a generic one.

```
public class ReservationException extends Exception {

  public static final String generic =
    "General exception fault.";

  public ReservationException() {
    this(generic);
  }

  public ReservationException(String message) {
    super(message);
  }
}
```

Problems in adequate exception handling are typically noted by their absence rather than by poor deployment. Look for meaningful points in process control where adding exception handling makes sense. If the sample code provides an exception class, consider whether extending it would clarify risky operations specific to the application. If it does not, provide at least one for context. Finally, as a general rule, avoid using exceptions to handle data validation, unless the code gives you no other reasonable choice. Exception handling, by definition, is a controlled deviation from the normal flow of control followed by code that only runs in the event of that deviation. Consequently, exception code may run up to an order of magnitude slower than inline code covering the same operations and using expected entry and return points.

Design Impediments

In the application code you receive, you may find one or two methods that, based on the instructions you are given, pose more hindrance than help in completing the assignment. Obstacles of this sort may be the result of hastily written code, where the central principles of object-oriented programming—data encapsulation, polymorphism, access control, inheritance—were not given adequate forethought, leaving subsequent programmers some form of maintenance headache. The easiest way to approach such problems is to break them down into four steps. First, identify the ideal or conventional technique to complete the code. Second, determine that it cannot be used. Third, consider the less-attractive options. And fourth, implement the least of those evils. Chances are there won't be a right choice, but simply two or more bad ones that sacrifice different virtues.

Consider a parent class whose public methods make frequent use of a variety of private methods, which are intended to spare any programmer who wants to write a subclass some burdensome details of implementation:

```
public class DoDirtyWork {

    // record key
    private Object key;

    public void addRecord() {
    // private method
```

```
        checkDataIntegrity();
    // private method
      handle = getObjectID();
      try {
        // code that changes fields the subclass
        // wants left alone
      }
      catch(Exception ex) {}
    }
  }
```

Let's say a subclass of `DoDirtyWork` needs the two private methods at the beginning of `addRecord()`, but wants to override the processing within the `try` block.

```
public class MyWork extends DoDirtyWork {
  public void addRecord() {
    super.addRecord();
  // now what?
    ...
  }
}
```

The desired actions are `private` and, from the point of view of the subclass, impossible to get at without executing the unwanted code. Assuming that the work of the parent class within the `try` block could be reversed, the subclass has two ugly choices:

- Call the parent's `addRecord()` method to first perform the integrity check and get a copy of the record's key. Then set the values altered by the parent's `try` block back to their original state in the remainder of the overriding method.

- Copy the private methods into the subclass using the parent source code, including any necessary private fields and other dependencies to make the calls work.

Neither of these choices represents inspired object-oriented work. They may be all the more difficult to realize because they require abusive programming to solve the problem. But they do pose very different potential problems, and the justification chosen for either approach will depend on which problems are deemed least severe.

In the first approach, the chief danger is exposure to concurrent accesses. Assume for one reason or another that the overriding version of `addRecord()` cannot be made `synchronized`. Thread R calls the overridden method in the parent class, which changes state data and then returns. Before Thread R can revert state back to the original values, it is preempted by Thread W, which accesses those values through a different method and writes them to another record. In this specific case, Thread W's subsequent behavior may be indeterminate. In the best case, it is preempted again by Thread R, which then has a chance to rectify the situation. In the worst case, data gets corrupted in one record or possibly all subsequent records.

The second approach, copying the relevant source from `DoDirtyWork` into `MyWork`, severs the chain of inheritance. The parent class has its private methods modified, possibly to account for the use of a more efficient data structure or to introduce other hidden fields that expand the versatility of the class. Because the changes occur to private members and methods, there is no reason `MyWork` shouldn't compile, and it could be a long time before the disconnect in logic is detected. Any attempt to subclass `MyWork` leads to the same dismal choice as before.

A case like this has no good answer, much less a right one. It is more likely that the solution you choose here will influence the remainder of the project. A problem of this type may well be covered in the follow-up exam; examine the problem carefully and choose from the alternatives you can devise, rather than take the first work-around that comes to mind.

Thread Safety

Making data threadsafe is just one of two considerations in implementing an effective multithreading strategy. Achieving thread safety means guaranteeing serial access to the data on some level. Serial or *synchronized* access to data guarantees that any number of concurrent operations, which share access to the data and may modify it, do not interfere with each other. Another way of saying this is that the object that contains or wraps the data usually assumes a passive or defensive role against concurrent access. In a two-tier database model, the database portion assumes this role. Based on how data is safeguarded, the server code is responsible for managing and applying incoming client requests to data retrieval and storage in a manner that acknowledges such limits.

In practice, the balance between these processes can shift considerably, depending on the design goals of the application. If the database permits only one access at a time of any kind to the entire data structure, then there is no possibility of corrupting the data through conflicts in concurrent requests. But global enforcement of data safety comes at a price—a very limited potential for performance, which may become unacceptable as data operations take more time to process. There's no advantage to improving server efficiency if requests are prepared faster than the database can accept and process them. But for small databases supporting very basic requests, serially ordered access to all data is easy to program and maintain and is a viable approach for many situations.

Achieving greater performance requires data access below the level of the entire data structure coupled with a technique for processing requests that corresponds to how deeply the data is exposed. The finer the granularity of the access, the more sophisticated the techniques available to exploit it. And of course the more complex the strategy, the greater the burden on the developer to ensure it is implemented and maintained correctly. Simply put, a scheme for multithreading that offers optimal performance is not right for all occasions. The cost of such a scheme must be justified by the potential benefits it can return. Some of those schemes are covered here and some in the following chapter.

Synchronizing on the Data Structure

Synchronizing data access has to occur on some level, but it can take many forms. Some container types guarantee threadsafe access as part of their structure. For other containers, the same result can be achieved within a code block that invokes synchronization on the data object as a precondition to the block's execution.

```
...
public void modifyRecord() {
  synchronized (theData) {
    //modify the record
  }
  ...
}
...
```

This approach is not as stifling to performance as it might first seem. Calls to the `Object` class' `wait()` and `notify()` methods within a synchronized block can be used to defer operation as desired, allowing thread control to change hands based on some conditional state. By using a series of wait/notify conditions with each potential data change, some degree of interleaving is possible, again depending on which threads are subsequently eligible to run. Without the use of `wait()` and `notify()` (and `notifyAll()`), the `synchronized` qualifier confers exclusive access to the executing thread on the lock of any `Object` class's (instead of Thread class) it operates in or declares. If that declared object encapsulates the data, serialized access is achieved for the duration of that block.

The programmer also has the option of synchronizing the methods that access the data structure to achieve the same effect; methods and blocks both acquire the object lock before they operate. Synchronizing on the method may seem to make simpler and "cleaner" code, but there are, as always, trade-offs. A long method that is synchronized may wrap process-intensive code that doesn't need an object lock. In extreme cases, such methods that access several major resources can create a deadlock condition by calling on competing processes. But employing a large number of synchronized blocks could be just as inefficient. Acquiring the lock over several code blocks in the same method is certainly slower than acquiring it once, but the difference may be marginal. The bigger danger is in synchronizing on objects other than the one represented by `this`, which can also create deadlock. However, in choosing to synchronize methods rather than code blocks, the programmer must ensure that non-synchronized method operations don't rely on data that synchronized methods actively manipulate. Conversely, non-synchronized methods can't be allowed to change data that synchronized methods are supposed to handle.

Other rules to bear in mind about synchronized methods:

- Calls from one synchronized method to other synchronized methods in the same object do not block.

- Calls to a non-synchronized method, in the same object or elsewhere, also do not prevent the complete execution of the calling method.

- Synchronization is not inherited, nor does the compiler require the keyword in an overriding method. An abstract class that supports a synchronized abstract method will compile, but the declaration is not meaningful. The abstract synchronized method aside, a `super.method()` call to a synchronized parent can create a block the programmer is not expecting.

Data Structure

Java 2's Collections API, located in `java.util`, offers containers that by default are not threadsafe. Each of these containers is supported by a static method in the `Collections` class that returns serialized control in the form of an interface reference that wraps and "backs" the original container type.

```java
public class DataStore {
   private HashMap hm;
   private Map map;

   public DataStore() {
   // "raw" access
     hm = new Hashmap();
   // threadsafe access
     map = Collections.synchronizedMap(hm);
     ...
   }
}
```

The key to ensuring serial access is to eliminate any reference to the "raw" class. Otherwise, the means for accessing the container is open to a developer's determination.

```java
public class DataStore2 {
   private Map map;

   public DataStore2() {
     map = Collections.synchronizedMap(new HashMap());
     // threadsafe access only
     ...
   }
}
```

The philosophy behind this support is twofold. If protection against concurrent access is not required, the container form can be used as is; to make it threadsafe, the entire object should be synchronized. In fact, the API documentation goes so far as to insist on using a synchronized reference to the container whenever multithreaded operations will rely on it.

This does *not* mean that synchronizing on a container protects it completely at all times, only that individual operations are guaranteed to be atomic. Most of the time, in practice, we rely on multiple operations to complete a single task, e.g., reading a record, modifying it, and writing back to the data store. The programmer must still devise a strategy for how records are handled during compound operations: whether the record is locked for the duration or may change asynchronously, whether the user is notified of other current locks or the latest change simply writes over any previous modifications, etc.

This all-or-nothing rationale behind container synchronization merely rests on the idea that requiring the developer to design a more granular thread-safety scheme, in the name of optimal performance, is not typically justified by an application's actual requirements. It may be better to achieve performance through other means, such as faster hardware or a more efficient VM. Less complicated programming strategies that do not involve defensive techniques can also aid performance. These include reducing file accesses, partitioning data structures in memory, or perhaps applying a design that would permit read-only threads to run asynchronously (while write-oriented threads are queued and scheduled for execution). But if optimal performance remains a central concern, nothing beyond advice prevents developers from writing their own interleaving schemes and applying them to native container types.

Data Elements

Each thread can be required to synchronize on the record objects it wants to write or modify. As a general rule, synchronizing on an object other than the one currently executing can be dangerous. Any code block that synchronizes on one autonomous object and then calls a method that threads its own attempt to synchronize on that same object runs the risk of creating a deadlock condition, hanging the system.

The alternative is to synchronize all the methods in a record object (and maintain complete encapsulation), but again this is only part of the entire scheme needed. The developer must still guarantee that each new record will receive a unique ID and will get written to a location in the container that is not already in use. Some container types inherently guarantee this, based on the record ID as a key, which then maps to its value pair; other structures do not. An ordered container, such as a linked list or a low-level file using a random-access pointer, should be wrapped so that acquiring the record's unique ID and adding the record are atomically executed, ensuring no conflicts with other record inserts. With respect to an actual file, the programmer must then also account for the space left by a deleted record and determine when best to reorganize files that fill up with null records.

Supporting New Features

Any feature you are expected to add to the existing code may imply, through its own requirements, a preferred way to implement threadsafe operations and still provide scalable performance. The considerations for achieving performance in the project assignment are, again, a decision each candidate will have to make based on the solution they feel most comfortable justifying. The following examples are intended to suggest potential threading strategies for the assignment, based on supporting features such as:

- Search and replace
- Sorting
- A record "lock"

Each of these features rests on a means for getting a list of records from the database, ignoring elements that fail to match the search criteria, and modifying those that succeed. In the case of a search-and-replace request, it isn't possible to know ahead of time whether the executing thread will only read (no matches), sometimes write, or always write. To avoid blocking the entire database, we need some way to list through the data and release records once they are no longer needed. An optimal solution for performance would also permit other threads to act on records not yet needed by the current thread but still on the list.

This kind of job has been supported by the `Enumeration` interface, which can be used to list the contents of a `Vector` or another ad hoc container type that implements it. The Collections framework provides an eventual successor to `Enumeration` called `Iterator`, which offers a tighter binding to all the container types in `java.util`. An `Iterator` knows how to remove elements from the container type and updates itself accordingly; an `Enumeration` has no such association with its container. But an `Iterator` cannot cope with modifications made by another `Iterator` or any other process that modifies the database; the program must ensure that records cannot be added or deleted while a list is running.

Sorting can be even more demanding, because elements are required until the sort is complete. One workaround that avoids blocking for the duration of the process is to copy the contents to sort into a temporary container and return the results from there. Using this same technique to hold records pending an update, sometimes called a "dirty buffer," can lead to improved performance. Write processes must be confined to using the dirty buffer, which only offers synchronous access. The original buffer is always readable. A copy of all dirty records remains in the original buffer but is marked "read-only" until the dirty buffer writes it back. Such writes must then take place while client write requests are blocked.

Ultimately, adding some type of state reference to the record object is required to track interested threads, iteration lists, buffer assignments, or even simple locks on a record while it is being added, updated, or deleted. This can take the form of a wrapper around the record that includes, for example, a `Vector` of thread references. The methods of the controlling database must be updated to wait or notify based on record state, including a means to update the set of active references.

Chapter Summary

The programming assignment requires each candidate to extend code that is supplied with the project and make it threadsafe. In our example, illustrating the potential development of a simple database, we've shown how some very simple oversights in design can lead to problematic development for future programmers—a context very close in purpose to what the assignment poses. In particular, when multithreaded design is not considered as a factor in initial design, the developer assumes a burden in retrofitting an effective scheme.

Working from a design using interfaces or abstract classes can also be problematic. It's important to note up front any missing elements, like exception lists, as well as signatures with narrow scope. Without a thoughtful review, any limitations may not surface until implementation is well under way, possibly forcing a hack work-around or, worse, a rewrite.

Achieving thread safety can be as simple as guaranteeing synchronous access to the entire data structure. Providing it in such a way as to optimize concurrent access increases the potential for performance but at the cost of adding considerable complexity to the overall project. There is such a thing as "too much" performance, from the perspective of the cost in time and future maintenance to achieve it.

Chapter 17

Writing the Network Protocol

One simple way to address the requirement for making a threadsafe database is to synchronize on it as a whole. The data cannot be corrupted by concurrent write requests if they're all forced to stand in line. At the same time, it's clear that the "bullet-proof" approach comes at a high price. If the database grows to any appreciable size, or if many requests require iterating over the entire record set, performance perception may suffer. And if the project assignment requires adding a feature that depends on "granular" access, some accommodation will have to be made for a complex scheme anyway. To that end, the previous chapter outlined some general points for designing such a system. The code bundled with the assignment may also influence those choices, so the best defense is a broad view of the options.

Whatever method you choose to manage the application, it's always good design to maintain independence between the server that encapsulates the database (or any application it will serve) and the database itself. Ideally, the application and all classes related to its operation should present themselves in as few references as practically attainable within the server code. As the exchange point between all possible clients and the data, the application server already has plenty of functionaries to manage. The initial design goal for it should be to maintain the cleanest possible separation of role-players. One assumption we will maintain in this chapter is that the database has been "wrapped" in such a manner.

Concurrency, or designing for multithreaded access, is only part of the puzzle. We have to make our decision early as to how we are going to institute inter-VM operations. If we want to build incrementally, we can define a network communication protocol, set up a loop to handle incoming requests, and add a scheduling system for the actual jobs. In the world of "request–response" Internet services, this is solid and well-trod ground. Java's object serialization facility lightens the load a bit, making it possible to send single objects over the network that contain all the details of a given request. There are lots of details to implement and document in this manner, but the developer then can build in new services one by one, verifying operations along the way. With a little planning, new request types can be written as classes that conform to a general interface contract, making it a simple matter to incorporate new jobs into the client-server scheme.

But if we want to avoid the details of how services are provided and focus solely on *what* services to provide, we need another approach. To make one VM's call on another VM's resources appear as a matter of detail—an important concept in distributed computing—we need an API that renders the need for a communications protocol transparent to the programmer. That convenience, of course, exacts its own costs, the first of which is defining client requirements in advance. To take advantage of RMI's services, a de facto network protocol and object transport system, we forego the ability to tinker with and refine services. Redefining a client service with RMI would mean rewriting and recompiling the service objects and the client code, which would get tedious quickly. We have to know what we want in advance so that RMI is doing what it does best: hiding the details of remote resources and expediting requests.

We'll discuss each method in turn in this chapter, weaving in the discussion of threading where appropriate, and saving for last some approaches to job scheduling that would apply equally well to both models.

Client-Server from Scratch

Java makes building the network aspect of a simple client-server application easy. The explosive rise in Web server deployment has made communicating over the network, by way of requesting "pages" of data, such a pervasive model that the JDK provides an entire library of tools to adopt it. This rapid change in the way most of us use computers has brought with it some devaluation of the term "client-server." A client-server system signifies the potential for a persistent connection between two machines; the dividing line between who processes what is somewhat negotiable. Basic Web servers are arguably better described as "request-response" information servers. Electronic commerce and other forms of facilitating browser access to a back-end database or other interactive facility are blurring this distinction more and more, but HTTP servers are so widespread and cheap to implement that people will continue to develop and extend them—and live with their restrictions. Until Web servers that can track clients across their individual requests come into wide use, attempts to implement "true" client-server will largely remain restricted to individual development efforts.

One product that integrates "session tracking" into its client handling now is Java Web Server. If the browser permits the server to write "cookies," or state information, to the browser's local disk, the server can then track the status of the client throughout a multi-stage request. More information is available online at http://www.sun.com/software/jwebserver.

Server Operation

A server's fundamental job is to run indefinitely, listening for and servicing requests. To reach the server, a client must know the name of the machine the server runs on, the *port* or channel it listens to, and the correct way to state a request. For widely popular service types, these last two elements usually assume the status of convention by way of a standards committee, such as the Internet Engineering Task Force (IETF). The user community relies on such committees to provide consensus or an authoritative message for agreed-upon standards and to make the information available to the public. You usually don't have to find a Web server by its port number, for example, because a "well-known" port (80) has been agreed upon and is even assumed by browsers unless you direct them explicitly to another port.

HTTP servers also use a standardized protocol to which clients adhere in order to receive the services they want. It is common for these types of servers to "speak" across the network in clear text, which makes testing and debugging much easier. The minimum request that a Web server would honor, once a client connects to it, looks like this:

```
GET /
<A blank line and carriage return signal a completed
request.>

. . .
```

Here the server is instructed to transmit the default, or "home" page in its root document directory, using version 1.0 of the HTTP protocol. If we were to telnet into a Web server instead of using a browser and submit this request, we'd get a stream of raw HTML code as a response. The browser simply formats the response according to the HTML tags that are part of the response.

This paradigm is so widely used that most of the needed behavior is already encapsulated in the java.net classes:

```java
import java.net.*;
import java.io.*;

public class Server implements Runnable {
  public final static int WK_PORT = 2012;
  protected int port;
  protected ServerSocket service;
  private String message = "Hello client!";

  public Server(int port_request) {
    if (port_request < 1024 || port_request > 65535) {
      port = WK_PORT;
    }
    else {
      this.port = port_request;
    }
    try {
      service = new ServerSocket(port);
    }
    catch (IOException ioe) {
      System.out.println("Error: Port " + port +
      "was not available.");
    }
    System.out.println("Port " + port +
    " is up and running.");
  }

  public void run() {
    InputStream receiving;
    OutputStream sending;
    while (true) {
      try {
        Socket client = service.accept();
```

```
            sending = client.getOutputStream();
            receiving = client.getInputStream();
            // insert code to accept client input
            // return request information, if any
            sending.write(message.getBytes());
          }
          catch (IOException ioe) {
            System.out.println("Could not accept client " +
            "request or establish streams.");
          }
        }
      }

    public static void main(String args[]) {
      Server svr = new Server(WK_PORT);
      svr.run ();
    }
  }
```

After establishing itself as a port listener, a Server creates and maintains incoming connections within its own thread of execution. At the same time, it's also possible to run multiple Server instances on different ports of the same machine. Our code checks to see whether a legal port number is entered: on Unix systems, ports below 1024 are reserved for the super-user. A TCP/IP stack supports 64K ports, making 65535 the upper limit. We also chose to catch the IOException that would be thrown if a Server instance attempted to start on a port already in use, in order to clarify the nature of this fault to the user. We could do more, of course, if we did not want the instance to terminate on this error. We also want to think about how we might protect the database itself; not a straightforward task to accomplish while also maintaining platform independence.

Within the run() method itself we've written just enough client-response code to test correct runtime behavior; no attempt at threading client requests has been made yet. Once a request does connect, ServerSocket returns an object that encapsulates the client's connection and the means for opening lines of communication between the two. This information is then managed by the Socket reference client, which invokes input and output streams to facilitate client-server communication. There is of course no need to open an InputStream if the socket has no reason to listen to the client.

To test this initial version, there's no need to write any Java at all. Java's networking library runs over TCP/IP as the transport protocol, which means Java network code can communicate with other TCP/IP-based applications, like Telnet. Telnet is a mainstay tool of Unix systems and is more than likely available and in your command path. You can then do the following:

```
$ javac Server.java
$ java Server &
$ telnet localhost 2012
Hello client!
```

On a Windows machine, you must start the Server in its own window, then telnet to it through another window. Also, be sure a TCP/IP stack has been configured and is currently active among the list of network drivers. You can check this in the Control Panel by clicking the Network icon and browsing the Configuration panel's list of drivers.

Connecting Clients to the Server

Our bare-bones server code above is not very interesting, but it gives us the first building block we need. As we further define the model for connecting multiple clients and threading the requests they carry, we want to think about mapping out the various tasks and developing a working set of class relationships. One of the first things to consider, since we know we will have to thread client requests, is to encapsulate each client connection in its own object running on its own thread. The server code must then provide a way to:

- Remember each client.

- Check the state of each client and its request regularly.

- Restore resources used by the client when done.

As each of these tasks appears to grow more complex or involve more than one basic job, you want to think again about forming classes to divide responsibilities economically. Before we get too deeply engrossed in class design, however, we want to establish how the client will call for the services provided by the application.

Communications Protocol

A communication protocol, such as HTTP, defines how the client and server communicate with one another. An HTTP server supports a variety of service-call keywords, like GET and POST, which any client browser may issue. These service calls are transmitted to the HTTP server via the communication protocol, which the server understands. The server recognizes these keywords as signals to invoke the corresponding method call.

If we were to write our own application from the ground up, this is probably where we would want to start; by determining what services our application should provide, we may quickly define a communication protocol to implement, however small, that specifies how to service client requests. Other communication protocols might include FTP, Gopher, and DayTime protocols. In a well-disciplined design environment, making such decisions early makes it possible for some aspects of client and server development to continue in parallel.

Define the Operations

In the project assignment, if we decide to build the client-server interaction from scratch, we will need to document:

- The action represented by each service code

- The data, if any, that must follow the code

- The data, if any, that the server should return

- Expected behavior if the data are inconsistent with the request or response

- What to do in "corner cases," or events that result from system operation the request cannot control

This last point is especially important from a maintenance perspective. Anticipating odd but plausible situations early in design helps future maintainers to avoid patching problematic situations with exception handling or some other cumbersome workaround, when no one wants to alter an otherwise acceptable design. How will the program behave if a find operation returns a null pointer? What if a record we want to delete has already been purged? The more specific and detailed our understanding of system behavior in these cases, the plainer the coding tasks become.

Let's assume our database application wants to make available a minimum complement of services, for the sake of illustration. Some of the issues addressed in the list above are only noted in part here and in the subsequent code example. The assignment documentation should strive to be thorough in this respect.

Add   Given a `String` array that conforms to the record type, this command prompts the database to convert the array into a record and return the unique ID assigned to it. The client is responsible for knowing the record layout and providing appropriate data.

Modify   Given a `String` array that conforms to the record type, this command prompts the database to update a record that is specified by its ID. Modify does not protect against multiple concurrent updates—the last change supersedes all previous changes.

Delete   Given a unique ID, this command removes the associated record from the database. Requests to delete a record that has already been purged are ignored.

Find   Given a single `String`, this command returns a list of all records that have matching data in at least one of their fields.

Scheme   This command returns the type and width of all columns used by records in the database to the requesting client.

Implement the Protocol

Interfaces are an ideal repository for static data such as codes that specify the legal calls a client can make to the server. Any class that implements the interface gains access to its list of constants, which in this example are nothing more than "named" integer values, similar to what one would expect in a C language header file. In the example below, we use integers as placeholder values for each operation we define. These values are sometimes called *magic numbers*, and it's helpful to use hexadecimal notation to express them. Notice, below, how we've used expressions like 0xA0A1, for the simple advantage of making the value more memorable. It could also be useful for debugging, where values extracted from the compiled code are often expressed in hex.

```
/**
 * Services specifies the various operations the client
```

```
     * may call on the application to provide.
     *
     * @author Mobile Conferencing IT.
     */
    public interface DataServices {

      /**
        * The ADD_RECORD command prompts the database to
        * include the data that follows it as a new record.
        * The client is responsible for the data provided
        * conforms to the record's fields.
        */
      public static final int ADD_RECORD = 0xA0A1;

      /**
        * MODIFY_RECORD must be followed by an existing record
        * ID and the intended modifications.
        */
      public static final int MODIFY_RECORD = 0xB0B1;

      /**
        * DELETE_RECORD must be followed by a record ID. It
        * prompts the database to purge the indicated record,
        * or ignore the request if the record is no longer
        * resident.
        */
      public static final int DELETE_RECORD = 0xD0D1;

      /**
        * FIND_RECORDS is followed by a String representing
        * the match criteria. The database is prompted to find
        * every match among the available records and return a
        * list of "hits" or a null pointer.
        */
      public static final int FIND_RECORDS = 0xF0F1;
```

```
/**
 * SCHEME requires no arguments and prompts the
 * database to list the column names and widths that
 * compose each record.
 */
public static final int SCHEME = 0xFFFF;
}
```

Thinking ahead for just a second, an additional benefit of the interface is that it gives us a document from which to extrapolate "job" classes, which might operate on a separate thread from the client that initiates it. Each type of operation could be contained in a class that implements something like a Job interface, and the job itself could run as a thread in a group, along with other threads that perform the same function. We can look for ways to achieve some economy of threads, in one scenario, if we somehow bundle certain jobs to run concurrently against the data store (because they don't change anything), while others must observe a strict queue. We'll develop this is idea further once we have had a chance to explore both this approach and RMI in full.

The Client/Request Structure

As mentioned above, the server should keep an account of all current client connections, check their connection status and the progress of their requests, and recoup server resources once a connection terminates. An intuitive first step on the first objective is to separate out client connections and requests and give them their own classes. Using the Socket reference returned by accept(), we can construct a Client instance and read the service call written by the remote machine to form a Request. Setting up the server to juggle concurrent instances is simple. All the Client class has to do is implement Runnable, construct a thread for itself, call its own start() method, and execute its central processes from that point, thereby keeping the listener loop free of the details and self-documenting a map of the object's life.

The Client class can absorb more detail by managing the creation of its associated Request object. A Request should consist of the action the remote client wants to perform, along with the data needed to support it. On its face, it may seem extraneous to form a separate object that uncouples the client's connection from its own request; it certainly isn't essential. But in this case, we are thinking ahead a little to how we will handle a data request. The request itself is only one part of the client object, so is it necessary to include posting the request within the same thread that governs the client's connection state? One advantage of breaking out the request as a separate object is that the full client object won't have to participate fully in a scheduling model the server might employ to expedite or regulate requests. A Client object could, in one configuration, simply observe its Request and wait for notification of the request thread's termination, indicating it has run its course. The Client then receives any return data by way of the notification update, which is passed back over the stream to the remote client. Figure 17.1 illustrates this relationship.

FIGURE 17.1 The client/request structure

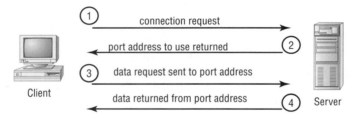

An alternative approach might be to make Request an inner class of Client, avoiding the overhead of the Observer notification model and the burden of negotiating field access between the two. Once data has been sent back to the remote client, the Client can close its data streams and flag itself for removal. The request object, focussed solely on getting processed and passing return data back, can be scoped and de-referenced by the server during a routine check.

This brings us to our second objective: to have the server support some form of client tracking. A container suffices to store object references, but we will also want to query each stored element to determine its current state. The least cumbersome way of accomplishing this is to add a boolean flag to the contained elements that indicates whether their purpose has been served. Client objects will close their own streams, so in normal processing we don't have to worry about connections staying open. If this were a full-fledged application, we would need to check for client connections that fail while their requests are in progress and respond accordingly.

The elements of the Server class that derive from our discussion are included in this code fragment:

```java
public class Server implements Runnable {
  private Vector connections;
  private Vector jobs;
  private Client clientTmp;
  private Request request;
  private Database dbs;
  private ServerSocket listener;
  ...

  public Server(int port) {
    listener = new ServerSocket(port);
    //stores client connection
    connections = new Vector();
    //stores request portion of client
    jobs = new Vector();
    //loads the database into memory
    dbs = new Database("reservations.ser");
    Thread t = new Thread(this);
    t.start();
  }

  public void run() {
    while(true) {
      try {
        clientTmp = new Client(listener.accept(), dbs);
        request = clientTmp.getRequest();
        connections.add(clientTmp);
        jobs.add(request);
        clientTmp = null;
        request = null;
      }
      catch(IOException ioe) {
        System.out.println(
```

```
            "Listener aborted irregularly");
            ioe.printStackTrace();
        }

        Iterator connectList = connections.iterator();
        Iterator jobList = jobs.iterator();

        while (connectList.hasNext()) {
          clientTmp = (Client)connections.next();
          if (clientTmp.isDone()) {
            connectList.remove(clientTmp);
          }
        }
        while (jobList.hasNext()) {
          request = (Request)jobs.next();
          if (request.isComplete()) {
            jobList.remove(request);
          }
        }
      }
    }
    ...
}
```

There are more than a few blanks to fill in for this class; they are left as development exercises for those who wish to complete the code. To keep this illustration brief, we have left a few things undone that would make the overall design more elegant. We are currently maintaining Client and Request objects in separate vectors; as intimately related as the two objects are, a tighter association between the two is a necessity.

The last portion of the run() method satisfies our third objective: to provide some form of cleanup for expired connections and jobs. If we wanted to keep the server's loop focussed on efficient listening, we could perform vector monitoring through a separate Cleanup class and run it on its own thread. Vectors are already internally synchronized, so we wouldn't have to worry about removing elements while the listener is trying to add a new one. But if we wanted to use wait() and notifyAll() to pre-empt the cleanup thread when either vector is unavailable, we'd still have to synchronize on them. Neither the compiler nor the runtime allows `wait()` and `notify-All()`, except within a synchronized block of code; there is no cross-check in the compiler to see whether the object in question "really" needs it.

The `Client` class below is also incomplete, but illustrates the features that have been discussed. It encapsulates the streams connecting the server's machine to the remote client, instantiates its request as a discrete object, and implements an `Observer` for keeping tabs on the request's progress. This is by no means the only choice. Using a Beans-oriented approach, our connection object could implement an event listener to be notified of changes in the `Request` object, thereby taking advantage of Java's built-in event handling mechanism. In the sense that the request portion of a client represents its "model," and the connection portion a type of "view," there are really a variety of ways to consider capturing the relationship effectively—one of which would be an MVC type of pattern. These techniques have the advantage of being more flexible. The `Observer/Observable` interface/class pair has the advantage of being easy to implement and ideally suited to the immediate problem. The `boolean` flag *done* can be set to true once the data returned from the database call, if any, has been written back to the remote machine. With a few basic modifications, however, this class could also support a persistent connection to the server, using its `run()` method as a loop for handling successive service requests.

```java
public class Client implements Runnable, Observer {
  protected Thread runner;
  private InputStream incoming;
  ObjectInputStream objInput = new
    ObjectInputStream(incoming);
  private OutputStream outgoing;
  ObjectOutputStream objOutput = new
    ObjectOutputStream(outgoing);
  private Request req;
  private boolean done = false;
  private Object returnData;
  private Database db;

  public Client(Socket connection, Database db) {
    try {
```

```
            incoming = connection.getInputStream();
            outgoing = connection.getOutputStream();
            req = new Request(this, objInput.readObject(), db);
            runner = new Thread(this);
            runner.start();
        }
        catch(IOException ioe) {
            System.out.println("Couldn't open socket streams");
        }
    }

    public Request getRequest() {
        return req;
    }

    public boolean isDone() {
        return done;
    }

    public void update(Observable request,
    Object retData) {
        returnData = retData;
    }

    protected void finalize() {
        incoming = null;
        outgoing = null;
        runner = null;
    }

    public void run() {
        while (!isDone())
        {
            try {
                objOutput.writeObject(returnData);
                objOutput.flush();
```

```
      }
      catch (IOException ioe) {
        System.out.println(
        "Couldn't write return data back to the client");
        ioe.printStackTrace();
      }
    done = true;
  }
  ...
}
```

This class implements the `Observer` method `update()`, which is then called by any `Observable` that has added this class to its list of listeners. As design patterns go, it is similar to the way event handlers work and is very useful when one object needs to base its behavior on the state change in another object. Also notice the assumption that the client's request is sent as a single `Request` object, reducing the "protocol" for client-server communication to a single `readObject()` call. Since this class has no role in dealing with data other than as a middleman, it only requires an `Object` reference to pass it back and forth.

The last class fragment we have roughed out in this preliminary sketch is `Request` itself. This class extends `Observable` so it can register its "owner's" interest in knowing when the job has completed. `DataServices` is implemented for access to the service codes. At the end of the thread run, the request notifies its client of any data that may have been returned when the call to the database finished. The `boolean` field `completed` is also set to true to expedite de-referencing the thread used by this object.

```
public class Request extends Observable
implements Runnable, DataServices, Serializable {
  protected int command;
  protected Object data;
  protected boolean completed = false;
  protected transient Thread runJob;
  private database db;
```

```java
public Request(Client owner, Object obj, Database db) {
  Request req = (Request)obj;
  command = req.getCommand();
  this.db = db;
  data = req.getData();
  runJob = new Thread(this);
  addObserver(owner);
  runJob.start();
}

public int getCommand() {
  return command;
}

public Object getData() {
  return data;
}

protected void setData(Object dbReturn) {
  data = dbReturn;
}

public boolean isComplete() {
  return completed;
}

public void run(){
  switch(getCommand()) {
    case ADD_DATA: db.add((String[])getData());
                   break;
    case SCHEME:   Object obj = db.getListScheme();
                   break;
  // remainder of service calls
  }
  setChanged();
  notifyObservers(getData());
  completed = true;
}
}
```

Since we have a limited number of data calls, a simple switch on `getCommand()` will suffice. But if the command list is going to grow to any size, it makes sense to start thinking about a parent class that all requests can subclass or perhaps even an interface they can all implement; see Figure 17.2 for one such arrangement. Another way to maintain uniform communication between client and server, regardless of the service requested, is to encapsulate all the relevant objects into one, perhaps in a `Response` object. This technique almost trivializes the argument that straight VM-to-VM communication over streams requires the developer to maintain a special protocol. Allowances have to be made for threads and other objects that do not serialize—notice that `Request` implements `Serializable` but marks its `Thread` reference `transient`—but hiding the details of transmitting objects over the wire is worth it.

FIGURE 17.2 A flexible parent class

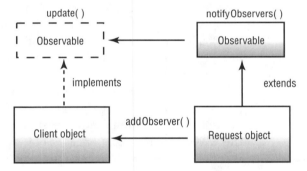

Limitations of the Model

Before object serialization was added to Java, one of the chief complaints about the JDK, regardless of its newcomer status, was its lack of a ready-to-use persistence model. Before the arrival of an object serialization facility, in order to commit an object type to a stream, programmers had to break the object into its constituent parts. Once an object was "unrolled" into integers, floats, byte arrays, and so on, it could be placed on the stream, one `writeUTF()` call at a time. Reading those values back in was, of course, the same call-intensive and order-sensitive process. The methods that were written to handle this were little more than hand-coded "object protocols."

The process wasn't ugly just because it was tedious and prone to error; it was ugly because there was no way to assure that any two people would even write the same class to the stream in the same way. Every object mapping was a potential exercise in lengthy, detail-oriented, throwaway code. Most work-arounds, such as trying to share object-serial maps in advance of the classes themselves, simply defeated the benefits that a "network-aware" language was supposed to offer.

Now, object serialization makes the task relatively easy. Where it is possible to abstract the types sent over the network so that as few objects as possible are part of the transmission, the resulting code is very straightforward and easy to read. With a small application, such as the one the project assignment will require you to write, building a quick-and-dirty protocol and defining a few object types to communicate to send back and forth may be all you really need. But there is a limit to how effective a "state-oriented" communication scheme can be. In general, the constraints of passing objects between autonomous VMs are the constraints of version control and updating.

Once we commit an object to the stream, its state is fixed. It's like sending a letter, in the sense that the information it contains is only current for so long. The more volatile the information, the less useful the letter is, especially if its delivery is slow or the recipient doesn't read it right away. If that object is being sent to a file, our only concern is keeping the stored data current. But if it is going to another VM, keeping both VMs in sync on the object means limiting object communication to state-oriented updates, making sure neither VM would need to change the object while it is in transit, or making sure that the changes aren't material to inter-VM communication.

The usual style of communicating through streams is a procedural one: the client sends a request, the server sends a response. If we want to develop an exchange that feels more interactive or reflect several turns the exchange might take, the script might be made more elaborate, but it remains tied to a synchronous model. As the communication becomes more complex, we end up with a new protocol on our hands. This has been a predominant objection among developers who see the ease of serializing individual objects but remember the lesson of writing individual objects into serial form by hand. Serialization alone relies on the programmer to maintain the protocol for communicating. Eliminating one layer of tedium—the atomic level of persistence—merely shifts the problem to higher ground. In the absence of a set way to communicate multiple objects between any two machines, we must still distribute the protocols, and the class files that embody them, to cast serialized objects back to their correct type.

Remote Method Invocation (RMI)

The end goal of Java's serialization facility is to simplify the task of persisting objects. Saving objects to a file or to another VM is now a straightforward, standardized, sometimes even trivial process. To call RMI, an alternative networking approach serves our immediate purpose in discussing the Developer's Exam assignment, but ultimately there's no qualitative comparison worth making. Object serialization is a useful but one-dimensional facility; RMI, on the other hand, is a full-grown architecture for distributed computing, and is scalable to far more complex tasks than the request–response style of programming our project requires at a minimum.

Serialization handles the details of writing object-level protocols so the programmer can send objects to a stream without worrying about their elemental structure or ordering. In much the same way, RMI provides a means for distributing objects as services so that a remote service request looks as much like a local one as we can manage. This overcomes at least one potential limitation in the approach we just discussed: Rather than send an object back and forth between VMs, we station it in one place. The VM responsible for serving the object declares it "exportable" and puts it where an RMI "object server" can call on it when a request comes in.

To use the object's services, the remote client must first obtain a reference to it. In order to do that, the client must of course know where to find the object, what it is called, and what method calls it provides. Once that information is acquired, however, RMI takes care of the rest:

- Object serialization

- Object transport, using its own "wire protocol"

- Exception handling specific to network errors

- Security management

Taking advantage of all these services requires some forethought. The developer must consider which objects to serve based on the applicability of their services to remote access. Although the risks of distributed computing are similar in nature to straightforward protocol-based communication, trying to make these variances transparent through RMI casts some murkiness over the exception process, possibly making it seem complex. Network connections can be severed physically or logically. The client or server may go down or drop the connection. The occasional extreme latency in network transmissions may cause a timeout just before a request is fulfilled. Any of these can disrupt the expected flow, leaving the server's current state and the client's understanding of it uncertain. The elegance of RMI is a fine thing, but we do not want to inherit a spate of exceptions on every remote call just to achieve it.

A Model RMI Transaction

For a client to be able to call on an object that resides on a remote machine, it must first have a reference to it. To retrieve the reference and use it, the client has to know substantially more about the object than we need to know to find a Web page. The only concise way to do this is to embed that lookup information in the client code. It is possible to find and determine remote services at runtime, but short of wanting to write an object browser in and of itself, we do not want to explore remotely available services and determine their facilities in runtime, before using them. We just want to use them, so advance knowledge of the available method calls is essential. Before changes in the JDK 1.2, RMI facilitated this discovery through a custom pair of classes called *skeletons* and *stubs*. These two classes derived directly from the class file of the remote object.

When the remote client calls on an object, it does so by way of a lookup. This lookup is coded into the client, as are the explicit calls to the object's methods. If the lookup succeeds, the RMI server returns the remote object's stub, which acts as a stand-in for the remote object's class and methods. Upon a call to any one of these methods in pre-1.2 code, the stub sends the request to the skeleton reference, which resides on the server side. The skeleton retrieves the operations of the local object that the client is interested in and maintains a `dispatch()` method to coordinate routing the object's response back through the stub. This method of internal communication-by-proxy is still available in the JDK 1.2, but RMI changes in the current release have brought the skeleton's role into the `RemoteObject` class.

The current JDK release changes the structure of RMI to make room for new features such as activatable objects. Before Java 2, the skeleton retrieved methods from the remote object as Operation objects, which are now deprecated. The tool that creates the skeleton and stub classes, the rmic compiler, now provides a flag (rmic -v1.2) to create stubs that are not backward-compatible with 1.1 RMI code.

The communication between stub and skeleton (whether discrete or part of RemoteObject) takes place over RMI's remote reference layer, the "wire protocol" we referred to earlier, which in turn relies on the transport layer already provided by TCP/IP. But the point of all this layering is to render the mechanics of network communication as transparent as possible, freeing the programmer to focus on the semantics of routine method calls. Figure 17.3 shows a logical view of an RMI-based interaction. In this diagram, the remote object is a Request, through which the client can call the same services we provided through the protocol interface shown earlier in the chapter.

FIGURE 17.3   An RMI-based interaction

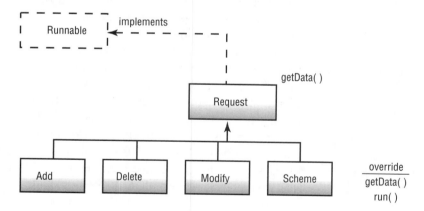

Implementing RMI

Once the questions surrounding proper design have been settled, writing the code for RMI requires several steps, but it is not overly complicated. In this example, we'll redesign the `Request` class as an object our client will access to enter a transaction request. We need to provide both the client and server resources. The `Request` class now assumes the dimensions of a protocol similar to `DataServices`, but has the advantage of being self-describing in its implementation:

```java
import java.rmi.*;
public interface RemoteRequest extends Remote {
  public void add(String[] newRecord)
    throws RemoteException;
  public void modify(Object id, String[] changes)
    throws RemoteException;
  public void delete(Object id)
    throws RemoteException;
  public String[][] find(String match)
    throws RemoteException;
}
```

`Remote` is a "tagging" interface, like `Serializable`. All it does is identify implementers of this interface to the VM as objects that are eligible for remote access. It's also necessary for each abstract method to declare throwing `RemoteException`, the parent class for all the processes that can go wrong during a remote invocation.

The class that implements `RemoteRequest`, which we will name `Request`, must meet three conditions. First, it needs the semantics that are peculiar to identifying an object in a remote context: its hashcode, `toString()` representation, and so on. Second, it must give the host VM a way to export it to the object server providing its lookup service. The easiest way to satisfy both requirements is by extending `UnicastRemoteObject`, which provides an export method the VM can call automatically when binding the object to its object server. This class also inherits its remote identification semantics from its parent, `RemoteObject`. Third, `Request` must explicitly provide a default constructor that throws `RemoteException`:

```java
import java.rmi.*;
import java.rmi.server.*;

public class Request extends UnicastRemoteObject
implements RemoteRequest {
```

```
public Request() throws RemoteException {
  super();
}

public void add(String[] newRecord)
throws RemoteException {
// code to add a record to the local database
}
...
}
```

If this class for some reason must extend something else, UnicastRemote-Object also supports a static export() method that takes the current object as an argument. This call can be added to the constructor:

```
UnicastRemoteObject.export(this);
```

Once the remote interface and implementing class are complete, we can generate the skeleton and stub classes that will be used to manage the communication endpoints between client and server. The tool that does this, rmic, takes the implementing class (not the .java source) as its argument and produces class files using the same name, but with _Skel.class and _Stub.class suffixes:

```
$ javac RemoteRequest.java Request.java
$ rmic Request
$ ls *.class
RemoteRequest.class
Request.class
Request_Skel.class
Request_Stub.class
```

RMI respectively calls on or distributes each class once a remote request occurs. The only requirement for these classes is that they reside in the same package space as the class they are generated from. To accommodate classes that are part of a package, the -d flag for rmic works the same as it does for javac.

The server code that sponsors the **Request** object is responsible for binding it to an RMI server. This service is launched through a tool bundled with the JDK called `rmiregistry`. This registry is really just another server like the one built early in this chapter. It sets itself up on an available port and waits for request from any client, local or remote. It functions as a registry by tracking all remote objects that any local VM binds to it. Since it operates autonomously from any VM on the same system, the VM must be given the port address of the registry. By default, `rmiregistry` attempts to use 1099 as its service port, but an optional one can be provided by passing the appropriate argument.

RMI for Java 2 adds a very interesting feature to its repertoire: the ability to launch the registry of one machine on demand, by way of a remote object request. The current registry has to run all the time, potentially taking up resources when it has no work to do. The JDK provides another tool, `rmid`, which behaves similarly to a Unix daemon or NT service, polling for requests to start up the registry when needed. A tutorial on activation is supplied with the JDK documentation. From the root directory for the documentation, locally or online, it is available at `docs/guide/rmi/activation.html`.

To bind a remote object to the registry, the server must first implement security. This step is a precaution against the client trying to pass an argument type with less than honorable intentions through the object server back to the application server. RMI does not mandate the use of a security manager, but it will refuse to load new classes coming from the client without one.

If we wanted the `Request` class to host its own registration code, we could add a main method to implement security and call `Naming.rebind()`. The `rebind()` method takes two arguments, a URL-style `String` representing the remote object's location, and a reference to the remote object itself:

```
public class Request extends UnicastRemoteObject
implements RemoteRequest {
...
  public static void main(String args[]) {
    System.setSecurityManager(new RMISecurityManager());
    try {
      // assume port 1099
      String URL = "rmi://www.objserver.net/DataRequest";
```

```
        Naming.rebind(URL, new Request());
    }
    catch(IOException ioe) {
        // the parent exception to both RemoteException
        // and MalformedURLException; rebind() throws both
        ioe.printStackTrace();
    }
  }
}
```

The Naming class has a static bind() method, but in practice it is not often used. bind() throws one more exception than rebind() does, called AlreadyBoundException, which directly subclasses Exception. Both methods are intended for the same purpose, but the rebind() method does not complain if its object reference wasn't already bound before being called, so it's provided to refresh either a "null" or existing object registration. The rebind() method requires less exception handling code than the bind() method.

The registration process by no means limits us to a single instance of the remote object type, but each instance does have to be uniquely named and individually registered.

In a system of any complexity, it would make sense to compose a single remote object through which other server resources could then be accessed. This "single resource" could even be the application server itself, providing a remote public interface to clients while reserving its internal operations— calls to the database, thread scheduling, and other local tasks—behind the scenes. This would certainly reduce name-space confusion when writing the client code. Under less than ideal circumstances, client-side programmers would have to document all of the object URLs required or add them and recompile code as they become available; this gets tedious quickly. The server-side developer, with good planning and design, can encapsulate all the required services through one remote reference and avoid that situation.

Any way it's handled, using an incremental approach to adding RMI services means extra work. The new services have to be written and compiled, new stubs and skeletons generated, new registration code added, and client code modified to use them. We're almost back to where we started with creating elaborate protocols! Design and include all the necessary remote objects before implementing them, and there will be less to remember and maintain.

All this work on the server side translates to a relatively trivial coding task for the client. The client must be able to cast a remote reference to its class, although it may not use the class reference to instantiate objects of that type; it must instead use the Naming class to look up the object via an RMI protocol handler and the correct URL:

```
public class ClientSide {
  Request myRequest;
  String [][] schema;
  ...
  public void issueRequest() {
    try {
      myRequest = (Request)Naming.lookup(
        "rmi://www.objserver.net/DataRequest");
      // port 1099 assumed
      schema = myRequest.listScheme();
    }
    catch(AccessException re) {
    // A RemoteException subclass - for illustration
    }
    catch(RemoteException ae) {
    // all remote accesses throw this
    }
    catch(NotBoundException nbe){
    // an Exception subclass thrown if the lookup fails
    }
  ...
  }
  ...
}
```

The client code then calls methods on the myRequest reference just as if it were a local object. RMI handles all the subsequent details. Here we've also laid out in detail the exceptions that a call to lookup() requires us to catch. Often these are ignored in example code by catching RemoteException, the parent class to most exceptions thrown when using RMI. Taking this shortcut also obscures the opportunity to recover from specific faults. On an AccessException, for example, a specific message pertaining to what action was denied could be crucial information to debugging. If we just catch the parent class, we can get an exception name and a stack trace if we want them, but no further information that could be provided in an exception-specific catch clause.

Limitations of RMI

Glossing over exceptions in complex, distributed code is a mild symptom of one of the more severe limitations of choosing RMI in any project: it can be exceptionally hard to debug a complex distributed application, particularly if the client and server are multithreaded. RMI renders many underlying operations transparent to the application code, which is a great advantage in many ways. It's not RMI's fault that it's easy to defeat proper exception handling by catching parents and super-parents. Nonetheless, that fact that runtime bugs can be obscured by the lack of a robust reporting mechanism may influence the perception that somehow RMI is at fault. However transparent RMI renders remote services at the code level, there is a deeper responsibility that the developer must take for a proper and thorough implementation of RMI's services. It is not a "pop-in" replacement for a more straightforward, if less robust, technique for writing proprietary serialization schemes.

Step-tracing through an RMI problem can be a technically overwhelming task without the right tools—assuming anyone has them. A debug walk-through in this environment means being able to walk through the stacks of two (or more) independent VMs, each of which is running simultaneously and quite possibly threading its activities among local and remote tasks. That said, there's no reason RMI programming must be overly complex, but it's easy to slip into bad habits and take a few shortcuts just to get something up and running. If multithreading is added as an afterthought, the application could well be at risk. The protocol-based approach we took earlier in the chapter makes us write more of the ground-level code by hand, but there is always only one VM acting on a serialized object at a time, which is easier to isolate.

Another condition any RMI implementation has to look out for is the way remote requests enter the server's local threading scheme. It's possible for Client A to look up Remote Reference B, which calls on Server Object C, on which some other server-local object is synchronizing. Without carefully negotiating the asynchronous requests of remote clients with what the server wants to execute locally, the potential for deadlocking the server and hanging the VM is high. Again, this problem goes back to design and properly accounting for interaction on the server side.

Various newsgroups and mailing lists have discussed RMI's performance extensively. The range of experiences reported in these forums is almost exclusively comparative and seems to vary from much faster than CORBA to a degree or two slower, depending on the design and type of implementation. But it's difficult to determine where the true mean in experiences lies: it's far easier to write toy code and benchmark it than it is to invest in a full-fledged example and gauge experience in production.

We can certainly infer that serializing entire objects, when only a small part of the data needs to be sent, plays a part in reports of sluggish performance, a point that brings us to a major difference between RMI and CORBA. RMI can pass objects by value, whereas CORBA—a model predicated on distributed code among heterogeneous systems—only passes values by reference. The developer has to be aware that passing a 10MB Vector is just as easy as passing a 15-character byte array, where RMI is concerned. Careful design, again, is imperative to keep track of exactly what kind of information (and how much of it) the completed system will send over the wire.

A full appreciation of RMI starts with understanding the functional differences between a local object and a remote one. With those characteristics fully understood, the benefits of the architecture can be weighed more effectively against its potential costs. At the same time, RMI is not so complex that experimenting with it will take substantially longer than writing straight "object protocol" code, once the functional steps are committed to memory.

More on Threads

Up to this point in our discussions about the Developer's Exam, we've addressed threading on a tactical level, suggesting a few possible ways to deploy them, but without creating a robust, working model of any one type. These hints and code fragments reflect an underlying philosophy to provide ideas and initial explorations that will help set the stage for the requirements of the project assignment. Providing some ready-made templates for implementation toward a generic project might be more to the point, but it would not help you to justify your work, as will be required on the follow-up exam. You must be able to articulate the relative merits of your work against other possible choices, and for that, a survey of possible answers is better preparation than a given few.

At the same time, concurrent programming, and Java threads in particular, are respectively multiple-volume and book-length subjects in their own right. It's not easy to simply "survey" threading strategies, so in this chapter's final section we will take a look at one thread-pooling strategy that may prove to be a useful complement to building the network server.

Sharing Threads

One complex aspect of writing a multithreaded application server is choosing a way to define how client requests will run. A request to the server implies a temporary need for its resources, which can be restored and allocated to subsequent requests—if we remember to reclaim them. But when that resource is a thread, a notably finite resource on any system, extra caution is warranted. Threads are not intended, by their nature, to be instanced, run, and de-referenced without some regard for the system-level resources involved in maintaining them. We can demonstrate this by creating a thread *pool*, or a collection of thread references that are continually "re-referenced" as their current tasks run their course, and compare that technique side by side with an application that creates new threads on demand and de-allocates them when their execution tasks complete.

Intuitively, we should expect to conserve a substantial amount of resources. As the need for more threads increases, the cost of object creation and garbage collection should increase, perhaps rising proportionately with the number of threaded tasks submitted. In a pooled-resource model, our thread-creation costs are incurred up front. After that, we reuse those resources continually, avoiding object creation and destruction in favor of referencing and de-referencing `Runnable` objects. It also stands to reason that the more efficient the arrangement for managing the thread pool, the more time or system-level resources can be conserved, up to some hard limit.

Another important point to make about threading: Just because an object is `Runnable` doesn't mean it needs a thread. `Runnable` is just an interface. It is a contract to implement a `run()` method, and an agreement into which any class may enter. By itself, the `run()` method is not especially significant. If a subclass of `Applet` were to implement `Runnable`, calling its `start()` method would not invoke threaded behavior. What makes a `Runnable` object so potentially powerful is that one of the `Thread` class' constructors will accept one as an argument. It is the `Thread` class itself that contains the tools necessary to endow a `Runnable` with its own line of execution, and only a thread construction that ties up system resources.

To demonstrate all of these points, and to give you something more to think about in preparation for the project assignment, we've provided (in the following sample code) the `ShareThread` class. Discussion follows the code.

```
/**
 * ShareThread is a poolable thread resource capable of
 * accepting and and executing small Runnable jobs
repeatedly.
 *
 * @author Sybex Certification Study Guide authors
 */
public class ShareThread extends Thread {
  private Runnable workToDo;

  /**
   * Sets this "pooled thread" instance as a daemon so
   * the program can exit if this is the only thing left.
   */
  public ShareThread() {
    setDaemon(true);
  }

  /**
   * execute() waits until the internal Runnable
```

```
 * reference is null, then assigns it a new job.
 *
 * @param Runnable - an object that requires
 * a thread resource
 */
public void execute(Runnable job) {
  synchronized(this) {
    while(workToDo != null) {
      try {
        wait();
      }
      catch(InterruptedException ie) { }
    }
    workToDo = job;
    notifyAll();
  }
}
/**
 * executeIfAvailable() checks once to see if no job is
 * pending. If not, a job is assigned, the boolean flag
 * set to true, and all waiting threads notified.
 *
 * @param Runnable - an object that needs its run()
 * method called.
 * @returns boolean - indicating whether a job was
 * successfully assigned
 */
public boolean executeIfAvailable(Runnable job) {
  boolean executed = false;

  synchronized(this) {
    if (workToDo == null) {
      workToDo = job;
      executed = true;
      notifyAll();
```

```
        }
      }
    return executed;
  }

  /**
   * A "snapshot" check whether a job is currently
   * assigned. Not reliable beyond the moment of the test
   *
   * @return boolean - indicates whether a job is
   * assigned.
   */
  public boolean available() {
    return (workToDo == null);
  }

  /**
   * Rejects any thread that is not owned by the current
   * instance. Waits until a Runnable job is assigned,
   * then calls its run() method directly, acting as its
   * surrogate Thread instance. Signals for another job
   * by dereferencing the current one. Terminates when
   * no more user-level jobs are available.
   */
  public void run() {
    if (Thread.currentThread() == this) {
      Runnable job = null;
      for (;;) {
        synchronized(this) {
          while (workToDo == null) {
            try {
              wait();
            }
            catch(InterruptedException ie) {}
          }
          job = workToDo;
```

```
            notifyAll();
          }
          job.run();
          workToDo = null;
        }
      }
    }
  }
```

This is a very simple subclass of Thread with just four methods and one constructor. All the constructor does is call setDaemon() and set it to true. Daemon threads are a special case; any application that has them may exit if only daemon threads are currently running. There are two methods that attempt to run a submitted job, execute() and executeIfAvailable(). Both synchronize on the current ShareThread instance. execute() waits until workToDo loses its current reference, then assigns it a new one. executeIfAvailable(), on the other hand, tests workToDo to see whether it is set to null during the current synchronized execution. If so, workToDo is given a new job. This is a one-shot attempt that makes the method appear clumsy. At the same time, it returns a boolean indicating success or failure in assigning a new job, so the responsibility is on the programmer to write a proper loop and test it.

Then ShareThread's run() method does an interesting thing. It synchronizes on its own instance, immediately returning if any thread other than the correct instance of ShareThread tries to run it. The method then waits until workToDo acquires a reference, rather than loses one. When that condition occurs, the new job is immediately reassigned to a temporary variable created within run(). Just after calling notifyAll(), workToDo is de-referenced again so that either execute method can assign a waiting job to it. But outside the synchronized block, the temporary variable calls run() directly on the Runnable object it now refers to. Since the current instance of ShareThread is already a thread, the job does not require a thread of its own.

The call to job.run() illustrates that the run method itself has no inherently threaded properties. If a job is called and executed within another threaded instance, it performs the same way as if it had constructed its own threaded instance, minus the costs of object creation. The jobs that are submitted to this class could be any object that implements Runnable, such as the Request class, minus its thread instantiation code.

This class lends itself well to a round-robin approach to satisfying data requests. Round-robin techniques don't scale well, unless more "robins" can be added easily. In this situation, that's precisely the case. The more requests that are expected, the more `ShareThread` objects that could be created to meet demand. Of course, the limiting factor will still lie in the ability of the database to expedite requests.

As a final demonstration, the code below is suitable for `ShareThread`'s `main()` method. It compares the time needed for a given number of `ShareThread` objects to execute a number of "joblets" against the time needed for the same number of jobs to instance their own threads and run individually. Use this code and experiment with a variety of pooled thread and joblet-count combinations. When you are satisfied that there is a clear difference in performance between the two, consider applying this model to your future project assignment.

```java
public class ShareThread {
...
  /**
   * Test facility that compares pooled threading to
   * straight threading of every submitted job. Launch
   * this program with the following syntax:
   * <PRE>java ShareThread <num_threads> <num_jobs> <job>
   * num_threads is how many threads to pool.
   * num_jobs is total number of Runnable jobs to queue.
   * job is a class that implements Runnable</PRE>
   */
public static void main(String args[])
throws Exception {

      //timing variables
    long startPool, startThreads, stopPool, stopThreads;

    final int totalJobs = Integer.parseInt(args[1]);
    final int threadPool = Integer.parseInt(args[0]);
    // runnables accounts for mult. job types submitted
    final int runnables =
      Integer.parseInt(args.length - 2);
```

```
Runnable[] joblets = new
  Runnable[totalJobs * runnables];

// populates the joblets array with number of jobs
// requested times the total Runnable types given
for (int i = 0; i < runnables; i++){
  Class cls= Class.forName(args[i + 2]);
  for (int j = 0; j < totalJobs; j++) {
    joblets[(totalJobs*i)+j] = (Runnable)
    (cls.newInstance());
  }
}

System.out.println("Running " + joblets.length +
  " jobs in " + threadPool + "worker threads.\n");
//begin timer on threadpool
startPool = System.currentTimeMillis();

ShareThread[] workers = new ShareThread[threadpool];
for (int i = 0; i < workers.length; i++) {
  workers[i] = new ShareThread();
  workers[i].start();
}

// simple looping strategy to assign a job to any
// available worker instance
int iLoop = 0;
int jLoop = 0;
while (iLoop < joblets.length) {
  while (!workers[jLoop].executeIfAvailable(
    joblets[iLoop])) {
    jLoop++;
    if (jLoop == workers.length) jLoop = 0;
  }
  Thread.yield();
  jLoop = 0;
```

```
        iLoop++;
      }

      // another simple loop to see if all workers are idle
      // if so, we're done
      for (iLoop = 0; iLoop < workers.length; iLoop++) {
        while(!workers[iLoop].available()){
          Thread.yield();
        }
      }
      stopPool = System.currentTimeMillis();
      System.out.println("Pooling all joblets took: " +
        (stopPool - startPool) + " milliseconds.\n");

      System.out.println(
        "Now giving each job a thread.\n");

      // Use a threadgroup to monitor all threads
      ThreadGroup group = new
        ThreadGroup("Threaded joblets");
      startThreads = System.currentTimeMillis();

      // Launch a thread for each joblet, and track all
      // joblet completions as a group to stop the clock.
      for (int i = 0; i < joblets.length; i++) {
        Thread thr = new Thread(group, joblets[i]);
          t.start();
      }
      while(group.activeCount() > 0) {
        thr.start();
      }

      stopThreads = System.currentTimeMillis();
      System.out.println("Threading all joblets took: " +
        (stopThreads - startThreads) + " milliseconds.\n");
    }
  }
```

The test class doesn't need to be much, just enough to cause a tick or two. As the number of jobs scales, the threaded test won't have any problem chewing up time. With pooled threads, make sure the sample `Runnable` can burn a few cycles, or you may get a few test runs that report taking no time. Here's an example test:

```java
public class Tester implements Runnable {
  public void run() {
    double val = getX() * getY();
  }

  private double getX() {
    return 3;
  }

  private double getY() {
    return 4;
  }
}
```

Chapter Summary

Building the application server brings together at least one aspect of each of the major components in a client-server environment. While the choices for network communication are relatively few, they are very different—and each technique has its own range of strengths and limitations. Building a network protocol between client and server is easy, but is limited to a synchronous exchange of objects between the two VMs and doesn't allow for interaction between them beyond what has already been scripted into the code. Object serialization hides the details of committing objects to a stream, but still requires us to handle writing objects in over the network in a sequence we have to define; there's no getting away from writing a proprietary protocol.

RMI makes everything look very simple from the client perspective. Instead of instantiating objects that exist on a remote server, we simply look them up to start using them. Each object we work with is otherwise transparent in its remoteness. Each object always resides on one machine, virtually eliminating the problem of state inconsistency that could arise with overly complex interactions in which objects themselves are being passed back and forth over the wire in serial form. At the same time, RMI hides so many layers of detail that when something goes wrong it can be difficult to find. Not the least of the obstacles is determining which VM originated the problem. RMI requires considerably more planning and design consideration before implementing. Casual oversights in RMI mean lots of maintenance later on, and lots of class rewrites and recompiles if we try to fix problems wholesale.

Once the choice of network technique has been made, however, we can give more thought to how threading plays a role in the whole scheme. This is admittedly a lot trickier to contend with in an RMI scheme, and multithreading questions should be pursued early in an RMI scheme rather than late.

As a final note, when looking for an efficient way to deal with lots of short requests to the application, consider using a thread pool to conserve object creation and destruction.

Chapter

18

Designing the User Interface

Lots of programmers who focus on writing business applications like to write the user interface first. The simple fact is that most people can absorb far more information in less time from a well-designed picture than they can from a well-written technical document. End users, particularly those who are removed from the process of programming, usually see a program's effectiveness in the form of the interaction it offers. Screen shots still sell far more programs than any other single marketing tool.

One of the more important decisions made within many corporate development efforts is not just the choice of a programming platform, but which "builder tool" to standardize on. The rise of rapid application development (RAD) tools, fourth-generation languages (4GL), and "integrated development environments" (IDE) is all based on the perception that direct visual feedback promotes faster and easier code writing than the code-compile-test cycle of a pure-text environment. One result of these developments seems to be that developers, like users, are just as interested in what programs will look like as what features they offer.

The GUI doesn't mean much, of course, unless it helps get the work done. Nor does it make sense to write application logic based on how the presentation will be structured. Java's Swing library addresses this issue in a very smart way: by decoupling the responsibilities of data presentation and manipulation into two different class groups. One outcome is that the data model, once developed, places no real constraints on the potential views of it, and vice versa. Since the cohesion between data and graphic elements has already been spelled out, development of the GUI in Swing could begin with either part, or it could progress in parallel in a team environment, without generating any fundamental concern for bringing the two together.

Another beauty of Swing is that this fundamental design pattern, often described as "loosely based on Model-View-Controller (MVC)," is repeated throughout the library. Once you understand Swing's particular take on this pattern, which we will call "model-delegate," most of what's left to know is a question of details. We won't worry about a comprehensive class review; exhaustive treatments of Swing are available elsewhere. We will focus instead on four topics we do not see covered in detail by others and that will directly benefit you in preparing for the project assignment. Once you have the basics down, you can reference the Swing library as necessary and absorb the details you need to develop the client you want.

See the section, "Write a User Interface," in Chapter 15 for a brief definition of the MVC design pattern and how Swing departs from it.

Assuming you'll have to build the client the same way you did the network server—from the ground up—there are four points to address that will assist you in writing your GUI and defending it on the follow-up exam:

- Defining the GUI's requirements
- How Swing components and models work
- Event handling and coding style
- Event handling and threading

Defining the GUI's Requirements

There's an even better tool for modeling a graphic user interface than a drag-and-drop code builder: pencil and paper. The single best recommendation we can make on designing your program's appearance is to just draw what you'd like to see on the screen. You can create a sketch for one or two GUI layouts in the time it takes your computer to boot, and a sketch is likely to capture more of your requirements and create less of a distraction than finding the proper widget in a draw program (unless, of course, you are already expert with one). Since there is usually less investment in designing on paper, it's easier to throw away bad ideas (one of the more important design principles we know). Unless you already have the digital art skills or an existing template for the kind of display you want in hand, a legible drawing makes a very reasonable initial reference document.

Here's a simple, four-step plan:

1. Identify needed components.

2. Sketch the GUI and a resizing.

3. Isolate regions of behavior.

4. Choose layout managers.

Identifying Needed Components

However austere the AWT's list of components might seem, it does have the advantage of economically describing the graphic objects in use on the most popular windowing systems today—Motif, Windows, and MacOS. It's therefore quite simple for virtually all GUI developers to express basic visual ideas in those terms: buttons for actions, checkboxes for toggles, lists for specified choices, text fields for arbitrary input, and so on. A microwave control panel, for example, is easy to conceive as one or more groups of buttons and a display for the time. The front of a tower computer translates easily—were we inclined to design one graphically—into a grid of 5¼" device faces; a tall, thin panel of status lights; a column of 3½"-wide device faces; a power button; and so on.

User interfaces are not much different once the requirements are defined. But it can be difficult, having identified the needed pieces, to verbalize how they should lay on the page and how they should respond to a window resizing. The menu belongs at the top; we know that. Generally speaking, if there is a primary display area—whether graphic, tabular, or document-oriented in presentation—we will want to devote any extra available space to it on a resize. Beyond those two principles, we need more information about what our application is. Let's assume for the sake of an illustration that we want to build a mail client in Java, and our first design review will concern the visual layout for a large number of departmental users. We know we will want to display a directory structure for sorting stored mail. Users will expect a table or list element to show mail items in the current directory; a text display for the current item being read; and a "status" area for updates on the client's background actions—downloading new messages, signaling new mail, and so forth.

Sketching the GUI

In our example in Figure 18.1, we profile the appearance of a typical mail client. The interface requires an area where we can review our directory tree of sorted mail in folders, which we placed to the left. We also want an area at the bottom of the frame for displaying status messages on the client's current attempt to send or retrieve mail. A dynamic display area for the list of pending incoming mail is located to the right of the tree structure and on top of another dynamic area that displays the current mail item. We want the detailed list of pending mail to be laid out by column and to show the column names in a button. We expect that experienced users will get the idea to click on a column name and infer from the results that a sort has taken place. As a provision for user preferences, we also want to allow the column size to be modified by dragging the column button's border.

FIGURE 18.1   Mail Client window

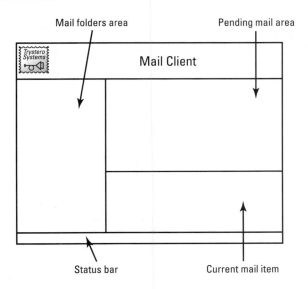

To get these ideas to paper, we sketched out a fairly conventional diagram with a menu bar on top, a flush-left panel with a tree-like figure drawn in, and a bottom bar with some sample text. The dynamic space we have split in two regions, showing multiple-column support for the pending mail list but a blank border area for the current mail item. We have split this area into equal parts so that a resize will better demonstrate who is acquiring the new space and in which direction.

Figure 18.2 shows the intended effect of the resize. In our example we wanted the mail item currently being read to assume as much available area as it could, on the presumption that the user resizes the window to get as much text to show as possible. While some users may in fact want a larger font for status messages or a dynamic font for the menu, we've chosen not to tie such preferences to the default behavior of dragging a window corner.

FIGURE 18.2 Mail Client window resized

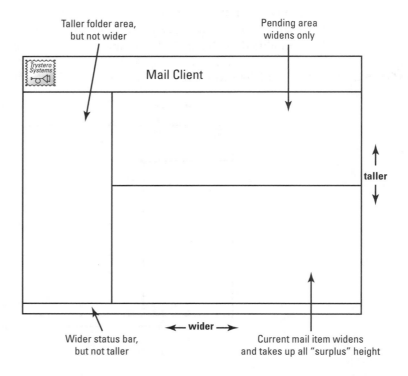

Taller folder area,
but not wider

Pending area
widens only

Mail Client

Trystero
Systems

taller

← wider →

Wider status bar,
but not taller

Current mail item widens
and takes up all "surplus" height

Along the horizontal axis, we want the bottom section to allow the status message area to use as much space as available, but without usurping the minimum space needed by the small icons. In the menu, we've followed the convention that the "Help" or "About" menu list appears flush-right on the frame (the menu components are not illustrated in the figure above). The displays of both the current mail item and the pending mail list could grow to the right but won't impinge on the tree (folders) view. Along the vertical axis, our tree area could take all the space the menu and status bars would allow. In our display area, the intention is to allow the current mail item view to resize as needed; the pending mail list would, however, remain fixed.

Isolating Regions of Behavior

Hopefully the description given of the behavior shown in the figures, combined with your knowledge of the AWT layout managers, already tipped you off to some appropriate layout choices. There is, of course, no single answer or "right" choice to make for the entire screen. Any reasonably sophisticated interface requires multiple layout managers and panels to contain the management behavior to its prescribed area, and there is no one formula for ordering or nesting those panels to get the desired effect. Yet neither is there a completely neutral way to describe the behavior we want. It probably wasn't hard to tell we already were thinking in terms of `BorderLayout` when we wrote the description above, in particular by our attempt to avoid saying "north," "south," "center," and so on. And this result is, in fact, exactly what we should expect; if we can articulate the screen behavior we want, the isolation of one region from the next and the tool needed to achieve the intent should be virtually self-evident.

This mail client breaks down very cleanly into the geographical areas provided by the Border layout manager—the default management scheme for an AWT frame—or Swing frame or window. The south will contain a status bar and small icons, and the tree will go in the west, leaving the center with the two dynamic areas. The center and south need a little more work to negotiate space allocation among the contained elements. In the south, the message bar and icons can first be contained by a panel. The panel, which is then added to the south, can adopt its own Border layout (instead of its default Flow layout), putting the message element in the panel's center and the icons in the east. Putting the icons in the east ensures that the icons get as much horizontal space as they require, and the center grabs all remaining space for messages. In the center, we add another panel with a Border layout manager, putting the mail list in its north and mail item in the center.

This is a decent first cut, but a second look will tell us we might have to rethink things as we refine the scheme. Just because we do not want the mail list to resize on a window control doesn't necessarily mean we don't want the user to have some control over setting the height requirement altogether. Also, if this window can't fit the messages listed in it, we'd like to have a scrollbar. If it has more space than it needs, a scrollbar that can't move but takes up space is a bit of an annoyance, but a price we pay with AWT components. The remaining option, before Swing, was to write our own.

The west can hold the tree we want without further help, but adding a panel first and then adding the tree to the panel is not a bad idea. It is one way of leaving options open to modifying that area of the border scheme rather than just the contained component itself. Getting in the habit of composing graphic areas this way, so that they can be added to a larger "component-container" frame and hooked in—we're whispering a loose definition for a JavaBean here—is an honorable way to build task-specific, reusable components. As we're about to discuss, however, Swing components already do that work for us.

Choosing Layout Managers

When you do come across limitations in the layout model, it's not a time to worry. The default layout managers, along with Grid, are widely applicable to several visual design objectives and are relatively simple to use. Whether they will suffice to handle a particular requirement well is a good first question to ask. In most cases, you should probably consider several alternative layout schemes to ensure you are choosing a simple approach that provides enough flexibility for some foreseeable changes. It's very nice to have choices for future improvements, but there is also a limit to how much versatility is a benefit. For example, if a programmer is required to survey a variety of open-ended alternatives that could have just as easily been left static, the benefit of flexibility may be wiped out by the cost of too many subtle decisions.

If you do have complex requirements and a compelling reason to implement them fully—for example, to successfully complete a Certification Exam—there are very powerful layout tools available in the JDK. The Programmer's Exam already tests your understanding of the fundamentals of the AWT layout managers. Chapter 9 provides some background and Java philosophy on layout management, then explores the five managers in detail. In this chapter's "Using Layout Managers" section, we complement that discussion by looking at a special-purpose manager, CardLayout, and then the Swiss Army knife of layout managers, GridBagLayout.

Using Swing

As mentioned in Chapters 14 and 15, the Swing library brings several new dimensions to graphic programming in Java. The first structural feature worth noticing is Swing's adaptation of a design pattern known as Model-View-Controller (MVC). In that pattern, the data, presentation, and data controls are decoupled from each other. Separating these roles into discrete classes allows the data to provide a generic interface to all possible views so that any number of views can form their data descriptions from a single, centralized source. Each view can then visually describe the model according to the set or subset of data that it is most interested in. The term that best describes Swing's view of this arrangement is *model-delegate*. The important concept to enforce by this renaming is that Swing employs a two-role version of MVC: the data model and the view controller.

The controller function is already built into Java by way of its event-handling facility, but Swing even takes that a step further by taking full advantage of JavaBeans' architecture in its components. For the purposes of our discussion, Beans can be oversimplified a little: they are characterized by a series of "properties" that are simply a class's existing field members supplied with a pair of formulaic get/set method signatures. Should you pick up a comprehensive book on Swing, you'll undoubtedly notice numerous references to the "properties" of each component. Beans are also designed to communicate state changes to their properties, not just that they've passed over by a mouse or been iconified. Other interested Beans can listen to these "fired" changes and behave appropriately. For example, if the listening Bean has an identical property, it can match the change. This might result in a change to the color of one component that would cause a whole group of components to change together. The advantage of this scheme is that changes in one Bean can be *bound* to changes in another, making it possible for one Bean to act as a "controller" for any component that wants to subscribe to the service.

As a further step, Beans can be configured to veto changes sent to them, rejecting values that exceed a normal range for the target Bean or whatever rule that Bean institutes. Of course, this process only has value to the sending Bean if it can learn whether its target accepts or rejects a change, and then it can respond. The sending Bean may wish to "roll back" to the previous state if the target Bean cannot comply or, in the case of multiple targets, the sender may attempt to set all target Beans to the last agreed-upon state. See Figure 18.3 for an illustration of each of these Bean-style events.

There's more to the total makeup of Beans, but much of the rest deals with managing them in a builder tool, which we don't have to worry about. The following sections discuss two component types that are particularly important to us: tables and lists. In keeping with Swing's model-delegate paradigm, we'll examine both aspects of these components: the way they present themselves and the way they hold the data that is used to create the presentation. It's also worth noting how Swing takes advantage of a structural model we discussed in Chapter 16. Swing relies heavily on interfaces and abstract classes in promoting its components, often providing a reference implementation model, either for recommended use or as a guide in building your own. As for toolkit design, this is a practice of the first quality. Take time to look around the source code for some of these classes and make some notes on how it's been implemented.

FIGURE 18.3 Three Bean event models

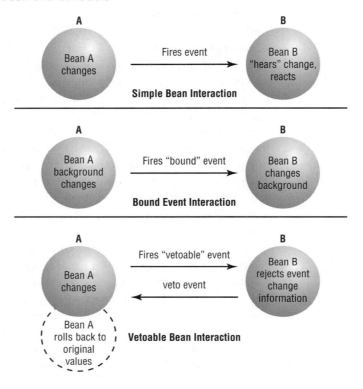

In the following sections, we take a look at two data-intensive Swing component types: tables and lists. As it stands, the organization of these two types is very similar. We're confident a structural overview of these two types and their support classes will fill in the blanks for you on the third component type, trees, leaving the implementation details of that type for you to master at your convenience.

Tables

The organization of classes for representing tabular data breaks down into three principal subgroups: the widget JTable, the table model, and the table column model. A list of the support classes for each, particularly the models, will give you a sense of the consistency of structure that will also apply to lists and trees. The following lists of relations are not all-inclusive lists.

JTable (**Class**)

- JTableHeader (class)

- TableCellEditor (interface)

- TableCellRenderer (interface)

- DefaultTableCellRenderer (class) (implements TableCellRenderer)

TableModel (**Interface**)

- AbstractTableModel (abstract class) (implements TableModel)

- DefaultTableModel (class) (extends AbstractTableModel)

- TableModelEvent (class)

- TableModelListener (interface)

TableColumnModel (**Interface**)

- TableColumn (class)

- DefaultTableColumnModel (class) (implements TableColumnModel)

- TableColumnModelEvent (class)

- TableColumnModelListener (interface)

A table in Swing uses the column as its smallest organizing unit; a table does not model itself at the cell level. Columns make sense, because they organize a specific data type, give it a descriptive name, and track important properties (such as field width). The TableColumn class itself represents a column. The interface TableColumnModel, as the name implies, provides the semantics for collecting a series of TableColumn objects together to represent a table row or record. This interface requires implementation for nineteen methods altogether; fortunately, DefaultTableColumnModel provides a standard implementation and includes event "firing" methods that broadcast changes in column behavior—deletion, addition, order change, selection change, and margin change. The event and listener classes associated with table columns are what you would expect—a means for generating column-oriented event objects and getting notifications when they occur.

The general and more important model is TableModel itself. TableModel adds a layer of control on top of column objects, which allows an implementation of the interface to return information on its table—row count, column count, and column names among them. Information reported on columns is not tied to what `TableColumnModel` reports, which makes it possible to report columns with non-unique names or to hide columns. `TableModel` also adds methods for accessing rows and cells.

One aspect of model-view relationships that may take some getting used to is that data model representations maintain column order independent of the view. When we want to rearrange data on the view level, for example, we don't want to be restricted to the model's internal arrangement of columns. We may decide we would rather have last names before first names or states before postal codes. Conversely, we do not want casual reorganization of the display to generate work for the model, forcing it to rearrange itself to reflect what the user sees. Therefore, there are always two accounts of what the data looks like: the order in which the widget table presents it and the order in which the underlying model maintains it. There is no obligation for either to match its arrangement to the other. The good news is that `TableModel` doesn't have to listen to events in the view regarding column activity. The better news is that indexing by column or row through any of the supporting classes follows the view. The mapping between the view and the model is hidden from the programmer so that the view can serve as a guide.

Be wary, however, of the three exceptions where the *model's* index order is maintained rather than the *view's*. If you decide to dig around a bit, bear in mind that the model's indexing of columns is kept in three places:

- `TableModel` in its entirety

- The `TableColumn` field `modelIndex`

- `TableModelEvent` constructors that get their values from `TableModel`

It's not required that you explicitly build models to create a `JTable`. You have the option to do so, of course, and it will make sense when you are thinking ahead to multiple types of presentation that can be based on one model of data. Otherwise, `JTable` is smart enough to accept hard-coded data or row–column dimensions in integer or `Vector` form and then construct default models using the inferred dimensions. One element that may not be immediately apparent is that `JTable` can also be constructed with a `ListSelectionModel` to support column and row selection. Details on `ListSelectionModel` are included with the discussion on lists.

Lists

There are three big changes between AWT and Swing lists. First, JList can contain any object as an item. The only requirement is some means must be provided for drawing a representation of the object if a toString() conversion would not suffice. This is a vast improvement over the Strings-only support of List. Second, where the AWT List enforces "pick-style" or multiple selections at random points on the list, JList supports range selection. Range selection is defined by its *anchor* (or initial selection) and its *lead* (or the last element pointed to when a selection is completed). Third, like all other Swing components, JList has no built-in scrollbar. To incorporate one, an instance of JList must be passed as the argument to a JScrollPane constructor. From that point forward, JScrollPane acts as a viewport to the list view, only providing scroll elements to the pane if the horizontal or vertical reach of the list's contents exceeds the viewable area.

The pattern of support classes for lists is quite similar to that for tables. However, lists have one less dimension to manage, so there are fewer roles to flesh out into classes. Nonetheless, these should look very familiar:

JList (**Class**)

- ListCellRenderer (interface)
- DefaultListCellRenderer (class)

ListModel (**Interface**)

- AbstractListModel (abstract class) (implements ListModel)
- DefaultListModel (class) (extends AbstractListModel)
- ListDataEvent (class)
- ListDataListener (interface)

ListSelectionModel (**Interface**)

- DefaultListSelectionModel (class) (implements ListSelectionModel)
- ListSelectionEvent (class)
- ListSelectionListener (interface)

Providing modeling support for lists is quite simple, but it's good design form to model the list's selection state separately from the arrangement of list data itself, in the same manner that column behavior is de-coupled from the overall data management for tables. A few properties are worth noting when dealing with selection behavior. `selectionMode` allows the programmer to define single-element, single-range, or multiple-range selection as the allowed behavior. Naturally, a selection of one item is just a special case of a range, one whose `anchor` and `lead` point to the same index value. `valueIsAdjusting` indicates whether the list object is currently firing events. This can be a useful state-check condition if you want to wait on new actions to the list until the current changes have been broadcast.

As with AWT `List` events, the broadcast of an event change does not necessarily mean a list selection has changed from its previous value. The only thing we can infer from receiving a list selection event is that some action took place on the `JList` and the item state might have changed as a result. In order to learn exactly what happened, we have to look at the event object itself; we cannot rely on the fact of an event alone to make decisions.

`ListModel` looks suspiciously like the beginnings of a `Vector`, as it supports two properties—`elementAt` and `size`. Its method list only supports these properties and the requisite methods for the Beans registration model—`addListDataEventListener()` and `removeListDataEventListener()`. As expected, the abstract class implementation `AbstractListModel` augments this with methods for firing changes to interested listeners. The `DefaultListModel` class bears out our hunch—it's almost a pure `Vector`. If you can handle questions on `Vector` for the Programmer's Exam, you'll have no problem mastering the `DefaultListModel`.

This implementation will change in future releases of Swing. One motivation is to tie Swing in more tightly with the Collections framework. In the meantime, any Java programmer who works with data structures or Beans has come across a `Vector` before, so it's familiar territory. To keep up to date on this and other Swing developments, you can browse `http://java.sun.com/products/jfc/tsc/`.

Using Layout Managers

Applying layout managers is all about matching the component behavior required with the manager that best provides it. As mentioned above, the only purpose of this section is to make sure your kit of layout managers is complete. Here we fully describe—expanding on the discussion in Chapter 9—the use of the two more advanced layout managers from the AWT, and show some sample code for demonstrating CardLayout and the beginnings of a scheme for learning how to manage a GridBagLayout. If you have already taken the time to learn the default layout managers, you're aware that it takes a few coding attempts to get a full sense of each layout manager's capabilities. With CardLayout, things are straightforward—just off the beaten path of layout managers. Learning GridBagLayout is an investment of your time and focus. It is something you should definitely look at twice before you think about applying it to your project assignment.

CardLayout

CardLayout differs from the other layout management in the ways it works. Instead of negotiating the screen's real estate among the contending preferred sizes of all the components, it organizes in layers. Though component overlap represents a misstep in layout among the other four managers, in Card it's expected behavior. Consequently, Card is the only layout manager that supplies a navigation scheme to flip through the number of cards made in a given container. Cards also link tail-to-head, so that flipping past the last card brings up the first in the series. The methods first(), last(), next(), and previous() each take the layout's parent container as an argument and are self-evident in action.

To add each component to a card, both the component and its constraints object must be specified in the add() argument of the container. In the case of CardLayout, the constraints object must be a String object; if it isn't, the method will throw an IllegalArgumentException. This String name is entered into a table as a key to the card with which it is associated. Calling the show() method with this key then allows for direct access to any card in the set. Listed below is a brief program to display a random card in the stack. Each card is a button with its number as a label. The program shows a card, waits an interval, and then picks another at random. The horizontal and vertical insets as well as the number of buttons wanted are entered at the command line like so:

```
$ java CardShow 5 5 25

import javax.swing.*;
import java.awt.*;
```

```java
public class CardShow extends JPanel
implements Runnable {
  private CardLayout clo;
  JButton jb[];

  public CardShow(int hgap, int vgap, int nbut) {
    clo = new CardLayout(hgap,vgap);
    setLayout(clo);
    jb = new JButton[nbut];

    for (int i = 0; i < jb.length; i++) {
      jb[i] = new JButton("Button: " + i);
      String number = new String(""+i);
      add(jb[i],number);
    }
  }

  public void run() {
    while (true) {
      try {
        Thread.sleep(1250);
      }
      catch(InterruptedException ie) {}
      String rand = "" +
        (int)(Math.random() * jb.length);
      clo.show(this, rand);
    }
  }

  public static void main(String args[]) {
    // horizontal gap
    int horGap = Integer.parseInt(args[0]);
    // vertical gap
    int verGap = Integer.parseInt(args[1]);
    // # of buttons
    int numButtons = Integer.parseInt(args[2]);
```

```
        CardShow cs = new
          CardShow(horGap, verGap, numButtons);

        JFrame jf = new JFrame("Flash Card");
        Container con = jf.getContentPane();
        con.add(cs, BorderLayout.CENTER);
        jf.pack();
        jf.setVisible(true);
        Thread t = new Thread(cs);
        t.start();
    }
}
```

GridBagLayout

Getting accustomed to layout managers is sometimes a chore. Spending the time to mentally associate a layout class's methods and field controls with its presentation takes a fair amount of practice and patience, especially when the components or their containers manifest what seems like competing behavior. GridBagLayout, of all the layout managers, is the one that is the most demanding in this regard. It is often deemed overly complex, hard to get accustomed to, and difficult to manage. It is the only layout manager with a separate helper class, GridBagConstraints, for dealing with the thirteen different behavioral variables it adds to the usual constraints of preferred size and minimum size. Unfortunately, GridBagConstraints only provides two constructors: a no-arg constructor that sets default values for all the layout variables, and another that requires the implementer to provide a default for every one of them. The latter, of course, is recommended for use only with a GUI builder tool that automates the process of setting those values. But in order to deal with each of these variables individually, a GridBagConstraints object must be constructed and default values changed by setting field values as desired. It sounds bad.

The value of GridBag is that it provides a way to achieve highly specific layout designs that the other existing managers might roughly approximate, but only at the cost of a far more complex arrangement of containers and components. The various constraints are not difficult to understand in the proper context; they take getting used to, of course. However, with a few helper classes of your own, learning to use GridBag by experimentation can become a very manageable process. As with any tool that provides a disarming number of controls, the key to using GridBag effectively is to first turn only the knobs that do work in broad strokes before resorting to the controls that provide fine adjustments.

`GridBagLayout` divides its given area into abstract cells (regions). Unlike `GridLayout`, which allots the same amount of space to each cell and one cell to each component, GridBag's components may vary in width and height, respectively, by occupying an arbitrary number of rows and columns. The height of each row is then determined by the height of the tallest component in it. The width of each column is the width of its widest component. This can get tricky, because the developer does *not* get to define the dimensions of a unit cell; the required size of the largest component does that.

Each component occupies a cell "region" or some number of contiguous columns and rows. The resulting shape is a solid rectangle—ells, snakes, and hollow boxes are not supported. The upper-leftmost cell it will occupy defines a component's location. This value is set using the `GridBag-Constraints` fields `gridx` and `gridy`. The component's `gridwidth` (number of columns) and `gridheight` (number of rows) are stored in variables with those names.

Some care has to be taken to assign components with incompatible needs to different columns or rows—if it's practical. It's quite possible that a desired arrangement will, nonetheless, create a sizing conflict; the result being that some components will get more space than they want. To alleviate the problem, there are further controls that separate a component's size from the size of its allotted region. If a component gets more space than it wants, it can set the variable `fill` to indicate its preference—accept surplus horizontal or vertical space, accept both, or accept none. None (keeping the current size) is the default. Furthermore, if the component should stick to one edge or corner of its region, a second variable, `anchor`, will set its alignment to one of eight compass points or center it.

So far we've covered the "broad-stroke" variables that `GridBag-Constraints` offers. These include setting the cell of origin, the component's dimension in rows and columns (remember, these are arbitrarily sized), and the instructions for sizing and positioning the component if its region is too large. The four grid variables can be set to one of two more possible values we have not mentioned yet—RELATIVE and REMAINDER. A component whose grid variables are set to RELATIVE will be next to last in its column or row. REMAINDER is then the final component for a given row or column. These options return some measure of convenience to developers. The extent of travel along either axis can be set without having to count out discrete cell units. By the same token, adding a new component can be much simpler.

In a GridBag, rows and columns maintain responsibility for resizing behavior. To change that behavior, the programmer must use `GridBag-Constraints`, which is tied to the definition of one or more components. Each time a component wants to set the behavior of its row and column through `GridBagConstraints`, there is a potential for conflict with other components that want the same row or column to behave differently. But since there is no master control, there must be a way to determine which component's instructions are heeded. With GridBag, it's the last component to set row- and column-sizing behavior that gets heard.

To visualize what this means, imagine a dozen audio speakers in a movie theater, with six speakers on each wall to either side of the screen. Each speaker has its own equalizer and volume controls. There's also a master volume control for the left and right walls in the projection room, but the knob's been broken off. Rather than replace the knob, the theater's electrician elected to wire every speaker on the left to adjust the master volume for the left. The master volume, in turn, now adjusts all the speakers on the left. With respect to resizing, the situation is similar.

When a resize occurs and there is more space than the sum of all the widest and tallest components for each column and row require, the surplus is divided according to the relative *weight* of each row and column. We say "relative" because the values that are assigned as "weight" only matter with respect to the values assigned to every other column or row. If we assign a relative weight of 5 to all columns, they will divide surplus space equally, just as if every number given was 100. The potential confusion that arises comes from the fact that weight is set through a component—there's no way to do it from a "master" row or column object. In practice, this means you should set a non-zero `weighty` for, at most, one component in each row and leave `weighty` at zero for all other components in the same row. Similarly, set a non-zero `weightx` on, at most, one component in each column and leave it at zero for all the others. Furthermore, make sure that you choose components that occupy only a single row (when setting `weighty`) and column (when setting `weightx`). If you choose to leave all the weights at zero for a row or column, then that row or column will not change size at all when the available space changes.

The remaining applicable values available through `GridBagConstraints` do the fine-tuning. The value `insets` sets a pad of pixels around the component relative to its containing region. The variables for internal padding, `ipadx` and `ipady`, set the number of pad pixels relative to the component's border.

Assuming you want to use a GridBag—and you should if it offers the services you need—one way to cut down the workload of setting up constraints is to write small arrays that keep associated values together (`gridx` and `gridy`, `height` and `width`, `anchor` and `fill`). This is also a case where a short substitution for typing out `GridBagConstraints.HORIZONTAL` and the like will make it far easier to read the resulting code.

```
public class GBC {
  public GBC(int location[], int area[], int size[]) {
    GridBagConstraints gbc = new GridBagConstraints();
    gbc.gridx = location[0];
    gbc.gridy = location[1];
    gbc.gridwidth = area[0];
    gbc.gridheight = area[1];
    gbc.fill = size[0];
    gbc.anchor = size[1];
  }
}
```

If some amount of fine-tuning is expected for each component, or the developer simply wants more flexibility, other options can be added in the form of overloaded constructors. We recommend that weight (because it is not specific to a component but to a column or row) be set explicitly in the main body of code, where it will be noticed. Alternatively, it could also be invoked with a special constructor.

In the `main()` method defining the class, setting up an array that groups associated values together makes maintenance and fudging the numbers a lot easier.

```
public class BentoBox {
  public static void main(String args[]) {
    final int NONE = GridBagConstraints.NONE;
    final int BOTH = GridBagConstraints.BOTH;
    final int CENT = GridBagConstraints.CENTER;
    final int NORT = GridBagConstraints.NORTH;
    final int VERT = GridBagConstraints.VERTICAL;
    final int HORZ = GridBagConstraints.HORIZONTAL;
    GBC gbc = null;
    JButton jb1 = null;
    JButton jb2 = null;
    ...
```

```
      // gridder lays out location, area, and size in
      // two-element integer arrays; this is cosmetic to
      // allow the programmer to eyeball the values for
      // each component.
      public int gridder[][] =
        { {0, 0}, {3, 2}, {VERT, NORT},
          {3, 0}, {2, 2}, {VERT, NORT},
          {0, 1}, {4, 4}, {HORZ, CENT},

        };

      JFrame jf = new JFrame("Bento Box Designer");
      Container box = jf.contentPane();
      box.setLayout(new GridBagLayout());

      // sample additions
      gbc = new GBC{gridder[0], gridder[1], gridder[2]};
      jb1 = new JButton("Tskimono");
      // fine-tuning for jb1 here
      box.add(jb1, gbc);

      gbc = new GBC(gridder[3], gridder[4], gridder[5]);
      jb2 = new JButton("Rice");
      // fine-tuning for jb2 here
      box.add(jb2, gbc);

      gbc = new GBC(gridder[6], gridder[7], gridder[8]);
      jb3 = new JButton("Tempura");
      // fine-tuning here
      box.add(jb3, gbc);
      ...
      jf.setSize(300, 400);
      jf.setVisible(true);
    }
  }
```

This technique is not an example to put to regular use; it merely illustrates a quick technique for experimenting with GridBagLayout to get familiar with its basic behavior. We've taken several shortcuts here. To avoid repetitive recompiling, the ideal solution would be to set up the grid data in a file and build a library of templates. Using a basic component like a JButton makes it simple to rough out the desired dimensions through experimentation. The messiness of the setup code is a reflection of the priority placed on presenting the grid data in as readable a format as possible.

Notice for example that the first row of data in the *gridder* array shows a component located at (0,0), taking up three columns and extending down two rows. Following that, another component is placed at (3,0), taking up the next four columns and extending down five rows. The result so far is depicted in Figure 18.4. With a grid of values visually presented like this, we can check for overlap fairly easily and verify the integrity of the layout. Once assured of a proper arrangement, adding in consideration for weight and pixel padding is far easier to manage.

FIGURE 18.4 Preliminary grid layout of BentoBox

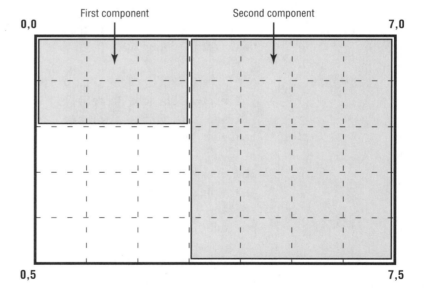

Event Handling and Style

Beginning with the change in event handling introduced in the JDK 1.1, the style of event-handling code has been a matter of some discussion in various circles. Talk about Java GUI development does not seem to generate a lot of thoughts on the question of code reuse, which doesn't seem altogether unreasonable. Application interfaces are often complex and customized enough that they don't lend themselves to a great deal of extension. If some effort has been invested up front in creating Bean-style components that could then be reapplied as modular units to other design requests, this might not be the case. But, as noted at the beginning of this chapter, many interfaces are written right away, so people can begin discussion on the topic of visual presentation right away. Quite often they are built from toolboxes provided by a RAD program. When they are built by hand, the focus on quick development precludes modular building, in most cases.

To expedite this sort of development in event handling, but also in other areas where the ability to write quick helper classes saves a lot of time, the JDK 1.1 introduced the concept of inner classes. Inner classes allow the programmer to embed one or more classes inside a "top-level" class. The benefits include the following:

- Convenient and elegant way to expose multiple implementations of the same interface (typically listeners) from what is superficially a single class

- Common access to import and package statements

- Common access to private variables across classes

- Self-describing class relationships

- Perceived reduction in name-space cluttering (especially with anonymous inner classes)

- Some reduction in class file size

NOTE

Inner classes may also appeal intuitively to students of Alonzo Church's lambda-calculus, the underlying mathematical model for the Lisp programming language. Lisp programming is based on the notion of a list; when an element in a list requires further definition, the definition is written "inline" in the code. If the definition itself includes elements that require more refined definition, it too is described inline. This has the effect of making Lisp code look like an extended outline of elements depending from other elements. In an extended form, inner classes perform this same function of naming and encapsulating a class's "sub"-behavior.

For custom event handlers, as one example, it makes sense to allow the developer to separate the class that contains event-handling code away from the rest of the class but at the same time show the tight relationship between the two by inserting one inside the another. A brief example might look like this:

```java
public class MyFrame extends JFrame {
  private Container cont;
  private JButton jb;

  public MyFrame() {
    super("Inner Class Model");
    cont = getContentPane();
    jb = new JButton("Send Query");
    jb.addActionListener(new EventHandle ());
    cont.add(jb);
  }
  ...
  // inner class to deal with this one little thing
  class EventHandle implements ActionListener {
    public void actionPerformed(ActionEvent ae) {
      System.out.println("Query Sent.");
    }
  }

  public static void main(String args[]) {
    MyFrame mf = new MyFrame();
    mf.pack();
    mf.setVisible(true);
  }
}
```

This implementation is straightforward and clean, and its conveniences are clear. The separator between GUI code and event-handling code clarifies the source code a bit and would also allow us to incorporate another inner class implementing the same kind of listener, but with different behavior for another component. Moreover, if the programmer were using an event adapter class, the benefit would be even more apparent. We don't want to implement, say, all five methods of `MouseListener` if we're only interested in `mouseClicked()`, but we don't want our main class to extend `MouseEventAdapter` for the privilege of avoiding null methods either.

But just as we have room in Java for static code (anonymous method blocks, which have their uses and abuses), we also have a provision for anonymous inner classes (classes that are defined as part of their instantiation). Here is a partial example drawing on the complete code model from above. In this case, an anonymous inner class is used three times: once to define the `ActionEvent` class, once to define a `Thread` that would execute a query on a remote database, and once more to define a `Runnable` that restores a label from "Working" to "Ready" and re-enables the container.

```
    ...
    JLabel status = new JLabel("Ready");
    JButton button = new JButton("Query me");

    // anonymous class 1
    button.addActionListener(new ActionListener() {
      public void actionPerformed(ActionEvent ae) {
      status.setText("Working");
      setEnabled(false);

      // anonymous class 2
      Thread queryJob = new Thread() {
        public void run() {
          try {
            //invoke query on remote VM
          }
          catch(InterruptedException ie) {}
          SwingUtilities.invokeLater(new Runnable() {
            // #3
            public void run() {
```

```
                    status.setText("Ready");
                    setEnabled(true);
                }
            });
        }
    };
    queryJob.start();
});
...
```

The application this code was excerpted from works fine, but it is a bit lengthier. We replaced several lines of code with our comment "invoke query on remote VM," which mitigates the concern we felt, wondering how quickly a programmer could find a bug in this code if a bracket or semicolon were accidentally deleted. While the code has managed to convey a variety of processes in a few lines, the thing that has been ignored is the readability and maintainability of this code. In return for a marginal savings in memory, file space, and number of code lines, the code here has sacrificed a simple style that would be far easier to read and modify when necessary. As it stands, the first thing a new programmer to this code must do is assure themselves that all the brackets match up and that this code will in fact compile.

Style matters. Clarity matters. It's possible to do a little worse than the snippet above, with a few anonymous array instantiations, but for purposes other than entertainment, this is a style that doesn't read well and is unusually fragile. When used as a crutch rather than a complement, anonymous inner class code can quickly get out of hand.

The secret of a powerful tool is in its proper use. When anonymous inner classes are kept short and to an immediate purpose, they can be quite beneficial. Having the ability to write one on the fly to capture a listener definition saves the programmer a considerable amount of time in choosing a name, writing a separate class, and working out the issues of variable access. The following code:

```
...
button.addActionListener(new ActionListener() {
  public void actionPerformed(ActionEvent ae) {
    status.setText("Query is pending");
    setEnabled(false);
    runQueryOnThread();}});
...
```

is easy to read, understand, and maintain, and it takes nothing away from the example code above. We have immediate access to top-level references and methods, and we remove what could rightly be called the baggage of naming something that realizes no advantage from being named. Furthermore, all the important elements of a class's behavior end up in a single source file. In the final analysis, anonymous classes are open to abuse precisely because they are so powerful. When their use is backed by a compelling programming need, there is no need to avoid them.

Event Handling and Threads

So far, we have discussed threads in conjunction with each major application component of the project assignment. Threading has a place in the GUI as well, and as with the database and the network server, there are certain caveats we must be aware of when adding threaded functionality to the client program. Let's imagine we are thinking about the application from the end user's viewpoint. We see a button that sends an already-formed query to the server. Knowing that the request may take some time, we'd like to have the GUI be able to accept other types of input while that process churns in the background. Thinking we know something about threading, we might suggest that a separate thread be used to manage the remote request while another allows us to continue working. We come to the conclusion that allotting a thread to each functionally independent button would make for a very efficient interface.

It sounds right in concept, but it doesn't necessarily translate directly into correct implementation. So far, it hasn't been part of our objective to read deeply into Swing's architecture, but adding some context here is helpful in understanding why threading with AWT or Swing components is risky. We want to justify the correct implementation with a refresher on the mechanics of paint routines. Refer back to Chapter 12, "Painting," for the full background.

In the AWT, all paint requests route through a single AWT thread. Either the system or the user can signal a call to paint the screen through various mechanisms. The system does so to initialize the screen or when it detects damage to the graphics area. The user can interject by way of a call to `repaint()`, which calls `update()`, which in turn "schedules" a paint request on the same thread the system uses to refresh or repaint. The upshot of all this is that screen appearance is kept up to date by the most recent request received to update the screen. In a special case, if the over-loaded version of update() is called (which allows the user to specify a clip region for painting), then the update() call taken up by the painting thread comprises a union of all clips to be painted, not just a "whitewash" request to cover all previous requests. In a very large or complex screen area, this approach may save some processing time.

It's a little different with Swing. A Swing component calls attention to itself as a painting target when any of three calls are invoked on it: paint(), setVisible(true), or pack(). Obviously, pack() is not a paint call, but because it does perform a recalculation of a component's size, which is prefaced by a call to invalidate(), a subsequent system call to paint() is inevitable. Without going into detail here, paint order is important to Swing components; lightweight components have problems dealing with overlap and neighboring with heavyweight components that become more complicated if one component paints out of turn. If one component's call to be painted goes on a separate thread, it runs the risk of violating the order the RepaintManager wants to follow. If the RepaintManager happens to do its part at the right time, no problem will manifest. It's when the autonomous thread paint request kicks in out of turn that screen behavior may be indeterminate. Let the underlying paint system do its own work.

There is a second issue with threading and Swing that has to do with sending off requests that may not return at a convenient interval to the event dispatch thread, such as a request to a remote database. The SwingUtilities class provides two key static methods to support cases where we don't want to hold things up while our job is in state, and where we do. The invokeAnd-Wait() and invokeLater() methods each take a Runnable argument. While the former blocks on the event dispatch thread until it completes its Runnable assignment, invokeLater() returns immediately once it posts its job, so that local processing can proceed while the Runnable contends normally for process time.

The trick to running a proper request using invokeLater() is shown in the previous code snippet. In that example, once the query button is pressed, a thread is defined and instanced to handle the actual query. This is followed by a call to invokeLater(), which defines a Runnable process that restores GUI interaction and sets the label back to its "Ready" message. The job to reset the GUI returns immediately, restoring the event dispatch's control of its own process queue, while the query thread itself is started and sent on its way. If we were to lock up the dispatch thread for the duration of our database call, our GUI would not be able to repaint or update in any way until that call returned.

Since a remote network connection plays a significant part in your project, it's worthwhile to investigate these two methods in detail and familiarize yourself with their operations.

Chapter Summary

Putting together a sketch of what a GUI should look like, along with the desired behavior on a window resizing, is an excellent tool for articulating the exact screen requirements you want. For a basic interface, the component choices are, and should be, fairly simple. Choose the components, assess how the overall window should behave, assign behavior to each region of the screen, and choose the layout managers that can implement that behavior. As a general rule, putting components into panels before they are added to layout regions adds a layer of flexibility to layout management.

Although they were not discussed at length in this chapter, you should plan, at a minimum, to write some kind of menu system for your GUI, taking advantage of keyboard accelerators and other Swing features to provide reasonable ease of use to your client.

If you are not already conversant with the model Swing uses to structure components and underlying behavior, defer the project assignment for a time. Get familiar with, at the very least, the differences between AWT components and their "J" counterparts. Do not consider yourself ready until you feel you can articulate the structural differences between AWT and Swing architecture, which is bound to come up in the follow-up exam for certification. You should be able to do the following:

- Explain Swing's model-delegate structure.

- Identify the roles of a model, listener, event, and view.

- Describe each layout manager.

- Offer a scenario for which each layout manager would be ideally suited.

- Explain the importance of the events dispatch thread.
- Apply anonymous and inner classes appropriately.

Unless the requirements for writing the GUI are rigorously defined, it's unlikely a mechanical check will suffice as an evaluation. With that in mind, you should be prepared to justify your solution on aesthetic, as well as functional, terms.

Chapter

19

A Second Example: A Trouble-Ticket System

In this second example, we will take a nuts-and-bolts approach to exam preparation and code more examples of the major pieces. If you are unfamiliar with one or two of the major areas touched by the assignment—Swing development, say, or RMI implementation—these examples can help accelerate your own practice work. We will also take a closer look at the administrative and scoring details of the exam. To do this, we downloaded our own assignment and wrote a solution, so that we could match our discussion to the degree of difficulty we saw.

The Java 2 Developer's Exam, as exams of this type go, is not overly complex or subtle. The focus is competence in applying programming, design, and integration skills over a broad range of libraries and problem domains. The power of object-oriented design, of course, is that breaking a job into self-contained pieces is easy. The question lies in effective partitioning of the overall goal, but this is already answered by the assignment requirements. Some elements in the assignment code require fixing, but they are plainly disclosed in the exam notes—no hidden surprises. The top-level objectives are straightforward, and although there are one or two obstacles to extending the code that may appear novel to some candidates, they require less time in thinking than implementation to solve.

Rather than parallel the exam's major requirements by a survey of techniques, as we did in the previous scenario (Chapters 15 through 18), now we will build the major elements of a client-server application of our own, from the ground up. As in the previous example, we will leave some integration details as user exercises. The exam's starter code is simple, so we will leave the previous example's discussion as a sufficient review of the problems that can arise. The download assignment we received asked us to clear up some deprecated methods; we also had to add a `synchronized` modifier to one method and delete another. So we are not concerned with putting land mines in sample code for you to sniff out. Write correct code to begin with, and you'll have less to remember about code that's not quite right.

In this example, we'll generate requirements for a technical-support service request, or "trouble-ticket," system. We'll write much of the application in a manner typical to simple prototyping, by:

- Specifying the data we need to store.

- Building a graphic interface to model its use.

- Writing code to serve the data.

- Allowing the client to communicate to a remote server.

In the spirit of code reuse, we will also look for ways to abstract a general design from our effort. We want to create a solution that not only fulfills the requirements at hand, but also helps us to see the larger problem domain and write a solution for it. Many initial design efforts begin this way, by inferring the general from the specific. Once you do things this way several times, you'll gain the experience necessary to start thinking about domains first and specifics second, otherwise known as *program architecture*.

We have chosen not to detail the code assignment particulars, even though we've seen them; we would be poor instructors (our first job) if we just gave answers to tests. Ultimately, we do want you to learn, by means of this assignment, how to work through a simple instance and see the more general problem set. If you can achieve that, completing the assignment will be a question of how well you understand the choices you make in execution, not merely correct operation. And if you are clear and consistent in your execution, you will have met the goal of the exam itself—to test your development skills, rather than your programming skills.

Having said that, the exam download fee is $250, prepaid. We'd prefer it if you didn't spend the money only to find out the exam is too much for you (or perhaps not as complicated as you hoped). So before jumping into the second example, we review below some assignment notes from the download we received.

More on Exam Requirements

Unlike the 1.1 Developer's Exam, the Java 2 assignment download does not include a test harness. Each submission is tested by an examiner for correct operation and meeting minimum requirements. Then the source code is reviewed for clarity, form, and design, and marked against criteria that are weighted according to their importance. Because there is no longer a mechanical test, delivering an assignment the examiner can easily use and test will have greater impact on the final score than before. Readable, easy-to-find documentation is essential. Clearing the hurdles of a mechanical test is still necessary, but now the candidate has more flexibility in choosing how to do it.

One point that was not clear in the previous exam was whether the provided code could be directly modified. In the Java 2 administration, the candidate may expressly modify the existing code, not simply add to it or subclass it. The exam requires the candidate to return both original and modified source code files in the submission.

The point system for grading the assignment breaks down into these categories and weights:

Category	Points
General Considerations	72
Server Design	37
User Interface	20
Documentation	10
Data Conversion Program	10
Object-Oriented Design	6
Total	**155**

Elements important to the server design category include adding a record-locking scheme and enhancing the search capability. Developing the user interface accounts for about 13 percent of the total points. If you are new to Swing, however, you will end up spending more time on this piece than the point value suggests. You can do some very nice things with Swing, but doing them quickly without experience is a different matter. The data conversion task requires you to take a delimited ASCII file data and turn it into a binary file format usable by the application. The submission fails if this tool is not provided.

General considerations receive about half the total weight and overlap some with other categories. They include the following elements, which are weighted from 5 to 20 points each:

- Ease of using the submitted assignment, including documentation. (15 points)

- Consistent and logical problem solving. (20)

- Adherence to JavaSoft coding standards. (15)

- Code that is clearly laid out and would be easy to maintain. (7)

- Exception handling applied in a consistent manner. (10)

- Using JDK library classes in favor of writing new ones for a limited purpose. (5)

The key compulsory requirements are as follows:

- The submission must include a README file that documents how the program is started. The grader cannot adjust or edit the JAR's contents in order for the program to execute.

- The submission must be sent as one JAR file, but may contain multiple JAR files.

- The program must be able to run on any Java 2 platform. Sun's reference platform engine is the expected test platform.

- The program can require command-line arguments, but the parameters themselves are limited to:

  - The server's host or DNS name

  - The application's server port number

  - The name of any data file(s)

  - `java.rmi.server.codebase` property value

  - The security manager policy (if any)

Remember that the examiner is not looking for "best" programming choices. There are no ideal choices they are looking for. The examiner's job is to assess how *clear and consistent* each candidate's approach to completing the assignment has been.

Assignment: Build a Trouble-Ticket System

Let's say we have been working with several start-up companies, and they all seem to have a common need: None of these companies has a systematic process for resolving internal technical support problems. To get support, staff members must call an engineer whose primary role is development, external customer support, or monitoring production systems. In other words, solving problems that do not directly affect customer satisfaction is often a matter of competing for already strained resources.

Maintaining responsiveness to such problems, as a result, is typically governed by political rather than technical priorities. The focus of the response, once arranged, is to quickly restore the individual's ability to be productive; no one tracks whose time is required or how much is used. Tracking tech support is viewed as simply another secondary assignment.

Since there is no formal record keeping of problems, assignments, or resolution—much less a centralized way to enter, modify, or view such records—hiring additional engineers to fulfill technical support needs is difficult to justify (except during an ongoing crisis). To establish and maintain an efficient operation, the resource managers of these companies must find a way to:

- Match the right expert to technical problems to improve turnaround time.

- Correlate widely reported symptoms to their source, thereby reducing duplication of effort.

- Sort the outstanding problems by priority and allocate resources first to the most important ones.

- Allow for distributed record entry into the database, relying on each person's responsibility to report problems.

Most start-ups, however, can't afford and don't want complex trouble-ticket systems for internal use. The organization's staffing can change rapidly, along with ownership of various projects. One of the few remedies available is to distribute the responsibility (and benefits) of the system. Start-up groups are also more inclined to use tools that require little learning, achieve specific objectives, and impose few requirements. They are more likely to use a tool if they can adapt it to their needs quickly.

We want to prototype a trouble-ticket system that will work on all of our customers' existing systems, one that we can modify as their needs are better identified, and that we can enhance without significant rewrites. We do not want to compromise our own rapid time-to-market objectives by simply adding flexibility (i.e., complexity)—we just want our code to be open to future requirements.

Our solution requires a simple client-server structure. Naturally, the server itself must allow for concurrent user connections, accommodate searches for specific data and, of course, protect against concurrent writes to the same record. We also want to keep the client-server connection scheme generic, for two reasons. One: to maintain a single communications model for all customers, so that a change to the data set does not change the code that connects the client and server. We must abstract the data from the data transport model. Two: for centralization. We know start-up companies want to outsource or contract technical support whenever they can. If we leave open the possibility of using our client as a *monitor*, we will be able to add features that let us manage several of these databases, regardless of their individual schema, from one location. If our clients like the tool and use it, the next thing they need is technical support that doesn't take away from their business focus. We will already know how they see their data, a crucial advantage in pursuing other consulting opportunities.

After surveying several of these companies for interest, we decide on a simple, generalized data scheme for our prototype, depicted in the following table:

Field	Data Type
Record Number	Integer
Reporting Person	String
Location	String
Time of Report	String (Date)
Engineer	String
Category	String
Complaint	String
Status	String

We will use fundamental data types, and start out with an internally delimited ASCII file to help model the graphic client interface. Once the logical elements are set, the ASCII data can be converted into a format that suits our server code. For now, we'll follow this form:

RECNUM|REPORT|LOCAT|TIME|ENGIN|CATEG|COMPLT|STATUS

Sample records would look like this in file:

```
001|Sayers|DEN|03/28/00 10:21|Wort|Network|T-1 is
down|CLOSED
002|Padula|EDI|04/01/00 13:30|Markson|Office|No
cookies|PENDING
003|Hunter|DEN|04/03/00 10:15|Brown|Server|Backups
failing|CLOSED
004|Cramer|MPT|04/09/00 08:59|Ramirez|Workstation|U-10
down|IN-PRO
005|Lewis|BRM|04/11/00 21:48|Unassigned|Database|Locked
table|OPEN
006|Gant|SFO|04/15/00 14:15|Unassigned|Office|Loud
whining|CRITICAL
```

GUI Development

The centerpiece of our graphic interface will naturally be a table—a
JTable, that is, since we are using Swing components. For the sake of depict-
ing a monitor-oriented approach to the client, we'll also include a JTree in
the prototype, as shown in Figure 19.1. This experiment will give us a chance to:

- Consider another graphic model to use for viewing multiple data-
  bases.
- Connect actions to tree nodes for use as "stored procedures."
- Help us think about alternative layouts as the GUI develops.

FIGURE 19.1 A simple box diagram to show relative position and layout

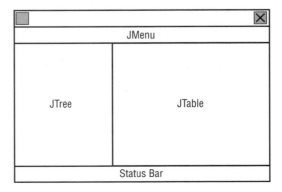

All Swing components inherit from `java.awt.Container`. This means it is possible to contain other components inside any `JComponent`, not just `String` objects—ample motivation to look past AWT widgets. This feature comes to mind because some of the data fields described so far—such as `Location`, `Engineer`, or `Status`—might have a fixed or constrained list of values. The graphic client can simplify data entry and validation in those cases by displaying a choice list instead of a text field. Furthermore, if we can get the data scheme to carry this information, then we can adjust the graphic table to reflect not only the header and field length, but also the most suitable component for displaying it. Swing was built to meet these kinds of needs, so we'll take the opportunity to learn how while building the client code.

The visual aspect, or *View* is easy to represent, but we are literally just scratching the surface of the code we'll need. We'll want to put more thought into the *Model*, or the way we expect to contain our data. A `JTable` model is defined by an implementation of the `TableModel interface`. If we want to exploit more capability than the `DefaultTableModel` provides—a simple `Vector` of `Vectors`—we can specify our own `TableColumnModels`. In short, plenty of work can be developed on the client side even before the actual data is determined. If we exercise a little forethought and focus on modular design, we might be able to handle even substantive changes in the data structure without altering the basic design of our GUI code.

Database/Server Development

The bulk of our back-end project consists of serving our data over the network; we'll start this discussion at the design level, using Java's Remote Method Invocation (RMI) API. We could also use object serialization to develop a protocol for conversing in objects between client and server—the exam allows either approach—but using RMI will give us a reason to talk about interfaces, a favorite topic. We don't have much more to say on using serialized objects over `Sockets` anyway, beyond our coverage in Chapter 17; but we nonetheless recommend that approach to candidates who do not want to learn RMI just to pass the exam.

There are advantages to using straight sockets. For one, it's easy to wrap an existing data layer in an object and pass it between systems. And there are drawbacks. It's cumbersome to manage the exchange as the "protocol" used between client and server gets more detailed (or more "meaningful," if you will). The logical extreme of this development is the dreaded "proprietary" protocol—a communication scheme that's useful, but usually isolated from widespread use. Developers must always consider the consequences of expending effort on schemes of their own when a standard one will suffice. If there is no compelling benefit to a specialized implementation, why spend the time and money? With Java specifically, it's necessary to ensure that client and server each have access to class files for all serialized objects, so that the objects themselves can be cast to their original type.

What RMI does for us in this regard is not a silver bullet. It simplifies programming the client-side logic, by requiring us to define the remote interface to the server in advance. Actual implementations can vary from client to client. One possible way to think about this is to have a single RMI server that exports multiple interfaces to the same database—in short, continue adding features to the database, but make them available through multiple interfaces. Then, add them to clients in the form of an interface collection. Figure 19.2 illustrates this approach.

FIGURE 19.2 Serving a collection of RMI objects to a remote client

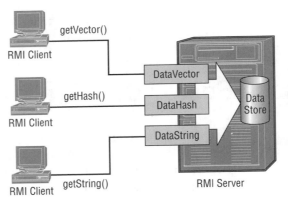

This isn't any faster to code; it's simply more flexible. We're far less likely to get locked in to one way of doing things. In any event, the key is what happens to the client code. A client that accesses remote resources through RMI initiates the process through an RMI request. As long as the connection request works, remote method calls look the same as local calls: the programmer sees no difference in writing an implementation. That's all there is to it—to avoid the problem of everyone generating their own protocols, RMI provides a generic transport for serialized objects. We don't have to worry about the *order* of communication as much, but we do have to consider whether the remote service provides a *complete* interface. As long as we're thinking about flexibility for the future—perhaps creating a database of databases in a later phase—implementing RMI is good practice.

If the "database of databases" notion seems like overkill to you, it would be for the Developer's Exam assignment. But consider the number of distributed-database schemes in use today—naming services like the Domain Name Service (DNS), electronic mail relay systems, Web servers that index other Web servers, even inverted-tree file systems. There's good reason for targeting that strategy and using it: inherent scalability.

We'll start our server development with a basic schema and include the functions necessary to support data entry and retrieval. Our discussion will center on incorporating search and record-locking features and on dealing with concurrent access. As instructors, we have found that multithreading is new territory for many students when they take Sun's preparatory Java courses, and we assume that this is generally true among programmers as a whole. Those who are familiar with multithreaded programming sometimes struggle with Java's "non-deterministic" thread scheduling, which we'll touch on as well.

Our goal at the end of this chapter is to have a database scheme supported with remote services.

Client-Server Logic

With the graphic end of the client roughed out, and once the server code is in place, all that would remain would be to tie the graphic client to our RMI client logic. As mentioned above, remote method call semantics are no different from local method calls, once the server connection is made. We'll simply tie the data given by the user via the GUI to a client request, then pass the response from the server back up. The overall model is the same: The user manipulates a Controller (graphic widget) to change the Model (data table), which makes the requested changes and updates the View (as illustrated in Figure 19.3). Aside from network latency or other performance aspects, there's no functional difference to the user—the local data model is "merely" being updated by a data source on another computer.

FIGURE 19.3 A data transaction using a remote data source

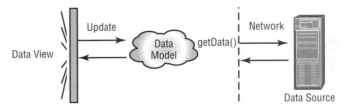

Delivering the Finished Assignment

Another development aspect that comes up frequently in Sun Java courses is confusion over the use of the JAR tool supplied with the Java Development Kit. One of this book's authors is fond of saying the JAR specification amounts to "tar semantics, pkzip format." Certainly users of the Unix `tar` command will grasp JAR quickly, since the command-line syntax is virtually the same, but it is not a complex syntax by any means. The most obvious benefit of using JAR is it provides an archive format that will work on any system with a JVM or a WinZip extraction tool. That amounts to platform-independence!

There are some minor potential pitfalls in bundling your assignment you may not have encountered with JAR files yet. We'll go over some of the particulars, including a proper `CLASSPATH` environment variable; you can assume you'll have to document its use for someone else as part of the exercise. Finally, we'll cover the administrative details of uploading the exam and recommend a simple structure for organizing your code and including the necessary documentation. We cover these essentials in Chapter 23, "Preparing the Upload."

Chapter

20

GUI Prototyping

In the first assignment scenario, we focused on the elements of layout management and on broad topics in GUI design. In this chapter we divide and conquer the elements of Swing, focusing on the pieces essential to completing the exam and techniques that promote effective, maintainable design:

- Events and properties
- Tables
- Trees
- Menus and Actions
- Panes
- Utility methods

We conclude with a discussion of inner classes—in particular, the anonymous form. We want to distinguish between the code you should strive to write and the code you most often see in demo source or other Java examples in the literature. Heavy reliance on anonymous inner classes helps to expedite a peripheral task and conserve page or screen space. It does not necessarily showcase best practice; following best practice can be bulky in print. It's important to remember that clarity of design and economy of expression are not always the same thing. Our moral is that, as a rule, the urge to write brief code should follow, not precede, the need to present it clearly.

Events and Properties

The event model is far more conspicuously intertwined in Swing than in the AWT. To the 13 listener interfaces defined in `java.awt.event`, Swing adds 23 more in `javax.swing.event`, which defines notifications for everything from content changes in a data model to an undo operation. This technique of separating the definition of listening from any one class is the foundation for Swing's take on the well-known Model-View-Controller (MVC) design pattern.

The MVC pattern separates and encapsulates these roles from each other, clearly defining the interface of each. Messaging among them then takes place by some form of callback, a technique in which one object has a reference to the other. If access is direct, then one object simply makes method calls on that reference. Indirect access is necessary when sender and receiver have no prior knowledge of each other. The solution is a common third reference, known as a listener (or adapter or delegate) object, which the sender knows about and the receiver contains or implements as part of its own interface. One such MVC implementation that uses callbacks for communication might look like Figure 20.1.

FIGURE 20.1   An MVC layout

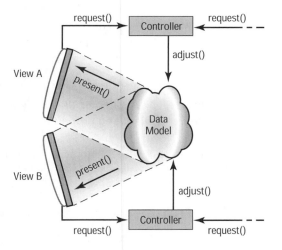

Swing changes the commonly understood roles of MVC by changing the nature of its implementation. Models and views still communicate by way of event-driven messaging, but controls are instead collapsed into the view that uses them. Controls are made accessible as properties—values within an object whose state can be accessed or changed through a method pair. We can change a JTable's view, for example, by changing the underlying model and firing an event the table listens to. We can only change a data cell's mutability, however, by directly acting on the view itself. Figure 20.2 illustrates that relation.

FIGURE 20.2 A JTable data update and controller update

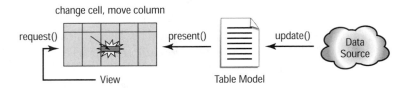

There are, as we said, 36 listeners and listener interfaces defined in `javax.swing.event` and `java.awt.event`. We can also create new events (by subclassing) and event objects (by implementing `java.util.EventListener` and extending `java.util.EventObject`). The only thing that functionally separates data and property management in a complex Swing component, therefore, is a well-defined model for event handling. But there is a support structure for handling property changes as events: it's part of the specification for JavaBeans.

See Figure 18.3 in Chapter 18, "Designing the User Interface," for a depiction of JavaBean event and property change dynamics.

The `java.beans` package contains interfaces and classes that comprise the entire library for passing property-change notifications between two classes:

- `PropertyChangeListener` (interface)

- `PropertyChangeSupport`

- `VetoableChangeListener` (interface)

- `VetoableChangeSupport`

The primary goal of these interfaces and classes is to provide support for bound and constrained property changes. Binding a property in one object to a property of the same type in another object has the effect of keeping those values consistent. A constrained property is usually a bound property as well, but also knows how to behave if the target property rejects the change issued by a source (hence the term "vetoable").

Any value that we encapsulate with a get/set method pair can be treated as a property, according to the JavaBeans specification. (An is/set method pair for boolean properties is supported as an alternative.) Communicating a property change between objects is supported by way of a PropertyChangeListener. The PropertyChangeSupport and VetoableChangeSupport classes supply the needed listener registration methods, so any class that wants to treat its property changes as events only has to include a PropertyChangeSupport object in its body, wrap the registration methods in its own add/remove pair, and add a firePropertyChange() call to the given property's set() method. Here's an example using a boolean property value:

```java
import java.beans.*;

/**
 * A demonstration class that knows how to broadcast its
 * active property value.
 *
 * @author The CJ2CSG Guys
 */
public class Monitor
{
  private PropertyChangeSupport pcs;
  private int powerOn = 1;

  public Monitor() {
    pcs = new PropertyChangeSupport();
  }

  /**
   * Registers listeners interested in the "active"
   * property of this object by wrapping a
   * PropertyChangeSupport reference.
   *
   * @see java.beans.PropertyChangeSupport
   */
  public void
  addPropertyChangeListener(PropertyChangeListener p) {
    pcs.addPropertyChangeListener(p);
  }
```

```java
/**
 * De-registers listeners interested in the "active"
 * property of this object by wrapping a
 * PropertyChangeSupport reference.
 *
 * @see java.beans.PropertyChangeSupport
 */
public void
removePropertyChangeListener(PropertyChangeListener p)
{
  pcs.removePropertyChangeListener(p);
}


/**
 * Returns true if the object is currently active,
 * false if not.
 */
public boolean isActive() {
  if ( powerOn == 0) {
    return false;
  }
  return true;
}


/**
 * Changes the value of the active property. This
 * method ignores calls that do not change the current
 * value, in order to avoid firing property changes
 * unnecessarily.
 *
 * @see java.beans.PropertyChangeSupport
 */
public void setActive(boolean active) {
  if ((active == true) && isActive()) {
    return;
  }
```

```
      if ((active == false) && !isActive())
        return;
    }
    pcs.firePropertyChange("active", isActive(), active);
    if (active) {
      powerOn = 1;
    }
    else {
      powerOn = 0;
    }
  }
}
```

Notice that the name of the `active` property derives only from the methods using that word in their identifiers. The property's data type is determined through method signatures as well, hiding the actual implementation in the class. This technique is in accordance with the way Bean properties are analyzed in a builder-tool environment by the `Introspector` class. Property identification relies on correct naming and method declaration; by the same token, we have far more flexibility in representing data to the public interface.

For details on the required syntax to support properties, including support for `int` and `boolean` primitive parameters, see the JavaBeans specification at http://java.sun.com/beans/docs/spec.html.

The `firePropertyChange()` method requires that both old and new property values be passed as parameters. There's no real need for a bound property to pass the old value; the listener, however, has the option to validate that parameter if desired. The old value is necessary in a vetoable change, though; without it, the issuing object wouldn't be able to roll back and maintain the same state as its vetoing target. Also, notice that the object maintains the actual support; what defines the property as bound is the use of the `firePropertyChange()` call.

Both Support classes now have overloaded registration methods in the Java 2 Software Developer's Kit. Originally, the only parameter was a Property-ChangeListener; now a property name, given as a String, can be included. The first version is intended for invoking the listener on any property change. The second specifies firing a change only when the named property is affected.

A bound recipient implements the PropertyChangeListener interface and gathers property-change information from the PropertyEvent object it receives in a call to propertyChange():

```
public class Pager
implements PropertyChangeListener
{
  ...
  public void propertyChange(PropertyChangeEvent pce) {
    Object old = pce.getOldValue();
    Object new = pce.getNewValue();
    String name = pce.getPropertyName();
    if name.equals("active") {
      if (((Boolean)new).booleanValue() == false) {
        issueAlert();
      }
      else {
        issueOK();
      }
    }
  }
  ...
}
```

The versatility of this approach to property changes isn't lost on Swing. SwingPropertyChangeSupport is available in the javax.swing.event package to assist with binding properties across components. However, Swing makes stringent demands to accommodate the sensitive nature of the single thread used for updating components in a Java GUI. Intense event dispatching can cause contention or blocking on the system thread, creating the same problem with refreshing the screen that occurs if we use event code to call `paint()` directly instead of `repaint()`. Any code that might block on the AWT's thread is risky code, because it can interfere with the GUI's ability to update itself. Therefore, the `SwingPropertyChangeSupport` class is intentionally thread-unsafe. De-synchronizing any code that issues events, of course, has the added benefit of improving performance.

`PropertyChangeSupport` and its Swing subclass provide a ready-made tool for sharing data of any kind across multiple components. Sharing controller-oriented values between two tables, for example, so that one data model can update another, is one possibility. Chaining data propagation in this way allows for filtering or other intermediate operations as well. Figure 20.3 illustrates this kind of collaboration.

FIGURE 20.3 Treating a data update as a property-change event

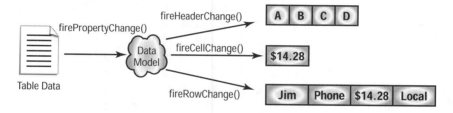

The key benefit to this approach is loose coupling among components that may be related only by their common task. Relating components through neutral event types makes it easier to avoid combining objects together, although it is perhaps not as intuitively compelling as using inner classes. We'll have more to say on that later.

Building a *JTable*

Swing seems to lend itself to writing a lot of "glue" code. There is a temptation to take advantage of the library as it is, combine the available components as needed, and rely on the fact that the important hookups between models and views have been done for us.

A `JTable`, for example, has three core internal models, dealing with its data structure (`TableModel`), the state of its column order and the column members

(TableColumnModel), and list selection behavior (ListSelectionModel). A JTable updates its view by capturing the event objects these models fire. All told, a JTable listens to six different event types, through the following interfaces:

- TableModelListener
- TableColumnModelListener
- ListSelectionListener
- CellEditorListener
- Scrollable
- Accessible

Each of these listener types has an event object counterpart, which is briefly described here. There are five different TableModelEvent constructors, each of which requires arguments at varying levels of granularity, so a TableModel can issue notifications ranging from a complete table refresh down to a single cell update. TableColumnModelEvent objects specify changes to the column structure of the table, including changes in column order, added or removed columns, and width changes. A ListSelectionEvent object reports which rows are included (or excluded) after the user or program has selected a range of rows to highlight. For example, if a user chooses a range of records in order to sort or delete them, a ListSelectionEvent gathers that collection and provides an index for it.

A CellEditorEvent object is created when editing on a cell completes or is cancelled. The Scrollable interface allows a JTable to be manipulated by any scrolling container (JScrollPane, JScrollBar, JViewport). Finally, the Accessible interface gives all implementing Swing components means for returning an AccessibleContext object. These objects are hooks that support using a Swing interface through some form of assistive technology, such as a Braille reader or magnified-font monitor. Figure 20.4 depicts the requirements a JTable adheres to just by listening.

FIGURE 20.4   JTable's interface implementations

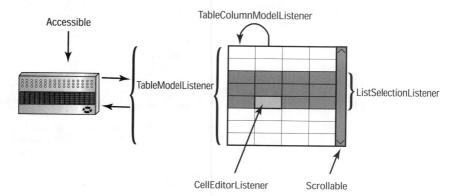

These interfaces are supported by various default classes located in `javax.swing.table`. They provide adequate behavior for many common uses, so that implementing a simple subclass is not tedious work. For starters, here is a subclass that simply extends the list of available constructors:

```java
import java.awt.*;
import javax.swing.*;

public class VSTable extends JTable {

  public VSTable(int r, int c) {
    super(r,c);
  }

  public static void main(String args[]) {
    VSTable vst = new VSTable(3,6);
    JFrame jf = new JFrame();
    Panel pan = new Panel();
    pan.add(vst);
    jf.addWindowListener(new WindowCloser());
    jf.setContentPane(pan);
    jf.pack();
    jf.setVisible(true);
  }
}
```

This code produces the example shown in Figure 20.5. We've merely provided a constructor that requires a row and column integer pair. Under the premise that extending a class interface doesn't break it, we've produced a form where `main()` only constructs and assembles objects. `VSTable` may change as we add features to it, and we can reuse the `main()` method for testing.

FIGURE 20.5 A `JTable` constructed with row and column values only

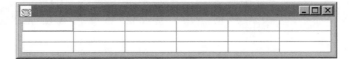

Also incorporated in this class is a simple `WindowCloser` utility, written as follows:

```
import java.awt.event.*;
import java.awt.*;

/**
  * Closes a window.
  * Subclass this to define more event handling.
  *
  * @author The CJ2CSG Guys
  */
public class WindowCloser extends WindowAdapter {
  public void windowClosing(WindowEvent wevt) {
    Window window = wevt.getWindow();
    window.setVisible(false);
    window.dispose();
    System.exit(0);
  }
}
```

This routine explicitly releases the system's windowing resources. There is a more direct way to do this, as explained in the following note, but we have added this class to show a simple object with potential for reuse, either by itself or through subclassing.

You may have noticed in some applications that the JFrame window goes away when dismissed, but the session that spawned it may not return the prompt as expected. A JFrame's closing behavior is defined by the javax.swing.WindowConstants interface. The default choice, HIDE_ON_CLOSE, accounts for this "hanging" behavior. It can be changed to DISPOSE_ON_CLOSE or EXIT_ON_CLOSE with JFrame's setDefaultCloseOperation().

To make a table of less trivial value, we need to take hold of the models directly. Since the Developer's Exam focuses on data functions through the GUI, we'll concentrate on the key player for that, the TableModel interface and its all-purpose implementation, AbstractTableModel.

Using *AbstractTableModel*

As the driver for any JTable view, the TableModel incorporates all the behavior necessary to maintaining data that is current and accurate. Developers who choose to implement the TableModel directly must also manage the event firing to all listeners, especially the JTable itself. Otherwise, it is far simpler to make a concrete subclass of AbstractTableModel and use it as a JTable constructor parameter. Default initialization code in the JTable takes care of the rest. At a bare minimum, the developer must implement:

- public int getColumnCount()

- public int getRowCount()

- public Object getValueAt(int row, int col)

Implementing these abstract methods makes for a concrete subclass, but is not enough to make the table editable. Overriding the following methods as well will give the developer a more useful degree of control:

- public boolean isCellEditable(int row, int col)

- public void setValueAt(Object obj, int row, int col)

- public String getColumnName(int index)

- public Class getColumnClass (int index)

Overriding `setValueAt()` carries with it the responsibility of calling
`fireTableCellUpdated()`, which in `AbstractTableModel` calls
`fireTableChanged()` on the model's current listeners. Here's an example:

```
import javax.swing.table.*;

/**
 * A model for a trouble-ticket system using the
 * following schema and data representations:
 * <CODE>
 * <OL>
 * <LI>RECNUMBER int
 * <LI>REPORTER  java.lang.String
 * <LI>LOCATION  java.lang.String
 * <LI>TIMEOFRP  java.lang.String
 * <LI>ENGINEER  java.lang.String
 * <LI>CATEGORY  java.lang.String
 * <LI>COMPLAINT java.lang.String
 * <LI>CTSTATUS  java.lang.String
 * </OL>
 * </CODE>
 *
 * @author The CJ2CSG Guys
 */
public class TroubleTicketModel
extends AbstractTableModel
{
  private String[] schema = { "Record Number",
    "Reporter", "Location", "Time of Report", "Engineer",
    "Category", "Complaint", "Status"};

  private String[][] rowData = {
   {"001", "Sayers", "Denver", "15:30 04/01/00", "Wort",
    "Network", "T-1 is down", "In Process"}
   };
```

```java
public TroubleTicketModel() {
}

/**
 * Returns the number of columns in the schema.
 */
public int getColumnCount() {
  return schema.length;
}

/**
 * Returns the number of rows in the table.
 */
public int getRowCount() {
  return rowData.length;
}

/**
 * Returns the value at the given cell as an Object.
 *
 * @return java.lang.Object
 */
public Object getValueAt(int r, int c) {
  if (rowData[r] != null && schema[c] != null) {
    return rowData[r][c];
  }
  return null;
}

/**
 * Sets the value at a given cell and notifies
 * listeners.
 */
public void setValueAt(Object obj, int r, int c) {
  if (rowData[r] != null && schema[c] != null) {
    rowData[r][c] = obj.toString();
```

```
      fireTableCellUpdated(r,c);
    }
  }

  /**
   * Turns on editing for all cells, excepting the
   * column that holds the record number.
   */
  public boolean isCellEditable(int r, int c) {
    if (c == 0) {
      return false;
    }
    return true;
  }

  /**
   * Returns the name of any column, given its
   * index in the model (not the current view).
   *
   * @return java.lang.String
   */
  public String getColumnName(int index) {
    return schema[index];
  }

  /**
   * Returns a Class representation of the common
   * class of any column.
   *
   * @return java.lang.Class
   */
  public Class getColumnClass(int index) {
    return String.class;
  }
}
```

With this in place, we can write a quick `main()` method to view the work so far.

```
import javax.swing.*;
import java.awt.*;

public class Test
{
  public static void main(String args[]) {
    JFrame jf = new JFrame("Trouble Ticket Table");
    JTable jt = new JTable(new TroubleTicketModel());
    JScrollPane jsp = new JScrollPane(jt);
    jf.getContentPane().add(jsp, BorderLayout.CENTER);
    jf.setDefaultCloseOperation(JFrame.EXIT_ON_CLOSE);
    jf.setSize(650,75);
    jf.setVisible(true);
  }
}
```

Figure 20.6 shows the output of this code.

FIGURE 20.6   Using `JTable` to display a `TroubleTicketModel`

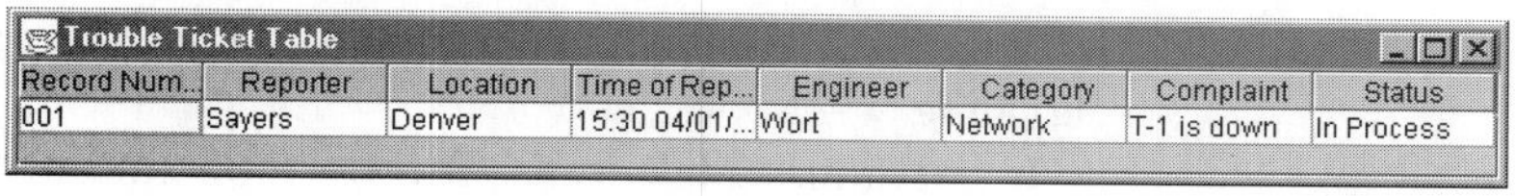

We haven't yet worked on the cosmetics, things like setting column widths nicely. To manage that, we need a `JTableHeader`. Adding one is easy enough: just add a `jt.setTableHeader(new JTableHeader())` call to the code above and start experimenting. The beginning of a table prototype is in the works.

With that formula established, the real work remains: hooking a data feed into the model, and extending `JTable` to add view features we need. You're invited to create a more aesthetically pleasing table view and supplement the model with live data to see how things work.

Building a *JTree*

Like a JTable, a JTree is complex enough to warrant its own library of support classes. It is becoming more widely used in GUI designs, typically as a drill-down or focus-oriented controller, or as an indexing tool for things like e-mail messages and, of course, files.

But JTree is not as well-defined a listener as JTable, as it only implements the Scrollable and Accessible interfaces. The primary use for a JTree is outlining any data structure that lends itself to hierarchical order. It could be used to diagram, say, the operations of a recursive descent parser, but it is more readily useful as an indexing tool.

Trees consist of a series of nodes, from which other nodes, called children, depend. A node that cannot have children is called a leaf; otherwise it is called a branch. A node is principally identified two ways: by its path, the route that links it back to the root; and by its row, the area it uses for display similar to a List element.

Aside from defining user actions for adding and removing nodes, the most common event type associated with a tree is selection. In our trouble-ticket system, for example, we might want to associate a different display or action with each kind of node we present. If a user clicks on a child of the Reporter node, we might want to display contact information for that person, or perhaps limit the table display to the trouble items reported by that person.

To get the visual effect first, we can mock up a tree using the Default-MutableTreeNode class.

It might also make sense for our table model to alter the node population of the tree using the data it receives to update the tabular view. A tree model could listen to property changes issued by the table model. The table model could filter the data before firing it, or the tree model could filter the table data. Or instead of adding this work to either class, where the fit is arbitrary, we could instead perform the translation work through an event adapter, whose only job is to create tree data out of table data. Keeping two models separated this way makes it possible to keep changes in the bootstrap code and out of the component code. Figure 20.7 is a logical diagram of this interaction.

FIGURE 20.7   Updating a tree outline with table data

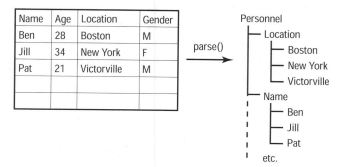

Name	Age	Location	Gender
Ben	28	Boston	M
Jill	34	New York	F
Pat	21	Victorville	M

parse() →

```
Personnel
  ├─ Location
  │     ├─ Boston
  │     ├─ New York
  │     └─ Victorville
  ├─ Name
  │     ├─ Ben
  │     ├─ Jill
  │     └─ Pat
  │ etc.
```

Creating a reusable mock-up of a tree display can take a little doing. Rather than embed some static data in a demo class that makes a JTree, we decided to take an extra step and write one that could accept input in the form of a property file. Property files present data in the form of key-value pairs, where the key is always a String (and in our example, so are the values). Our file sample looks like this:

```
Location=Chicago New York Parkersburg
Reporter=Padula Hunter Gant Anonymous
Engineer=Wort Brown Carrigan None
Category=Network Office Workstation
```

We treat the key as a parent node and the values as children, once the file contents are read in. To do that, we create (in the following code) a class called TreeSetup to take any file that's written as a "bundle" of properties and convert it to a series of parent and children elements.

```java
import java.io.*;
import java.util.*;
import javax.swing.tree.*;

/**
 * TreeSetup converts a properties file into a set
 * of parent and child nodes. Each key in the file
 * becomes a parent, and each value is a child to its
 * key.
 *
```

```java
 * @author The CJ2CSG Guys
 */
public class TreeSetup
{
  private PropertyResourceBundle prb;
  private String filename;

  /**
   * Accepts a String filename and converts it to a
   * PropertyResourceBundle.
   *
   * @see java.util.PropertyResourceBundle
   */
  public TreeSetup(String filename) {
    this.filename = filename;
    FileInputStream fis = null;
    try {
      fis = new FileInputStream(filename);
      prb = new PropertyResourceBundle(fis);
    }
    catch (FileNotFoundException fnfe) {
      System.err.println(filename + " was not found");
      System.exit(1);
    }
    catch (IOException ioe) {
      ioe.printStackTrace();
      System.err.println(
        "Error trying to open input stream");
      System.exit(1);
    }
  }

  /**
   * Returns a Vector of String values, given
   * a String key as a parameter.
   */
```

```
public Vector getChildren(String node) {
  StringTokenizer st = null;
  Vector vec = new Vector();
  String children = prb.getString(node);
  st = new StringTokenizer(children);
  while (st.hasMoreTokens()) {
    vec.addElement(st.nextToken());
  }
  return vec;
}


/**
 * Returns a Vector of Strings representing
 * each key found.
 */
public Vector getParents() {
  Enumeration enum = null;
  Vector vec = new Vector();
  enum = prb.getKeys();
  while (enum.hasMoreElements()) {
    Object key = (String)enum.nextElement();
    vec.addElement(key);
  }
  return vec;
}
}
```

The Vector returned by getParents() contains all the keys in the file. Passing each element of that Vector, as a String, into getChildren() will then return a Vector containing the key's values. Finally, we write (in the next code sample) a SampleTree class to create a DefaultTreeModel by passing the property file name as a parameter to the TreeSetup constructor, and using that object to create DefaultMutableTreeNode instances.

```
import java.util.*;
import javax.swing.*;
import javax.swing.tree.*;
```

```java
public class SampleTree
{
  private DefaultMutableTreeNode[] nodes;
  private TreeSetup tsu;
  private DefaultMutableTreeNode root;
  private DefaultTreeModel dtm;

  public SampleTree(String schema) {
    root = new DefaultMutableTreeNode("Trouble Fields");
    tsu = new TreeSetup(schema);
    Enumeration enum = tsu.getParents().elements();

    while (enum.hasMoreElements()) {
      String category = (String)enum.nextElement();
      DefaultMutableTreeNode parent;
      parent = new DefaultMutableTreeNode(category);
      root.add(parent);
      Enumeration enum2;
      enum2 = tsu.getChildren(category).elements();

      while (enum2.hasMoreElements()) {
        String child = (String)enum2.nextElement();
        parent.add(new DefaultMutableTreeNode(child));
      }
    }

    dtm = new DefaultTreeModel(root, false);
  }

  public DefaultTreeModel getSampleTreeModel() {
    return dtm;
  }

  public static void main(String args[]) {
    if (args.length == 0) {
      System.out.println("Provide a valid property " +
```

```
            "file name and try again");
          System.exit(1);
        }
        SampleTree st = new SampleTree(args[0]);
        DefaultTreeModel tm = st.getSampleTreeModel();
        JTree jt = new JTree(tm);
        JScrollPane jsp = new JScrollPane(jt);
        JFrame jf = new JFrame("Sample Tree");
        jf.getContentPane().add(jsp);
        jf.setDefaultCloseOperation(JFrame.EXIT_ON_CLOSE);
        jf.pack();
        jf.setVisible(true);
      }
    }
```

The resulting work takes the sample file listed above and displays it in a
Jtree like the one in Figure 20.8.

FIGURE 20.8   A JTree that displays the contents of the file sample

The work we did here was neither trivial nor rocket science, but the result
is a tool for creating any two-tier tree display quickly from a file—well worth
the effort for a prototype tool.

JMenus, JButtons, and Actions

The Swing library seems particularly thoughtful when it comes to providing conveniences for common GUI-based tasks. It's easy to create a single action as an object and bind its behavior to a ready-made Swing widget. Action objects encapsulate their behavior so that multiple widgets can reference them. An icon on a toolbar, a menu choice, or even a KeyStroke can all use the same object for processing. Using KeyStroke objects goes beyond the requirements of the Exam, but they can make the GUI friendlier for users who favor keyboard input over the mouse. This section therefore includes a sidebar on combining Action and KeyStroke objects through any JComponent.

The Action interface extends the ActionListener interface by adding methods that make it a list of properties, including its own "enabled" state, and a source of PropertyChangeEvents. The additional methods are:

- add/removePropertyChangeListener()

- is/setEnabled()

- public Object getValue(String key)

- public void putValue(String key, Object value)

The putValue() and getValue() pair support a hash-based collection for storing any number of properties as key-value pairs.

Making "Hotkeys" in Swing

All JComponents have a registerKeyboardAction() method that takes the following parameters:

- An ActionListener that is invoked

- A String for an actionCommand property

- The KeyStroke that invokes the ActionListener

- A focus condition that the JComponent must satisfy, expressed as an integer constant

Based on the component's focus condition, the programmer can supply a "hotkey" through this method. `Action` implements `ActionListener`, so an `Action` object can bind to any `JComponent`. The focus conditions available in `JComponent` are:

- `WHEN_FOCUSED`

- `WHEN_IN_FOCUSED_WINDOW`

- `WHEN_ANCESTOR_OF_FOCUSED_COMPONENT`

This last condition allows for binding `KeyStrokes` to a `JFrame`.

Classes must meet the same requirements in order to implement `Action` (or subclassing `AbstractAction`) as for `ActionListener`. `Action` implementations are different in that they allow for direct containment by a `JComponent`, although only `JMenu`, `JToolBar`, and `JPopupMenu` know how to contain, display, and listen to them. Here's a simple look at creating an `Action` and binding it to a menu (the result of the following code is shown in Figure 20.9).

```
import java.awt.event.*;
import javax.swing.*;

/**
 * This subclass of AbstractAction serves as a prototype
 * for creating simple Action objects. No provision is
 * made for icons - just a String value so the containing
 * component has something to display.
 *
 * @author The CJ2CSG Guys
 */
public class SampleAction extends AbstractAction
{
  private String message;

  /**
    * Passes the supplied String to the parent class;
    * also maintains a copy locally.
    */
```

```java
      public SampleAction(String output) {
        super(output);
        message = output;
      }

      /**
       * Sends the Action message to stdout.
       */
      public void actionPerformed(ActionEvent ae) {
        System.out.println(message);
      }

      /**
       * A bootstrap test. Adds the object to a JMenu.
       */
      public static void main(String args[]) {
        SampleAction sa = new SampleAction(args[0]);
        JFrame jf = new JFrame("Action Test");
        JMenuBar jmb = new JMenuBar();
        jf.setJMenuBar(jmb);
        JMenu jm = new JMenu("Sample");
        jmb.add(jm);
        jm.add(sa);
        jf.setSize(100,100);
        jf.setVisible(true);
        jf.setDefaultCloseOperation(JFrame.EXIT_ON_CLOSE);
      }
    }
```

FIGURE 20.9   Adding an Action to a JMenu

The JDK 1.3 version of javax.swing.AbstractButton supports the method setAction(Action act). Now its subclasses can retrieve property values and changes from an Action object, and adjust to its enabled state.

Take another look at the TreeSetup class from the last section. This same code could be used to create a quick menu prototype, using a file that lists Menus as keys and MenuItems as values. It won't have much in the way of interesting functionality, but it will provide a quick means for choosing how to visually arrange menu items.

It makes sense to rename TreeSetup to something more general, such as WidgetSetup, to suggest wider usage. As practice, write a SampleMenu class that reads from a menu property file and builds a GUI menu for you.

Panes

Swing panes all provide some form of containment service. The services they provide vary widely, from delegated layout managers (content pane), to specialized "layout managers" (JSplitPane, JScrollPane) and dialog boxes (JOptionPane, JTabbedPane, JFileChooser), to embedded layers that have no class of their own (the "glass pane" in the JFrame). The content pane is something everyone who writes a Swing application must use, and JFile-Chooser is a straightforward class, so we briefly discuss here two of the panes you might not think to use: JSplitPane and JOptionPane.

JSplitPane

As the name suggests, a JSplitPane holds two other components and provides an adjustable divider service. A JSplitPane is not a layout manager subclass, but contains layout behavior just the same: it has its own rules regarding minimumSize and preferredSize requests from the components it contains. JSplitPane looks at minimumSize on a resize request, ensuring that one component does not encroach on the other's needed space. The range of the divider's location is normally fixed by the minimum sizes of the components in the pane, but is adjustable.

Other properties of JSplitPane include:

- orientation–HORIZONTAL_SPLIT or VERTICAL_SPLIT

- dividerSize–in pixels

- dividerLocation–current position

- minimumDividerLocation–left/bottom minimum size

- maximumDividerLocation–right/top minimum size

Now we're ready to put the tree, table, and simple menu together for a first look, which we create with the following code:

```java
import java.awt.*;
import java.awt.event.*;
import javax.swing.*;
import javax.swing.tree.*;

/** A bootstrap class that combines our table and tree,
 * in a split pane, along with a trivial menu that is
 * backed by an Action.
 *
 * @author The CJ2CSG Guys
 */
public class Prototype
{
  public static void main(String args[]) {
    JFrame jf = new JFrame("SplitPane Test");

    TroubleTicketModel ttm = new TroubleTicketModel();
    JTable jta = new JTable(ttm);

    SampleTree st = new SampleTree("sample");
    DefaultTreeModel tm = st.getSampleTreeModel();
    JTree jtr = new JTree(tm);

    SampleAction sa = new SampleAction("PROTOTYPE");
    JMenuBar jmb = new JMenuBar();
```

```
jf.setJMenuBar(jmb);
JMenu jm = new JMenu("Sample");
jmb.add(jm);
jm.add(sa);

JSplitPane jsp = new
  JSplitPane(JSplitPane.HORIZONTAL_SPLIT, jtr, jta);

jf.getContentPane().add(jsp, BorderLayout.WEST);
jf.setDefaultCloseOperation(JFrame.EXIT_ON_CLOSE);
jf.setSize(650,200);
jf.setVisible(true);
  }
}
```

The result is shown in Figure 20.10. We didn't spend time refining appearances in this first round, but now we have a quick look at our elements. Most of the adjustments to appearance can be made in the bootstrap code, meaning less focus on changing class behavior and more on experimenting with it.

FIGURE 20.10 Menu, table, and tree together in one JFrame

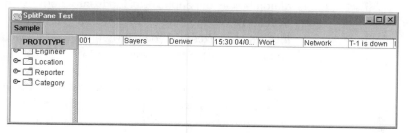

The final exercise left for you here is to produce a GUI prototype like this one, relying only on a property file for input. With a little more effort, you can load sample data from that file, then store it off to another file into Object format, assuming the data itself is Serializable. With those tools in hand, you are free to fuss over various appearances and data formats, each of which is maintained as a file for later use. It's more work up front, but down the road that effort will pay off each time we have an opportunity for reuse.

JOptionPane

The JOptionPane class encapsulates several conventional dialog-box formats, but with one clear advantage: it is not necessary to declare a Frame and bind to it (more on that in a moment).

JOptionPane defines five message types:

- ERROR_MESSAGE

- INFORMATION_MESSAGE

- WARNING_MESSAGE

- QUESTION_MESSAGE

- PLAIN_MESSAGE

Each of these types maps to a prepared display format. These formats can be associated one of two ways: using a confirmation request that locks the underlying frame (a modal dialog), or a dismiss-on-demand style that does not interfere with the application (a non-modal dialog). These behaviors are respectively enabled by the static methods showconfirmDialog() and showMessageDialog().

A superficial way to curb user perception of a slow program is by popping a dialog box as the application loads into memory. In the time it takes a user to dismiss the widget, the application can get a lot done. Dialogs are also useful for throwing exception data where the user expects to see it: on top of the application, not in the session window.

Add the following code snippets to the Prototype class as a way to experiment, and compare your perception of speed before and after these changes. The dialogs that pop up are depicted in Figure 20.11.

```
...
JOptionPane.showMessageDialog(null, "Tree created",
      "Program Note", JOptionPane.INFORMATION_MESSAGE);
...
JOptionPane.showConfirmDialog(null, "Load the GUI?",
      "Roll Call!", JOptionPane.YES_NO_CANCEL_OPTION,
      JOptionPane.QUESTION_MESSAGE);
...
```

FIGURE 20.11   JOptionPane's (a) information and (b) question dialogs

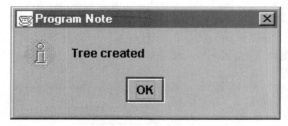
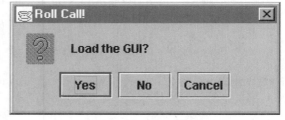

(a) information dialog   (a) question dialog

Final Thoughts on Code Style

If you pick up a book devoted to explaining Swing and look through the sample code, chances are you will notice heavy reliance on anonymous inner classes. Among the most commonly used forms is something like this:

```
import javax.swing.*;

public class GUIFrame extends JFrame {
  public GUIFrame() {
    ...
    addWindowListener(new WindowAdapter() {
      public void windowClosing(WindowEvent we) {
        System.exit(0);
      }
    });
  }
  ...
}
```

This construction can be hard to unravel on first sight, so we'll break it down. GUIFrame's constructor invokes addWindowListener() so the frame can listen to its own window events. The parameter is an object of type WindowAdapter. This class implements the WindowListener interface by providing null code for each declared method. WindowAdapter itself isn't interesting, as a result, but convenient. It saves us the trouble of writing null method bodies ourselves for each method (i.e., window event actions) we don't care about. We can just extend WindowAdapter anonymously, override the methods we need, and move on to the next task. If we were to diagram this class relation, it might look like Figure 20.12.

FIGURE 20.12 A relation diagram with an anonymous inner class

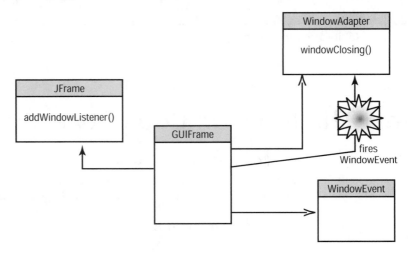

"Throwaway" classes like this are useful when there is little or no reuse potential for the code. They fulfill a necessary function without forcing the programmer to create a separate class file or a name. And Java's inner class scheme gives the programmer a way to express both concepts quickly. In the statement above, WindowAdapter is subclassed on the fly—the compiler recognizes this instruction by the open bracket after the constructor call. WindowAdapter's windowClosing() method is then overridden by adding a System.exit() call. The parameter list is closed normally, with a closing parenthesis and semicolon, and that's all there is to it.

The class that has been defined here is nameless and only available to GUIFrame. The compiler in this instance would generate a class file named GUIFrame$1.class, reflecting a composite of:

- The top-level class name

- The $ symbol, which delimits the outer and inner class

- An index number the compiler assigns to each anonymous inner class in a top-level class

The compact expression of the form also makes it popular in printed examples. In the majority of `JTable` illustrations we've come across in other works, all the elements that help compose the sample table are anonymous inner classes. And while convenience and brevity are staples of the periodical world, those virtues don't necessarily equate to best practice or elegance in design. They take up less space, and they seem quite clever, but they're also contagious. A quick look at the JFC code bundled with the JDK 1.2, for example, shows the same `windowClosing()` routine hard-coded into every demo class that has a `JFrame`.

It's not wrong. But what if the routine in question needed updating? Let's say the authors wanted to use `JFrame`'s `setDefaultCloseOperation()` instead, or `windowClosing()` became deprecated (ok, that's very unlikely, but you get the idea). The maintainer(s) would have to change and recompile every source file that used it. If one class contained this code, on the other hand, and every demo used it, one class change and recompilation would square everything. Which maintenance model would you prefer?

The goal of object-oriented programming should be to create reusable classes. And while allowing for code reuse often means planning ahead, there's no requirement that it be expensive or time consuming. Closing a window is a small example, compared to what this chapter has covered, but it certainly isn't a one-time task; creating a reusable service class isn't that much extra work, and it's certainly easier to read and extend later. It's worth your long-term programming efforts to find small economies of abstraction where you can, so you don't find yourself reinventing the wheel with every new project.

Chapter

21

Building the Database Server

One of the three main architectural requirements of the exam is to use either RMI or socket programming to connect the client GUI and the server database. We've chosen to focus on RMI in this scenario, so we can leave out discussion of serializing objects and socket programming—for which there are many online examples—and focus instead on topics "above the transport." Details of database operation won't concern us much either; in the end, the only implementation that will matter is the one provided on the exam, and it is not intended to challenge anyone with even minor experience in database programming.

Database Requirements

In addition to the choice of RMI or socket programming, two other architectural requirements are written into the Developer's Exam we received. One: the resulting application must allow for either local or networked access to the database. Two: the client must be able to access all the public methods provided in the exam's database code. The access requirement sounds sticky. The GUI client must connect at start-up, based on user choice, to either the local VM or a remote one. One way to interpret this requirement is to launch client and server code from a single bootstrap program, such that the server always has a built-in client; the client can connect to that or to any remote data server, without restriction. By the same token, every client would then need to have a server attached to it for this approach to work, which does not sound like great design.

After some thought, we inferred that the real reason for the requirement was to ensure that the developer deals with thread safety in the received database, and not just in the RMI code alone. It's an interesting problem; the straightforward solutions are ugly, but the elegant ones are code-intensive. Given, those options, defending a solution is likely to be far more important in scoring than the solution itself, so pick the method that suits you best.

The second requirement tells which operations must work in our application. These operations consist of:

- Retrieving the schema
- Getting a total record count
- Retrieving a record based on its key

- Matching a record based on a search string
- Adding a record
- Modifying an existing record
- Deleting a record
- Closing the database

In addition to these operations, three more must be added and made accessible to client control:

- Locking a record based on its key
- Unlocking a record based on its key
- Matching against multiple records based on multiple criteria

The developer may write a subclass or directly modify the provided code. Either approach will have benefits and drawbacks; it's the developer's job to defend the choice made and demonstrate awareness of those strengths and weaknesses.

Implementing RMI

As discussed previously, RMI makes it possible to export to other virtual machines the interface of a concrete object on the local machine. RMI hides the details of object serialization and network communication, and places the bulk of the preparation for remote access on the server-side. Client code that calls a local method, as a result, does not look substantially different from code that makes remote calls. After the client initiates a lookup to the remote objects that it is interested in, remote and local calls will, in fact, look the same.

The interactions between an RMI client and the server objects it uses can go a long way to help define the category of network communication they engage in. We call this scheme *client-server* largely because of its long association with centralized database resources and multiple concurrent users. Many contemporary computing models employ similar schemes, but the term "client-server" would be meaningless if it simply referred to any two machines communicating over a network.

To give a client access to server resources, we first build an interface that extends the Remote interface. Remote is a tagging interface, meaning it has

What Exactly Does Client-Server Mean?

The term "client-server" suffers from a fair amount of dilution and misinterpretation, to where in some contexts it means any interaction between two machines. We find it helpful to maintain distinctions among the terms *client-server, distributed computing,* and a more recent term, *request-response.*

Client-server interaction most often describes a structure for permitting access to a centralized data store that the clients can manipulate in some way: by adding or deleting records, initiating complex queries, etc. This interaction for the most part is not what is usually meant with static-content services like HTTP, sometimes referred to as a request-response service. Some people will contend that Web content is in fact becoming more dynamic, and to the degree that a Web server is really a graphical front-end to a fully functional database, it's a reasonable contention. At the same time, most HTTP servers distribute one type of content, possibly with multiple views, to all subscribers, until the server side changes that content. Information about the user may shape the data, but the user's range of options for gathering data based on their own input is typically very limited.

Distributed computing is a separate beast altogether: it refers to the process of breaking down a job into parts, and garnering the resources of very many or very specialized systems to process the parts and return them. Possibly the largest distributed computing model working today is the SETI (Search for Extraterrestrial Intelligence) Project based in UC Berkeley's Space Sciences Laboratory. At this writing, more than two million subscribers have volunteered computer time to that project.

no methods of its own we must implement. Much like the `Serializable` interface, which only identifies the objects the virtual machine may convert to a stream of bytes, `Remote` is only used to flag its implementing classes as available for export.

```
import java.rmi.*;

/**
 * Defines database operations available to remote
```

```
    * clients.
    *
    * @author The CJ2CSG Guys
    */
public interface DBServer extends Remote
{
  /**
    * Retrieves the column structure of the records in the
    * implementing database.
    *
    * @returns array of Field objects
    */
  public Field[] getSchema() throws RemoteException;

  /**
    * Returns the total number of records currently in the
    * implementing database.
    */
  public int getRecordCount() throws RemoteException;

  /**
    * Returns the Record associated with the record
    * number.
    */
  public Record getRecord(int key)
  throws RemoteException;

  /**
    * Given a String to match against, returns the first
    * exact match found in the implementing database.
    */
  public Record matchOne(String match)
  throws RemoteException;

  /**
    * Accepts a String array and adds it as a Record to
```

```
 * the implementing database.
 */
public void addRecord(String fields[])
throws RemoteException;

/**
 * Modifies the disparate fields in the Record that
 * matches the parameter Record's key value.
 */
public void modifyRecord(Record rec)
throws RemoteException;

/**
 * Deletes the record with the same key value as the
 * one provided by the parameter Record.
 */
public void deleteRecord(Record rec)
throws RemoteException;

/**
 * Closes the database.
 */
public void close() throws RemoteException;

/**
 * Locks the Record with a matching key, provided it is
 * not locked.
 */
public void lock(int key) throws RemoteException;

/**
 * Unlocks the Record with a matching key. This method
 * currently offers no protection against an unlock()
 * attempt that was not preceded by a lock().
 */
public void unlock(int key) throws RemoteException;
```

```
    /**
     * Given a String with multiple matching criteria,
     * returns an array of records that match exactly all
     * the criteria given.
     */
    public Record[] matchAll(String matchList)
    throws RemoteException;


}
```

All methods in a Remote-extending interface must declare RemoteException in a throws clause. RemoteException extends IOException, appropriately enough, but is also a useful front for any problems the client has using the method.

We can proceed one of two ways from here. To make our remote object available only while its server process is active, we can implement the above interface in a concrete class that also extends java.rmi.server.UnicastRemoteObject. To keep the object available over time, but only use system resources as needed, we can extend the java.rmi.server.Activatable class instead. Objects that are Activatable rely on a daemon process (or service) to wake them when a client request is pending. They can also maintain changes to data using the MarshalledObject class.

Exporting with *UnicastRemoteObject*

To walk through both approaches in a short amount of space, we'll use an interface with a single method:

```
import java.rmi.*;

/**
 * Describes a remotely available interface for
 * retrieving a count of records.
 *
 * @author The CJ2CSG Guys
 */
public interface RecordCounter extends Remote
{
```

```
   /**
    * Returns a total number of records.
    */
   public int getRecordCount() throws RemoteException();
 }
```

...and we take our first pass by extending UnicastRemoteObject:

```
import java.rmi.*;
import java.rmi.server.*;

/**
 * RecordCountImpl is a UnicastRemoteObject
 * implementation, so it will only be available while its
 * server process is up and running.
 *
 * @author The CJ2CSG Guys
 */

public class RecordCounterImpl
extends UnicastRemoteObject implements RecordCounter
{
  private static int requests = 0;
  private int count = 0;

  /**
   * Constructors must throw RemoteException, therefore
   * the default constructor must be declared explicitly.
   */
  public RecordCounterImpl() throws RemoteException {

  }

  /**
   * Returns zero; increments the local "request" counter
   */
  public int getRecordCount() throws RemoteException {
```

```
      requests++;
      return count;
   }


   /**
    * Returns total count of remote requests made during
    * uptime. Available only to local objects.
    */
   public int getRequestCount() {
      return requests;
   }
}
```

The only thing that takes us out of our way here is the default constructor, which is required because the parent constructor throws `RemoteException`. This class always returns a count of zero, but maintains a separate counter for how many times the count value has been requested. This current value of requests is only available to another local object. This simple technique creates the separation that we want to maintain between database and client access. Now we need a server application that can export this object to the outside world.

```
import java.rmi.*;
import java.rmi.server.*;
import java.net.*;

/**
 * A bootstrap class for launching the RecordCounter
 * service.
 *
 * @author The CJ2CSG Guys
 */
public class BootUnicast
{
   public static void main(String args[]) {
      System.setSecurityManager(new RMISecurityManager());
      try {
```

```
          RecordCounterImpl rci = new RecordCounterImpl();
          Naming.rebind("RecordCountServer", rci);
        }
      catch(RemoteException re) {
        re.printStackTrace();
        System.err.println
        ("Creation error: RecordCounterImpl");
      }
      catch(MalformedURLException mfe) {
        mfe.printStackTrace();
        System.err.println("Malformed URL: " +
                              mfe.getMessage());
      }
    }
  }
```

Loading classes across the network, either from client to server or vice versa, is not permitted without an appropriate SecurityManager installed. If we do not install a SecurityManager, class loading is restricted to only what is available on the local CLASSPATH.

From the implementation of the remote interfaces, we can then create the files that act as endpoints between client and server on RMI's transport system. These proxy files, known as *stubs* and *skeletons*, are generated for each concrete type. Once we start the rmiregistry, we can run our UnicastBoot class and wait for client requests. Here's a throw-away client that indicates a successful remote call by popping a JOptionPane:

```
import java.rmi.*
import java.awt.event.*;
import javax.swing.*;

/**
 * A bootstrap client to prove the remote service works.
 *
 * @author The CJ2CSG Guys
 */
public class CountClient
```

```
    {
      public static void main(String args[]) {
        RecordCounter rc;
        try {
          rc = (RecordCounter)Naming.lookup
                      ("//localhost/RecordCountServer");
        }
        catch(RemoteException re) {
          re.printStackTrace();
          System.err.println
            ("Error accessing remote object");
        }

        JFrame jf = new JFrame("Count Client");
        JButton jb = new JButton("Request Count");

        jb.addActionListener(new ActionAdapter( {
          public void actionPerformed(ActionEvent ae) {
            try {
              rc.getRecordCount();
              JOptionPane.showMessageDialog(jf,
                "It's still zero", "Count Request",
                JOptionPane.INFORMATION_MESSAGE);
            }
            catch (RemoteException re) {
              re.printStackTrace();
              System.err.println
                ("Error getting record count");
            }
          }
        });

        jf.getContentPane().add(jb, BorderLayout.SOUTH);
```

```
    jf.setDefaultCloseOperation(JFrame.EXIT_ON_CLOSE);
    jf.pack();
    jf.setVisible(true);
  }
}
```

Notwithstanding a few details—setting the server's CLASSPATH properly, making sure the stubs and skeletons aren't in it, and creating a policy file—this model covers a general RMI scheme as supported by `UnicastRemote-Object`. Creating a policy file is discussed in the next section. The rest of the client-server work deals with more operations, including threading. Chapters 16 and 17 provide an adequate foundation on threads for the purposes of the exam.

Exporting an *Activatable* Object

If we want to support on-demand activation of an RMI server resource, we need to subclass `Activatable` instead. Setting an RMI server object to be `Activatable` means that no server resources are committed to making that object available except when it is in use by one or more clients. Requirements for extending `Activatable` start right with its constructors. The daemon or service process that runs on the server (`rmid`) uses the provided constructor to perform an on-demand or lazy instantiation of the `Activatable` object. If the remotely available object stores data that it wants to save to a file between uses, a `MarshalledObject` instance is required to manage that data. Passing an `Object` as a parameter to a `MarshalledObject` constructor has the effect of serializing its state, which can then be retrieved through the object's `get()` method. The tools needed to store state data between remote calls are an `Activatable` object's `restoreState()` and `saveState()` methods, and a stream that points to a backing store, such as the file system. Figure 21.1 illustrates the differences in state action between the two remote types.

FIGURE 21.1   (left) A UnicastRemoteObject state using rmiregistry and (right) an Activatable using rmid

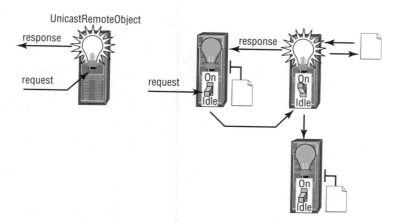

Server implementation of either type is transparent to the client. The server-side implementation is free to choose either model, or switch from one to the other, with no impact to client code. Here is a sample implementation using Activatable in place of UnicastRemoteObject:

```java
import java.io.*;
import java.rmi.*;
import java.rmi.activation.*;

/**
 * This class implements the RecordCounter as an
 * Activatable object. It persists the request counter
 * between uses.
 *
 * @author The CJ2CSG Guys
 */
public class RecordCounterImplAct extends Activatable
implements RecordCounter
{
  private File dataStore;
  private static Integer requestCount;
  private static int requests = 0;
  private int count = 0;
```

```
/**
 * Constructor passes activation ID and integer (0) to
 * the parent class. Persists the request counter to a
 * file between uses.
 *
 * @see java.rmi.activation.ActivationID
 */
public RecordCounterImplAct(ActivationID
activate, MarshalledObject ser)
throws RemoteException, IOException
{
  super(activate, 0);
  try {
    dataStore = (File)ser.get();
    if (dataStore.exists()) {
      restore();
    }
    else {
      requestCount = new Integer(requests);
    }
  }
  catch (ClassNotFoundException cnfe) {
    cnfe.printStackTrace();
    System.err.println
      ("Error: Trouble finding File class?");
  }
}

/**
 * Increments the request counter after each call.
 * Returns zero.
 */
public int getRecordCount() throws RemoteException {
  FileOutputStream fos;
  ObjectOutputStream oos;
  File f = dataStore;
```

```java
    try {
      fos = new FileOutputStream(f);
      oos = new ObjectOutputStream(fos);
      requests = requestCount.intValue() + 1;
      requestCount = new Integer(count);
      oos.writeObject(requestCount);
      oos.close();
    }
    catch(IOException re) {
      re.printStackTrace();
      System.err.println("Error: Saving requestCount.");
    }
    return count;
  }

  /**
   * A separate method for restoring the serialized
   * object, to make the constructor more readable.
   * It makes sense to balance the code separation with a
   * save() method.
   */
  protected void restore()
  throws IOException, ClassNotFoundException {
    File f = dataStore;
    try {
      FileInputStream fis;
      ObjectInputStream ois;
      fis = new FileInputStream(f);
      ois = new ObjectInputStream(fis);
      requestCount = (Integer)ois.readObject();
      ois.close();
    }
    catch (IOException ioe) {
      ioe.printStackTrace();
      System.err.println
        ("Error: Restoring requestCount");
    }
  }
}
```

The majority of this code performs simple serialization and deserialization and the associated housekeeping for exception conditions. The `ActivationID` provides a unique identity for this service once it has been exported. There are several options for retrieving a unique ID; we use `Activatable.register()` in our bootstrap code. The `register()` method returns a `Remote` stub, which is cast back to the implementation type and exported via the `Naming` utilities `bind()` or `rebind()`. Also, because we wish to write a file locally, we need to set a policy. Java 2 comes with a binary called `policytool`, which helps the programmer create an access rule without mastering the syntax required, but that's overkill for what we want to show here. A simple "wide-open" policy will suffice for demonstration (justifying it on the exam might be a stretch!):

```
grant { permission java.security.AllPermission }
```

Finally, the bootstrap code spends most of its effort constructing various activation objects needed to build up to registering our service.

```java
import java.io.*;
import java.util.*;
import java.rmi.*;
import java.rmi.activation.*;

public class BootStrapAct
{
  // If this doesn't work, might as well fault and exit.
  public static void main(String args[]) throws
    IOException, ActivationException, RemoteException
    {
    RecordCounter rc;
    ActivationDesc ad;
    ActivationGroupDesc agd;
    ActivationGroupDesc.CommandEnvironment ace = null;
    ActivationGroupID agi;
    File store = new File("Requests.ser");
    MarshalledObject serData;

    System.setSecurityManager(new RMISecurityManager());
```

```
      Properties props = new Properties();
      props.put("java.security.policy", "policy");

      agd = new ActivationGroupDesc(props, ace);
      agi = ActivationGroup.getSystem().registerGroup(agd);

      serData = new MarshalledObject(store);
      ad = new ActivationDesc(agi, "RecordCountServer",
        ".", serData);

      rc = (RecordCounter)Activatable.register(ad);
      Naming.rebind("RecordCountServer", rc);

      // No reason to hang around; rmid is in charge now
      System.exit(0);
    }
  }
```

Record Locking

Solutions for record locking in the Developer's Exam do not need to be elaborate. The principle applied and the operation that expresses it must be sound but not bulletproof against the unknown. Part of the reason for this is that, taken as a whole, most programmers do not have a lot of experience in multithreaded environments. The other part of the reason is that the developer is expected to make less than elegant choices in an imperfect situation, then document his or her awareness of the solution's limits.

The exam requires the candidate to demonstrate control over overlapping safety mechanisms: the synchronized method calls already in the assignment source, and a method that will flag a data element as unavailable if it is in use by a client. A rigorous programmer with a great imagination can easily turn this aspect of the exam into a black hole, so don't read too much into the requirement.

The lock() and unlock() methods are intended as public methods, and so are required to be made available for use by the GUI client. From that perspective, a few different approaches to implementation are possible. Each associated figure shows a possible evolution to the strategy.

- Active client: Highlighting a row locks the record (Figure 21.2).

- On-demand client: Locking is integral to all add/delete/modify operations (Figure 21.3).

- Lazy client: Requests are queued; notification occurs on a subsequent thread (Figure 21.4).

Each model has its advantages and disadvantages. As a general rule, the more "active" the strategy, the less appropriate it is for large numbers of users. The more passive the strategy, the more "available" the database seems, at least under moderate use. Passive strategies also typically require more careful designs, as each sub-process takes on a thread of its own, and "deference" is sorted out among competing processes.

For each strategy, some tactic can usually be applied to mitigate drawbacks. An active client (illustrated in Figure 21.2) can be supported with a timer thread. If the client senses no user activity in the course of a timed loop, the client can release the lock and notify the user through a modal dialog. Or the server can host the timer, possibly polling the client for signs of life as well, and reclaiming locks only when the connection client appears to die.

FIGURE 21.2 Record locking for an active client

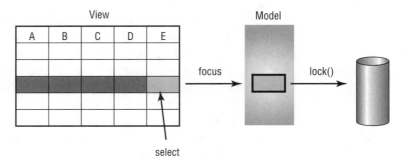

On-demand clients, such as the one in Figure 21.3, can suffer from lengthy blocks under heavy usage, blocking the GUI application until some action is resolved. Swing actually prevents this kind of behavior in an RMI server environment, by not allowing remote calls to take place on the GUI's event dispatch thread. To work around this, remote calls that need to run on

this thread can be encapsulated as `Runnable` objects. `SwingUtilities`
`.invokeAndWait()` and `SwingUtilities.invokeLater()` each accept a
`Runnable` parameter, which they can then execute synchronously or asynchronously, respectively, on the AWT event dispatch thread.

FIGURE 21.3   Record locking for an on-demand client

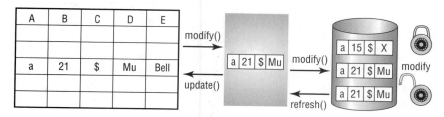

Lazy clients (diagrammed in Figure 21.4) are our closest strategy for
record locking as it might be modeled in a relational database. Relational
database management system (RDBMS) designers have to concern themselves with record locks that can occur during a large join operation, making
it computationally expensive to assess which records are in use and which
are free. Notification in such environments is usually required to be as quick
as possible, separate threading or not. The usual solution: more memory,
faster CPUs, more efficient storage systems. To achieve a similar effect for
this assignment, look to build a server algorithm that queues jobs, similar to
the model we described in Chapter 17, and uses a publish-subscribe or event-
delegation model to notify the client.

FIGURE 21.4   Record locking for a lazy client

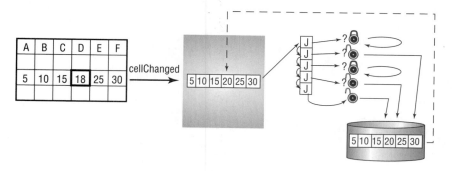

Chapter Summary

As an exam candidate, you will have to support a fundamental list of data-oriented operations in a client-server environment. Most details for server-side storage have been decided in the assignment source code, so it's really up to you to decide what kind of design you can best defend. There are two possibilities for RMI-based networking: export the object using `UnicastRemoteObject`, so that it is always up and running; or extend the `Activatable` service class and set up a `MarshalledObject` to persist the data between uses. Remember to follow the documentation guidelines for instituting security, writing a policy file, and refresh your understanding of how the CLASSPATH can interfere with proper RMI behavior.

Record locking ensures that one change operation on a record can't be interrupted by another change to the same record. Without that guarantee of serially ordered (or `synchronized`) operations, the integrity of the data could be lost. It is the developer's job to provide for efficient concurrent access without jeopardizing data. Manipulating records as discrete objects is one way to provide for threadsafe operation. In a client-server arrangement, it's tempting to synchronize the client at the moment it requests access to the remote object, but truly threadsafe code must center on the shared data itself.

Chapter

22

Connecting Client and Server

In this chapter, the focus of our discussion turns back to architectural issues. So far, we've covered each piece of the Developer's Exam as a substantial collection of related details. Now that we are looking at ways to connect the two major components—the client and the server—it's time to consider some design-level strategies we can apply to the assignment as a whole.

It's easy, on a first reading, to mistake the exam for a collection of related but separate requirements: write a conversion tool, replace some deprecated methods, write a GUI, add a locking feature, and so on. Certain other requirements, like configuring the server application so that a client can connect locally or remotely, can add to this sense of fragments creating a whole.

We want to introduce the idea of a near-universal solvent for many of these tasks: notification-based objects. The chapter starts with a primer on the subject, so if you are comfortable with the foundation, feel free to skim forward. By chapter's end we will have covered:

- Notification basics

- Using Bean conventions

- Event adapters

- Remote notification

- Distributed notification

Also, some of you may be new to the term *design patterns*. A design pattern is an arrangement of classes by their relations and working collaborations. Properly used, design patterns help provide a structure to solve a well-known problem and help reduce programming effort. You do not need to know any patterns to pass the Developer's Exam, but chances are you've seen one and simply didn't know it had a name. If you are in the habit of writing reusable code, you are almost certainly applying a pattern to do it—you just may not know there is a formal term that describes it.

We will call the family of patterns described below *event notification* patterns.

Notification Basics

Notification is a form of object-oriented messaging for which Java programming is a remarkably good fit. As discussed in Chapter 20, event-driven coding is a staple form of communication among AWT and Swing widgets. The pattern they use is also the foundation of Sun's JavaBeans specification, which describes a few fundamental roles that are played out time and time again in different contexts and arrangements. These fundamental roles are:

- Event object
- Event handler
- Event source
- Event target

Event objects define and encapsulate an action or state change that took place in some other object, an *event source*. An event source creates event objects and sends them to other objects it tracks as listeners, otherwise known as *event targets*. An object can become a target in one of two ways:

- It acquires a reference to the event source and "registers" its interest. Java `Components` do this through a source's `addXXXListener()` method. Targets that implement the same interface the source uses for event-firing receive events through a method call on that interface. Figure 22.1 depicts this interaction.

- It acquires a reference to another object that knows how to register to the source. From the point of view of the target, this intermediary is known as an event handler. See Figure 22.2.

How the final target responds once it receives the event object may depend on the event object's content, or the target's function, or both, or neither. In other words, the resulting behavior could be anything within the range of the target's abilities, and that's the point. Any two objects can talk, either directly or through a handler. If the intermediary also happens to translate, filter, or perform some other service, we call it an *event adapter*. Figure 22.3 demonstrates a substantive event adaptation.

FIGURE 22.1 A simple callback relation

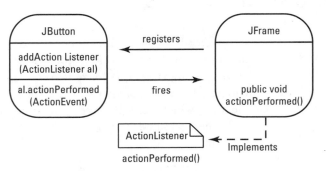

FIGURE 22.2 An indirect callback

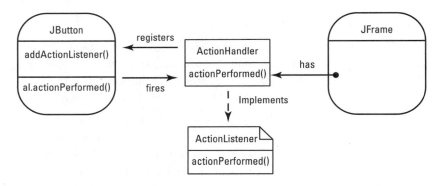

FIGURE 22.3 Adaptive event behavior (multiplexing)

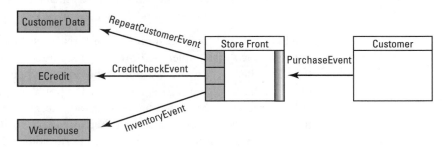

Notification is such a flexible, and therefore powerful, object-oriented strategy that it is modeled in a variety of ways. Some frequently described and widely documented variations of this general construct include:

- Model-View-Controller: discussed in Chapter 20 with respect to Swing.

- Observer-Observable: a collaboration focusing on the relation of one observable to many observers; a generic notification model.

- Publish-Subscribe: describes a source of continuous events, and listeners that use policies or filters to "discriminate" among the event types.

- Callbacks: a term coined in Motif/X window programming to describe one widget's interest in another widget's property or state changes.

These models vary based on how they stress (or de-emphasize) two high-level aspects all notification schemes share: *coupling* and *context*. Coupling is an expression of how *tight* or *loose* the objects become when they share a notification scheme. An example of a tight relation is two objects that must maintain mutual references in order to communicate. A context defines an environment the objects operate in. It can be a containment system (the **BeanContext** library, an EJB container), a communications framework (Lotus' InfoBus), both (a builder tool), or something as simple as the Virtual Machine environment itself.

The broader the context is, the more general the notification strategy becomes, and therefore the looser the couplings between objects. The more deterministic the context, the more it defines the available roles. Coupling may get tighter as well, but with the added benefit of sharing more meaningful information.

For more information on these technologies, here are some sources:

- Bean Context Services: the `java.beans.beancontext` package
- InfoBus: `http://java.sun.com/beans/infobus/index.html`
- Enterprise JavaBeans: `http://java.sun.com/products/ejb`

Using JavaBean Conventions

The JavaBean specification is not a notification pattern; it's a naming convention. In a runtime environment, Beans only care about two things: events and *properties*, which can be communicated from one Bean to another Bean by way of a special-purpose event. A property is any value in an object that has been encapsulated by a get/set or is/set method pair. If a Bean is also an event source, it supports a method pair to add listeners to and remove them from its registry.

A JButton will send an ActionEvent to all its listeners when a user clicks it, for example, but there is nothing "GUI-driven" about how it does so. Shown next is a Monitor class that has no visual appearance but supplies the same event behavior we just described for JButton. It also has an alert property that, when re-set by way of a setAlert() call, fires an ActionEvent.

```java
import java.awt.event.*;
import java.util.*;

/**
 * Monitor maintains a single alert property.
 * When some other object changes the value of alert,
 * it fires an ActionEvent.
 *
 * @author The CJ2CSG Guys
 */
public class Monitor
{
  private Vector listeners = new Vector();
  private String alert;

  /**
   * Registers an action listener to this object.
   * Ignores repeat registrations.
   */
  public void addActionListener(ActionListener acl) {
```

```
    if (!listeners.contains(acl)) {
      listeners.add(acl);
    }
  }

  /**
   * De-registers an action listener from this object.
   * Ignores repeat de-registrations.
   */
  public void removeActionListener(ActionListener acl) {
    if (listeners.contains(acl)) {
      listeners.remove(acl);
    }
  }

  /**
   * Sets the alert property of this object.
   * Fires an event if the value changes,
   */
  public void setAlert(String alert) {
    if (!alert.equals(this.alert)) {
      this.alert = alert
      notifyListeners();
    }
  }

  /**
   * Returns the alert property value.
   * @returns java.lang.String
   */
  public String getAlert() {
    return alert;
  }

  private void notifyListeners() {
    ActionEvent ae;
    Vector copy;
    Enumeration enum;
```

```
int evt = ActionEvent.ACTION_PERFORMED;
ae = new ActionEvent(this, evt, alert);
copy = (Vector)listeners.clone();
enum = copy.elements();

while (enum.hasMoreElements()) {
  Object obj = enum.nextElement();
  ActionListener al;
  al = (ActionListener)obj;
  al.actionPerformed(ae);
}
}
}
```

We used get/set and add/remove method pairs to adhere to the Java-Beans convention. We'd do this if we intended to treat Monitor as a Bean, however, there's no other benefit to doing this. If we deployed Monitor as a Bean, we could use the java.beans.Introspector class to load it, break it down using the Reflection API, and use the "reflected" data to build Descriptor objects. Descriptors provide hooks into event and property types, as well as into the whole Bean. Figure 22.4 illustrates the two-step process of reflecting and introspecting a Java class.

FIGURE 22.4 The Monitor class gets reflected and introspected.

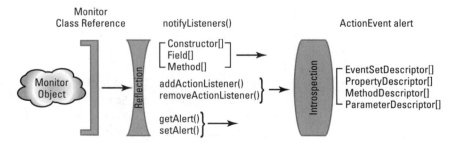

If none of this matters to us, we can use any method names we want. The class behavior would remain the same; it just wouldn't have a Bean-aware public interface.

WARNING   The descriptor classes in java.beans are designed to support low-level controls in Bean-aware graphical builder tools. Because descriptors rely on reflection data, they can be used to manipulate a Bean's appearance and operate on it at an extra "level of remove." Some programmers use these descriptors in their applications to analyze objects on the fly and to experiment with adaptive behavior. As with any powerful tool, using these techniques in mainstream applications can lead to inadvertent exploits in your own code. They are not recommended tools for routine development.

Event Adapters

Adapters provide the glue to any event-notification scheme. Their purpose in life is simple: make it possible for any two objects to communicate. In the simplest of deployments, an event adapter brings two or more classes together because it knows enough about both interfaces to provide translation, or filtering, or whatever function that closes the loop between would-be source and target.

Identifying adapters, in objects as in real life, is often a matter of simply changing one's perspective. To a car with an empty tank, for example, a human being is a useful adapter between itself and a station gas pump. The human can establish a hookup between the two and remove it when the tank is full. In that sense, neither the gas pump nor the car must change their behavior to complete the model.

As an exercise in thinking more about adapters, consider the list of firing methods supported by DefaultTreeModel and AbstractTableModel and shown in Table 22.1. What form of adapter would you write so that each model informs the other of changes to its state?

TABLE 22.1   Firing Methods in Two Data Models

AbstractTableModel	DefaultTreeModel
fireTableCellUpdated()	fireTreeNodesChanged()
fireTableChanged()	fireTreeNodesInserted()

TABLE 22.1 Firing Methods in Two Data Models *(continued)*

AbstractTableModel	DefaultTreeModel
fireTableDataChanged()	fireTreeNodesRemoved()
fireTableRowsDeleted()	fireTreeStructureChanged()
fireTableRowsInserted()	
fireTableRowsUpdated()	
fireTableStructureChanged()	

The straightforward approach seems so obvious that many people regard it as trivial: Encapsulate instances of the two classes in a new class, then add the code necessary to make them work together. And if you give this some thought, you'll realize that you write "adapter code" all the time. In the following example, one class encapsulates a JButton and JPanel and provides an interaction through an event:

```
public class Adapter implements ActionListener {
  private JButton jb;
  private JPanel jp;

  public AdapterPanel(JButton but, JPanel pat) {
    jb = but;
    jp = pat;
    jb.addActionListener(this);
  }

  public void actionPerformed(ActionEvent ae) {
    System.out.println("Button pressed");
  }
}
```

That's all there is to a simple adapter. A little reflecting on this idea will bring you to the conclusion that an adapter strategy is the central premise of all event-driven coding. Calling it an adapter only makes it easier to communicate what's going on.

An easy way to start building a library of adapters is to write a class that implements the listener for a component you want to learn more about. These classes become the functional equivalent of the Adapter classes in the java.awt.event library, with the exception that your classes will do something. We find it convenient to use JOptionPane dialogs for this purpose, especially when working with an unfamiliar component. The following code implements a few tree listeners for experimentation. Note how each event-handler method simply pops a dialog box to acknowledge a successful event-driven operation.

```java
import javax.swing.*;
import javax.swing.event.*;

/**
 * A sample listening class--on our way to building an
 * adapter.
 *
 * @author The CJ2CSG Guys
 */
public class ListeningTree
implements TreeModelListener,
        TreeExpansionListener,
        TreeSelectionListener
{
  // Abbreviation for long identifier
  private int MSG = JOptionPane.INFORMATION_MESSAGE;

  /**
   * Part of TreeExpansionListener
   * Posts the event toString() to a dialog box
   */
  public void treeCollapsed(TreeExpansionEvent tee) {
    JOptionPane.showMessageDialog
```

```
       (null, tee.toString(), "Tree Collapsed", MSG);
}

/**
 * Part of TreeExpansionListener
 * Posts the event's toString to a dialof box
 */
public void treeExpanded(TreeExpansionEvent tee) {
  JOptionPane.showMessageDialog
  (null, tee.toString(), "Tree Expanded", MSG);
}

/**
 * Part of TreeSelectionListener
 * Posts the image of the tree's new state to the
 * dialog box.  Currently hangs the tree.
 */
public void valueChanged(TreeSelectionEvent tse) {
  JOptionPane.showMessageDialog
  (null, tse.getSource(), "Value Changed", MSG);
}

/**
 * Part of TreeModelListener
 */
public void treeNodesChanged(TreeModelEvent te) {
  JOptionPane.showMessageDialog
  (null, te.getSource(), "Nodes Changed", MSG);
}

/**
 * Part of TreeModelListener
 */
public void treeNodesInserted(TreeModelEvent te) {
  JOptionPane.showMessageDialog
  (null, te.getSource(), "Nodes Inserted", MSG);
```

```
    }

    /**
     * Part of TreeModelListener
     */
    public void treeNodesRemoved(TreeModelEvent te) {
      JOptionPane.showMessageDialog
      (null, te.getSource(), "Nodes Removed", MSG);
    }

    /**
     * Part of TreeModelListener
     */
    public void treeStructureChanged(TreeModelEvent te) {
      JOptionPane.showMessageDialog
      (null, te.getSource(), "StructureChanged", MSG);
    }
  }
```

In experimenting with a JTree, we now have a way to see which of our actions on the GUI trigger which method calls on this class. For the purposes of prototyping, a class like this could act as default behavior for a GUI that is being assembled. It might be reasonable to subclass it; throughout the course of development, the dialog boxes could serve as a checklist for all event methods that must be handled before the code is complete.

Remote Notification

Event notification schemes can be created on the local VM with a small amount of effort. RMI's design goals include, among other things, allowing the programmer to ignore most semantic differences between local and remote method calls. Taking those two points in hand, it isn't that hard to put together a callback setup that runs over the network—a notification scheme using RMI.

The easiest way to do it is to build the notification scheme on the server, then export the object that the client is most interested in. The exported class provides a registration model that accepts a listener interface type the client maintains locally. When the exported object happens to fire an event, the client's handler method is called back just as if the source were local.

The bulk of the work is on the server side, obscuring the details of implementation from the client. Figure 22.5 shows the classes needed to develop a remote callback. The heart of the operation is the DataProxy class, which is the only object exported from the server side. In this view we suggest that the DataProxy object could be an event target for the DataSource. DataProxy implements the interface of remotely available calls (Data-Interface) and extends UnicastRemoteObject. The Client class represents the outmost encapsulation of the client-side logic: it implements the ClientListener interface so it can register interest in the DataProxy class.

FIGURE 22.5 Remote notification using RMI

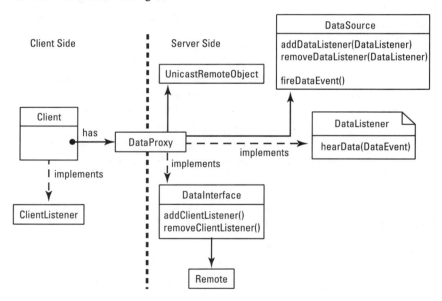

DataProxy must be setup to listen to and receive DataEvent objects from DataSource. This callback relation is server-local only. DataProxy then uses this notification to trigger a call to its listeners, including, of course, the Client that has registered interest in his events. The Client class could be a client-side event adapter that knows how to re-broadcast the events it receives. Or by the more direct approach, the Client class could be replaced by a subclass of DefaultTableModel.

Using Distributed Notification

With a bit more work, we could upgrade our remote notification scheme into a *distributed* notification scheme. In remote notification, we simply put the event source and target together on the server but export the target for remote client access and hookups.

In a distributed model, we want notification to work in both directions: from the server to all clients, and from all clients to the server. The class roles don't change that much from the remote approach, but there are better ways to visualize the domain. Publish-Subscribe seems to be the right model, because its structure is designed to push a steady stream of event messages from multiple sources, then allow each Subscriber a View on to the messages board.

This "newsflash" approach to event messages is particularly well suited for keeping clients updated each other's doings. Any candidate who wants to go above and beyond the call of duty for the Developer's Exam assignment, for example, should feel free to establish "server-active" record locking; that is, the server notifies all clients which records in the database are locked and reminds them when the records are released. Once you've grasped all the roles that need to be incorporated into this scheme, instituting "server-push" notification isn't that bad. The difficult part is developing a clear but comprehensive map of all the classes and their relations:

- News (interface)
- Subscriber (Remote interface)
- NewsService (Remote interface)
- Subscriptions (maintained by the NewsService)

Figure 22.6 outlines the top-level relations. The client accesses remote services through the Subscriber interface. The notification scheme can be made more interesting through the Subscription class, for example by using preference objects and news filters ("sports and weather only"). Once you've assembled a working structure of this order, you'll be able to do whatever you please to complete the developer assignment.

FIGURE 22.6   Elements of a distributed notification scheme

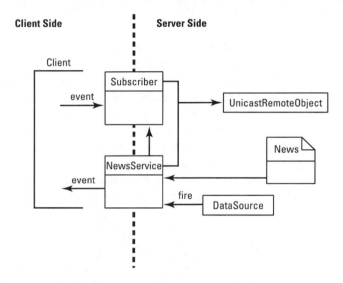

Chapter Summary

Notification schemes can be as simple or as complex as you like. Base your design on the needs at hand, but remember that notification schemes are easy to build and provide a lot of flexibility when they are chained together. Remember to write simple adapters to get two unlike classes to collaborate. They can seem tedious to write at times; it's easy to conclude, especially after some long hours of coding, that we're just writing another class that "doesn't really *do* anything." Sooner or later, however, classes have to be brought together somewhere. We've seen constructors that require a hundred or more lines to incorporate all the necessary objects being used, and such code is often a telltale sign that people have resisted the tedious work until it's unavoidable. The same holds true for `main()` methods that go on for more than a page; if the bootstrap code is that involved, it's because there are no relations among the needed classes to leverage. You can write those relations into the code now, or you can try and remember what the intent was six months later, when you're busy with other things.

Chapter

23

Preparing the Upload

The final submission to Sun must be packaged as a single JAR file. The rules for correct packaging listed in the Developer's Exam assignment are strict but not complex. In concluding this second scenario, this chapter models a sample submission by reviewing the tools needed, `jar` and `javadoc`, and by adding a few pointers on keeping a submission clean and easy to read. The topics included are:

- Submission requirements
- Using `javadoc`
- Adhering to file structure rules
- Using the `jar` tool

Oddly enough, the written instructions don't specify how or where to upload the assignment. There are instructions at `http://suned.sun.com/USA/certification/devregistration.html`, which state the upload should be done at the same location from which the candidate initiated the download. The page is located on `http://www.galton.com/~sun` and is restricted by password access. Make sure to record the login and password given to you for the download!

Submission Requirements

The completed assignment must include the following elements:

- All source code: new, modified, or unchanged
- All compiled class code
- HTML documentation on all source code
- Notes on each working program
- A top-level README file

All elements must be bundled together in a single JAR file, with an "appropriate directory structure." The main JAR may contain other JAR files, which is how we recommend the client/GUI and server/database applications be presented.

All source code must be run through `javadoc` so the examiner can verify through a browser the candidate's proper application of comments. The assignment also requires the candidate to supply a text or HTML file for each working program in the submission. There should be three of these files altogether: one for the GUI, one for the server program, and one for a data-conversion utility the candidate is asked to write. This utility must accept a flat table of records, provided in the assignment instructions, and store it to a file format that is usable by the code Sun provides.

The flat-file format used for the assignment is similar to the one we described as our practice data. We avoided following Sun's data format, however, to preserve the integrity of the exercise. The candidate must deduce and apply the correct binary format only by reading the details of the data routines—a task that is as real-world as it gets.

The most important piece of documentation is the README file. It must be a single file in ASCII format, it must be named README or README.TXT, and it must reside in the root directory of the uploaded JAR file. README must include the following information:

- How to execute each program, including command-line syntax

- A list of the files submitted, along with directory location and brief purpose for each

- A special note that points to any and all files that document the design of the submission, including any justifications

Without these elements, the submission fails, so it's well worth the effort to cover these guidelines carefully, and take your time on the packaging process. Sun does allow a candidate to submit twice under the same fee, but it would be a waste to fail on not following instructions.

Using *javadoc*

As mentioned in Chapter 14, javadoc output in the JDK 1.2 can be directed to an alternative format, known as a *doclet*, if desired. Several switches in javadoc's command-line syntax support that usage, but we will focus on documentation using Sun's default HTML format and style sheets. Table 23.1 presents a select overview of options.

TABLE 23.1 javadoc Options for Standard HTML Output

Option	Comment
-overview <file>	Reads in an HTML overview file.
-[public | protected | package | private]	Sets level of scope to document.
-1.1	Creates 1.1-style documentation.
-sourcepath <pathlist>	Location of source code. Useful for references to classes in other package structures or JAR files.
-classpath <pathlist>	Location of user class files. Useful for references to classes in other package structures or JAR files.
-verbose	More information on javadoc processing (mostly process time on loading reference classes and parsing the source files).

javadoc verifies the compilability of all the source files indicated as a necessary pre-condition for parsing the comments. Not only will it fail to produce documentation if the source can't compile, javadoc will abort if any one source file in the list is not correct. Warnings are issued for bad tag information, such as @see and @link tags that don't link up to qualified class names, and so on.

Among the helper files that `javadoc` generates is what's known as a cascading style sheet, `stylesheet.css`. This document provides the default values for fonts and colors in all the HTML pages generated. It plugs into every page by way of a `<LINK>` reference, so changes made in `stylesheet.css` will affect all pages in the same directory. This allows any developer who wants the default document structure but possibly different cosmetic values to make changes in a single file and have those changes "cascade" to every associated HTML page.

Run the following command to install documentation pages in your current directory (use a backslash in place of the slash for Windows platforms, of course):

```
$ javadoc -sourcepath <path_to_source>/*.java
```

File Structure

If you principally work with Java at the command line, you may have run into some annoying problems with the CLASSPATH environment variable. Dealing with this value is often a headache for novices, and for good reason: how CLASSPATH works is not always intuitive.

The usual obstacle is an entity known as the *default package*. It applies to every Java class that does not declare its own package structure, and appears to resolve to the current directory—except when the source is in the same location. When a class that explicitly declares a package shares a same directory as its source, strange things seem to happen. The effect is to collapse the "unnamed" package (the current directory) and the CLASSPATH pointer (locations of all "named" packages) together, forcing a name collision that the runtime interpreter won't try to resolve.

An easy way to resolve this conflict is by locating the source directory and the root package directory within a common parent. This way, there is no package-name collision to interfere with runtime execution. This scheme facilitates runtime and compilation use as well. The command line invocation here assumes `Code.java` has declared package `this.that`.

```
$ javac -d .. Code.java
```

This creates the class file `../this/that/Code.class`, relative to the `src` directory, as shown in Figure 23.1.

FIGURE 23.1 Directories for source and compiled code

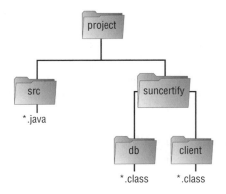

From the same directory, the code can be run as follows:

```
$ java -cp .. this.that.Code
```

This same approach works well under the submission requirements. The JAR file acts as a directory point of its own, under which you can create `src` and `suncertify` (the top-level package name for the exam source). Add a `docs` directory at this level to store the class and application notes. If you want to take advantage of the Java 2 runtime's ability to execute a JAR file directly, create `server.jar`, `client.jar`, and `converter.jar` and place them here as well. Finally, if RMI is the mechanism for connecting client and server over the network, a `policy` file should be included at this directory level too. Figure 23.2 shows the complete file layout.

FIGURE 23.2 File distribution for the submission

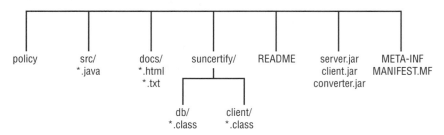

Writing the README file

README.TXT doesn't have to be fancy, just clear and to the point. Possibly, the submission rules are so insistent on proper form because the file might be extracted programmatically; in any case, it's a good idea to be thorough and in the right place. Here's a mockup of a submission given as a guide:

```
Java 2 Developer's Submission
Candidate: Cuppa, Joe
This JAR contains the following files:

server.jar - an executable JAR file that launches an RMI
    data server.

    Please read the notes on this application in the docs
    directory before executing.  This application will run
    with the command-line invocation:

    $ java -jar server.jar

client.jar - a Swing client that connects to the server.
    Run this application with the following command-line
    invocation:

    $ java -jar client.jar <server_name>

    See the notes on client.jar in the docs directory for
    more details.

converter.jar - a tool that takes the flat file record
    format given in the Exam and converts it to a file the
    server code can read.  Run this application with the
    following command-line invocation:

    $ java -jar converter.jar records.txt
```

docs/ - .html files for the source, and text notes on the design of these applications.

src/ - All .java files for new and modified code, as well as unmodified code that was provided with the exam.

suncertify/ - top-level directory package. All class files are contained in the subdirectories db/ and client/.

policy - sets the permissions for the RMI server. Do not move this file.

records.txt - a flat file of records ready for conversion using converter.jar. This file should reside in the same directory as the application.

Using the *jar* Tool

The jar binary is a bridge between two worlds: the syntax of the Unix `tar` command, and the file storage mechanics of PKZip. Since traditional `tar` doesn't offer compression but has always been free, this is a nice combination of virtues, at least for Unix users already familiar with the syntax. `jar` now represents a single-image compression utility for any platform that Java can run on, making it a nearly universal file format. Command options are listed in Table 23.2.

TABLE 23.2 jar Command Options

Option	Comment
-c | -x | -u	Create, extract from, update
-v	Verbose
-m	Named manifest file
-f	Named .jar file

TABLE 23.2   jar Command Options *(continued)*

Option	Comment
-t	Create a table of contents
-0	Use zero (no) compression
-M	Do not create a manifest
-C dir	Find files in the dir directory

The jar command requires the manifest file (-m) and JAR file (–f) to appear on the command line in the same order as their respective option flags are declared.

A key selling point for the JAR format is its *manifest* specification. By providing certain tags in the manifest, the packager can signal a particular kind of usage or delivery. For example, there is a tag to specify whether a contained class file is a JavaBean. Other tags are used to "sign" the jar for purposes of authentication and to assign it a control number used for version checking. Yet another tag is available to support a feature known as *package sealing*. With package sealing in place, the JAR itself mandates that all associated classes working with the JAR must be contained in it—a control against class-spoofing.

The tag we are interested in allows any Java 2 interpreter to execute a main method within the JAR, without extracting the associated class file or even knowing its name. Furthermore, execution of the class is treated as though it resided in the current directory, so the syntax for adding command-line arguments is maintained. Here's a simple demonstration:

```
public class JARTest
{
  public static void main(String args[]) {
    System.out.println(args[0]);
  }
}
```

After compiling this code, we write one line into a file called `manifest`:

```
Main-Class: JARTest
<empty line in the file here>
```

We include that file in the JAR image, then execute the JAR using the run-time interpreter's –jar flag:

```
$ jar cfm test.jar manifest JARTest.class
$ java -jar test.jar Hello
Hello
$
```

Applying this technique to your deliverables keeps the structure of your submission clean, and keeps the necessary files the examiner must handle down to a minimum.

Chapter Summary

A well-thought-out and carefully prepared deliverable doesn't make up for inoperative code, but given the time and attention the examiner must now pay to evaluating your work, keeping things clean and simple is best. If you're interested in maxing out on the points an examiner can attribute to good form, you'll also pay close attention to thorough documentation in the source. If you have a flair for individual presentation, there's no rule that says you must stick to the exact style of `javadoc`–experiment with the style sheet if you're not in a great hurry.

Chapter

24

Thinking About the Follow-Up Exam

In this last chapter, we review some key topics presented in Chapters 18 through 23 and present a short, FAQ-style list of questions and answers. The spirit of the mock exam questions presented in the Programmer's Exam section was to acquaint you with the style and difficulty level of those test questions. In this chapter, instead, we're posing questions to help prepare you to defend your project's implementation, which of course will vary with each developer and will invariably involve making some subjective judgments.

Preparation Questions

Rather than attempt to mirror the exam questions, we have more or less fed ourselves a list of questions that we hope will broaden your sense of what you should be prepared to discuss. Some of the discussion here will raise awareness on points that, strictly speaking, aren't tested in the project assignment, but it may provide an explicit way to justify a design choice or two that you, the developer, have intuitively grasped.

What are the choices for data structures?

Review the classes in `java.util` and consider using arrays where practical. The conventional wisdom is that the better you understand your data, the clearer the choices become for a type of storage. With the addition of the Collections framework to Java 2, however, switching container types to meet new requirements has become very simple. (Collections is described in Chapter 8.) It's now possible to move data from one kind of container to another with a minimum of conversion work. Knowing the benefits of each container type aids the selection processing, but it's also important to know that such decisions can be changed more readily if necessary.

Each container type has its own most suitable usage. Arrays are fast, but once their length is set, they're fixed for the life of the program run. It's possible to copy from one array to another with more room using `System.arraycopy()`, but if that turns out to be a common operation, a `Vector`, which does the copying for you, is a tidier choice. `Vector`s will acquire memory space for more elements each time they reach capacity, but they don't trim themselves automatically; in a storage environment with high activity, vectors may require a lot of checking, and tuning for capacity and expansion may prove problematic.

Key-value structures like `HashMap` offer constant-time performance, meaning the time needed to add or access records doesn't scale along with the size of the table, assuming it is proportioned correctly. As long as operations against the table are predominantly simple ones, `HashMaps` perform well. Upon a non-key search, however, the developer must typically iterate through the entire structure, which does take time proportional to the number of elements. A structure such as a linked list may take time up front to sort elements as they are added. This work greatly speeds up the time taken to iterate over the list. Pre-sorting elements makes it possible to select a small range of the list's contents in cases where the search follows the sorting criteria of the structure itself.

While each container type has specific advantages, it may not be clear in some cases that one is a better choice than another. In such cases, the best defense is to know the strengths of each type and justify your choice based on the features you find most useful for the task at hand. Simplicity is a reasonable justification, too, provided you acknowledge that simplicity is important to you, and the performance price you might have to pay is acceptable. Ease of maintenance is an even better reason in many situations.

Is implementing *Runnable* better than extending *Thread*?

Because threading is built into Java, there may be some confusion among programmers about the relationship between the `Thread` class and the `Runnable` interface. It's not uncommon to come across classes that extend `Thread` and do nothing more than override the `run()` method. Compared to classes that merely implement `Runnable` and provide a code body for `run()`, these operations may seem synonymous in every important regard.

However, consider that we normally subclass to alter or specialize the function of a parent class. In cases where we extend JDK classes just to override a method or two, it's typically because the class is designed to be used that way, such as an exception or the `Applet` class. With respect to `Thread`, which merely houses a null implementation of the `Runnable` interface, there's no practical motivation to extend the class if all that's intended is to add `run()` code. It's just one method, and, if no other behavior in `Thread` is going to be changed, it's not worth sacrificing the one opportunity we have to extend a parent class.

Isn't comparing object serialization to RMI an apples-to-oranges analysis?

Yes . . . and no. As technologies, they do not compete with each other for attention. Object serialization is a fundamental Java facility; RMI is Java's architecture for distributed computing. Both are bound to evolve a bit more. For object serialization, evolution most likely means improvements of its basic features. For RMI, it means cooperating in the larger, industrial world of distributed computing that includes not only heterogeneous systems but heterogeneous code as well. The fact that RMI makes ample use of serialization demonstrates the different playing fields in which they both operate.

But so far as choosing a way to talk VM-to-VM is concerned, both are likely candidates for the job, until some requirements are established. Serializing objects by hand and establishing the patterns for sending them back and forth between two machines is neither elegant nor necessarily reusable work. It can, however, be quickly implemented, tested, and deployed on limited-scale projects with short build times. If it's determined that future needs will have to be addressed through inter-VM communication, it's easy enough to add a method to the proper class that encapsulates a new "object protocol" for communication with other machines. It's not difficult, other than checking to ensure that all values intended to cross the wire are serializable.

RMI is a means for establishing object control from a single location. It avoids the potentially messy effects of simply passing around state information from machine to machine and risking version control. Since the remote user's semantics for invoking a remote reference are very similar to calling a local one, most of the details are hidden once RMI is implemented. But RMI's power comes at a very definite cost: Among those issues, the one that arguably damages perception of RMI's efficacy the most is its ability to pass objects by value, rather than by reference. RMI makes it possible to pass large objects remotely without thinking about the cost of bandwidth, and so some will invariably argue that RMI itself is inefficient. Developers clearly fall into three camps on questions of this ilk. One side argues that a good programming environment saves users from themselves; another argues that it's unfair to fault a tool for abuse by those that wield it. Still another side argues that a technology is only effective if it is easily understood and deployed. Rather than pick sides, we simply point to a systems engineering truism: Pick a tool that best fits the task at hand, and don't forget to understand it first.

If the care in design for proper RMI is not something a project assignment can tolerate, ground-level object serialization is available. Like the many dumb terminals we see still heavily populating shop floors and financial desks, object serialization may not be groundbreaking stuff, but it does the job at a reasonable price. Good enough is good engineering.

How elaborate should an exception class structure get?

It's possible to create as many shell exceptions as one wants, as a cheap and easy way to describe the variant conditions that represent non-routine code execution for an application. It might be easy to infer from the cumbersome naming of certain JDK classes, such as `ArrayIndexOutOfBounds-Exception`, that naming is in fact important enough to support, and that the expense of developer convenience is not too high a price to pay for it. Bearing in mind that some of these classes were never intended to be caught or managed by users—all exceptions that extend `RuntimeException` fall into this category—we have to take any emphatic importance on naming with a grain of salt. Yes, we want to know what an exception is about, and ideally we can get the idea from the name alone. A more substantive policy, however, might be to simply name unique exceptions when there is a potential need to catch them and write alternate code to execute when it occurs.

Provide new exceptions whenever the application should, under unusual conditions, inform the user, save current data, and offer alternate ways to continue or exit. This helps to define exceptions by necessity rather than using them merely to spell out a problem through a class name. Also consider the possibility that the exception class itself might add methods to enable context-specific processing, thus avoiding rewrites of the same catch code over several related classes.

How many ways can you set up "listener" relationships? Which one is best?

Several patterns are already implemented in Java, including:

- Observer/Observable
- Event handling, as implemented in the AWT package

- "Model-delegate" (an MVC variant) in Swing, which is 50 percent event handling

- Beans' style change listeners, which are nothing more than a standardized set of event handlers

The proliferation of these patterns in Java reveals the increased use of objects that rely on event notification to monitor changes. Three of these listener schemes deal primarily with GUI components in one form or another, although Model-View-Controller as a pattern needn't be strictly defined as having a visual component. Views can just as easily be called filters where they offer a narrow perspective on the model at hand, and the filter could just as easily be an interpreter or parser. Whatever the case, several strategies are available to incorporate listening in one form or another, and if you're persuaded that it works well enough that the graphic components shouldn't hog all the fun, a little research will show you how these techniques work.

One place you may be inclined to experiment with "callbacks," as they are often informally termed, is between the client and server in your project assignment. Assuming the assignment's main objectives don't prohibit this, the easiest thing to experiment with is the `Observer/Observable` interface/class pair in `java.util`. The class that implements `Observable` does most of the work, tying its inherited methods to state changes elsewhere in the class so that ultimately a call to its own `notifyObservers()` is made. This method then calls `update()` in any class that implements `Observer` and has registered interest in the notifying `Observable`. The two knocks on this pattern are: The observed class must extend `Observable`, which may not be feasible if it must subclass something else; and the use of events and listeners is more widely accepted and accomplishes the same goal.

The event handling model for the AWT and the change-listener format for Beans follow the same model as the Observer/Observable pattern. Swing, with its model-delegate structure, also takes advantage of the Beans specification by instituting change listeners and event-firing mechanisms as a way to bind changes in one part of a component's supporting tools to another. The nice part about the Beans model (which is essentially the AWT's) is that it doesn't require you to create full-fledged Beans to take advantage of it. At the same time, the features that allow the developer to create modular components are easy enough to adopt so that maintaining compatibility with Bean adaptation is usually a good idea. If there is no best way to establish listening between classes, there certainly seems to be a most popular one: the Beans model.

How do I know which layout manager to use?

Consider the type of behavior each layout manager supports. Consider the possibilities of mixing each with the behavior of different components. Then consider the additional permutations of nesting one container within another, each with its own layout manager. There are lots of variations, some of which ultimately produce the same effect. So far as the end user is concerned, whatever brings the GUI to its most effective presentation is suitable. End-user satisfaction should be a developer goal as well, but also remember that someone has to maintain the resulting code.

The only recommendation we can make is to offer all the required functionality in the most maintainable form possible, for applications that may be in service for a while. The overlap in behavior between one layout manager and another is often accounted for by the constrained situation in which a choice will be made. Border layouts are ideal where each set of components wants to occupy a fixed peripheral space and "serve" what's going on in the center. Flow layouts are best when each component should be laid out in the order it is specified, and a single layout rule (e.g., "center everything") is sufficient. Grid layouts offer a quick "control console" feeling and automatic equal-weight distribution to every column and row. Card layout is clearly different, useful for information that may "stack" well, but don't overlook the JTabbedPane in Swing, which gives the user control of the tabs. GridBag offers a great deal of flexibility, but mastering its behavior is by far the most challenging of the five layout managers.

If the topmost layout strategy is unclear, one simple strategy is to build up to the containing frame. Components that share space or work together in some cohesive way will typically suggest by their function an appropriate layout scheme. As these groups are placed in panels, it may make sense to combine two or more panels into another panel; nesting multiple containers is honorable. Once the major panels are assembled, it's very likely that one of two schemes will apply to the topmost container: Border or GridBag. GridBag, in a nutshell, allows you to vary components' dimensions by the rows and columns they reside in; if you have no need for this kind of flexibility, use Border.

Which design patterns are most useful in this kind of project?

At the risk of sounding evasive, whichever design patterns help you get the job done are most useful. While using design patterns competently to complete the project assignment will most likely lead to tighter code that an experienced programmer can readily appreciate, it's hard to say abstractly when to apply one. Using design patterns in a formal sense requires some amount of playing around with them and working up your own practical uses for them. In much the same way that it's difficult to teach someone an application when they have no need for it, design patterns are far more useful when they can provide a solution for problems you already have in mind. If you know what they are, how they're commonly referred to, and how they solve specific problems, that is a good start. With some preparation and experience, it's more likely that articulating a specific objective may lead to a design pattern you know about and can apply to the situation.

Looking for a place to plug one isn't likely to help produce better code. But you can find plenty of opportunities just by reading some source in the JDK itself. `Observer/Observable` represent a class design pattern, as does MVC. Any time you come across a class with the term *factory* in its name, you're looking at a class built with that pattern in mind. Studying these classes along with a primer on design patterns will help you understand what's going on: Design patterns are simply solutions to very common problems in object-oriented programming.

That said, it's not necessarily true that formal schooling with design patterns is the only way to learn how to use them. For experienced programmers, many design patterns may seem to be generic articulations of code they've had in their toolboxes for years. Giving them specific names merely makes it easier to talk about them; it's the proper application of design patterns in code that makes them powerful.

Some knowledge of the formal conventions for design patterns may make it easier for some candidates to discuss their programming rationale on the follow-up exam. A working knowledge of the patterns mentioned above will go a long way toward preparing the candidate, as they are among the most prevalent patterns in the JDK. Look for signs of often-repeated words in class names: It's your best hint that a pattern is lurking underneath.

The seminal book on design patterns is *Design Patterns: Elements of Reusable Object-Oriented Software* by a group of authors known as the "Gang of Four": Erich Gamma, Richard Helm, Ralph Johnson, and John Vlissides. More and more literature on Java and design patterns is coming out regularly, including design patterns that take particular advantage of Java.

When does it make sense to use *protected* and default scope?

Look for a compelling need to use either. Even though the project assignment may employ a package structure for the code provided, it's unlikely you'll be looking at a problem in choosing the best scope for a certain variable or method. Variables and methods that are `protected` are only accessible to subclasses and other classes sharing the same package. Members and variables that have no scope modifier are only visible to other package members. Subclasses outside the package do not have access to package-private resources, while subclasses inside the package do.

The value of these scopes is to allow direct access for "local" classes into important package resources, while blocking access to out-of-package programmers altogether, or blocking those that aren't extending the class in question. Typically, a package-private identifier is available within a package to allow some package-specific operations to take place more readily than they could through the normal public interface.

A good place to study the use of `protected` identifiers is the AWT, where there are a lot of class interrelations. A good place to start investigating this for yourself is the **Component** class. Unless you intend to write something as complex as a windowing toolkit or similar package, chances are you won't have a real need for either scope. Good design starts with enforcing encapsulation wherever possible and breaking encapsulation (an evil) only where it allows a greater good to prevail. If it shouldn't be `public`, goes the general rule, make it `private`. If `private` seems restrictive, *keep* it `private`; resist the urge to open things up until there's a truly compelling need. Only if being `private` prevents related classes from doing their job without adding a lot of code, consider whether access outside the package would ever be warranted. If so, then use `protected`. Otherwise, choose default scope.

What we really want to challenge is the nature of the question. Learning programmers want to know how best to use the tools they encounter, and so they ask questions in the form of the one that heads this section. The better question we want programmers to ask is, "Why should I make all fields private?"

Our first objective in developing new classes is to preserve encapsulation. A class is properly encapsulated when its data are only available through the class's public "interface." When we say interface in this context, we mean the methods that permit access to the state of a class instance or object. Consider what happens to a class that uses a vector for internal storage and allows direct access to it, possibly in the name of greater performance. Along comes a better type of storage for the class developer's purpose. Now if the developer wants to swap out the vector for this new type, all the subsequent code that relies on this class will break. If, instead, some methods, such as `getContainer()` and `setContainer()`, are used to govern access to the data container, the developer is free to internally implement fields at will, leaving other programmers with a consistent, unchanging interface.

Encapsulation promotes maintenance. You can find several Java articles that demonstrate how much faster a field access is than a method call, but if you want to keep code maintenance simple, you'll acknowledge the difference and stick to proper encapsulation. A class can add methods to the interface without breaking its contract to existing users, and it can change the body of a method. So long as method signatures remain consistent, encapsulated classes provide the greatest protection to their users.

Why would we take a hit in performance, especially if our code seems to run unacceptably slow? First, of course, we have to determine whether method calls really are holding things up. Knowing that field accesses are faster than method calls is a dangerous bit of information if it's regarded in a vacuum. We have to know through profiling or other analysis where our compute time is being spent. Even if method calls proved to be our biggest expense, we still must consider whether breaking the public interface—a drastic step—is warranted. But it's a simple matter if access is initially more restrictive than not. We can simply change a private member to the appropriate scope and document this variance. If fields start out as public or protected, however, and we make them private, we've now broken the public interface, and our users to date have to address the consequences of that. Maintenance is easier if we start out with a conservative view of encapsulating fields.

In various portions of this guide, we've stated our case that you can't over-estimate the importance of using interfaces to declare method calls when designing your application. Assuming you've been persuaded, you're also aware that an interface has no support for instance variables, since an interface bears no relation to any one instance. The point of an interface is to separate design from the details of implementation. Once you've fixed on a specific field type and given access to other classes, you've anchored your design in a specific implementation. If there's never a case for changing that specific field type, there's no problem. In this situation, we must admit that performance outweighs flexibility of design.

In short, keep fields private. If the application runs correctly but is too slow, and performance is critical, consider allowing field access. If you can afford to wait, however, the best of all worlds is coming in the form of improved VMs, which include a just-in-time (JIT) compiler to execute code faster. Sun's HotSpot includes features such as the ability to "inline" simple accessor/mutator methods. From a design point of view, the long-term problem is creating an engine that runs with proper efficiency, rather than "tricking out" the design to achieve better performance by forsaking ease of maintenance.

Doesn't an abstract class let the developer specify more behavior than an interface?

If specific behavior is what you want, yes. The point of an interface, in one respect, is that it really doesn't tie you down to very much. Earlier in this chapter, we discussed the run() method in Thread that is merely a null implementation of the Runnable interface. The fact is, run() has next to nothing to do with the Thread class. We can implement run() in any class we want. We can also call any object's run() method directly from another thread; bypassing Thread.start() simply means that we don't set this process off on its own execution context. In other words, there's nothing about the run() method by itself that carries threaded behavior with it; it's just a hook, a method that when used as directed taps into the Virtual Machine's multithreaded engine. If we don't honor the proper form for using the run() method, it's just a name. An abstract class, on the other hand, has at least some concrete behavior, some "real" definition to it.

If you're unsure about this assertion, review the section "Sharing Threads" at the end of Chapter 17. In the code sample for that section, look closely at the `run()` method of `ShareThread` and the call to `job.run()` near the end of that method. Notice that no call is made to `job.start()`. Yet `job` references an object that implements `Runnable`. Walk through the code until you see the logic behind this call.

One view on the abstract class is that it should contain the code that will be common to every subclass, but leave abstract those methods that rely on a local implementation to fulfill its commitments to other implemented methods in that class. If we have an abstract class `Currency`, for example, all methods pertaining to exchange for goods or services may be implemented. The methods that describe the local currency, however, which are called by the methods that describe exchange, still must be implemented locally for the class to be useful. This is the idea behind classes like the AWT's `Container` and `Component`, which define the vast majority of AWT operation, but leave some important methods to be defined by actual components. Outside of toolkit development, abstract classes could also be used as a "convenience class" to capture information that interfaces cannot—implementations of non-public methods, constructors, overrides of inherited methods—and could be useful as a kind of "concrete reference" for an intended subset of extending classes.

But this type of use should not necessarily be construed as affording the kind of control that interfaces lack. The true power of interfaces lies in remaining as abstract as possible. Consider this:

```
public interface Payment {
  public Double getAmount();
  public Account getAccountInfo();
}
public interface Account {
  public Double getBalance();
  public String getName();
}
public interface Payable {
  public Account deductPayment(Payment pmtOut);
```

```
}
public interface Receivable {
  public Account addPayment(Payment pmtIn);
}
```

With three exceptions, these preliminary interfaces rely completely on abstract definitions to describe a rudimentary ledger-entry system. If we need to add behavior as we further define the details, all we have to do is add the name of that method to the interface list, and we've broken no code. What we have done is set the stage to describe relationships for the classes that implement these interfaces. We've also started declaring their responsibilities for participating in this framework appropriately in a minimum of time. In this manner, we could go through a couple of design passes without ever worrying about updating concrete code as we make potentially sweeping changes.

Abstract classes are convenient for conveying ideas that are more concrete than design-oriented. Interfaces, by contrast, keep details from bogging down the design effort. Chances are an interface that seems to do nothing but name methods simply hasn't been developed aggressively enough. Some schools of thought go so far as to propose that *every* parameter and return type in a method be represented by an interface, for both maximum flexibility and to preserve the precious single opportunity each class has to inherit from another.

Chapter Summary

The follow-up exam determines whether candidates can demonstrate their command of Java's core libraries and submitted code well enough to defend it in a series of essay questions. The above questions are simply intended to provoke some thoughts on what kinds of topics might be fair game for the exam itself. Candidates might be expected to offer several alternatives to a problem that is posed generally, and to state the various attractions and drawbacks of each alternative. They might then be asked to correlate the previous question to a situation in the exam itself, detail how the problem was solved, and explain why they chose that approach.

The best preparation for this kind of exam is to have a reasonably broad overview of how the project assignment might be solved, as well as a particular interest in completing it in a manner that suits the candidate's style. The easiest way to answer subjective questions is to stick to your natural inclination for problem solving. In the context of an exam like this, there are wrong factual answers; it would be bad to conclude that synchronized methods are faster than synchronized blocks, or that arrays take up more memory than Vectors. But in justifying an approach that has proven to work, the remaining element is whether the code as it appears on paper corresponds to the candidate's accounting for it, and whether its implementation remains consistent with their judgment.

Appendices

Appendix

A

Answers to Test Yourself Questions

Chapter 1 Test Yourself

1. A signed data type has an equal number of non-zero positive and negative values available.

   A. True

   B. False

   Answer: B. The range of negative numbers is greater by 1 than the range of positive numbers.

2. Choose the valid identifiers from those listed below.

   A. `BigOlLongStringWithMeaninglessName`

   B. `$int`

   C. `bytes`

   D. `$1`

   E. `finalist`

   Answer: A, B, C, D, E. All of the identifiers are valid.

3. Which of the following signatures are valid for the `main()` method entry point of an application?

   A. `public static void main()`

   B. `public static void main(String arg[])`

   C. `public void main(String [] arg)`

   D. `public static void main(String[] args)`

   E. `public static int main(String [] arg)`

   Answer: B, D, E.

4. If all three top-level elements occur in a source file, they must appear in which order?

   A. Imports, package declaration, classes.

   B. Classes, imports, package declarations.

   C. Package declaration must come first; order for imports and class definitions is not significant.

D. Package declaration, imports, classes.

E. Imports must come first; order for package declaration and class definitions is not significant.

Answer: D. This order must be strictly observed.

5. Consider the following line of code:

```
int[] x = new int[25];
```

After execution, which statement or statements are true?

A. x[24] is 0.

B. x[24] is undefined.

C. x[25] is 0.

D. x[0] is null.

E. x.length is 25.

Answer: A, E. The array has 25 elements, indexed from 0 through 24. All elements are initialized to zero.

6. Consider the following application:

```
1. class Q6 {
2.    public static void main(String args[]) {
3.       Holder h = new Holder();
4.       h.held = 100;
5.       h.bump(h);
6.       System.out.println(h.held);
7.    }
8. }
9.
10. class Holder {
11.    public int held;
12.    public void bump(Holder theHolder) {
13.       theHolder.held++; }
14.    }
15. }
```

What value is printed out at line 6?

A. 0

B. 1

C. 100

D. 101

Answer: D. A holder is constructed on line 3. A reference to that holder is passed into method bump() on line 5. Within the method call, the holder's held variable is bumped from 100 to 101.

7. Consider the following application:

```
1. class Q7 {
2.   public static void main(String args[]) {
3.     double d = 12.3;
4.     Decrementer dec = new Decrementer();
5.     dec.decrement(d);
6.     System.out.println(d);
7.   }
8. }
9.
10. class Decrementer {
11.   public void decrement(double decMe) {
12.     decMe = decMe - 1.0;
13,   }
14. }
```

What value is printed out at line 6?

A. 0.0

B. −1.0

C. 12.3

D. 11.3

Answer: C. The decrement() method is passed a copy of the argument d; the copy gets decremented, but the original is untouched.

8. How can you force garbage collection of an object?

   A. Garbage collection cannot be forced.

   B. Call `System.gc()`.

   C. Call `System.gc()`, passing in a reference to the object to be garbage-collected.

   D. Call `Runtime.gc()`.

   E. Set all references to the object to new values (`null`, for example).

   Answer: A. Garbage collection cannot be forced. Calling `System.gc()` or `Runtime.gc()` is not 100 percent reliable, since the garbage-collection thread might defer to a thread of higher priority; thus B and D are incorrect. C is incorrect because the two `gc()` methods do not take arguments; in fact, if you still have a reference to pass into any method, the object is not yet eligible to be collected. E will make the object eligible for collection the next time the garbage collector runs.

9. What is the range of values that can be assigned to a variable of type `short`?

   A. It depends on the underlying hardware.

   B. 0 through $2^{16} - 1$

   C. 0 through $2^{32} - 1$

   D. -2^{15} through $2^{15} - 1$

   E. -2^{31} through $2^{31} - 1$

   Answer: D. The range for a 16-bit `short` is -2^{15} through $2^{15} - 1$. This range is part of the Java specification, regardless of the underlying hardware.

10. What is the range of values that can be assigned to a variable of type `byte`?

    A. It depends on the underlying hardware.

    B. 0 through $2^8 - 1$

    C. 0 through $2^{16} - 1$

D. -2^7 through $2^7 - 1$

E. -2^{15} through $2^{15} - 1$

Answer: D. The range for an 8-bit byte is -2^7 through $2^7 - 1$. Table 1.3 lists the ranges for Java's integral primitive data types.

Chapter 2 Test Yourself

1. After execution of the code fragment below, what are the values of the variables *x*, *a*, and *b*?

```
1. int x, a = 6, b = 7;
2. x = a++ + b++;
```

   A. *x* = 15, *a* = 7, *b* = 8

   B. *x* = 15, *a* = 6, *b* = 7

   C. *x* = 13, *a* = 7, *b* = 8

   D. *x* = 13, *a* = 6, *b* = 7

   Answer: C. The assignment statement is evaluated as if it were:

```
x = a + b; a = a + 1; b = b + 1;
```

   Therefore, the assignment to *x* is made using the sum of 6 + 7, giving 13. After the addition, the values of *a* and *b* are actually incremented; the new values, 7 and 8, are stored in the variables.

2. Which of the following expressions are legal? (Choose one or more.)

   A. `int x = 6; x = !x;`

   B. `int x = 6; if (!(x > 3)) {}`

   C. `int x = 6; x = ~x;`

Answer: B, C. In A, the use of ! is inappropriate, since *x* is of int type, not boolean. This is a common mistake among C and C++ programmers, since the expression would be valid in those languages. In B, the comparison is inelegant (being a cumbersome equivalent of if (x <= 3)) but valid, since the expression (x > 3) is a boolean type and the ! operator can properly be applied to it. In C, the bitwise inversion operator is applied to an integral type. The bit pattern of 6 looks like 0...0110 where the ellipsis represents 27 0 bits. The resulting bit pattern looks like 1...1001, where the ellipsis represents 27 1 bits.

3. Which of the following expressions results in a positive value in *x*? (Choose one.)

    A. int x = -1; x = x >>> 5;

    B. int x = -1; x = x >>> 32;

    C. byte x = -1; x = x >>> 5;

    D. int x = -1; x = x >> 5;

    Answer: A. In every case, the bit pattern for –1 is "all ones." In A, this is shifted five places to the right with the introduction of 0 bits at the most significant positions. The result is 27 1 bits in the less significant positions of the int value. Since the most significant bit is 0, this represents a positive value (actually 134217727). In B, the shift value is 32 bits. This will result in no change at all to *x*, since the shift is actually performed by (32 mod 32) bits, which is 0. So in B, the value of *x* is unchanged at –1. C is actually illegal, since the result of x >>> 5 is of type int and cannot be assigned into the byte variable *x* without explicit casting. Even if the cast were added, giving

    byte x = -1; x = (byte)(x >>> 5);

    the result of the expression x >>> 5 would be calculated like this:

A. First, promote *x* to an `int`. This gives a sign-extended result, that is, an `int` –1 with 32 1 bits.

B. Perform the shift; this behaves the same as in A above, giving 134217727,which is the value of 27 1 bits in the less significant positions.

C. Casting the result of the expression simply "chops off" the less significant eight bits; since these are all ones, the resulting `byte` represents –1.

Finally, D performs a signed shift, which propagates 1 bits into the most significant position. So, in this case, the resulting value of *x* is unchanged at –1.

4. Which of the following expressions are legal? (Choose one or more.)

A. `String x = "Hello"; int y = 9; x += y;`

B. `String x = "Hello"; int y = 9; if (x == y) {}`

C. `String x = "Hello"; int y = 9; x = x + y;`

D. `String x = "Hello"; int y = 9; y = y + x;`

E. `String x = null;int y = (x != null) && (x.length() > 0) ? x.length() : 0;`

Answer: A, C, E. In A, the use of `+=` is treated as a shorthand for the expression in C. This attempts to "add" an `int` to a `String`, which results in conversion of the `int` to a `String`—`"9"` in this case—and the concatenation of the two `String` objects. So in this case, the value of *x* after the code is executed is "Hello9".

In B, the comparison (`x == y`) is not legal, since variable *y* is an `int` type and cannot be compared with a reference value. Don't forget that comparison using `==` tests the values and that for objects, the "value" is the reference value and not the contents.

C is identical to A without the use of the shorthand assignment operator.

D calculates `y + x`, which is legal in itself, because it produces a `String` in the same way as did `x + y`. It then attempts to assign the result, which is "9Hello", into an `int` variable. Since the result of `y + x` is a `String`, this is not permitted.

E is rather different from the others. The important points are the use of the short-circuit operator `&&` and the conditional operator `?:`. The left operand of the `&&` operator is always evaluated, and in this case the condition (`x != null`) is false. Because this is false, the right part of the expression (`x.length() > 0`) need not be evaluated, as the result of the `&&` operator is known to be false. This short-circuit effect neatly avoids executing the method call `x.length()`, which would fail with a `NullPointerException` at runtime. This false result is then used in the evaluation of the conditional expression. As the `boolean` value is false, the result of the overall expression is the value to the right of the colon, which is 0.

5. Which of the following code fragments would compile successfully and print "Equal" when run? (Choose one or more.)

   A. `int x = 100; float y = 100.0F;`
   `if (x == y){ System.out.println("Equal");}`

   B. `int x = 100; Integer y = new Integer(100);`
   `if (x == y) { System.out.println("Equal");}`

   C. `Integer x = new Integer(100);`
   `Integer y = new Integer(100);`
   `if (x == y) { System.out.println("Equal");}`

   D. `String x = new String("100");`
   `String y = new String("100");`
   `if (x == y) { System.out.println("Equal");}`

   E. `String x = "100";`
   `String y = "100";if (x == y) {`
   `System.out.println("Equal");}`

   Answer: A, E. Although `int` and `float` are not assignment-compatible, they can generally be mixed on either side of an operator. Since `==` is not assignment but is a comparison operator, it simply causes normal promotion, so that the `int` value 100 is promoted to a `float` value 100.0 and compared successfully with the other `float` value 100.0F. For this reason, A is true.

The code in B actually fails to compile. This is because of the mismatch between the `int` and the `Integer` object. The value of an object is its reference, and no conversions are ever possible between references and numeric types. Because of this, the arguments cannot be promoted to the same type, and they cannot be compared.

In C, the code compiles successfully, since the comparison is between two object references. However, the test for equality compares the value of the references (the memory address typically) and, since the variables *x* and *y* refer to two different objects, the test returns false. The code in D behaves exactly the same way.

Comparing E with D might persuade you that E should probably not print "Equal". In fact, it does so because of a required optimization. Since `String` objects are immutable, literal strings are inevitably constant strings, so the compiler re-uses the same `String` object if it sees the same literal value occur more than once in the source. This means that the variables *x* and *y* actually do refer to the same object; so the test (x == y) is true and the "Equal" message is printed. It is particularly important that you do not allow this special behavior to persuade you that the == operator can be used to compare the contents of objects in any general way.

6. What results from running the following code?

```
1. public class Short {
2.    public static void main(String args[]) {
3.       StringBuffer s = new StringBuffer("Hello");
4.       if ((s.length() > 5) &&
5.          (s.append(" there").equals("False")))
6.          ; // do nothing
7.       System.out.println("value is " + s);
8.    }
9. }
```

A. The output: `value is Hello`

B. The output: `value is Hello there`

C. A compiler error at line 4 or 5

D. No output

E. A `NullPointerException`

Answer: A. The effect of the **&&** operator is first to evaluate the left operand. That is the expression (`s.length() > 5`). Since the length of the `StringBuffer` object `s` is actually 5, this test returns false. Using the logical identity false AND X = false, the value of the overall conditional is fully determined, and the **&&** operator therefore skips evaluation of the right operand. As a result, the value in the `StringBuffer` object is still simply "Hello" when it is printed out.

If the test on the left side of **&&** had returned true, as would have occurred had the `StringBuffer` contained a longer text segment, then the right side would have been evaluated. Although it might look a little strange, that expression, (`s.append(" there").equals("False")`), is valid and returns a `boolean`. In fact, the value of the expression is guaranteed to be false, since it is clearly impossible for any `String-Buffer` to contain exactly "False" when it has just had the `String` " there" appended to it. This is irrelevant, however; the essence of this expression is that, if it is evaluated, it has the side effect of changing the original `StringBuffer` by appending the text " there".

7. What results from running the following code?

```
1. public class Xor {
2.    public static void main(String args[]) {
3.       byte b = 10; // 00001010 binary
4.       byte c = 15; // 00001111 binary
5.       b = (byte)(b ^ c);
6.       System.out.println("b contains " + b);
7.    }
8. }
```

A. The output: b contains 10

B. The output: b contains 5

C. The output: b contains 250

D. The output: b contains 245

Answer: B. The eXclusive-OR operator ^ works on the pairs of bits in equivalent positions in the two operands. In this example, this produces:

```
        00001010
        00001111
    XOR --------
        00000101
```

Notice that the only 1 bits in the answer are in those columns where exactly one of the operands has a 1 bit. If neither, or both, of the operands has a 1, then a 0 bit results.

The value 00000101 binary corresponds to 5 decimal.

It is worth remembering that, although this example has been shown as a byte calculation, the actual working is done using int (32-bit) values. This is why the explicit cast is required before the result is assigned back into the variable *b* in line 5.

8. What results from attempting to compile and run the following code?

```
1. public class Conditional {
2.   public static void main(String args[]) {
3.     int x = 4;
4.     System.out.println("value is " +
5.       ((x > 4) ? 99.99 : 9));
6.   }
7. }
```

A. The output: value is 99.99

B. The output: value is 9

C. The output: value is 9.0

D. A compiler error at line 5

Answer: C. In this code, the optional result values for the conditional operator, 99.99 (a `double`) and 9 (an `int`), are of different types. The result type of a conditional operator must be fully determined at compile time, and in this case the type chosen, using the rules of promotion for binary operands, is `double`. Because the result is a `double`, the output value is printed in a floating-point format.

The choice of which of the two values to output is made on the basis of the `boolean` value that precedes the ?. Since *x* is 4, the test (x > 4) is false. This causes the overall expression to take the second of the possible values, which is 9 rather than 99.99. Because the result type is promoted to a `double`, the output value is actually written as 9.0, rather than the more obvious 9.

If the two possible argument types had been entirely incompatible— for example, (x > 4) ? "Hello" : 9—then the compiler would have issued an error at that line.

9. What is the output of this code fragment?

```
1. int x = 3; int y = 10;
2. System.out.println(y % x);
```

A. 0

B. 1

C. 2

D. 3

Answer: B. In this case, the calculation is relatively straightforward, since only positive integers are involved. Dividing 10 by 3 gives 3 remainder 1, and this 1 forms the result of the modulo expression. Another way to think of this calculation is $10 - 3 = 7, 7 - 3 = 4, 4 - 3 = 1$, 1 is less than 3, therefore the result is 1. The second approach is actually more general, since it handles floating-point calculations, too. Don't forget that for negative numbers, you should ignore the signs during the calculation part, and simply attach the sign of the left operand to the result.

10. What results from the following fragment of code?

```
1. int x = 1;
2. String [] names = { "Fred", "Jim", "Sheila" };
3. names[--x] += ".";
4. for (int i = 0; i < names.length; i++) {
5.    System.out.println(names[i]);
6. }
```

A. The output includes `Fred.` with a trailing period.

B. The output includes `Jim.` with a trailing period.

C. The output includes `Sheila.` with a trailing period.

D. None of the outputs show a trailing period.

E. An `ArrayIndexOutOfBoundsException` is thrown.

Answer: A. The assignment operators of the form *op=* only evaluate the left expression once. So the effect of decrementing *x*, in —*x*, occurs only once, resulting in a value of 0 and not –1. Therefore, no out-of-bounds array accesses are attempted. The array element that is affected by this operation is "Fred", since the decrement occurs before the += operation is performed. Although `String` objects themselves are immutable, the references that are the array elements are not. It is entirely possible to cause the value `name[0]` to be modified to refer to a newly constructed `String`, which happens to be "Fred".

Chapter 3 Test Yourself

1. which of the following declarations are illegal? (Choose one or more.)

A. `default String s;`

B. `transient int i = 41;`

C. `public final static native int w();`

D. `abstract double d;`

E. `abstract final double hyperbolicCosine();`

Answer: A, D, E. A is illegal because "default" is not a keyword. B is a legal transient declaration. C is strange but legal. D is illegal because only methods and classes may be abstract. E is illegal because abstract and final are contradictory.

2. Which one of the following statements is true?

    A. An abstract class may not have any final methods.

    B. A final class may not have any abstract methods.

    Answer: B. Any class with abstract methods must itself be abstract, and a class may not be both abstract and final. Statement A says that an abstract class may not have final methods, but there is nothing wrong with this. The abstract class will eventually be subclassed, and the subclass must avoid overriding the parent's final methods. Any other methods can be freely overridden.

3. What is the *minimal* modification that will make this code compile correctly?

```
1. final class Aaa
2. {
3.     int xxx;
4.     void yyy() { xxx = 1; }
5. }
6.
7.
8. class Bbb extends Aaa
9. {
10.     final Aaa finalref = new Aaa();
11.
12.     final void yyy()
13.     {
14.         System.out.println("In method yyy()");
15.         finalref.xxx = 12345;
16.     }
17. }
```

    A. On line 1, remove the final modifier.

B. On line 10, remove the `final` modifier.

C. Remove line 15.

D. On lines 1 and 10, remove the `final` modifier.

E. The code will compile as is. No modification is needed.

Answer: A. The code will not compile because on line 1, class `Aaa` is declared final and may not be subclassed. Lines 10 and 15 are fine. The instance variable `finalref` is final, so it may not be modified; it can only reference the object created on line 10. However, the data within that object is not final, so there is nothing wrong with line 15.

4. Which one of the following statements is true?

   A. Transient methods may not be overridden.

   B. Transient methods must be overridden.

   C. Transient classes may not be serialized.

   D. Transient variables must be static.

   E. Transient variables are not serialized.

   Answer: E. A, B, and C don't mean anything, because only variables may be transient, not methods or classes. D is false because transient variables may never be static. E is a good one-sentence definition of transient.

5. Which one statement is true about this application?

```
1. class StaticStuff
2  {
3.      static int x = 10;
4.
5.      static { x += 5; }
6.
7.      public static void main(String args[])
8.      {
9.          System.out.println("x = " + x);
10.     }
11.
12.     static {x /= 5; }
13. }
```

A. Lines 5 and 12 will not compile, because the method names and return types are missing.

B. Line 12 will not compile, because you can only have one static initializer.

C. The code compiles, and execution produces the output x = 10.

D. The code compiles, and execution produces the output x = 15.

E. The code compiles, and execution produces the output x = 3.

Answer: E. Multiple static initializers (lines 5 and 12) are legal. All static initializer code is executed at class-load time, so before `main()` is ever run, the value of *x* is initialized to 10 (line 3), then bumped to 15 (line 5), then divided by 5 (line 12).

6. Which one statement is true about this code?

```
1. class HasStatic
2. {
3.      private static int x = 100;
4.
5.      public static void main(String args[])
6.      {
7.          HasStatic hs1 = new HasStatic();
8.          hs1.x++;
9.          HasStatic hs2 = new HasStatic();
10.         hs2.x++;
11.         hs1 = new HasStatic();
12.         hs1.x++;
13.         HasStatic.x++;
14.         System.out.println("x = " + x);
15.     }
16. }
```

A. Line 8 will not compile, because it is a static reference to a private variable.

B. Line 13 will not compile, because it is a static reference to a private variable.

C. The program compiles, and the output is x = 102.

D. The program compiles, and the output is x = 103.

E. The program compiles, and the output is x = 104.

Answer: E. The program compiles fine; the "static reference to a private variable" stuff in answers A and B is nonsense. The static variable x gets incremented four times, on lines 8, 10, 12, and 13.

7. Given the code shown, and making no other changes, which access modifiers (`public`, `protected`, or `private`) can legally be placed before `aMethod()` on line 3? If line 3 is left as it is, which keywords can legally be placed before `aMethod()` on line 8?

```
1. class SuperDuper
2. {
3.     void aMethod() { }
4. }
5.
6. class Sub extends SuperDuper
7. {
8.     void aMethod() { }
9. }
```

Answer: On line 3, the method may be declared private. The method access of the subclass version (line 8) is default, and only a private or default method may be overridden to be default. The basic principle is that a method may not be overridden to be more private. (See Figure 3.2.) On line 8 (assuming line 3 is left alone), the superclass version is default, so the subclass version may stand as it is (and be default), or it may be declared protected or public.

8. Which modifier or modifiers should be used to denote a variable that should not be written out as part of its class's persistent state? (Choose the shortest possible answer.)

A. `private`

B. `protected`

C. `private protected`

D. `transient`

E. `private transient`

Answer: D. The other modifiers control access from other objects within the Java Virtual Machine. Answer E also works but is not minimal.

The next two questions concern the following class definition:

```
1. package abcde;
2.
3. public class Bird {
4.    protected static int referenceCount = 0;
5.    public Bird() { referenceCount++; }
6.    protected void fly() { /* Flap wings, etc. */ }
7.    static int getRefCount() { return referenceCount; }
8. }
```

9. Which one statement is true about class `Bird` above and class `Parrot` below?

```
1. package abcde;
2.
3. class Parrot extends abcde.Bird {
4.    public void fly() {
5.       /* Parrot-specific flight code. */
6.    }
7.    public int getRefCount() {
8.       return referenceCount;
9.    }
10. }
```

A. Compilation of `Parrot.java` fails at line 4, because method `fly()` is protected in the superclass, and classes Bird and Parrot are in the same package.

B. Compilation of `Parrot.java` fails at line 4, because method `fly()` is protected in the superclass and public in the subclass, and methods may not be overridden to be more public.

C. Compilation of `Parrot.java` fails at line 7, because method `getRefCount()` is static in the superclass, and static methods may not be overridden to be non-static.

D. Compilation of `Parrot.java` succeeds, but a runtime exception is thrown if method `fly()` is ever called on an instance of class `Parrot`.

E. Compilation of `Parrot.java` succeeds, but a runtime exception is thrown if method `getRefCount()` is ever called on an instance of class `Parrot`.

Answer: C. Static methods may not be overridden to be non-static. B is incorrect because it states the case backwards: Methods actually may be overridden to be more public, not more private. Answers A, D, and E make no sense.

10. Which one statement is true about class `Bird` above and class `Nightingale` below?

```
1. package singers;
2.
3. class Nightingale extends abcde.Bird {
4.    Nightingale() { referenceCount++; }
5.
6.    public static void main(String args[]) {
7.      System.out.print("Before: " + referenceCount);
8.      Nightingale florence = new Nightingale();
9.      System.out.println("  After: " + referenceCount);
10.     florence.fly();
11.   }
12. }
```

A. The program will compile and execute. The output will be
Before: 0 After: 2

B. The program will compile and execute. The output will be
Before: 0 After: 1

C. Compilation of `Nightingale` will fail at line 4, because static members cannot be overridden.

D. Compilation of `Nightingale` will fail at line 10, because method `fly()` is protected in the superclass.

E. Compilation of `Nightingale` will succeed, but an exception will be thrown at line 10, because method `fly()` is protected in the superclass.

Answer: A. There is nothing wrong with `Nightingale`. The static `referenceCount` is bumped twice: once on line 4 of `Nightingale`, and once on line 5 of `Bird`. (The no-argument constructor of the superclass is always implicitly called at the beginning of a class's constructor, unless a different superclass constructor is requested. This has nothing to do with modifiers, but is covered in Chapter 6, "Objects and Classes.") Since `referenceCount` is bumped twice and not just once, answer B is wrong. C says that statics cannot be overridden, but no static method is being overridden on line 4; all that is happening is an increment of an inherited static variable. D is wrong, since `protected` is precisely the access modifier we want `Bird.fly()` to have: We are calling `Bird.fly()` from a subclass in a different package. Answer E is ridiculous, but it uses credible terminology.

Chapter 4 Test Yourself

1. Which of the following statements is correct? (Choose one.)

A. Only primitives are converted automatically; to change the type of an object reference, you have to do a cast.

B. Only object references are converted automatically; to change the type of a primitive, you have to do a cast.

C. Arithmetic promotion of object references requires explicit casting.

D. Both primitives and object references can be both converted and cast.

E. Casting of numeric types may require a runtime check.

Answer: D. C is wrong because objects do not take part in arithmetic operations. E is wrong because only casting of object references potentially requires a runtime check.

2. Which one line in the following code will not compile?

```
1. byte b = 5;
2. char c = '5';
3. short s = 55;
4. int i = 555;
5. float f = 555.5f;
6. b = s;
7. i = c;
8. if (f > b)
9.    f = i;
```

Answer: Line 6. The code b = s will not compile, because converting a short to a byte is a narrowing conversion, which requires an explicit cast. The other assignments in the code are widening conversions.

3. Will the following code compile?

```
1. byte b = 2;
2. byte b1 = 3;
3. b = b * b1;
```

Answer: No. Surprisingly, the code will fail to compile at line 3. The two operands, which are originally bytes, are converted to ints before the multiplication. The result of the multiplication is an int, which cannot be assigned to byte b.

4. In the code below, what are the possible types for variable result? (Choose the most complete true answer.)

```
1. byte b = 11;
2. short s = 13;
3. result = b * ++s;
```

A. byte, short, int, long, float, double

B. boolean, byte, short, char, int, long, float, double

C. byte, short, char, int, long, float, double

D. byte, short, char

E. int, long, float, double

Answer: E. The result of the calculation on line 2 is an int (because all arithmetic results are ints or wider). An int can be assigned to an int, long, float, or double.

5. Consider the following class:

```
1.   class Cruncher {
2.     void crunch(int i) {
3.       System.out.println("int version");
4.     }
5.     void crunch(String s) {
6.       System.out.println("String version");
7.     }
8.
9.     public static void main(String args[]) {
10.      Cruncher crun = new Cruncher();
11.      char ch = 'p';
12.      crun.crunch(ch);
13.    }
14.  }
```

Which of the statements below is true? (Choose one.)

A. Line 5 will not compile, because void methods cannot be overridden.

B. Line 12 will not compile, because there is no version of crunch() that takes a char argument.

C. The code will compile but will throw an exception at line 12.

D. The code will compile and produce the following output:
int version

E. The code will compile and produce the following output:
String version

Answer: D. At line 12, the char argument ch is widened to type int (a method-call conversion) and passed to the int version of method crunch().

6. Which of the statements below is true? (Choose one.)

   A. Object references can be converted in assignments but not in method calls.

   B. Object references can be converted in method calls but not in assignments.

   C. Object references can be converted in both method calls and assignments, but the rules governing these conversions are very different.

   D. Object references can be converted in both method calls and assignments, and the rules governing these conversions are identical.

   E. Object references can never be converted.

   Answer: D

7. Consider the following code. Which line above will not compile?

```
1. Object ob = new Object();
2. String stringarr[] = new String[50];
3. Float floater = new Float(3.14f);
4.
5. ob = stringarr;
6. ob = stringarr[5];
7. floater = ob;
8. ob = floater;
```

   Answer: Line 7. Changing an Object to a Float is going "down" the inheritance hierarchy tree, so an explicit cast is required.

Questions 8–10 refer to the class hierarchy shown in Figure 4.12.

FIGURE 4.12 Class hierarchy for questions 8, 9, and 10

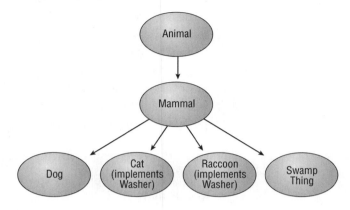

8. Consider the following code:

```
1. Dog       rover, fido;
2. Animal    anim;
3.
4. rover = new Dog();
5. anim = rover;
6. fido = (Dog)anim;
```

Which of the statements below is true? (Choose one.)

A. Line 5 will not compile.

B. Line 6 will not compile.

C. The code will compile but will throw an exception at line 6.

D. The code will compile and run.

E. The code will compile and run, but the cast in line 6 is not required and can be eliminated.

Answer: D. The code will compile and run; the cast in line 6 is required, because changing an `Animal` to a `Dog` is going "down" the tree.

9. Consider the following code:

```
1. Cat sunflower;
2. Washer wawa;
3. SwampThing pogo;
4.
5. sunflower = new Cat();
6. wawa = sunflower;
7. pogo = (SwampThing)wawa;
```

Which of the statements below is true? (Choose one.)

A. Line 6 will not compile; an explicit cast is required to convert a Cat to a Washer.

B. Line 7 will not compile, because you cannot cast an interface to a class.

C. The code will compile and run, but the cast in line 7 is not required and can be eliminated.

D. The code will compile but will throw an exception at line 7, because runtime conversion from an interface to a class is not permitted.

E. The code will compile but will throw an exception at line 7, because the runtime class of wawa cannot be converted to type SwampThing.

Answer: E. The cast in line 7 is required. Answer D is a preposterous statement expressed in a tone of authority.

10. Consider the following code:

```
1. Raccoon rocky;
2. SwampThing pogo;
3. Washer w;
4.
5. rocky = new Raccoon();
6. w = rocky;
7. pogo = w;
```

11. Which of the following statements is true? (Choose one.)

A. Line 6 will not compile; an explicit cast is required to convert a `Raccoon` to a `Washer`.

B. Line 7 will not compile; an explicit cast is required to convert a `Washer` to a `SwampThing`.

C. The code will compile and run.

D. The code will compile but will throw an exception at line 7, because runtime conversion from an interface to a class is not permitted.

E. The code will compile but will throw an exception at line 7, because the runtime class of w cannot be converted to type `SwampThing`.

Answer: B. The conversion in line 6 is fine (class to interface), but the conversion in line 7 (interface to class) is not allowed. A cast in line 7 will make the code compile, but then at runtime a `ClassCastException` will be thrown, because `Washer` and `Swampthing` are incompatible.

Chapter 5 Test Yourself

1. Consider the following code:

```
1. for (int i = 0; i < 2; i++) {
2.    for (int j = 0; j < 3; j++) {
3.      if (i == j) {
4.        continue;
5.      }
6.      System.out.println("i = " + i + " j = " + j);
7.    }
8. }
```

Which lines would be part of the output?

A. i = 0 j = 0

B. i = 0 j = 1

C. i = 0 j = 2

D. i = 1 j = 0

E. i = 1 j = 1

F. i = 1 j = 2

Answer: B, C, D, F. The loops iterate *i* from 0 to 1 and *j* from 0 to 2. However, the inner loop executes a continue statement whenever the values of *i* and *j* are the same. Since the output is generated inside the inner loop, after the continue statement, this means that no output is generated when the values are the same. Therefore, the outputs suggested by answers A and E are skipped.

2. Consider the following code:

```
1. outer: for (int i = 0; i < 2; i++) {
2.   for (int j = 0; j < 3; j++) {
3.     if (i == j) {
4.       continue outer;
5.     }
6.     System.out.println("i = " + i + " j = " + j);
7.   }
8. }
```

Which lines would be part of the output?

A. i = 0 j = 0

B. i = 0 j = 1

C. i = 0 j = 2

D. i = 1 j = 0

E. i = 1 j = 1

F. i = 1 j = 2

Answer: D. The values of *i* appear set to take the values 0 to 1 and for each of these values, *j* takes values 0, 1, and 2. However, whenever *i* and *j* have the same value, the outer loop is continued before the output is generated. Since the outer loop is the target of the `continue` statement, the whole of the inner loop is abandoned. So for the value pairs, this table shows what happens:

i	j	Effect
0	0	Continues at line 4
1	0	Prints at line 6
1	1	Continues at line 4
2	1	Exits loops at line 1

Therefore, the only line to be output is that shown in D.

3. Which of the following are legal loop constructions? (Choose one or more.)

A.
```
1. while (int i < 7) {
2.    i++;
3.    System.out.println("i is " + i);
4. }
```

B.
```
1. int i = 3;
2. while (i) {
3.    System.out.println("i is " + i);
4. }
```

C.
```
1. int j = 0;
2. for (int k = 0; j + k != 10; j++, k++) {
3.    System.out.println("j is " + j + " k is " + k);
4. }
```

D.
```
1. int j = 0;
2. do {
3.    System.out.println("j is " + j++);
4.    if (j == 3) { continue loop; }
5. } while (j < 10);
```

Answer: C. In A, the variable declaration for *i* is illegal. This type of declaration is permitted only in the first part of a `for()` loop. The absence of initialization should also be a clue here. In B, the loop control expression—the variable *i* in this case—is of type `int`. A `boolean` expression is required. C is valid. Despite the complexity of declaring one value inside the `for()` construction, and one outside (along with the use of the comma operator in the end part) this is entirely legitimate. D would have been correct, except that the label has been omitted from line 2, which should have read `loop: do {`.

4. What would be the output from this code fragment?

```
 1. int x = 0, y = 4, z = 5;
 2. if (x > 2) {
 3.    if (y < 5) {
 4.       System.out.println("message one");
 5.    }
 6.    else {
 7.       System.out.println("message two");
 8.    }
 9. }
10. else if (z > 5) {
11.    System.out.println("message three");
12. }
13. else {
14.    System.out.println("message four");
15. }
```

A. message one

B. message two

C. message three

D. message four

Answer: D. The first test at line 2 fails, which immediately causes control to skip to line 10, bypassing both the possible tests that might result in the output of message one or message two. So, even though the test at line 3 would be true, it is never made; A is not correct. At line 10, the test is again false, so the message at line 11 is skipped, but message four, at line 14, is output.

5. Which statement is true about the following code fragment?

```
 1. int j = 2;
 2. switch (j) {
 3.    case 2:
 4.      System.out.println("value is two");
 5.    case 2 + 1:
 6.      System.out.println("value is three");
 7.      break;
 8.    default:
 9.      System.out.println("value is " + j);
10.      break;
11. }
```

A. The code is illegal because of the expression at line 5.

B. The acceptable types for the variable j, as the argument to the switch() construct, could be any of byte, short, int, or long.

C. The output would be only the text value is two.

D. The output would be the text value is two followed by the text value is three.

E. The output would be the text value is two, followed by the text value is three, followed by the text value is 2.

Answer: D. A is incorrect because the code is legal despite the expression at line 5. This is because the expression itself is a constant. B is incorrect because it states that the switch() part can take a long argument. Only byte, short, char, and int are acceptable. The output results from the value 2 like this: First, the option case 2: is selected, which outputs value is two. However, there is no break statement between lines 4 and 5, so the execution falls into the next case and outputs value is three from line 6. The default: part of a switch() is only executed when no other options have been selected, or if there is no break preceding it. In this case, neither of these situations holds true, so the output consists only of the two messages listed in D.

6. Consider the following class hierarchy and code fragment:

```
                    java.lang.Exception
                              \
                    java.io.IOException
                      /                \
java.io.StreamCorruptedException    java.net.MalformedURLException
```

```
1. try {
2.     // assume s is previously defined
3.     URL u = new URL(s);
4.     // in is an ObjectInputStream
5.     Object o = in.readObject();
6.     System.out.println("Success");
7. }
8. catch (MalformedURLException e) {
9.     System.out.println("Bad URL");
10. }
11. catch (StreamCorruptedException e) {
12.     System.out.println("Bad file contents");
13. }
14. catch (Exception e) {
15.     System.out.println("General exception");
16. }
17. finally {
18.     System.out.println("doing finally part");
```

```
19. }
20. System.out.println("Carrying on");
```

What lines are output if the constructor at line 3 throws a
`MalformedURLException`?

A. Success

B. Bad URL

C. Bad file contents

D. General exception

E. Doing finally part

F. Carrying on

Answer: B, E, F. The exception causes a jump out of the `try` block, so
the message Success from line 6 is not printed. The first applicable
catch is at line 8, which is an exact match for the thrown exception.
This results in the message at line 9 being printed, so B is one of the
required answers. Only one `catch` block is ever executed, so control
passes to the `finally` block which results in the message at line 18
being output; so E is part of the correct answer. Since the exception
was caught, it is considered to have been handled and execution continues after the `finally` block. This results in the output of the message at line 20, so F is also part of the correct answer.

7. Consider the following class hierarchy and code fragment:

```
                    java.lang.Exception
                             \
                       java.io.IOException
                       /               \
java.io.StreamCorruptedException    java.net.MalformedURLException
```

```
1. try {
2.    // assume s is previously defined
3.    URL u = new URL(s);
4.    // in is an ObjectInputStream
5.    Object o = in.readObject();
6.    System.out.println("Success");
7. }
```

```
 8. catch (MalformedURLException e) {
 9.   System.out.println("Bad URL");
10. }
11. catch (StreamCorruptedException e) {
12.   System.out.println("Bad file contents");
13. }
14. catch (Exception e) {
15.   System.out.println("General exception");
16. }
17. finally {
18.   System.out.println("Doing finally part");
19. }
20. System.out.println("Carrying on");
```

What lines are output if the methods at lines 3 and 5 complete successfully without throwing any exceptions?

A. Success

B. Bad URL

C. Bad file contents

D. General exception

E. Doing finally part

F. Carrying on

Answer: A, E, F. With no exceptions the try block executes to completion, so the message Success from line 6 is printed and A is part of the correct answer. No catch is executed, so B, C, and D are incorrect. Control then passes to the finally block, which results in the message at line 18 being output, so E is part of the correct answer. Because no exception was thrown, execution continues after the finally block, resulting in the output of the message at line 20, so F is also part of the correct answer.

8. Consider the following class hierarchy and code fragment:

```
                java.lang.Throwable
              /                     \
     java.lang.Error          java.lang.Exception
            /                          \
java.lang.OutOfMemoryError         java.io.IOException
                              /                    \
      java.io.StreamCorruptedException    java.net.MalformedURLException
```

```
1. try {
2.     // assume s is previously defined
3.    URL u = new URL(s);
4.     // in is an ObjectInputStream
5.    Object o = in.readObject();
6.    System.out.println("Success");
7. }
8. catch (MalformedURLException e) {
9.    System.out.println("Bad URL");
10. }
11. catch (StreamCorruptedException e) {
12.    System.out.println("Bad file contents");
13. }
14. catch (Exception e) {
15.    System.out.println("General exception");
16. }
17. finally {
18.    System.out.println("Doing finally part");
19. }
20. System.out.println("Carrying on");
```

What lines are output if the method at line 5 throws an
OutOfMemoryError?

A. Success

B. Bad URL

C. Bad file contents

D. General exception

E. Doing finally part

F. Carrying on

Answer: E. The thrown error prevents completion of the try block, so the message Success from line 6 is not printed. No catch is appropriate, so B, C, and D are incorrect. Control then passes to the finally block, which results in the message at line 18 being output; so option E is part of the correct answer. Because the error was not caught, execution exits the method and the error is rethrown in the caller of this method, so F is not part of the correct answer.

9. Which *one* of the following fragments shows the *most* appropriate way to throw an exception? Assume that any undeclared variables have been appropriately declared elsewhere and are in scope and have meaningful values.

A.
```
1. Exception e = new IOException("File not found");
2. if (!f.exists()) { // f is a File object
3.    throw e;
4. }
```

B.
```
1. if (!f.exists()) { // f is a File object
2.    throw new IOException("File " + f.getName() +
      " not found");
3. }
```

C.
```
1. if (!f.exists()) {
2.    throw IOException;
3. }
```

D.
```
1. if (!f.exists()) {
2.    throw "File not found";
3. }
```

E.
```
1. if (!f.exists()) { // f is a File object
2.    throw new IOException();
3. }
```

Answer: B. A would give misleading line number information in the stack trace of the exception, reporting that the exception arose at line 1, which is where the exception object was created. C is illegal since you must throw an object that is a subclass of `java.lang.Throwable`, and you cannot throw a class, only an object. D is also illegal, as it attempts to throw a `String`, which is not a subclass of `java.lang.Throwable`. E is entirely legal, but it is not as good as B since E doesn't take the effort to clarify the nature of the problem by providing a string of explanation.

10. The method `risky()` might throw a `java.io.IOException`, `java.lang.RuntimeException`, or `java.net.MalformedURLException` (which is a subclass of `java.io.IOException`). Appropriate imports have been declared for each of those exceptions. Which of the following classes and sets of classes are legal? (Choose one or more.)

    A.
    ```
    1. public class SomeClass {
    2.    public void aMethod() {
    3.      risky();
    4.    }
    5. }
    ```

    B.
    ```
    1. public class SomeClass {
    2.    public void aMethod() throws
    3.      IOException {
    4.      risky();
    5.    }
    6. }
    ```

    C.
    ```
    1. public class SomeClass {
    2.    public void aMethod() throws
    3.      RuntimeException {
    4.      risky();
    5.    }
    6. }
    ```

    D.
    ```
    1. public class SomeClass {
    2.    public void aMethod() {
    3.      try {
    4.        risky();
    5.      }
    6.      catch (IOException e) {
    ```

```
 7.          e.printStackTrace();
 8.        }
 9.    }
10.  }
```

E.
```
 1. public class SomeClass {
 2.   public void aMethod()
 3.     throws MalformedURLException {
 4.     try { risky(); }
 5.     catch (IOException e) {
 6.       // ignore it
 7.     }
 8.   }
 9. }
10.
11. public class AnotherClass
12.   extends SomeClass {
13.   public void aMethod()
14.     throws java.io.IOException {
15.     super.aMethod();
16.   }
17. }
```

Answer: B, D. A does not handle the exceptions, so the method aMethod might throw any of the exceptions that risky() might throw. However the exceptions are not declared with a throws construction. In B, declaring "throws IOException" is sufficient, because java.lang.Runtime-Exception is not a checked exception and because IOException is a superclass of MalformedURLException, it is unnecessary to mention the MalformedURLException explicitly (although it might make better "self-documentation" to do so). C is unacceptable because its throws declaration fails to mention the checked exceptions—it is not an error to declare the runtime exception, although it is strictly redundant. D is also acceptable, since the catch block handles IOException, which includes MalformedURLException. RuntimeException will still be thrown by the method aMethod() if it is thrown by risky(), but as Runtime-Exception is not a checked exception, this is not an error. E is not acceptable, since the overriding method in anotherClass is declared as throwing IOException, while the overridden method in aClass was only declared as throwing MalformedURLException. It would have been correct for the base class to declare that it throws IOException and then the derived class to throw MalformedURLException, but as it is, the overriding method is attempting to throw exceptions not declared for the original method. The fact that the only exception that actually can arise is the MalformedURLException is not enough to rescue this, because the compiler only checks the declarations, not the semantics of the code.

Chapter 6 Test Yourself

1. Consider this class:

```
1. public class Test1 {
2.    public float aMethod(float a, float b) {
3.    }
4.
5. }
```

Which of the following methods would be legal if added (individually) at line 4?

A. `public int aMethod(int a, int b) { }`

B. `public float aMethod(float a, float b) { }`

C. `public float aMethod(float a, float b, int c) throws Exception { }`

D. `public float aMethod(float c, float d) { }`

E. `private float aMethod(int a, int b, int c) { }`

Answer: A, C, E. In each of these answers, the argument list differs from the original, so the method is an overload. Overloaded methods are effectively independent, and there are no constraints on the accessibility, return type, or exceptions that may be thrown. B would be a legal overriding method, except that it cannot be defined in the same class as the original method; rather, it must be declared in a subclass. D is also an override, since the *types* of its arguments are the same: Changing the parameter names is not sufficient to count as overloading.

2. Consider these classes, defined in separate source files:

```
1. public class Test1 {
2.    public float aMethod(float a, float b) throws
3.    IOException {
4.    }
5. }
```

```
1. public class Test2 extends Test1 {
2.
3. }
```

Which of the following methods would be legal (individually) at line 2 in class `Test2`?

A. `float aMethod(float a, float b) { }`

B. `public int aMethod(int a, int b) throws Exception { }`

C. `public float aMethod(float a, float b) throws`
`    Exception { }`

D. `public float aMethod(float p, float q) { }`

Answer: B, D. A is illegal because it is less accessible than the original method; the fact that it throws no exceptions is perfectly acceptable. B is legal because it overloads the method of the parent class, and as such it is not constrained by any rules governing its return value, accessibility, or argument list. The exception thrown by C is sufficient to make that method illegal. D is legal because the accessibility and return type are identical, and the method is an override because the types of the arguments are identical—remember that the names of the arguments are irrelevant. The absence of an exception list in D is not a problem: An overriding method may legitimately throw fewer exceptions than its original, but it may not throw more.

3. You have been given a design document for a veterinary registration system for implementation in Java. It states:

"A pet has an owner, a registration date, and a vaccination-due date. A cat is a pet that has a flag indicating whether it has been neutered, and a textual description of its markings."

Given that the `Pet` class has already been defined, which of the following fields would be appropriate for inclusion in the `Cat` class as members?

A. `Pet thePet;`

B. `Date registered;`

C. `Date vaccinationDue;`

D. `Cat theCat;`

E. `boolean neutered;`

F. `String markings;`

Answer: E, F. The Cat class is a subclass of the Pet class, and as such should extend Pet, rather than containing an instance of Pet. B and C should be members of the Pet class and as such are inherited into the Cat class; therefore, they should not be declared in the Cat class. D would declare a reference to an instance of the Cat class, which is not generally appropriate inside the Cat class itself (unless, perhaps, you were asked to give the Cat a member that refers to its mother). Finally, the neutered flag and markings descriptions, E and F, are the items called for by the specification; these are correct items.

4. You have been given a design document for a veterinary registration system for implementation in Java. It states:

   "A pet has an owner, a registration date, and a vaccination-due date. A cat is a pet that has a flag indicating if it has been neutered, and a textual description of its markings."

   Given that the Pet class has already been defined and you expect the Cat class to be used freely throughout the application, how would you make the opening declaration of the Cat class, up to but not including the first opening brace? Use only these words and spaces: boolean, Cat, class, Date, extends, Object, Owner, Pet, private, protected, public, String.

   Answer: public class Cat extends Pet. The class should be public, since it is to be used freely throughout the application. The statement "A cat is a pet" tells us that the Cat class should subclass Pet. The other words offered are required for the body of the definitions of either Cat or Pet–for use as member variables—but are not part of the opening declaration.

5. Consider the following classes, declared in separate source files:

```
1. public class Base {
2.    public void method(int i) {
3.       System.out.println("Value is " + i);
4.    }
5. }
```

```
1. public class Sub extends Base {
2.    public void method(int j) {
3.      System.out.println("This value is " + j);
4.    }
5.    public void method(String s) {
6.      System.out.println("I was passed " + s);
7.    }
8.    public static void main(String args[]) {
9.      Base b1 = new Base();
10.     Base b2 = new Sub();
11.     b1.method(5);
12.     b2.method(6);
13.   }
14. }
```

What output results when the main method of the class Sub is run?

A. Value is 5
   Value is 6

B. This value is 5
   This value is 6

C. Value is 5
   This value is 6

D. This value is 5
   Value is 6

E. I was passed 5
   I was passed 6

Answer: C. The first message is produced by the Base class when b1.method(5) is called and is therefore Value is 5. Despite variable *b2* being declared as being of the Base class, the behavior that results when method() is invoked upon it is the behavior associated with the class of the actual object, not with the type of the variable. Since the object is of class Sub, not of class Base, the second message is generated by line 3 of class Sub: This value is 6.

6. Consider the following class definition:

```
1. public class Test extends Base {
2.    public Test(int j) {
3.    }
4.    public Test(int j, int k) {
5.       super(j, k);
6.    }
7. }
```

Which of the following are legitimate calls to construct instances of the Test class?

A. Test t = new Test();

B. Test t = new Test(1);

C. Test t = new Test(1, 2);

D. Test t = new Test(1, 2, 3);

E. Test t = (new Base()).new Test(1);

Answer: B, C. Since the class has explicit constructors defined, the default constructor is suppressed, so A is not possible. B and C have argument lists that match the constructors defined at lines 2 and 4 respectively, and so are correct constructions. D has three integer arguments, but there are no constructors that take three arguments of any kind in the Test class, so D is incorrect. Finally, E is a syntax used for construction of inner classes and is therefore wrong.

7. Consider the following class definition:

```
1. public class Test extends Base {
2.    public Test(int j) {
3.    }
4.    public Test(int j, int k) {
5.       super(j, k);
6.    }
7. }
```

Which of the following forms of constructor must exist explicitly in the definition of the `Base` class?

A. `Base() { }`

B. `Base(int j) { }`

C. `Base(int j, int k) { }`

D. `Base(int j, int k, int l) { }`

Answer: A, C. In the constructor at lines 2 and 3, there is no explicit call to either `this()` or `super()`, which means that the compiler will generate a call to the zero argument superclass constructor, as in A. The explicit call to `super()` at line 5 requires that the `Base` class must have a constructor as in C. This has two consequences. First, C must be one of the required constructors and therefore one of the answers. Second, the `Base` class must have at least that constructor defined explicitly, so the default constructor is not generated, but must be added explicitly. Therefore the constructor of A is also required and must be a correct answer. At no point in the `Test` class is there a call to either a superclass constructor with one or three arguments, so B and D need not explicitly exist.

8. Which of the following statements are true? (Choose one or more.)

   A. An inner class may be declared `private`.

   B. An inner class may be declared `static`.

   C. An inner class defined in a method should always be anonymous.

   D. An inner class defined in a method can access all the method local variables.

   E. Construction of an inner class may require an instance of the outer class.

Answer: A, B, E. Member inner classes may be defined with any accessibility, so `private` is entirely acceptable and A is correct. Similarly, the `static` modifier is permitted on a member inner class, which causes it not to be associated with any particular instance of the outer class. This means that B is also correct. Inner classes defined in methods may be anonymous—and indeed often are—but this is not required, so C is wrong. D is wrong because it is not possible for an inner class defined in a method to access the local variables of the method, except for those variables that are marked as `final`. Constructing an instance of a `static` inner class does not need an instance of the enclosing object, but all non-static inner classes do require such a reference, and that reference must be available to the `new` operation. The reference to the enclosing object is commonly implied as `this`, which is why it is commonly not explicit. These points make E true.

9. Consider the following definition:

```
 1. public class Outer {
 2.    public int a = 1;
 3.    private int b = 2;
 4.    public void method(final int c) {
 5.      int d = 3;
 6.      class Inner {
 7.        private void iMethod(int e) {
 8.
 9.        }
10.      }
11.    }
12. }
```

Which variables may be referenced correctly at line 8?

A. *a*

B. *b*

C. *c*

D. *d*

E. *e*

Answer: A, B, C, E. Since `Inner` is not a `static` inner class, it has a reference to an enclosing object, and all the variables of that object are accessible. Therefore A and B are correct, despite the fact that *b* is marked `private`. Variables in the enclosing method are only accessible if those variables are marked `final`, so the method argument *c* is correct, but the variable *d* is not. Finally, the parameter *e* is of course accessible, since it is a parameter to the method containing line 8 itself.

10. Which of the following statements are true? (Choose one or more.)

   A. Given that `Inner` is a non-static class declared inside a public class `Outer`, and appropriate constructor forms are defined, an instance of `Inner` may be constructed like this:

   ```
   new Outer().new Inner()
   ```

   B. If an anonymous inner class inside the class `Outer` is defined to implement the interface `ActionListener`, it may be constructed like this:

   ```
   new Outer().new ActionListener()
   ```

   C. Given that `Inner` is a non-static class declared inside a public class `Outer` and appropriate constructor forms are defined, an instance of `Inner` may be constructed in a static method like this:

   ```
   new Inner()
   ```

   D. An anonymous class instance that implements the interface `MyInterface` may be constructed and returned from a method like this:

   ```
   1. return new MyInterface(int x) {
   2.    int x;
   3.    public MyInterface(int x) {
   4.      this.x = x;
   5.    }
   6. };
   ```

Answer: A. Construction of a normal (that is, a named and non-static) inner class requires an instance of the enclosing class. Often this enclosing instance is provided via the implied `this` reference, but an explicit reference may be used in front of the new operator, as shown in A.

Anonymous inner classes can only be instantiated at the same point they are declared, like this:

```
return new ActionListener() {
  public void actionPerformed(ActionEvent e) { }
}
```

Hence, B is illegal; it actually attempts to instantiate the interface `ActionListener` as if that interface were itself an inner class inside `Outer`.

C is illegal since `Inner` is a non-static inner class, and so it requires a reference to an enclosing instance when it is constructed. The form shown suggests the implied `this` reference, but since the method is `static`, there is no `this` reference and the construction is illegal.

D is illegal since it attempts to use arguments to the constructor of an anonymous inner class that implements an interface. The clue is in the attempt to define a constructor at line 3. This would be a constructor for the interface `MyInterface` not for the inner class—this is wrong on two counts. First, interfaces do not define constructors, and second, we need a constructor for our anonymous class, not for the interface.

Chapter 7 Test Yourself

1. Which one statement below is true concerning the following code?

```
1. class Greebo extends java.util.Vector
2.    implements Runnable {
3.      public void run(String message) {
4.        System.out.println("in run() method: " +
```

```
5.              message);
6.      }
7.  }
8.
9.  class GreeboTest {
10.     public static void main(String args[]) {
12.        Greebo g = new Greebo();
13.        Thread t = new Thread(g);
14.        t.start();
15.     }
16. }
```

A. There will be a compiler error, because class `Greebo` does not correctly implement the `Runnable` interface.

B. There will be a compiler error at line 13, because you cannot pass a parameter to the constructor of a `Thread`.

C. The code will compile correctly but will crash with an exception at line 13.

D. The code will compile correctly but will crash with an exception at line 14.

E. The code will compile correctly and will execute without throwing any exceptions.

Answer: A. The `Runnable` interface defines a `run()` method with `void` return type and no parameters. The method given in the problem has a `String` parameter, so the compiler will complain that class `Greebo` does not define `void run()` from interface `Runnable`. B is wrong, because you can definitely pass a parameter to a thread's constructor; the parameter becomes the thread's target. C, D, and E are nonsense.

2. Which one statement below is always true about the following application?

```
1.  class HiPri extends Thread {
2.     HiPri() {
3.        setPriority(10);
```

```
4.    }
5.
6.    public void run() {
7.      System.out.println(
8.        "Another thread starting up.");
9.      while (true) { }
10.   }
11.
12.   public static void main(String args[]) {
13.     HiPri hp1 = new HiPri();
14.     HiPri hp2 = new HiPri();
15.     HiPri hp3 = new HiPri();
16.     hp1.start();
17.     hp2.start();
18.     hp3.start();
19.   }
20. }
```

A. When the application is run, thread hp1 will execute; threads hp2 and hp3 will never get the CPU.

B. When the application is run, all three threads (hp1, hp2, and hp3) will get to execute, taking time-sliced turns in the CPU.

C. Either A or B will be true, depending on the underlying platform.

Answer: C. A is true on a preemptive platform, B is true on a time-sliced platform. The moral is that such code should be avoided, since it gives such different results on different platforms.

3. True or False: A thread wants to make a second thread ineligible for execution. To do this, the first thread can call the yield() method on the second thread.

A. True

B. False

Answer: B. The yield() method is static and always causes the current thread to yield. In this case, ironically, it is the first thread that will yield.

4. A thread's `run()` method includes the following lines:

```
1. try {
2.   sleep(100);
3. } catch (InterruptedException e) { }
```

Assuming the thread is not interrupted, which one of the following statements is correct?

A. The code will not compile, because exceptions may not be caught in a thread's `run()` method.

B. At line 2, the thread will stop running. Execution will resume in, at most, 100 milliseconds.

C. At line 2, the thread will stop running. It will resume running in exactly 100 milliseconds.

D. At line 2, the thread will stop running. It will resume running some time after 100 milliseconds have elapsed.

Answer: D. The thread will sleep for 100 milliseconds (more or less, given the resolution of the JVM being used). Then the thread will enter the Ready state; it will not actually run until the scheduler permits it to run.

5. A monitor called `mon` has 10 threads in its waiting pool; all these waiting threads have the same priority. One of the threads is `thr1`. How can you notify `thr1` so that it alone moves from the Waiting state to the Ready state?

A. Execute `notify(thr1);` from within synchronized code of `mon`.

B. Execute `mon.notify(thr1);` from synchronized code of any object.

C. Execute `thr1.notify();` from synchronized code of any object.

D. Execute `thr1.notify();` from any code (synchronized or not) of any object.

E. You cannot specify which thread will get notified.

Answer: E. When you call `notify()` on a monitor, you have no control over which waiting thread gets notified.

6. If you attempt to compile and execute the application listed below, will it ever print out the message In xxx?

```
1. class TestThread3 extends Thread {
2.   public void run() {
3.     System.out.println("Running");
4.     System.out.println("Done");
5.   }
6.
7.   private void xxx() {
8.     System.out.println("In xxx");
9.   }
10.
11.   public static void main(String args[]) {
12.     TestThread3 ttt = new TestThread3();
13.     ttt.xxx();
14.     ttt.start();
12.   }
13. }
```

A. Yes

B. No

Answer: Yes. The call to xxx() occurs before the thread is registered with the thread scheduler, so the question has nothing to do with threads.

7. True or False: A Java monitor must either extend Thread or implement Runnable.

A. True

B. False

Answer: B. A monitor is an instance of any class that has synchronized code.

Chapter 8 Test Yourself

1. Given a string constructed by calling s = new String("xyzzy"), which of the calls listed below modify the string? (Choose all that apply.)

   A. s.append("aaa");

   B. s.trim();

   C. s.substring(3);

   D. s.replace('z', 'a');

   E. s.concat(s);

   F. None of the above

   Answer: F. Strings are immutable.

2. Which one statement is true about the code below?

   ```
   1. String s1 = "abc" + "def";
   2. String s2 = new String(s1);
   3. if (s1 == s2)
   4.    System.out.println("== succeeded");
   5. if (s1.equals(s2))
   6.    System.out.println(".equals() succeeded");
   ```

   A. Lines 4 and 6 both execute.

   B. Line 4 executes, and line 6 does not.

   C. Line 6 executes, and line 4 does not.

   D. Neither line 4 nor line 6 executes.

   Answer: C. Since *s1* and *s2* are references to two different objects, the == test fails. However, the strings contained within the two string objects are identical, so the equals() test passes.

3. Suppose you want to write a class that offers static methods to compute hyperbolic trigonometric functions. You decide to subclass `java.lang.Math` and provide the new functionality as a set of static methods. Which one statement below is true about this strategy?

    A. The strategy works.

    B. The strategy works, provided the new methods are public.

    C. The strategy works, provided the new methods are not private.

    D. The strategy fails, because you cannot subclass `java.lang.Math`.

    E. The strategy fails, because you cannot add static methods to a subclass.

    Answer: D. The `java.lang.Math` class is final, so it cannot be subclassed.

4. Which one statement is true about the code fragment below?

    ```
    1. import java.lang.Math;
    2. Math myMath = new Math();
    3. System.out.println("cosine of 0.123 = " +
    4.    myMath.cos(0.123));
    ```

    A. Compilation fails at line 2.

    B. Compilation fails at line 3 or 4.

    C. Compilation succeeds, although the import on line 1 is not necessary. During execution, an exception is thrown at line 3 or 4.

    D. Compilation succeeds. The import on line 1 is necessary. During execution, an exception is thrown at line 3 or 4.

    E. Compilation succeeds, and no exception is thrown during execution.

    Answer: A. The constructor for the `Math` class is private, so it cannot be called. The `Math` class methods are static, so it is never necessary to construct an instance. The import at line 1 is not required, since all classes of the `java.lang` package are automatically imported.

5. Which one statement is true about the code fragment below?

```
1. String s = "abcde";
2. StringBuffer s1 = new StringBuffer("abcde");
3. if (s.equals(s1))
4.    s1 = null;
5. if (s1.equals(s))
6.    s = null;
```

A. Compilation fails at line 1, because the `String` constructor must be called explicitly.

B. Compilation fails at line 3, because *s* and *s1* have different types.

C. Compilation succeeds. During execution, an exception is thrown at line 3.

D. Compilation succeeds. During execution, an exception is thrown at line 5.

E. Compilation succeeds. No exception is thrown during execution.

Answer: E. A is wrong because line 1 is a perfectly acceptable way to create a string, and is actually more efficient than explicitly calling the constructor. B is wrong because the argument to the `equals()` method is of type `Object`; thus any object reference or array variable may be passed. The calls on lines 3 and 5 return false without throwing exceptions.

6. True or False: In the code fragment below, after execution of line 1, sbuf references an instance of the `StringBuffer` class. After execution of line 2, sbuf still references the same instance.

```
1. StringBuffer sbuf = new StringBuffer("abcde");
2. sbuf.insert(3, "xyz");
```

A. True

B. False

Answer: A. The `StringBuffer` class is mutable. After execution of line 2, sbuf refers to the same object, although the object has been modified.

7. True or False: In the code fragment below, after execution of line 1, sbuf references an instance of the StringBuffer class. After execution of line 2, sbuf still references the same instance.

```
1. StringBuffer sbuf = new StringBuffer("abcde");
2. sbuf.append("xyz");
```

A. True

B. False

Answer: A. The StringBuffer class is mutable. After execution of line 2, sbuf refers to the same object, although the object has been modified.

8. True or False: In the code fragment below, line 4 is executed.

```
1. String s1 = "xyz";
2. String s2 = "xyz";
3. if (s1 == s2)
4.    System.out.println("Line 4");
```

A. True

B. False

Answer: A. Line 1 constructs a new instance of String and stores it in the string pool. In line 2, "xyz" is already represented in the pool, so no new instance is constructed.

9. True or False: In the code fragment below, line 4 is executed.

```
1. String s1 = "xyz";
2. String s2 = new String(s1);
3. if (s1 == s2)
4.    System.out.println("Line 4");
```

A. True

B. False

Answer: B. Line 1 constructs a new instance of String and stores it in the string pool. Line 2 explicitly constructs another instance.

10. Which would be most suitable for storing data elements that must not appear in the store more than once, if searching is not a priority?

A. `Collection`

B. `List`

C. `Set`

D. `Map`

E. `Vector`

Answer: C. A set prohibits duplication while a list or collection does not. A map also prohibits duplication of the key entries, but maps are primarily for looking up data based on the unique key. So, in this case, we could have used a map, storing the data as the key and leaving the data part of the map empty. However, we are told that searching is not a priority, so the proper answer is a set.

Chapter 9 Test Yourself

1. A Java program creates a check box using the code listed below. The program is run on two different platforms. Which of the statements following the code are true? (Choose one or more.)

```
1. Checkbox cb = new Checkbox("Autosave");
2. Font f = new Font("Courier", Font.PLAIN, 14);
3. cb.setFont(f);
```

A. The check box will be the same size on both platforms, because Courier is a standard Java font.

B. The check box will be the same size on both platforms, because Courier is a fixed-width font.

C. The check box will be the same size on both platforms, provided both platforms have identical 14-point plain Courier fonts.

D. The check box will be the same size on both platforms, provided both platforms have identical check-box decorations.

E. There is no way to guarantee that the check boxes will be the same size on both platforms.

Answer: E. Java makes no guarantees about component size from platform to platform, because it uses each platform's own fonts and component appearance. The whole point of layout managers is that you don't have to worry about platform-to-platform differences in component appearance.

2. What is the result of attempting to compile and execute the following application under JDK 1.2 or later?

```
1. import java.awt.*;
2.
3. public class Q2 extends Frame {
4.    Q2() {
5.       setSize(300, 300);
6.       Button b = new Button("Apply");
7.       add(b);
8.    }
9.
10.    public static void main(String args[]) {
11.       Q2 that = new Q2();
12.       that.setVisible(true);
13.    }
14. }
```

A. There is a compiler error at line 11, because the constructor on line 4 is not public.

B. The program compiles but crashes with an exception at line 7, because the frame has no layout manager.

C. The program displays an empty frame.

D. The program displays the button, using the default font for the button label. The button is just large enough to encompass its label.

E. The program displays the button, using the default font for the button label. The button occupies the entire frame.

Answer: E. A is wrong because the constructor is called from within its own class; the application would compile even if the constructor were private. B is wrong because the frame has a default layout manager, which is an instance of BorderLayout. If you add() a component to a container that uses a Border layout manager, and you don't specify a region as a second parameter, then the component is added at Center, just as if you had specified BorderLayout.CENTER as a second parameter. (Note, however, that explicitly providing the parameter is much better programming style than relying on default behavior.) C is wrong because in JDK 1.2 the button does appear; it takes up the entire frame, as described in E. Answer D would be true if frames used Flow layout managers by default.

3. What is the result of compiling and running the following application?

```
1. import java.awt.*;
2.
3. public class Q3 extends Frame {
4.    Q3() {
5.       // Use Grid layout manager.
6.       setSize(300, 300);
7.       setLayout(new GridLayout(1, 2));
8.
9.       // Build and add 1st panel.
10.      Panel p1 = new Panel();
11.      p1.setLayout(
12.         new FlowLayout(FlowLayout.RIGHT));
13.      p1.add(new Button("Hello"));
14.      add(p1);
15.
16.      // Build and add 2nd panel.
17.      Panel p2 = new Panel();
18.      p2.setLayout(
19.         new FlowLayout(FlowLayout.LEFT));
20.      p2.add(new Button("Goodbye"));
21.      add(p2);
22.   }
```

```
23.
24.   public static void main(String args[]) {
25.     Q3 that = new Q3();
26.     that.setVisible(true);
27.   }
28. }
```

A. The program crashes with an exception at line 7, because the frame's default layout manager cannot be overridden.

B. The program crashes with an exception at line 7, because a `Grid` layout manager must have at least two rows and two columns.

C. The program displays two buttons, which are just large enough to encompass their labels. The buttons appear at the top of the frame. The "Hello" button is just to the left of the vertical midline of the frame; the "Goodbye" button is just to the right of the vertical midline of the frame.

D. The program displays two large buttons. The "Hello" button occupies the entire left half of the frame, and the "Goodbye" button occupies the entire right half of the frame.

E. The program displays two buttons, which are just wide enough to encompass their labels. The buttons are as tall as the frame. The "Hello" button is just to the left of the vertical midline of the frame; the "Goodbye" button is just to the right of the vertical midline of the frame.

Answer: C. A is wrong because *any* container's default layout manager can be replaced; that is the only way to get things done if the default manager isn't what you want. B is wrong because there is no restriction against having a single row or a single column. What really happens is this: The frame contains two panels—p1 occupies the entire left half of the frame and p2 occupies the entire right half (because the frame uses a grid with one row and two columns). Each panel uses a Flow layout manager, so within the panels every component gets to be its preferred size. Thus, the two buttons are just big enough to encompass their labels. Panel p1 uses a right-aligning Flow layout manager, so its single component is aligned to the far right of that panel, just left of the vertical center line. Panel p2 uses a left-aligning Flow layout manager, so its single component is aligned to the far left of that panel, just right of the vertical center line. Thus, the two buttons end up as described in answer C. D and E are incorrect because the buttons get to be their preferred sizes.

4. What is the result of compiling and running the following application?

```
1. import java.awt.*;
2.
3. public class Q4 extends Frame {
4.    Q4() {
5.       // Use Grid layout manager.
6.       setSize(300, 300);
7.       setLayout(new GridLayout(3, 1));
8.
9.       // Build and add 1st panel.
10.      Panel p1 = new Panel();
11.      p1.setLayout(new BorderLayout());
12.      p1.add(new Button("Alpha"),
13.        BorderLayout.NORTH);
14.      add(p1);
15.
16.      // Build and add 2nd panel.
17.      Panel p2 = new Panel();
18.      p2.setLayout(new BorderLayout());
19.      p2.add(new Button("Beta"),
```

```
20.          BorderLayout.CENTER);
21.       add(p2);
22.
23.       // Build and add 3rd panel.
24.       Panel p3 = new Panel();
25.       p3.setLayout(new BorderLayout());
26.       p3.add(new Button("Gamma"),
27.          BorderLayout.SOUTH);
28.       add(p3);
29.    }
30.
31.    public static void main(String args[]) {
32.       Q4 that = new Q4();
33.       that.setVisible(true);
34.    }
35. }
```

A. Each button is as wide as the frame and is just tall enough to encompass its label. The "Alpha" button is at the top of the frame. The "Beta" button is in the middle. The "Gamma" button is at the bottom.

B. Each button is as wide as the frame. The "Alpha" button is at the top of the frame and is just tall enough to encompass its label. The "Beta" button is in the middle of the frame; its height is approximately one-third the height of the frame. The "Gamma" button is at the bottom of the frame and is just tall enough to encompass its label.

C. Each button is just wide enough and just tall enough to encompass its label. All three buttons are centered horizontally. The "Alpha" button is at the top of the frame. The "Beta" button is in the middle. The "Gamma" button is at the bottom.

D. Each button is just wide enough to encompass its label. All three buttons are centered horizontally. The "Alpha" button is at the top of the frame and is just tall enough to encompass its label. The "Beta" button is in the middle of the frame; its height is approximately one-third the height of the frame. The "Gamma" button is at the bottom of the frame and is just tall enough to encompass its label.

E. Each button is as tall as the frame and is just wide enough to encompass its label. The "Alpha" button is at the left of the frame. The "Beta" button is in the middle. The "Gamma" button is at the right.

Answer: B. The frame is laid out in a grid with three rows and one column. Thus each of the three panels p1, p2, and p3 is as wide as the frame and one-third as tall. The "Alpha" button goes at North of the top panel, so it is as wide as the panel itself (thus as wide as the frame), and it gets to be its preferred height. The "Beta" button goes at Center of the middle panel, so it occupies the entire panel (since there is nothing else in the panel). The "Gamma" button goes at South of the bottom panel, so it is as wide as the panel itself (thus as wide as the frame), and it gets to be its preferred height.

5. You would like to compile and execute the following code. After the frame appears on the screen (assuming you get that far), you would like to resize the frame to be approximately twice its original width and approximately twice its original height. Which of the statements following the code is correct? (Choose one.)

```
1.  import java.awt.*;
2.
3.  public class Q5 extends Frame {
4.     Q5() {
5.        setSize(300, 300);
6.        setFont(new Font("SanSerif", Font.BOLD, 36));
7.        Button b = new Button("Abracadabra");
8.        add(b, BorderLayout.SOUTH);
9.     }
10.
11.    public static void main(String args[]) {
12.       Q5 that = new Q5();
13.       that.setVisible(true);
14.    }
15. }
```

A. Compilation fails at line 8, because the frame has not been given a layout manager.

B. Before resizing, the button appears at the top of the frame and is as wide as the frame. After resizing, the button retains its original width and is still at the top of the frame.

C. Before resizing, the button appears at the bottom of the frame and is as wide as the frame. After resizing, the button retains its original width and is the same distance from the top of the frame as it was before resizing.

D. Before resizing, the button appears at the bottom of the frame and is as wide as the frame. After resizing, the button is as wide as the frame's new width and is still at the bottom of the frame.

E. Before resizing, the button appears at the bottom of the frame and is as wide as the frame. After resizing, the button retains its original width and is about twice as tall as it used to be. It is still at the bottom of the frame.

Answer: D. A is wrong because every frame gets a default Border layout manager. Since the button is placed at South, it is always as wide as the frame, and it gets resized when the frame gets resized. Its height is always its preferred height. Note that of the three plausible answers (C, D, and E), the correct answer is the simplest. The point of this question is that when a container gets resized, its layout manager lays out all the components again.

6. The following code builds a GUI with a single button. Which one statement is true about the button's size?

```
1.  import java.awt.*;
2.
3.  public class Q6 extends Frame {
4.    Q6() {
5.      setSize(500, 500);
6.      setLayout(new FlowLayout());
7.
8.      Button b = new Button("Where am I?");
9.      Panel p1 = new Panel();
10.     p1.setLayout(
11.       new FlowLayout(FlowLayout.LEFT));
```

```
12.       Panel p2 = new Panel();
13.       p2.setLayout(new BorderLayout());
14.       Panel p3 = new Panel();
15.       p3.setLayout(new GridLayout(3, 2));
16.
17.       p1.add(b);
18.       p2.add(p1, BorderLayout.NORTH);
19.       p3.add(p2);
20.       add(p3);
21.    }
22.
23.    public static void main(String args[]) {
24.       Q6 that = new Q6();
25.       that.setVisible(true);
26.    }
27. }
```

A. The button is just wide enough and tall enough to encompass its label.

B. The button is just wide enough to encompass its label; its height is the entire height of the frame.

C. The button is just tall enough to encompass its label; its width is the entire width of the frame.

D. The button is just wide enough to encompass its label, and its height is approximately half the frame's height.

E. The button's height is approximately half the frame's height. Its width is approximately half the frame's width.

Answer: A. The only lines of code that matter are 9, 10, 11, and 17. The button is added to a panel that uses a Flow layout manager. Therefore the button gets to be its preferred size.

7. An application has a frame that uses a Border layout manager. Why is it probably not a good idea to put a vertical scroll bar at North in the frame?

A. The scroll bar's height would be its preferred height, which is not likely to be high enough.

B. The scroll bar's width would be the entire width of the frame, which would be much wider than necessary.

C. Both A and B.

D. Neither A nor B. There is no problem with the layout as described.

Answer: C. With a Border layout manager, any component at North (or South) is as wide as the container and as tall as its own preferred height. A vertical scroll bar needs plenty of play in the vertical direction, but it does not need to be very wide. The problem produces a scroll bar that is both too wide and too short to be useful, so the correct answer is C. With a Border layout manager, vertical scroll bars are most useful at East and West; horizontal scroll bars are most useful at North and South.

8. What is the default layout manager for an applet? for a frame? for a panel?

   Answer: The default layout manager for panels and applets is Flow; the default for frames is Border

9. True or false: If a frame uses a Grid layout manager and does not contain any panels or other containers, then all the components within the frame are the same width and height.

   A. True

   B. False

   Answer: A. The Grid layout manager ignores the preferred size of its components and makes all components the same size. If the frame contained any panels, then the components within those panels would be likely to be smaller than those directly contained by the frame. However, the question explicitly states that the frame does not contain any panels.

10. True or false: If a frame uses its default layout manager and does not contain any panels, then all the components within the frame are the same width and height.

A. True

B. False

Answer: B. The default layout manager is Border. Components at North and South will be the same width; components at East and West will be the same height. No other generalizations are possible.

11. True or false: With a Border layout manager, the component at Center gets all the space that is left over, after the components at North and South have been considered.

    A. True

    B. False

    Answer: B. Almost, but not quite. The component at Center gets all the space that is left over, after the components at North, South, East, and West have been considered.

12. True or false: With a Grid layout manager, the preferred width of each component is honored, while height is dictated; if there are too many components to fit in a single row, additional rows are created.

    A. True

    B. False

    Answer: B. The question describes a hodgepodge of layout manager attributes.

13. For each of the following descriptions, select the layout manager or managers to which the description applies:

    A. Uses rows and columns of potentially unequal sizes.

    B. Constrains all components to the same sizes.

    C. Can resize some components along one axis while leaving them unchanged along the other when the container is resized on both axes.

    D. Can leave all component sizes unchanged regardless of container size changes.

E. Can align components that are separated by other components that do not share the same alignment.

F. Can simulate at least two other layout managers.

G. Lays components so only one is visible at a time.

Answer: A = GridBag
B = Grid
C = Border and GridBag
D = GridBag and Flow (also arguably Card)
E = GridBag
F = GridBag
G = Card

Chapter 10 Test Yourself

1. True or False: The event delegation model, introduced in release 1.1 of the JDK, is fully compatible with the 1.0 event model.

A. True

B. False

Answer: B. The two event models are incompatible, and they should not appear in the same program.

2. Which statement or statements are true about the code listed below?

```
1. public class MyTextArea extends TextArea {
2.   public MyTextArea(int nrows, int ncols) {
3.     enableEvents(AWTEvent.TEXT_EVENT_MASK);
4.   }
5.
6.   public void processTextEvent(TextEvent te) {
7.     System.out.println("Processing a text event.");
8.   }
9. }
```

A. The source code must appear in a file called MyTextArea.java.

B. Between lines 2 and 3, a call should be made to super(nrows, ncols) so that the new component will have the correct size.

C. At line 6, the return type of processTextEvent() should be declared boolean, not void.

D. Between lines 7 and 8, the following code should appear:
return true;

E. Between lines 7 and 8, the following code should appear:
super.processTextEvent(te);

Answer: A, B, E. Since the class is public, it must reside in a file whose name corresponds to the class name. If the call to super(nrows, ncols) is omitted, the no-arguments constructor for TextArea will be invoked, and the desired number of rows and columns will be ignored. C and D are attempts to create confusion by introducing concepts from the 1.0 model; in the delegation model, all event handlers have void return type. E is correct because if the suggested line is omitted, registered text listeners will be ignored.

3. Which statement or statements are true about the code listed below?

```
1. public class MyFrame extends Frame {
2.    public MyFrame(String title) {
3.      super(title);
4.      enableEvents(AWTEvent.WINDOW_EVENT_MASK);
5.    }
6.
7.    public void processWindowEvent(WindowEvent e) {
8.      System.out.println(
9.          "Processing a window event.");
10.   }
11. }
```

A. Adding a Window listener to an instance of MyFrame will result in a compiler error.

B. Adding a Window listener to an instance of MyFrame will result in the throwing of an exception at runtime.

C. Adding a Window listener to an instance of `MyFrame` will result in code that compiles cleanly and executes without throwing an exception.

D. A Window listener added to an instance of `MyFrame` will never receive notification of Window events.

Answer: C, D. The code will compile and execute cleanly. However, without a call to `super.processWindowEvent(e)`, the component will fail to notify its Window listeners.

4. Which statement or statements are true about the code fragment listed below? (Assume that classes `F1` and `F2` both implement the `FocusListener` interface.)

```
1. TextField tf = new TextField("Not tricky");
2. FocusListener flis1 = new F1();
3. FocusListener flis2 = new F2();
4. tf.addFocusListener(flis1);
5. tf.addFocusListener(flis2);
```

A. Lines 2 and 3 generate compiler errors.

B. Line 5 throws an exception at runtime.

C. The code compiles cleanly and executes without throwing an exception.

Answer: C. Lines 2 and 3 construct instances of the listener classes, and store references to those instances in variables with interface types; such assignment is perfectly legal. The implication of answer B is that adding a second listener might create a problem; however, the delegation model supports multiple listeners. The code compiles cleanly and runs without throwing an exception.

5. Which statement or statements are true about the code fragment listed below? (Assume that classes `F1` and `F2` both implement the `FocusListener` interface.)

```
1. TextField tf = new TextField("Not tricky");
2. FocusListener flis1 = new F1();
3. FocusListener flis2 = new F2();
```

```
4. tf.addFocusListener(flis1);
5. tf.addFocusListener(flis2);
6. tf.removeFocusListener(flis1);
```

A. Lines 2 and 3 generate compiler errors.

B. Line 6 generates a compiler error.

C. Line 5 throws an exception at runtime.

D. Line 6 throws an exception at runtime.

E. The code compiles cleanly and executes without throwing an exception.

Answer: E. Lines 2 and 3 construct instances of the listener classes, and store references to those instances in variables with interface types; such assignment is perfectly legal. The implication of answer C is that adding a second listener might create a problem; however, the delegation model supports multiple listeners. The code compiles cleanly and runs without throwing an exception.

6. Which statement or statements are true about the code fragment listed below?

```
1. class MyListener
2. extends MouseAdapter implements MouseListener {
3.    public void mouseEntered(MouseEvent mev) {
4.       System.out.println("Mouse entered.");
5.    }
6. }
```

A. The code compiles without error and defines a class that could be used as a Mouse listener.

B. The code will not compile correctly, because the class does not provide all the methods of the MouseListener interface.

C. The code compiles without error. The words implements MouseListener can be removed from line 2 without affecting the code's behavior in any way.

D. The code compiles without error. During execution, an exception will be thrown if a component uses this class as a Mouse listener and receives a mouse-exited event.

Answer: A, C. Since the class extends `MouseAdapter`, and `MouseAdapter` implements the `MouseListener` interface, the `MyListener` class implicitly implements the interface as well; it does no harm to declare the implementation explicitly. The class can serve as a Mouse listener. In response to mouse events other than mouse entered, the listener executes the handler methods that it inherits from its superclass; these methods do nothing.

7. Which statement or statements are true about the code fragment listed below? (Hint: The `ActionListener` and `ItemListener` interfaces each define a single method.)

```
1. class MyListener implements
2.   ActionListener, ItemListener {
3.   public void actionPerformed(ActionEvent ae) {
4.     System.out.println("Action.");
5.   }
6.
7.   public void itemStateChanged(ItemEvent ie) {
8.     System.out.println("Item");
9.   }
10. }
```

A. The code compiles without error and defines a class that could be used as an Action listener or as an Item listener.

B. The code generates a compiler error on line 2.

C. The code generates a compiler error on line 7.

Answer: A. Multiple interface implementation is legal in Java. The class must implement all methods of both interfaces, and this is indeed the case. Since the class implements the `ActionListener` interface, it is a legal Action listener; since it also implements the `ItemListener` interface, it is also a legal Item listener.

8. Which statement or statements are true about the code fragment listed below?

```
1. class MyListener extends MouseAdapter, KeyAdapter {
2.    public void mouseClicked(MouseEvent mev) {
3.       System.out.println("Mouse clicked.");
4.    }
5.
6.    public void keyPressed(KeyEvent kev) {
7.       System.out.println("KeyPressed.");
8.    }
9. }
```

A. The code compiles without error and defines a class that could be used as a Mouse listener or as a Key listener.

B. The code generates a compiler error on line 1.

C. The code generates a compiler error on line 6.

Answer: B. This class attempts multiple class inheritance, which is illegal in Java.

9. A component subclass that has executed `enableEvents()` to enable processing of a certain kind of event cannot also use an adapter as a listener for the same kind of event.

A. True

B. False

Answer: B. A component, whether or not it has explicitly called `enableEvents()`, can have an unlimited number of listeners, and those listeners may be adapter subclasses.

10. Assume that the class `AcLis` implements the `ActionListener` interface. The code fragment below constructs a button and gives it four Action listeners. When the button is pressed, which Action listener is the first to get its `actionPerformed()` method invoked?

```
1. Button btn = new Button("Hello");
2. AcLis a1 = new AcLis();
3. AcLis a2 = new AcLis();
```

```
 4. AcLis a3 = new AcLis();
 5. AcLis a4 = new AcLis();
 6. btn.addActionListener(a1);
 7. btn.addActionListener(a2);
 8. btn.addActionListener(a3);
 9. btn.addActionListener(a4);
10. btn.removeActionListener(a2);
11. btn.removeActionListener(a3);
12. btn.addActionListener(a3);
13. btn.addActionListener(a2);
```

A. a1 gets its `actionPerformed()` method invoked first.

B. a2 gets its `actionPerformed()` method invoked first.

C. a3 gets its `actionPerformed()` method invoked first.

D. a4 gets its `actionPerformed()` method invoked first.

E. It is impossible to know which listener will be first.

Answer: E. There are no guarantees about the order of invocation of event listeners.

Chapter 11 Test Yourself

1. A text field is constructed and then given a foreground color of white and a 64-point bold serif font. The text field is then added to an applet that has a foreground color of red, background color of blue, and 7-point plain sans-serif font. Which one statement below is true about the text field?

   A. Foreground color is black, background color is white, font is 64-point bold serif.

   B. Foreground color is red, background color is blue, font is 64-point bold serif.

   C. Foreground color is red, background color is blue, font is 7-point bold serif.

D. Foreground color is white, background color is blue, font is 7-point bold serif.

E. Foreground color is white, background color is blue, font is 64-point bold serif.

Answer: E. Since the text field does not specify a background, it gets the same background as the applet: blue. The text field's foreground color and font are explicitly set to white and 64-point bold serif, so these settings take effect rather than the applet's values.

2. You have a check box in a panel; the panel is in an applet. The applet contains no other components. Using `setFont()`, you give the applet a 100-point font, and you give the panel a 6-point font. Which statement or statements below are correct?

   A. The check box uses a 12-point font.

   B. The check box uses a 6-point font.

   C. The check box uses a 100-point font.

   D. The check box uses the applet's font, because you can't set a font on a panel.

   E. The check box uses the panel's font, because you did not explicitly set a font for the check box.

   Answer: B, E. Since you have not explicitly set a font for the check box, it uses the font of its immediate container.

3. You have a check box in a panel; the panel is in an applet. The applet contains no other components. Using `setFont()`, you give the applet a 100-point font. Which statement or statements below are correct?

   A. The check box uses a 12-point font.

   B. The check box uses a 6-point font.

   C. The check box uses a 100-point font.

   D. The check box uses the applet's font.

   E. The check box uses the panel's font, because you did not explicitly set a font for the check box.

Answer: C, D, E. The panel does not explicitly get its font set, so it uses the applet's font. The check box does not explicitly get its font set, so it uses the panel's font, which is the applet's font.

4. You want to construct a text area that is 80 character-widths wide and 10 character-heights tall. What code do you use?

   A. new TextArea(80, 10)

   B. new TextArea(10, 80)

   Answer: B. The number of rows comes first, then the number of columns.

5. You construct a list by calling new List(10, false). Which statement or statements below are correct? (Assume that layout managers do not modify the list in any way.)

   A. The list has 10 items.

   B. The list supports multiple selection.

   C. The list has up to 10 visible items.

   D. The list does not support multiple selection.

   E. The list will acquire a vertical scroll bar if needed.

   Answer: C, D, E. The first parameter (10) specifies the maximum number of *visible* items. The second parameter (false) specifies whether multiple selection is supported. A list always acquires a vertical scroll bar if the number of items exceeds the number of visible items.

6. A text field has a variable-width font. It is constructed by calling new TextField("iiiii"). What happens if you change the contents of the text field to "wwwww"? (Bear in mind that i is one of the narrowest characters, and w is one of the widest.)

   A. The text field becomes wider.

   B. The text field becomes narrower.

   C. The text field stays the same width; to see the entire contents you will have to scroll by using the

D. The text field stays the same width; to see the entire contents you will have to scroll by using the text field's horizontal scroll bar.

Answer: C. If a text field is too narrow to display its contents, you need to scroll using the arrow keys.

7. Which of the following may a menu contain? (Choose all that apply.)

   A. A separator

   B. A Checkbox

   C. A Menu

   D. A Button

   E. A Panel

   Answer: A, C. A menu may contain menu items, check-box menu items (*not* check boxes!), separators, and (sub)menus.

8. Which of the following may contain a menu bar? (Choose all that apply.)

   A. A panel

   B. A frame

   C. An applet

   D. A menu bar

   E. A menu

   Answer: B. Only a frame may contain a menu bar.

9. Your application constructs a frame by calling `Frame f = new Frame();`, but when you run the code, the frame does not appear on the screen. What code will make the frame appear? (Choose one.)

   A. `f.setSize(300, 200);`

   B. `f.setFont(new Font("SansSerif", Font.BOLD, 24));`

   C. `f.setForeground(Color.white);`

   D. `f.setVisible(true);`

E. `f.setSize(300, 200); f.setVisible(true);`

Answer: E. A newly constructed frame has zero-by-zero size and is not visible. You have to call both `setSize()` (or `setBounds()`) and `setVisible()`.

10. True or False: The `CheckboxGroup` class is a subclass of the `Component` class.

    A. True

    B. False

    Answer: B. The `java.awt.CheckboxGroup` class is not a kind of component.

Chapter 12 Test Yourself

1. How would you set the color of a graphics context *g* to cyan?

   A. `g.setColor(Color.cyan);`

   B. `g.setCurrentColor(cyan);`

   C. `g.setColor("Color.cyan");`

   D. `g.setColor("cyan");`

   E. `g.setColor(new Color(cyan));`

   Answer: A. The 13 pre-defined colors are static variables in class `Color`, so you access them via the class name as you would any other static variable. The name of the color-setting method is `setColor()`, not `setCurrentColor()`.

2. The code below draws a line. What color is the line?

   1. `g.setColor(Color.red.green.yellow.red.cyan);`
   2. `g.drawLine(0, 0, 100, 100);`

   A. Red

   B. Green

   C. Yellow

D. Cyan

E. Black

Answer: D. This question tests your knowledge of static variables as well as the `Color` class. The `Color` class has 13 final static variables, named `red`, `green`, `yellow`, and so on. These variables happen to be of type `Color`. So `Color.red` is the name of an instance of `Color`. Recall from Chapter 3, "Modifiers," that there are two ways to access a static variable: via the class name, which is the preferred way, or via a reference to any instance of the class. Thus one (non-preferred) way to access the `green` static variable is via `Color.red`, because `Color.red` is a reference to an instance. Thus `Color.red.green` is a legal way to refer to the `green` static variable. Similarly, the preferred way to refer to the `yellow` static variable is `Color.yellow`, but it is legal (although very strange) to reference it as `Color.red.green` `.yellow`, because `Color.red.green` is a reference to an instance. And so on. The answer would still be cyan if the color were set to `Color.red.white.red.black.cyan.magenta.blue.pink` `.orange.cyan`.

3. What does the following code draw?

```
1. g.setColor(Color.black);
2. g.drawLine(10, 10, 10, 50);
3. g.setColor(Color.red);
4. g.drawRect(100, 100, 150, 150);
```

A. A red vertical line that is 40 pixels long and a red square with sides of 150 pixels

B. A black vertical line that is 40 pixels long and a red square with sides of 150 pixels

C. A black vertical line that is 50 pixels long and a red square with sides of 150 pixels

D. A red vertical line that is 50 pixels long and a red square with sides of 150 pixels

E. A black vertical line that is 40 pixels long and a red square with sides of 100 pixels

Answer: B. The `setColor()` method affects only *subsequently drawn* graphics; it does not affect *previously drawn* graphics. Thus the line is black and the square is red. The arguments to `drawLine()` are coordinates of endpoints, so the line goes from (10, 10) to (10, 50) and its length is 40 pixels. The arguments to `drawRect()` are *x* position, *y* position, *width*, and *height*, so the square's side is 150 pixels.

Some readers may feel that a different answer is appropriate: "None of the above, because you never said that g was an instance of `Graphics`." This is legitimate; the real issue is what to do when you have this reaction during the Certification Exam. Always bear in mind that the exam questions are about Java, not about rhetoric. The exam tests your knowledge of Java, not your ability to see through tricky phrasing.

4. In the illustration shown, which shape (A or B) is drawn by the following line of code?

   ```
   g.fillArc(10, 10, 100, 100, 0, 90);
   ```

   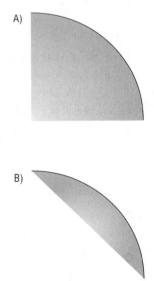

   A)

   B)

Answer: A. The `fillArc()` method draws pie pieces, not chords.

5. Which of the statements below are true? (Choose one or more.)

   A. A polyline is always filled.

B. A polyline cannot be filled.

C. A polygon is always filled.

D. A polygon is always closed.

E. A polygon may be filled or not filled.

Answer: B, D, E. A polyline is never filled or closed; it is just an open run of line segments. A polygon may be filled (the `fillPolygon()` method) or not filled (the `drawPolygon()` method).

6. True or False: When the GUI thread calls `paint()` in order to repair exposure damage, the `paint()` method must determine what was damaged and set its clip region appropriately.

A. True

B. False

Answer: B. When there is damage to be repaired, the GUI thread passes to `paint()` a graphics context whose clip region is already set to the damaged region. Java was built this way to make sure that programmers never have to determine damaged clip regions. In fact, programmers never have to do anything at all about exposure damage, provided all drawing is done in `paint()` or in methods called by `paint()`.

7. Your `mouseDragged()` event handler and your `paint()` method look like this:

```
1. public void mouseDragged(MouseEvent e) {
2.    mouseX = e.getX();
3.    mouseY = e.getY();
4.    repaint();
5. }
6.
7. public void paint(Graphics g) {
8.    g.setColor(Color.cyan);
9.    g.drawLine(mouseX, mouseY, mouseX+9, mouseY+9);
10. }
```

You want to modify your code so that the cyan lines accumulate on the screen, rather than getting erased every time `repaint()` calls `update()`. You know that your program's window will never be obscurred, minimized, nor otherwise damaged. What is the simplest way to proceed?

A. On line 4, replace `repaint()` with `paint()`.

B. On line 4, replace `repaint()` with `update()`.

C. After line 7, add this: `super.update(g);`

D. Add the following method:
```
public void update(Graphics g) {paint(g);}
```

Answer: D. This is a standard technique whenever you don't want `update()` to wipe the screen before calling `paint()`. All the diagonal cyan lines will remain on the screen; the effect will be like drawing with a calligraphy pen. Answers A and B (on line 4, replace `repaint()` with `paint()` or `update()`) will not compile, because both `paint()` and `update()` require a `Graphics` as an input. Answer C is serious trouble: `super.update(g)` will clear the screen and call `paint(g)`, which will call `super.update(g)`, and so on forever.

8. What code would you use to construct a 24-point bold serif font?

A. `new Font(Font.SERIF, 24, Font.BOLD);`

B. `new Font("Serif", 24, "Bold");`

C. `new Font("Bold", 24, Font.SERIF);`

D. `new Font("Serif", Font.BOLD, 24);`

E. `new Font(Font.SERIF, "Bold", 24);`

Answer: D. The signature for the `Font` constructor is `Font(String fontname, int style, int size)`. The font name can be one of `"Serif"`, `"SansSerif"`, or `"Monospaced"`. The style should be one of `Font.PLAIN`, `Font.BOLD`, or `Font.ITALIC`, or a combination of these.

9. What does the following `paint()` method draw?

```
1. public void paint(Graphics g) {
2.    g.drawString("question #9", 10, 0);
3. }
```

A. The string "question #9", with its top-left corner at 10, 0

B. A little squiggle coming down from the top of the component, a little way in from the left edge

Answer: B. The y-coordinate parameter passed into `drawString()` is the vertical position of the baseline of the text. Since the baseline is at 0 (that is, the top of the component) only descenders will be visible. The string "question #9" contains one descender, so only a single descending squiggle from the *q* will be seen.

10. What does the following `paint()` method draw?

```
1. public void paint(Graphics g) {
2.    g.drawOval(100, 100, 44);
3. }
```

A. A circle at (100, 100) with radius of 44

B. A circle at (100, 44) with radius of 100

C. A circle at (100, 44) with radius of 44

D. The code does not compile.

Answer: D. The signature for `drawOval()` is `drawOval(int x, int y, int width, int height)`, where *x* and *y* define the upper-left corner of the oval's bounding box, and *width* and *height* define the bounding box's size. The question points out the common misconception that *x* and *y* define the center of the oval.

Chapter 13 Test Yourself

1. Which of the statements below are true? (Choose none, some, or all.)

   A. UTF characters are all 8 bits.

   B. UTF characters are all 16 bits.

   C. UTF characters are all 24 bits.

   D. Unicode characters are all 16 bits.

   E. Bytecode characters are all 16 bits.

   F. None of the above.

   Answer: D. UTF characters are as big as they need to be. Unicode characters are all 16 bits. There is no such thing as a bytecode character; bytecode is the format generated by the Java compiler.

2. Which of the statements below are true? (Choose none, some, or all.)

   A. When you construct an instance of `File`, if you do not use the file-naming semantics of the local machine, the constructor will throw an `IOException`.

   B. When you construct an instance of `File`, if the corresponding file does not exist on the local file system, one will be created.

   C. When an instance of `File` is garbage collected, the corresponding file on the local file system is deleted.

   D. None of the above.

   Answer: D. All three statements are false. Construction and garbage collection of a `File` have no effect on the local file system.

3. True or False: The `File` class contains a method that changes the current working directory.

   A. True

   B. False

   Answer: B. The `File` class does not provide a way to change the current working directory.

4. True or False: It is possible to use the `File` class to list the contents of the current working directory.

   A. True

   B. False

Answer: A. The code below shows how this is done:

```
1. File f = new File(".");
2. String contents[] = f.list();
```

5. How many bytes does the following code write to file `dest`?

```
1. try {
2.   FileOutputStream fos = newFileOutputStream("dest");
3.   DataOutputStream dos = new DataOutputStream(fos);
4.   dos.writeInt(3);
5.   dos.writeDouble(0.0001);
6.   dos.close();
7.   fos.close();
8. }
9. catch (IOException e) { }
```

   A. 2

   B. 8

   C. 12

   D. 16

   E. The number of bytes depends on the underlying system.

Answer: C. The `writeInt()` call writes out an `int`, which is 4 bytes long; the `writeDouble()` call writes out a `double`, which is 8 bytes long, for a total of 12 bytes.

6. What does the following code fragment print out at line 9?

```
1. FileOutputStream fos = new FileOutputStream("xx");
2. for (byte b=10; b<50; b++)
3.   fos.write(b);
4. fos.close();
```

```
5. RandomAccessFile raf = new RandomAccessFile("xx", "r");
6. raf.seek(10);
7. int i = raf.read();
8. raf.close()
9. System.out.println("i = " + i);
```

A. The output is i = 30.

B. The output is i = 20.

C. The output is i = 10.

D. There is no output because the code throws an exception at line 1.

E. There is no output because the code throws an exception at line 5.

Answer: B. All the code is perfectly legal, so no exceptions are thrown. The first byte in the file is 10, the next byte is 11, the next is 12, and so on. The byte at file position 10 is 20, so the output is i = 20.

7. A file is created with the following code:

```
1. FileOutputStream fos = new FileOutputStream("datafile");
2. DataOutputStream dos = new DataOutputStream(fos);
3. for (int i=0; i<500; i++)
4.     dos.writeInt(i);
```

You would like to write code to read back the data from this file. Which solutions listed below will work?

A. Construct a FileInputStream, passing the name of the file. Onto the FileInputStream, chain a DataInputStream, and call its readInt() method.

B. Construct a FileReader, passing the name of the file. Call the file reader's readInt() method.

C. Construct a PipedInputStream, passing the name of the file. Call the piped input stream's readInt() method.

D. Construct a RandomAccessFile, passing the name of the file. Call the random access file's readInt() method.

    E. Construct a `FileReader`, passing the name of the file. Onto the `FileReader`, chain a `DataInputStream`, and call its `readInt()` method.

Answer: A, D. Solution A chains a data input stream onto a file input stream. D simply uses the `RandomAccessFile` class. B fails because the `FileReader` class has no `readInt()` method; readers and writers only handle text. C fails because the `PipedInputStream` class has nothing to do with file I/O. (Piped input and output streams are used in inter-thread communication.) E fails because you cannot chain a data input stream onto a file reader. Readers read `chars`, and input streams handle bytes.

8. True or False: Readers have methods that can read and return `floats` and `doubles`.

    A. True

    B. False

Answer: B. Readers and writers only deal with character I/O.

9. You execute the code below in an empty directory. What is the result?

```
1. File f1 = new File("dirname");
2. File f2 = new File(f1, "filename");
```

    A. A new directory called `dirname` is created in the current working directory.

    B. A new directory called `dirname` is created in the current working directory. A new file called `filename` is created in directory `dirname`.

    C. A new directory called `dirname` and a new file called `filename` are created, both in the current working directory.

    D. A new file called `filename` is created in the current working directory.

    E. No directory is created, and no file is created.

Answer: E. Constructing an instance of the `File` class has no effect on the local file system.

10. What is the result of attempting to compile and execute the code fragment below? Assume that the code fragment is part of an application that has write permission in the current working directory. Also assume that before execution, the current working directory does *not* contain a file called `datafile`.

```
1. try {
2.    RandomAccessFile raf = new
3.       RandomAccessFile("datafile" ,"rw");
4.    BufferedOutputStream bos = new
5.       BufferedOutputStream(raf);
6.    DataOutputStream dos = new
7.       DataOutputStream(bos);
8.    dos.writeDouble(Math.PI);
9.    dos.close();
10.   bos.close();
11.   raf.close();
12. }
13. catch (IOException e) { }
```

A. The code fails to compile.

B. The code compiles, but throws an exception at line 4.

C. The code compiles and executes, but has no effect on the local file system.

D. The code compiles and executes; afterward, the current working directory contains a file called `datafile`.

Answer: A. Compilation fails at lines 4 and 5, because there is no constructor for `BufferedOutputStream` that takes a `RandomAccessFile` object as a parameter. You can be sure of this even if you are not familiar with buffered output streams, because random-access files are completely incompatible with the stream/reader/writer model.

Appendix

B

Programmer's Final Exam

If you have mastered the content of Part I of this book, and if you have done well on the sample questions at the end of each chapter, you are probably in good shape to take the Programmer's Exam. To make sure, try the following sample test, which is your final exam for the first part of this book.

For best results, simulate actual test conditions as closely as possible. Get one piece of blank, unlined paper out of your printer. Close all your books. Except this one! (You didn't close this one, did you?) But don't look at any pages outside of this appendix. If temptation is a problem for you, or if you just prefer to do things on a computer, insert the CD-ROM that came with this book and take the test electronically.

This final exam has 50 questions. You have one hour and forty minutes. The answers can be found at the end of this appendix. Good luck!

NOTE   The CD-ROM supplied with this book contains a Java program that allows you to test yourself, with these questions and the ones from each chapter. Appendix C describes how to take the test on your computer.

1. In the code fragment below, what are the legal data types for the variable "answer"?

```
byte b=1;
char c=2;
short s=3;
int i=4;
float f=5f;
answer = b*c*s*i*f;
```

A. byte

B. char

C. short

D. int

E. float

F. double

G. long

2. What does the following code print out?

```
1. try {
2.    int i = -5 % -3;
3.    System.out.println("i = " + i);
4. }
5. catch (Exception e) {
6.    System.out.println("TROUBLE"); }
```

A. i = 2

B. i = 3

C. i = –2

D. i = –3

E. TROUBLE

3. When you run the following application, which component is responsible for painting the pixel at the extreme bottom-right of the interior of the frame?

```java
import java.awt.*;
class A {
  private final static String[] regions = {
    BorderLayout.NORTH, BorderLayout.WEST,
    BorderLayout.SOUTH, BorderLayout.EAST,
    BorderLayout.CENTER };
  public static void main(String[] args) {
    Frame f = new Frame();
    f.setSize(800, 800);
    for (int i=0; i<regions.length; i++) {
      Scrollbar s =
        new Scrollbar(Scrollbar.HORIZONTAL);
      f.add(s, regions[i]);
    }
    f.setVisible(true);
  }
}
```

A. The scrollbar at North

B. The scrollbar at South

C. The scrollbar at East

D. The scrollbar at West

E. The scrollbar at Center

4. Which of the following statements is/are true?

    A. The RandomAccessFile class does not provide a method that positions the file's file pointer.

    B. The RandomAccessFile class provides a method that positions the file's file pointer relative to the beginning of the file.

    C. The RandomAccessFile class provides a method that positions the file's file pointer relative to the current file pointer position.

    D. The RandomAccessFile class provides a method that positions the file's file pointer relative to the end of the file.

5. Pick all the true statements.

    A. If a thread wants to call wait() on an object, the thread must own that object's lock.

    B. There is a method that you can call on an instance of the Thread class that puts the instance to sleep for a specified number of milliseconds.

    C. At the moment when a thread is notified, it automatically gets the lock of the object for which it was waiting.

6. In the code fragment below, what is the value of *k* after line 3 executes?

```
1. int i = -1;
2. int j = i >> 3;
3. int k = j & 129;
```

    A. −1

    B. 0

    C. 129

    D. A very large negative number

    E. A very large positive number

7. What happens when you attempt to compile and execute the following application?

```
1. class XXX {
2.    public static void main(String[] args) {
3.       String s1 = "abcde";
4.       String s2 = "abcde";
5.       s1.toUpperCase();
6.       if (s1 == s2)
7.          System.out.println("YES");
8.       else
9.          System.out.println("NO");
10.   }
11. }
```

A. Compiler error.

B. The program prints out "YES".

C. The program prints out "NO".

8. In the code below, does line 7 compile?

```
1.  class Outside {
2.     private final float i = 1.23f;
3.
4.     void amethod(float j) {
5.        class Inside {
6.           void innerFoo() {
7.              float k = i + j;
8.              System.out.println("k = " + k);
9.           }
10.       }
11.    }
12. }
```

A. Yes

B. No

9. What statement or statements is/are true concerning the following code?

```
1. class X {
2.    public static void main(String[] a) {
3.       try {
4.          short s = 0x00FD;
5.          byte b = (byte)s;
6.          System.out.println("b = " + b);
7.       }
8.       catch (Exception e) {
9.          System.out.println("TROUBLE!");
10.       }
11.    }
12. }
```

A. It generates a compiler error at line 4.

B. It generates a compiler error at line 5.

C. If the cast on line 5 were omitted, then line 5 would not compile.

D. The code compiles and prints "b = 0".

E. The code compiles and prints "b = –2".

F. The code compiles and prints "b = –3".

G. The code compiles and prints "TROUBLE".

10. What happens when you run the following application?

```
1. class Q extends Thread {
2.    public void run() {
3.       for (int i=0; i<1000; i++)
4.          System.out.println(i);
5.    }
6.
7.    public static void main(String[] args) {
8.       Q that = new Q();
9.       that.run();
10.      for (int j=999; j>=0; j--)
11.         System.out.println(j);
12.   }
13. }
```

A. The code concurrently counts up to 999 and down from 999.

B. The code first counts up to 999, and then counts down from 999.

C. The code first counts down from 999, and then counts up to 999.

11. When you run the following application, which component is responsible for painting the pixel at the center of the interior of the Frame?

```
import java.awt.*;
class A {
  public static void main(String[] args) {
    Frame f = new Frame();
    f.setSize(801, 801);
    Scrollbar sbar1 =
      new Scrollbar(Scrollbar.VERTICAL);
    f.add(sbar1, BorderLayout.WEST);
    Scrollbar sbar2 =
      new Scrollbar(Scrollbar.HORIZONTAL);
    f.add(sbar2, BorderLayout.NORTH);
    Button btn = new Button("PushMe");
    f.add(btn, BorderLayout.CENTER);
    f.setVisible(true);
  }
}
```

 A. The horizontal scrollbar

 B. The vertical scrollbar

 C. The button

12. What happens when you attempt to compile the following code?

```
1. class Xyz {
2.   protected String toString() {
3.     return super.toString();
4.   }
5. }
```

 A. Compiler error at line 2

 B. Compiler error at line 3

 C. No compiler error

13. What is the effect of attempting to compile the following code and then execute the Child application?

```
1. public class Papa {
2.    int i;
3.    Papa(int j) { i = j; }
4. }
5.
6. class Child extends Papa {
7.    Child() { i = 5; }
8.    public static void main(String[] args) {
9.      new Child();
10.   }
11. }
```

A. Compiler error at line 6.

B. Compiler error at line 7.

C. Compiler error at line 9.

D. The code compiles but throws an exception when the application is executed.

E. The code compiles and executes with no problems.

14. What is the result of attempting to compile and execute the following application?

```
1. public class X {
2.    public static void main(String[] args) {
3.       int i = Math.ceil(-Math.PI);
4.       System.out.println("i = " + i);
5.    }
6. }
```

A. Compiler error at line 3.

B. The code compiles and prints out a value of 3.

C. The code compiles and prints out a value of 4.

D. The code compiles and prints out a value of –3.

E. The code compiles and prints out a value of –4.

15. Which statement or statements is/are true about the following code, when run as an application?

```
 1. class X {
 2.    public static void main(String[] args) {
 3.       try {
 4.          int i = (-1 >> 65535) + 1;
 5.          int j = 5 / i;
 6.          System.out.println("End of try block");
 7.       }
 8.       catch (Exception e) { System.exit(0); }
 9.       finally { System.out.println("FINALLY!"); }
10.    }
11. }
```

A. The program doesn't print anything.

B. The program prints "End of try block".

C. The program prints "FINALLY".

16. Does the following code compile? If not, where is the first compiler error?

```
1. interface Inter { }
2.
3. class A implements Inter { }
4.
5. class B extends A {
6.    A a = new B();
7.    Inter i = a;
8. }
```

   A. The code compiles without error.

   B. Compiler error at line 6.

   C. Compiler error at line 7.

17. Which of the following code fragments generate compiler errors? Select all that do.

   A. `boolean boo = true;    int i = boo;`

   B. `byte b = 5;    char c = b;`

   C. `char c1 = 'a';    short s = c1;`

   D. `long lon = 1L;    float f = lon;`

   E. `float f1 = 2L;    long lon1 = f1;`

18. Which of the lines are printed out by the following application?

```
1. import java.io.IOException;
2. class SubEx extends IOException { }
3.
4. class A {
5.   public static void main(String[] args) {
6.     try {
7.       thud();
8.     }
9.     catch (IOException x) {
10.      System.out.println(
11.        "main() caught IOException");
12.    }
13.    catch (Exception x) {
14.      System.out.println(
15.        "main() caught Exception");
16.    }
17.  }
18.
19.  static void thud() throws IOException {
20.    try {
21.      throw new SubEx();
22.    }
23.    catch (IOException x) {
24.      System.out.println(
25.        "thud() caught IOException");
26.      throw new SubEx();
27.    }
28.    catch (Exception x){
29.      System.out.println(
30.        "thud() caught Exception");
31.    }
32.  }
33. }
```

A. "main() caught IOException"

B. "main() caught Exception"

C. "thud() caught IOException"

D. "thud() caught Exception"

19. True or false: All methods in all event listener interfaces in the java.awt.event package have the same return type.

A. True

B. False

20. The following application displays a frame that contains several components. Which component is responsible for painting the top-left pixel of the frame's interior?

```java
import java.awt.*;
class A {
  public static void main(String[] args) {
    Frame f = new Frame();
    f.setSize(600, 300);
    Panel top = new Panel();
    top.setLayout(new FlowLayout(FlowLayout.RIGHT));
    top.add(new Checkbox("Cbox"));
    f.add(top, BorderLayout.NORTH);
    Panel left = new Panel();
    left.setLayout(new GridLayout(1, 2));
    left.add(new Scrollbar(Scrollbar.VERTICAL));
    left.add(new Button("Button"));
    f.add(left, BorderLayout.WEST);
    f.setVisible(true);
  }
}
```

A. The checkbox

B. The scrollbar

C. The button

D. The "top" panel

E. The "left" panel

21. What is the result of attempting to compile the following code?

```
1.   class OutThing {
2.
3.     class AnInner {
4.       public int i;
5.     }
6.
7.     public static void main(String[] args) {
8.       AnInner aninn = new AnInner();
9.       aninn.i = 15;
10.    }
11.  }
```

A. The code compiles without error.

B. Compiler error on line 4.

C. Compiler error on line 8.

D. Compiler error on line 9.

22. When application A is run, two threads are created and started. Each thread prints a message just before terminating. Which thread prints its message first?

```
class A {
  private Thread t1, t2;
  public static void main(String[] args) {
    new A();
  }

  A() {
    t1 = new T1();
    t2 = new T2();
    t1.start();
    t2.start();
  }
  class T1 extends Thread {
    public void run() {
      try {
        sleep(5000); // 5 secs
      }
      catch (InterruptedException e) { }
      System.out.println("t1 done");
    }
  }
  class T2 extends Thread {
    public void run() {
      try {
        t1.sleep(10000); // 10 secs
      }
      catch (InterruptedException e) { }
      System.out.println("t2 done");
    }
  }
}
```

A. t1

B. t2

23. If a Java program imports a large number of classes, what is the
runtime impact?

    A. There is no impact at runtime.

    B. There is a slight impact at runtime.

    C. There is a moderate impact at runtime.

    D. There is a significant impact at runtime.

24. Which of the lines below are printed out by the following application?

```
1. import java.io.IOException;
2. class SubEx extends IOException { }
3.
4. class A {
5.    public static void main(String[] args) {
6.       try {
7.          thud();
8.       }
9.       catch (SubEx x) {
10.         System.out.println("main() caught SubEx");
11.      }
12.      catch (IOException x) {
13.         System.out.println(
14.            "main() caught IOException");
15.      }
16.      catch (Exception x) {
17.         System.out.println(
18.            "main() caught Exception");
19.      }
20.   }
21.
22.   static void thud() throws IOException {
23.      try {
24.         throw new SubEx();
25.      }
26.      catch (SubEx x) {
```

```
27.          System.out.println("thud() caught SubEx");
28.          throw new IOException();
29.      }
30.      catch (IOException x) {
31.        System.out.println(
32.          "thud() caught IOException");
33.        throw new IOException();
34.      }
35.      catch (Exception x){
36.        System.out.println(
37.          "thud() caught Exception");
38.      }
39.    }
40. }
```

A. "main() caught SubEx"

B. "main() caught IOException"

C. "main() caught Exception"

D. "thud() caught SubEx"

E. "thud() caught IOException"

F. "thud() caught Exception"

25. What happens when you attempt to compile the following code?

```
1. class A          { static void foo(int i) {}; }
2. class B extends A { void foo(int i) {}; }
```

A. Compiler error at line 1

B. Compiler error at line 2

C. No compiler error

26. Consider the following class definition:

```
class Parent {
  void abcde(int i) throws IOException {
    if (i>10) throw new IOException();
  }
}
```

Which of these methods would be allowed in a subclass of `Parent`?

A. `protected void abcde(int i) throws IOException`

B. `private void abcde(int i) throws IOException`

C. `void abcde(int j) throws IOException`

D. `float abcde(int i) throws IOException`

E. `void abcde(int i)`

27. What is the value of the following expression?

`Math.round(Math.random() + 2.50001);`

A. 2

B. 3

C. It is impossible to say.

28. What one statement is true about the following code?

```
1. Map map = new HashMap();
2. map.put("key", "Hello");
3. map.put("key", "Goodbye");
```

A. Line 3 generates a compiler error.

B. An exception is thrown at line 3.

C. After line 3 executes, the map contains one entry: the string "Hello".

D. After line 3 executes, the map contains one entry: the string "Goodbye".

E. After line 3 executes, the map contains two entries.

29. A computer is manufactured and shipped to Tibet. When the computer's operating system is installed, it is told that it is in the Tibet locale. When the computer executes the following line, what encoding is used by the File Reader?

```
FileReader fr = new FileReader("8859_1");
```

A. Tibetan

B. U.S. ASCII

30. What happens when you try to compile and execute the following application, invoked by typing **java Switcheroo 1**? (Choose all that apply.)

```
1. class Switcheroo {
2.   public static void main(String[] args) {
3.     long i = 0;
4.     try {
5.       i = Integer.parseInt(args[0]);
6.     }
7.     catch (Exception e) { }
8.
9.     switch (i) {
10.       case 0:
11.         System.out.println("zero");
12.       case 1:
13.         System.out.println("one");
14.       default:
15.         System.out.println("default");
16.     }
17.   }
18. }
```

A. Compiler error.

B. The program prints "zero".

C. The program prints "one".

D. The program prints "default"

31. Which of the following statements are true? Choose all correct answers.

   A. You can directly read text from a FileReader.

   B. You can directly write text to a FileWriter.

   C. You can directly read `ints` and `floats` from a FileReader.

   D. You can directly write `longs` and `shorts` to a FileWriter.

   E. You can directly read text from a RandomAccessFileReader.

32. In the code listed below, how many key-value pairs are contained in the map after line 6 executes?

```
1. Map map = new HashMap();
2. map.put("1", "1");
3. map.put("2", "2");
4. map.put("3", "3");
5. map.put("1", "3");
6. map.put("4", "1");
```

   A. 1

   B. 2

   C. 3

   D. 4

   E. 5

33. If a superclass and a subclass are in two different packages, can the subclass override a protected method of the superclass?

   A. Yes

   B. No

34. Which of the following code fragments throw `ArithmeticException`?

A. `int i=1; i = i<<32;`

B. `int i=1; i = i>>1;`

C. `int i=1; i = i>>>1;`

D. `int i=1; int j = i>>>1; int k = i/j;`

E. `int i=0x7FFF; i *= 5;`

F. None of the above

35. Does the code below compile?

```
1.  class SubEx extends Exception { }
2.
3.  class Parent {
4.    void foo(int i) throws Exception {
5.      if (i > 20)
6.        throw new Exception();
7.    }
8.  }
9.
10. class Kid extends Parent {
11.   void foo(int i) throws SubEx {
12.     if (i < 20)
13.       throw new SubEx();
14.   }
15. }
```

A. Yes

B. No

36. Consider the following code:

```
1. interface Inter { }
2. class A { }
3. class B extends A implements Inter { }
4. class C extends B {
5.    public static void main(String[] args) {
6.       A a = new A();
7.       B b = new B();
8.       C c = new C();
9.       if (a instanceof B)
10.        System.out.println("Hello");
11.      if (b instanceof A)
12.        System.out.println("Hello");
13.      if (c instanceof C)
14.        System.out.println("Hello");
15.      if (c instanceof Inter)
16.        System.out.println("Hello");
17.    }
18. }
```

When you run class C as an application, which of the following lines execute? (Choose all that apply.)

A. Line 10

B. Line 12

C. Line 14

D. Line 16

37. True or false: It is legal to instantiate a class that contains abstract methods, provided you do not call any of those abstract methods.

A. True

B. False

38. What happens when you try to compile the following code and execute the Dolphin application?

```
1. class Animal { }
2. class Mammal extends Animal { }
3. class Cat extends Mammal { }
4. class Dolphin extends Mammal {
5.    public static void main(String[] args) {
6.       Mammal m = new Cat();
7.       Animal a = m;
8.       Dolphin d = (Dolphin)a;
9.    }
10. }
```

A. The code compiles with no errors and runs without throwing any exceptions.

B. Compiler error at line 6.

C. Compiler error at line 7.

D. Compiler error at line 8.

E. The code compiles without error but throws an exception at line 6.

F. The code compiles without error but throws an exception at line 7.

G. The code compiles without error but throws an exception at line 8.

39. How many objects are created by the code listed below?

```
1. String s1 = "abc";
2. String s2 = s1;
3. String s3 = "abc";
```

A. None

B. 1

C. 2

D. 3

40. Which of the following is/are true?

   A. A static method may be overridden by a static method.

   B. A static method may be overridden by a non-static method.

   C. A non-static method may be overridden by a static method.

   D. A non-static method may be overridden by a final non-static method.

41. The code below creates a button and a scrollbar, and adds them to a frame.

```
1.  Frame frame = new Frame();
2.  frame.setSize(450, 450);
3.  Panel pan1 = new Panel();
4.  pan1.setLayout(new GridLayout(2, 1));
5.  Panel pan2 = new Panel();
6.  Button b = new Button("B");
7.  pan2.add(b);
8.  pan1.add(pan2);
9.  Scrollbar bar =
10.    new Scrollbar(Scrollbar.HORIZONTAL);
11. pan1.add(bar);
12. frame.add(pan1, BorderLayout.NORTH);
13. frame.setVisible(true);
```

What is the button's height?

   A. The button's preferred height

   B. Something other than the button's preferred height

42. What does the following code print out?

```
1. byte b1 = -5;
2. int i = 0xff;
3. byte b2 = (byte)(b1 ^ i);
4. b2++;
5. System.out.println(b2);
```

A. 4

B. −4

C. 5

D. −5

E. 6

F. −6

43. What method/methods of the KeyEvent class provide X and Y information about the event?

A. There are no methods that provide this information.

B. `int getX()` and `int getY()`

C. `Point getXY()`

D. `void getXY(Point p)`

44. Which of the following statements is/are true?

A. After a blocked thread becomes unblocked, it must enter the Ready state before it can run.

B. After a sleeping thread wakes up, it must enter the Ready state before it can run.

C. After a waiting thread gets notified, it must enter the Ready state before it can run.

D. After a waiting thread gets notified, it must acquire the lock of the object for which it was waiting, before it can run.

45. Does the following line of code compile?

```
byte b = 5;
```

A. Yes

B. No

46. What one statement is true about the following code fragment?

```
1. byte b1 = 32;
2. byte b2 = 3;
3. int i = 5 << (b1+b2);
```

A. The code generates a compiler error at line 3.

B. The code throws an exception at line 3.

C. After line 3 executes, the value of *i* is 0.

D. After line 3 executes, the value of *i* is 5.

E. After line 3 executes, the value of *i* is 40.

47. Consider the following class definition:

```
class Parent {
  void abcde(int i) throws IOException {
    if (i>10) throw new IOException();
  }
}
```

Which of the following methods would be allowed in a subclass of
Parent? (Choose all permitted methods.) Note: EOFException is a
subclass of IOException.

A. void abcde(byte i)

B. void abcde(byte i) throws Exception

C. float abcde(byte i) throws EOFException

D. void abcde(byte i) throws EOFException, IOException

E. static void abcde(int j) throws IOException

48. What happens when you try to compile and run the following application? (Assume `java.awt.Button` is imported.)

```
 1. class Z extends java.awt.Label {
 2.    private static double d;
 3.
 4.    public static void main(String[] args) {
 5.      Inner inny = new Inner();
 6.    }
 7.
 8.    class Inner extends Button implements Runnable {
 9.      Inner() { d = Math.PI; }
10.      public void run() { }
11.    }
12. }
```

A. Compiler error at line 5.

B. Compiler error at line 8.

C. Compiler error at line 9.

D. The code compiles but throws an exception at runtime.

E. The code compiles and runs without throwing any exceptions.

49. Consider the following class definition:

```
class Parent {
  void abcde(int i) throws IOException {
    if (i>10) throw new IOException();
  }
}
```

Which of the following methods would be allowed in a subclass of Parent? (Choose all permitted methods.) Note: EOFException is a subclass of IOException.

A. void abcde(int i)

B. void abcde(int i) throws Exception

C. void abcde(int j) throws IOException

D. void abcde(int i) throws EOFException

E. void abcde(int j) throws IOException, EOFException

50. What happens when you attempt to compile and execute the following application?

```
1. class Duck {
2.    private int i;
3.
4.    private void printOtherDucksI(Duck otherDuck) {
5.       System.out.println("Other = " + otherDuck.i);
6.    }
7.
8.    public static void main(String[] args) {
9.       Duck d1 = new Duck();
10.      Duck d2 = new Duck();
11.      d1.printOtherDucksI(d2);
12.    }
13. }
```

A. Compiler error at line 5.

B. Compiler error at line 11.

C. Exception thrown at line 5.

D. The application prints out: "Other = 0".

Answers to Programmer's Final Exam

1. **E, F.** The result of the multiple arithmetic is either `int` or the widest of the operand types, whichever is wider. Here the widest operand type is `float`, which is wider than `int`, so the result type is `float`. The variable "answer" may be `float` or any type that is wider than `float`. The only type that is wider than `float` is `double`.

2. **C.** We repeatedly subtract the right operand (–3) from the left operand (–5), until the magnitude of the result is less than the magnitude of the right operand (–3). Thus –5 – (–3) = –2.

3. **B.** Some of these horizontal scrollbars (the ones at West, Center, and East) will look very strange, but that isn't relevant to this question. Whenever there is a component at South of a Border Layout, that component manages the bottom-right pixel.

4. **B.** The RandomAccessFile class has a `seek(long position)` method, whose argument is the desired offset from the beginning of the file. There are no methods for seeking relative to the current position or the end of the file.

5. **A.** A thread must own the lock of an object it attempts to wait on; otherwise an exception will be thrown. B is incorrect because the `sleep()` method is static; it always puts to sleep the currently executing thread. C is incorrect because a notified thread enters the Seeking-Lock state; at the moment of notification the lock is never available, because the thread that called `notify()` still holds it.

6. **C.** After line 1, *i* is a negative `int` with a 1 in every bit position. It doesn't matter how many bit positions are shifted in line 2; since the >> operator preserves the sign bit; the result is still an `int` with a 1 in every bit position. AND'ing with 129 in line 3 yields 129, since (all 1's) AND anything = anything.

7. B.   The call on line 5 does not modify the original string; it only creates a new uppercase string, which soon gets garbage collected because there are no references to it. The string on line 3 is put in the literal string pool. Line 4 does not create a new string; it reuses the one in the literal pool. That is why the comparison on line 6—which tests whether the two arguments are references to the same object, as distinguished from two objects that have the same contents—is true.

8. B.   If an inner class (`Inside`) is contained within an enclosing method (`amethod()`), then the inner class may only access the variables of the enclosing method if those variables are final. Line 7 attempts to read `j`, which is not final.

9. C and F.   Line 4 compiles because the compiler allows literal assignments to `bytes`, `shorts`, and `chars` without requiring an explicit cast. The cast on line 4 is required, because a `short` is wider than a `byte`. At runtime, no exception is generated; the original 16-bit value is truncated to an 8-bit value (FD = 1111 1101) by having the high-order half discarded. To determine the value of this two's-complement number, invert all bits: 0000 0010. Then increment: 0000 0011. This is binary 3, so the value of FD is –3.

10. B.   This code does not start up any new concurrent threads. To do that, it would have to call `start()`, not `run()`.

11. C.   The horizontal scrollbar occupies the entire width of the frame and gets to be its preferred height. While we do not know what the exact preferred height of a scrollbar is, the scrollbar can't possibly occupy the center pixel, because for that to be the case, the preferred height would have to be 400 pixels—a very unreasonable height for a horizontal scrollbar. A similar argument applies to the vertical scrollbar: we might not know exactly how wide it is, but it is certainly much narrower than 400 pixels, so it too does not occupy the center pixel. So the horizontal scrollbar is a narrow strip across the top of the frame, and the vertical scrollbar is a thin strip along the left of the frame. The button at Center occupies the entire remainder of the frame, so the button must own the center pixel.

12. A. The toString() method in class Object is public. Methods may not be overridden to be more private.

13. B. Since the Papa class has a non-default constructor, it does not get an invisible do-nothing default constructor. Thus, the constructor for class Child (on line 7) will not compile, because it invisibly attempts to call its superclass default constructor.

14. A. The ceil() method's return type is double (even though the value in integral). So the assignment at line 3 requires an explicit cast.

15. A. (−1 >> anything) is −1, so after line 4, i is 0. Line 5 divides by zero, so an ArithmeticException is thrown. The JVM terminates in the exception handler on line 8, so the finally block never executes.

16. A. Line 6 is OK because the new type (A) is a superclass of the old type (B); for such an assignment, casting is not required. Line 7 is OK because the new type (Inter) is an interface that the old type (A) implements explicitly.

17. A, B, C, E. A generates an error because booleans are incompatible with all other primitive types. B generates an error because, despite intuition, char is not wider than byte; the byte type can represent negative values that cannot be represented in the char type. C fails for a similar reason: short is not wider than char; the char type can represent large positive values that cannot be represented in the short type. D compiles because the float type is wider than the long type (float has less precision but uses magnitude and exponent formats that gives it greater range, even though longs are 64 bits and floats are only 32 bits). Since float has a greater range of values than long, E fails to compile.

18. A and C. The thud() method throws a SubEx. The first appropriate handler is at line 23, because SubEx extends IOException. Line 24 prints out "thud() caught IOException". The exception handler then throws a new SubEx, which is caught by the calling method (main()). The first appropriate handler is at line 11; it prints "main() caught IOException".

19. A. This is true. All the methods have `void` return type.

20. D. Since the "top" panel occupies the frame's North region, the upper-left pixel must be managed by either the "top" panel or one of its child components. The "top" panel contains only one child: a checkbox that lies at its far right side. So the upper-left pixel lies in unoccupied territory of the "top" panel.

21. C. A static method may not instantiate a non-static inner class in the ordinary way.

22. A. First, `t1` starts up and begins a 5-second sleep. Then `t2` starts. It looks like `t2` causes `t1` to sleep an additional 10 seconds, so you might think t2 finishes first. Actually, the `sleep()` method is static; it always causes the currently executing thread to sleep. So `t2` goes to sleep for 10 seconds. After 5 seconds, `t1` wakes up and finishes first. Note that invoking static methods using instance references in this way would normally be very bad style.

23. A. `import` just tells the compiler about class name abbreviations. There is no impact at runtime.

24. B and D. The `thud()` method throws a `SubEx`, which is caught at line 26. So line 27 prints out "thud() caught SubEx". The exception handler then throws an `IOException`, which is caught by the calling method (`main()`) at line 12. The exception handler there prints "main() caught IOException".

25. B. A static method may not be overridden by a non-static method.

26. A, C, E. A is allowed because it overrides a default-access method with a protected one; thus the method becomes more public. B attempts to make the method more private, which is not allowed. C is a straightforward example of overriding. D alters the return type, which is not permitted. E is allowed because a subclass method is not required to throw exceptions that the superclass version throws.

27. B. `Math.random()` returns a number greater than or equal to zero and strictly less than zero. If the value is greater than 0.99999, the full expression rounds to 3; otherwise the expression rounds to 2.

28. D. If you attempt to add a value to a map, and your key is already in use, the new value replaces the old value. Here the new value is the string "Goodbye" and the old value is the string "Hello". Note that there is only one instance of the literal string "key" (seen on lines 2 and 3), because of Java's literal string pool.

29. A. When you construct a FileReader using the one-arg form of the constructor, the argument is the name of the file to be read. The reader uses the computer's default encoding, which is Tibetan. The file reader will read from a file named 8859_1.

30. A. The argument to `switch` must be `byte`, `short`, `char`, or `int`, so line 9 does not compile.

31. A, B. Only A and B are true. Readers and writers are exclusively for text. There is no RandomAccessFileReader class.

32. D. If you attempt to add a value to a map, and your key is already in use, the new value replaces the old value. This happens on line 5, so after line 5 executes there are still three pairs in the map. Then line 6 executes, adding a fourth pair.

33. A. A protected method of any superclass in any package may be overridden, provided the subclass's version of the method is protected or public. Default or private access would not be allowed.

34. D. The only way to generate `ArithmeticException` is to perform integer division by zero. The shift in answer D results in a value of zero for `j`.

35. A. If a subclass overrides a method, the subclass version may only throw exceptions that are the same as, or subclasses of, the exceptions thrown by the overridden version. Here the overridden version throws Exception. The subclass version throws SubEx, which is a subclass of Exception.

36. B, C, D. If the right argument of instanceof is a class name, then the result is true if the class of the left argument is the same as, or is a subclass of, the right argument. If the right argument of instanceof is an interface name, then the result is true if the class of the left argument implements the interface.

37. B. Any class that contains one or more abstract methods must be declared abstract, and an abstract class may not be instantiated.

38. G. The code compiles without error: the assignments on lines 6 and 7 are up the inheritance hierarchy, so no cast is required. The cast on line 8 is required because Dolphin is a subclass of Animal. An exception is thrown at line 8 because the object referenced by a is an instance of class Cat, which is not compatible with class Dolphin.

39. B. Line 1 creates a string object. Line 2 creates a second reference to that string. Line 3 appears to create a different object, but because literal strings are taken from the literal pool without duplication, line 3 only creates a third reference to the same object.

40. D. A and B are false because static methods may not be overridden. C is false because a non-static method may only be overridden by a non-static method. D is legal.

41. A. The button is added to pan2, which uses a Flow layout manager. This is the only relevant fact, because Flow layout honors preferred size.

42. C. The code inverts all the bits in b1 and then increments the result. This is exactly how you take the negative of a two's-complement number.

43. A. Key events do not provide X/Y information.

44. A, B, C, D.   A, B, and C are true because after a running thread leaves the Running state (no matter whether it blocks, sleeps, or waits), it must enter the Ready state before it can run. D is true because `wait()` gives up both the CPU and the lock, so the lock must be re-acquired.

45. A.   The code attempts to assign a literal `int` to a `byte`. Ordinarily a cast is required to assign an `int` to a `byte`, but because "5" is literal, the compiler allows the assignment. (The assignment would also be allowed if *b* were a `short` or a `char`.)

46. E.   (`b1 + b2`) is 35. Before the shift is executed, the second argument (35) is reduced modulo the bit-size of the argument to be shifted (5, an `int`). Since an `int` is 32 bits, the shift is not 35 positions but 35 % 32 = 3 positions. Thus line 3 is equivalent to `int i = 5 << 3;`, so *i* is 40.

47. A, B, C, D.   The superclass method takes one `int` as its argument. The methods in A, B, C, and D all take `byte` arguments. This does not constitute overriding, so the return types and exception types do not matter; all four methods are legal. E is illegal because an instance method may not be overridden by a static method.

48. A.   A non-static inner class may not be used with ordinary syntax inside a static method. Line 5 would have to be modified as follows:

```
Z.Inner inny = new Z().new Inner();
```

49. A, C, D, E.   An overriding method is allowed to throw exceptions, provided each exception is either the same class as one thrown by the superclass's version, or is a subclass of one thrown by the superclass's version. The only choice here that violates this rule is B, which throws a superclass of the exception type thrown by the overridden method.

50. D.   The point of this question is the granularity of the `private` access modifier. It restricts access to instances of the same class. Another way to say this is that `private` means private to the class, not private to the instance. In line 5, one Duck reads private data of another Duck, which is perfectly legal.

Appendix C

Using the Test Program

The CD-ROM supplied with this book contains Java programs that allows you to test yourself. The questions from each chapter are available in the test tool, which provides a format that allows you to simulate taking the real Java Certification Exam and to make a reasonable estimate of whether you are sufficiently prepared for the exam. In addition, the CD-ROM includes the complete Programmer's Final Exam from Appendix B, plus another 150 sample questions not available anywhere else. These allow you to make the best possible determination of your readiness for the real thing.

The Real Test

First, we'll discuss the real test program, since it differs somewhat from the tester, but is the one you will have to use when you take the exam "for real." You will see immediately that the user interface is different. The real test uses a native Windows interface that differs in appearance from any variation that the tester will offer. However, in addition to the inevitable differences of windowing system, the overall layout differs a little. We will take a little time to describe the overall appearance of the real test system.

The real test uses a scrollable area to present the body of the question and the answer choices. This question area occupies most of the screen. Beneath the question area are at least three buttons: Next, Previous, and Help. The Help button gives help on using the test system, not on the questions. Next and Previous step between questions, but the Next button sometimes changes to More. This change occurs when a question is long enough that you must scroll to see the whole question and all the answers. After you have pressed the More button, or have scrolled down the page far enough to have seen the whole question with all its answers, the button changes back to Next. The diagram in Figure C.1 shows the approximate layout of the real test system's main screen.

In many cases, there will be another button at the bottom of the screen, labeled Exhibit. When a question uses sample code that is particularly long, that code will generally be provided as an exhibit rather than in the body of the question. Press the Exhibit button and you will see a new window that contains the supporting example code. To close the window, click the Close button in the window border in the normal way.

FIGURE C.1   Sketch of the main screen of the real test

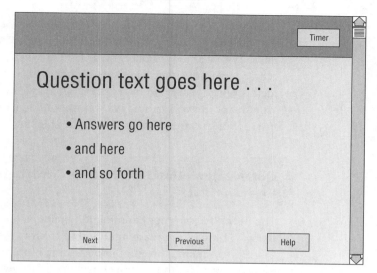

When you have stepped through all the questions the real test system offers, you see a review page showing all the questions and indicating any you have left unanswered or that you marked for later reconsideration. This page provides facilities for you to return to these questions to complete them.

Upon completion of the real test, which is strictly timed, you are presented with your mark on paper. You do not find out the correct answers, or even what specific questions you got wrong. Instead, the test gives you a breakdown of your scores by each group of objectives, so that you get some indication of the areas you should study further before you retake the exam.

In addition to the main test system, the real test allows you to have a "trial run" working with the test system to become familiar with it. During that phase you are given questions that are entirely unrelated to Java, so do not worry about getting them right!

Another facility allows you to make comments about the questions if you wish, although you will probably want to concentrate on your answers.

The Supporting Instructions

Before you take the test, you will be presented with some instructions and advice on how to take the test. These instructions are mostly obvious, but reflect things that have been of concern to candidates in the past. The idea is not to trick you into getting an answer wrong, but to determine whether or not you know Java well enough to isolate the correct answer. The instructions text you will see is in the sidebar.

Conventions Used in the Sun Certified Java Programmer Examination

The Java Programmer Examination includes the conventions described below. Some of them are intended to shorten the text that is displayed, therefore reducing the amount of reading required for each question. Other conventions help to provide consistency throughout the examination.

Conventions for Code

The code samples that are presented for you to study include line numbers. You should assume that the line numbers are not part of the source files, and therefore will not cause compilation errors.

Line numbers that begin with 1 indicate that a complete source file is shown. In contrast, if line numbers start with some other value, you should assume that the code you see is relevant to the question. You can assume that the omitted code would cause the code sample to compile correctly, and that it does not have any unexpected effects on the code in the question. So, for example, you should not choose an answer that says "The code does not compile" based only on the fact that you do not see a required import statement in the code sample that is presented.

In general, code of eight lines or less will be presented in the body of the question. If more than eight lines are needed, the code will be presented as an exhibit, and you will need to click the "Exhibit" button to see the code. Since you generally cannot see both the exhibited code and the question simultaneously due to limited screen size, you should read the question first, and use notepaper as necessary when considering an answer.

Conventions for Questions

When a question includes a code sample and asks "What is the result?" or something similar, you should consider what happens if you attempt to compile the code and then run it. This type of question admits the possibility that the code might not compile, or if it compiles, that it might not run. You should assume that all necessary support is given to the compilation and run phases (for example, that the CLASSPATH variable is appropriately set). Therefore, you should only examine possible causes of error in the information that is presented to you, and ignore information that is omitted.

Some of the possible answers use a form like this: "An error at line 5 causes compilation to fail." If you see this, you should consider whether the line in question is either a syntax error, or if it is inconsistent with some other part of the program and therefore misrepresents the program's clear intent. You should choose an answer of this type if the root of the problem is at the specified line, regardless of where any particular compiler might actually report an error.

Some questions might ask "Which answers are true?" or something similar. If an answer is worded like "An exception can be thrown," or "An exception may be thrown," then you should choose this answer if what it describes is possible, rather than disregarding it because the situation does not always occur. In contrast, if an option discusses something that "must" occur, then you should choose it only if there are no conditions under which the observation is untrue.

In multiple choice questions that require you to pick more than one answer, you will be told how many options to choose, and the options will be presented as checkboxes. In questions that require you to pick only one answer, the possible answers will be presented with radio buttons that effectively prevent you from selecting more than one answer.

Note that even after reading this sidebar, you should read the version provided on the day you take the test. It is possible that the text might be updated, and since the time you take reading the instructions is not part of your test time, you owe it to yourself to make this extra effort in preparation.

Now that you have a sense of the format of the real test, let's discuss the tester that is provided on the CD with this book.

The Tester

There are several differences between the real program and the tester. First and foremost, the questions are different! While we have sought to cover the same ground as the real test and to make the questions of comparable difficulty, you must appreciate that this is not the "real thing." There is no point in learning the answers to these questions by rote—that will only give you inappropriate confidence and will not provide you with actual answers to the real test.

The appearance of the tester main window on a Windows system is shown in Figure C.2.

FIGURE C.2 Screen shot of the tester main screen

In the tester, the questions are presented in a text area in the upper part of the main window, with the answer options presented in the lower part. If the question is a long one, the upper area will offer you a scrollbar as necessary.

The tester provides five buttons at the bottom of the window, and to the right is a timer. The timer allows you to determine how long you took to answer a set of questions.

The buttons provided are marked Next Unanswered, Next, Previous, Clear Answer, and Mark. The first three of these buttons are for navigating the question set; Next and Previous are self-evident, while Next Unanswered checks the question set to find the next question that you have not yet answered.

The Clear Answer button removes all marks from a question so that the Next Unanswered button will consider it to be unanswered. You can use this if you decide to skip a question for now but want to be able to come back to it easily.

The Mark button stops the test and timer and marks the questions. Unlike the real test, the tester gives you complete feedback on all the questions, including the correct answers and explanations. To give this feedback, the tester uses two additional windows. One pops up automatically when you press the Mark button. A screen shot of this window is shown in Figure C.3.

FIGURE C.3   The marking window

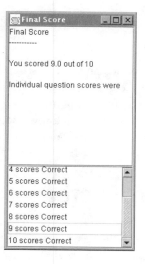

Notice that the marking window is divided into two regions. At the top is a text area that states your mark and the total number of questions you were asked. Beneath this is a scrollable list that indicates your score on a question-by-question basis. If you select one of the lines in this list, you are presented with a second window containing a text area that tells you either that you got the question correct, or what the correct answer is. An example of this is shown in Figure C.4.

FIGURE C.4   The explanation window

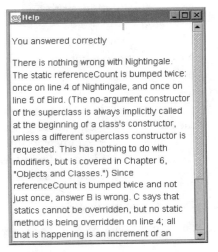

Notice how the first line indicates the correct answer or answers. If you got the question right, this line simply says so. The explanation text appears on the following lines.

Now that you know broadly what to expect when you run the tester, let's take a look at how to start the program and the options that it offers.

Running the Tester

The tester is written for the Java 2 Platform. It uses a Swing interface and can be run directly from the CD-ROM. Each chapter has its own tester, and there is another for the final exam and each set of 50 bonus questions. Each tester is supplied as an executable JAR file.

If you have a Windows system, simply insert the CD into your drive, use Explorer to locate the tester JARs in the directory /tests, and double-click

the icon for the test you want to take. The chapter tests are called `Chapter01`
`.jar` through `Chapter13.jar`. The file `final.jar` contains the programmer's final exam from Appendix B; `Bonus.jar` is a set of 150 sample questions exclusive to the CD-ROM.

If your host OS doesn't recognize executable JAR files, simply issue a
command of this form:

```
java -jar /mnt/cdrom/tests/Chapter01.jar
```

and substitute the path to your CD-ROM drive for `/mnt/cdrom` part as
necessary.

When you press the Mark button, the timer at the bottom-right corner of
the display will stop, showing you how long you spent on the questions.

Imposing a Time Limit

You can run the test in timed mode; the tester will move forcibly into marking mode if you take too long. To invoke this behavior in the tester, define
the property `testTime` when you start the program. This value should be
specified in minutes, and to approximate the conditions of the real exam you
should give yourself between 1.5 and 2 minutes per question. To define this
property, you must start the programs manually (you cannot do the double-
click trick), so start the tester with a command like this:

```
java -jar -DtestTime=90 d:\tests\Final.jar
```

This would give you one and a half hours to complete the test.

Answering the Questions

The questions presented by the tester are all multiple choice; some take
only a single correct answer, and some allow zero or more selections. You
can tell if you are allowed only a single answer to a question because the
answers will be presented to you with round radio buttons. To select an item,
click the body of the text for that answer.

If you see square check boxes, you can select any number of options, from
none to all that are shown. You can think of this type of question as a collection of true/false questions based on the same topic. Because true/false is
generally considered to be pretty easy—giving you a 50 percent chance of

success simply by guessing—you will not be surprised to know that you must get *all* parts of the question correct to score the mark.

In the Summer 2000 rewrite of the real exam, this was changed. If you must make multiple selections in that test, you will be told exactly how many items to select. Naturally, this makes things a little easier for you. However, we chose to make some of our sample questions a bit harder, to ensure that you really are as well prepared as you can be.

As with any test, you must read each question carefully. We have tried to make the questions unambiguous, but inevitably some uncertainties will remain. Although it is practically impossible to eliminate ambiguity from natural language (if it weren't, then lawyers would be unemployed), the questions on the Java Certification Exam have been subjected to extensive review and correction by many people; therefore, you can reasonably expect your interpretation of a question to match the intended one.

Good luck!

Although Swing is a powerful and fully featured GUI toolkit, it does have some bugs—more so in the earlier versions, and particularly on Windows platforms. Some of these may affect the tester. Most of the time, the worst that you will suffer from this is that the display might look a little odd, especially where something is highlighted. If this happens, you can probably ignore the effect, but if not, you will often find that a slight resize to the window will fix the problem. Another effect that might cause more trouble is that you might not get a scrollbar for some long questions. If you think part of a question is missing, this might be the case. Again, a small resize will usually fix the problem. Of course, an updated version of Swing (that is to say, an updated JDK) might provide a better and more permanent fix.

Appendix

D

The Certification Initiative for Enterprise Development

The Sun Certified Programmer's Exam has been very well received, and has won industry-wide support based on the validity of both the objectives and the questions. Much of this support results directly from the fact that the test is hard, and as such proves something worthwhile about you when you hold the certification. This general recognition led to an appropriate desire on the part of other vendors to be part of the success and relevance of Java certification. In consequence, some major players set up an organization called jCert, with the goal of creating the "Certification Initiative for Enterprise Development." The initiative aims to provide a suite of certification options that are essentially comparable in difficulty and relevance, but that focus on particular vendor's tools at the appropriate points. The slogan "Certified Once, Valued Everywhere" is used by the jCert organization to convey the consistency of value.

The initiative is open to new members, but as of June 2000, the jCert organization consisted of Sun, iPlanet (the Sun/Netscape Alliance), IBM, Oracle, BEA Systems, Novell, Hewlett-Packard, and Sybase. At that time, most of the member companies had not finalized their examinations. Because of this, we can really only describe the structure of the initiative, and outline the broad intent of the participant companies. To help you get the general picture, we have listed the objectives for the core exams and for the vendor examinations from IBM, since that company seems to be furthest along the road and has offerings that appear to be stable. You should refer to the jCert Web site, and the Web sites of the individual participants, to get up-to-date details on the various vendors' examinations.

The jCert organization site acts as the home for the entire initiative. The site is located at `http://www.jcert.org/` and includes descriptions of the initiative and links to the certification program information of the individual members of the group.

The Structure of the Initiative

The initiative is composed of three levels of examinations, some of which are specific to particular vendors, and others of which are common to the initiative as a whole. Each level constitutes a certification in its own right, so you can get the benefit of fulfilling part of the overall certification before you complete the whole thing.

You must take the three levels in order, but you may change vendors between the levels if that suits you. The Level I exam is always the "Programmer" exam—that is, the standard Sun Microsystems certification that is the topic of the first part of this book. So, all the hard work and preparation you put into achieving your programmer certification is of value regardless of where you choose to seek your next level of certification.

The second and third levels both consist of two exams each. In each case, one exam is common across the whole initiative and the other is vendor-specific. The name of the certification you receive reflects the vendor-specific examination you chose to take at that level. If, for example, you took one of the IBM exams at the second level, you could call yourself an "IBM Certified Solution Developer." At the third level, if you chose an iPlanet examination, you would become an "iPlanet Certified Enterprise Developer."

One important point is that the Sun Microsystems Developer and Architect certifications are not part of this initiative. Rather, the focus of these two programs is independent of both tool and vendor, so if you have no interest in proving skills with a particular vendor's products, these exams might be a better choice for you.

The Second-Level Exams

Since the first step on the road to jCert certification is always Sun Microsystems' "Programmer" exam, we will not discuss that here. Instead, we will go right ahead and describe the basic format of the second-level, or "Certified Solution Developer," exams.

There are three main areas of coverage in the Level II exams. These are:

- Your ability to use JDBC to access and manipulate data
- Your ability to develop and deploy applications in a heterogeneous networked environment (such as the Internet)
- Your understanding of object-oriented principles, your ability to apply these principles, and your ability to work with JavaBeans components

You must take two exams to gain the second level of certification.

The Common Exam at Level II

The first of the exams is common to the initiative as a whole and is produced by IBM. This exam covers object-oriented analysis and design (OOAD) skills, rather than Java programming skills. You will also be expected to demonstrate proficiency in Unified Modeling Language (UML). The exam title is "Object-Oriented Analysis and Design with UML;" it has two identifying numbers: Test 486 or 1Z0-513. The detailed objectives listed for the exam are listed here in six categories.

Development Process

Apply iterative and incremental processes.

Schedule project activities based on use cases.

Exhibit the ability to trace requirements both forward and backward through OOAD artifacts.

Utilize use cases to drive other project activities.

Apply the appropriate OOAD activities for a given situation, based on their strengths and weaknesses.

Control and coordinate the interfaces between packages.

Organize the project team responsibilities based on OOAD artifacts.

Requirements Modeling

Identify skills and resources needed to write use cases.

Identify actors for the system.

Identify use cases from a requirement document and/or domain expert and extract business rules for the domain.

Develop and interpret a use case model using the UML notation.

Write use cases that focus on the problem domain.

Write use cases using the terminology of the target audience.

Derive subsequent OOAD artifacts from use cases.

Use a prototype of the user interface for customer feedback when appropriate.

Architecture

Develop view-model-persistence layered architectures and understand how the layers should interact.

Use package diagrams when appropriate, creating and interpreting contractual interfaces and dependencies between packages.

Use cohesion and coupling effectively when grouping classes into packages.

Use deployment diagrams effectively.

Apply brokering to build flexible systems.

Consider issues related to scalability, performance, transactions, and concurrency.

Static Modeling

Identify domain objects, services, attributes, and their relationships using different techniques, including "parts of speech."

Determine when a new class is needed.

Choose good names for classes and methods.

Describe the business concept and role that each class represents in the domain model.

Develop and interpret UML class diagrams, including the effective use of aggregation, generalization, and delegation.

Effectively interpret and develop associations in class diagrams, including stereotypes, qualified associations, cardinality of associations, and association classes.

Maintain encapsulation of attributes and visibility of operations effectively.

Recognize and exploit polymorphism.

Create, interpret, and exploit interfaces.

Interpret class diagrams from different perspectives, including subclassing and subtyping.

Create and interpret CRC cards as appropriate.

Dynamic Modeling

Focus on behavior while modeling the domain.

Include an appropriate level of detail in diagrams.

Effectively assign responsibilities to appropriate classes.

Develop UML interaction diagrams (sequence and collaboration) to satisfy requirements.

Interpret interaction diagrams, including the use of iterations, conditionals and concurrency.

Recognize complexities early in the project and resolve them in an iterative and incremental fashion.

Determine when to use state diagrams.

Develop and interpret UML state diagrams, including the use of events, guards, actions, and super state.

Determine when to use activity diagrams.

Develop and interpret UML activity diagrams, including concurrency, iterations, and conditionals.

Design and Implementation Techniques

Design for reuse.

Given its definition, apply a pattern.

Refactor classes to distribute responsibilities and behavior.

Carry OOAD artifacts forward into implementation.

Resolve implementation issues and update OOAD artifacts

You will probably notice that some of these objectives are rather broad in scope. Of course, this is a rather different exam from the Programmer test that you have probably spent much time studying for. Fortunately, IBM provides an online sample test that allows you to get a reasonable idea of the scope of the test. The pre-tests can be found by following the link at `http://www` `.jcert.org/sponsors.html` for IBM, which takes you to the IBM site that handles Java certification issues. The pre-test for test 486 can be found via the links for any of the "IBM Certified Solution Developer" tests. At the time of writing, this takes you to:

`http://www-4.ibm.com/software/ad/certify/sam486a.html`

One point about the IBM sample test site. You will be required to register before you can take the sample test. There's no cost involved, but they do give you a user id and password (which you can't control) and the password is splendidly secure—which means it's utterly impossible to remember; mine is poxp6cd7 (I'm not telling you my username ☺). Since the site doesn't seem to provide any means of recovering a forgotten password, you'll either have to re-register each time you use the site, or you really do need to make a note of the login information they provide.

The Vendor-Specific Exams at Level II

The second exam is the vendor-specific one, which will test core aspects of your skills in creating applications, but will also examine your ability to make efficient use of the vendor's tool while performing the programming work.

The vendor exams all cover comparable material, but of course since they deal with your ability to use the vendor's tool, there will be significant variations in the material. The general objectives for all vendor-specific Level II exams can be summarized as follows:

- Use the tool effectively for coding, testing, version control, and deployment, including appropriate use of JAR files and Beans components.

- Be able to create applications that use either JDBC or forms-based database access.

At the time of writing, you had a choice of three vendor-specific exams at Level II: two from IBM and one Oracle.

The IBM tests are numbered 282 and 494. Test 282 covers development with IBM VisualAge for Java, while test 494 covers IBM WebSphere Application Server, Standard Edition, V3. What follows are the objectives for these exams:

The IBM VisualAge for Java Exam

The IBM exam number 282 covers IBM VisualAge for Java. These are its objectives:

Construct and Deploy Java-Based Solutions, Including Applications, Applets, and Servlets

For a given situation, choose the appropriate type of Java program (Application, Applet, or Servlet) and assess their basic technical requirements.

Deploy Java code and associated files for Applets, Servlets, and Applications.

Access Databases and Use Remote Method Invocation (RMI) in the Development of Java-Based Solutions

Access databases using Data Access Beans, JDBC, SQLJ.

Connect database query results to forms or UI controls.

Use VisualAge for Java to aid implementation of RMI.

Use Visual Programming and the Existing Library of JavaBeans to Create Java-Based Solutions

Add JavaBeans to the Composition Surface.

Create connections in the Composition Editor and recognize meaning of the different types and appearances of connections.

Change the properties and parameters of connections.

Explain how and when to promote Bean features.

Modify Bean settings and understand the resulting changes that occur on the composition surface and in generated code.

Reorder connections and understand the effects.

Tear off properties of a JavaBean and understand the resulting changes that occur on the composition surface and in generated code.

Use Variables on the Composition Surface and understand the results on the composition surface and in the generated code.

Use and modify Visual Beans.

Use the Morph Into function on the Composition Editor.

Apply appropriate Bean given a required functionality (such as, use proper Visual Bean for required user interface).

Use the Visual Composition Editor to specify, change, and configure the layout and layout manager of a Visual Bean.

Identify and change the tab order of Visual Beans.

Create or consume re-usable panels (i.e., forms).

Use Object Factories and understand the results on composition surface and generated code.

Understand how and when to use the Beans List.

Create and use Quick Forms.

Create Re-Usable JavaBeans using VisualAge for Java

Use the BeanInfo Page to create and modify JavaBean features (properties, events, methods) and be aware of what code is generated in the class and its corresponding BeanInfo class.

From the BeanInfo Page, create new Event Sets and Listeners, know what methods are generated, and be able to make use of them.

Create Property features using the various attributes a property can have (e.g., bound, constrained, expert, etc.) and be able to make use of them.

Set and use Property Editors and Bean Customizers.

Develop Java-Based Solutions Using VisualAge for Java

Write and modify Java code using the editors and editing aids provided by the IDE.

Understand the purpose of various Smartguides and be able to make use of them.

Make use of IDE features which aid Internationalization.

Import and export source code, resources, class files, and repository files.

Execute and test Applets, Applications, and Servlets from within the VisualAge for Java Environment.

Set the classpath in VisualAge for Java with each of the available techniques and explain the advantages and disadvantages of each technique.

Use the debugger to set and modify breakpoints, step through code, inspect variables, change the value of variables, etc.

Use the WebSphere Test Environment, Servlet Launcher, and JSP Monitor to execute and test servlets and JSPs.

Create Packages, Projects, Classes, Interfaces, methods, and fields.

Identify and resolve Java code errors, using facilities of the IDE.

Use the Code Management Facilities of VisualAge for Java

Access and manage repositories.

Implement version control for the different types of program elements, and use the 'compare' and 'replace with' functions of the IDE.

Understand the difference between the repository and the workspace.

Use Features of VisualAge for Java to Improve Development Productivity

Use and understand purpose of Console Window.

Identify and distinguish visual cues and clues.

Use the IDE's browsers to navigate and find information by making use of the features of the IDE such as bookmarks and search functions, as well as the different pages of each of the browsers.

Change the properties of browsers to display desired information.

Change and save the properties, settings, and options associated with the workspace.

Use the Quick Start Window.

The IBM WebSphere Application Server Exam

The IBM exam number 494 covers the WebSphere Application Server, Standard Edition. These are its objectives:

Overall Application Design

Determines the mechanism for managing client-specific state (e.g., Cookies, URL rewriting, hidden tags, HTTP sessions, etc.).

Designs a layered solution from a given multi-tiered architecture.

Designs and develops a solution to manage the decoupling of model from presentation.

Designs and develops model persistence using JDBC.

Controller Development

Designs and develops Java Servlets conforming to the JSDK 2.1 or JSWDK 1.X Specification.

Builds threadsafe, multi-user server-side programs.

Uses HttpSession objects to manage client-specific data on the server.

Knows when and how to use Cookies appropriately.

Knows when and how to use Security APIs appropriately.

Writes code to handle error conditions.

Builds and uses Java components to communicate between application layers (e.g., JavaBeans).

Examines HttpServletRequest objects in order to process client requests.

Sets properties of the HttpServletResponse and HttpServletRequest objects for controlling presentation content and application behavior.

Presentation Development

Modifies/constructs Web pages, to provide dynamic content using JSP.

Understands the JSP 1.0 Specification.

Configuration/Deployment

Knows IBM WebSphere Application Server architecture and terminology (e.g., startup sequence, plug-in, admin server, managed servers, property storage, etc.).

Installs and configures the IBM WebSphere Application Server.

Defines and/or configures Application Servers, Virtual Hosts, Web Applications, Web Resources, load-by-classname (invoker servlet), file server servlet, JDBC drivers, JSP enablers, Datasources, named servlets, Servlet Engines, and Web Paths.

Configures Session Manager options.

Uses Tasks, Types, and Topology configuration pages in the Administrative Console.

Starts, stops, and restarts Application Servers, Web Applications, and Servlet Engines.

Troubleshooting

Directs application and AdminServer trace outputs.

Interprets trace and log files to locate and solve problems.

Familiarity with tracing and debugging facilities.

Identifies and resolves concurrent programming issues.

Identifies misbehaving servlets and JSPs.

Identifies performance tuning opportunities.

Other Vendor Exams at Level II

At the time of writing, the only other jCert participant to offer reasonably stable information about a second-level test was Oracle. Their Level II test was actually available in two forms, one being phased out by the other, which was in beta test. Oracle's tests are based on the JDeveloper product, and the tests were being upgraded from Release 2 to account for Release 3. The codes for these versions are 1Z0-502 and 1Z1-512 respectively.

The Third-Level Exams

To achieve the designation "Certified Enterprise Developer," you must complete the third level of examinations, in addition to the first two. As with Level II, you must pass one common exam and one vendor-specific one. In this case, the common exam is owned by the jCert group, rather than by IBM.

The Common Exam at Level III

The Level III common exam covers the following broad areas:

- J2EE functional areas (the APIs)
- Security
- Enterprise JavaBean construction and deployment
- The EJB model (security, transactions, and so forth)

Although this exam is essentially a product of the jCert initiative, the details of the exam are not available from the `jcert.org` Web site. Instead, you can find this information at the IBM site, under IBM exam number 483. The test is called "Enterprise Connectivity Test with Java 2 Enterprise Edition." As with the other exams, IBM provides a sample test that will give you a feel for the type and difficulty of the questions. The objectives for this exam are divided into these six areas:

Java 2 Enterprise Edition (J2EE) Architecture

Select and apply appropriate J2EE technologies to design the desired multi-tiered architecture.

Evaluate tradeoffs in designing distributed systems.

Use given design patterns to encapsulate enterprise services in a multi-tiered application.

Assign responsibility to appropriate layers to optimize maintainability, scalability, and performance.

Web Component Development

Construct Web pages to provide dynamic content using JavaServer Pages (JSPs).

Design and develop Java Servlets conforming to the Java Servlet Specification, including Servlet life cycle, classes, and interfaces.

Coordinate and manage session state, including cookies, HttpSession, and URL rewrite.

Implement threadsafe server-side logic.

Implement robust controller logic within a framework which supports effective error handling.

Separate responsibilities between Servlets, Enterprise JavaBeans (EJBs), and JSPs.

Enterprise JavaBean (EJB) Development

Select and understand types of EJBs.

Design EJB home and remote interfaces.

Design logic compatible with EJB lifecycle and state behavior, including creation, activation, passivation, and removal.

Develop Entity EJBs with container-managed persistence (CMP) or bean-managed persistence (BMP).

Understand exceptions in the context of distributed objects and container managed transactions.

Develop EJBs with bean-managed transactions, including UserTransaction and session synchronization.

Client Development

Customize payment processing.

Understand the issues of client-side programming, including application, servlet, and EJB clients.

Use Java Naming and Directory Interface (JNDI) to obtain references to services and publish available resources.

Use the UserTransaction type in a client application.

Connectivity Services

Select and use alternative distribution technologies, including remote method invocation (RMI), Java Messaging Service (JMS), and common object request broker architecture (CORBA).

Understand RMI issues for J2EE application design, including serialization, RMI-IIOP, and RemoteException.

Use JDBC 2.0 to access relational databases, including driver and statement selection.

Understand implications of JDBC 2.0 standard extension features on application design, including DataSources, connection pooling, and transaction management.

Assembly and Deployment

Package EJBs for portable deployment.

Understand content of the deployment descriptor and identify which architecture roles use which sections.

Assemble EJBs for deployment, including transaction demarcation and isolation level.

Establish security in a J2EE application.

The Vendor-Specific Exams at Level III

As with the Level II certification, the second exam at Level III is vendor-specific and relates to the use of the vendor's tools in complex development scenarios. Generally, the objectives of these exams will cover the following areas:

- Development of client and server components of an application using the tools and the following technologies and APIs: EJB, JSP and servlets, JDBC, connection pooling, transactions, and security.

- Test and deploy the application using the tools. Monitor and administer the application for best performance and reliability using the tools.

At the time of writing, exams or preliminary information were available for three vendor-specific exams at Level II, one each from IBM, Oracle, and iPlanet. Novell also offers the IBM exam under its own banner.

The IBM Vendor-Specific Exam

The IBM test is number 495, covering development with IBM WebSphere Application Server, Advanced Edition, V3. These are the objectives for this exam:

Application/Component Design

Designs and develops a solution that decouples model from presentation.

Identifies appropriate Enterprise JavaBean (EJB) type to solve a given business problem.

Uses appropriate design patterns to encapsulate services in an EJB application.

Web Component Development and Testing

Designs and develops Java Servlets conforming to the JSDK 2.1 Specification.

Builds and tests server-side logic which is threadsafe concurrent web application environment.

Manages end-user state using HttpSessions and cookies.

Implements robust controller logic within a framework supports effective error handling.

Uses methods of HttpServletRequest and HttpServletResponse interact with HTTP data streams.

Modifies/constructs Web pages to provide dynamic content using JSP 1.0.

Enterprise JavaBean (EJB) Development and Testing

Implements stateful/stateless Session Beans.

Implements container-managed persistence (CMP) Entity Beans.

Implements bean-managed persistence (BMP) Entity Beans.

Uses EJBContext to coordinate with the EJB container.

Uses client proxy to interface with EJBs.

Uses Java Transaction API (JTA) to control transaction demarcation.

Understands and works with Java Enterprise APIs to connect to EJBs.

Development and Testing of Applications with VisualAge for Java, Enterprise Edition, V3

Uses the WebSphere Test Environment to test Web applications within VisualAge for Java.

Uses VisualAge persistence to map CMP fields to existing database schemas.

Uses VisualAge EJB test client to unit test EJBs.

Uses EJB Development Environment in VisualAge for Java.

Selects and uses appropriate Access Bean(s) in order to provide client access to EJBs.

Configuration, Deployment, and Management of Applications

Manipulates transactional behavior of EJBs (e.g., isolation levels, transaction attribute).

Declares security policies on enterprise applications.

Uses WebSphere Administrative Console and related property files to configure and deploy an application.

Configures HttpSession management options.

Configures multi-node applications using Servlet Redirector and application server models/clones.

Uses the resource analyzer tool to identify performance tuning opportunities, connection pooling characteristics, etc.

Uses WebSphere trace facilities and log files to debug Application Server and Admin Server problems.

Identifies misbehaving servlets, JSPs, and EJBs.

Configures workload management selection policies.

Other Vendor Exams at Level III

Two other vendors had preliminary information about their exams at the time of writing, these are Oracle and iPlanet. The Oracle test is based on the Oracle Internet Platform product. The code for this exam is 1Z0-505, and it is called "Enterprise Development on the Oracle Internet Platform."

The iPlanet exam is called "iPlanet Application Server 6.0" and is identified as 310-540. If you take this route, you will be able to call yourself a "Sun/Netscape Alliance Certified Enterprise Developer."

Index

Note to the Reader: Throughout this index **boldfaced** page numbers indicate primary discussions of a topic. *Italicized* page numbers indicate illustrations.

D

M

Q

R

r mode, 444
\r prefix, 10
race conditions, 502
RAD (rapid application development) tools, 576
radio groups, 374, *375*
raising exceptions, 145
random() method, 251
RandomAccessFile class, **444–448**
range of data types, **8–9**
range selections from lists, 587
read() methods
    in DataInputStream, 452
    in FileInputStream, 449–450
    in InputStream, 156
    in RandomAccessFile, 446–448
    in Reader, 457–458
readability
    importance of, 607
    overloading for, 176
    in sample assignment, **503**
Reader class, 457–458
readers, **456–457**, *460*
    encodings for, **460–462**, *461*
    serialization for, **462–464**, *463*
readLine() method, 459
README files
    in exam, 609
    writing, **695–696**
ready thread state, 216, *217*
rebind() method, 560–561, 666
RecordCounter class, 657–658
RecordCounterImplAct class, 663–665
records
    in databases, 508, 514
    defining, **512–513**
    locking, **667–669**, *668–669*

recordTotal() method, 514
rectangles, **406–407**, *407*
reduction of right-hand operand, **49–50**
references. *See* object references
Reflection API, 678
regions
    in Border layout manager, **298–305**, *298–299, 301–306*
    for GridBag components, 592
register() method, 666
registerKeyboardAction() method, 640
registry, binding objects to, 560
relational databases, 508–509, 648, *648*
relationships in object-oriented design, **173–174**
RELATIVE feature in GridBag, **329–332**, *331*
RELATIVE grid variable, 592
relative paths for files, 439
reliable protocols, 465
REMAINDER feature in GridBag, **329–332**, *331*, 592
remainder operator, **40–41**
Remote interface, 654–655
Remote Method Invocation (RMI), 465, **555–556**
    for database servers, **653–657**
    in exam, 487–488
    implementing, **557–563**
    limitations of, **563–565**
    vs. object serialization, **702–703**
    proxy files in, 660
    for remote notification, **683–685**, *684*
    in sample assignment, **500–501**
    transaction model for, **556–557**, *557*
    in trouble-ticket system, **613–615**, *614*
remote notification, **683–685**, *684*
RemoteException class, 558, 563, 657
RemoteObject class, 558
RemoteRequest interface, 558
removeActionListener() method, 677
removeListDataEventListener() method, 588

S

#

Z

#